NEW GRANADA:

TWENTY MONTHS IN THE ANDES.

BY ISAAC F. HOLTON, M.A.,

PROFESSOR OF CHEMISTRY AND NATURAL HISTORY IN MIDDLEBURY COLLEGE.

WITH MAPS AND ILLUSTRATIONS.

NEW YORK:

HARPER & BROTHERS, PUBLISHERS,

FRANKLIN SQUARE.

1857.

PREFACE.

The botanist can not study the productions of the torrid zone without a strong desire to see with his own eyes the regions of perpetual summer. This desire grows from year to year, but each succeeding year generally binds him closer to local duties and his home. In the case of the author, this centripetal force had not developed itself in due proportion to its antagonist, and a visit to the tropic world was the result.

His attention was directed more particularly to New Granada by the scantiness of botanical information on a region so profusely rich in plants. Not even a catalogue of a collector had appeared since the results of Humboldt's visit, at the beginning of this century, were given to the world.

Nor were the sources of general information on that republic much more copious or recent. Our libraries were found to contain several works on Colombia, written during that terrible struggle with the mother country which terminated, or, rather, took on a chronic form in 1825, but not a volume was to be found which had been written since New Granada had taken her place among the nations. No answer could be found to the inquiry what effect thirty years of liberty had produced on a land that had been till that time sealed up from all the world by Spanish despotism. This void in our geographical information was the determining cause of the journey narrated in this volume.

Thus my task was commenced with a more correct estimate of the need of the undertaking than of its difficulty. A want of reliable facts began to produce its inconveniences even before leaving our shores, impeded the journey at every stage, and afterward still more embarrassed the composition of the narrative. The observations of earlier travelers, who resided in the country for some special object, or hurried through it ignorant alike of the genius and the language of the people, were so frequently erroneous, that I did, perhaps, not often enough distrust my own conclusions when different from theirs. In addition to these old works, accident has lately thrown in my way a small book, entitled "Bogotá in 1836–7. By J. Steuart. Printed for the author by Harper & Brothers, 82 Cliff Street, 1838." I had heard of this book in South America, but all my search for it in libraries and book-stores had been in vain. I know of no other copy in the United States.

No Spanish-American nation has furnished a larger proportion of authors than New Granada; still, their works are neither numerous nor easy of access. The "Semanario de la Nueva Granada," published in Bogotá in 1810, various scientific papers by Boussaingault, and a pamphlet by President T. C. Mosquera, have been freely used. On the latter I have relied for the names of many animals and some plants. Plaza's history has been carefully examined, and Acosta's sometimes referred to. Public documents were supplied with exceeding kindness by those officers who had them in their power, both at Bogotá and elsewhere. It is to be regretted that neither the Granadan legation in the United States, nor the consulate at New York, were able to add any thing to these stores collected abroad.

Many individuals have kindly aided in promoting the accuracy of the work, whose favors, though gratefully remembered, can not be enumerated here. To no North American does it owe more than to that gentleman, merchant, and scholar, Alexander I. Cotheal. Señor Julio Arboleda was never applied to in vain. Señor Escipion García-Herreros contributed some valuable and elaborate observations on civil law, and a compendium of the history of the last attempt at revolution, both of which deserved a better fate than to be reduced to such mere abstracts as alone could find room in a volume of travels.

But to no one individual, nor, indeed, to all others, does the work owe so much as to Señor Rafael Pombo, secretary of the Granadan legation. And this zeal was owing, not to a friendship to the author, to whom he was a stranger when his aid was first sought, but to a noble love for his country. May that country thank and reward him; for his faithfulness, accuracy, promptness, and zeal transcend all mere thanks of mine.

It was a calamity that the book was put in type at a time when Señor Pombo was absent from the country. The author's distance from the printers also tended to increase the number of verbal errors, which, notwithstanding an almost marvelous accuracy on their part, will be noticed by the Spanish scholar. As most of these occur rightly spelled in the Appendix, it is hoped that they will not sensibly impair the utility of the book. The translation of the phrase *Dominus vobiscum*, the expressions *Que entren para dentro*, and *Por siempre*, are perhaps the most important not thus corrected.

But there is another class of errors which no proof-reader can correct, and the number of which no one will ever know. So many are the motives for misleading the traveler—so many the errors that, once set down for truth, are never re-examined—that it can not be possible that this work shall be exempt from them. The indulgent reader will pardon them.

The author claims of the publishers the right to make one more acknowledgment of obligation, and that is to themselves. The liberality with which they have acceded to every wish of his, involving outlays far beyond what was at first intended, is one of the most pleasing circumstances in the retrospect of the long and unremitted toil this day concluded. And if succeeding travelers shall find in the book that aid which the writer sought in vain, and the philanthropist shall feel his best sympathies aroused for one of the most liberal and free nations on the face of the globe, that toil will not be unrewarded.

Middlebury College, October 15th, 1856.

CONTENTS.

CHAPTER VII.

HONDA AND GUADUAS.

CHAPTER VIII.

PLAIN OF BOGOTÁ.

CHAPTER IX.

POSADA AT BOGOTÁ.

CHAPTER X.

BOGOTÁ.

CHAPTER XI.

FOREIGNERS IN BOGOTÁ.

CHAPTER XII.

THE BOGOTANOS.

CHAPTER XIII.

RELIGION AND CHURCHES OF BOGOTÁ.

CHAPTER XIV.

CHURCHES OF BOGOTÁ.

CHAPTER XV.

PÁRAMO AND POLITICS.

CHAPTER XVI.

MONTSERRATE AND THE BOQUERON.

CHAPTER XVII.

THE PRISON, THE HOSPITAL, THE GRAVE.

CHAPTER XVIII.

THE VALLEY OF THE ORINOCO.

CHAPTER XIX.

CONGRESS, CONSTITUTIONS, INSTITUTIONS, AND WEATHER.

CHAPTER XX.

THE FALLS OF TEQUENDAMA.

CHAPTER XXI.

BALLS AND BULLS.

CHAPTER XXII.

THE BRIDGE OF PANDI.

CHAPTER XXIII.

IBAGUÉ.

CHAPTER XXIV.

THE BACK TRACK.

CHAPTER XXV.

CROSSING THE QUINDIO MOUNTAINS.

CHAPTER XXVI.

A CAUCAN FAMILY.

CHAPTER XXVII.

ROLDANILLO AND LAW.

CHAPTER XXVIII.

GRAZIER LIFE.

CHAPTER XXIX.

GRAZIER SPORTS.

CHAPTER XXX.

THE GRAZIER AT HOME.

CHAPTER XXXI.

THE PASTURES IN THE FOREST.

CHAPTER XXXII.

BUGA AND PALMIRA.

APPENDIX.

ILLUSTRATIONS.

ERRATA.

Page 37, line 3, *for* two, *read* twenty-two.
Page 117, line 37, *for* Losa, *read* Loras.
Page 273, line 5, *add*, This was Boza.
Page 529, line 23, *for* Candelaria, *read* Caloto.

NEW GRANADA.

CHAPTER I.

INTRODUCTORY.

A tropical Scene.—Position of Vijes.—Valley of the Magdalena.—The Cauca.—Seclusion of its Valley.—Aim of the Work.—Origin of Character.—Influence of Latitude on Value of Time.—Effect of Altitude on Temperature.—Religious Monopoly.—Ancestry.—Language.—Plan of the Work.

I HAVE just come up from a refreshing dip in the cool mountain stream, and have thrown myself leisurely on the rude and not too clean bank of earth and stone that forms a seat along the front of the lime-burner's hut, under the piazza.

Here sits the tenant of the cottage on a large fragment of rock, destined some day for the fire, shaping a section of the stem of a bush into a wooden spoon. He uses for this the universal tool, the machete—a knife about twenty inches long, that the peasant rarely fails to have in a sheath belted to his waist.

His little girl has slipped on her camisa, perhaps the only garment that she possesses, in honor of my coming. The little monkey has hardly improved her appearance by the operation; for the garment, though not so black as her skin, is infinitely inferior to it in cleanliness. She is doing as her father does, and has taken a large piece of wood, and is busy, with a dull case-knife that has lost its handle of horn, hacking at random, to make, as she tells me, a spoon.

The older daughter and her mother are busy at a little fire built at one end of the piazza. They are broiling some rather suspicious-looking pieces of beef, and roasting peeled plantains, for the family lunch, which the laboring class convert into a frugal noonday meal whenever they have the means at hand. The little boy, undisfigured by clothes or dirt, is busy investigating the foreigner, but at the same time seems to have a special anticipatory interest in the operations of his mother.

We are a little higher than the point of a triangular plain that spreads out eastward to the river. The western angle, near us, is occupied by a village of huts, some of which merit the name of houses, arranged around the Plaza, or public square, that is almost never wanting from a Granadan village. The little stream in which I have been bathing receives, just below, a tributary from a gorge at my left, skirts the village on the north, having also a dozen or more houses on its left bank, makes its way among cane-fields, plantain-patches, uncultivated lands and forest for a mile or two, and loses itself in the yellow current of the river, and hurries off to the north to reach the Caribbean Sea. That river is the Cauca, and the village is Vijes.

Beyond the river are low lands covered with forest, and in the farthest east the blue summits of the Quindio Mountains, which separate this most secluded valley from that of the Magdalena.

The nook of Vijes is separated from the rest of the world by the river and forest on the east, and on all other sides by a high range of steep rocky hills, with grass-covered sides, and crowned at the summit with dense forest. Over these the road down the river from the south climbs in laborious zigzags, or quingos, as they call them, while, proceeding down the river, it finds room to squeeze itself in between the hill and the river, or, when hard pressed, climbs along the steep side to pass a difficulty and to descend again. I used the word *road*, but I fear it will mislead the reader: a road might imply travelers—might be understood to mean a path on which two mules could always pass each other. The word *trail* would better convey the idea to a Western man.

All this scene lies before us now, owing to the slight elevation of the flat spot in the gorge of the hills where this hut stands. It is bathed in the brilliant but not burning rays of a vertical sun—a scene of quiet beauty, so far out of the way of travel that probably not an eye that reads these lines has seen, or will ever see, the original that I am trying to delineate.

And why shall I not commence, here and now, those random sketches that I have so long been promising my friends? Well, this shall be the beginning.

Now let me fix the geography of the place I am dating from. New Granada occupies the northwest corner of South America, and extends from a little north of the Isthmus of Panama to the neighborhood of the equator. It is the central fragment of the three into which Colombia was divided in 1830, and comprises one half of the whole.

The Pacific receives no large river from South America. The Atlantic receives most of the water from New Granada through the Amazon, Orinoco, Magdalena, and Atrato. Nine tenths of the population live on the Magdalena and its tributaries. Of these the Cauca is by far the largest. This and the Magdalena flow northward for many hundreds of miles in valleys parallel to each other, having between them the Quindio Mountains.

It will best suit us to view the Cauca as having its origin in the lofty and cold regions between the provinces of Popayan and Pasto. From the volcano of Puracé, southeast of the ancient town of Popayan, flows a stream that justly merits the name of Rio Vinagre, as ten thousand parts of its waters contain eleven of sulphuric acid and nine of hydrochloric, or one part in five hundred of pure acid. Even after turning directly north, and taking the name of the Cauca, no fish can live in its sour waters for leagues. Farther down it enters a broader valley, and becomes a quiet but turbid navigable river, lined always on its right bank, and often on both, by muddy and tangled forest. Thus the considerable towns of Palmira and Cali, which are opposite each other, and eighteen miles apart, are at quite a distance from the river, Palmira on the left banda, or side, and Cali on the right. The word *banda*, then, is not equivalent to bank, for it embraces a space much farther from the water.

Soon after passing Cali the western hills crowd down to the river, and in a nook of them lies Vijes, with its fertile, half-cultivated plain, and limpid, babbling brook. Farther down are Buga and Cartago, both east of the river, and lastly old Antioquia; but here the river has begun to form a series of rapids, becoming more violent below, as it plunges into gorges where no road nor foot-path can follow it, and shuts out all hope of commerce here finding an outlet either by land or water, by steamboat or rail-road, by canoe or pack-mule.

At last comes a pause in the rapid career of the Cauca when

it has nearly reached the level of the sea, and it turns northeast, and joins its turbid stream with the turbid stream of the Magdalena, and both proceed north to the sea. But the lower navigable portion of the river has no neighborhood with the upper. No man goes down there to see his friends, buy goods, or sell his produce.

The natural outlet for the commerce of this fertile valley, then, is forever closed. What are its substitutes? First, the pestiferous sea-port of Buenaventura, on the Pacific, lying just west of Vijes. The land roads to Buenaventura terminate at Juntas, at the forks of the Dagua, from whence there is tolerable navigation when the river is not too high or too low. He that comes down to Juntas from the Cauca probably will find no boats, and can go no farther by land. He that comes up from Buenaventura may find no mules, and can go no farther by water. There may be a detention of a week at Juntas in either case. Hence Buenaventura has no commerce, and even the steamers that run down the Pacific coast from Panamá do not stop there. The shortest road from Bogotá to Buenaventura is to leave the principal road of the Cauca at a point east of Vijes, cross the river by a private ferry, and begin to scale the Western Cordillera by a crazy path from this very spot. Three or four hours of terrible climbing will bring you to where little streams are running toward the Pacific.

The other outlet to the scanty trade of the valley is over the Quindio Mountains. About ten days' packing, in the best of weather, brings it to the Magdalena, two miles below Honda; but if it would reach the port of Cartagena, it must be by a farther mule carriage from Calamar of 65 miles, a distance more than twice as great as from here to Juntas. Was there ever, then, such an out-of-the-way place? Must not human life and human nature, though essentially the same in Labrador and Guinea, exhibit here some very unique and singular phases? We shall see.

Human nature is indeed every where the same in its essence, but infinitely diversified by the modifying power of external circumstances. Unlike instinct, that scarcely yields to the strongest influences, human nature bears the impress of the slightest inappreciable perturbing forces. Ancestry, soil, climate, occupation, bodily constitution, all have their power. But almost every where all these are borne down and modified, if not neutralized, by the resistless power of the great world of European civilization, which circulates through all the arteries of travel, so that the most minute ramifications receive their share. So the traveler who would study the power of local influences on men must go where travelers are not wont to go, nor foreign influences to penetrate. He must set himself leisurely down in a foreign land, with a foreign language, a foreign climate, a foreign religion, a foreign and local literature and commerce, or none at all.

Such study does Vijes afford to the Anglo-American and Protestant. He comes from a scene where life is a battle, a truceless warfare with adversity and competition, and where not even the dead can rest in peace unless deposited where commerce will locate no new railroad, or health and convenience demand no new street. He comes where winter can never overtake the sluggard, where the maxims of Poor Richard have never been heard of, where it is cheaper to make a field than defend a lawsuit, and easier to raise a new baby than cure a sick one; and where even the sacred office is a quiet monopoly, undisturbed by the severe but salutary strifes which arise from planting two or three doctors and two or three churches in the same village.

Here, then, let us observe dispassionately what is before our eyes, trace effects back to their causes, and estimate the various moral forces that have for their resultant the Granadan character. I will try to serve you as the eye serves the body, by laying before you pictures of the fidelity of which you shall have no reason to doubt; and if I ever draw any conclusions for you, it will not be because some superior sagacity is needed to arrive at them, but rather because they are too obvious to be ignored.

Vijes (or Biges, for the orthography is uncertain) has a latitude of about 3° 45′ N., so you may consider it situated on the equator. The sun ought therefore to set at six invariably; but as it always goes into the clouds when it is about an hour high, the people make no account of it afterward. They say the sun "goes in" about five, but never speak of its setting. Twilight ends between half past six and seven, so it appears quite like a natural sunset at about five; and no one notices whether the sun is vertical or not at noon; so that all the diversities that you derive from the annual changes of the sun's declination are unknown here. It may be that even this has its bearing on character. Let a man with us lose a day by the high water, or by the negligence of an attendant, and if he feels that winter is approaching, or spring coming on, or any other season whatever, he grows desperate; but a Granadino sees day after day run away like so much Croton water, without concern, for there is an indefinite quantity of the same yet to come. The entire absence of clocks and watches aids this illusion. I do not know that in the entire population of this little triangle (1160) there is one of either. Nor is the want much felt. Things go on well enough without. What an absurdity to measure the time a man works, when you are only concerned in the amount of work he does! Some surgeons are wont to cut off arms and legs by the watch, but I never yet heard it proposed to pay them by the minute.

We are at an altitude of about 3540 feet above the ocean. This is below the lowest limit of wheat and the potato. In the rare instances in which we see potatoes or bread, they result from trade with higher lands, where the sugar-cane can not be cultivated, and perhaps not even maize. We can do very well without their wheat and potatoes, but they need the product of the cane both for food and drink; so a commerce between the cold lands and the warm is inevitable.

I know of no reason that our valley should be colder for being higher, unless it is that a greater thickness of the crust of the earth separates us from the central fires; but the fact can not be questioned. Select a beautiful day in the beginning of June in New York, and correspondingly earlier for any point south, and it will show you all the variation to which the thermometer is exposed in this paradise in all the year. To come to figures, the lowest I have ever seen it is 65°, and the highest is 86°, with one exception of 89°. But the heat of such a day is more supportable here than there, for we have only about ten hours of sunshine, preceded and followed by deliciously cool nights.

The weather affects national character, directly by means of dress, and indirectly through agricultural products. The most important of them in this respect is the plátano, which, with bad taste, we represent by the English word plantain. The plantain saves man more labor than steam. It gives him the greatest amount of food from a given piece of ground, and with a labor so small that that of raising it to the mouth after roasting is a material part of it. "New Granada would be something," says my neighbor Cáldas, "if we could exterminate the plátano and the cane: this is the parent of drunkenness, that of idleness."

But among all the influences of which we are to trace the effects, none is more powerful and widespread than that of religion. I must deal with this tenderly; for I am a Protestant, and may be suspected of hostility to the Romish religion in itself. Still, I ought to speak about it honestly, whether I incur suspicion or not; but my theological objections to it as a religion of forms are distinct from my political ones as a monopoly of worship. True it is, that by law this monopoly, which has continued since the first Spaniard entered the country, ceased on the 30th of August, 1853, but, in effect, it must continue till other churches have been brought into competition with that hitherto established by law, and, till lately, the only one tolerated. You must be prepared, then, to find the priests here much worse than in Ireland and Germany, where competition insures a better article, and still less can they compare with those of the United States, which are to the mass of Catholic clergy as the apples in a prize exhibition are to those of our ordinary orchards.

In speaking of the influences of climate, I should have alluded to the common impression that the passions of the inhabitants of the torrid zone are much more violent than those of northern races. Nothing could be more untrue and more improbable than that the blood should flow in fiercer torrents through the veins of the languid sons of the tropics than in our own. All the difference in morality is more than explained by the influence of priestly example, vows of celibacy, and the confessional, and by the want of restraint either from conscience or public opinion.

The remaining influences that modify character here are less in amount perhaps, but still appreciable. Ancestry, or principles and habits handed down from father to son, hold perhaps the next place; and the ancestry of this people has been peculiar. I am constrained to admit that the *Conquerors*, as they here style the first Spanish invaders, were a sanguinary and remorseless race. The best families retain this blood nearly pure, but it is only on rare and terrible occasions that the ancient ferocity comes to light in some popular outbreak. The remaining classes present all possible variations between the white, the negro, and the aboriginal; only this last element is scarcer here than in any other part of New Granada, probably because the conquerors treated the Indians with more severity here than any where else. They found the valley tenfold more populous perhaps than it now is; and what did they do with all the inhabitants? I dare not try to answer this question. Both the Indians and the negroes were of a mild, loving character, and if the negro element has survived the Indian, it may be because they had to buy the negroes, where the Indians cost them nothing but the catching, like the dodo of the Indian Isles.

To make the isolation of this valley the more complete and impassable, its beautiful language, the Spanish, bears the same relation to the principal European tongues that an island does to a continent. An uneducated man may get along very well with one language, provided that be German, English, or French; but to be limited to the Spanish, a language remarkably deficient in periodical literature, in original books, and in translations, is to be cut off from the world by a wall of circumvallation.

Such is the country we have for our study; but what course shall our investigations take? The worst, perhaps, would be the form of a diary, passing repeatedly over the same ground, and detailing such things as strike the traveler's fancy. Such a work is easy of execution, amuses as well as any other, but does not so well subserve the purposes for which travels are generally read. I would much prefer the analytic method of Tschudi, discarding entirely all relations of time, and giving the results in a purely geographical treatise; but I distrust my powers to make such a work interesting, even if readable. I choose, therefore, a middle course. If it is necessary for any one to be precise about dates, and the order of time, or the number of times of visiting such and such places, let him consult the itinerary in the appendix; if not, let him confide himself to the writer, who will bring him here over a way that he might have come.

One word farther as to the persons that will figure in the narrative. It has been the custom of some English travelers in Spanish countries to take great liberties with the characters and circumstances of their hosts. One, for instance, after dining with a former bishop of Popayan, not only speaks with due commendation of the bishop's wine, but also the beauty of the bishop's mistress! To avoid a practice that hardly comports with my notions of hospitality, without, at the same time, depriving my readers of my most accurate and reliable observations, I shall sometimes change the names of persons where I have to say something disagreeable of them. And if, through the officiousness of any meddler, any frailty of a man whose bread (plátano) I have eaten shall become more widely known, I protest that it shall not have been by any legitimate use of my book, and that I would sooner have suppressed a dozen facts than that one should be thus dishonorably used. For the rest, I trust to difference of language, distance, seclusion, and my honest artifices to cover, like the cloak of charity, a multitude of sins.

But, farther, fiction has no place here. I have been eye-witness of all the things that I profess to have seen, and, from respect for the reader, as well as for truth's sake, I will never tamper with facts.

CHAPTER II.

SABANILLA.

First View of New Granada.—Perpetual Snow.—Rio Hacha.—Goajiro Indians.—Santa Marta.—Mouth of the Magdalena.—A Native.—Port Officers, and the Passenger without a Passport.—Sabanilla School.—Collecting the Revenue.—Rotation in Office.

My first view of New Granada was on the 21st of August, 1852. You have here, good reader, one date on which you may rely; remember it well: perhaps you may not get another in the whole book. The sun had not yet reached our horizon, even had there been no clouds in it, when the captain called out that there was land in sight. I did not believe him, but came out to confirm with another observation the strange fact that some men will lie even when the truth would serve them equally well.

I doubted my eyes as much as I did the captain's words, so improbable was what I saw. Imagine a mass of the whitest clouds heaped one upon another in the south, tinged with a delicate rose-color wherever the rays of the sun, yet unrisen on us, could reach them, while deep recesses in other places presented yet the obscurity of night. I look for one unsupported mass, some impossible crag for the captain to explain, but can not find one, and I begin to doubt his mendacity this once.

True, it is not impossible that land should be in sight. Unquestionably we should see it were the horizon clear of clouds, an event we can never expect in the tropics. At a distance of 50 or 100 miles from the coast the mountains are said to rise to the height of 24,000 feet, and, of course, are capped with perpetual snow, but what can they have to do with the unearthly spectacle before me? Once admit that it is but cloud that I see, and the vision takes its place among the sublimest sunrises I ever saw; but call it earth, and Homer would scarce dare invent such an Olympus for his gods.

A strange optical illusion still kept up my incredulity. These masses appeared to be towering up some 10 or 15 degrees, rising out of the clouds resting on the sea at a point that we count the horizon, that is, where the sea disappears from view by reason of its convexity. I took a little sextant from my state-room to measure the altitude of the highest peak, and it gave me but 3° 12′. Even this I doubted till confirmed by the captain's quadrant.

But clouds are not so brief as morning views of snow-capped Andes. It is not on every voyage that this glorious sight is vouchsafed, and soon, too soon, the clouds shut it in forever.

We were now sailing westward nearly parallel with the coast, and opposite us to the southeast was the province of Rio Hacha. Little communication by land has this province with the rest of the world. Around the base of these mountains lives a fierce tribe of unsubdued Indians, the Goajiros. When arms have failed against the savages, the Spaniards have been wont to resort to missionaries to subjugate them. Even these have failed with the Goajiros, who would make the priest load his own shoulders with the things his peons had brought, and thus conduct him to their borders. Still they treated with great kindness a lady who was shipwrecked on her voyage from Maracaibo to Santa Marta, a Señora Gallego, if I recollect aright. I had hoped ere this to secure some letters from her detailing her adventures and the character of the Goajiros, but now fear they will never meet the public eye.

One curious custom of the Goajiros I suspect may have extended to other tribes. A maternal uncle was counted a nearer relative than the father. The reason given by one of them was this: "The child of a man's wife may be his or it may not; but beyond a peradventure the son of the daughter of his mother must be his nephew." I am inclined to think that in some nations of South American Indians, not only property, but also crowns, have descended according to this very unconfiding law.

At length we are nearer shore, and now we can see land that looks like earth, and not like heaven; but it looks desolate enough. It seems to be a bare, dry ridge of mountain, without trees, herbage, water, or inhabitants. Why is it that we expect perpetual verdure in the tropics, and imagine that vegetation, which knows no other rest than from want of water, could possibly attain the freshness of that which has just thrown off the weight of four months' snows, and has so much less time to get its year's growth in? We are expecting impossibilities; but he who approaches Santa Marta near the close of the dry season, as we now do, with these notions, must be disappointed indeed.

After passing a point of land, we looked southeast, and at the bottom of a bay that serves for a roadstead rather than a harbor, we saw Santa Marta. The Cathedral was distinctly visible, rising from a mass of houses, but I had no nearer view.

Nature seems to have denied the interior of New Granada any good outlet for commerce. The Santa Marta people think that there the coast is most accessible from Bogotá, but I can not readily believe it. Occasionally the Magdalena steam-boats of the Santa Marta Company pass the bar of the river and the small space of open sea necessarily crossed to reach the town, and *they say* they do it without danger, but they rarely venture it.

The unfortunate traveler bound for Bogotá, whose impatience leads him to leave his vessel at Santa Marta, has first some leagues to go by land, then to take a canoe or small boat over ponds and through narrow channels, till he counts himself happy to reach Remolino. Brief happiness, if he finds no steamer there! I have seen Remolino, and should judge that a detention there would be worse than a residence in one of our prisons in dog-days. The town, when I visited it, had been recently overflowed—no uncommon occurrence, I should judge, by the eight-inch dike that promises defense to the town from the river.

Santa Marta, I am told, has no good harbor. Though sheltered from the prevailing wind from the northeast, still ships will drag their anchors rather than face the gusts that come down the mountains back of the town. As for piers, where a ship may lie to discharge and take in freight, you must not expect such a thing in South America.

At Santa Marta you leave the mountains, and at length, in following on west, you lose the land entirely if the weather is not very clear. After some hours, a fringe of bushes appears on your left, suggesting rather the idea of a submerged thicket than a shore. At length the ship enters muddy water—she is sailing across the mouth of the Magdalena. The fresh water, even when surcharged with mud, is lighter than sea-water, and floats on the surface; but here may be seen a rare phenomenon. The tawny flood that is spreading over the top of the sea strikes against the south side of the vessel, but can not pass under. In place of it boils up clear sea-water on the north side. It remains unmixed with the fresh water so long as you can see it.

Parti-colored water is a rare sight. He who has once well seen it at the mouth of the Missouri does not soon forget it. He wonders how it is possible for a visible distinction to remain so long between two rivers flowing in the same bed. The limpid Mississippi is quietly flowing south, when, of a sudden, the yellow Missouri bursts in upon it like a race-horse, so that the muddy water seems to gain the centre of the river at a single bound. They boil into each other, still without mixing. Here you see far within the clear water a patch of mud, like a squadron of an adverse army far in advance of the main body of the attacking party; there a piece of clear water refusing either to retreat or mix with the less pure masses around it, till you seem to imagine a moral force within that keeps up the lines of distinction so sharp and clear.

Off the mouth of the Magdalena, the wonder would be invisible but for the intervention of the vessel. You are told that there is a flood beneath a flood, but you could see nothing did not the keel of the ship hold back the water of the river, to let that of the sea come up with the same shades of color, the same contrasts and well-defined lines, as in the Father of Waters.

At length there appears over the low trees a large white building. It is the custom-house (aduana) of Sabanilla. It gives you good hopes of the country to see so fine a building, for it appears, at least, good enough for a second-rate port in the United States.

The flag of our Union is hoisted to call a pilot, and in due time a boat is seen approaching. It is something to see a new face after a voyage of twenty days; but to see one of another race and nation in his own home, unaltered by travel, is enough to excite a deep interest in any one who is just beginning his foreign wanderings. The boat contained the pilot, his little son, and a negro. The pilot and his boy had on enough clothes, and dirty enough, but the negro was half naked, and of a stupid, vacant countenance. I could not refer the other two to any one of the five races of man, but it seemed as if three of them, at least, had contributed to the blood in their veins.

Now the word is given, and the anchor is let go! It is an event in a man's life, when, for weeks, he has been moving, with no visible object to mark his progress or fix his situation, whose ideas of locality have all been cooped into the space of a few yards, to find his ship, so long a world by itself, again part of the great world. Yes; our position is fixed, and what we see now we shall see to-morrow in the same places. We are twenty or thirty rods from a shore that runs north and south along the foot of a low, green hill, covered with sparse woods. On that hill, southwest of us, is the pretentious, unoccupied custom-house, and at the foot a group of sheds, and a little wharf where boats can land; there is none for ships. I ask for the town, and they show me a few acres of low flat land and low thatched roofs two miles south. There is Sabanilla, and the nearest residences of men.

Scarcely had the anchor reached the bottom, when another boat approached, with a more numerous company of health-officers and custom-house men. Contrary to all the predictions of the captain, they pronounced me free to go ashore when I liked. For a fortnight, no occasion had been lost of impressing on my mind that I was to be taken off the ship by a file of soldiers, carried to prison, kept there till the vessel was ready to leave, and then put aboard again. So much was the captain's mind exercised by this, that he declared he would never carry another passenger without seeing that his passport was in due form, and the first item of his report to the collector, of the contents of his ship, was, "One passenger without a passport."

Meanwhile I strained my eyes shoreward to catch the first glimpses of tropical vegetation. I had indeed seen, in passing before the mouth of the Magdalena, some stems of plantains, and masses of Pistia and Pontederia, detached from the low, marshy banks of the Magdalena; but the curiosity excited by this earnest was in no way to be gratified by any thing yet visible in the common-looking woods that lined the hill-side west of the harbor, the Nisperal.

No sign of human labor was visible, save the showy custom-house and its attendant hovels, nearer than the dingy town. What could be the peculiar merits of the favored spot that attracted all the population away from the centre of business? I was determined to see, and got into a boat that was going up there. I found it a piece of salt marsh, a few inches above high water, covered with one-story cottages, built of mud, and thatched with cat-tail flags—Typha. All of them appeared alike, made generally of two rooms, both adjoining the street, one only having an outside door. The unglazed windows, each covered with a grating, built out a little way into the street, the reja, gave it a dreary, prison-like aspect. These projecting rejas let out the head of the tenant, so as to see up and down the street. Occasionally they catch the head of the passer-by on a sharp corner, but not so often as I should expect. A salutary fear of this accident becomes habitual with him.

The town of Sabanilla is as dense as any factory village, and as much more homely than they can be as mud and thatch is worse than brick and slate. Not a tree, bush, or weed is found in the streets; but a few steps brought me to an opening in a fence, where I pounced upon a bush in flower—the first green thing within reach of my hands. It was Laguncularia racemosa, a common Antillan Combretate shrub. I fell at once to dissecting its peculiar fruit. It left a permanent mark on my bright new knife from its corrosive juice.

A little farther on I saw the papaya—Carica Papaya—well translated by the word papaw. Unfortunately, we have applied the name to a very different plant, the Asiminia triloba, that has nothing in common with the true papaw. The branchless tree, ten feet high, with the flowers, often unisexual, clustered about the summit of the almost hollow stem, is at once recognized by any one who has a previous idea of this peculiar genus. I find there are other species of them, but if any of them have the strange property of making meat tender, it is unsuspected here. I found later a Jamaica gentleman, who "knew of a man" who used the leaves to pack meat in for this purpose, but I would like to see the matter made the subject of scientific experiment.

The next thing that caught my eye was huge Cactate stems, on the sand-hill back of the town. They are triangular, and ten feet high. I have never found flowers on them, but one of them must be the famous night-blooming Cereus grandiflorus, or an allied species.

It seems as if all the houses or huts of Sabanilla might be taverns or stores. A remarkable prevalence of bottles and absence of casks strikes you on entering the stores. The first place I went into was a large, almost vacant room, the house, perhaps, of some custom-house officer. I saw an object on the floor that I took for a large monkey at the first glance, but, to my disgust, a second view showed it to be a baby, naked, and of the precise color of the earth of the floor on which it was crawling. A similar specimen of the same species I saw in another house swinging in a hammock, a piece of dry hide being placed under the child.

The next house I entered was formally "placed at my disposition," which simply means that I am welcome. Its inhabitants seemed to be a woman, who may have been a widow (you can never tell widows here); her son, a customs' guard; and Joaquin Calvo, M.D., a custom-house officer. They kindly proposed to procure me a horse to go next day to Barranquilla, distant about eight miles, directly up the river.

Some horsemen rode past while I was sitting with them, and fairly started me to my feet with the flaming colors of their ruanas. Those of the better class may be regarded as striped shawls, woven of thread cotton, with a few inches of seam left unsewed in the centre to admit the head. The name of poncho, by which we best know them, must not be used in some parts of the country, and is little used any where. The heavier article, made of two thicknesses of flannel or blanket, often thick enough to shed water, is called a bayeton. Ruanas may cost from two to five dollars; a good bayeton, an article no traveler should be without, costs about eight dollars. When made of India-rubber cloth it is called an encauchado.

One hut of two rooms had the shop in one room, and the other served as a family room and for the public school. This consisted of about a dozen boys. It is contrary to law to have girls and boys in the same school, and as it is only large places that can maintain two public schools, girls must generally learn as they can at home, or, as is too often the case, go ignorant. I now look at Sabanilla with a more experienced eye, and conclude that it is the meanest town that I have seen in New Granada, and its school is also the poorest. Here I saw naked boys in school. Elsewhere it would not be allowed. The teacher was a mere boy, and the school was almost completely destitute of books. But it is a credit to such a town to have a school at all, when it has no church.

I walked down from Sabanilla to the custom-house wharf. The most striking thing on the way is the mangrove-tree, Rhizophora Mangle, called here mangle. The roots branch out from some way up the stem, and the fruit stays on the trees till some time after the seed has sprouted, and its radicle, escaping the rind of the fruit, hangs dangling in the air over the water and mud where it buries itself when it drops.

I picked up here the acridly poisonous fruit of the manchinael-tree, Hippomane Mancinella. Both this and chamomile are called here manzanilla, a diminutive of manzana, an apple. It may be the poison of the tree that makes it fatal to sleep under its shade, but I should not like to sleep out of doors at any place where it would grow. Here, too, a violently stinging plant of the same order, Cnidosculus stimulosa, had wellnigh "stimulated" my fingers.

The custom-house, as I said, is a beautiful large white building, with an inclined plane leading up to it from the miserable little wharf, to which goods must be brought in lighters. Not a bale of goods has ever traveled up to the custom-house, nor can I see that a single room of it has ever been of use to the nation. Had the money been spent in building a ship-wharf instead of an inclined plane, and a large store-house on the wharf, it would have been of great service to commerce. But other nations have their follies; and one, at least, builds custom-houses where the revenue is less than the cost of collecting.

The custom-house hill would make a fine site for a city but for the want of water. Sabanilla is supplied by boats, that go to a point where the river is fresh, pull out a plug, let in as much as they want, and return with it washing their feet. The supply of eatables is more mysterious to me. I heard of a farm some three miles off; but beyond that papaw and a young cocoa palm, I saw not the first approximation to cultivation.

Under the hill, at the wharf, the low sheds belong to a foreign firm in New Granada, and are rented to the government. Here I saw the collector and inspector passing goods. Their swords and pistols were lying on the table by them, and their attendants were ripping open every bale, broaching every cask, opening every box, and weighing all things, wet and dry. Such is the law. The inspector placed the weights on the scale, and the collector recorded their several weights. If the weights of the several parcels were nearly equal, the vigilance of the officers would relax a little after probing, ripping, and broaching some fifty parcels.

I do not suppose smuggling is impossible at Sabanilla, but its chief difficulty is not in the seal on the main hatch and the watchman on board, but rather in the uninhabited state of the country around the landing. Much, however, may be done by bribery, and many officers will be found open to it. In the short interval that our vessel lay in the harbor, I believe nearly all the officers of the port were changed. The displaced collector asked my certificate that he was not intoxicated when he visited us, and I readily gave it.

CHAPTER III.

BARRANQUILLA.

Ride to Barranquilla.—First Spot in the Tropics.—Lizards.—Mail-carrier.—Town.—Government of New Granada.—Governor.—Prison.—Church.—Boat Expedition.—Bongo.—Poling.—A Night with Bogas and Musquitoes.—Caña de la Piña.—Harbor of Sabanilla.

THE next day was my ride to Barranquilla. I started early to avoid the heat, and took a cup of coffee at the house where they offered me the horse. I never tasted so good coffee before in my life, and I am sorry to say that, in all my subsequent travels, I have not seen another cup like it. There was a fragrance about it that I should like to meet again.

This ride might be called one of the epochs of my life. A botanist feels a growing desire to visit the tropics every time that he examines or arranges plants from the sunny lands. The difficulty of gratifying the desire generally grows with its growth and strengthens with its strength, and remains for life a case of stable equilibrium or equal balance of centrifugal and centripetal forces. In my case the centripetal force had proved too weak, and here I was traversing the space I had so long desired to enter. It was like an illimitable conservatory. The little bead-peas, Abrus precatorius, lay scattered on the ground. They are familiar to many at the North from their beauty. They are of a bright red, with a round black spot. I was surprised not to find more Aroid plants, for I saw but one climbing against the trunks of trees, and of this I barely found one flower. I saw a beautiful passion-flower—apparently Passiflora quadrangularis—picked it, and threw it away again. In short, the day seemed filled to the brink with a tide of happiness which seemed every moment ready to overflow.

It is said that the traveler retains for life a peculiar affection for the first spot where his feet have pressed a tropical soil. Certain it is that my mind turns back with strong longings from the happier scenes that now surround me to the Lower Magdalena. I may be obliged to confess it is a dry, sterile, desolate region, with inhabitants few and far between, and of the ruder cast of Granadinos; but I love it, and always shall, next to the rocky little farm that I first called *home*. But what a contrast!

The farm in Westminster, Vermont, could boast the best assortment of rocks, the finest and tallest snow-drifts, and the most diminutive trout I ever knew, while my new love was blazing with a tropical drought and burning sand, a very paradise for lizards.

The lizards were numerous, but not large. They are not well studied, for there is a strong belief that some of them are venomous. Even Dr. Minor B. Halstead, of Panamá, believes that it was a lizard that bit a man whom he saw dead with a venomous wound; and they tell strange stories of a lizard in Bogotá that they call salamanqueja. *They say* that a body of soldiers drank from a jar of liquor, and all died. They found, on examination, a salamanqueja at the bottom of the jar. I believe them all harmless. They are not easily caught, although their long tail seems to serve no other purpose than as a handle to take them by, just as Cuba or Panamá would be to the Model Republic.

In the day's ride I found no houses except at a small town called La Playa—the beach. It has a small Plaza—the almost universal centre of a Spanish town, with a few miserable huts ranged around it. Sabanilla has no Plaza. Towns here are laid out by authority, and are rarely irregular or straggling. The Plaza is sometimes paved, and is generally the seat of a weekly market, almost always on the Sabbath, so as to secure a better attendance on the church on that day.

Soon after leaving La Playa, I fell in with the mail-carrier. He was on a mule, on a saddle somewhat resembling a saw-horse. The four horns were very convenient to hang things on. On one of them hung perhaps the cheapest pair of shoes possible. They call them albarcas. They were mere soles of raw hide, with a loop to put the great toe through, and perhaps some leather thongs to tie them on with. His hammock helped to cushion his saw-horse, and from one side projected his sword. He was bearer of the weekly mail from Barranquilla to the custom-house at Sabanilla.

In all my ride I saw nothing of the river, and but one field, and that contained nothing but maize. The first symptom of approaching Barranquilla was that my companion stopped by the road-side to dress himself. Next, the heads of palms appeared, the first I had seen in my trip, except a low species. Those now before me were cocoas growing in the gardens of Barranquilla. Like the mail-carrier, I too had my toilet to make; for the lady at Sabanilla had taught me to roll my coat up in my handkerchief, wrapping it in diagonally, and tying the two free corners around my waist. I stopped at the very edge of the town to put it on.

Barranquilla looks much better than Sabanilla, for the houses are all whitewashed, according to law, and some of them are of two stories. I did not at once learn the first radical distinction between houses as tiled or thatched. It seems to be thought that the best possible thatched house is inferior to the poorest tiled one. At this place the thatch appeared to be cat-tail flag —Typha; but farther up, it is of the same leaves as the Panamá hats—iraca, Carludovica palmata. In all cases thatch is called paja, straw.

I came up mainly to deliver letters of introduction from the Granadan minister in the United States to the governor, and to Señor José María Pino, one of the chief merchants of this region. I found the latter in his warehouse, where he received me very politely, offering me a glass of wine. I capitulated for lemonade. He insisted on my spending the night in town, and furnished me a guide to Mrs. Creighton's house, the only decent stopping-place in town, where I paid at the rate of eighty cents a day. Here he did me the honor of a call in the evening.

Barranquilla boasts a private school and a public school for boys, but no school for girls that we could call one. Even two girls, taught in the same house, would make a school, according to the governor's report, which states the number of female schools in the province to be about five, and the number of scholars some twenty or twenty-five. The public schools are all professedly on the Lancasterian plan, and the variations are deteriorations, not improvements. A great clumsy wheel, five feet in diameter, with the written alphabet on its circumference, is the most useless part of the furniture. The teacher here is a young man, but of some education, and, among other accomplishments, can read a little English.

New Granada is divided into one state, two provinces, and three territories; in 1851 these contained one hundred and thirty cantones, subdivided into eight hundred and sixteen districts, and seventy aldeas or hamlets. These last have the local government concentrated into fewer hands than in the districts.

I give the modern political divisions once for all, and the officers, etc. These need a thorough study, in order to understand any thing about the country, for it is useless to try to translate some of them. The national government is called Gobierno, its executive Presidente, and its Legislature Congreso. The provincial government is Gobernacion, its executive Gobernador, and its Legislature Camera Provincial. The executive of a canton is Jefe Político: it has no Legislature. The executive of a district is the Alcalde, and the Legislature Cabildo. The district is Distrito, formerly called Distrito parroquial and Parroquia, or parish. Vice-parroquia is a parish dependent on another for occasional services of its cura, or parish priest, who was, till September, 1853, an officer of the distrito as much as the alcalde is. There are no parroquias nor vice-parroquias now.

To sum this up in a table, it is as follows:

Nacion	Capital Nacional	Presidente	Congreso	Gobierno.
Provincia	Capital Provincial	Gobernador	Camera Provincial	Gobernacion.
Canton	Cabezera	Jefe Político	————	Jefetura.
Distrito	Cabeza	Alcalde	Cabildo	Alcaldía.

Aldea is a partially organized distrito; Territorio is a partially organized provincia: both are thinly inhabited, while the Estado de Panamá has conceded to it more independence from the central authority than have the provinces.

Barranquilla is the seat of gobernacion or provincial government for the province of Sabanilla. I had a letter for the previous governor, and called with it on the present incumbent, Señor Julian Ponce, and had a very interesting call, but declined his invitation to dine with him, fearing to incommode him.

The gobernacion always gives employment to one or two men besides the governor. He was appointed by the president formerly, and appointed the head of the government of the canton (jefe político), and he, in his turn, the chief of the district (alcalde). Perhaps New Granada is governed too much. The gobernacion here occupies the lower story of the governor's house.

This has been the arrangement, but much is changed in the new constitution. The cantones have no legal existence or officers. Many officers appointed are now to be elected. Among these are the governors, who are still to be the agents of the president, though they may be his personal enemies. Thus they may interfere in any national matter, as mails or military movements. I fear this can not last.

I visited also the provincial prison. It has a hall, with two rooms on each side. The keeper (*alcaide*) was at work making shoes. He was the first man that I saw at work on land in the country. If I saw any other work here, it was sawing boards, by two men, using a rude contrivance to elevate one end of the log so that one could stand partly beneath it. The prison was not very full nor very clean, but the most objectionable feature was that the windows of two rooms opened on the street. No prison here is made of any thing stronger than rammed earth or unburned bricks. Of course, the volition of the prisoner must have much to do with the duration of his captivity in such a pen. The laws of different provinces differ as to whether the prisoners shall be fed at the cost of the province. In all, they beg from the windows whenever they can.

My only other call of interest was at the church. I was first conducted to an old priest, who had a sort of study in an upper room of the church. He assures me that things have gone wrong ever since the King of Spain lost his power here. He is the only man that I have found that had the frankness or imprudence to avow this opinion. As the Cuban government is now the only remaining specimen of Spanish domination in the New World, we can not easily appreciate too highly the loss that New Granada suffered at the overthrow of the power of Spain.

We descended to the church, my hat being carefully removed before crossing the threshold. It is a vast shell, with an earth floor. The principal altar is at one end, but along both sides are placed secondary altars that are rarely used for mass. There are no seats in this church. The priest stated that the town greatly needed a larger and better church, though this is but half filled even on special occasions.

The organ particularly attracted my attention. It was of parlor size, but had outside it two huge pairs of bellows that require two men to blow them. The carpentry around the organ was rather coarse, but it was ornamented with a row of trumpet-shaped pipes, projecting horizontally from the front, and the front row of the remaining pipes had faces painted on them, long and narrow, like the reflection of the face from the back of a spoon. The cura has an assistant.

On my return I had quite a discussion with our captain as to whether I was expected to pay for my horse. As he was a professed hater of the Spanish race, I wished to prove him wrong. I waited the result, and was at length asked 80 cents for the bare use of the horse, a lazy animal. It was precisely what the captain paid for a guide, a horse, and his maintenance.

I went again to Barranquilla by water. I was anxious to see the Canal of Piña, that connects the waters near Sabanilla harbor with those of the Magdalena. I agreed with the patron, or captain of a bongo, or gigantic canoe, to take me there for $1 20. The bongo was loaded with goods from the custom-house for some merchant in Barranquilla. It had a little piece of deck at the stern, but the only protection of the goods from the weather was some dry hides that were spread over them. The crew consisted of a huge black man, who was patron, another a little blacker and smaller, and a mulatto. The patron had a little naked son on board. The ordinary watermen are called bogas.

We pushed off from the custom-house wharf. The only means of moving the bongo, besides the patron's paddle (*canalete*), were long poles (*palanca*), to which a fork of a different wood was tied, and smaller poles, to which a hook (*gancha*) had been tied in the same way. The boga applies the fork of the palanca to the muddy bottom, and the other end to the naked chest where it joins the shoulder, and thus gives motion to the boat by walking toward the stern. The rate may be considered nearly three miles an hour. We soon arrived at Sabanilla. At the custom-house the bongo can come up to the wharf, even when fully loaded, and drawing, perhaps, three feet of water, but here we could only come within eight feet of the end. I went through the town for a ripe plantain to eke out my supper, but in vain. There was not one in town. I then returned to the bongo. To go on board, I must either wade, go in a boat, or on the shoulders of a man. I chose the latter, and had my feet wet for my pains. The bogas had not yet appeared. At length one of them came, and told me that he could get me some plantains. I gave him a half dime. He returned and informed me that he found he was *mistaken*, so he had filled a bottle with the half dime.

At length we pushed off. We went to the east, and even a little northward of east, now through narrow channels, now through broader expanses of water, having little or no current to contend with. All the way on our left could be heard the roar of the ocean surf, into which, farther up from Sabanilla, boats are sometimes carried and lost. We were in the middle of one of these broad places about 10 P.M., when the anchor went down with a sullen plunge, and we went to bed. They allowed me the sail for my bed, pillow, counterpane, musquito-net, and roof, and it served its purposes well. Bogas are as unconscious of musquitoes as a rhinoceros. They unrolled pieces of matting, called estera, and slept on them without covering. It is exactly such as is used for matting floors. They wondered where my matting was.

When I waked it was still dark, but we were moving. First we were passing a dark channel almost overarched by trees. At dawn it was through a floating meadow of tall grass-weeds and splendid bulbous flowers. Later, the ground grew firmer and the water more shallow. Then we met a boat fast in the channel. There was another boat behind ours. Those of the bogas of the three boats who wore any clothes took them off, and all jumped into the water and pushed the boats past each other. "And this," said I, as the bogas continued wading and pushing the boat half a mile, "this is a constriction on the main artery of the commerce of New Granada!" The Canal of Piña is cut through soft alluvial ground. It ends within six miles of the sea, and might be deepened sufficiently for the passage of steam-boats for $100,000.

We at length emerged from the narrow channel into the real Magdalena, broad, rapid, and turbid like the Mississippi at St.

Louis, although, even above this, part of its waters had joined the ocean through chasms of the embankment, which prolongs its northern bank so as to carry the river many miles along the coast, as a mill-race carries water along the bank of a river.

Now our difficulties commenced. The poles could not be applied to the bottom of the river. The edge was of floating marsh and drift-wood. With poles, hooks, and the patron's paddle, the problem was to hug the shore and push up stream. Repeated efforts often were necessary to pass a projecting log. Hours were thus consumed in advancing a few miles of capital steamboat navigation. At length we entered another narrow channel, and an hour or two more brought us to the steam-boat, a mile below Barranquilla. Leaving the bongo there, I walked up to the town.

A day or two after, I witnessed the departure of the first steamboat that had left Barranquilla for a month. No hour of starting was fixed, except it was to be "as soon as the passengers had got on board." Accordingly, trunks and packages, on the heads and shoulders of men, were early seen coming down from the city, and, what was to me surprising, four or five carts, although I had supposed there were but two pair of wheels in town. At length the passengers were on board, and the plank taken in at 8. The next operation was to take in a few fathoms of chain and raise the anchor. The next thing was to turn round in a channel no wider than the boat's length. All this took some time. Then came the waving of handkerchiefs, as the boat moved down stream for some hours to the lower end of the island that lies in front of Barranquilla. It arrived opposite the starting-place a little before night.

The only difficulty in the location of a city at Sabanilla is the want of water. The natural difficulty must be much less than at Cartagena, and it can be easily remedied by a steam-pump or wind-mill. The climate must be healthy, I think, and, if agriculture were duly stimulated in the region, there could be no lack of supplies.

The harbor is the western edge of an estuary, into which the Magdalena empties. Like the Mississippi, this river brings down an immense amount of sediment. This causes a bar at the mouth. Here it meets the trade-wind and current from the east, and is compelled to deposit its sediment, not at right angles with the river, and parallel with the coast, but in a direction determined by the combined action of river, wind, and sea-current. Little or no fresh water passes through the harbor. The harbor is exposed somewhat to the winds from the north, and is not deep enough for large vessels. In value it is intermediate between those of Santa Marta and Cartagena, but might be made far more useful than either, were the Canal of Piña opened, as it will yet be.

CHAPTER IV.

CARTAGENA.

Entrance to a splendid Harbor.—A walled City and a finished City.—Consul Sánchez.—Mule Travel.—La Popa.—Turbaco.—Arjona.—The Dique.—Mahates.—How the Duke *did* a Yankee.—Calamar.—A Dance.

THE navigator who sails from Sabanilla to Cartagena has both wind and current in his favor. As he nears its white walls, he wonders to have finished his voyage so soon. He has not finished it. He must pass the town entirely to reach Boca Grande, the large mouth of the harbor. This he can not enter, for it was closed up by a costly wall completed in 1795, because the entrance was too near the city and too wide. This entrance they now would gladly free from obstructions, but the commerce of Cartagena is at present so small, that the measure, though often proposed, has never been attempted.

Still you must proceed to the west, and, passing the Isle of Tierra Bomba, you take in the pilot, and enter the Boca Chica, little mouth; and, passing between two forts, you are in the harbor of Cartagena. Facilis est descensus: it was easy sailing down from opposite Cartagena to Boca Chica; but now the city is out of sight, and you have the wind against you, and you find the voyage longer than you thought a little before.

You anchor at an inconvenient distance from town. Will commerce never demand decent wharves here? What would Boston or New York be without wharves? How would Liverpool dispense with her docks? You land on a boat-wharf as free from commerce, perhaps, as the Battery at New York; passing through a thick wall, you are at last in Cartagena.

It is the first and only walled town I have ever seen. I look at its defenses with amazement. They seem to have cost as much as all the buildings within them. A good, well-equipped railroad to the Magdalena would have cost much less. First, here is an island entirely walled in, except that certain waste grounds, that would have made the wall too irregular in its form, were left between it and the sea. These are not at present worth a dollar to any body. Then there is, southeast of it, another island, the suburb of Jimaní (Gethsemane), that has its wall, its gate, its defenses, and bridge; and then there is, outside of this, the detached fort of San Felipe de Barajas, on Mount San Lazaro, a steep detached rock, in which the works are cut, unfortunately attacked by Vernon in his siege.

I can only speak of these works as a layman. Next to their cost, the most observable thing is the compactness they give the town. Cartagena is finished—has been so a long time; it looks as if it might have been a hundred years. Room is precious within fortifications, so the streets are narrow, the houses of two stories, and the plazas small. Withal, there is an air of neatness about it, notwithstanding that rain-water is sold by the cask, that really does one good to see.

Scarce as space is within the city, the walls furnish an exceedingly delightful promenade. Every where you find water on one hand, and the old, sleepy town on the other. There is another fine walk on the beach, between the walls and the water, where those who do not fear sharks too much may take a nice sea-bath. I saw little use made of either of these facilities, perhaps because my stay was so short. For the same reason, I saw none of the many pretty drives that there are in the neighborhood of the city. If you are to go to the interior, you must here take leave of all wheeled conveyances, unless it may be in Bogotá.

I love Cartagena, and for many reasons. Not the least is, that it is the residence of that model of American consuls, Ramon Leon Sánchez. Mr. Sánchez is an annexed citizen of the United States, having been a Spanish subject in Florida. Speaking both languages with facility, for a long time a resident of Cartagena, an experienced merchant and a polished gentleman, if any thing is wanted to enable him to serve his countrymen, it must be the will to do so, and of this will I have never heard of any one that has yet found him lacking. Never had I more need of a friend than when I arrived in Cartagena without a single letter, for I had not anticipated a visit to this city; but letters would be of little use if all men were like Mr. Sánchez. From all the letters that I carried to South America, there did not result one half so much pleasure or profit as I have experienced in the bosom of that excellent family. Mr. Sánchez has long been consul here. Were the office a more profitable one, it would doubtless, ere this, have been taken from him to reward some maker of stump speeches or puller of wires, who, leaving his family and interests in the United States, would hastily come and gather as many dollars as the length of his harvest would permit.

Cartagena has suffered numerous sieges that I can not stop to enumerate. That by Admiral Vernon in 1741, commemorated in Thomson's Seasons, is the one that will most interest the Englishman or American. The last, in 1841, was witnessed and endured by the family of Mr. Sánchez.

I took leave of Cartagena with great regret, and a strong desire to revisit it, or to meet elsewhere Mr. and Mrs. Sánchez, and the amiable sister of the latter; and my memory of those brief happy days stands in strong contrast with much that I have seen this side of there. To one who arrives here inexperienced in wheelless traveling, the advice and assistance of the good consul is invaluable. It seems incredible that your two trunks will ever be mounted on the back of a mule. You are told to have them even in number, each pair of equal size and weight, and not much to exceed one hundred pounds each; and if you neglect this, dear is the penalty you pay. An article of freight may exceed the ordinary limits, and, with time and money, it will reach its destination, but to the traveler such detention would be worse than the entire sacrifice of his baggage.

Every trunk ought to have a water-proof cap, covering it entirely except the bottom, or, in default of this, it must be encumbered with an encerado. This is a stiff, sticky cloth, water-proof with pitch or paint. It is tied on with a rope that you do not pretend to untie with your own hands. I have paid eighty cents per trunk for encerados and ropes.

You must own the ropes that tie on the encerados. The peons will steal them if they can, for they have a great propensity to stealing any thing of the nature of string. Nothing would be secure from them, from a needleful of thread to a cable. The ropes for the hammocks and encerados are called incorrectly lazo, which means running-knot or noose. Ropes of raw hide, rejo, are sometimes used to tie encerados, and always to tie the cargas to the mule. These ropes are furnished with the beasts. Whip-lashes are made generally of slender rejo, so *the lash* is translated by rejo.

Provisions for the journey are often put in cubical cases of nearly two feet on a side, made of leather, and lined within; these are called petaca. If roughly made and not lined, they are atillos.

Your next concern is to secure cattle—bestias—a term that includes horses, oxen, female mules (mulas), and male mules (machos). If the number you require be five or more, you pay for the number you hire, and the hired man—peon—is paid by the owner of the cattle; if the number be less, the peon is paid for as an additional bestia. Thus four beasts cost you the same as five. It would be difficult to force them to make an exception to the rule, if not impossible. The peon is to feed himself and his cattle from his employer's purse; he is also your servant to bring you water to wash, hang your hammock, etc.; indeed, the limits of his rights and duties are not well defined. At the ferry you pay your fare and that of your baggage; he pays his and that of the cattle, if the boat helps them to swim.

Your peon can not load his mules alone, but only in an emergency will call on you to hold one trunk against the side of the animal while he puts on its fellow and ties them together. A load is called a carga, and its two component halves, tercios. The peon throws his ruana over the mule's head to cover his eyes so that he will stand still. Then he puts on a pair of cushions called an enjalma. Next he brings one tercio or half load, and places it against the animal's side, where some one must hold it while he places its fellow—compañero—on the opposite side, and ties them together.

When all are loaded, it will be prudent for you to see the peon and cargas safe off before losing sight of them. You need not keep with them all day, but it makes a great difference whether you are before or behind them. If you go before, they travel rather better; but it may happen, if you pass at 5 o'clock a place where there is to be a ball or a frolic, that something will happen to some of the cargas that will render it impossible for them to reach the place where you are innocently waiting for them. Your best remedy will be to believe all the peon says, but watch him better next time; and count yourself happy if your bedding do not line his nest on a night you have to do without it, or if you get it again uninfested with bloodthirsty parasites.

You now pass out of the gate into an open space that lies between the walls and the suburb of Jimaní. This you cross diagonally, pass a second gate, moat, drawbridge, and bridge-head, and you have before you, on your left, the sharp rock of San Lazaro, hewn into a fort. Farther on, you have, on the right, a suburb of mud and thatch, and on the left, the high, convent-crowned hill, La Popa, *the stern*, which first caught your eye in coming up from Boca Chica. The convent is deserted, and the place has been the seat of some slack military operations.

Unfortunately for Cartagena, La Popa commands its defenses. To include it would be to double their cost, already a hundred-fold more than it ought ever to have been. Any detached fortification there would be but to make the fate of the city dependent on the taking of it; so it seems to me that it would have been better not to have fortified Cartagena on the land side, but to have invested the cost of the walls in endowing free-schools. I was sorry not to have visited the top of La Popa, but I do not consider that I have yet seen Cartagena.

Next comes a pond that I suspect is brackish, La Laguna de Tesca. Your peon will tell you strange stories of the viviparous fish—manatí—with women's breasts, found there. It is the Manatus Americanus, a mammal. This is Herndon's cow-fish, a staple article of food on the Amazon, but not often caught here. No wonder that its meat is not like fish, for it is no more a fish than a seal or a whale is. Near here I saw a pale-green succulent bush for the first time in my life. When I saw it I exclaimed, "This can be no other than Batis maritima!" The plant is considerably diffused over the Antilles, and I had wondered at not meeting it at Sabanilla. I have seen it since under the very walls of Cartagena, growing in company with the low, straggling, abominably thorny bush that bears the burning beans or nicker-beans, Guilandina Bonduc. Batis was first described by Browne in 1756; but the true nature of the plant has remained an enigma up to a short time before I saw it, when Dr. Torrey discovered that it belonged to the neighborhood of the Euphorbiate and Empetrate orders.

Farther on we came to Ternera, a small collection of houses, near which I gathered the singular flower of Hura crepitans, a large, handsome Euphorbiate tree, with milky juice. The beautiful fruits sometimes reach the States under the name of sand-boxes. They generally explode with a great noise, when there remains nothing but seeds and chips.

Now we leave the flat, level ground, and rise the hill to Turbaco. Probably no spot in New Granada in sight of the sea affords so agreeable a residence as Turbaco. Here the monopod hero, Santa Anna, fights cocks, and waits the moving of the waters in Mexico. Some of the wealthier inhabitants of Cartagena have country-houses here, and, among others, the British consul, Mr. Kortright. Here ends the carriage-road, and you feel as if you might also add, here ends civilization. I had hoped to see some mud volcanoes within four miles of here, and was much disappointed in not being able to stop.

Turbaco is called nearly two and a half leguas from Cartagena. It is easy to translate legua by league, and call it three miles. An old Spanish league, indeed, was three marine miles = 3.459 statute miles, but other leagues have been used from 2.6 miles to 4.15. The common old Castilian legua was 3.4245 miles; the present legal legua Granadina is 3.10169 miles.

Unless you can find two measures given, you can in no case be sure of what league is used. I follow this rule: understand all leagues to be common Castilian ones unless there is evidence to the contrary. A league is an hour's journey of a baggage-mule in good weather, with an ordinary load and no drawbacks. You can never calculate on performing more than this, but you will find a thousand good reasons for making less. So I call Turbaco eight miles from Cartagena.

At Turbaco you turn and take your last look of the sea. Who can tell whether it may not be a last look indeed? So long had I dwelt on the sea, that taking leave of it was like taking a last view of home. To gaze on the fading hills of Navesink was nothing in comparison. At this moment my mind reverts to that last view, in a tropical twilight, with a tenderness that I feel at scarce another retrospect of all my life. An American is scarce away from home in any spot where the tide flows.

A long night-ride, in which a French gentleman in the India-rubber business was fortunately my companion, and unfortunately my baggage was not, brought me to Arjona. As I never saw the place, having entered long after dark, and left it before daylight, I can say little, except that it has a plaza and quite a number of houses, and a posada, or stopping-place, where it was quite difficult to make a supper. We gave our horses post-meat, the usual treatment of hired horses in New Granada. In plain English, we left them tied, starving, as we could do no better. A man who lets you his horse never expects you to feed it more than to sustain life, and the letting of a horse is often prudently coupled with the condition that, if it die from any cause whatever, the loss shall be yours. I would not like to lend or let a horse to a Granadino without this slight provision for the animal's comfort.

Our posada, or stopping-place for the night, was a tienda or small shop. These tiendas may be considered as a house with two rooms, one of which has a counter run across it before the front door, and behind the counter another door, opening into the other room—sala, or parlor, as I will call it. The sala is the dancing-room and sleeping-room, and generally also the dining-room. We ate, as an exception, in a sort of shed, which connected the house with the kitchen.

I had first slept in a hammock in Barranquilla, and I am ready to pronounce it one of the cheapest luxuries known. To read in, by day or night, no bed can equal it. You can vary your posture as you please, on your back or side, diagonally or parallel, and you never find it hard, and I, for one, never tire of it. Many complain that the constant use of the hammock injures their chest, tending to roll them up into a ball;

but I have thus far experienced no such inconvenience. And although they say that there are in this country bed-bugs more formidable than any we know, they never molest one in a hammock; nor do fleas, with all their agility, manage so often to take up their quarters with you as in a bed.

Apropos to fleas and bed-bugs, I propose to do justice to the former when I bring my narrative up to Cartago in this happy valley, but as to bed-bugs I have not seen one. The Cimex lectularius is said not to live at a greater altitude than 5817 feet. Nor have I, with all annoyances, goats included, suffered so much in any night in New Granada as in my penultimate night in our dear native land, when I relighted my candle in the small hours, held it under my tormentors, and, to use the words of a poet whom I can not quote well from memory, I "gave to grease and vengeance" so many of these hateful creatures as nearly to extinguish it. For the convenience of more unfortunate travelers, I will mention that the Spanish call these novelties that disturb our peace chinches. Query: Is it mere coincidence that the same word (derived from cimex) is used in the Southwestern States for these same insects?

Beds are unknown in this country except, so far as I have seen, in Cartagena or near Bogotá. The traveler's usual bed is to lay his bayeton and ruana on the poyo, or bench that runs round the principal apartment of a house—the sala. At the very best, he has a square frame allowed for a bedstead, and nothing more on it than a thickness of the estera—matting used for carpets—laid on a raw hide, stretched as tight as a drum-head. All the addition your host thinks of offering you is a red pillow in a pillow-case open at both ends, trimmed doubtless with some sort of edging or embroidery.

Our bill here was sixty cents for our supper; nothing for the hammock they lent me, and nothing for the posts to which our horses were tied. Early indeed were we on our way, and, had not my companion been a baquiano, as they call a man familiar with a road or with any operation (in law-English, an expert), my great haste would have been bad speed. As it is, some five leagues beyond Arjona represent themselves to my mind as a series of man-traps and horse-traps, with one pond of the most stupendous frogs I ever heard or heard of.

The first thing we shall recognize on the road will be the Dique. So they name a crooked canal that they have laid out from Calamar, on the Magdalena, to the tide-water near Cartagena. I imagine the day is past when such a work could greatly benefit the commerce of the Magdalena, even were it perfected, as it never will be. It has absorbed a great deal of capital, which has shared the fate of most Granadan operations—for I have not yet learned the Spanish word for *dividend.*

This opening is partly natural and partly artificial. Its creation was one of the works of Spanish policy to make of Cartagena (a defensible place) the emporium of the country, instead of suffering a city to grow up at the natural outlet of trade, but a bad spot to fortify. It was destroyed by the same power in the war of independence. It has been partially reopened on a shorter line, making only one hundred and five miles from the Magdalena to Cartagena. Even were the work completed, it would not probably yield enough to keep it in repairs, unless the post of Sabanilla were again closed by law. From near this post boats still go occasionally to Cartagena.

At the Dique is a ferry, where every passer who does not live in the province of Cartagena is obliged to pay a dime. When the canal is low and fordable, as now, this tax is called peaje; were the canoe necessary, it would be pasaje; and, were the water bridged, it would be pontazgo. Its chief use is to replenish the provincial treasury, and to drive off commerce and travel to the rival ports of Sabanilla and Santa Marta. These tolls were once part of the national revenue; now, with great imprudence, they are put into the power of the provinces, and they often, as in the present instance, use them to their own detriment.

Mahates or Mate, as they generally call it, is quite a place, 34 miles from Cartagena. It is cabecera of a canton. It lies on low ground, and the traveler who thinks of stopping over night must be forewarned that the Dique keeps them well stocked with musquitoes. At Arjona there were none. I found a poor dinner rather dear there too.

At Mahates I discovered once the most amusing imposition by which I was ever victimized. I must tell it to you, though you laugh at me. Well, at nine o'clock one night, I leaped off a steam-boat that was about making fast at Calamar, on her way down the Magdalena. Breathless, I sought Joaquin Duque, with a letter for him in my hand. In a quarter of a minute I found him, put the letter into his hands, telling him, at the same time, I was a "cabinet courier" of the United States, and that I must be in Cartagena without loss of time.

"How many animals do you need?" he asked.

"Three."

"Three animals, Catalina," he said, turning to his wife; "quick! find Lorenzo!"

Catalina ran one way, and Joaquin another, and in two minutes more both cattle and peon were engaged.

"Will you start now?" asked the *duke*.

"No; but at three in the morning."

By this time the boat had been fastened, the plank put out, and leisurely up came a Congressman on his way home from Bogotá. He was a personal friend of Duque, and they had a good hearty hug. Then came two more Congressmen, then three more, all friends of Joaquin Duque, and all needing animals for saddle and carga. I had not been any too quick in engaging mine.

I hung my hammock and musquito-net in Duque's house, and slept till three, and then found nobody within call. Daylight came—six, seven, and eight. I stormed, and the *Duke* answered *presently*. The truth was, he had so many animals to get off that he could not find enough. Saddles, too, were wanting, as many of the travelers had brought none. He dared not offend his personal friends by sending me off before them on so frivolous a pretext as that his word was pledged.

But animals (horses and asses—no mules) were assembling, and I took some strange substitute for breakfast. It may have been an enormous quantity of chocolate, with boiled eggs, without bread or any thing else. It did not occupy my attention. I paid well for it—20 cents. Just then Duque inquired if I did not want a *gentle* horse. I replied, "A *gentle horse* for a *cabinet courier*, forsooth! Vaya!" Then I found a man who had a carga and a half was about fixing his half carga as a sobre-carga, a middle load, over the top of one of my light cargas.

I called out, "To whom am I indebted for this present, and what shall I do with it when I get home?" They took it off.

My horse was saddled, and I saw a peon putting my bridle on another horse. I called to him to put it on my horse.

"I know it is your bridle," said the *duke*, "but your horse is not used to such. I will give her the bridle she is used to."

I was too mad at the delay to notice any thing else. We were off at 9. I paid $4 80 each for my carga beasts, and $5 60 for that which I rode.

Well, at Mahates I took off the saddle to rest her a bit, and I was horrified. She was a walking skeleton—skin and bone—minus a good piece of skin on the back.

"Your horse never will reach Arjona," said a by-stander. "She is *destroncada*."

I know of no English for destroncada, but I knew its meaning too well. It might designate the condition a gun would be in after it had successively lost its stock, lock, barrel, and ramrod.

Just then a peon of Duque's arrived. He brought the pleasing intelligence that one of my baggage-beasts had given out, and that one of my cargas was some leagues behind.

"Tell me nothing of my cargas," I replied; "but if you do not wish it to cost Señor Duque all he is worth, do you look me out a horse without a moment's delay."

This was precisely what he was going to do. The price of an animal from Mahates to Cartagena is perhaps $1 50, and better animals at that than at Calamar at $5 60. So the duke gained some $4 by the services of poor Rackabones, who really had gone remarkably well considering her condition. I confess I was angry enough for an instant, but my wrath gave place to mirth when I discovered what sort of "bridle she had been used to." It was no bridle at all, but merely a head-stall with reins attached to it! Duque had got short of bridles for some of his friends who had neglected to bring their own, and, not daring to offer them this thing, had ingeniously borrowed mine.

As to my cargas I never took pains to inquire. I never doubted that it was *not* my beast that gave out, as my cargas were considerably under weight. Either they selected for mine the weaker beasts, or, one of the others failing, they changed him for mine. Now I have told my story, not for the amusement of those who sit at home to laugh at me, but for the benefit of any poor wight that may have to follow my steps. Let such "avoid entangling alliances" when he is in a hurry, and see that his peon has nothing to do with any man with whom he is unacquainted, and particularly let him learn to be, what I shall never become, a judge of horseflesh.

But let us be off from Mahates, a place of dear dinners and cheap horses. We enter next a rolling country, covered with wood all the way to Arroyo Hondo. Here we see the moro, the fustic of the Magdalena. It is, I suppose, Morus tinctoria—a small tree. Sections of the trunk are put on mules and carried to the Magdalena.

Arroyo Hondo is not worthy of the name of a village; but the remaining cluster of houses, bearing the lovely name of Sapo (toad), is altogether poorer yet. There was not another house till we came to Calamar. We are now on level ground. Possibly it is sometimes inundated. Here again is the Dique, with a bridge over it; a well-built lock lifting up from the Magdalena, a guard-lock, and the river itself. This last cheers us. If we can live here till the first steam-boat comes up, we then shall have a respite from our sufferings and fatigues. But I know of nothing you will have to see here except it be some new palms back of the town, and the Spanish moss, that I believe to be the same as that of Mississippi—Tillandsia usneoides. They here call it salvaje.

Fortunately, I have never spent much time in Calamar, but here I witnessed the drollest dance imaginable in the open air. I saw a light down a street running back from the river, and heard a strange thumping of a tamborine, accompanied by vocal exercises, that might be called singing or squalling, as you please. A dense crowd readily made way for me, and I reached the dancers. I found the lights were on tables where they sold cakes, sweets, and rum. The dancers used unadulterated moonlight. An old negro and his partner were in a most interesting attitude. She was dancing *ad libitum;* he, almost inclosing her in his arms, but not touching her at all, was following her motions as he could. He was in a stooping attitude, so as to bring his arms on a level with her waist.

CHAPTER V.

THE MAGDALENA STEAMER.

Steam on the Magdalena.—The Barranquilla.—Mouth of the Cauca.—Lady Passenger left.—Houses.—Bogas and their Women.—Banco and its Ants.—Its Priest as industrious.—Puerto Nacional.—Fertility of Ichthyophagi.—San Pablo.—An opening for Practice.—Water-drinking and Drinking-water.—Geography.—Geographer lost in the Woods.—On a Sand-bar.

STEAM on the Magdalena has a long infancy. Bolívar arbitrarily rescinded the first contract, giving a monopoly of it to Mr. Elbers; a second was afterward given him, which he forfeited by delays in the execution of it.

It has been since open to free competition, but the boats were all owned at this time by two companies. The Santa Marta Company had the government for a partner, and, whenever it overtook a mail-canoe, carried the mail. The rival interests of Cartagena and Barranquilla maintained the other line, which had no aid from government. Both have since gone down, and an English company, which put on boats wholly unfit for the river, and mismanaged them as none but non-residents could do, must probably follow.

Still, the enterprise will succeed whenever it shall be put in the right hands. The fare up is $96 from Barranquilla to Honda, and the returning fare $24. Freight enough can be had for several boats at $19 per ton up, and $16 down.

No happier sight can greet the eyes of a traveler in a dull, mean village like Calamar, on a flat plain, with uninteresting vegetation, than the approach of the steamer he is waiting for. The little naked urchins, clothed in their own skins of nankeen variegated with dirt, shout "*Vapor!*" the women get their bottles ready, and the lords of creation slowly rise from a recumbent posture and walk down to the bank.

It fell to my lot to be passenger in the Barranquilla, then under the command of Captain Chapman, an experienced navigator of the sea with sails, but little versed in river craft. Like the

Mississippi boats, those of the Magdalena have but one story for passengers. The deck belongs to the engineers, firemen, and bogas. These last make capital deck-hands. Their chief is called contramaestro; ours bore the name of Pedro, and a strange combination he was of savage and civilized man. He could talk a little English. You are at once brought in contact with him, as he takes charge of the baggage, all of which he *will* put in his hold. As a particular favor from Captain Chapman, mine was rescued from his clutches and carried up to the cabin.

You should be aware of this arrangement of your baggage before entering the boat. It will often be nearly as much as a thing is worth to get it out of a trunk in a hold that has only a notched timber, at most, for a ladder. If there be much baggage —and every man has a right to two cargas, four trunks—yours may be deeply buried up sometimes, and moved about, from time to time, as unfortunate passengers, seething in that damp, dark oven, with a dim light, tumble it over in search of some stray trunk. These visits to the bodega, as they call the hold, are terrible. You are covered with perspiration, and ready to drop, and at length make up your mind to do without the most indispensable articles rather than go to that purgatory for them.

The Manzanares has a ladies' cabin on the same floor as the deck, and, if there are ladies there, they remain by themselves, and eat with the gentlemen of their company. The Barranquilla has a little triangular space at the stern that bears the name of ladies' cabin. It is very small indeed, but, as they have very rarely any female passengers, they make it answer. We had only two little girls and their servant, and these slept in the principal cabin. There are no berths. They would impede the circulation of air. They give you a cot-bedstead, and, if you need any bedding, you will probably have it with you. In a large boatful there will always be some scrambling for the best places, and, if the captain does not interfere actively, the whole cabin will be obstructed by beds soon after 6. The rule is not to locate any beds before 8. I hung my hammock, with its musquito-net, and had a very comfortable night's rest. The musquito-net of a hammock is a large bag inverted, with a couple of sleeves for the cords of the hammock to pass through.

We are early risers on steamers. We first roll up our bedding, and put it where it will not be in danger of being disturbed. An attendant takes away the cot. Next comes, with us, the washing; but the Granadinos are not in a hurry for this operation, nor is it always essential to them. It is a little difficult to get water, and often more so to obtain a towel, here not called *toalla*, but only *paño de manos.* They are generally made of sheeting, but are embroidered with red at the ends.

You are next invited to take a drink of anisado. Omitting the *d* in words terminating in *ado*, they unite the *a* and *o* into a diphthong like *ou* in *thou.* *Anisado* is thus clipped into *anisáu.* It is a sort of rum, distilled, I am told, from the seed of Anethum Fœniculum, called anis. It is much used on the Magdalena. It takes the place of a cup of chocolate, which is not easily prepared on board at this hour. I have seen coffee used as a better substitute.

Breakfast comes about 10. It is spread in a small space between the cabin and the captain's house, that has a roof over it, but is open at the sides. Among other luxuries, they put on the table some square soda-biscuit, and butter, that is eagerly dipped out with spoons by persons who scarcely know the article by name. It is universally called, in New Granada, mantequilla, a diminutive of manteca, its lawful name, here reserved entirely for lard. There is an infinite variety of stews, of beef, kid, fowl, etc. The most essential vegetable with me was rice, for plantains were dealt out to us with a very sparing hand, while the bogas were denied rice and bread altogether, and compelled to eat plantains.

It was interesting to see the bogas preparing their dinner. The beef they used is cut up, when on the carcass of the ox, into ropes of meat, that are rubbed in salt, and hung on a pole to dry. This they call tasajo, and a pile of it is enough to sicken one by the mere sight of it. This they cut up in pieces, and stewed in a large iron pot mounted on three stones on a fire built on deck. Three stones thus arranged—tulpas—are the ordinary fire-place of the peasantry here; in a boat they are, of course, placed on a box of earth. They threw in pieces of green plantain till the disgusting broth threatened to run over. When done, they used the carapax of a turtle for a platter, and dipped out the mess, and attacked it with fingers and wooden spoons, till soon they would be scraping the ribs of the turtle. Nothing could sicken me more unless it were a cannibal feast; but one of the passengers told me he would rather have a part of their dinner than of ours.

Fish is a popular food here, but seen rarely on the boat; it is too cheap. On the rivers it is only surpassed in cheapness by plantains. It is supposed, contrary to the opinions of Dr. Mussey, that fish-eating tends to increase the population. The captain showed me a passenger, a resident of Remolino, who looked as if he might live to see his progeny greatly increase, telling me that he had already some twenty children by the same wife, and that this fecundity was owing to the ichthyophagous habits of the family!

We have not yet been over the whole boat. The captain's house is a little room, with two little closets, between the dining space and the chimney. The dining space would accommodate about twenty, but they seldom have so many passengers. There is a considerable space of open air around the chimney, and then succeeds the pilot-house. The pilots are picked out from among the bogas, and are utterly incompetent for their duties. The captain and the engineer divide the pilot's responsibility between them. The pilots are chosen because they know the river, its rocks and channel, but the engineer keeps a look-out, and stops and reverses without waiting for orders to do so. Forward of the pilot-house is a large space covered with awning: this is the general sitting-room of the passengers. They sometimes annoy the pilot by cutting off his look-out, or, rather, he annoys them by calling on them to move.

The engineer has a little house of his own down on deck. His name was Salt, and he was a man far superior to what we expect of such a post. On another boat, whenever it was lying still, we had the pleasure of the company at table of the American engineer, his English mate, and his Irish mate's assistant, together with a nice-looking negro that was employed on the boat in some capacity. The captain can not put himself high above his engineers when they can command nearly equal wages and need equal abilities; but they err exeeedingly in taking captains that have no river experience, good seamen on merchantmen, but who have never seen Council Bluffs.

Dinner, when it comes, is but a repetition of breakfast. It is hasty judging of national character by the conduct at the table of a steam-boat, especially when so many nations are represented as here. I have seen boats on Western waters with as much piggishness at table; but it could hardly be worse served. Richard, the steward, was a well-meaning Jamaica negro, but his two assistants are very stupid Indian boys. I heard a passenger scolding one of them, and I asked him what he had done. He replied, "I called for a knife, and, as he was bringing it, he used it to scrape his arm with; when I complained of that, he wiped it on his pantaloons." It is exceedingly difficult to secure good waiters. Ours can hardly understand good Spanish, or make themselves understood.

The river banks present little variety. It seems much like the scenery or want of scenery of the Lower Mississippi, but the water, I think, is never so low as to show such elevated banks as we see there. We conclude, then, that at high water the Mississippi immensely exceeds the Magdalena in depth. It is also wider, and its width is more uniform, and its channel far more crooked. After this lapse of time I can recollect no difference of color between the Magdalena and the Lower Mississippi. We make no stops except for wood, or so rarely that each one will be chronicled as an event.

On Wednesday the boat set out from Barranquilla, and tied up for the night at Remolino, the station of the Santa Marta boats. They call the distance 6 leagues. My rule makes it 21 miles; but if the leagues are new ones, it is much less. They attribute the smallness of the journey to a late start, and delays in getting out of that little arm of the river on which Barranquilla stands. On Thursday, before reaching Calamar, they came 8½ leagues, say 28 miles.

They wood but about once a day, and at wood-piles of their own. A wood-agent on board discharged so much of the clerk's duties as he was going up, that I long mistook the real clerk for a passenger. At night they often tied up to a bank far from any house. We come to more signs of cultivation as we ascend the river.

On Friday we stopped at a small town on the west bank. We found here the head of the distrito represented by a barn-like edifice, with a roof of thatch and walls of sticks, designed to let in the light and air, but keep out all animals as large as a hog. In this last office they failed for want of a door. So I saw in this very prison a mother with about the same number of offspring that John Rodgers had. The grunting parent of little swine lay stretched in the abundant black dust, contented with her lot. Happy the prison that witnesses no sadder scenes! But when a biped is detained here, it is, of course, with his locomotive apparatus locked in between two logs—the stocks. So, as a man that does not possess "the thumb and first finger of the right hand" can not vote, a man that has lost both legs can not be imprisoned here until a new apparatus is invented to hold him.

A group of various colors, all ages, and both sexes, and in every possible stage of nudity, gathered on shore to look at us. From these I select the wife and child of a fustic-cutter as a favorable example. She is carrying two baskets of ivory-nuts in positions which the reader is challenged to imitate. The sleeveless garment that covers as much of her as she thinks necessary is called a camison, an augmentative of the word camisa, as it is nearly twice as long as that garment, which would be useless without another garment to eke out its scantiness. There would be more fidelity, but less beauty, had the artist colored their bodies according to nature, diversifying the skin of the little one with the parti-colored patches with which Nature and the accidents of the day had combined to adorn it.

THE FUSTIC-CUTTER'S FAMILY.

One of the passengers has pointed out a plantation of cacao chocolate-trees. But I am astonished at the boundless contiguity of shade that is interrupted here and there at long distances by the merest bits of patches of plantains or cane. When the white man came to the New World to curse it, the banks of the Magdalena are said to have been one continuous village from Sabanilla to Honda. The cupidity of the Conquerors exterminated its happy inhabitants.

On Saturday morning a passenger pointed out what I should have taken for an arm of the river coming in at the foot of an island. But, though the color was the same, the surface was strewn with fragments of vegetation, when none were descending the Magdalena. It was the Cauca, escaped from its long and terrible conflict with the rocks above, and now pacified to the same stately gait as the Magdalena and the Mississippi.

By Saturday noon we reached the head of the island opposite Mompos, formerly spelled Mompox. This is stated as 40½ leagues from Barranquilla, say 148 miles in four days (for we went no farther that day), or, throwing out a day for hinderances and stoppages, 50 miles a day.

Mompos is called the hottest place on the river. Up to here some little influence of the sea-breeze is felt, and above, the increase of altitude diminishes the heat: here the sum of these restraining influences on the sun's power is at a minimum. The population is about the same in number as at Barranquilla, but very different. It is a very old town, and a very religious one. The churches are quite numerous, and in a far higher condition than the solitary barn-like edifice in Barranquilla. The schools are not correspondingly advanced, though a girls' school of the higher class was to open the day I left (Sunday).

I visited the cemetery, one of the best in New Granada. The iron fence in front of it is of Granadan workmanship, and was much admired by Bolívar. The inscription over it signifies, Here are the limits between life and eternity.* There is within it a very small chapel, as there is in every cemetery of the least pretensions. Most of the best tombs were brick vaults, called bóvedas, built like ovens, with the foot against the wall. Some of them are beautifully set off with miniature steeples.

* Aquí confina la vida con la eternidad.

There are some monuments in the ground also, but none of either are of a high class of merit.

Mompos is a town of jewelers and bogas. It stands on an island. Perhaps its insular position, making so much land accessible to it by canoes, has been the origin of its greatness. The steam-boat landing is at the upper extremity of the town, above the head of an uninhabited island. Farther down, in front of the older part of the town, is the ordinary landing of market-boats. An open space adjoining is protected on the river side by a wall three feet high, the use of which I can not conjecture. It is the market-place. I dread the description of the markets of New Granada, and of all that I saw in this I will mention only the fruit of the Anacardium occidentale, a huge tree called caracoli, which we may translate cashew. It is a kidney-shaped nut, with an acrid milk in its rind. The stem of this nut becomes a mass of pulp longer and smaller than a pear, but it is sour, astringent, and disagreeable.

At this spot I once witnessed an exciting scene. A French lady was going up the river in the steamer Nueva Granada to join her husband in Bogotá. A French family with which she was acquainted was descending, on their way to "la belle France." She came on board the Manzanares to chat with them, as the boats lay side by side all night. They talked in the morning till, before any of them were aware of it, her boat had left and was beyond hail. Poor woman! She had not even a bonnet to her head nor a dollar in her pocket. Two remedies were suggested: one, to take a canoe and follow after the Nueva Granada with the vain hope of overtaking her. The other appeared more feasible—to take a horse and ride up on shore, as there was a slight bend in the river above; but there was no horse at hand. Hundreds became interested in her case, and I in their sympathy. She was unknown and a foreigner—nothing but *a passenger left.* It might have moved the mirth of a crowd on our docks, but here all were anxious. For half an hour nothing else was thought of, and all eyes were turned up the river. At length the Nueva Granada appeared round the point, and one universal *viva* broke from the anxious crowd. Whether you take this as a testimony in favor of poor human nature, which has many amiable traits in common with that of gregarious animals, or in favor of Granadan nature in particular, it is honorable to the Momposinos.

Here we saw the last of certain loaves of bread more than a foot in diameter, and about a quarter of an inch thick, very white and tender, but quite insipid. They are cassava, made of the starch of a poisonous Euphorbiate root, the Manihot utilissima. The root also comes on the table quartered and boiled, under the name of yuca, but is not to be confounded with the Liliate genus Yucca. It is a slow-growing herb or herbaceous shrub, and is nearly a year in coming to perfection. It rarely flowers, and I have never seen them digging its roots. For a substitute for flour, it is grated and then washed in cold water.

I went into two gardens in Mompos, and was surprised to see so many familiar things. The most universal was the common balsam or lady's slipper of our gardens, Impatiens Balsamina. I saw the Oleander in flower and fruit, and but one new thing, a Polygonum, which they call bellisima, a climbing vine with a large, permanent petaloid calyx. It would be a splendid acquisition to our gardens.

These gardens were the courts of two-story houses. Most of the plants were in pots around the court or patio. Perhaps, as these were the first regular houses I was in, I may as well describe them. A house with but one entrance from the street is called a casa claustrada. That one grand entrance is the porton, and the space that leads to the inner door is the zaguan. The zaguan is always paved. The pavement is often of brick. Sometimes it is of small stones, with mosaic figures in it of vertebræ of oxen or swine. It leads into one corner of a square space within the house that has no roof. In the Bible this is called the court, and here the patio. A walk—the corredor—runs entirely around it. The corredor is separated from the patio by a balustrade called pretil. The rooms generally open into the corredor, and only the front has windows that do not look into the patio. If the house be of two stories, the stairs, which are of brick edged with wood, are placed in a recess in one corner of the corredor. In a two-story house, casa alta, the lower rooms facing on a street are either used for stores or rented to poor people, and then they have no connection with the patio. These families, who have no rights out of their narrow rooms save in the streets, are a nuisance to the neighborhood. Poor things! decency is a luxury beyond their means.

No houses have more than two stories. The casa baja—one-story house—is more common and more convenient, if not damp; but the casa alta is more pretentious, and is preferred. Another radical distinction is into tiled and thatched houses. Thatch is cooler, but exposed to fire, and sure to decay and let in the rain when you are unprepared for it. Tile is called teja, and in the plural tejas or texas. Thatch is called paja, straw, because in Spain it was made of the culms of grasses. Here it is generally of the leaves of a pandanate plant, Carludovica palmata, which bears the names of iraca, jipijapa, and nacuma. The so-called Panama hats are made of the young leaves of this plant, which are split fine and dipped in boiling water to make the shreds cylindrical.

These hats are generally a week in braiding, and the fineness and price are in proportion to the skill of the braider. The average price, as first sold, is estimated at eighty cents. The finest have been sold at $50, and even $100. A hat of this kind should be called by metonymy *thatch* rather than "*tile.*" The mature leaves are sold standing by the proprietors of the ground for thatch. They spring from the ground on smooth petioles eight feet long. The blade looks like that of a palm leaf, but the flowers have a striking resemblance to ears of maize. I know of no warm lands in New Granada where this useful plant does not grow.

We left Mompos about 8 on Sunday morning, instead of 6, as had been intended. They often have to hunt up slack and careless passengers who would otherwise be left. Such delays astonish, amuse, and vex. We took in tow a champan—a large flat-boat with an arched thatched roof. It had its crew of bogas. Their women came down to see them off. As they sat on the shore, I was struck with the fact that their skirts were all blue. I soon found that this color is almost universal in New Granada among the lower classes, whether from taste or from the abundance of indigo I know not; but this row of women probably had cause for looking blue. It is likely that they had danced all night, and mayhap attended mass this morning, and now had come down to take farewell of the men whose last cuartillo they had helped spend, and who were now taking to the river for more money to be spent in the same way.

Before the day of steam, it used to be impossible to engage a crew from below to go above Mompos, nor would any from above go lower down, so that every champan was delayed at Mompos till a new crew had been shipped, provisioned, and got off with no small ado.

A little above Mompos is Margarita, on the same large island. A more paradisaical place to look at I have not seen in New Granada. There is no clump of houses, but a long street of many miles, with houses on the west side of it fronting the river, and buried in orange-trees. In the middle of this long succession of ruralities stands the church. To add to the beauty of the scene, every few rods, gathered on the very brink of the river, were groups of little sons of Adam and daughters of Eve, in all stages of dress, from that before the fig-leaves to that in which modest painters drape their figures. Margarita is about fifteen miles above Mompos. The population of the district is 1827.

More than thirty miles now pass with no noticeable place, but amazing multitudes of children at the water-side under the green trees. Then we come to Banco, on the east side of the river, fifty miles above Mompos. Here we arrived in the afternoon, and stopped to wood. A large, unfinished church, roofless and floorless, filled with vegetation, stands as a monument of ambition, and perhaps to date the decline of Romish power.

Here I saw a great curiosity. It was a long procession of ants, every one with a bit of green leaf in his mouth. I understate the matter. There ran through the grass a well-beaten road, like a sheep-path, six inches wide—a very Cumberland road for ants. It was thronged with busy travelers, all of whom were hastening from home, or returning with about half an inch squaie sheared out of a leaf. I followed on to see their nest. It was curious to see their broad highway passing under logs, stones, and brush-heaps. I followed it for a long distance into the woods, and then gave up in despair. These ants are called arrieros—the same word that means muleteer. They are a terrible pest. It is thought that ant-eating animals generally reject this species, on account of four strong, sharp projections on the body. They can carry a grain of maize, and I am sure that to load a whole colony would demand many bushels. Woe to the orange-tree that they have determined to shear of its leaves! The best, if not the only defense, is to make the trunk inaccessible to them by water. Some even manage to surround their house with a stream of water, and others are driven to despair by domiciliary visits, clearly in violation of the Constitution of 1843, but which neither parchment nor architecture have strength to resist.

I was once sitting in the evening in a house near Tuluá, and fancied I saw something whitish moving on the floor. I examined, and found a broad stream of rice flowing from a large jar under a bed; each grain was in the jaws of an arriero. Long before morning the jar would have been empty, for the diligent thieves work night and day, without even stopping Sunday. The only hope for the rice was to hang it up in what the sailors call a true-lover's knot by a hair rope. In the end, the jar fell and broke, and the enemy bore off the contents. But, on the whole, I am surprised that so resistless an enemy should do no more damage in a country.

I saw where the ants' highway crossed a human foot-path. Of course, many of the little folk must be crushed under the feet of the lords of creation. There their green loads were left, for no ant picks up the load of another. I found that if the antennæ of one of these ants were removed, he no longer had the power of finding his way. Whether it is by smell, or by some analogous sense, I know not, but it is not by sight. I have effaced the path of ants with a little chocolate oil, too little to impede the feet of the insect, and only for an ant's length in extent. On each side were gathered a crowd, at a loss to find their way, although their antennæ could nearly meet in the middle. At length some formic Columbus set the example, others followed, and the way was re-established.

But let us go back to the boat.

"Do you see that handsome young man—*bueno mozo*—leaning against the post?" asked a fellow-traveler.

I looked, and saw a nice young man, with a sort of stock on. It is called sotacuella. It is a plain parallelogram, about two inches wide, more fit for a badge than any thing else, and is often, if not always, of what is called worsted-work. This, and the tonsure—a carefully-shaved spot on the crown as large as a dollar—are intended to be permanent marks of the sacred position of the wearer.

"Well," he continued, "that is the Cura of Banco. Young as he is, they tell me that he has twelve children that are known to be his."

And a friend that passed Banco some time after mentioned incidentally that he witnessed the baptism of a new-born child of the cura there.

Let not the reader start with incredulity, nor turn with a disgust unmingled with pity from the natural explanation of this phenomenon. Let us bear in mind, in the first place, that his crime here is not disgraceful in an unmarried man, be he clergyman or layman. Second, that the anticipation of a chaste marriage is one of the main safeguards of virtue in either sex. I was talking with an intelligent man on this point, and he laughed heartily at a story I told him. It was of a man who had reached the age of eighty without ever having been outside of the gates of Bagdad. The calif, professing a desire to have a proof of the tranquillity of his reign inscribed on a tomb, forbade his ever leaving the city on pain of death. Early the next morning, he sent to inquire for the octogenarian, but he had run away during the night. Generally, the young aspirant for the priesthood is no novice in the school of debauchery, but his very vow of chastity would insure its violation, if he were so.

Again, the confessional is the cause of this evil perhaps even more than the celibate. The priest is to know the sins of his flock both in deed and of thought. If he suspects a timid one of passing over in silence what she ought to confess, it is his duty to question her, and hers to answer. The Protestant pastor can not take the first step toward undue familiarity without turning his back on his professional duty. The Catholic priest may nearly have completed the ruin of a soul committed to his charge before even he himself is fully conscious of the nature of his designs.

Lastly, the position of the female is by no means hedged about by those stern laws of decorum established among us. Her sin brings her into no lasting disgrace, no total exclusion from society. I should judge that the shame of her position is more like that of a young man in New England, or possibly even less.

So, take it for all in all, a chaste priest here must be an exceedingly rare phenomenon. It would be scarce possible for human ingenuity or satanic malice to place a man in a position where his fall would be more inevitable or irrecoverable. I have asked two persons just now what proportion of the priests are unfaithful to their vow. One replied, "About 99 per cent." I knew him to be a friend to the priests. I knew that the other was not, and his reply must be received with a grain of allowance. It was, "Of the secular clergy (parish priests), 98 per cent.; of the regulars (monks), 102 per cent. Thus," says he, "the excessive licentiousness of the monks is enough to offset any casual instance of chastity in the seculars."

Nor is this liberty of the priests always ill received by the people. A woman below here was expressing her horror at the idea of a married clergy, and I asked her whether she would prefer the Banco priest to a married man faithful to his wife. She replied, "Yes; for the sacraments from the hands of a dissolute priest would retain their validity, but not from those of a married one."

In these days the cura of the isle of Taboga, near Panamá, has been making arrangements to avail himself of the new law of civil marriage. He has lived with the woman he wishes to marry many years, and they have children. All this has excited no complaint, for men consider their families safer with a priest that lives so. But the first step toward legal marriage has excited a great hubbub. Even the Panamá Star came out with a leader in English against him. And, to crown all, the Substitute for the Bishop of Panamá, who is in exile, informed him that he would depose him if he proceeded, so the poor couple came to the conclusion that they must go on as before.

I hear no complaint from the people of the unchastity of their priests. Probably they act on the principle of Æsop's entangled fox, who would not have the half-sated flies driven away lest a hungrier swarm should open new avenues to the vital flood. Many years since, indeed, a priest in Bogotá had a peculiar *penchant* for innocent and artless girls. When he was found to have brought trouble into five or six of the first families of the capital almost simultaneously, their indignation broke out against him, and he was sent to Rome to be judged. When sufficiently penitent or sufficiently punished, he was sent back to exercise his sacred functions in Cartagena.

But I am tired of this painful topic, which, however, I could not honestly pass by in silence. The steamer is off at last from Banco, and the motley throng at the landing has again given place to the magnificent, interminable forest.

Up the stream we go. Settlements become thinner, and the groups of children rarer and smaller. At last we stop and make fast to the bank. The forest is so dense that there is hardly a place for the boga to set foot when he leaps ashore to make fast. Here grows an immense quantity of a Heliconia, called by the people Lengua de vaca—Cow-tongue. It is of that group of families including the plantain, arrow-root, and ginger. This is the most frequent genus, with those broad, horizontal, veined leaves, which, with those of the Palms and the Pandanates, are the only striking marks that the scenery, of which it makes a part, is certainly tropical.

On again the next day. All day we go without stopping except to wood. I can not understand how these fertile banks can remain, washed almost weekly by the waves from steam-boats, but without commerce, and nearly without inhabitant. No American would have anticipated such a state of things, so do we cling to the maxim of political economy that travel begets traffic. The first change in the passenger-list was in the addition of our names at Calamar. Next we lost our little girls and their nurse, and some other passengers, at Mompos. We may have added a name or two there. Now we have reached Puerto Nacional, or Puerto Ocaña, as it is often called, and we must suffer some losses, one of which I shall long regret.

It is that of Señor Gallego and his son Ricardo. Señor Gallego was a political exile from Venezuela, perhaps Governor of Maracaibo under Paez. He is going to establish himself at Cúcuta, on the very edge of Venezuela. He was coming from Curaçoa, and had applied in vain for permission to come the nearest way and bring with him his family, who are at Maracaibo. He has before him some severe land-travel—40½ miles to Ocaña, 71½ to Salazar, and 100 more to San José de Cúcuta.

We stopped in an open field at a distance of three fourths of a mile from the town of Puerto Nacional. There is a deserted house at the upper end. I made the circuit of the field, where I found a climbing fern of a genus occasionally met at home; it was Lygodium hirsutum. A little way above the field was the mouth of a small river that determined the site of the landing at the nearest good bank. The steward (whom I intend to immortalize a few pages farther on) had started in a boat up the little river to the town before I was aware of it. I walked up half way, and was rewarded with a number of curious plants; but it was time to return before coming in sight of the town, so I only saw the *port of the* "*Port* of Ocaña."

President T. C. Mosquera states that he has repeatedly seen the thermometer at Puerto Nacional at 104° in the shade—the highest he has ever seen in New Granada. This he elsewhere gives as the *mean* temperature, although he has stated 86° 6′ as the highest mean temperature of New Granada. Codazzi gives 81° for the mean temperature at Puerto Nacional, which I think is none too low.

Here would be a fine chance for an industrious negro to enrich himself in the ivory-nut trade. These nuts are not the fruit of a palm nor a tree, but of a stemless Pandanate, with leaves like the cocoa-nut tree. It is unisexual, and the staminate plant is represented on the following page. The fruit grows near the surface of the ground, and at Sabanilla, where most of it is exported, it costs about two cents a pound, and ought to sell for twice that, at least.

The figure placed beside the plant to mark its size is a native of the banks of the Magdalena in full dress. He is an approximation toward the mestizo—half negro and half Indian, but neither you nor he will ever know the exact proportions in which the blood of three races are mingled in his veins. His hat is called, as to its shape, raspon; as to its material, de palma, rama, or cuba, being made from palm-leaves, and not of jipijapa. In structure it is de trenza, being braided in a strip and sewed, as many are at the North. If you disdain to call the rest of his dress pantaloons, it must be called tapa, which term, howev-

IVORY-NUT PLANT.

er, designates any quantity less than this, down to the size of half a fig-leaf. In his right hand, with his paddle—canalete—he holds his machete, which he can not do without, and which he is too lazy to belt around him. The humble attempt at a tassel in which the sheath terminates teaches us that man, even in his most primitive state, loves ornament.

The machete is not for defense against either man or beast. He cuts the tangled vines with it as he traverses the forest. It is his axe. This, with his canoe, lines, hooks, and nets, are all his stock in trade. Add to what is here enumerated a camisa and a hammock, and you have his entire wealth. He wishes no more. His fish has cost him no more trouble than to go out and dig a hill of potatoes. His plantains come easier still.

Why then should he work? Indolent and amiable, he might be made a good citizen by properly taxing and educating him. Armed as you see him with the machete, he never fights unless driven to it by the extreme of outrage, and then only in a mob —never alone. But when a Granadan mob is once thoroughly aroused, it will commit great outrages. He loves, perhaps not wisely, but too well, as I should infer from the census of 1851, which records that, in the distrito of Puerto Nacional, there were 32 married women and 67 births that year. "This great fecundity," says Ancísar, "is to be attributed to the vast quantities of fish they consume." The former marriage-fee of $6 40 is said to have caused much illegitimacy.

Now comes another entire day, with only one stop in the edge of the dense forest for wood. Above here no steamer can safely run at night. At dark we made fast to the western bank in tall grass, where they cautioned me against snakes, and I knew no better then than to heed their counsel. I succeeded, however, in bringing down a stem of caña brava, which should mean *wild cane*. It is a gigantic grass, the stem of which is herbaceous and not hollow. Sections of it, when young and juicy, make admirable pickles, crisp and tender, having no taste except what they derive from the vinegar and other condiments. The ripe stems serve to make fences and houses, being more than an inch in diameter. When in fruit, the panicle at the top of the stem is of great beauty, particularly when the wind carries all the peduncles to one side, waving them like the streamer of a lance. The whole height of the stem is from 12 to 20 feet.

I have said nothing about the alligators; but now, as we are soon to take leave of that abundant and interesting animal, I must give him a paragraph. The caiman is an animal of the same genus with the crocodile and the alligator. They infest the middle Magdalena to an incredible extent, and in the lower part they are as common as the alligator is in our Southern waters. They disappear entirely before reaching Honda; but on the sand-bars here there were sometimes half a dozen to be seen at once. Swimming is not to be thought of; and even women washing on the shore, unprotected by a fence, are sometimes carried off.

Musquitoes also reach a maximum in the middle Magdalena, and disappear entirely before reaching Nare. As *mosquito* means gnat, I did not learn the Spanish for the larger torment to which we give that name (mis-spelling it) till the seventh month of my journeyings in New Granada. It is zancudo—long-legs.

Next day we came to San Pablo, one of the most considerable places on the river. It is about seventy-four miles above Puerto Nacional, and two hundred and one and a half miles above Mompos. We stopped some time on account of some accident to the engines. The place seems larger than Banco, and far more pleasant than any little place on the river except Margarita. The steward here attempted to buy some cocoa-nuts, but the owner thought it more agreeable to lie in his hammock than to climb for them. The difficulty was arranged by a boga from the boat climbing the tree, and the luxurious proprietor secured the *utile* without sacrificing the *dulce far niente*. I drank the milk of one of these nuts, but it did not please me. It was insipid, with little or none of the peculiar flavor of the nut, but rather resembling milk and water when the water preponderates. I might have formed a different judgment of it had I been suffering with extreme thirst. On the whole, the cocoa-palm—Cocos nucifera, coco—has seemed to me ornamental rather than useful in New Granada; but the tree should only be judged of by the sea-shore, for it leaves the level of the sea with reluctance, and is the first useful plant that forsakes man in his ascent of the mountains.

Here too I met, outside of the town, an abundance of a fruit-tree, smaller and more slender than an apple-tree, with a smooth bark like the button-wood (Platanus occidentalis), and a fruit about the medium size of an apple, crowned, like it, with the remains of the calyx. It is the guava—Psidium pomiferum—called here guayabo, and the fruit guayaba. As a general thing, the names of trees are masculine, and end in *o*, while the fruits are feminine, and end in *a*. Thus an orange-tree is naranjo, and an orange naranja. The name of a place where things grow ends in *al:* thus this guava orchard is a guayabal. I never saw or heard of a naranjal, for no man has orange-trees enough to deserve the name. The interior of a guava is hard pulp, full of seeds, surrounded by a harder seedless portion. Both are eaten, and often also the skin, though this is generally rejected, and sometimes also the outer portion. There are other Psidia here, but this is the most abundant fruit in all New Granada. I have never seen it cultivated, nor is it eaten extensively, except in jellies and conserves. Such preserves are sold put up in square boxes which might hold a pint, and which looked as if they might have been made with a broad-axe. The instrument used in their construction was probably a cooper's adze. The fruit is eagerly eaten by swine, and is often so abundant as to be of importance on this account.

Another small tree attracted my attention, perhaps the only rosaceous plant of the low country, or tierra caliente. No English terms satisfy me for the four gradations of altitude, tierra caliente, tierra templada, tierra fria, and páramo. The cessation of the cocoa might mark the upper limit of tierra caliente, the banana may cease with the tierra templada, and barley and potatoes with the tierra fria. The uncultivable land above is páramo. Now there are many blackberries, the strawberry, and some species of cratagus and spiræa in tierra fria, and I have even found a blackberry down to the edge of the tierra caliente; but here was a rosaceous tree belonging to tierra caliente only. It was Chrysobalanus Icaco, here called icaco. It is a plum, used in one of those innumerable kinds of sweetmeats called dulce. I described the flesh of the preserve as cotton and sirup, and my hostess suggested that a third ingredient was atmospheric air; but, after disposing of the sarcocarp, the endocarp easily resolved itself into three valves under a gentle force of the teeth, leaving the seed in the mouth, a miniature almond, on which alone, I think, the icaco relies for the popularity it enjoys.

Just as I was leaving this tree, after our long detention was over, a man came to me to prescribe for his sick wife. I was glad that the summons of the boat saved me farther excuse; but, if a man aims at popularity here, he might well bring with him a small stock of medicines, and particularly those used in mitigating the penalties that outraged nature visits on licentiousness.

Arrived on board, I found a new fruit to attract my attention.

I should have called it a crazy orange, but it bears the name of limon dulce—sweet lemon. It is an orange with a thick rind, green even when ripe, and filled with a copious gummy oil, that obliges you to wash your hands as soon as you peel one. This alone greatly reduces its value, and its insipid sweetness has little attraction for Northern palates, but people here value them more than oranges. The carpels separate from each other much more readily than those of the orange. It must be a variety of Citrus Limetta or Citrus Aurantium.

For some time after leaving San Pablo our voyage seemed to be without events to chronicle. Day passes after day without receiving or leaving a passenger or an article of freight. Once a day we stop for wood. Perhaps the space of an acre has been cut over, and may have been cultivated, but has again run up to weeds. Two miserable sheds—ranchos—serve to protect the occupants, who can not be called a family, from dew and rain. A part of a raceme of plantains, the staff of life, hang under one roof, and a few ears of maize constitute the remainder of their store. All their furniture is summed up in a few coarse earthen vessels (perhaps made on the spot), and some of totuma or calabasa. This last is a huge fruit of the gourd family, and has given origin to the English word calabash. The name ought not to be applied to the totuma, which is a much smaller fruit, made only into dishes and spoons, all made of half a fruit or less; but the calabasa needs but a small opening made into it, and it is cleaned out by rinsing with water if the orifice be too small for the hand. In a word, calabashes are substitutes for kegs, jugs, and bottles; totumas for dishes, bowls, and spoons. Ask for a totuma of water, and they will give you what you need to drink. Ask for a calabasa of water, and they will propose to lend you or sell you a calabasa to hold a supply of water to take with you.

Totumas grow on the Totumo, Crescentia Cujete, a tree about the size of an apple-tree. The first I saw was at Barranquilla, where I was nearly knocked down while chasing a butterfly by bringing my head in contact with a fruit of nearly the same size, which had escaped my notice by being of the same color as the leaves. A section of a small one answers for a spoon; bowls made of halves of larger ones are sold at from one to three cents apiece. In Pasto they ornament and varnish them, and then they are sold all over the country at a much higher price.

As you ascend the river population decreases. The villages grow smaller, and you forget to inquire their names, even when they are few and far between. There is also a sensible diminution in the proportion of children, suggesting an infant mortality equaled only in the vicinity of still-slops and "pure country milk."

Mountains appear in the distance, now on one hand and now on the other, gradually coming nearer and nearer, till at length they are seen on both sides at once, a sure indication that the alluvial region of the Magdalena is narrowing as we ascend. There is now and then a bluff of thirty feet in height, but I have generally seen the banks of a height varying from eight feet to two or three. The width of the river has diminished one half, till it is less than the Ohio or the Hudson at Albany. The current has been growing a little more rapid, but here at last is something new. The river is compressed by rocks on both sides, and for a few rods is quite rapid. This is the Angostura de Nare—the Narrows of Nare. It is the eleventh day of the trip, and our confinement has just reached the term of a Liverpool voyage.

The river widens again, and soon the boat enters the mouth of a smaller river of clear water. It is the River of Nare, and we make fast to the bank. It is so long since we have seen any clear water, that the passengers eagerly seize on it.

O formose puer! nimium ne credas colori!

I doubt very much the superiority of the new beverage. I doubted then; I distrust now. Many who ascend the Magdalena are taken sick at Nare or soon after, and some die there. I suspect that the clear water has something to do with this. At all events, there can be no better water in the world to drink than the turbid streams of the Magdalena and the Missouri. The steam-boats keep their water in large jars of brown earthenware, holding perhaps half a barrel or more. They are called tinajas. There are always two or more, so that the water has time to settle. Sometimes there is a filter made of porous stone, holding two gallons, which lets it drip slowly into the tinaja beneath.

The luxury of cold water is and must always be unknown here. Deep wells and uniform springs retain the average temperature of the year, which, in the temperate zone, is much lower than that of a summer's night; so the earth treasures up for us, at home, the coolness of winter for the refreshment of our summer-heats, but in the tropics this resource fails us. To get cool water, we must ascend the mountains till the air becomes so cool that the water almost ceases to be a luxury.

There are no houses at the mouth of the Nare. There were only a store-house—bodega—and a wood-shed. Both are since leveled to the ground, and boats now stop only at the town, half a mile or so above. While waiting for dinner I went up to the town. It is the last mentionable place before you get to Honda. It is a desolate range of mud huts, and a wretched plaza, with a small church on it, as usual. It is all the worse for having a back street and cross streets. We found the people dressed up because it was Saint Somebody's day. This made the bad place look somewhat better. One little fellow, who was too small to need clothes, attracted my attention as a remarkably fine specimen of a frequent disease, said to be produced by earth-eating, called jipitera: such a person is called a barrigon, from the great enlargement of the abdomen. No sooner did he see my four eyes (spectacles included) bent on him, than he ran bellowing into the house.

After dinner I went out to look for plants. I went far and found few. The land road from Antioquia Medellin and Rio Negro terminates at Nare, or at a dépôt—bodega—on the Nare a mile or two up. The boundary of the province of Antioquia itself crosses the Nare some distance up, extends down the north bank to the Magdalena, and follows the west bank of the Magdalena down for some leagues. The spot we are on is in Mariquita, a name which is a diminutive of that of the Virgin. The provincial Legislature has just tried, by an unconstitutional law, to change the name to Marquetá. The limits between Antioquia and Mariquita have never been settled. It will be seen below why I wish to establish my good character for *geography*.

Well, I started up toward the Bodega de Antioquia by land. I found a little path, impracticable for mules, and followed it a mile without finding any thing worth seeing except some monkeys scrambling over the tree-tops. An awkward chap is the monkey, sprawling his five long limbs (his tail is prehensile) in different directions, holding on by one, two, or more of them, and reaching off amazingly for new points of attachment. That old lady, with one of her lovely progeny clinging to her in affectionate embrace, tranquilly imbibing its nourishment, has no scruples of delicacy at exhibiting her rarest feats of climbing thirty feet above our heads. But bring the monkey down to the ground, and chain him, cage him, or turn him loose, and you make him a chattering idiot, a mischievous fool, and the most utterly disgusting creature ever made in caricature of man.

I was turned back by the approach of night. I had returned nearly to the boat, and the sun had "gone in" so long that it yielded no indication of the points of the compass, when I suddenly lost my path. I retraced my steps to a spot that I knew I had passed in going, and then turned boatward and lost my way at the same point. I grew alarmed, for night was on me, and my pocket compass was in New York! Just as I had made my third attempt to extricate myself by *a posteriori* investigations, and was in the full tide of speculation as to the nocturnal occupations of the tenants of the wilderness, from the musquito to the "tiger" and "lion" of South America, I saw two of my fellow-passengers gunning.

How came I lost? The path probably made one turn that I had taken without observing it. Before I came to the river again, that, too, had turned in the same direction, and when I saw it my error of meridian was confirmed. In returning, all my caution was aroused. I took not a step at a venture, and, when my road turned again directly to the boat, I would not follow it a step, for it carried me in a direction opposite to that indicated by my imagination.

We were under way in the morning with a diminished number of passengers. We were just eight men and two boys. A fine view, this, of the passenger business on the main thoroughfare of New Granada! A longer interval than usual, too, had passed since the last boat; not less, I think, than three weeks.

We had left Nare three hours behind us when we ran plump into a sand-bank. Here I did injustice to Captain Chapman, and I am sorry for it. He was a good seaman, and had omitted nothing he could contribute to the comfort of his passengers, and to mine especially; but he knew nothing of low water on the Ohio. I, who have been on more bars than I hope ever to be again, looked on his operations with perfect amazement, till I came to the conclusion that he wished to stay there. Once we were fairly afloat, but one awkward manœuvre fixed us. The next that I saw, twenty bogas stood in three feet of water, on the lower side of the boat—which lay obliquely to the stream—pushing against the current. They carried out hawsers, and they slipped. They tied them better, and broke them. The spar with which a resolute Ohio captain would crawl over two feet of dry bar, was unknown to them. There we lay, and we lay all day.

At night we were notified that we were to leave the boat early next morning in the champan that had been towing more than a week at our stern filled with idle bogas. Now commenced a packing-up, and it was like the sack of a city for confusion. All languages were put in requisition. One question would begin with "Where is—," the next with "Donde está—," another with "Ou est—," "Wo ist—." Only the Italian was precluded from the use of his mother tongue. It was at bedtime only that the Babel became quiet, and our twelfth day on the boat was at an end.

CHAPTER VI.

THE CHAMPAN.

Bogas.—Farewell to Steam.—Trying to be "down sick."—The Hammock.—Our Prison.—On short Allowance.—Plank-making.—Platanal.—Chocolate.—Buena Vista.—On Shore.

THE champan, which had been forgotten for so many days, early became the object of universal attention. It had been intended for the short distance not navigable by steam, and it was only after great diplomacy that terms could be found on which all parties could agree for a greater amount of service. No task is more disagreeable than to negotiate with bogas, and this

THE CHAMPAN.

morning the bargain was to be reconcluded. In the course of the discussion, the bogas made a show of returning the baggage to the boat, selecting for the demonstration some light, bulky articles.

It is time now to describe the champan. It is much larger than a bongo, being, in fact, a flat boat with an arched roof—toldo (the same word describes also a musquito-bar, a bed-curtain, and a tent), woven of poles and thatched with palm leaf. The ends are open to the air; the width of the boat is about 7 feet, and the length of the covered part may have been 15 or 20 feet. It contained but one article of freight, a hogshead of crockery, but our baggage seemed to nearly fill it. One passenger, however, contrived to keep a portion of the floor free from trunks by spreading his bed down upon it. As for myself, I paid little attention to matters, as I was suffering from a distressing diarrhea, the result, perhaps, of the beautifully clear Nare water with which we regaled ourselves. I ate nothing this morning before starting; the others took only a cup of chocolate.

A Bogotá Yankee and his son remained with his large and varied lot of freight on board the steamer. There were eight of us, then, consigned to the tender mercies of an uncivilized horde of bogas, most of them absolutely naked, governed by a patron of a little higher grade, who, with his woman—patrona—occupied the open stern—popa—of the boat; and all that represented the owners of the boat—captain, clerk, steward, cook—all was supplied by Richard (the steward—a Jamaica negro) and Manuel, a stupid Indian boy, who scarce understood any Spanish! I complained of this to the captain, but he told me that even what he did was a favor and not an obligation, done at a great expense, and that it was optional to take the champan or wait the rise of the river in the boat. My complaint, then, was groundless.

It is time now to introduce to the reader these seven fellow-prisoners and victims with whom I was now brought into so close and involuntary an intimacy. They were,

1. A little Granadan of the name of Lara, who lived in Honda. He spoke Spanish only.

2. A Frenchman who had been in Jamaica, and spoke English and Spanish well. He was a sort of apothecary.

3. His son, a thievish little rascal, speaking Spanish and French. He would read all the children's tracts I would lend him, and stole from under my mattress some anti-Catholic tracts I had there, which I did not think best to lend.

4. Another Frenchman, a Bogotá tailor—a nice man—speaking French and Spanish.

5. A fine young Italian, named Dordelli, nephew to a merchant in Bogotá. He was going from there to establish a branch of his house in Cúcuta. He was a naturalist and my especial friend. He spoke French and Spanish.

6. A Dutch violinist, who had been in the United States with Sivori, and was now going through the American Tropics. He was a gentlemanly man, but unprincipled and miserly to excess. He spoke Low Dutch, German, English, French, and a little Spanish.

7. His companion, a pianist, an easy, over-generous man, who had given up all the financiering operations to his more penurious partner; he spoke the same languages, and also Latin to me when we wished the Frenchman, No. 2, not to understand us.

There never had been very strict discipline on the steam-boat. Here there was and could be none except that of the patron over the bogas. These all assembled in the front open space, the proa—forecastle; and one of them began a prayer, which all the rest finished. I could never determine whether this prayer was in Latin, Spanish, or Lengua Franca.

Then most of them sprung to the roof, seized their palancas (described on page 39), and commenced pushing against the bottom of the river, and walking toward the stern, shouting, Us! us! us! us! us! us! us! till they could go no farther. Their cry was tremendous. Oh for some method incapable of exaggeration, like the photographic process, to record it and compel belief! A pack of hounds may make as much noise in some given half hour as a crew of bogas, but these continue it, only with the intermissions of eating and crossing the river, from daybreak till night. They shout, and jump on the toldo over your head till you might fancy them in battle and repelling boarders.

Sad indeed was the sight to me, sick and dispirited, to see the boat slowly disappearing around a bend of the river. Barbarism was carrying me away from civilization, and when or how was I destined to see its like again? I turned and went in, for a horizontal position and quiet were the only remedies in my power. Horizontal position and quiet! how could I obtain either? I found Lara's bed empty, and I lay down on it. I lay there till he came, and, fearing to lose his ill-founded claim, requested me to leave it. I found another space as large, which Richard had been busy in, now unoccupied, and I would have at once spread my hammock on it as a bed, but the little French boy was asleep on it, and I would not disturb him. While waiting for him to waken, his father took formal possession of the spot in question by unrolling his bed on it. None had leisure to sympathize with me, and I roused myself, and I roused the boy too, and called to Richard to sling my hammock.

"No hammock can be slung in this champan," says the Frenchman.

"But I must lie down, for it is impossible for me to remain up longer," I replied.

No others offered any objection, and the hammock was soon slung, in nobody's way, close up under the toldo, over a pile of baggage at the side of the boat, and I was in it. I wish my best friend might some day receive, in recompense for some great and good action, an equal gratification. I was as much out of the way of all the rest as though I had fallen overboard and drowned, and it was all the same to them. I remained in my hammock, with little intermission, twenty hours, and rose entirely recovered.

And here I feel it my duty to detain my reader while I pay a debt of gratitude to my hammock. High in the scale of physical comforts I place the hammock. A clean bed in the filthiest hovel, no refuge for the odious bug, unscalable by the nimble flea, it offers a glorious sleep to the traveler, when sleep would be impossible without it. Hung up in the forest between two trees, I have slept dry and warm when the rain was falling in torrents. When musquitoes in clouds have presented their bills like hungry creditors, I have taken refuge beneath its impassable toldo, and converted their threats into soporific music. Many is the time, by night and by day, that I have read to keep awake, or read to get asleep, in my hammock without feeling any of those inconveniences of holding my book, having my head too low, or a violent bend in the neck, or any other disagreeables that attend on reading in bed. But were there such a thing as a hot night in New Granada (one of those oven-like nights that has driven many of my readers from their beds to sprawl themselves—unpoetic objects—on hard floors), then the hammock could show itself in its transcendency; but till I return to the land of long days and short nights, this virtue must lie dormant in my dear hammock, like all the imaginable virtues of an infant.

My saddle-bow shall always have a place to tie my hammock. I hope never to be without a hammock again. No house should be finished without abundant facilities for hanging them, for the only inconvenience of a hammock is its length, and the necessity of two points of attachment at sufficient distance and height from whence to depend its length. What feats, both of ingenuity and climbing, have I performed in places where it was "impossible to hang a hammock!" But let us return to the champan.

A boat 30 or 40 feet long, with baggage piled on both sides, with an alley-way of less than three feet in the middle, would be a tolerable prison for seven men, a boy, two servants, the patron, the patrona, and an uncounted lot of bogas, although these last had no rights under or aft of the toldo. But there was a sad drawback on this. There were three beams running across the top of the boat, from side to side, too low to creep under and too high to step over, so that, in fact, we were penned up like animals in a cattle-show.

Such was our home, or our prison, from Monday till Saturday. Once or twice a day we came to land when the bogas' dinner was boiled enough, but as soon as it was eaten they prayed again, and on they went again with an us! us! us! us! us! us! uh! ! ! jumping and screaming. One black rascal had a string tied round his waist, and tied to it his trunk key. So he has clothes, it seems, somewhere; but when a man has put every rag he has in the world into his trunk, in what pocket shall he put his key? A knotty question, which the fellow seems to have solved completely.

But the most amazing problem of political economy I ever tried to solve is how to nerve a naked vagabond up to almost superhuman exertions, day after day, in a land where starvation is impossible. The boga's task used to be to push his huge champan against a violent current up stream, from Mompos to Honda—a month's dire task of twelve hours' dreadful labor every day, except two or three accustomed stops, where neither promises, threats, blaspheming, nor pistols could start him a particle; but you may as well inquire why a man will be a poet, a naturalist, or a book-maker, with the certainty of hard labor and bad pay, as a boga. *Boga nascitur.*

The truth seems to be that our boga is a great sensualist. He has his finery and embroidered shirts, and he must have his dances and drinking frolics. We may suppose him, then, to arrive home with an amount of money that the upland Indian never has seen; but his old debts, and one or two *benders*, make short work with it. Then he resorts to borrowing till that resource is exhausted, and again he must get a champan; but I must forewarn my readers that the borrowing part of the business will not go far, for the credit system is not well understood in low latitudes. So the river-craft is based on the vice and improvidence of its victims. I see many analogies between bogas, the deck-hands of the Mississippi, and common sailors. The Millennium would involve the reconstruction of many classes of society.

Generally, in all parts of the Magdalena, one bank is steep and the other shallow. The champan chooses the latter, and, when it changes to the other side of the river, we must cross it. All the men on the toldo jump down forward, and each one takes his paddle—canalete. Then we have an intermission of the noise till they are again at their poles. Some of them stand in the proa all the time, and push there. These occasionally exchange the pole for the hook—gancha—and thus, at times, manage to pass a small turn of steep bank, and save crossing the river twice, which is always effected with a great loss of ground.

One of the greatest trials of life used to be to manage the bogas in ascending from Mompos to Honda. It is almost impossible to hurry them; sometimes they desert, sometimes rebel. The laws now give you even less control of them than formerly; and, unless the navigation of the Magdalena is specially protected, it is quite likely that it may be impeded, delayed, and rendered more costly by the change. The tendency of the ultra-republicanism now springing up is to protect the vagabond, but this must soon reach its limit.

We always ate while the boat was going, and, as the kitchen was nothing but a frame filled with earth in the popa, with tulpas, our meals could not, even had we wished it, been simultaneous with those of the bogas. In fact, we preferred taking their meal-time for a little ramble on shore. In one of these rambles with Dordelli I came upon two men at work, a really strange sight in this land. With the most shocking substitute for axes they had cut down a large tree, hewn it four-square, and were now cutting a deep groove on the upper side, like a trough. They showed me a similar but deeper groove on the under side, and told me that when these two grooves met in the middle they would have two *planks*—a hard way of making lumber. I think they were to make part of a champan. This was the only instance of men at work that I saw between Cartagena and Bogotá, except one man making a fish-net at a town on the Magdalena.

We were gone longer than we expected, and found the company all waiting for us. We had left them under the impression that they were going up to a house to buy provisions, which they did not. They were little satisfied with our delay, as the bogas had been fighting while they were waiting, and it was feared that they would go no farther for some hours. However, in a little while they prayed again, and were in as good starting order as ever. After this they contrived their midday halt generally on an island, or in shallow water, where they would wade ashore to eat, leaving us in the boat.

But of nothing can I complain so much as of the Jamaica negro, Richard, who was our steward. He seemed determined to carry economy to the utmost. He had now turned cook, though I imagine any one of our number would have shown more science in the matter. Nothing was to be had. Frequently the whole meal for eight of us was a single fowl and hard crackers. Nay, he even complained that the "gentlemen used too much sugar in their coffee" (milk we had none in all the voyage), and undertook the task of sweetening it for us. As for fruit or other luxuries, there was none to be had. Save a green pineapple that I saw at one of our stopping-places, I saw neither fruit nor fruit-tree after leaving San Pablo. And here we were, almost without resources, and with no remedy but to advance.

At length the conduct of the Frenchman, No. 2, became intolerable. At one of our scant meals of one chicken, he, in virtue of his post next the popa, seized on nearly half of it for himself and his boy. I came next, and then Dordelli, but we always passed it on without taking any; this time it came back to us with one diminutive joint of a wing, which Dordelli took; it was no object to either of us, and I fasted till the next meal. To prevent the recurrence of this injustice, the pianist at the next meal took his seat by the Frenchman. Certainly so little of manly fairness could not have been found in any class of people that I have any knowledge of.

About this time a tree on the banks attracted my attention from its frequency and its singular port. It was sometimes 30 feet high, with a hollow stem, and large peltate leaves on the extremities only of the branches. The flower resembled an immense catkin of a willow or birch. They call it guarumo. It is Cecropia peltata.

Once again we all went ashore in hopes of buying something to eat. After passing through a skirting of wood, we came to a platanal or plantain-field. I know of nothing in nature more majestic than a platanal. The real stem of the plátano, Musa paradisiaca, is not developed, but a false trunk of fibrous footstalks of leaves rises 10 feet high, and is 6 or 8 inches in diameter. It is important to know whether the fibre of this huge herbaceous stem can be made into paper. It is sometimes used for strings. The blades of the leaves are 6 or 8 feet long and 2 feet wide. Horses eat them greedily. The plants are about a dozen feet apart, and when one is cut down a shoot springs up that again matures in about a year. From the summit springs out a spike of flowers that develops into a raceme (racimo) of fruit three feet long, and as heavy as a man can conveniently carry. The fruits are seedless, an inch in diameter or more, and, in the *harton*, 8 inches long. The skin comes off readily, and, when ripe, the fruit is good both raw and every way it can be cooked. It is roasted for bread, and tastes something like cake or sweet potato, but softer and sweeter than the last. It is generally eaten green, roasted or boiled, and is then insipid, and to me abominable.

The banana, *guineo* (Musa coccinea and M. sapientium), is known in our Northern cities. As a fruit it is better than the plantain, but is insipid when cooked, and is useless when not ripe. It grows like the plátano, but the stem is purple, and the fruit shorter. It is not much cultivated. There is a belief that it will kill one to eat guineos and drink spirits too soon thereafter. I never tried it. There are other species or varieties of Musa, but they are little cultivated. The dominico, said to be Musa regia, is very good, but smaller, and, to my taste, inferior to the banana. It is useless to enter a platanal in hopes to find ripe fruit in it. I never have seen a single raceme in my life that I have not been directed to. The reason must be improvidence; they raise rather fewer than they need, so that they are generally eaten as soon as they get their growth.

We proceeded half a mile through the platanal, and came to a house or hut where lounged and sat two or three half-naked lazy mortals. Here I saw, for the first time, the cacao-tree which yields chocolate. The first thing that strikes the beholder is the strange way that the fruit is stuck against the side of the tree or the larger limbs, projecting horizontally, as if stuck endwise on a peg. The flower, too, would be curious were it larger, having some little extras about it, as Byttneriate flowers generally have; but they are small, and, in the cacao, white. The fruit is six or seven inches long, and three or four in diameter. It is ribbed like a melon, but never opens. It is knocked off when it appears to the eye to be ripe; two or three, perhaps, from a tree, are as many as will be ripe at the same time. Children carry them in their hands to a central heap, that grows from day to day, till enough is collected to make a batch.

Then come the man, his wife, all the boys and girls, all the babies and dogs. The effective force surrounds the pile. Two of them draw their machetes, and begin opening the fruit. They apply the word mazorca equally to an ear of Indian corn or a fruit of cacao, only the granos of one are on the outside and those of the other within. The man gives the mazorca three cuts lengthwise, not so deep as to injure the precious seeds within, and tosses it over to the softer sex and smaller fry. They tear it open with their claws, and find within the thick fleshy rind a central cavity, from the centre of which rose a column with the seeds attached; but when ripe, the whole is reduced to a pulp, in which the large seeds are packed so compactly that they alone, if thrown in loosely, would be more than sufficient to fill the entire cavity. These they separate a little from the pulp, and throw them into a tray, upon a skin, or on some plantain leaves. The pulp is as agreeable in taste as any fruit we have, but, as it is difficult to get a spoonful from a fruit that contains a pint of seeds, it is not worth the trouble of eating. They often suck it off the seeds as they get them out. If the seeds are to be loaded on a mule, they are put into a guambía, a bag made of net-work. As the meshes are large enough to let potatoes through, it requires some management to fill it with seeds of cacao. First you put in pieces of plantain leaf, and upon them the quantity of cacao they will hold. Pieces of leaf are added to the edges of the first, overlapping freely, till, when it is full, the whole guambía appears lined with leaf. Arrived home, they are put into a trough—canoa—and left to ferment till the seed is freed from what appears to be an aril or false covering. Then it is spread on a skin in the door-yard to dry.

It is prepared by grinding on a warm, flat stone, by the application of another stone, held, like a rolling-pin, in both hands, but not rolled. The stone has under it a place to put coals, and it is heated to about 120°. Maize is always ground on this stone. The cacao is first ground alone, and then with a coarse sugar, to which dried bread is sometimes added, for a cheap article for the poor. This kind I have sometimes eaten in bulk. Cho-co-lá-te is made into tablas, or cakes, of from an ounce to an ounce and a half, the quantity to which two ounces of water are to be added for a cup. They are boiled together, generally in a small brass jar—olleta—and, before pouring out, as much of it is reduced to foam as possible by making a grass-stem, on which portions of the roots are left, to revolve rapidly, as in beating eggs.

The cacao loves the tierra caliente. Its price varies exceedingly, being often dearer than in New York, and sometimes ten cents per pound, or less. It is never so cheap as to be an unprofitable crop. It is generally sold in the seed, and ground by the family that use it.

In all these days we saw but one town. It was Buenavista, near the mouth of the Rio Negro, that rises below and west of the great plain of Bogotá. A wagon-road may yet follow this river down, and near here may be the future port of Bogotá. At present there is here only a large, straggling town of mud and thatch. I saw a champan partly made here, from which it is inferrible that there are here men who work sometimes. I saw, too, a garden that had been, but the gate was broken down, and the whole area was filled with tall weeds. The utter neglect of horticulture is inexplicable, but may arise from the impossibility of preserving the crop from theft. Except the garden of Don Miguel Cáldas, at Bolivia, in the hills above Vijes. many miles from any ordinary inhabitants, the few gardens I have seen have padlocks. Be it as it may, there are no garden-thieves at Buenavista. Children are very scarce here: in all the upper river they have been very few—a striking contrast to the crowds that lined the banks of the lower river. The absence of children may explain the grass-grown, desolate quiet of these towns, which seem like decayed places that have no future.

On Friday the river became more tortuous and rapid. On our left, on the west bank of the river, and not very far from Honda, we saw a mountain range of the boldest description. High on the summit were enormous perpendicular precipices, seen in clear profile against the sky. Rarely can we place ourselves in a situation to get a profile view of a single precipice, but the top of a distant mountain-ridge so set off looks more like cloud than rock.

We have passed several avisperos. I know not whether they are nests of wasps or hornets; but the bogas show them great respect, passing them in entire silence. Should we unfortunately disturb them, we would have to fall back and let them get quiet again, unless we could cross over and pass on the other side.

About this time we passed Conejo, where Richard's reign and our torment were to have commenced, had the boat not grounded. From here it would have been quite tolerable, and it may even have happened that the boat would ascend entirely to the Vuelta, which a good, light-draft boat ought to reach at any time in the year. Some boats leave the passengers to make their way from Conejo or La Vuelta as they can. Ours carried us to the very head of navigation.

At last, on Saturday morning, I was called from my hammock and asked to decide whether I would submit to another day's imprisonment or walk to Honda. It did not take me long to decide. The two Hollanders were of the same mind, and we hastily closed our seventeen days' voyage with a cup of chocolate and a hard, dry cracker, and leaped ashore.

CHAPTER VII.

HONDA.

Bodega and Bodeguero.—Crusoe's Long-boat.—Men of Burden.—Wonderful Bridge.—Municipal Suicide.—Salt.—A universal Swim.—A petrified City.

So sudden was my exit from the boat that I did not even know on which bank we were. As Honda is on the left bank, I supposed we were on the same, but I found it otherwise. We are at La Vuelta de la Madre de Dios—the Turn of the Mother of God. La Vuelta is the farthest that steamers ever go, but they say that boats can go up to the foot of the Honda rapids if they have sufficient power.

At La Vuelta there is but a mere shed or a small house. Were it healthy, it would be an admirable place for a farm, for the land ought to be fertile, and it is a convenient place to embark or disembark. There is a good road, as they call it, all the way from here to Bogotá. With good beasts, the journey from here to Guaduas could be made in a day.

Travelers now often come up, with their baggage, on mules from La Vuelta to Honda. It is better to engage them at once for Guaduas if possible, or, if not, to Pescaderias, opposite Honda, where they will stand the best chance of finding cattle, and where I have seen better accommodations for travelers than ever I found in Honda. Should you go up by water, if you have much baggage, it had better be left on the east bank, and not taken into Honda.

We struck off directly from the river through a variegated country, over an old mule-road. Soon we found high hills between us and the river. Monkeys were climbing over the trees, and various flowers covered the ground. A little grass-like plant here first met my eye, that I have found every where since. It is noticeable in having its upper leaves (bracts) white at the base. It is the Dichromena ciliata.

We had walked some miles before we came to any of the few houses that are found on the road. Then we entered a pasture through an open gate with a roof on the top. I was surprised at this, but I learned, from further observations, that all gates here have roofs. Doors, gates, and bars all have the name of puerta. A pair of bars is puerta de trancos, and a gate puerta de golpa. It is often very inconvenient to the traveler not to know some such phrases, which, being perhaps local, are not to be found in dictionaries or phrase-books. These last I have found very deficient for Granadan use, being generally composed for the longitude of Madrid.

We began to wonder, after going six or eight miles, whether it might not be possible that we had made some false turn, and were getting into the interior, when a roaring drew us a little to the right, and there was the river, rushing and tumbling over the rocks, so that we wondered how the poor champan was ever to get past this point, called Quita-palanca.

We reached the foot of the rapids unexpectedly. We found there a small collection of cottages, a good-sized rough storehouse, and a magnificently-planned government structure, either in ruins or unfinished. It bore the inscription of BODEGA DE BOGOTÁ on the arch over the door.

The keeper of the bodega is a character. It was at a later period I came in contact with him. I had some baggage coming to be deposited, and, to hasten matters, I began by unsaddling my own beast, and putting in my saddle and bridle before the peon got in. Then I called out the little thin old man from his breakfast.

"What's this in here?" says he, pointing to the intruding articles.

"It is only my montura," I replied. This term includes saddle, bridle, halter, and whatever else may belong to your saddle-horse.

"Take it out," he cried; "it has no business in there till it has been entered."

I was greatly diverted by the zealous strictness of the only man I have ever found here with any system at all, and would gladly have spent half an hour in resisting his mandate, but time pressed. My peon took out the saddle, the old man counted it, and it was put back as before. At another time I greatly scandalized the good bodeguero by changing my linen there. He said all he could to induce me to change my purpose and not my camisa; but necessity, though she knows no law, is a keen logician. I argued with him, working diligently with my hands the while, till we had nothing to argue for.

Near the bodega, under a large tree, I saw the sections of an immense sugar-boiler. They were six or eight in number, and were destined for Cuni, two days' journey in the mountain. To carry one of them there would be a task comparable only with that of transporting one of Hannibal's elephants or a piece of Napoleon's artillery over the Alps. But all the region through which they have been brought is a fine sugar country, and here the concern has been lying for years like a stranded whale. Some transportation transactions that begin here are to be compared with the movement of a small army. One piece was so heavy that the cargueros (as human beasts of burden are called) are said to have eaten a cow a day. The heaviest load ever carried to Bogotá by a single carguero is said to have been carried by a woman. It is given at 216 pounds; but there is always an uncertainty about translating weights.

The carguero, like the boga, has a more laborious calling than any known in the United States, and the philosophy of his attachment to it is even more difficult than that of the boga. He is a native of a higher, colder clime, and of a more industrious race. Nor is he always a poor man. Colonel Santamaria tells me he was once *riding* a sillero or saddle-man, who, from a summit, pointed out a farm of his on which he had a tenant. They are of Indian blood, mixed or unmixed, and go naked from the waist upward, and from the middle of the thigh downward. The weight is supported by two straps across the chest. I am told the carguero's wife meets him on the last day of his journey, brings him food, and takes his load.

I met them once as I was coming down from Bogotá, stringing along the road for hours, with boxes of all imaginable shapes, and found here at the bodega the fountain from which the stream flowed. It was the machinery of some kind of a factory.

After hallooing "Paso!" and "Pasero!"—ferry and ferryman—till we were tired, we started out a dilatory ferryman, who took us across to a large sandy beach. He is obliged to carry the neighbors gratis, and pay the province something for the privilege of charging a half dime and extorting a dime when he can from all others. This pasaje is an item of provincial revenue that ought to be centralized, as they say, for it is drawn from the pockets of inhabitants of other provinces rather than of their own. This particular ferry is the worse off, as it is on no traveled road, so that the Hondeños are almost the only ones that cross, and they cross gratis. The delays of this ferry, and, still more, its vexations, are a reason for going straight on to Pescaderias instead of going into Honda at all. The ferry there is bad enough, but this is worse. You can walk from the bodega to the Pescaderias, and a very pleasant walk it is, especially in the morning. You may find, on low bushes, some Sterculiate flowers and fruits, both of a peculiar structure. The flowers, an inch across, are red, and will remind you a little of the mallows. The fruit, of which you can not fail to find some old ones, are an inch long, and curiously twisted. It is a Helictres.

At the beach, on the Honda side, is a row of cottages, chiefly, I think, of bogas, and a considerable warehouse. This is the bodega of Honda, or, it is better to say, of Ibagué and Santa Ana. Here lie some old guns, that seem to have been left in a military movement for want of land transportation. They will never move again till they are sold.

A short, steep hill, with a paved road, led up to a dry, sunny, uncultivated plain, extending nearly to Honda. Here I first met a Lantana, a genus that has followed my steps every day since. It was a Verbenate shrub, three or four feet high, with a flat disk of flowers, looking almost like Labiate flowers, but the fruits were small berries. The unexpanded flowers were red, the young flowers orange, and the older ones yellow. The plain was bounded on the east by the river, roaring over a rocky bed, and absolutely unnavigable. President Herran, however, once ventured down it in a boat, on an occasion when time seemed of more moment to him than safety. A railroad is purposed around the rapids, through Honda, but I fear it will not pay, if executed.

On the west was the range of almost perpendicular bluffs which surprised me so the day before with their fantastic forms. On the north they come down to the river. Beyond the plain, on the south, was Honda, and, back of it, another high hill comes down to the river.

The road descends by a pavement to a very old stone bridge across a little dry ravine, and immediately after enters the ancient city of Honda. Here once united two currents of trade, flowing toward Spain from the lofty cities of Bogotá and Quito. The robbery of Indians, that once enriched these cities, is over: their trade with Spain is done. No trade from Quito seeks the Magdalena, and the scanty exports and imports of Bogotá are beginning to creep along the base of the mountain on the opposite side of the river. No wonder, then, that ten steps in the old city show it to be decayed. Many a rich old house is reduced to a roofless ruin, hedging in tall weeds with walls of thick, rough masonry. Honda is all stone and tile, so that never had an obsolete old place harder work to tumble down, and it would not have succeeded without the respectable aid of a few earthquakes.

The richest specimen of earthquake-architecture I ever saw is the bridge over the Gualí, a noisy river that runs right through the middle of the town. This was formerly spanned by two bridges made of hard stone and a mortar almost as hard. Of the upper one the abutments remain, and a fragment of one pier. The other has undergone so many cataclysms, that no description, ground-plans, and elevations would explain to an architect its present condition, and no geological investigations and speculations of which I am capable could lead me to satisfactory conclusions as to what had happened to it. It had broken down, been mended with wood, burned, and remended; so the track of the bridge is of three different dates. Part is strong enough to bear two loaded elephants abreast, and part so weak that all horsemen are required by law to dismount, and every beast to be unloaded. Part of the masonry leans up stream, and part down stream; and one piece, shaped something like an old tin lantern, has puzzled me a dozen times to decide whether the axis of the cone were originally horizontal or vertical.

But there is one more wonder about the bridge. So anxious are the provincial Solons to consummate the utter ruin of Honda, that they have imposed a peaje of a dime on each tercio of merchandise that passes the bridge, while on the other side is an unobstructed portage from the smooth water above the rapids to that below. Altogether, I should like dearly to pack up this victorious rival of the tower of Pisa in a box, and send it to New York; but they can not spare it, for the rapid Gualí is never fordable, and I fear it will be a long time ere another bridge will span it.

Above the bridge you turn to your left, then to your right, then go up hill through narrow streets, and then down hill through a narrower one, to come to a wide, straight street, the upper end of which terminates on a smooth beach at the junction of a small stream with the Magdalena, at the very head of the rapids. Above here the river is navigable for days without more obstruction. This upper point is the market-place, and the straight street is probably the newest part of the city.

In coming up, we had the Magdalena near us all the while, at the left, with no street between us and the river. At first we had only one tier of inconsiderable houses on our right; then there was a back street west, then a little plaza, then a church, and back of it a little hill with houses on it; then a street up the north bank of the Gualí, in ruins; then a street on the south bank, with some good houses, some ruins, and a plaza in front of the barracks and cantonal offices; then a high hill with a pleasant street or two running along the top, with another plaza and another church; lastly, another branch of the town, mostly cottages of mud and thatch, runs up a fine piece of intervale along the north side of the small stream which bounds Honda on the south. It runs at the foot of a very high hill, coming down to the very bank of the Magdalena. This quiet vale pleases me much, for the cottages have space around them that a little labor might convert into the prettiest gardens in the world. The heart of the town, on the other hand, just south of the bridge, is a dense mass of stone houses and crooked, rough-paved streets, crowded in between a hill and two rivers—a perfect petrifaction.

To me the chief attraction of Honda is because it is the residence of two as excellent gentlemen as ever a traveler would wish to meet with in a strange land. I allude to Mr. J. H. Jenney, of Boston, and Mr. Treffrey, an Englishman, who has lived a long time in New Granada, and is married to a native of the country. To both these gentlemen I am indebted for almost every thing it was possible for me to need or for them to bestow. The presence of such men in a foreign land is a source of national pride, too often mortified by the unworthy representatives of the Anglo-Saxon race dispersed over the world. I had no letters to either, and, at my first visit, Mr. Jenney was from home. I directed my steps to Mr. Treffrey, and was welcomed with a cordiality that put me entirely at my ease. He took me to breakfast with him, hunted up Mr. Jenney's keys, and at once installed me solitary master of the best house in Honda, as I should judge.

To relieve me of the care of housekeeping, he showed me a place where I could take my meals. A traveler here would call Mr. Jenney's house my posada, and the place where I ate, my fonda. It would be hard to translate these words by hotel and eating-house, but they are the nearest approximations we have here. The fonda would not have been considered entirely unexceptionable by Northern moralists, inasmuch as the lady hostess had a few illegitimate children playing about the house; but travelers must get over their scruples, or manage them as best they may.

I found the house spacious and exceedingly comfortable, though far inferior to what the society of its master and the hospitality of his table afterward made it. It had a date-palm growing in the narrow patio, or court, and reaching up nearly as high as the roof. All the rooms were in the second story, and communicated by means of a gallery—corredor—running around the court. Balconies overhung the narrow streets, and gave an opportunity of seeing what was going on in town.

I went to the fonda four times a day; early and late for chocolate and sweetmeats—dulce—and at about 10 and 4 for my meals. These were generally beef, with yuca and plantains. Fish are very plenty here, for you will see, of a morning, men and boys with three or four huge ones, as much as they can carry, balanced over their shoulder on a stick, or propped up by another stick leaning against a wall. They labor under the demerit of being cheap, and our fondista would not feel that she is giving her guests their money's worth if she set fish before them. There is a smaller species, however, possessing the same merit as the round clam (quahog, Bostonicé) has in New York—it is dearer. I preferred the larger kind. They are frequently dried, and I have met them in the market of Bogotá.

In the market I saw a curious mineral for sale, which I at first took to be marble. It was of a dirty reddish-white color, and with a grain like sandstone, and was broken in pieces. I inquired its use, and learned that it was salt. Most of the salt is from Cipaquirá. They take water from a salt spring, and dissolve impure rock salt in it till the water is saturated. It then settles and is decanted into earthen jars over a furnace. These are supplied with brine till they are full of a mass of conglomerated salt. The jars are then broken, and the mass within—moya—broken into pieces of a good size for loading on the backs of mules. No cover is used to protect this load from the rain, which, however, does not greatly diminish the huge compact masses. Nearly all salt springs and mines are national property, and the salt is made by contract, and sold by the government at prices fixed by law. This monopoly has many enemies, and the government would gladly abolish it, but their revenues are already too scanty. I saw, in another place, some moyas made in smaller jars: these I knew to be contraband, made secretly, without paying the excise duty.

At night Mr. Treffrey sent four men down for my baggage. It made me ache to see my heavy trunks mounted on a man's back for a two miles' porterage. I paid two of them a dime each; the other two demanded a dime and a quarter. All agreed that the difference was just, though they did not deny that the weight was equal. Soon after they arrived a collector came in for peaje for two bales of merchandise. I had two bales of paper for drying plants: it was not merchandise, and they let it pass.

Honda is a forwarding town rather than mercantile. One industry, however, is carried on here, that is fast growing in New Granada—cigar-making. It is but recently that the free cultivation of tobacco has been permitted. Tobacco culture used to be limited to two places: Ambalema, a town above Honda, on the same side of the river, the richest town in the province of Maraquita, and Palmira, in the Cauca. Each cultivator took out a license to raise so many plants, and if he exceeded the number a heavy fine followed. No peasant dared raise any for his own use. I can not see how the multiplication of cigars or the reduction of price can benefit the world, but the abrogation of this monopoly has certainly given a great impulse to industry in this region. The abolition was begun by Mosquera, but accomplished by President López, his successor.

The next day was Sabbath, but I had not yet learned that he who would go to mass must go early, so I have always found the churches closed. It was rather a busy day, for it seemed as if all the population were bent on a public swim. The little river has its congregation when it has any water. The Magdalena is much frequented just where the rapids begin, and again at the mouth of the Gualí. The Gualí itself, between the bridge and the Magdalena, was the resort of a few quiet ones, but the liveliest scenes were in the rapid current just above the bridge. There were full-grown men and large boys stark naked, young girls in the same state, and women of all ages with their bodies more or less covered with a blue skirt.

The better bred of these would come down under an umbrella to shade them from the sun, a servant following with a skirt, a sheet, and a totuma. The bather would throw the sheet over her, and emerge from it in the skirt. Next the body is covered with soap, and the hair filled; this is then converted into lather. Then follows a pouring of water from the totuma for a long time without intermission. If any children are to be washed, now is the time to take them in hand. After this, they plunge into the stream, if they choose, and thus pass the time they have to spend in the water. Again they envelop themselves in the sheet, which now serves for a towel as well as a dressing-room, and at length they emerge from it nearly dressed. The servant rinses the skirt in the river, wrings it, and puts it and the other wet clothes into a tray, which she carries home on her head. Thus the lady has secured a good swim in the open river without any violation of decorum. But it would not be fair to the reader to leave him to imagine that all these details are the result of one day's observation. It would be difficult to find the hour in all the week in which some of these scenes are not going on.

Back of Honda are plains of different elevations, extending to the west to the base of the Quindio Mountains. In these plains are the silver mines of Santa Ana, which I had not time to visit. I walked out more than a mile, and had a strong desire to go farther, especially as I saw before me what looked exactly like a great embankment for a railroad. It was the edge of a higher plain, but it was very difficult to undeceive myself. Here I met Don Diego Tanco on foot, and we walked back speaking of the military operations that these plains had witnessed in the revolutions of New Granada, and particularly of a battle there last year. He afterward sent me an invitation to dinner by a deaf mute; but I had no idea that I was concerned in the paper he was showing round the table, and did not discover the fact till too late.

I called on Señor Tanco one evening. I found no place to knock, neither at the porton, at the foot of the stairs, nor yet at the head of them. Señor Tanco told me the custom was to advance till the visitor meets some one. I found a little monkey chained to the top of the stairs, that manifested, as usual, a lively desire to bite me. Within I found the family, partly in the balcony, and the rest near the windows. I was much pleased with my call.

I experienced a material kindness at Señor Tanco's hand on the eve of leaving Honda. I had found a young chap at the Bodega de Bogotá who would take my cargas and myself to Guaduas, where he lived. The bargain was struck, but it remained to be seen whether, in all Honda, I could borrow or hire a saddle. I was about giving up in despair, when Señor Tanco came forward to my relief with the spontaneous offer of his saddle, which I gladly accepted.

The start was to be an early one, and the men were all engaged who were to carry my baggage to the upper ferry, and Gregorio, the peon, had engaged the ferryman to be at his post at daybreak. I then bought some chocolate and bread for my breakfast. They have a convenient pouch or pocket to sling over the shoulder, called a carriel. Some have locks to them; some are highly ornamented. As a substitute for this useful article, I now bought a little bag, here called a mochila, and elsewhere a guambía.

Guambía, as I said before, often means a large sack or net, in which things are carried on a mule's back. Mochila often means a money-bag, more properly called talega, capable of holding five or ten pounds of cash; while again a purse to carry in the pocket is called bolsa, and the pocket itself bolsilla.

Early next morning came Gregorio and the cargueros, and soon all my effects were on the bank, where the ferryman ought to have been. After a tedious delay he came, smoking his cigar, and a fisherwoman, who seemed to have been long at her fishing, sent her little girl to beg a light of him. So we crossed over to Pescaderias.

Las Pescaderias—the fisheries—was lately but a little collection of huts. Now Don Santos Agudelo is building a warehouse, and a large house that will serve as a hotel. All the mules that travel between Honda and Guaduas are kept at Guaduas, and if a man would go there, he must either send up for mules, or take some that have brought a load down, and are going back empty. It is quite common to send a messenger on foot to Guaduas, and wait till he can find mules and a peon, and return with them. Now Pescaderias is the point to secure a passage up with the least inconvenience. Honda has the advantage of good landings above and below the rapids, while those on the eastern bank are both steep and stony. Honda needs a good bridge across the Magdalena, and a new bridge across the Gualí, and then it would recover its pristine importance. A bridge is already projected, but I doubt if the Magdalena will ever be bridged here; and, if not, Honda is a doomed city.

I had some terrible ideas of the mountain-road to Bogotá, and of passive submission to the fantasies of my mule. This last thing has been wrongly represented. You should select the path for your mule just as you would for your horse at home; but, at home or abroad, when you come to a difficulty in your path, you must, after ordering your animal to pass it, let him do so in his own way, without pulling at the bit. The doctrine, as ordinarily stated, endangered my neck unnecessarily. The mountain mule possesses no miraculous instinct that will lead him to encounter a less difficulty now, to save him from a greater one farther ahead.

How a baquiano would have stared at seeing me come down the first broad inclined plane of rock, dipping like the roof of a house at about thirty degrees! He would have thought me mad, while I was only carrying out my theory of "passive obedience" without flinching; and I supposed, too, that there were plenty of worse places ahead, that would test my faith in mulishness still more severely. The rock was a spur that runs down to the river, over which we climbed, because going round is contrary to the old Spanish theory. Several more we pass, keep up the river some miles, and then boldly launch forth into the sea of mountains on the left.

Before doing this I must breakfast. Gregorio had a companion, to whom he committed the baggage, and devoted himself to aiding my breakfast. I had chosen a simple one as the beginning of my semi-bivouac life. It was bread and chocolate. We stopped at a house that had a fire burning back of it. Into one of my little tin pails he put a pint or more of water, and two balls—tablas—of chocolate, unwillingly obeying me in the strange proportions and large quantity, for half a tea-cup of water and one tabla of chocolate seemed to him all that an ordinary stomach could master. While this was going on, I noticed a colony of wasps that had taken possession of a cavity under or in the walls of the hut, from which it was too much trouble to dislodge them.

Breakfast over, we soon began to ascend, but not rapidly. We came to Las Cruces, a place where a more experienced traveler would have ordered a better breakfast than I had, and lost two or three hours in waiting for it. He would also have run great risk as to the variety of the larder, with a dead certainty against him as to the cuisine. To cook for one's self is a great annoyance, and eating at houses by the way is very uncomfortable, wasteful of time, and not very cheap. Could we only afford the meat-biscuit, or reduce beef to a dry powder, it would settle the question in favor of the independent plan. On the whole, I would advise making provision for four days between Honda and Bogotá before leaving home, providing *every thing* except sugar, chocolate, and water.

After leaving Las Cruces there was a long spot of nearly level road. I gave my mule into Gregorio's hands, to be more independent. I passed under a beautiful Bignoniate vine, covered with large purple blossoms, that I wished in New York. I came to another plant with stiff, thorny leaves, much like those of the century-plant. The inner leaves were red, and within is a dense head of flowers six inches in diameter, which give place to scores of fruits as large as a finger. It bears the name of piñuela, and is one of the best fruits of the land, being among the sweetest in the world, with a good supply of a very agreeable acid. The drawbacks are that each fruit must be peeled—and the operation covers the fingers with sirup—and that there is rather an abundance of seeds. These are said to have been the original carat weights, and the plant is the Bromelia Karatas. It makes a formidable hedge, and it often costs more to cut your way with a long machete to the centre of a vigorous plant than all the fruits are worth. I have seen where boys have cut a sort of dog-hole to creep in, six or eight feet under the leaves, and it seemed to me an operation worthy of Baron Trenck. There is another species or variety, I know not which, that is so acrid as to blister the lips. I have seen another species in the West Indies, with the flowers in a spike, instead of down at the roots of the leaves in a head. This is Bromelia Penguin. Next an Oxalis carried my thoughts home again.

Now we began rising more rapidly, till the prospect became magnificent, and, for the first time since leaving New York, I found the luxury of cool water. At last the wished-for and dreaded moment arrived when my ascent for the day was at an end. I was standing on the Alto del Sargento, 4597 feet above the level of the sea. Honda, being 718 feet above the sea, lay

3879 feet beneath me, while on the other side was a continuous descent of 1000 feet to Guaduas. And now the ridge I was to descend was to shut out the Magdalena from view. My farewell to my native shores cost me not a sigh; the last glimpse of the masts of my vessel fading in twilight, and, weeks afterward, the chimneys of the steamer disappearing at a turn of the river, went nearer my heart; but now I was to sever the *last* link that bound me to all my heart holds dear. I dismounted. I gazed on the immense valley far beneath my feet, with the tawny Magdalena winding through it, so that I could have watched the progress of a steam-boat from this point for one or two days without ever losing sight of her for half an hour.

And all this wide space looked like untouched forest, just as it appeared to the first of the Conquerors that ever climbed to this point. What vegetable wealth, if not mineral also, has lain here undeveloped for more than 300 years! And how much longer ere civilized industry will be sending precious woods down the Magdalena, and planting orange-groves and plantain-fields? There, in the distance, is a gently-swelling hill, its sides and its top all buried in primeval forest. Who has ever drunk from the springs that must gush out of its sides? And to what purpose is the mill-stream that murmurs past its base?

Then I turned my eyes to the future, as if I stood on the threshold of my fate for good or ill. Who can tell the joy and sorrow that shall mingle in my breast if I ever live to return homeward, and look down from this point again on a river flowing 600 miles straight toward home? Shall I survive the dangers of the way—the crumbling precipices, the hidden serpents, and, more than all, the seductions of Saxon and un-Saxon vices that too often bury body and character in a common grave?

I have stood there again, but a dense cloud filled all the space to the opposite mountains, and under those clouds lay two hostile bands of men, expecting soon to engage in deadly conflict for the key of the Magdalena. My previous fears for a distant and unknown future were now exchanged for an anxiety for the day.

Nothing is so apt to be exaggerated as danger. I met a soldier, who assured me that the firing between the two forces was about commencing when he left. As this weighed little with me, he added that to cross to Honda would be impossible, and equally so to procure a morsel of food, either at Pescaderias, or even by proceeding down to La Vuelta. Here was a less evil than being shot, but a more certain, and, therefore, a more serious one; but as I determined to go on, I bought a live fowl, and my peon secured half a dried fish at a house which we passed. These we tied to the top of the baggage, and proceeded. We arrived at Pescaderias in time to find the defense of Honda abandoned, and Melo's troops in victorious possession. Instead of whistling bullets exchanged between the two banks, I suffered no farther evil than a detention all night on the eastern bank, and a fast of 24 hours.

There can be no better medicine for gloomy reflections than the sight that met my eyes as I turned my back on the Magdalena. Instead of a boundless wilderness, there lay at my feet a happy valley, green with grass, cane, and maize, and dotted with cottages and fruit-trees, and, at the eastern edge a large town, with its paved streets, crowded houses, and white church fronting me. Such is the valley of Guaduas, a paradise as to temperature and fertility, where heat and cold are unknown, the thermometer being always between 70° and 76°. It is said to be unhealthy from dampness, but on this point I am not satisfied. I think it must be founded in imagination.

I stopped at one of the cottages on the way, and asked for water. A woman was sitting on the ground or a low stool braiding a palm-leaf hat, and her little daughter was beside her. They offered me dulce, which I declined. I waited there till my peon came up, and continued descending. It was now raining in the valley, and the shower at length reached us. We took shelter in a deserted cottage, near which I saw a beautiful Amaryllis in flower, perhaps "a garden flower run wild." Here I took my India-rubber encauchado, and also my gun. And now I found out a naughty trick of Gregorio's. He had taken a fancy to speculate a little in the huge dried fishes of Honda, and, finding my cargas rather light, he added a venture of his own. It was in contact with one of my blankets, which, when the fish became moistened with rain, became fishified, to my long discomfort. I remonstrated, and he placed some leaves of old thatch between the fish and my bedding.

From here my way was steep downward, in a road often slippery with rain, and, encumbered with my gun and encauchado, I continued a victim to my doctrine of passivity. At length I reached the plain without a fall, and soon was at the house of Mr. William Gooding. He kindly found room for my baggage in an empty house of his, and for myself at his table, thus defrauding the negress Francisca of her lawful prize. Every stranger that arrives in Guaduas is at once referred to this enterprising woman for bed, or board, or beasts to continue his journey. She will always promise you beasts; and, what is more, she will have them, if not at the time she sets, at least soon after.

I left Don Diego's montura, according to agreement, with his cousin, Señor Gregorio Tanco. He keeps a school here, about which I distrust both my recollections and impressions very much, so different are they from any thing I have seen since. First, girls went there, or at least I understood Mr. Gooding's little girls to say that there was where they went, and that, among other things, they learned *coser*, to sew. As *cocer** means to cook, and *coser* was new to me, I came near adding another ridiculous impression to my blunders about this school. I never elsewhere in New Granada knew a man to have any thing to do with a female school. Second, I believe boys went there. Now I can not think that the two sexes were permitted to attend the same school. Third, it seemed to me a good school. My opinion now is that the daughters of Mr. Gooding went and studied in the sitting-room of la Señora de Tanco.

In Guaduas I came also unexpectedly upon a female public school, but I did not go in.

When the peon had delivered the saddle and the accompanying letter, I wished to pay him off, so I called out, "Gregorio!" Señor Tanco, of whom I had just taken leave, reappeared, thinking I was calling him. Then I found that he was a tocuyo of my peon; that is, he had the same Christian name—nombre. Of the surname, apellido, they make little account. Tocuyo is often used in the vocative. Cristoval Vergara, when he calls Cristoval Caicedo, does not say Cristoval, but Tocuyo.

In paying Gregorio, I had a difficulty from not understanding the meaning of suelta, or plata suelta—small money, change.

* *C* has the sound of *s* lisped, and is often pronounced exactly like *s*.

He wanted suelta, for his mules had fasted three days without a mouthful—a fact I now do not doubt—and his home was far from town. I thought he wanted additional pay, and told him I paid him all I agreed to, and, over and above, had paid his ferriage and the freight on his fish. I think the price was six dollars—it may have been but five—for three mules and peon. So we parted.

The week I spent with Mr. Gooding's family was the first bright spot in my peregrinations. Some of the family spoke English, and I never have had any Spanish lessons more pleasant than those I received from the little folk there. At his table I learned the word guarapo, which here signifies a fermented solution of sugar, resembling new cider in taste and properties. In the Valley of the Cauca the same word is applied to simple cane-juice, either fresh or boiled. Guarapo is a cheap drink for peons, at the rate of eight quarts for a dime, and is not despised by gentlemen travelers at wayside inns at double that price.

Guaduas contains one of the two Houses of Correction—Casas de Reclusion—of New Granada. They have three orders of penitentiaries, according to the nature of crimes—Forced Labors, Presidio, and the House of Correction. Where the law would condemn a man to either of the two former, a woman or youth is sent to the House of Correction for a longer period, so that the proportion of boys and females here is large to that of men. Through the kindness of General Acosta, Jefe Politíco pro tem., who alone had power to grant admission to visitors, I was conducted all over the establishment. It was an extinct Franciscan convent, founded in 1606. These buildings make excellent prisons without any alteration. All public buildings, with scarce an exception, were originally built for convents, or have been seized on by the monks.

I found the inmates making cigars and cigar-boxes, and sawing out boards for these by hand. The discipline seemed excellent. The matron appeared to be well fitted for her task. To one of her punishments I ventured to object, as being hardest on the most sensitive or least depraved. It was shutting them up in the public coffin, in which corpses are taken to the grave, and then taken out to be buried.

There are some criminals here whose cases would be great

novelties in a criminal calendar. One was pointed out to me who conspired with a priest. She killed a man for whom she was *housekeeper;* and the priest testified to having married her to him in private before his death. She hoped to inherit his property, and share it with the priest.

Another woman and her daughter were there for a series of horrid cruelties practiced on unfortunate persons of their own sex that fell into their power. It seemed to be without motive, something like the case of a woman in New Orleans of whom I have read. This mother and daughter left one of their mutilated victims at the door of the hospital when they supposed she could never speak again. I think, too, that after their imprisonment a skeleton was discovered walled up in their house.

Guaduas was the residence of the father of the best-known writer of New Granada, Colonel Joaquin Acosta, as he is known on his title-pages, although he was a general when he died. He has done much for the geography and history of his country, especially while minister at Paris. There he collected and translated into Spanish numerous memoirs of Boussaingault, and abridged and republished the only scientific periodical ever published in New Granada, the "Semanario." He put in the church at Guaduas the only town-clock that I know of that has two hands in all the country. Part of his valuable library has become national property. His widow, an English lady, still resides here. The immense estate of his father is divided, I am told, between his family and his half-brother, General Acosta.

General Acosta is said to be a man of immense wealth. It is a pity that he has arrived now at the evening of life without ever marrying. Such a circumstance is far more common here than it ought to be. He is one of the most hospitable men in all the land. "Many persons," says Steuart, "are in the habit of partaking of General Acosta's hospitalities, and then of abusing him afterward," an example which he accordingly imitates; I can not.

I ate at his table one of the most characteristically Granadan dinners I ever saw. Among other articles too numerous and strange for me to enumerate, was one called bollo, which I took to be a white, tender, insipid root. It proved to be a preparation of maize, wrapped in the husks of the same and boiled.

It could not have been a favorable time for a botanist when I was at Guaduas, being just at the close of the dry season. In one excursion I went out on the north side of the river that runs through the place, intending to cross it far above, and come down a road that ran along its south bank. When I had gone up as far as I wished, I found a place where a hut had once stood, and the little path by which its occupants had brought water from the brook. Here I was within less than two rods of the road; but I had not taken my machete. After nearly an hour fruitlessly spent in trying to penetrate the thicket, I found night was coming on, and I gave myself up for foiled, and made an immense circuit over a horrid tract of rough grassy hills, and thus reached town.

In connection with Guaduas I must notice the guadua itself, the most indispensable plant of all New Granada after the plantain, the cane, and maize. It might be called the *lumber-tree*, for it supplies all our fencing except walls of brick, rammed earth, and, rarely, of stone, and also the wood-work of most houses, and whatever is made of boards at the North. It is an enormous grass, like the bamboo of the Eastern tropics, growing, however, to a less height, only 30 or 40 feet. The slender foliage is of inconceivable beauty, comparing with that of other trees as ostrich feathers do with goose-quills. The stem is about 6 inches in diameter, with joints about 20 inches apart. The thickness of the wood is nearly an inch.

When poles or slats are wanted, the stem is split into four, six, or eight parts. For boards for the top of a coarse table, bench, or bedstead, it is opened and flattened out, splitting almost at every inch of width, but not coming entirely apart. For a dish, candle-case, grease-pot, or extemporaneous vessel for carrying drink to a company of hunters or laborers, it is cut off just below the partitions. Such a receptacle is called a tarro. Tarros of double capacity are made for bringing the domestic supply of water for a family, by taking a piece two joints long, with a septum at each end and one in the middle. A hole is made in the upper and middle septa, and if they be used for carrying molasses, a bung can be put in, or an orange used for a stopper. Bottles of a single joint are used for holding castor oil, etc. In short, the uses of the guadua are innumerable. I met the lumber of it as far down as Sabanilla, and saw some bad specimens of the tree near Cartagena.

The guadua starts from the ground with the full diameter, or nearly so, but the joints are at first very short. Some trees send out branches, and they are long, straggling, and terribly thorny. Others grow with a diameter of only two inches, and make good poles for bringing down oranges, every one of which has to be torn from the tree, or it decays without falling. The cavities of the guadua often contain water. It is erroneously believed that the quantity increases and diminishes with the phases of the moon. Stones are said also to be found in these joints. This might be expected, but I never found an authentic instance, and doubt the fact. The only instance believed to occur under my own observation was certainly false, as the stone was an ordinary one.

I must state one other thing about the guadua which is unusual in the vegetable kingdom here, but very common at the North. It is apt to take entire possession of the ground on which it grows. Now a square mile covered with the same species, say a pine, an oak, or the beech, an acre covered with the same species of grass, or whortleberry, or other plant, is no uncommon thing at the North, but in the tropics it is quite different. Plants are not gregarious here, still less exclusive. I have seen the guava grow in natural orchards where most of the trees in a considerable space were Psidium, but even this is rare, and in general you can not expect, where you have found a plant you want, to find others of the same species near it. If I wish to find a second lime-tree, for instance, it is of no more use to look in the neighborhood where I found the first than in any other. But a guadual is a considerable space, almost always near a stream, where scarce the smallest intruding plant is permitted. The guadua might be cultivated to great profit, but I never knew of but one attempt at it. The flower and seed are so rare that few botanists have ever seen it.

One night Mr. Gooding's little daughters showed me a luminous coleopterous insect about an inch long, called here cocuyo. It was a snap-bug of the size and form of the largest known at home as the Elater ocellata, which closely resembles it except in the luminous faculty. They had three of them prisoners in "houses" made by splitting a piece of cane and cutting a cavity in it for each one, so that the walls of their cell serve them for food. They shine continuously, except when at rest, with a light no brighter than the instantaneous flash of the best of ours. But their light is of two distinct and beautiful colors, red and a yellowish green. I do not know if this depends on sex. It is generally believed that you can call the cocuyo to you by whistling, but the experiments I witnessed in the Cauca were adverse to this conclusion. I think it is Elater noctiluca.

I passed a Sabbath at Guaduas. At early dawn the plaza in front of the church was nearly filled with country people of all shades, from Indian and negro to white, with all imaginable productions of all altitudes. A Sunday market is a great annoyance to any decent family. It is so particularly to Mr. Haldane of Palmar, whose very name is suggestive of stiff Scotch Presbyterianism. He applied to Archbishop Mosquera to suppress the Sunday market at Guaduas, but he told him that it was the best day for a market, as these poor peasants could not spare two days to come to town, and Sunday being a holiday, they were bound to hear mass on it. There being two priests here, they have two masses, and the market-people may take charge of each other's goods in turn during the mass. The archbishop laughed at the scruples of the good Scot, and applied to him the sobriquet of "Bishop of Guaduas."

I attended here the first mass I heard in New Granada, having always before gone too late. A little daughter of Mr. Gooding went with me. She left her hat at home, and put on her shoulders a black shawl, which, on entering the church, she put on her head, and sat down flat on the floor. I felt a pang to see the amiable, intelligent child assimilated with the masses around her in dress and posture. The men never sit on the floor. If there be benches, men alone sit on them; and, if not, they stand: the women never stand. There are times when all must kneel, or be counted impious; at these times the bells peal, and the buyers and sellers in the market all uncover, at least. A Protestant who remains covered is liable to have things thrown at him, but would be protected by law. No resident Protestant has ever attempted to resist these requisitions of superstition, as far as I have learned. A traveler like myself, can generally escape compliance without inconvenience; but I hold that they have a right to insist on our uncovering in church, though in the rare cases that a lady wears a European bonnet—gorra—it is rather inconvenient.

Before describing the mass I will premise that the church, like almost all the others I have seen here, besides a gorgeous or gaudy altar at the end, had others of inferior splendor extending all along down the sides, looking not unlike a row of highly-ornamented mantle-pieces. Peculiar merit is ascribed to some of these side-altars. Over each was generally an image, sometimes a picture, covered by one or two curtains that roll up at the top by pulling a string. All the images are painted to the life, and dressed often absurdly, and the pictures often have jewels or finery stuck upon them, to the great injury of the few that are of merit. One form of the Crucifixion disgusts the stranger particularly. You get the impression that it was painted absolutely nude, and that some person, shocked at the indecency, has sewed on a piece of muslin. I have no doubt, however, that, on removing the real muslin, painted drapery would be found under it.

The mass is essentially the key-stone of the ancient and once gorgeous fabric of Romish worship. In theory it professes to be the creation of the body of Christ by a power given to a consecrated priest. This body is declared to be divine, not human—God, not man. Eating this body is the mass.

The ceremony of the mass varies slightly with times and seasons, as to the color of garments worn by the priest (paramentos), in the color of the altar decorations (ornamentos), and in some details of the words used; but it varies still more as to whether it is said or sung, low mass or high mass. Low mass requires only a priest, and a little boy for an assistant; but in a high mass two principal assistants are necessary, at least, and I think others may also have a part. A fluent priest will say a mass in 25 minutes, but it requires sometimes two hours to sing one; but the general plan and actions of both are the same.

The preparations are washing the hands and dressing, with some prayers, in a room adjoining the church, called the sacristía—vestry. The sacristía almost always opens out of the church at the right-hand farther corner. Once only I knew one behind the church, so that it was under the main roof, and not in a lean-to, as it generally is. From the sacristía the priest issues, robed, and bearing the cup, which is always of gold, or is gilt within. On it lies a silver plate—patena—like a cover, and on the plate something looking like a thin square book and an embroidered cloth. Among other things said and read is part of an epistle; this reading is on the right-hand side of the altar, nearest the sacristía. After this the priest crosses over to the other side, and, among other things, reads some in the Gospel. I have seen the nigh (left) side of a horse called the Gospel side.

The book (missal) is then placed obliquely, so that the priest can read standing in the middle of the altar. Now he opens the cover on the cup. Instead of paper, it contains a folded cloth. He unfolds it, and finds in it a white wafer of the size of a notarial seal, stamped with a cross. He lays this on the plate. He empties out of the cup a sort of salt-spoon, and perhaps a miniature dust-pan, both of silver. He then wipes the cup carefully and covers it. He goes to the right (Epistle) side of the altar. The attendant takes a miniature tea-pot off a tray of the size of a snuffer-tray, which he holds under the priest's fingers and pours water on them. He then empties the water caught in the tray on the floor, and the priest wipes the tips of his fingers on a towel, which the attendant kisses.

Then the priest proceeds to read immediately the words of consecration, and the wafer becomes a *hostia*—becomes, as they suppose, *God*. The priest kneels to adore it, and then, standing with his back still to the people, raises it high above his head for all to adore. An attendant rings the altar bell, and all kneel. Often the bells in the belfry are also rung. If persons are in front of the church, they ought, at least, to take off their hats, even though they be at some distance, and occupied with business. After the hostia is raised, the priest in like manner raises the cup, into which a large glass of wine has been poured. At this time all noisy demonstrations possible are made. The organ peals its merriest notes in marches, dances, or waltzes. If there be cannon or platoons of soldiers in front of the church, they fire. A sort of rocket, called cohete, is often let off, that rises a little way in the air, and bursts with a report like a pistol. The smoke of gunpowder sometimes enters the church, and mingles with the odors of incense. Soldiers on parade may stand with their caps on, and the organist keeps his seat. The Protestant may keep his seat or his feet, though greatly to the distress of the devout, who would put him down perforce if the law would let them.

The priest breaks the hostia into three pieces, and, putting a small one into the cup, eats the other two. He scoops up any imaginary crumbs that fall in breaking the wafer with the plate if he have no scoop for the purpose, and puts them into the cup. He drinks the wine, rinses his fingers, first with unconsecrated wine and then with water, and drinks both rinsings, so as to be sure that not a consecrated particle has failed of its destination. He then wipes out the cup, returns the spoon and scoop, and, with a few more ceremonies, closes the performance.

It would take too much time to describe the movements of the attendants in a high mass. To swing the censer, to carry backward and forward two ciriales, tall poles of silver with candles on top, to hold up the tip of the priest's garment when he kneels, pouring water, handing the towel, ringing the altar bell, taking part in responses, moving the missal, singing part of the service, etc., all in the right time, is quite a trade to learn.

A mass may be said in the time it takes to read this account of it; and the high mass (where every word is sung or drawled, and where the choir sing the responses which the attendant otherwise makes) is often avoided on account of its length. Several times during the mass the priest turns toward the audience, or to where they would be were they present, and says Dominus vobiscum—peace be with you. The response is, Et cum spiritu tuo—and with your spirit. During the confession in the earlier part of the mass, the audience give three light blows on their breast. If the attendance be large, a strange, hollow, and impressive sound fills the church. At the close the priest says, Ite, missa est—go, it is sent, or dismissed (sc. *concio*, the meeting). Hence the word mass; in Latin, missa; Spanish, misa.

I visited the cemetery at Guaduas. It is a substantial inclosure, with a chapel in the middle. Most of the bodies are buried in the ground, but the bodies of the richer class are placed in the oven-like bóvedas. In one case a husband was immured in one, leaving another beneath him yawning for his widow. Here I saw the bóveda of the lamented Acosta, the mouth closed with a beautiful, soft rose-colored stone, which, if it would endure our climate, would be admired for monuments.

Coffins are little used in Guaduas. In the chapel I saw two coffin-shaped boxes painted black, with a skull and cross-bones in white on every side, just similar to that which I saw at the prison. Here, too, I saw, thrown about the grounds, fragments of little extemporaneous biers for very small children, and in one spot a little pillow and some coarse rags, that touched my heart with a feeling of compassion. The cemetery is a good one for this country, and was probably originated by Colonel Joaquin Acosta.

Another feature of Guaduas remains to be noticed. It is the fountain in the Plaza. It is a structure resembling a monument, and is surrounded with a wall about three feet high. In the front and ends of the monument are the mouths of iron tubes, from which issue streams of clear water, brought from the neighboring hill in an open, drain-like aqueduct, called an acequia. The fountain itself is called a pila; the same word is applied to a baptismal font.

The water-girls come here with a large earthen jar—múcura —slung so as to rest on their hips, and a long tube in their hand. The múcura is placed on the low wall, one end of the long reed —often terminating in a cow's horn—applied to the mouth of one of the iron tubes, and thus the stream conducted to the múcura. When a múcura is nearly full, a struggle often occurs between two expectants, each desirous to fit her horn to the spout as soon as the other leaves it.

On reaching the house the múcura is emptied into the tinaja, which is a much larger jar with a wide mouth. Each house has a sort of arch of burned bricks, built generally in the corridor, with holes to receive two or three tinajas. This is called a tinajera. The tinajera might sustain the same relation to the family circle here, if any thing does, that the sacred hearth does at the North. "Pro aris et focis," then, must be translated, in New Granada, "For the little saints' cupboards and the tinajeras."

I assume Guaduas to be almost exactly 1000 metres in altitude, or 3281 feet, with a mean temperature of 74°. The thermometer has very little range, and, if it be not too damp, there can not be on the face of the earth a more delightful climate. There is, however, some goître here; but I believe that a little iodine water, taken daily, would prevent it or cure it. I thought I saw a case of cretinism, but it may have been ordinary idiocy. Goître is called coto, and a person whose throat is thus ornamented is a cotudo.

But I must leave Guaduas. It is a curious illustration of the influence of the customs of a country on our own habits, that I took leave of my little friends, who had gained a large place in my heart by their amiable, affectionate, winning ways, by a salutation little known here—a kiss. After considerably more than a year's experience of Granadan life and ways, I met them again, to my great delight, with an equally earnest greeting—an embrace. I can not say that kissing is used at all here, but embracing is in almost universal use in case of long separations, with inferiors, superiors, and equals, with persons of the same sex or different. Some illustrations of this will occur farther on.

CHAPTER VIII.

PLAIN OF BOGOTÁ.

The Negress Francisca.—Ups and Downs.—Venta at Cuni, and Sausage there.—Villeta.—Great Tertulia and hard Lodgings.—Excelsior.—The Plain.—Traditions.—Fences.—The Orejon.—Battle-fields.—Market-people.—Fontibon.—Entrance to Bogotá.

OUR party from Guaduas consisted of the two musicians, who had also been waiting in Guaduas in order not to change too suddenly their temperature and altitude, and two persons who had arrived in a subsequent boat the night before. These were a Bogotano, a printer by the name of Martínez, and a boy from Caraccas named Páez, traveling under the protection of Martínez. Altogether we had 11 beasts, furnished by the enterprising negress Francisca—la negra Francisca, as they always call her. She meant to count us off into three parties, each with less than five beasts, and, consequently, each obliged to pay for a peon as an extra beast. She would send with us three peons, and we would pay for 14 beasts. We resisted. I sent back the peon that was putting my trunks in their encerados, saying that I should engage another set of mules and peon, and travel by myself. She gave in, and sent two peons, and received pay for but 11 beasts. She had great difficulty in counting the money. I had to pay extra for my saddle, which was, at last, a bad one. I have lost the minute I made of the prices; but I once paid $12 80 for three beasts and peon (four) from Bogotá to Guaduas, and $6 40 from Guaduas to the bodega below Honda. These were high prices.

We started at 9, having already breakfasted. So early a start is a rare proof of the activity of the negress Francisca, but I did not then appreciate it as I now should, after more experience in Granadan early breakfasts. We soon found our mules' backs making an angle of from 20° to 40° with the horizon while they climbed the paved zigzags—quingos—which at length took us to where we could see the valley beneath us like a map.

At this rate we might reach the altitude of Bogotá before night, but here came a change. We were at the beginning of an enormous descent, and we could plainly see that if the road had kept farther to the north, it might have wound round this great hill, and saved all the descent and most of the ascent. We were now at the Alto del Raizal. Once at the bottom, we recommenced the ascent, and to a still higher point. This was the Alto del Trigo. Trigo means wheat, and it is quite possible that wheat will grow here, for it is at an altitude of 6139 feet, according to Mosquera, my best authority on this road. We have risen, then, 2839 feet. Lewy calls it 4148 feet, a little less than a mile, which is probably a clerical error of 2000 feet. Mosquera makes a similar one of 3000 feet in the altitude of Guaduas.

Before I was aware, I had passed the hacienda—estate—of Palmar, the property of Mr. Haldane, the "Bishop of Guaduas." I was sorry not to have seen this excellent man, who, it is said, has suffered much for his want of the peculiar tact necessary in managing peons. It is supposed that his first difficulty originated from ejecting a tenant for living with a woman he was not married to. The ceremony had been dispensed with to save the fee, $5 60. One attempt seems to have been made to assassinate the family, but the fearless Scot was an overmatch for his numerous assailants. A new cane-mill was burned to the ground the day before he was to commence operations on a large field of cane just ripe: he lost his crop. Again he engaged in the culture of coffee, and the last I heard was, he was losing his entire crop for want of a will to gather it.

All around us was a confused crowd of hills, separated by deep, narrow valleys. Every where on the sides are cottages and fields, but no roads visible. Many of the fields were cane-patches—cañaverales. *Caña vera* would mean *true cane*, that is, *sugar-cane*. There must once have been a cane-field at Cape Cañaveral, on the coast of Florida, or Florída, as the name used to be before Andrew Jackson reformed the pronunciation. The cane is the most odious-looking crop that ever covered the ground. The scanty leaves on its rigid stalks are of a sickly yellowish green, and before the beautiful tassels can come out to wave in the breeze, the stalk is cut for sugar or horse-feed. Nor does the cañaveral improve on a closer acquaintance, as it is difficult to pass through it without endangering the face and eyes with the harsh, stiff foliage.

At the Alto del Trigo I gave my horse into the charge of Nepomuceno, the little peon of little Páez, and walked down the long hill to Cuni. Every step down hill is two steps lost. In descending I saw a tall brick chimney, that at once suggested thoughts of the North. It proved to be an establishment of Mr. Wills, an Englishman, who has bought the monopoly of supplying the province of Bogotá with spirits. He makes it of cane-juice, which he extracts by water-power. Mr. Wills has long lived here, speaks and writes the language well, is deeply interested in the financial prosperity of the country, and was once appointed fiscal agent to London. He did not go, however, as the creditors there expressed a preference that his salary should be added to their scanty dividends. The huge kettle at the Bodega de Honda was for this establishment.

Three women fearlessly waded across the brook at Cuni while I was about picking my way across on some stones. They entered the first house; I followed them, and saw there the most perfect specimen of a venta that I have ever seen. You would have called the room I entered, the tienda, a miniature grocery, but it was less and more. How they live on their slender sales I can not guess; but in this instance they had managed to get up almost a casa claustrada, a perfect house. Most ventas consist of but a single room except the tienda, with perhaps a little cooking-house in the rear. At Cuni there is a small place where you may ride into the patio, and there is food that could be sold for horses, but gentlemen rarely buy, even when stopping over night.

As I was determined to wait here till the company overtook me, I set myself to watch the women. They called for a cuartillo of ajiaco. A cuartillo is not a measure: no measures of capacity are ever used in New Granada, and very rarely any other weight than the carga of from 200 to 250 of our pounds—a mule-load. A cuartillo is a fourth of a dime, and is the smallest of our silver coin. Some other passers at this time showed me the only copper Granadan coin I have ever seen. Practically the cuartillo is subdivided into cuartos, but you must lay out your whole cuartillo at the same tienda. Most loaves of bread and tablas of cheap chocolate are made to sell at a cuarto. A half cuartillo is a mitad, a medio is a coin worth half a dime, and a real is exactly a dime. It is legally divided into ten centimos, but they are never used.

I may as well say what remains to be said on coins now. The legal meaning of the word peso is ten dimes, but the word is always used for eight dimes. The traveler must never doubt on that point, but he is very apt to on being told once only. If, after a *verbal* agreement, legal pesos of ten dimes are demanded, resist the demand; it is an attempt to cheat that they never would try on an experienced traveler. Dollars are always denominated pesos fuertes, duros, or fuertes, except at auctions and in law documents. A patacon is a coin of eight reals, or a transverse section of green plantain fried hard. An onza is a gold coin sold at about sixteen dollars. They have a piece a little heavier than our double eagle, called a condor.

Well, numismatics have kept us till the poor women's ajiaco is hot, and brought in and set in a wooden ring nailed to the counter to hold the round-bottomed totuma steady. It is a broth or stew, containing pieces of potato or plantain, and perhaps, if the seller be generous, a mouthful or two of meat. If you had any confidence in the cook, the composition would not be bad to take. There was a single spoon, of totuma or wood, in the dish, with which each one took a mouthful in her turn, till, too soon, alas! the totuma was empty. There had been in it only a moderate allowance for one, and perhaps it was a case where the richer of the three was dividing her little all with her neighbors.

A still more amusing meal might have been witnessed some ten years since on this spot. A New York hatter, just speaking a few words of Spanish, who has been tormented and half-starved by the abominated Granadan cookery, and especially persecuted with cumin-seed, has his eyes gladdened by seeing suspended in this same tienda some veritable sausages, relleno (Bologna sausage is salchicha). An idea has struck him. He has seen sausages cooked; nay, he is sure he can cook them. He will have one feast, cost what trouble it may. He purchases *quant. suff.*, paying in inverse ratio to the Spanish he can speak. This is the easiest part of the task. With greater difficulty he secures an olla—home-made earthen cooking vessel—an olla of any form in which frying would be possible. He is conducted by the astonished natives to a spot yet to be described, a Granadan kitchen. By broken Spanish and gesticulation he superintends operations they have never seen before. With the vigilance worthy of a man whose life has been attempted a dozen times with cumin-seed, he watches against the introduction of all heterodox ingredients, and of that in particular. A visible success crowns his efforts. Eagerly he sits down to a large table, made of boards, with a full dish before him of sausages cooked as well as any that ever came from his mother's kitchen. The first morsel is now between his teeth, and he discovers—oh, horrors!—that things can be put inside of a sausage!

Steuart describes his emotions as follows: "Then I had it dished, while my delighted orbs of vision followed the direction of the knife, which immediately divided in twain the much-prized morsel; but oh! horror of horrors! my delicious anticipations all vanished with one fell stroke, for it revealed to me the fact that this, too, had been plentifully besprinkled with the always used and never-failing cumin-seed!"

For myself, I must admit that I had reached Cuni without tasting any thing more abominable than their sausage. It was the only thing that I found myself absolutely incapable of eating. My difficulty was with the garlic; Steuart's failure was attributed by the natives to his not knowing the proper way to cook them.

At this same venta I too have dined with the loss of less than an hour in waiting, and with a bill of 6 dimes for two. It would prove one of the best places to pass the night on the road, but it is scarcely possible to avoid changing beasts at Guaduas, and passing a night there, so that, in a well-regulated journey, you must be here nearer midday. But an ascent toward Guaduas from this point between 2 and 4 P.M. was one of the warmest pieces of traveling I have ever done in the tropics.

At length our party arrived, and I mounted and proceeded. Soon I saw a piece of made road. It looked like the grading for a railroad, only it had a sharp elbow in it. Nobody traveled it, for it was much easier to go across it than follow it. None but a North American can give New Granada carriage-roads, for in the United States alone are extensive portions of new and *cheap* roads located every year. Some persons, like "Blind Jack" of Derbyshire, England, have a genius for locating roads, and such a genius is much needed here. The Granadino runs his road straight up the hill and down on the other side. The European, who rarely has a new road to make, and knows no want of money, digs straight through; the Yankee goes round, and the Granadino should learn of him.

Again we commenced ascending. On the Alto de Petaquero I found a neglected orange-tree, and as I liked the idea of oranges to be had for the gathering, I rode under, and with some trouble filled my pockets. To my surprise, I found them apparently of another species, with an exceedingly thick rind, and of a pulp so sour as to be entirely uneatable. They are good only when cooked with sugar, or the juice may be mixed with water and sweetened. This is the Naranja agria, Citrus vulgaris, often called the Seville orange.

Another steep descent brought us to Villeta, the only real town between Guaduas and the plain of Bogotá. Mosquera puts it at the altitude of 2635 feet, with a mean temperature of 77°.

So it is considerably lower than Guaduas, and we have lost all the climbing we have done to-day.

I find, in two measured descents that we make in ascending from Honda to Villeta, a loss of 4792 feet, lacking only 488 feet of a mile perpendicular. Add to this the descent from the Alto del Raizal, and that from the Alto de Petaquero, and we have a sheer loss of much more than a mile climbing up, and the same quantity of climbing down. We have no idea of such a waste of force combined in one useless ascent and descent. Let the principal highway of a nation be led by zigzags from the base of Mount Washington up to the summit, and down on the other side, and it would be *much less* than the useless descent in a journey of a day and a half, given in the mail-routes as 11 hours, say 31 miles! It is to keep this precious specimen of a national road in the power of the greatest city of New Granada that the province of Bogotá is made to extend down to Pescaderias, embracing a people that are as far removed from the Bogotanos in customs and interests as in climate.

Villeta stands on the banks of the Rio Negro, which empties into the Magdalena near Buenavista. The future carriage-road to the river may run through this place, but not through Guaduas. That, however, is in a broader, greener, and much more beautiful valley than this, and has the advantage of being cooler, so that, though farther from Bogotá, it is much more visited. Villeta yields much more sirup and sugar. But I must explain these terms. The sirup is thin and watery, and bears the name of *miel*. Molasses drained from sugar is *miel de purga*. Thick sirup is *amíbar;* all three are *melado*. Honey (which is not here a table article) must be specified as *of bees* to be understood—*miel de abejas*. All the sugar made in Villeta is of the cheap form, which is called *panela*. It is sirup sufficiently concentrated to "grain," or form fine crystals without giving rise to molasses. It is cast in the form of bricks. It is often one third the price of coarse brown loaf-sugar, which alone bears the name of *azúcar*, and sometimes is a dime and a half per pound. Faint approximations to white sugar are common, but any that would bear the name of loaf-sugar with us is very rare.

All this while we were waiting dinner at the best posada or venta in the place. I sallied forth over the rough-paved streets, and came to the Plaza and the church, with its rude-painted images, and coarse, flat-looking pictures. The aspect of the church was like that of Guaduas, but poorer. The only thing of interest that I saw was an Orchid flower lying at the feet of a saint. It was the second flower of that Order that I had seen in the country, but I did not venture to take it. Returning from church I came upon the school. It was taught by an intelligent lad of seventeen, dressed in neat but dilapidated clothes. The room was furnished after the Lancasterian plan, but the teacher seemed to have no idea of any thing farther than the mechanical processes of reading, writing, and praying. I have seen many such schools since: few are much better, none much worse.

I returned to dinner, but it was not ready. Time enough had passed to have slaughtered a bullock, and cooked a dinner from it and eaten it. I suspected that they designed detaining us all night, but when our baggage had passed on they gave up and brought in dinner. It was no great affair after all, but we finished it so as to mount about 5 o'clock.

We followed up the Rio Negro, crossed Guama bridge, passed Guayabal and Mauve. About here I learned a new fact in Natural History. It appears that some of our beasts can not drink with the bit in their mouth—a most vexatious circumstance, that has many a time since brought me to my feet at a most inconvenient spot, on the muddy bank of a stream. One thing I am sure of: any horse that I should ride much would acquire this useful accomplishment in one day were I sure of plenty of drinking-places; but where you hire a beast for two days it is for your interest to humor him.

It was now dark, and we would gladly have found our baggage halted, but they had passed on with a diligence as yet inexplicable. We now entered on the Salitre, a patch of road that is sometimes so bad as to cost half a day to pass what we unconsciously crossed after dark. At last we arrived at a venta filled with a noisy crowd, and there we found all our trunks piled up under the eaves in a heap. It consisted of a single room besides the tienda. Within, one or two tallow candles, in a rude wooden chandelier, shed a dim light upon a dense mass of men and women. I made my way through it to where two or three were sitting at a table playing a sort of cards unknown to

Hoyle in number, name, or form. Cups, cudgels, golds, and swords—espadas—were the four suits, and I believe the number of cards was 40.

But there was music too, vocal and instrumental, and, I believe, dancing. The principal musical instrument was the tiple, a diminutive of the bandola, which is itself a reduction of the common guitar. The length of this implement of torment is a little more than a foot, and I do not think the strings are ever shortened by *stopping* them, as in the guitar and violin. This banjo, jun., is easily played, when once in tune, by drawing your fingers across it in any manner, only keeping time. It costs only two or three dimes, and the number that infest the land, not only in the tiendas, but by the roadside, is dreadful. The tiple was accompanied by an alfandoque, a small joint of guadua, with numerous pegs across the cavity within. It contains some pebbles or grains of maize. In a word, it is the most stupendous rattle-box ever clutched by grown-up baby. The word alfandoque also applies to a composition of sugar, full of cavities, so that it crumbles in the mouth like the candy they call kisses; but alfandoque is in the size of biscuits.

The eagerness of our peons to press on was now explained. The traveler must guard against passing near night a place where there is a holiday or merry-making, if his baggage is in the rear. Some unforeseen accident will inevitably happen to beast or peon, and you will sleep without your baggage.

I was glad to retreat from the crowd, and, as I was doing so, I trod on something soft. Thinking it a dog or cat, I took off my foot immediately, but there came not up that instantaneous cry of brute anguish that I expected, but in its stead, an instant after, the wail of a naked babe, that its ostrich mother had left to creep beneath the feet of the unshod crowd, and now was under the heel of my heavy riding-boot!

I felt sick, and when we met in council I found we were all desperate. I alone had a hammock. Our baggage was so mixed, and the peons were so *busy*, that we had hard work to get our night fixings. The Hollanders declared that they would not sleep there. They took their bayetones and went to another house, and came back again. There was a trough of molasses in the back porch, with a cover on it. This made a bed for the little Venezolano. Martínez spread his duds (trastos) on the ground, with a mat set up on edge to keep the cold mountain wind off his head. Over him I hung in my hammock, and when I became accustomed to the noise, I slept like a prince.

I awoke in the morning, and found the Hollanders sleeping at last, packed in together like two pigs, on the rough stones in front of the house, one bayeton serving them for mattress, like a feather on a rock, while the other served as blanket. They did not complain so much of their bed as of that infernal serenade. The performers were partly dispersed abroad, and partly spread over the floor, sleeping in various attitudes.

Without waiting for even a cup of chocolate, we took leave of the venta with a polyglot of valedictories that would not be worth the trouble and erudition necessary to record them. Not far from here I passed a Cinchona bush in flower; it was a useless species.

We breakfasted, after passing Chimbi, at Escobal or Agualarga. The meal was of fried beef and fried eggs, with fried plantains. Soon after setting out again a fine rain came upon us. I put on my encauchado, and lent my umbrella. Soon we came to dry ground, where no rain had fallen, and then again we were in the rain. When it stopped, I found myself in Aserradero, a spot that strongly reminded me of home. There was a house more Yankee-looking than usual, some grass fenced in, and even the plants seemed to present a different aspect. One little flower that there attracted my attention would have interested me more had I then known its significance. It occurs in all places above a particular height, and marks the boundary of the tierra fria, the cold region, as we ascend. It is a flower just like a dandelion, but it is stemless; and if you would find the connection between the flower and leaf, you must dig for it. It is the achicoria of the natives, Aschyrophorus sessiliflorus. It extends down to a height of about 7900 feet above the level of the sea—a very respectable altitude.

Long before reaching here we could have seen the outer rim of the great plain of Bogotá rising before us like the walls of a fortress, and we seemed to be approaching a very difficult place to surmount them. If there is a good place, I have never heard of it. Such a discovery will be necessary to a railroad, unless the engineer can teach locomotives to climb like ants or jump like crickets. Even an inclined plane would be more difficult to make than a hoistway. Our zigzag road was now as steep as stairs, and turned continually. But never did I expect to see such a vegetation. As I ascended, it seemed almost to shift past me. Among the flowers were species of the green-house genera, Begonia and Fuchsia. A bush without flowers, but with large leaves and very large clusters of little berries or nuts, particularly puzzled me. It was the strangest reduction of a poppy, Bocconia frutescens.

At length the ascent remitted its severity, and then ceased entirely at El Roble. We found here a venta, at which we stopped a while. Even then I could not believe that we were at the altitude of Bogotá, but we were and more. It was now not much past noon, but since dark last night we had ascended more than a mile perpendicular! We are here at an altitude of 8858 feet, according to Humboldt, or more than 300 feet higher than the summit of Mount Washington. Then we came down a gentle slope without rock, and at last the vast plain burst upon our eyes. It is the strangest spectacle to the traveler; it seems incredible that, after such an ascent, level ground can be reached without hours of descent. Before us the plain stretched thirty miles to the eastward, and having an extent of about sixty miles from Suesca on the north to Cibaté on the south. It has been calculated to contain 1378.3312172 square miles, or 220,533 acres and a few square inches over.

All this vast plain has been leveled by water; few doubt but that it was once a lake. If not, it has been a hollow of unknown depth, now filled with alluvium. So strongly marked is the dividing line between the hills, that form the rim of the basin, and the plain within, that the idea of a lake rises involuntarily to the mind of the unreflecting, and he calls the knolls rising out of the plain near its edges *islands*, and the hills themselves *shores*.

The Indians had a tradition that Chia, Yubecayguaya, or Huitaca, a beautiful but malicious divinity, flooded it, driving the inhabitants to the mountains for their lives. Bochica, her husband, called also Zuhé and Nemqueteba, transformed her into the moon, struck the barrier ridge with his staff, made the Falls of Tequendama, drained the plains, and then retired to Sogomoso, where he reigned for 2000 years.

What was the height of the water of the supposed lake? Tradition, of course, will say that its waters were drained off. But of this I found no evidence at all, although in other lake plains north of here I can not doubt the fact. But if a lake was ever drained off the surface of the whole plain of Bogotá, it must have been very shallow indeed in proportion to its extent.

To the Bogotanos this plain is the joy of the whole earth, and the fact that nothing will grow here but wheat, barley, grass, and a few roots, weighs nothing with them. So chill is its climate that frost may visit it in any season of the year. A sufficient succession of cloudy days and clear nights might at any month congeal its whole surface. Now it stretched away before us almost a dead level, with patches of water toward the centre, but elsewhere so parched with drought that it seems an Illinois prairie in October, and the temperature corresponded. It never assumes all the verdure of an extra-tropical spring just escaped from the prison of winter, but by reason of the transparency of the air, the strong setting of the picture in a framework of mountain, and the indescribable roughness of the country just passed over, the impression made by this plain can neither be effaced nor described.

We began to trot, and I found my breath failing me. I was obliged to beg the company to slacken their pace, for I could not gather strength to pull my reins, and was very near falling.

We had passed our posada without seeing it, and had to return. It was a very unpromising affair as to the exterior, with not a window to the street, but on riding through the huge portal we found ourselves in a casa claustrada, with an enormous patio. All the doors of the establishment opened into it, even that of the tienda, which, in every other venta, opens into the street. A small yard, six feet square in the centre, protected some shrubs.

Some macaws—guacamayas, Ara glauca—and a monkey blind of one eye, helped to people the patio. But what most interested me was a bird a little less than a turkey, called a paují. It was remarkable for a sort of ventriloquial voice, at first appearing to come from a great distance, and then appearing rather to resemble the humming that a stick makes when rapidly whirled in the air. It was probably Ourax alector.

Our posada, which bears the name of El Botello (not the bottle—la botella), was in reality better than ordinary, and, were it provided with stables and horsefeed, would be almost a country inn. One thing it could not give me—a place to hang my hammock in-doors, and it was too cold in the corredor. They tried to make up a bed to satisfy me, but I found it very hard. We had a very tolerable dinner and breakfast, and, on the whole, I was much pleased with the place.

On arising in the morning I was surprised to find the whole patio filled with carga mules, which gave me an exalted opinion of the popularity of El Botello. Just at this moment an explanation comes to my mind after I had long forgotten the fact. Wednesday is market-day at the town of Facatativá, and this assemblage of beasts, laden chiefly with skins of miel, could occur on one morning only in the week. They must have been nearly a hundred in number.

I committed a great error in starting from here across the plain without greasing my face, and particularly my lips. Grease is a good preservative against the effects of sun and wind. The wind here is often very dry, and you may pay dearly for kissing it. I have had my lips bleed for weeks after passing it, even with the wind at my back all the way. Many protect themselves by cloth, as if against cold, but it seems to me less convenient, and even less agreeable, to be so bundled up.

We started late from El Botello, and in bad order. First, they had our baggage so thoroughly mixed that, to get at my two cargas on arriving at Bogotá, it was necessary to unload four beasts. All my exhortations at El Botello to put my property by itself were unavailing. Second, part of the mules were suffered to start before all were loaded. This was probably designedly done, to give the peons a chance to chat with the market-girls at Facatativá; and at last it happened that we found part of our cargas entirely without a peon, and were obliged to drive them through Facatativá ourselves, or risk losing them. One dodged between two houses into a field, and I had a hard ride to drive him out, as my poor mule preferred rather to share the spoil with him than to make haste, and I wore no spurs.

Then, again, when clear of the town, we resolved to halt and wait a reunion of all our forces; but here occurred a difficulty: not one of the party knew the word to use to command the mules to stop; not the Venezuelano, nor even the Bogotano. The word used here is *ō-ō-ís-te;* in other places, *sh;* in others, *chĭt-to-o*. We adopted a better expedient: we bought a half dime of maize on the stalk (it can scarcely ripen here), and threw it to the famishing animals, and they waited contentedly till the peons arrived with the remainder.

Facatativá is a large, poorly-built town, with a population chiefly of Indian blood. Its main support must be derived from the herdsmen of the great plain; perhaps as a place for an intermediate sale of miel and other articles, that are brought here from the tierra caliente on mules, and which can be carried on carts to Bogotá. A rude cart rumbling past El Botello quite excited me. The road here is even too good, for the cost spent on it would have done much toward making a wheel-road to the Magdalena. Carriages come out here to bring or meet travelers, who are made to pay roundly for it. The distance is stated as low as seven leagues; the post-office calls it nine. I reckon it as twenty-eight miles.

As we proceeded we noticed a saw-mill on the left, not far from Facatativá, and where trees and water-power would seem nearly equally scarce. I know of but one other in all the country. It is at Tequendama, and, like this, is accessible to Bogotá by wheels. In fact, carriages and carriage-roads seem a necessary prerequisite to saw-mills, and it is not strange that there should be none off this plain. And how many interests of domestic economy depend on the existence of saw-mills!

Near the mill I saw a fence made of the trunks of tree-ferns set up on end. I recognized them without difficulty, although I had not yet seen them growing. A botanist would fancy a fence of so strange a material; here it was merely economy, as the shell of the trunk seems quite durable. They call tree-ferns here palo-bobo, fool-wood.

Soon I caught at a passion-flower that was not a passion-flower, for it had assumed a form so distorted as to take the name of Tacksonia. This new Passiflorate genus has numerous species here, several of which yield a fruit known at Bogotá as curuba. Some of them are very fine when well sweetened. The seed is swallowed with the aril, which is the only edible part. The curuba of the Cauca is a real Passiflora, which, if not a variety of the P. quadrangularis, known in our green-houses, and here called the badea, is certainly close to it. Both are huge fruits, as large as a small watermelon; but of the badea you eat the walls of the fruit itself as well as the arils, while of this curuba, as of that of Bogotá, only the aril serves. The utter neglect of cultivation of fruits gives rise to all my doubts as to these being varieties, and what adds to my difficulty is that I never have been able to obtain a ripe badea.

Another Passiflora, probably P. ligularis, yields the granadilla, one of the very best fruits unknown to the New York markets. The walls of the fruit are thin, and, when broken open, are clear and dry; and the mechanical process of taking out the rich, juicy, sweet arils with a fork or spoon is in itself a very agreeable one. The granadilla, and all the Tacksonias, are plants of high lands, and only the badea and the Caucan curuba grow in Tierra Caliente. All are vines that will flower in our green-houses, but all cast their fruit there. Query: Would not P. quadrangularis perfect its fruit if kept at a temperature below 70°?

A few words more will finish all I have to say of the Passiflorate plants of this country. Several have very small fruits and flowers. One, with a large, pretty flower, has a tolerable fruit, with a very hard shell. Another, with a viscid calyx, has a fruit so thin that it is called paper granadillo—granadillo de papel. I found one Passiflora that was an erect bush, and another still was a *tree!* it was so high that I had to stand on my horse's back to reach the lowest limbs.

I noticed another vine on the plain terminated with enormous clusters of large, beautiful flowers. It was an Alstrœmeria. Other species grow here, but none so splendid. I found, also growing by the road-side, Tropæolum majus, known to children at home as "stertian," and also two or three other species. How came the stertian in our gardens? Who sent the seeds from this plain, and whither, and why? What merit has diffused the little vine over the world? Lastly, here an enormous herb, or a stout shrub, raises its head six or eight feet high, crowned with a profusion of cream-colored pendent solanate flowers eight inches long. It is Datura arborea, known as borrachero, or the intoxicator. There is a yellow-flowered variety, and another species with smaller red flowers—D. sanguinea—is cultivated in some patios in Bogotá.

The plain appeared so much like prairie that I often forgot myself. It is inclosed from the road by ditches, often made of two rows of deep square pits, alternating with each other, so that the idea of leaping it suggests instantly that of a broken bone. The arrangement is exactly that of two rows of cells in a honeycomb. Farther on I saw a man making or renewing a ditch of the ordinary description. He scooped the earth up with a paddle, or his hands, and put it into a piece of hide, in which he threw it upon the bank. At other places a thick, high wall of rammed earth—tapias—or of large unburned bricks—adobe—serves as a fence, but it must have a roof of burned tiles, or a protection of twigs of bushes, laid on transversely and covered with sod.

Fences are rare in this country. I reached Guaduas before learning the Spanish for fence. Very few indeed are of wood. I asked a man the reason of this, and he replied that wood would be stolen for fuel. I suggested that at home the study of the Bible in Sabbath-schools had been found an effectual preventive of petty thefts, when severer remedies of law, and other man-traps, had proved of no avail. He replied that he had been informed that we used mutilated copies of the Bible in these schools. He thought the measure questionable, even for so laudable an object as to protect fences. This man is one of the few gentlemen who still keep up their fasts, confess, and commune. He is an exception.

At one place, in an immense pasture, we saw hundreds of cattle, and some men on horseback examining them or catching some, but the scene of operations was too far from the road for me to observe them sufficiently. As the mode is different there and in the great plains east of Bogotá from that practiced here in the Cauca, I am sorry not to have seen both.

The rich proprietors on this plain are not highly respected by

THE OREJON.

the gentry of keener wits and lighter purses, who call them Orejones, or big-eared; but why, I really can not tell. They describe them as big, burly, brutal, and butcher-like, with a characteristic face recognized every where, and which marks the bearer as rich and stupid. But I have great fear of doing them an injustice, and an impression that a nearer acquaintance with them would bring out some excellent qualities.

The above sketch is by one of these characters, and is as bad as it well can be and be faithful, but faithful it is. It is exactly as I saw him when I found him paused on his steed near a low, tile-roofed venta on the Sabana, as they call the great plain.

Let us study him. In every feature of his face is written

OREJON; and the handkerchief tied on under his hat but makes the expression of his countenance the more pitiable. His broad jipijapa hat is covered with a case (funda) of red oiled cloth, and is held on by a borboquejo or string passing under the chin. His ruana is of wool, a mixture of a dingy color and bright stripes. His nether man is encased in zamarras of goat-skin with the hair on. They are made like the legs of pantaloons, connected only by the waistband. The feet are armed with a formidable spur, and thrust into brass or copper slipper-shaped stirrups, which cost from eight to twelve dollars. Into our ordinary stirrup of the north—estribo de aro, hoop-stirrup—he would not put his foot.

His Rosinante is of the meek, tame kind when he has no fear of the spur, but knows what it is to be severely ridden, and has more long fasts in the year than his master. Under the bridle is a halter—jáquima—the end secured to the saddle; it serves oftenest to confine the horse by the simple contrivance of pulling its broad, worsted-worked head-piece down over the eyes. Little is seen of the saddle save the well-filled pockets on which the rider's hands now rest, and the back strap—arretranca—so useful in riding down stairs to tierra caliente. Well, you have seen the worst of him. The best is, that in morals he is on a par with, or above the average character of those who speak so lightly of him.

Again we saw great stacks of wheat, and men thrashing wheat beneath the feet of mules, and others throwing it up against the wind, a primitive mode of separating it from the chaff. This plain is the great wheat-field of the republic; and, although in all the colder parts it will grow readily, it is only in these ancient beds of mountain lakes that the land is level enough to admit of the rude cultivation practiced here. Off the plain of Bogotá I have never seen a plow, and only once there have I seen one that threw up such a furrow that you could tell which way the plow had been drawn. In other words, the plow here is in the primitive state, an instrument for scratching, not for turning the soil.

Now we have on our right, near the *shore* of the plain, a small town, with its little church, not half a mile from the road. It is Serrezuela, the head of a little district of 1094 souls. Next we come to Cuatro Esquinas—the Four Corners. Here are several houses at the junction of our road with one from La Mesa, which enters the plain at Barro Blanco. This, too, is macadamized to the edge of the plain. We have been coming from the northwest, and La Mesa lies due west from Bogotá, so that this is the ordinary road for the Upper Magdalena, the Cauca, the Pacific, and Ecuador. Standing at the Four Corners, the road east goes to Bogotá; west, you go on the northwestern road to Honda and the Atlantic, and south, the road leads to the western and southern parts of New Granada. The north road leads to the little ancient Indian town of Funza, once the capital of the plain when Bogotá was only a watering-place. It is a pity that they had not pitched on the western side of the plain, where there must be more sun and less rain, so as to save me this long ride; but the copious cold streams rushing down to the plain from the eastern ridge drew the town to the junction of the last slope with the plain.

A little farther east an immense gateway gave passage to a road up to a building large enough for a railroad depôt. It was only an ordinary hacienda or farm-house. Large houses are a weakness of the Orejones, and they delight especially in a gate of magnificent proportions.

Now my eye catches a little white spot half way up the blue barrier of mountain before me. It must be the church of Montserrate. I now scan more clearly the ground beneath it, and see lying straight before me, and in full view, the city of Bogotá. It had lain hid so long on account of its dingy color, so closely resembling the hill behind it. Besides the dark-yellow front of the Cathedral, which rises in ample proportions, fronting the plain, you see little else than tiled roofs. A distant city is always a blotch upon the canvas. It has none of the beauty of a village, and is but a chaos of roofs mixed hap-hazard with steeples. How could it be otherwise? Still, the State-house at Boston, St. Paul's in London, St. Peter's in Rome, and the Cathedral at Bogotá, all give a character to the respective cities, as if they were the only buildings in them—they are, in fact, the only features they have.

The road advances straight toward the city till it meets the lowest part of the plain, the marshes through which the sluggish Bogotá creeps toward its only possible exit from the Sabana at the south. Here we turn almost north, and seek, for miles, a place to cross. We pass the hacienda of Quito, the owner of which lost much in my estimation by receiving full price for a horse too weak for me to ride, and which, indeed, I could hardly drive before me, as I ascended on foot the weary steeps from La Mesa to the plain; but he lets mules on a wholesale scale, and if he gave heed to reclamations, he would suffer a thousand impositions. Besides, if it is his portrait which I have given a few pages before, I am amply revenged.

The Dutchmen had preceded us on fresh horses, taken at Facatativá, and, as the road at last turned down to the river, the little Venezolano, who had not stopped to be acclimated at Guaduas, became too unwell to keep on; and Martínez, in whose charge he was, stopped with him at a venta to await the cargas, and I proceeded entirely alone.

But let us pause a moment at the causeway that leads straight toward Bogotá again, and is conducting us down to Puente Grande, the bridge over the Bogotá. Near where we stand the fates of two revolutions have been decided. Behind us, as we face the city, is the field of Santuario, two leagues from Bogotá, say 5½ miles. Here, on the 27th August, 1830, in the language of Samper,* "the fanatics of the plain threw themselves, in the name of the most holy Virgin," upon the troops of President Joaquin Mosquera, routed them, and placed the usurper Urdaneta on a dictator's throne. The reader must be cautioned that there was another battle of a Santuario in the province of Antioquia in October, 1829.

Turn your face again toward the bridge and Bogotá, and on your left is the field of Culebrera. Nay, the very ground under our feet has been drenched in human blood, for here where we stand died the revolution of 1840, in a vain attempt to pass this causeway and bridge on the 28th October. All Bogotá had been thrown into commotion by the approach of insurgents from Socorro. Priests and women had aided in the transportation of all the military stores to the Plaza, and the conversion of the eight blocks adjoining it into a citadel, when here, at the very threshold of the capital, "the Revolution of the Governors" breathed its last.

* Apuntos para la Historia, page 148.

The Bogotá, as we here pass it, is rather a marsh than a river. A small outlay, no doubt, would drain a large portion of it. Beautiful white cranes were flying over its shores in large numbers. They are called garza, and are probably Ardea alba. One species of fish alone is caught in this chilly, sluggish stream, and this has a sort of reptilian look, which belies its excellent flavor. They call it capitan. It is almost finless, and must be slow in its motions. How came it up here? When the ichthyology of the Andes shall have been studied, some curious facts will appear.

INDIANS GOING TO MARKET.

Nothing has touched my heart more than to see the poor people, women especially, loaded with articles that they carry to market. Once, when I saw a couple loaded like those before us, a whole day's walk from Bogotá, I could not restrain my tears. Look at this couple in raspon hats. The man wears nothing more, perhaps, except his pantalones and ruana, or he may have a scanty camisa besides. Except the mantellina under the woman's hat, and the camisa that extends but a little below her waist, she wears only a chircate, a piece of cloth, like a shawl, wrapped around her, and held in place by a belt called a maure. The fish they carry, with each a rush through its gills, are not uniform enough in their diameter to be the capitan —too large at the thorax—therefore I suspect they come from tierra templada. Their guambías then probably contain yuca or plantains. Happy they if they shall succeed in selling all they have, including the dog, whose own feet have brought him.

I passed these poor people at Puente Grande, and thought myself entering the suburbs of Bogotá, especially when I reached Fontibon. This is the head of a district of 1985 souls, separated from Bogotá by farms and marshes, and by what I thought was rather a long strip of road. This is the turning-point of many a little ride from the city, and a very convenient place to dispose of some loose change. Probably a billiard-table could be found, or a pack of cards, and possibly every other appliance of gambling known at this altitude.

Two circular enlargements of the road here excited my curiosity, but my inquiries were in vain. I subsequently learned that they are called las Vueltas de la Vireina: they were made for the turning-places for the carriage of the Viceroy's lady, which was too cumbrous to turn in the ordinary width of the road. After this, a sudden contraction of the road, as if a bridge with a high parapet, announced the entrance of Bogotá, which must mark the conclusion of this chapter.

CHAPTER IX.

POSADA AT BOGOTÁ.

A House at Bogotá.—Servants.—Abnormal Cookery.—A Visit to the Kitchen. —A Discovery.—Sickness.—Rooms and Furniture.—Food and Fruits.—A Love Affair.

THE reader surely can have no wish to know the precise names of those who for sixteen dollars per calendar month gave me shelter, food, and attendance, and all the other thousand comforts and annoyances incident to family life in Bogotá. That city has no hotel, and but one boarding-house, and as that is an English one, and has few inmates that do not speak English almost entirely, the very words "board" and "boarding-house" have scarcely an equivalent in the popular language. Perhaps, like the English word "self-government," these too may be yet transferred to the language to which the idea is now foreign.

The normal way of living here is to hire a house or a "habitation," and either eat at a fonda, have your meals sent in to you from a fonda, or hire a cook. This last implies either that you also go to market and have your provisions stolen at home, or send your cook to market to steal your money. The last is preferable, if the cook be not insatiable; but an alternation of evils is always better than the long continuance of the same, so you should at least make a part of your purchases. It is not wise to turn off a servant for peculation, for you may get in his place one who has been long out of employment, and who, consequently, has some months' back stealing to do. It would not be imprudent to take a servant into your service who has just been discharged for theft, for of all thieves an unsuspected one is the worst. In a word, any inquiry into the morals of your servants is simply ridiculous; you may rest assured that they have none.

From all these perplexities I was saved by a letter of introduction from Mr. Gooding to Don Fulano de Tal. This I delivered in person to la Señora Tomasa, his wife, in five minutes after the close of the last chapter. La Señora Tomasa is said to be the fattest woman in Bogotá, where obesity is not common. She is chiefly characterized by a head of black hair that always looks like a rat's nest, but there is no part of her whole person that is not in keeping with it. The worst of her is external; but a man with a strong mind and a strong stomach makes little account of externals. I followed Mr. Gooding's advice, and became at once her guest.

She showed me the house, which was a casa claustrada of one story, with a second patio behind the first, built only on two sides, and a third behind that, which has only a shed (XVIII.) on one side. The front is equal to about three house-fronts in a Northern city. It fronts the west, and the zaguan (1) is in the northwest corner. It is paved with stones of the size of a double fist. The door from the zaguan to the patio is very large, and is opened only to let in horses. It has a little door cut in it, and, as you pass, you must raise your foot and lower your head. This last I often forgot to do till I had received a blow.

CASA CLAUSTRADA.

1. Zaguan.
II. Corredor.
3. Sala.
4. Bed-room.
5. Tienda.
6. Dining-room.
7. Servants' Dormitory.
8. Guests' Room.
9. Host's Sleeping-room.
10 and 11. Proprietor's Rooms.
12. Passage.
XIII. Back Corredor.
14. Study.
15. Pantry.
16. Kitchen.
17. Passage.
XVIII. Shed for Horses.

The front was occupied by the sala (3), with its portraits of Mary and Joseph, and a nice image-closet, that contained a Dolores or la Dolorosa; that is, a Mary, with a dagger in her heart, her hands spread out, with a cloth lying across them, and her upturned eyes red with weeping. Some stuffed birds; two sofas, of chintz; a strange ottoman, that looked like the middle section of a trough, with flaring sides, and the matting on the floor completed the furniture. Carpets are not to be expected in ordinary houses here. But I forget an important and rather uncommon article—a good mantel-clock.

The adjoining bed-room (4) was devoted to the riding establishment of Don Fulano, his gun, his blunderbuss, and other precious articles. The windows of the parlor and this room opened to the street. The south side of the patio was occupied with a little dining-room (6), having no window, and a little room (7) with an unglazed window, where three servants slept. The east side had one large room (8), with a door and window, which became my quarters. Next was a passage (12) to the second court, closed with a leathern door by day and stout wooden ones at night. North of this was the family sleeping-room (9), which extended into the corner so as to leave no room for a window. On the north side were two little rooms (10 and 11) appropriated to Don Pastor, the landlord, who occasionally came to town and spent a night. All these windows were furnished with a reja, and with doors to them, and most of them, also, with glazed sash on hinges. Glass is almost a necessary to the rich here, but unknown to me in all other places in New Granada.

The first patio was paved, but had several plum-trees, cherished objects with Don Fulano, and some pots of flowers. Its corredor (II.) had a matting on the northern half, as this was more trodden by visitors and less used by servants than the rest. The second patio had an unpaved garden, with a fig-tree, a papaya, more plums, and a minute apple-tree half dead with cold. By way of annuals, there were potatoes and other esculents. The west side of this patio was occupied with my little study (14), an open corredor (XIII.), and a dirty pantry (15). A few steps led down to a still dirtier kitchen (16), to a little space (17) containing an oven, in which there never has been a fire, and to the door of the third patio. This is all paved, has a shed (XVIII.) and manger on the south side, with a door opening on a back street or vacant lot.

This place, designed to accommodate more horses than the house could hold of guests, was entirely in the occupation of a dog of the Newfoundland breed and feminine gender, whose offspring were held by the Señora at high prices, as they were difficult to raise at lower altitudes. These would do well but for the supposed nightly visits of the bats, who are said to keep them poor by sucking their blood. No one doubts these vampire stories, but some confirmation of them would be desirable.

While I was looking at these things, a servant-girl had placed on the parlor-table a little cup of chocolate, a slice of cake, and a saucer of sweetmeats. This was my dinner that day, as frequently happens on a journey. This over, I sallied out to meet my baggage, which, fortunately, was just entering town at the close of twilight. We proceeded to the little Plaza of San Victorino, and had halted for an instant, when I heard an English voice ask, "Is there an American here?" It was Mr. John A. Bennet, our excellent consul, who had learned that he had a countryman coming in the party. And I have never found him less prompt or less friendly to any stranger, even though he come, as I did, without any letters to him.

Thus I settled myself in the family of Don Fulano de Tal. A little cot-bed gave me a warmer embrace than my cold couch at El Botello. I awoke from it, and waited in the morning to see whether I was to eat in the house. While meditating on this, Ignacia, an Indian girl of 17 years, and a little over five feet in stature, came into my room and spread a cloth on my table. What else she put on I can not say, only first there was something that they called sopa, because it resembled soup in being eaten with a spoon. I can offer no conjecture as to the ingredients. Another dish was the ajiaco that we saw at Cuni: it contained potato, fluid a little thickened with something, and traces of meat. Another dish contained what comparative anatomy would call chicken, but the palate would conjecture might be lizard. But it is colored yellow. This is one of the inventions of Spanish cookery. It is often done with arnotto, called achiote or bija. It is Bixa Orellana. Some time afterward I objected to this addition, which only served to prevent the eye from judging of the real condition of things. La Señora named it cover-dirt (tapa-mugre), and banished it from her kitchen. My breakfast ended in chocolate.

My dinner seemed but a repetition of my breakfast, except that it ended in sweetmeats instead of chocolate. As to what occupied the butter-plate, I ventured to suggest that if the butter were on one plate by itself, and the other ingredients on another, I could perhaps make a mixture more in accordance with my own palate. The good lady tried to improve on my suggestion, but with indifferent success. So minute were the particles, and so intimate their dissemination through the butyraceous gangue, that it seemed as easy for the Ethiopian to change his skin. The result was, that though Bogotá furnishes a dozen kinds of good bread, I soon forgot the use of butter.

All bread is made in small loaves of 16 for a dime (a cuarto each). None is made in families, as far as I ever knew, nor have I yet seen a bakery. I suspect those that make it sell but a dollar's worth or so per day. There is little consumption for the article, as it is beyond the reach of the poor.

Only the last session at the table afforded unmingled pleasure. I can not call it a meal. It was but a single cup of chocolate, with a piece of bread or cake, a saucer of dulce—sweetmeats—and a silver goblet of cold water.

After a day or two I asked permission to come to the family table, which was acceded to with much satisfaction, but my little *tea* continued to be in my own room. The change of table gave my landlady a better opportunity to study my tastes, which she did with the diligence that I afterward gave to those of an armadillo. She spared no pains to gratify my palate. I am sorry she succeeded no better; but, while my pet starved to death, hers has survived. And, if variety would have sufficed, none could have excelled her; and my dishes were almost as exclusively mine as when I ate alone. Never was hostess more indefatigable, nor guest more uncomplaining in his sufferings. Suffice it that the experiments lasted the two months of my stay.

I dare not undertake to tell you of all the strange things I ate and attempted in this time. One of their dishes was blood thickened, seasoned, etc. This I would not eat. I based my refusal on the decision of the Council of Jerusalem (Acts, xv., 29); but they make nothing of that, for they seem to think that in decrees of councils, as in acts of Legislatures, the last is binding to the exclusion of all the others. Now, as the Council of Trent did not command, as I am aware, to "abstain from meats offered to idols, and from blood, and from things strangled, and from fornication," they can not be expected to be very scrupulous on such points.

One day I wanted to see the Señora, and she was in the kitchen. So I went in. Now, good reader, I am caught. I have been dreading these fifty pages the necessity of describing a kitchen. Well, I submit to my fate. Of course, the kitchen has no floor. A floor would be useless—nay, impossible. As well might you carpet a foundry. Second, it has no chimney. A chimney would not be impossible—there are several in Bogotá, but of what use are they? Smoke consists of creosote, acetic acid, and carbon. The last is perfectly inert, the first a valuable antiseptic, and the other an important condiment, and no harm can arise from an admixture of the three as in bacon. A portion of the roof is raised, so as to permit the egress of smoke and steam without admitting rain.

Most ordinary cookery is done in a sort of forge, having a series of little fire-places over which ollas can be placed. These are coarse earthen pots, often unglazed, and of various shapes and sizes. The olleta of cast brass, in which chocolate is made, resembles a quart pitcher in size and shape.

And now what is doing here? Petronila is busy at the grinding-stone bruising wet maize to dough. The Indian corn here never enters a water-mill, nor does it enter largely into Granadan cookery. La Señora is seated on a low stool; before her is a jar—tinajon—as large as the oil-jars in the Forty Thieves, each of which was capable of concealing a man in its capacious abdomen. It is mounted on three stones—tulpas—so that a fire can be put under it where it is and when she chooses. Here you see the convenience of dispensing with those troublesome contrivances, floors and chimneys. On her right hand is a tray of Petronila's freshly-ground dough, and a dish of peas (alverjas) or chick-peas (garbanzas—Cicer Arietinum). On her left is a tray containing part of the mortal remains of a pig, cut in pieces of about an ounce each, bone extra, and a pile of the green leaves of an Indian-shot plant—a Canna, called achira. It may be Canna Indica, and its leaves are used here, like those of other Marantate plants, for wrapping up things.

She takes half a leaf, puts in it a spoonful of dough, a spoonful of peas, and a piece of pork, folds the whole up, and deposits it in the tinajon. This she repeats till the ingredients are exhausted. Water is then put in. All Saturday night these little green packages of miscellany are boiling over a slow fire, and on Sunday morning La Señora's tienda is thronged with purchasers of tamales. Imagine a tamal now on your plate. You open it with fork or fingers, and you see what irresistibly strikes you as an accidental juxtaposition, not mixture, of heterogeneous matters, like the contents of a turkey's crop disclosed by the carving-knive. It is hard to overcome prejudice, but I have learned to eat tamales with relish, and have even perpetrated the pun, "No está mal, it is not bad." *No es tamal* would mean it is not a tamal. *Es* and *está* both mean *is*, but with a curious difference. *Es* refers to a permanent or essential condition, *está* to a temporary or accidental one. *Esta naranja es dulce, peró está agria: this orange is sweet, but it is sour*, means that it is of the sweet species, but not sweet yet because not ripe. *Soi mal* means I am wicked; *estoy mal*, I am sick.

But I have said nothing of Don Fulano; indeed, there is little to say. He is the reverse of his wife, a dry little Quiteño, rather neat, and as friendly as a man can be. He was a helpmeet for La Señora in the arduous task of pleasing her guest. Señor de Tal had but one weakness: after church, at which he was quite constant, he must go to the cock-fight every Sunday. He never lost large sums, for he could not afford to bet high. His only income was derived from his salary as shop-keeeper in a small dry-goods store. A sprightly little boy, of very inoffensive, affectionate manners, was all their family.

For a long time the southwest corner of the house (No. 5 of the plan on page 139) was a mystery to me. I thought it might be another kitchen, and, what seemed strange, there was evidently an immense amount of talking done there. One day Señora Tomasa called me to follow her through the crooked passage that led to it, with the air of one who was about to reveal a surprising mystery. On my left hand, in the passage, was one of those places like a blacksmith's forge, where much minor cookery is done; on the other were some huge tinajas, sheathed in hide, called also gacha or tinajon, filled with a nasty-looking, whity-yellow liquid, covered with the bubbles of an active fermentation. It was chicha, the great bane of the tierra fria—an Indian drink, compounded of maize, sirup, and water, that carries the Granadino just as far toward intoxication as he generally desires to go; for he differs from us in that he gets satiated before he gets drunk, and we only when we can swallow no more; and the difference is in his nature, not in his beverage, for, if he drinks aguardiente, it is all the same. Chicha mascada, prepared by chewing the maize, if it exists except in the imagination or credulity of travelers, must be rare indeed. Most persons here believe in its existence, but I know of no one that has seen it prepared.

Well, with a sudden turn of the passage I found myself in a tienda, behind a counter, and face to face with a goodly assembly of customers. Whether she wished to show me to them, or them to me, I know not, but she appeared highly satisfied, and must have appreciated my surprise. It was a tienda of the lowest kind, and would, at the North, have been a horrible nuisance. It was a damp evening, and the little space in front of the counter was wedged full of people, one of whom was torturing one of those horrid little abortions of the guitar, a tiple. In a brief space, procured at the expense of a greater condensation of the rest of the crowd, a forlorn couple were trying to dance. Others were talking, and totumas of the turbid fluid were passing from mouth to mouth. Others would force their way up to the counter, and expend a cuartillo in bread, chocolate, lard, and wood, receiving as a bonus a drink of chicha from the ever-open tinaja behind the counter. The oldest and largest of the servants, whose name it is blasphemy to utter lightly, is the presiding genius of this condensed bar-room for both sexes.

Of the cook I know nothing, except that, like all the rest of the servants, she rarely changes her camisa. One of them one day made her appearance in a clean camisa, and I took occasion to express so much admiration that the others felt constrained to follow suit.

Not to use terms for dress before defining them, I may as well here describe an ordinary peasant-dress throughout; nor is the task a long one. The camisa begins a few inches below the chin, and extends as far below the waist. It has an inch or two of sleeve, and a sort of collar, cape, or ruffle falling down from the upper edge—arandela. This is often embroidered with red or blue, but the garment, when clean, is white. The enaguas extends from the waist to a proper distance from the ground. As this may be the only other garment, an accidental loss of it might discompose even the least reserved of the wearers of it; so it is divided into two flaps by openings at the sides, and each one is secured to the body by a separate string, that of the forward lobe being tied behind, and the other in front; so the whole person, or enough of it, is scientifically covered, but the two garments do not overlap much. Add to the dress in-doors a woolen shawl—the mantellina—which, like the enaguas, should be always blue or black, and a man's palm-leaf hat, and you have the peasant Granadina in sufficient dress for street or church. In warmer climates, a thinner shawl or large handkerchief—pañolon—is substituted for the mantellina.

A girl named Petronila formerly made her appearance every morning, with her múcura and long tube, bringing water. I am sorry to say that, when a regiment stationed in Bogotá left for the south, she disappeared. These bodies of troops are said to be followed by more women than there are men in them.

While here I paid the common matriculation fee to a residence—an attack of the diarrhœa. The exciting cause was a brief dip in the icy waters of the Fucha, a mile or so south of the city, where others bathe almost by the hour with impunity. I am sorry that I must believe that the attack was prolonged by the interference of my medical advisers in my plan of treatment.

My disease involved a variety of privations besides that of locomotion, and impressed me with the idea that my motherly hostess had not the talent that we often find in kind ladies of her age. She fed me at first on sagú—arrow-root (hence, perhaps, our word *sago*), of which New Granada cultivates all it uses, and no more. If I found this insipid, the chicken-broth that succeeded it was not much less so, for the Andine cooks have an innate faculty of destroying the natural flavor of all meats. Turkeys are here reduced, by their process, to a viand as unpalatable as the rest.

One other little circumstance occurs to me: from some cause, I had occasion to spit frequently, and laid down a paper on the floor for a spittoon. La Señora sent in a mat as a substitute for the paper; and the Indian girl, after putting it just where I wished, spat on the floor beside it, and went out. Indeed, I had no other reason for using the mat than to keep myself from learning nasty tricks, for there was no way of saving my floors from my visitors, nor even from La Señora herself, although, for a wonder, I never saw her or any of her family smoke. The servants, I presume, smoked, but it is contrary to etiquette for a servant to smoke in the presence of superiors, or for a soldier to do so on duty. I never should have changed my boarding-place but for circumstances that connected me with a companion for traveling. He was a cachaco: the word indicates such young men as wear coats, and might include all English words from *buck* and *dandy* to gentleman. The cachaco in question, whom I will call Don Pepe (Pepe means José María), was an LL.D., a graduate of the Holy Ghost College of Señor Lorenzo Lléras (since Secretary for Foreign Affairs).

We commenced our life in common with three thievish servants, who professed to take charge of some horses said to be kept in some pasture near the city for us, but we soon succeeded in getting the two best off our hands. As for the other, Bentura (Buenaventura), nobody would have him, so we kept him.

We took rooms in a large casa baja, opposite the fonda of Doña Paz. She rented this house to let to guests, and she took us in hopes that we should frequent her table also. This did not suit Don Pepe, who alleged a want of neatness in her dining-room, indicative of still more in her kitchen. Of our rooms we could not complain. Besides a small bed-room, with a cowhide bed for Don Pepe and a cot-bed for me, who am too much of a Sybarite to sleep well on the soft side of a dry hide, we had a huge parlor, with three sofas, three tables, two chairs, and two looking-glasses, all of which might have been sold for between five and ten dollars in Chatham Square.

But now came a vermilion edict from Doña Paz that all who occupied her rooms must patronize her fonda exclusively. But we had found at another fonda a table more to my satisfaction than I have elsewhere found among the Spanish race. I explained to La Señora Margarita the necessity we should be under of leaving her table or finding new rooms. She assured me that she had no rooms fit for us; but she showed me an inner pantry, or store-room, that, besides communicating with the pantry, had a door opening into the sala, and another that opened upon what once was the corredor of a back patio. A portion of this corredor had been transformed into a snug little bed-room, at the expense of great ingenuity and very little money. I at once insisted on having the two rooms, and that night our two servants carried our *trastos*—effects, including monturas, trunks, atillos, and petacas—on their shoulders to the large room. The pantry door was locked, the sala door unlocked, and both keys delivered to me. The rooms were entirely transformed; for La Señora Margarita had set about it herself, and worked, she assured me, "like a demonio."

Don Pepe slept, as before, in a stylish cowhide bed in the large room with the baggage and servants; and as all the light came through glass doors from my room, of which they shut the blinds every night, they all slept as late as they chose, undisturbed by daylight. I was equally suited with my little room, that just held the indispensable cot-bed, bought expressly for me, a table, and a chair, with space on the walls to hang my maps. Here I was at the top of Fortune's wheel, and I expect nothing equal to it, or at all to be compared to it, in all my exile. I paid here, as before, sixteen dollars per calendar month.

I did have one cause of complaint on the first night. My pillow felt too much like a well-stuffed rag-bag. La Señora would have it righted as soon as mentioned; so we ripped it open, and behold! as much cotton, in solid wads, just as it came off the seed, as could possibly be got in. We picked loose a third of it, and filled the pillow nicely, and the lady probably jotted down in her note-book that los Ingleses are very particular about soft pillows.

La Señora was an Ibagueña—a native of Ibagué—quite a handsome matron, perhaps more prepossessing than any other that I have seen here; nor were my expectations disappointed, for she was a nice lady, excepting, perhaps, a violence of temper, which I never knew excited without cause, though occasionally it went beyond bounds. When she raged, it was like a sea or like a lioness — she never fretted. She kept a tienda and a fonda, both of superior order, and sold no chicha, and more brandy than rum. Her husband, who was a major on half pay or pension, appeared to be a confidential boarder, and her best friend rather than her liege lord. I do not know what his business was, but it may have been gambling. They had three fine little daughters, the oldest of whom went to a boarding-school a few blocks off, but occasionally came home of a Sunday morning. The second went to the same school as a day scholar. A strong-willed little boy, who had a great passion for riding a horse around the corredor, and a babe in charge of a wet nurse, completed the family record.

The house, which they rented of a friar, was a casa baja claustrada—a one-story house, with the rooms opening on the patio or court. It stood on the corner, and was much larger than usual. The corner room opened on both streets, but had nothing to do with the house, although it appeared to be a part of it, while the tienda, which appeared to belong to the next house, as seen externally, had its only inner door opening into a spacious refectory, where at first our meals were served with those of chance comers who paid by the meal. At my instance, we removed to the family-table in a separate dining-room. The husband had a room that served him for bed-room and office, far removed from the two rooms that served as dormitories for the lady, the children, and the nurse. Another room served for several female servants, including the shop-tender—cajera—while of other rooms I knew no destination. A fellow-boarder, a physician in poor health, a relative of Margarita, occupied still another room in the house. Back of the house was a large patio, divided in two by a high brick wall. One half was paved, and the other may have once been a garden, of which a fig-tree and a papaya seemed to be the only remains. In a shed at the back side was an oven, with a peep-hole made in the side.

Such were the premises where I found more physical comfort than in any other Granadan family. Our meals were two a day, at about 9 and 2. The latter nearly always included a dish called puchero, made of boiled beef, potatoes, and cabbage, not unlike a common boiled dish at the North. It was preceded by a soup, often with vermicelli, of which I seldom tasted. A delicious dish here was the terminal bud of the palm, but it seems almost a crime to destroy a stately tree for so insignificant a treat. It is eaten with butter, and commonly called palmiche. It is a little curious that, among all the strange Spanish dishes I found, the olla podrida never made its appearance. As to ask for it would be to commit myself to eating of it, I waited till it should come, but it never did.

We had a good supply of fruits, bought once a week at the market. On Friday, and sometimes Saturday, the last course was fruit just from market. An immense dish of strawberries, with sugar and milk; the curuba, before mentioned; a fruit tasting very much like a cucumber, and therefore called pepino; and bananas: such were the ordinary table-fruits.

The Granadinos do not understand eggs. They make them into an omelet, unpalatable to us, called tortilla: they fry them, but, in eating them, they break a hole in the centre of the yolk, and put in a good quantity of salt, and after all it seems as if they may have been fried in water. They offer you also what they call warm eggs—huevos tibios—which are eggs boiled in the shell: if they would offer you a bit of nice butter at the same time, you would relish them all the better. As for custard, pie, tart, and pudding, I believe these words have no equivalent in Spanish. I have once seen a thing that had the same anatomical structure as a pie, and bore the name of pastilla, but it was an outrage on the palate.

The pulse kind—Leguminosæ—yielded us a large and puzzling variety of food. It is all the worse for us that the English word bean means a different thing on the two sides of the Atlantic. The Vicia Faba—in French fève, in Spanish haba—is almost unknown with us, and is called Windsor-bean, broad-bean, coffee-bean, and horse-bean, but in England is called bean. The plant grows over two and less than four feet high. The Phaseolus vulgaris—in French haricot, in Spanish frijol, frisol, and judía—is from a plant less than two feet high (bush-bean), or more than four feet high (kidney-bean, cranberry-bean, or pole-bean), is almost unknown in England, and there called French-bean, but, in some families of the Yankee race, is one of the staples of subsistence. The garbanza, chick-pea, vetch, or fitch—Cicer Arietinum—is a seed about the size and shape of a common pea, but with a protuberance on it that seems to detract from its beauty. I do not like the taste so well as that of the pea. This also grows here, but is less used than the garbanza: it is called alverja—a name applied in Spain, I believe, to the chick-pea. To these add the Ervum Lens—lentil, ervalenta—here called lenteja, and you have the synonymy of these useful articles of food.

The arracacha is the root of numerous plants in different parts of the world, but all allied botanically to the parsnip and carrot. Those of New Granada are said to be Conium Arracacha, C. esculenta, and C. xanthorrhiza. Some, or all of these, are plants of the uplands, like the potato. I find them insipid; but, when severely pressed with hunger, I have found them delicious fried: I have never eaten them in houses except boiled.

One esculent unfortunately escaped my taste. Some may have noticed that our wood sorel, Oxalis violacea, has a scaly bulb, too small, however, to be worth eating. A species here, Oxalis tuberosa, is cultivated for its little corm or root, called oca, which is only about two inches long, and therefore could not be advantageously introduced at the North, although it grows where potatoes flourish. I have not mentioned the common Antillan yams, Dioscorea alata and D. sativa, here called ñame; they are not much cultivated away from the coast. I do not like them, except when served up like mashed potato.

But, if any thing tires the traveler in Bogotá, it will be the pantry, the kitchen, and the dining-room. It makes me feel mean to find my mind and pen dwelling so long and so earnestly on such topics. Perhaps it is an inevitable evil incident to keeping a soul yet in the flesh, which flesh must be kept up, in a land of heterodox cookery. I will now cheerfully close my views of domestic life here with a single incident, showing how we *lost* Bentura.

He was an unwholesome-looking chap, with a piebald skin; the two colors were not supposed to be those of his two parents, but owing to a cutaneous disease called carate. If it be not a form of leprosy (and it is not here so regarded), it seems to be a chronic ulceration *sui generis*. But let that pass. As we had nothing for him to do, he seems to have occasionally absented himself from Don Pepe's room of nights, and found more congenial quarters in one occupied by the shop-girl, the cook, and another servant of the feminine gender and the class called guaricha. Here his cough several nights reached the ears of the head of the family, and one day he recommended to Margarita that the *sick girl* have a sleeping-place where she would not disturb him. The truth came out that his friend was the saleswoman, a valuable servant, who had been with them for some years. My lady's fury knew no bounds. She insisted on Bentura's instant banishment. Unfortunately, Don Pepe had gone down to lower lands to thaw out, and I was unwilling to interfere in the matter till his return; so she consented that I might lock him fast into our large room all alone each night till Don Pepe returned. But solitude operates badly on some tempers, and next evening, about dark, "el carataso" waxed surly, and made some really insulting remarks to the mistress of the house, though he did not presume to deny any of the allegations against him. She screamed to her husband, and he ran to the spot armed with a spear. But I had overheard his speech, and ordered the thief to leave the house at once and forever, which he did before the spear came in sight.

CHAPTER X.

BOGOTÁ.

Streets of Bogotá.—Plan of the City.—Plazas.—Public Buildings.—Library.—Museum.—Observatory.—Preparations for Execution.—Cemeteries.—Plaza de los Martires.—Mode of Execution.—Victims of Morillo.

We are glad to escape again to the street, and now let us get our first impressions of the capital.

The very first impression that Bogotá makes is on the soles of the feet, and that is by no means an agreeable one. You feel that it is making a beast of you by compelling you to contend with pack-mules for passage along the cobble-stone pavement. There are no brick sidewalks, and few of flat stone. These are but two feet wide, and are highly prized by the mules: a string of them never fail to take possession of them when they come in their way.

Look at the houses. None are more than two stories; most are but one. They are whitewashed, but not white. They have a plenty of front, a large, ugly portal, and a few small grated windows, from which the female inhabitants seem to be constantly looking out like prisoners.

The poor live on the ground floors of the two-story houses, in tenements of one room, with no access to court or yard. It may seem incredible, but they have none of the outbuildings or domestic conveniences thought necessary elsewhere. There are no sewers—no drainage—and the ground floors are generally damp; hence the second floors are occupied by the rich, and so extremes meet. But here we come to a horse with his head in a door and his heels out in the middle of the street. We must make the circuit of them: every passer has done so for half an hour past. I never knew a horse, mule, or ass to kick in this country, though I am assured that they do.

The plan of the city was, in the main, laid out by nature. In the chapter before the last we were proceeding eastward, and had all the vast plain at our back, and our feet stood on the threshold of the city, at the very point where the plain begins to rise a little. In the following plan, an asterisk on the west side marks the place where the Honda road enters on it. What appeared like a bridge, with inscriptions on either side, is, in reality, no bridge at all, but rather a bar—as Temple Bar yet is in London—to show the entrance to the city. Its site is indicated by the termination of the two lines that represent the road. Just north, on the plain, is a detached square block, occupied by the spacious buildings where once was the Colegio

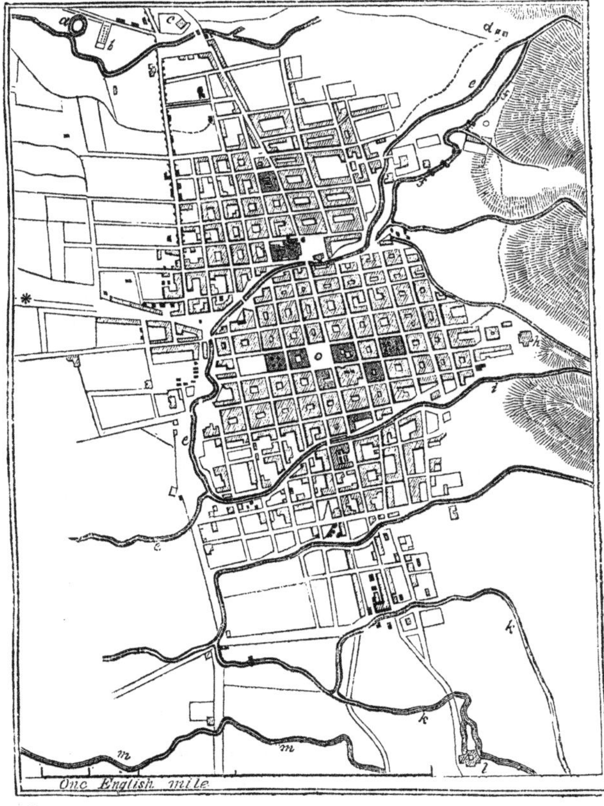

a. Cemetery.	*h.* Church of Egipto.
b. English Cemetery.	*i.* Rio San Agustin.
c. Convent of San Diego.	*k.* Aqueducts from the Fucha.
d. Quinta de Bolívar.	*l.* Powder-works (abandoned).
e. Rio San Francisco.	*m.* Rio Fucha.
f. Aqueducts for Water-power.	* Entrance of the Honda Road.

of Dr. Lléras, who has since been Secretary of State. Advancing, we enter the Carrera de Palacé, the widest street of the city and of New Granada. It was named for a battle-field of 1819. The streets generally bear the names of battle-fields or provinces. The Carrera of Palacé is short and funnel-shaped, and terminates in a small square, the Plazuela of San Victorino, ornamented by the principal fountain of Bogotá, represented by a small square block on the plan. It might have been copied from some Gothic tomb in Spain; has, of course, its inscription, its low fence around it—pretil—its numerous jets of water issuing from iron tubes, for which a crowd of girls in blue mantellinas and enaguas are contending, each striving to apply her own caña to the stream as the múcura of her neighbor is full.

A few paces beyond the fountain is a wall, seemingly low till you look over, when you see the River San Francisco (*e*) ten feet below you. It has come down through a deep cleft of the mountains, and flows southwest to this point, where it turns south, runs half a mile, and then flows west again, out upon the plain, in quest of the Bogotá. This river has made the city, and the principal ward or parish, Barrio del Catedral—Cathedral Ward—is shut in between the San Francisco and its tributary, the San Agustin (*i*), which comes down from another gorge, and flows nearly west, both before and after entering the San Francisco. An aqueduct—El Agua-nueva—is laid from the upper waters of the San Agustin nearly to the San Francisco, supplying various streets with water.

The barrios—wards—take their names from their parish churches. The central ward, Barrio del Catedral, then, is almost shut into an angle of the San Francisco by the San Agustin and the aqueduct. It contains seven parallel streets, running straight up the hill from the river to the base of the mountain, where the broken ground arrests them. These streets are crossed by eleven others, running south from the San Francisco to the San Agustin. Each block—calle—of each street has a number, and, in common language, also a name, by itself, but the names of the streets—*carreras*—are not used, although painted on all the corners.

The third of the streets that run east (counting from the north) crosses the San Francisco by the San Victorino Bridge, and enters the south corner of the Plazuela of San Victorino, a little south of the fountain. All the travel crosses the Plazuela obliquely to the southeast from the Street of Palacé to this bridge. I say all; but all teams of two or more bulls are arrested at this bridge, to the no small inconvenience of importing merchants, all of whom live in the Cathedral Ward. We cross this bridge, and we find a rill of water running down the centre of the street, which is concave, as Centre Street, New York, used to be in days of yore.

On the first block on the left hand, as you go up east, was once seen a flag-staff projecting obliquely over a porton: here floated, on special days, in 1852, the stars and stripes, for it was then the residence of our chargé d'affaires, Hon. Yelverton King.

Nearly opposite, but a little above, was once the Convent of San Juan de Dios—Saint John of God—or the Hospital monks. The convent church alone remains in the possession of the hierarchy: the rest is now national property, and used, as it professedly was before, as a hospital, now at the charge of the province.

We go directly east for five blocks, and let us then turn to the south and pause. We are at the business centre of the city. The street before us and behind us bears the familiar names of Calle Real and Calle de Commercio. We have traversed the Calle de San Juan de Dios; and the Calle de los Plateros extends up to our left. The view on the following page is from a daguerreotype by George Crowther, Esq., taken from the balcony of the American consulate, the house on the northwest of the four corners here. In it you face the south. Just one block before you, on the right, is the Plaza, and that tall building facing it is the Cathedral.

In front of the whole block, of which the Cathedral is part, is an elevated platform, the Altozano. It is broad and level, overlooking the Plaza, and descending to it by stone steps running the whole length. It is the most public place in Bogotá. The Church claimed, of course, the best building spot on the upper side of the Plaza for the Cathedral. It is not convenient for a Catholic church to stand in the centre of a block, as a side

STREET AND CATHEDRAL IN BOGOTÁ.

door, Puerta de misericordia — door of mercy — needs to open into a side street from the left-hand side of the church as you enter—the Gospel side; so the Cathedral has the north end of the west side of the Plaza. Next is a small, old, rich, neglected church, once the viceroy's chapel. The pulpit is overlaid with tortoise-shell and silver. Beyond is a plain building used as a custom-house.

If the government would erect a building on the south end of the block with a façade to correspond to the Cathedral, and connect the two fronts by a still higher central part, they might make the whole side of the square contribute to the glory of a capitol worthy of the great nation whose destinies are yet to be ruled there. But they have taken an entire block on the south side to erect a capitol, with its front on a side hill, where no architectural genius can make it more than the second building in the city. Its walls are as yet only up to the height of the first floor, and it is to be hoped that, ere another stone is laid, better counsels will prevail, and that it may be employed, as the north side is, for a range of stores.

On this side of the Cathedral, and separated from it by a street which we can not see, is a group of houses, which are a fair specimen of the better class of genteel houses in Bogotá. They hide the mercy-door of the Cathedral, while over its roof is seen the top of the cupola of San Carlos. They are stores below and dwellings above. The ground-floor has no windows. The first and second doors on the left are tiendas, while the third, partly hidden by two female figures, is the porton. Entering it, you pass through the zaguan to the patio, the stairs, and the rooms above. All this is shown by the door-posts and the width of the door.

Above, all the doors are windows, and all the windows doors. The balconies rarely approach each other so as to render a transit possible from one to another. Beneath the balconies is seen a side-walk of brick. Half of the city is furnished with them, but none of the others is as wide as that here seen. They barely permit the passage of two persons.

I have little to say of the figures in the street. In the group at the left, the nearest of the three is a type of the old ladies of Bogotá. She is of respectable conservative family, and if she did not wear that same round-topped felt hat in the time of the viceroys, she at least wore one like it. It became her fresh young face then better than it does now, when it proclaims to every passer-by, My mistress is not ashamed of being old. The bull is loaded with two guambías of potatoes from the páramo north of Bogotá. That basket on the woman's shoulders, farther forward and to the right, reminds me of some that I have seen at Choachí, but the bearer seems too tall to be an Indian.

Passing the Cathedral on our left, and the Plaza on our right, we have the foundations of the capitol, not seen in the plate, and on our left the pile of San Bartolomé, of which San Carlos, the Hall of Degrees, and the Libraries are parts. These we pass now, as they can not be entered from this street. On the next block on our right is the Colegio Militar, which we shall again visit. In the rear of this, and almost on the street below, is the Observatory, the oldest on the continent, nearer the equator, and at a higher altitude than any other. The building is now empty, unfurnished, and, to be adapted to modern instruments, would need a revolving roof.

Farther on, we cross the San Agustin by a little bridge. Then, on our right, is the Convent of San Agustin, the tower of which closes the view of the street in the engraving. The open space between it and the river is the Plazuela de San Agustin. A little farther on, on the third block, and on the upper side of the street, is the parish church of Santa Barbara, from which the Barrio south of the San Agustin takes its name.

Let us return again to the Plaza and take a view of it. It is paved, of course, with small stones. In the centre is a handsome statue of Bolívar, erected by his friend Pepe Paris. It is of bronze, executed in Italy, and in very good taste. Bolívar gave to Paris the Quinta de Bolívar, marked (*d*) on the Plan of Bogotá.

The lower and western side of the square is occupied by the only Northern-looking building in Bogotá. It is called Casa de Portales and Casa Consistorial. It contains the Halls of Congress, the office of the Secretary of the Treasury, and the General Post-office and also that of the city.

Let us go to the southeast corner of the Plaza and turn up east. On our left, as I said, is the Custom-house, and on the right the old convent of San Bartolomé, that has lately been in use as a national college. In the centre of this block they have contrived to insert the Church of San Carlos, called by some the centre of fanaticism for the nation, and the cradle of the revolution of 1851. The Hall of Degrees in this building is not only used for the public ceremonies of the college, but also for concerts. It is remarkable for its structure: one half the audience faces the other, and the platform is down between the two inclined planes occupied by the audience.

In this same building, too, with the entrance on the east side, is the National Library, to which the students of the college had also access. The nucleus is a very old library bound in parchment, to which there have been added a few thousand volumes in French, English, German, and other languages. In some departments it is quite rich. I noticed over fifty volumes on China alone. I would be glad to say more about it, but the librarian was an invalid, and neglected his duties sadly, and it was very difficult to find it open.

There is another library here that deserves a particular notice. It is one of the richest collections of pamphlets ever got together by the patient industry of any one man of limited means. It is the work of Colonel Anselmo Pineda, a man who has served his country in a more daring, but never in a more honorable manner. After binding and indexing them in the most thorough manner, he has presented them to the nation. Congress, in return, has voted him a small pension for life, minus certain taxes that are always assessed on pensions and salaries paid by government. There is no end to the attacks and defenses in Granadan pamphlets, handbills, and newspapers, all of which are here bound in and catalogued. There is no eminent man in the nation who is not assailed on some page of this library. Government has unwisely made it too accessible, and already has more than one theft occurred of documents that can never be replaced. It is to be hoped that this liberality will not continue.

Another room here is a cabinet of minerals and woods, the best in the nation. My first visit was brief, and I never was able to find it open again. Here, too, I recollect one piece of Vandalism, a portrait cut and ruined. Below is what is called the Museum proper. It contains birds, I believe, some insects, and also trophies, portraits, and relics of the heroes of the War of Independence. Here we see the banner with which Pizarro led on his handful of robbers to the plunder of Peru.

One room in this vast pile I have tried in vain to enter. It is the chapel—capilla—used by the students, I believe, but anciently used for the preparation of those who are on the eve of execution. It has been a beneficent regulation of the Church that no man should be executed who had not passed the previous night in a capilla. These capillas are generally recesses that occupy two sides of large churches, each of which has an altar of its own. One of these in Santo Domingo is fenced in with an iron railing, which seems to render it quite appropriate to such a use; but this little church in San Bartolomé opens on no street whatever, but into an inner court only, so that escape to the distant world is hopeless. Here some of the purest patriots that ever lived spent their last hours before they were shot by the direction of the fierce and brutal Morillo.

But let us leave this dismal old building, with its awful chapel, ambitious, ill managed, and now suspended school, its Hall of Degrees, libraries, cabinet, museum—all locked, and its fanatical church—always open. We proceed up the hill one step farther. Next above San Bartolomé, and still on our right, is the Palace, a common-looking house, but with two or three soldiers about the door, which fronts that of the libraries, cabinet, museum, and Hall of Degrees. Both open on a street running north and south. The basement corner of the palace near us is occupied by the palace porter, a man who has long held his place. You will note, as we go up the hill, that the windows of the principal story come nearer and nearer to the ground, till the last is not more than 7 or 8 feet high. Remember that window: Bolívar saved his life by escaping from it. A few steps farther up, look at the left. Here you see a large building, separated from the street by a high, stout fence. Is it not the ugliest building in Bogotá? Well, that is the Theatre, where shopmen, clerks, and guarichas turn players on the nights of Sundays and the other fiestas, when people have leisure to attend and they to perform. I have never been in, and can not say whether the interior corresponds to the exterior for beauty, but I see they care for ventilation, for there is an opening in the roof for the steam to escape, as in the roofs of kitchens.

Returning down to the Plaza, let us keep on west. On our right, after passing the piazza of the Casa Consistorial, we come soon to a door guarded with a sentinel or two. It is the provincial prison, an ill-regulated concern, not over clean; but we must look into it by-and-by. On the left, and a little lower down, is a very large house, devoted to the offices of secretaries of state. The rooms are arranged around two patios, one behind the other. Occasionally a sentry is seen here, out of respect, I suppose, to the War-office.

On our right, on the next block, is the nunnery of La Concepcion, that occupies two entire blocks of the heart of the city. The plan shows the east end to be built up, and the lower end left for a garden. It is a pity government had not found means of confiscating this fine property before severing the union of Church and state. One thing they can do yet: it is to open the street that ought to separate the vast, useless property into two blocks, when the lower one could not be devoted to the pleasures of a few idle, frolicking nuns. And this leads me to speak of another thing: the walking past a nunnery is always worse than elsewhere, because they never have a decent sidewalk.

And here, one block down, and opposite the garden of La Concepcion, is another nunnery, that of Santa Inés. Nunneries seem not to have their churches on the corners of streets, and, consequently, to have no "mercy doors;" or, rather, as it is a side door that you enter, that may be the "mercy door," and the principal door may be theoretically one that leads from the body of the convent into the church opposite the principal altar.

Let us return to the northeast corner of the Plaza, at the Cathedral. Looking up the street past the "mercy door," you may see, some distance up, a sentinel before the door of the Mint. This block, and those of the Palace and Cathedral, are darkly shaded in the Plan. The Mint is a very creditable establishment, under the superintendence of the only survivor of the ancient band of scientific men, most of whom were butchered by Morillo. Fortunately, Manuel Restrepo never fell into his power, and he still lives, the geographer of Antioquia, a historian of his country, the director of the Mint, and the very model of a gentleman.

Now let us turn north from the American consulate. The whole block, of which it is the southeast corner, is the property of the convent of Santo Domingo—St. Dominic—the richest in New Granada. All the stores and shops on the four streets that surround it are theirs, and, as if these did not yield enough, the part on the street by which we came up, past the hospital of San Juan de Dios, is built up into regular houses of two stories, with small patios. Here, too, the church is in the middle of the block, but the "mercy door" opens into the street last named by a passage between two houses.

Still farther north, we have the greatest stores of the capital on either hand, and its best walks beneath our feet, till we come to the bridge of San Francisco. One block lower down is the Bridge of Apes—Micos—then down, after the river turns south, is that of San Victorino, that we crossed first. There was once a fourth and upper bridge, but that has been carried away, and as it was not much needed, it has never been replaced. Except the Ape's Bridge and that at Honda, I know of no bridge in New Granada that is not of the most solid construction. All the wooden ones have rotted down centuries ago, and the flimsy stone ones, if ever there were such, have yielded to the force of earthquakes.

Passing the Bridge of San Francisco, we have on our left the Convent of San Francisco, and opposite it, on the right, the Plaza of San Francisco, with its fountain. The block in the Plan on the south side of the square represents the barracks of San Francisco, and the little block in the northwest corner is the Humilladero, perhaps the smallest church in New Granada, and the oldest not only in Bogotá, but in all the interior, dating, if I recollect aright, back to 1538.

Now look down the next street, and you see a bridge running over the street from the convent of San Francisco to the opposite building, of which I have not learned the history, but as it is a place used for female devotions, it has been unjustly called a nunnery. Perhaps it is malice to call that bridge the Bridge of Sighs, though, unless designed for tender meetings and partings, it is difficult to say why it was there. The church in this next building is called La Tercera, or of the Third Order of St. Francis, the first order being the monks, the second the nuns of Santa Clara, and the third married and unmarried persons of either sex who are inclined to a stricter religious life than laymen generally. On our right, opposite La Tercera, is a large and fashionable school of the widow of ex-President Santander. It is almost as strict as a convent.

On the next block but one north, on the left, is an old convent (darkly shaded in the Plan), taken away from the Jesuits, and converted into a poor-house—hospicio — which was in a miserable condition when I saw it. To fit it for a foundling hospital, it was necessary to cut a small door in the wall next the street. Open the door wide, and you will pull a chain and ring a bell within. You see a wheel 30 inches in diameter, with an opening in it. If a babe be put in, a turn of the wheel will bring it into the presence of a porteress within. She can not see out, and the depositor may walk off. She will never know her child, nor her child her. Could any thing be more convenient? The engraving on the opposite page, made probably from

THE FOUNDLING WHEEL.

description, gives the wheel of twice the true height, and omits the door. The artist has likewise taken the liberty of dressing the unfortunate mother in European costume.

Next you come to the parish church of Las Nieves — of Our Lady of the Snows— on your right, and a plazuela on the left, with a fountain. North of this the houses become sparse and mean, till they degenerate into huts. Then comes an open space with a muddy brook running through it. Across the brook is the little Franciscan convent of San Diego, marked in the Plan with the letter *c*. I shall show you no more convents, although there are enough more, both for monks and nuns. Fortunately, quite a number of them are suppressed.

From San Diego let us go west, and we soon enter upon the great plain again. Our road is bordered with deep ditches, the banks overgrown with bushes. This road leads past the elliptical Cemetery of Bogotá (*a*), which we must visit again. Just before reaching it we come to a neat cottage, with a bridge across the ditch. Behind the house is a garden with abundant roses. At the end of the flowery path is the gate of the English Cemetery (*b*). I copied and have lost the beautiful and appropriate inscriptions over the entrance in Latin and English. The grounds are overgrown with grass, and no walks are visible. In the centre stands the grave of a British minister. The monument has been surrounded by an iron fence, but each bar of it has either been broken off or wrenched out of the stone and carried off. It is said the depredators climbed over the gate through the narrow space under the archway.

Let us return to the Plazuela de San Victorino by the straight street running into it from the north. This street is called the Alameda, not because it is shaded with elms—álamos—but because a favorite walk near Madrid was so adorned. A curious bush grows along the ditches here. It seems to have long, compound leaves like sumach, with small leaflets, among which, along the petiole, grow some pretty little Euphorbiate flowers. It is Phyllanthus, and the seeming petioles are branchlets, and the leaves are simple.

Just before you reach the Plazuela of San Victorino, you find, on your right, what was once a Capuchin convent, but the church is now, since the Church of San Victorino went to ruins, the parish church of this barrio, and the rest of the building is put to a better use still. It is the Colegio de la Merced—the Public High School for girls of the province of Bogotá.

But now let us proceed down the river, past the Plaza and bridge, and we find an open spot on our right. It is the Plaza de los Mártires—Square of the Martyrs. Formerly it was the Huerta de Jaimes—James's Garden. This Jaimes was probably an early settler of Bogotá, though his extraction may have been English. The irregular string of black spots on the Plan represent a line of mean cottages, that look as if occupied by squatters on the largest square in Bogotá. The western wall of the square is a high garden fence, built, as usual, of rammed earth—tapias. The northern end seems to have been much acted on by the weather or some other cause. A few feet from this wall a bench is sometimes placed, and a man is seated on it. A file of soldiers is drawn up before him; a priest steps away from him; the command fuego!—fire—is given, and the poor mangled victim falls in the agonies of death.

The more humane, but more odious system of the garrote—strangling with a collar of iron—has been long since decreed by law, but the necessary mechanism has never been procured. It is, perhaps, the least objectionable mode of executing the last dreadful penalty of the law. The place where we stand is called patibulo, and the seat itself banquillo

Here suffered José Cáldas, José Lozano, José María Cabal, J. G. Gutiérrez (Moreno), Manuel Ramon Torices, Antonio María Palacio (Fajar), Count Casa-Valencia, Miguel Pombo, Francisco Ulloa, and other eminent men, all martyrs to liberty—all worse than assassinated by that butcher, Morillo, for many, if not all of them, were shot in the back! Pardon, reader, this long list, for the monument to their memory and to his undying infamy in the Plaza de los *Mártires* has not yet been erected.

It has been proposed to select another place for executions, and to retain the patriotic recollections of this unsullied in future; but executions are so rare here that they never seem to anticipate another.

Here ends our lesson on the geography of Bogotá.

CHAPTER XI.

FOREIGNERS IN BOGOTÁ.

Legations in Bogotá.—Our System.—Mr. King.—Mr. Green.—Mr. Bennet.—British and French Legations.—Venezuelan.—Legate of the Pope.—Spanish Obstinacy.—Granadan Courtesy.—Naturalization.

It is but just, on entering a foreign city, to salute first the representatives of our national authority. An American can scarcely be said to have come in contact with his own national government till he meets its representatives abroad; and here, so much of his comfort and respectability depend on their character, that the traveler can not but feel acutely alive to the manner in which their trusts are discharged; and, while it is the second duty of the writer to be grateful, his first is to be impartial.

Fortunately, I have nothing to do with any of the cases in which it has been said that blackguards and bullies have been sent abroad; for with, perhaps, the exception of President Pierce's commercial agent at St. Thomas, I have never met one that did not seem anxious to do all his duty, and as faithfully as possible. But it may be necessary, before testifying what I have seen, to make a few remarks on the American system of appointment of ministers.

Unless we can reform our system of removing and appointing officers, it is highly desirable that we abolish all embassies to the courts of civilized nations, and leave them to deal with us as they do with Morocco, Muscat, Burmah, and other barbarians, at our own capital. Under the present system, we must always have the poorest minister at every court. We must pay him for leaving his business at home, if he has any, with the probability that he will have to return home in four years or less, and generally with the intention of coming much sooner. You can not expect him to understand the language of the country where he is, and still less the spirit of the government and the character of the men with whom he has to do. With other nations diplomacy is a profession, and no man expects to be minister who has not served a due apprenticeship as attaché.

The English and French ministers at Bogotá were both married to South American ladies. Both are said to have used their posts for base purposes—one as a smuggler, and the other as a holder of a share in an enormous usurious claim that he urged to an unjust settlement. The English government had committed the farther and inexcusable error of appointing a Catholic to represent them at a Catholic court. This ought never to be, for in half the cases where the traveler should need protection, the minister might deem it a sin to act. I know of no valid objection to a Catholic embassador to Sweden or Prussia, or a Mohammedan sent to Rome or Naples, but to send a Mohammedan to Constantinople, or a Catholic to Spain, would be worse than to leave the post vacant.

It is a little curious that all our ministers to Bogotá have been natives of the Southern States. To this there can be no objection, as New Granada has abolished slavery, and an abolitionist would never need protection on account of his opinions. Mr. Yelverton P. King was a fine specimen of the Georgia gentleman, having with him his wife, and a son as secretary of legation. His hospitable board was spread for every respectable countryman, and the weary traveler would forget for a time that he was a stranger in a strange land; and to the Christian, who felt that he had none elsewhere to sympathize with him, the family of Mr. King was a treat not soon to be forgotten. As a minister, however, Mr. King was of necessity incompetent, from inexperience, ignorance of the Spanish language and of Granadan character, and he was too far advanced in life to begin.

His successor was an entirely different man. Mr. King came to enjoy the novelty of an Andine life, Mr. James S. Green to indemnify himself for the losses that his practice had suffered from his devotion to politics. His plans were well laid for this. Leaving his family in Missouri, he came and took board in Bogotá. Hospitality was no part of his plan, and, indeed, it would defeat it, and accordingly not even the 22d of February was allowed to make an exception. But as a minister, Mr. Green was at once able and faithful, and had he continued a few years at his post, there would be every prospect that he would become eminent in his profession; but he did not stay long enough to speak the language even moderately, and before he could begin to act independently of the advice of his countrymen, he returned.

But how do our affairs get on here amid all these changes? The answer is clear. The consulate of Bogotá does not pay its charges. No partisan could be rewarded with it; it is neither a loaf nor a fish; so it is left in the hands of Mr. John A. Bennet, who came here as a photographer, and, by virtue of Yankee versatility, has become a merchant of established character and of much influence with the Bogotanos. I risk little in conjecturing that no step has been taken by our ministers lately without his concurrence, and, as he is a safe adviser, and interested in the continuance of a good understanding between the two countries, all is likely to go well enough, whether the legation is vacant or filled.

But is there no remedy for this state of things? I see none so long as our foreign missions are or can be used as rewards for the friends of the President. I know of but one branch of national service that seems at all well managed, and that is the army. Would it not be well to detach lieutenants of engineers and artillery for secretaries of legation, and appoint to the more important embassies the best officers of the army? We need not fear a worse system than we now have, and, until some better system is adopted, nothing save a wholesome fear of our cannon can keep our embassadors from being the laughing-stock of veterans that have spent their days in this branch of their country's service.

The legation of Venezuela happens now to be very well filled here, and the minister is, I understand, contracting a matrimonial alliance while negotiating on other matters that arise. The Pope had also a legate here at that time—a live cardinal, walking our streets in purple robes. But it appears by the Gaceta Oficial of 7th October, 1853, that Monseñor Lorenzo Barili has ceased from his functions. He officially protested against the law authorizing marriages without the consent of the clergy. The government could not recognize his heavenly functions after the 30th August, nor his right to meddle with their local legislation. Government was ready to communicate with the representative of the sovereign of the States of the Church on any *international* matters that he might propose. Monseñor disdains exercising merely earthly functions. Señor Lléras desires to know at what time he will resign the immunities of an embassador, to which the cardinal distinctly replies that from that day forth he resigns them all. He has become an attaché to the French legation.

Spain has no representative in New Granada. It does not comport with the dignity of that proud weak power to acknowledge the independence of New Granada, and, in consequence, there is a practical non-intercourse between them. Had Britain been thus unwise toward her rebel colonies, what a valuable commerce must she have forgone by keeping her best market closed against her! Very few natives of Spain (Chapetones) are now to be found in all New Granada. Indeed, they have almost forgotten the very word Chapeton, and its counterpart Criollo, which used to designate natives of the country. Besides the citizens of adjoining republics, the most numerous foreigners in this country are English, French, North Americans, Dutch, and Germans. Of our countrymen there are some half a dozen here generally, and all of them respectable citizens. The English are more numerous, including some in the humbler walks of life.

A few of the foreigners have become naturalized citizens of the country; but, though naturalization is liberally encouraged, it is hardly an advisable step. To the great scandal of his Holiness, liberty of worship was long since conceded to the immigrant. His domestic effects and tools pass duty free. He is allowed a plot of land for himself, and one for each member of his family, to be selected from any public lands—tierras baldias—and I have even known government defend a long suit of ejectment against a naturalized citizen who claimed some land with cinchona on it.

But the protection to the alien is such as to make him slow to covet the privileges of naturalization. He is now equally protected in his worship, and exempted farther from forced loans—the bane of a country liable to revolutions. He is sometimes permitted to hold office, but can not be compelled, while to the citizen there is no liability more to be dreaded; for most minor offices have neither salary nor fees to reward them, while there is no escaping them but by a certificate of ill health, or by resigning, and getting the resignation accepted.

And the district officer is obliged to hold his office in the place designated as cabeza—head—of the district, and to be at it daily, often to the ruin of his private affairs. I have seen a man, therefore, earnestly beg of a doctor a certificate of ill health to escape being juez de distrito—parish judge; and this responsible office has, in two instances in my knowledge, fallen to the lot of men who could not read!

Farther, while the laws for protecting the person are the same for aliens and citizens, in the execution of them a crime against an alien is apt to be more certainly and severely punished if the representatives of his nation are at all competent. So it is a privilege, with this liberal government, to be an alien.

But, be the foreigner citizen or alien, the courtesy of government does not stop where his lawful claims end. The whole spirit of the government has always been liberal both to individuals and governments. There is the same difference between their dealings and common diplomacy as between the transactions of a merchant of the first class and the trader who professes to ask all that he can get. The Granadan government contemns the idea of overreaching or outwitting the party it deals with, or driving the closest possible bargain. The history of its dealings with the Panamá Railroad Company is full of instances of this; and my own testimony is, that the foreigner is treated as a guest rather than a stranger by all classes of officers, from tide-waiters to the President.

CHAPTER XII.

THE BOGOTANOS.

Houses.—Smoking.—Dinner at the Palace.—Coreographic Commission.—Lower Orders.—Market and Marketing.—Lesson in Spanish.

I CALLED on the day after my arrival at the house of a merchant there with a friend. We entered the zaguan of a casa baja, and advanced to the inner door, on which he struck one or two blows with the palm of his hand. A brief dialogue ensued with a servant who came to a door on the other side of the patio. It was "Quien?" "Yo." "Adelante"—"Who?" "I." "Forward." We pushed open the coarse, heavy square door. It resisted our push because of a stone hung to a peg over the door by a leather thong. The stone rises as the door opens, and its weight shuts the door as we release it. "Que entran por dentro" is the invitation to walk in. The sala is high and spacious, the floor is matted, and two or three cheap sofas extend along the sides of the room. Instinctively you look around for books or papers, but you see neither. The windows are high, and are furnished with glazed sashes, that open inward with hinges. The walls, of unburnt brick—adobe—or of tapias, are two feet through. In the thickness of the wall is a step as high as a chair, by means of which you can mount and seat yourself in the *jamb* of the window. Two persons thus seated and two more standing make a snug party. All windows are protected with a reja or grate, and no reliance is placed on the sash for protection.

The lady of the house came in, and we learned that the gentleman we wished to see was not in town. She ordered a servant to bring fire—candela. It was a brand from the kitchen, or else a coal in a massive silver spoon, and with it she handed round cigars. I declined, saying that I do not *know how* to smoke—No sé fumar.

She and my friend went to smoking. She was of about the middle age, rather coarsely dressed, as I should say, and seemed uninteresting, rather from the want of intelligence than from the lack of the elements of physical beauty. Her black-eyed daughter, whom I afterward saw rather by accident, as she was engaged with other company when I called, was scarce able to converse about *things*, and I cared little to converse about *persons*, so that, in spite of personal attractions, I tired of her as I would of a moving, speaking image.

But how can we expect conversational powers without reading? The young lady is, in fact, almost a prisoner. Her sole enjoyment and employment seems to be to seat herself in the window, and exchange salutations with those who pass. Should I ask her to take a walk with me, it could be little less than an insult. She can never go out but with her parents and brothers. In fact, she scarce ever enters the street except to go to church. Her school was a prison to her, her house is a prison, and what does she lose if she betake herself to a nunnery, as a prison from which she shall go no more out? In fact, the nunnery receives no prisoners without a respectable dowry, and perhaps it secures her as much happiness as she might find in the married state.

I did not see the young lady smoke, but I presume she does. Many assert that it is not disreputable for ladies to smoke; but it is said that many smoke secretly, but not openly, so that there must be some discredit about it. As for the practice of smoking with the lighted end of the cigar in the mouth, which prevails in the Tierra Caliente among the women, I have never seen it here. It probably is economical of tobacco, as none of the smoke wastes its sweetness on the outer air till it has deposited a part of its narcotic principle on the mucous membrane. Cigarillos, made by wrapping tobacco in paper, are rarely used; the ladies smoke unmitigated cigars.

The family may be safely said to live up to their means. I have thought that in New York there was a propensity to retrench in necessaries and spend too much in show. That failing is no less here. A former writer said that when Bogotá was in its glory, it was the abode of much ostentatious hospitality; but that since war and revolution have impoverished the nation, and the increased liberty of negroes and Indians have tended to the same result, there has been a retrenchment rather in the number than the splendor of their dinners.

The only dinner to which I was invited by the Bogotanos to whom I brought letters was at the Palace. It was styled a dinner "en familia," and the hour was six. I went a little before the time. I passed unquestioned the sentinel at the porton, went through the zaguan and corredor till I reached the stairs. In the corredor of the second story an officer was in attendance. He conducted me to one of the parlors. I believe I have been in six or eight of these rooms at different times. Most of them are carpeted, and all of them are comfortably, not splendidly furnished. No one of the rooms would strike one as extraordinary in the house of a gentleman of ordinary wealth. The receptions are all plain, and of due republican simplicity. At home the President appears like an ordinary citizen; but in the streets, his body-guard of lancers distinguish the "*Ciudadano Presidente*" from all other ciudadanos—citizens.

Both General López and his successor, General Obando, are old soldiers, who have often risked their lives in battle, sometimes for their country and sometimes against it. Both are dignified, soldierly men—Obando, perhaps, the more so, while, as a civil officer, I would form the higher opinion of López. He appeared interested in the development of the resources of the country. La Señora de López appears as well for her age as any lady I have seen in Bogotá, with one or two unusual exceptions. La Señora de Obando seemed to me more domestic, perhaps more of a Granadino, but less elegant.

At the meal there were in all about a dozen guests, but there was little about it characteristic of the country. I will mention only one dish: the short, thick, and reptile-looking fish of the Bogotá. These were wrapped in letter-paper and baked, and placed on the table in their original packages. During dinner the military band played in the patio.

On no family in Bogotá did I call with more pleasure than that of Colonel Codazzi, who lives three streets above the Cathedral. The colonel is Italian, and his lady a Venezolana, but the younger of their numerous and intelligent children are Bogotanos. In their parlors I saw them sewing, and at their table there was so little of pretense, that when I have happened in after my own dinner and before the close of theirs, I have never been able to resist their invitations to sit down with them.

Codazzi is the head of the Comision Coregrafica. His work on the geography of Venezuela, prepared and published at the expense of that government, is a model of geographical research. At the close of his duties there he undertook a similar task in New Granada, on which he has now been engaged some years. He has encountered incredible hardships, and at the present rate will in a few years have visited every part of the republic. He had then just returned from the provinces of Antioquia, Medellin, etc., having previously visited those north of the capital, not including those on the coast. He has since passed through the pestiferous region of Chocó, the coast of Buenaventura, and the provinces of Popayan and Pasto, besides a visit to the Isthmus, in which he gave advice to the explorers for a canal route which it would have been well for them if they had taken. The last and worst thing I ever knew of him was, that he, as well as Colonel Pineda, risked his precious life in putting down the revolution of Melo.

Codazzi is a man of the utmost enthusiasm, dauntless courage, and, I believe, a true friend. He has been accompanied at the charge of government by a number of assistants. The history of his tour at the North was published by one of them, Manuel Ancísar. Another gentleman, who has accompanied him on all his trips, is José María Triana, a young and persevering botanist. It is impossible to secure such men as are desirable for such an undertaking, but government has done its best, and so has the commission. They take latitudes, longitudes, and altitudes, and make other observations as best they may. And thus they are struggling on, year after year, with horrible obstacles from thickets, precipices, and, on the Pacific coast, from venomous serpents and fevers. Honor and success to them.

But let us take a look at the poorer classes. Why do so many of them live here? Of the 30,000 inhabitants of Bogotá, what a small portion have the means of comfortable subsistence! But why are there more men in New York than ever can obtain employment there? It is because vice is gregarious, and they would rather suffer for food than lose the excitement of the rabble. There are in Bogotá many that know what hunger and scanty fare mean. Among them are a large proportion of females, occupying a position more like that of the grisettes of Paris, only the latter far excel the *guarichas* of Bogotá in intelligence, wealth, comforts, attractiveness, and in morals.

The guarichas furnish an ample supply of wet-nurses at a very reasonable price, only that when they have gained the affections of their charge they abuse their advantage, as the heartless of that class are apt to do. Their own children are no obstacle, for, if they live, they can put them into the foundling wheel as soon as a good offer for their services occurs. Margarita treated some of her girls to a little recreation once. They went off to the Fucha to swim, taking with them the babe and wet-nurse, and also our two little girls, who are not old enough to learn any evil in such company. Well, there our *ama de pechos* saw her own babe and its father, and what else happened my little friends did not tell me. Next day our babe was crying, and the mother calling out to the nurse, who made no answer. She cried worse, and La Señora, in a fury, ran to the rescue. She found the babe all alone, clinging to the valance of the bed, and unable to get down. The nurse had decamped, bag and baggage!

I called on my washerwoman one day. She lives in a tenement on the ground floor of a casa alta. Cold as is the weather in Bogotá, the door is open to admit light, for she has no glass. To prevent the intrusion of prying eyes, a screen—mampara—is placed before the door. It is too high for a five-foot Indian to look over, and placed just so that we can run round it. The little room looks like a prison cell, only it has no grated window, nor loop-hole, nor breathing-hole, except the open door. Within is an inner cell, smaller than the outer, with no door, and all its light and air comes from the outer door. A table, as large and as high as an ottoman, a low stool, the seat of which is made of two equal surfaces descending to the centre like a trough, two or three little earthen dishes, the poyo or immovable seat built around the walls, pieces of raw-hide or mat for beds, and the mampara, are all her furniture. The wash-tub? It is the river. The ironing apparatus? Another woman does the ironing.

Where is her door leading into the patio? She has none, and can have none. A fine house would it be if any guaricha that chose to rent this miserable tenement could come into the patio. But what can she do? Where can she go? for modern improvements are not dreamed of, and sewerage there is none. She has no rights outside these two little holes, except in the streets, vacant lots, and by the river side. Blame not, then, the poor peasant women by the river side: they keep the laws of decorum as far as is in their power; and when you are sickened at the sight of filth in the street in a city 314 years old, washed by two rivers, and placed on a side hill to make drainage as easy as possible, let it be a motive to urge upon the gobierno of the province some such radical measures as health and decency demand.

The number of families living in this way exceed, perhaps, the number of well-living families in Bogotá. The ground floor is often regarded as not so healthy as the first floor, so each house has but one respectable family that has access to the patios. The front room of these lairs, excavated, so to speak, in the foundations of the best houses (the Vice-president's among the rest), are often used as shops by shoemakers, tailors, saddlers, etc., some of whose implements even occupy part of the street, to the inconvenience of every passer-by. Here you see a gamecock anchored to a peg by a string that has a segment of cow's horn, of the size of a napkin-ring, forming a sort of swivel-link in the middle, that the prisoner may not twist his cord up into knots. The bird is out here at board: his owner might not wish such an ornament in his own patio.

Bogotá has a daily market in the Plaza of San Francisco. It is, however, small, and resorted to mainly to supply accidental deficiencies and unforeseen wants. The great market-day of Bogotá is Friday, though the market really opens on Thursday in the principal plaza. On Friday the whole square is covered with sellers and their merchandise. They invade the steps of the Altozano, but the platform above is left free. The square is paved with cobble-stone, except two diagonal walks of flat stone, which are so arranged in some places as to form troughs to save the rain water to moisten the thirsty sole of some passer at night. One of them, near the northwest corner, almost deserves a place on the map of the city; and there are others in the city that I could avoid even now by my distant recollections of repeated disasters. A person who designs stopping in Bogotá should bring his lantern and a good pair of India-rubber shoes.

But I was speaking of the market. Wednesday, you remember, is the market-day of Facatativá. Many things sold or unsold there are transferred to the Plaza of Bogotá on Thursday. Here there is a stream of sirup, panela, yellowish loaf-sugar, fruits, etc., flowing toward Bogotá, along the great macadamized road, in bull-carts, and on the backs of men and beasts. Here an unfortunate descendant of the warlike Panches, that climbed up the steep height on Tuesday night, sat all day on Wednesday in the market of Facatativá, is taking his weary way, with his unsold back-load, twenty-eight miles more, and to-morrow he hopes to sell his load and start home.

At Cuatro Esquinas he meets others directly up from La Mesa by Barro Blanco, chiefly with the products of the cane. Why is not rum, the bane of man, among them? Because no man has a right to sell unimported spirits in this province that have not been distilled by Mr. Wills, and all his is brought from Cuni, and sold in his little shop near the Hospital. And from south and north, along the eastern edge of the plain, come other bands of marketers. Those mules from the north, entering the city near the Convent of San Diego, are loaded with moyas of salt, bought at the government store in Cipaquirá at two dollars per hundred weight. The beef for the market is much of it killed in the southern and meanest outskirts of the city. The ox spent the first three years of his life a bullock on the plains of Casanare, far to the east—three terrible years of alternate thirst and rain, of famine and flies. All this he survived, then the perils of the knife, then the journey through the mountains; and he has hardly got wonted to this colder climate, when, having waxed fat with the first peace and plenty he has ever known, he is cut off in the midst of his years. A good piece of him will constitute an important ingredient of Margarita's puchero for Saturday. His head has fallen to the share of some guaricha or peasant, his skin is already stretched out on the ground and made fast by pegs, his blood is cooking in twenty ollas at this moment, and in six days more every digestible particle of him except the gall-bladder will have been subjected to the action of the human stomach. How I hate carne menudo, as they call those parts of the animal that are not muscle. I could write feelingly, and give an especial philippic on mondongo—tripe—black pudding, and the udder of cows, only that it would make us all sick.

But no roads to market are more thickly crowded than those which come down through the mountains east. What multitudes I have met on them at different times! I meet them singly and in groups, all females, or with some men in company, leading or driving a bull with a rope in his nose, or themselves loaded with the productions of their little fields or of their labors.

And now, on Friday morning, let us go out and pass them in review. I have spent many patient and laborious hours with them, and even completed an enormous catalogue of their wares, which I was intending to weave into one of those easy metres so natural to Spanish and Italian, but, fortunately, perhaps, for the reader, I have lost the list. Nevertheless, to show you what I can do and what you have escaped, I will even give you a verse or two. I will take a favorite metre that they call Safico-adonigo, well known to Horace, and best illustrated by Canning's "Knife-grinder:"

"Needy knife-grinder, whither art thou going?
Rough is the road, thy wheel is out of order,
Cold blows the wind, thy hat it hath a hole in't,
So have thy breeches."

This metre taught me the laws of Spanish prosody, and the accents will all come right without writing, except where orthography always places them. The pronunciation will be given at the head of the Glossary at the end of the volume. I must forewarn the beginner farther, that when one word ends with a vowel and the next begins with one, the two are counted as but one syllable, as ò-ro|en pòl-vo, and càr-ne,e-stè-ras. Now here you have it:

Papas, tinajas, peces, alpargates,
Sal, cuentas, ocas, cueros, alfandoque,
Piscos, marranos, oro en polvo, fresas,
Losa y brevas.

Huevos, cabuya, plátanos, zarazas,
Múcuras, patos, piñas, carne, esteras,
Tunas, naranjas, azafran, frijoles,
Cal y tasajo.

M

There! with some twenty-eight more verses like these we might perhaps have a tolerable enumeration of the articles most ordinarily sold in the market of Bogotá, and as a reading-lesson for the future traveler in the Andes it would be very serviceable, though he might like a little more of the "dulce" mixed in with the "utile" in its composition.

But we must enter the market in plain prose. We approach the Plaza from the plain at the northwest corner. Along up toward the Cathedral extend collections of sugar and salt, the moyas broken into various pieces. Wooden scales, and stones for weights, enable the seller to weigh the articles to his own satisfaction, perhaps to the entire satisfaction of the buyer.

On our left hand, as we look toward Bolívar's statue, are some Indian productions, made of cotton, wool, and the fibre of a kind of century-plant yet to be mentioned. We advance toward the centre a rod or two, and turn up in front of the centre of the Cathedral. On our left are the sugar and salt aforesaid, on the right esculent roots and other vegetables; hens in eel-pot cages, eggs tied two and two, earthenware, and fish. Here is a collection: a turkey tied by one leg to a peg driven into the pavement, a pig similarly moored, and a babe almost naked. Advancing, we find fruits on both hands, till you come near the Altozano, and turn south. Here you fall in with sellers of imported goods, cloths, and calicoes. There are one or two tents or boxes with a roof. The occupant of one, seeing me busy with my pencil, desires me to record that he has gold dust for sale, which I have done (*vide supra*). Here are cylinders of matting five inches wide; those who sell it put it down and sew it. As we approach the south end we come to the meat department, and turn down between meat and dry goods. Then on our right comes the green grocery again, till we approach the Casa de Portales, where are found cordage and native manufactures of wood, cotton, wool, and other fibres that we noticed on entering. The arrangement is not, however, systematic, but rather geographical, or that which is congenial to the sellers. Each locates herself among her friends, and sells whatever she has brought; and here they remain, sitting or waiting all day. On Saturday morning you find the gallinozos scanning the whole field, and particularly where the meat was sold, leaving no substance unexamined. Lastly come the scavengers, a small squad of the presidio, under the guard of two soldiers. They sweep up the leaves that had served for wrapping-paper and all the rest of the refuse, and market is over.

I went to market once for string, and, as I had had no other opportunity of making practical experiments, I made the most of this. The first time the price asked was more than I had been told to give. I accordingly went off without making my purchase, after having offered what I had been told was proper. One of the girls took the balls of string, and followed me all over the market, where I must have spent more than half an hour. It was some time before I discovered her, and she was not aware of my discovery. She seemed to wait for me to apply to another for the same article, but I did not, and at length left to go home. Still the poor indiacita followed me some rods beyond the Plaza, when, finding me really going, she offered her balls at the usual price, and received her pay.

Overcharging strangers from richer nations is a fault of the mean and wicked every where. It vexes the traveler, who now submits, and now resists with more benefit to his successors than to himself; but I think, on the whole, there is far less of it in New Granada than might reasonably be expected; and if the market-people could only be made to husband their gains, one could not help loving them. But the tiendas where chicha is sold witness a great many sad scenes at the close of a market, and some of a disgusting character. Many reach home without a cuartillo of all their sales. Poor things! they need to be taught economy, and to desire nobler and more lasting gratifications than any they now know.

CHAPTER XIII.

RELIGION AND CHURCHES OF BOGOTÁ.

Doctrines of the Romish Church.—Miraculous Birth of Christ.—Baptism.—Relation of God-parents.—Confirmation.—Communion.—Rosary and Crown.—Family Worship.—Vespers.—Neglect of Religion.

Many intelligent persons are but little acquainted with the Romish religion. We propose to take a view of it as observers, not as theologians. It shall be by a candid statement of facts without comments, which here would be out of place; and if the reader charge me with irreverence, my plea is that I find no reverence among the faithful here, and the less can therefore be expected in me.

We wish to see some of the churches in the city of the Holy Faith, as certain devotees still call Bogotá, although the name of Santafé seems to have departed with the last of the viceroys that here ruled the New Kingdom of Granada. It is well first to be indoctrinated into the holy faith itself. I shall treat it briefly, and as a historian rather than a polemic.

The Romish Church—or the Church, as she styles herself, for she admits the existence of no other church—the holy Catholic Church professes not to teach, as many of her ignorant votaries believe, a salvation by mere ceremonies irrespective of any exercises of the heart; and yet to this we must except the doctrine that no unbaptized person can escape hell; while, save in some rare and dreadful case, no baptized person can go there. Baptism, the first and only absolutely essential sacrament of the seven, may be administered by a layman or a woman. It is accordingly often done, if the babe be weak, at once, by some intelligent person, but not with all the ceremonies. This is called "Echar agua"—to throw water. If the child lives, the priest performs all the other ceremonies of the sacrament with oil, salt, and spittle, with bell, book, and candle. The priest must have, when he applies the water, a mental or habitual intention to baptize, or the ceremony is void, and no future precautions, while this defect is not suspected and remedied, can save from hell. Priests have been guilty of this awful crime from sheer deviltry. But if the priest be drunk or stupid, and have no intention at all, it is habitual intention, and is valid. A godfather and godmother—padrino and padrina or madrina—are required, to whom the babe is ahijado or ahijada, according to the sex. This relation—padrinazgo—is a bar to matrimony, and a priest may have an ahijada in his house with as much propriety as a niece. The god-parents consider themselves bound in a sort of relationship to each other and to the parents, and for all the rest of life they call each other compadre and comadre. But when you find persons using these terms, you may not infer that there has been any baptism in the case, for these terms of endearment are often assumed by agreement between a gentleman and a lady.

God has so ordered that, with a proper education, the children of Christians become Christians with a good degree of regularity. Now the profession that the child makes at birth through the god-parents, it is proper that he should make by himself when he comes to years of discretion. And who can judge better than the parents when that time has come? The act is called confirmation, and we might naturally expect it to be performed at the age of from twelve to fifteen. But parents are rather apt to anticipate the age of discretion, and it has become quite common to confirm them about the time they begin to run alone. But the intervention of the bishop, or of some one with his powers, is necessary to this operation. I never witnessed it but once, when the brother of ex-President Herran (now Archbishop) confirmed a large number of children, some of them six or eight years old, and some unable to walk. There was nothing imposing in the ceremony. The bishop gives the child a pat on the cheek as a part of it.

But the most important part of religious training is the preparation for the first communion. When the time comes—say at fourteen—the child is withdrawn for a time from school and from all gayety, and put under the care of a priest. A chaste and pious one, if such can be found, is to be preferred where the catechumen is a girl. Some content themselves with merely seeing that the child knows all the catechism, and can pray; but one lady told me that her priest brought her so into the presence of God that she never was the same person afterward as before. She thinks this result would be more common if there were more good priests. This first communion is a great ceremony, but it is not necessary to describe it.

In doctrines they do not differ so greatly from other churches except as to the necessity of the sacraments to every comfortable escape from purgatory, and as to the existence of that doleful place fitted up expressly for Christians. They believe in the doctrine of the Trinity—the necessity of faith and repentance; but there is another doctrine to which they attach an importance that seems to me a little extravagant. It is to the perpetual virginity of Mary. It seems to me a delicate point to discuss, and I may only hint that they infer from it that her body never bore any anatomical marks of maternity whatever. From this they infer the miraculous *birth* of Christ, which was, in their opinion, necessary to the virginity of the Virgin. Decency forbids my quoting the words in which this doctrine is taught in the child's catechism. I will give, however, the conclusion—"just as a ray of light passes through glass without *breaking* or *staining* it." It is supposed that every person who does not believe this doctrine must be lost forever.

They say that the Virgin revealed to some one in a vision, after her death, the peculiar terms on which she lived with her husband, but to whom, or when, or why, I have never learned. But when I argue that, if matrimony be a sacrament, it must have been a dreadful sin in her to prostitute it to the mere purpose of saving her character, and escaping punishment on a false charge of unchastity, they have no answer for me.

The communion is swallowing a wafer, that, before consecration, was like a common white wafer, but which has been, by the act of consecration, really converted into the body of Christ. This, the *hostia*, is received from the thumb and finger of the priest into the mouth, and never is touched with unconsecrated hands. The communion of the priest is the mass. As the communion must be taken fasting, it follows that masses can be said only in the morning, and that the same priest can say but one mass in a day. To this last there is one exception. On the 2d of September each priest is bound to say three masses before breakfast. The mass has already been described at length.

Every Christian who is able is bound to hear mass every festival: to stay away is quite a sin. The next most important religious exercise is the rosary. This is a series of prayers represented by a string of beads of different sizes—cuentas. The company who are to be benefited by this exercise have one for their leader, who begins and says a prayer or two at the beginning, and then half of the Lord's Prayer, as is found in Luke. The rest say the other half. He says the first half of a Hail Mary—salve—and they the last half: so for nine more salves; but at the end of the tenth they say a Gloria Patri, and the party that ends that begins immediately on the Lord's Prayer, and the leader finishes. They say that they have finished the first casa—house—and have begun the second. The leader, when he has finished the second Gloria Patri, begins the third *Pater*, and thus they change till they have finished five casas, or fifty salves. Then they say some other things, and among them the creed, which is their longest prayer. The corona has ten casas like those of the rosary.

All families ought to pray the rosary at night, either at home or at church, but it is such a bore that men generally shirk out of it except on festivals. Some families pray only then, and a large majority not even then. The prayer-time at dusk is called la oracion, and the prayers then held in the church *vísperas* —vespers. The sound of the vesper-bell was the preconcerted signal of that dreadful massacre at Palermo known as the "Sicilian Vespers." The vísperas of any saint is the eve before his day, and even the whole day before.

Persons who pray can not, of course, have their thoughts fixed on the words of the prayer, nor is that necessary; but it is better to have them occupied with some profitable subject than in such thoughts as are apt to come to mind. Protestants would say that all the use of the rosary was to measure off the time to be spent in meditation, but I fear, should you teach this doctrine to the people, they would neither pray nor meditate much more. These prayers may be either in Spanish or Latin, and often, when a priest is leader, his half is in Latin and the rest in Spanish; but the words of the mass must always be Latin.

Two other ceremonies, or acts of devotion, that are first learned, are both known in English by the phrase "to cross one's self." Persignarse, derived from the Latin Per signum crucis, etc., is to say, in Spanish, "By the sign (touch your forehead) of the holy cross (touch your breast), deliver us (right shoulder) from our enemies (left shoulder). Amen." Santiaguarse is to make a cross in these four places, saying, "In the name of the Father, the Son, and the Holy Spirit. Amen."

I have said nothing of confession. It is a rare practice, and I have never seen it but once, although I have been in Bogotá at a time of year when the most confess. Few, indeed, of the more intelligent class ever confess, and, of course, these can not commune, neither do they fast. In fact, religion is in a great degree obsolete, especially with men. There is nothing to captivate the senses, no splendor, no imposing spectacles in the richest of their churches. It is simply ridiculous, like a boy's training with sticks for guns. Only once did I see any thing that was an exception to this, and that was la reseña, at the Cathedral; of that in its place. I will farther add that, after an acquaintance of more than 20 months among all classes and in different sections, I have met but three persons that I have known to fast from my own observation: they were all females, and one was a little school-girl.

Now, ladies and gentlemen, my lecture is over; let us sally forth to church. But, my dear madam, if you would not get us all into trouble, take a little of my advice about your dress. And, first, lay off that European bonnet—gorra, as they incorrectly call it. You may go bareheaded, wear a gentleman's straw hat, or borrow a round-topped, broad-brimmed beaver of one of the antiquated Bogotana grandmammas. Now take your best black silk petticoat, and tie it on outside of all your other clothes for a saya. Never mind your gay corsage: that will be hidden by the mantellina—a large black silk shawl, bordered with black ribbon, worn over your shoulders. The mantellina and saya bring down the lady almost to the level of the Indian woman, for she only differs from you in wearing the same fashions in flannel, black or blue. No tawdry finery can enter the house of God; there is no scope for display here.

CHAPTER XIV.

CHURCHES OF BOGOTÁ.

The City of Churches.—Clocks.—Advocaciones.—Las Nieves.—Bells.—Ara.—Nude Saints.—La Tercera.—Flagellation.—San Francisco.—Santo Domingo.—Clerical Dress.—Cathedral.—San Agustin.—Nunneries.

BOGOTÁ is pre-eminently the city of churches. With a population of 29,649, it has little short of 30 churches, while Paris, with its million of souls, has but about 50. Of the numerous churches there I have visited between 20 and 25, a feat that I doubt whether any other visitor has ever accomplished. But fear not that I will give the results of all this labor in detail. We must content ourselves with specimens that may give a general idea of them all, if such a thing is possible, where no two are more alike than the two most dissimilar churches in all the United States.

There are no new churches here: I know not their dates, but judge that most, if not all of them, were built before the beginning of the last century. I wish to take you to a church that never has been a part of a convent. And now it occurs to me for the first time that all these churches without convents must be small churches, and comparatively poor ones; so I must take the largest of them, Las Nieves. Starting from the Altozano, on the upper side of the Plaza, we go north. In three blocks we come to the River San Francisco, and cross it by the Bridge of San Francisco. Before us, on the left, is an immense pile, the Convent of San Francisco, with its church door almost facing us. Look on the tower just before us. Do you see that town clock, with a face of the same shape, and of but little larger size than that of the old family clocks of the last generation? Well, there are three town clocks in New Granada that I know of: that at Guaduas has two hands, and, I believe, strikes; that at the Cathedral, behind us, strikes, but has no dial; and this has *one* hand, and does not strike.

We continue on past the little Humilladero, La Tercera, and

the Hospicio, and on the next block but one, on the east side of the street, opposite a small vacant space, which is all the Plan shows of a plazuela and fountain, is the Church of Las Nieves. Our Lady of the Snows is, of course, the Virgin in one of her *advocaciones*, a word I can not understand nor translate. Take, as an instance of its use, Our Lady of Chiquinquirá. This is a town, 82 miles north of Bogotá, where, in 1586, a young girl was praying before an old, dilapidated, and much-abused picture of the Virgin in a kind of hovel. While gazing on it, it raised itself in the air, the gaping wounds in its canvas closed up, and it blazed out in new colors, and is now the most powerful in miracles of any picture or image in New Granada.

So there is the Virgin of the Ledge (La Peña), of the Queremal, of Concepcion, of Dolores (sorrows), Socorro (help), etc., etc. Each of these has its own form of representation, which is never varied. These have other churches dedicated to them than that in which the original image was placed, and the character and abilities of these different Virgins are very different. I said different Virgins; I should have said different advocations of the Virgin. A vow made to one is not payable to another. All these are used as names of females, as Concepcion, Dolores (masculine and plural, with adjectives in fem. sing.), Pilar, Ascencion, Nieves, etc., etc. But who Nieves is, or where and when she had her origin, I have not tried to ascertain.

Now for the church. The façade, like all the others, is decidedly homely, as I count homeliness, though admirers of the Gothic may not agree with me. In the belfry are the bells, tier above tier, fewer and smaller successively, till at the apex is one of the size of a magnificent cow-bell. They are not hung as ours are, but a string is tied to the tongue of each, and they are pulled without the intervention of any machinery. Of course, the largest are small, for they have been brought from Honda by mule or by carguero. There is no tolling, no solemn peals, but a rang-a-tang-tang on all occasions, and as in all the city there must be over 100 of them (Steuart says 1000), they can make considerable noise.

We enter, carefully taking off our hats as we cross the threshold, and the ladies covering their heads with their mantellinas. You are in a long room like a barn, open up to the top of the roof. Full in front of you stands the high altar, adorned with figures too numerous to describe. The one in the centre, the Virgin of the Snows, I suppose, is veiled with two curtains. When they are raised or lowered it is with great pomp and the ringing of a little bell. Of course, she is dressed with real clothes, and covered with tawdry finery, gilt paper, and ribbons; or, in some cases, with massive gold, real diamonds, and particularly emeralds. The face, too, must be painted and varnished, and adorned with long hair, probably from the head of some guaricha. Light hair, rare here, is preferred. The niche before which these curtains hang to cover her is called the camarin. Directly under this is the sagrario, a little cupboard, in which a large hostia or wafer is kept constantly in a costly apparatus, the custodia, where it is visible between two watch crystals. In honor of this, a light is kept constantly burning in the church. Not all churches can afford a custodia, as their price varies from $112 (the cheapest I know) to $16,000, the most costly that are made except to order. One, once belonging to the Jesuits in Bogotá, is said to have cost $60,000. The churches that have no custodia can keep no hostia, and they have no light burning in them.

Under this is a sort of shelf that contains, let into it, a consecrated stone, the ara, about 18 inches square, and only over this can mass be said. On this shelf are placed the missal-frame, and other traps used at mass.

All along down the sides are other altars, with their camarines and saints. It is quite desirable that there should be five at least. One of these is, in this instance, in a capilla, that projects out beyond the walls on the left-hand side. This particular chapel is remarkable for being used as a store-room for the twelve apostles, which are here all left to shiver in coarse shirts —all except the beloved disciple, who, in a very dilapidated robe, leans on the bosom of his Master in robes equally superannuated.

Directly over the door as we enter is the organ-loft. There are two pairs of bellows outside of the organ: it takes a stout man to blow them. Each is loaded with a heavy stone, and the man alternately lifts up the upper valve of each. The music is horrible. I may as well get through this at once by saying that in all New Granada I have heard but one good or even decent singer, an Italian monk. Even he had never studied music. On extra occasions secular singers are hired as at a ball, but they are poor at that, and, but for the performers of the military band, poor indeed would be the music on the most urgent occasion. Rarely is it better than none.

Often there are no seats in the church. In Bogotá there are generally a series, placed end to end, running down from the high altar to near the door on each side of the central line; so the occupants of the seats sit facing each other, 6 or 8 feet apart. The seats are occupied by men only: all females sit flat on the floor, or on a pellon carried by a servant. The pellon is a rug, like the finest that we lay at our doors for a mat, and is used for a bed, on the saddle, and for a seat in church. As the floor abounds in fleas, and creatures still more unclean are carried away from there—as all women spit on it, and as, in the uniformity of mantillas and sayas, it is difficult to find a friend or judge of a stranger, a crowded church is a disagreeable place for a lady. The men who do not get seats stand. No woman stands or sits on a bench, and no man sits on the floor. Only when they kneel are they all on a level. Now comes the signal for all to kneel: the little bell at the altar—the bells in the tower—the merriest strains of music, all mark the elevation of the hostia as the crisis of the mass. The women rise and the men sink, and all are together on their knees. This moment was once fixed upon by some assassins, one of whom was the officiating priest, to strike the fatal blow, that the victim might die adoring the hostia, and in the most favorable circumstances for salvation. The same motive seems to have guided another priest, who poisoned his victim with the communion hostia.

But we are tired of the church; let us return. We will not try to enter the scanty Church of the Poor-house, once a Jesuit convent. It is rarely opened, or, rather, I never knew its front door to be unbarred. So we proceed on to La Tercera. La Tercera means The Third. There are three orders of St. Francis. The first is of Franciscan friars, the second of the nuns of Santa Clara, and the third—Tercera Orden—is of men and women, who may marry and hold property. To join it is to promise an unusual strictness in religion, and you can, with more propriety, be buried in a friar's habit. The Tercera is hardly a Cofradía. This is an association paying a small sum statedly, like a burial society or benevolent association, for the sake of liberating each other's souls from Purgatory. These, in large places, often consist of men in the same line of business.

La Tercera is a sombre church. It is remarkable as destitute of both paint and gilding; but the carving is elaborate enough. I can hardly get a good idea of the use that is made of the convent which belongs to it, which is, you remember, joined to the Convent of San Francisco by a bridge. At stated times it is the theatre of *Ejercicios*. A company of women arrange about their board, and go in there, and are shut in. No one goes out, and no message comes in for nine days. Friends may die and they know nothing of it. To each is given a scourge (disciplina) and a cilicio—a contrivance made to press points of wire against the flesh. It looks like a flat chain, between one and two inches wide, made of small wire. The scourging is done in the dark, and each satisfies her own conscience. La Señora de Tal assures me that she has been through that mill, probably to ease her conscience after some great fault. Here I have frequently seen them praying in cross, as it is called, with their arms wide spread in the form of a cross, often displaying a large string of beads.

But we will proceed back toward the Plaza. The Humilladero on our left, and La Vera Cruz—the True Cross—in the middle of the Convent of San Francisco, on our right, must be passed, because they are, as usual, locked. We enter the Church of San Francisco. I first visited it, I believe, on Saint Francis's day. Never was decoration so elaborate; and the church itself was meant to be rich: the walls are covered with carvings, and almost the whole interior of the church is gilded with ancient heavy red gold. The crowd was enormous, and the ceremonies, as usual, stupid. A great many new figures and pictures were brought out. The explanations of many of them were written with chalk or soap on looking-glasses; and the number of these aids to reflection that are found among altar ornaments in New Granada is wonderful, but the most of them are cracked or otherwise damaged. I take one of these figures as an example. It was cut out of pasteboard, and painted, and set up on edge. The looking-glass below said, "Saint Francis, in order to convince a heretic prince, shows the hostia to an ass, which immediately kneels." I saw the church lighted up at night with more candles than I ever before saw in one room. The monks were climbing like ants in little galleries high up the wall, now hugging a saint for support, now climbing in or out of port-holes. They were lighting candles wherever they could reach. Now down comes a blazing candle: take care of your shaven crowns below! But, with all this blaze of candles, the church was darker (I noticed particularly) than our New York churches ordinarily are on a Sabbath evening.

I went into the convent: it was the first I ever visited. You do not meet so good treatment here as with the Agustinians, but the pictures will pay a visit. They are usually covered with large screens hanging by hinges from the top: on this day these were all drawn up. The pictures are a series, illustrating the life of Saint Francis. I am not sure now whether it begins before or after his birth. They are large, say five feet by six, but of no artistic merit. The most interesting one to me is Saint Francis preaching to the fishes. His audience are thrusting their faces out of the water, not "with ears erect" indeed, but with their large eyes staring out of their heads, and their mouths agape with a wonderful expression of credulity. A stork near the saint's feet is poised demurely on one leg, one eye fastened on the preacher, while the opposite one may be stealthily estimating the weight of some beloved object in the audience. I confess it reminds me of some things which I have seen at church before.

All these pictures are in the corredor of the principal patio. There are several other patios, some of them gardens that are absolutely uncultivated. I made some vain attempts to see the library. I fear they were ashamed to show it. I got, however, a glimpse of the kitchen and its productions. The room is spacious enough for a hotel kitchen, but of the fare I should be a poor judge. My taste certainly differs from that of the sleek brethren. Monasticism is not dead yet: some of the monks are quite young. I made them several calls, but got very little more insight into their life than at first.

We now recross the Bridge of San Francisco, and proceed

along the Calle Real to the Church of Santo Domingo. Saint Dominic's name is not very fragrant in New Granada, and very few children are named after him. In the Spanish of Robinson Crusoe, his man *Friday* bears the name of Dominic—Domingo—which means *Sunday*. Still, this unpopular saint of the Inquisition has the richest convent of monks in Bogotá. It owns all the block, and on two sides of it are the best business stands in the city. It had also, till recently, the right to the great gains of the church at Chiquinquirá, to the curacy of which they appointed their oldest monk, knowing that he could not hold the fat office long. This church is said to be rich in fine paintings, but those that interested me most were a series of smaller paintings than those in San Francisco, illustrating the life of Saint Dominic. There is horrible spelling in the inscriptions under them, *b* and *v* being inexplicably confused. One says, "God deliberating whether to send down war, plague, or famine to chastise the wickedness of men, Saint Dominic prevails on him to send, instead of either of them, the Inquisition."

A second shows the saint arguing with a batch of female heretics. Failing otherwise to convince them, he opens their eyes to behold the air over their heads filled with devils. Pity he ever had worse coadjutors in the work of conversion.

Here, in a third, are all the monks in the first Dominican convent, with their books open, singing their matins at midnight, when in comes the devil to stop them, and puts out all their lights. What a to-do! The day of friction matches is yet future; smoking has not yet come into vogue; the devil has had the audacity to extinguish even the light burning in honor of the hostia. Indeed, there may be no fire nearer than the distant kitchen, where monks are wont to keep a fire with the diligence of Vestals. Without a light they can not pray; and if the Prince of Darkness invade the chapel in spite of light and prayer, what will he not do when he has annexed it to his own dominions and silenced the holy strains? Here was an emergency, and a saint equal to it. In the picture you behold the Saint of Fire and Fagot producing a flame from his own breast to relight the candles.

Another shows us a dormitory where all the monks are on beds on the floor, sleeping, with their heads to the wall. The

Virgin has descended with a hisopo—a sprinkler, made of silver, and shaped like the doubly conical sieve of a watering-pot. A female companion attends her, unconscious of any impropriety in the transaction, bearing a pot of holy water. She goes round the room, sprinkling and blessing all but one, who "loses the blessing because he is not sleeping decently." This unlucky chap, instead of lying flat on his back, and straight, like all the others, has partly risen, and is watching the transaction—a fortunate circumstance, without which the world would have known nothing of it.

The church itself is spacious and rich, though not so indiscriminate a use is made of gold as in San Francisco. The main altar is not at the end of the church, but leaves quite a comfortable space behind it completely screened off.

I at first mistook for uncolored lithograph a small painting that is said to be worth one or two thousand dollars. It is by Vásquez. Gregorio Vásquez (Ceballos) was born in Bogotá, perhaps about the year 1700, and, if not the greatest painter that ever saw the New World, has, at least, been excelled by none that never saw the Old. The works of Vásquez are very numerous, and of quite unequal merit. Many of them have been carried abroad, and many others are lost or ruined, or nearly so, by neglect. In some, the very canvas is pierced with holes to attach jewels, lace, or muslin. The picture of which I speak is not a fair specimen of his powers of coloring, nor can it be fairly criticised, as it is covered with glass. It is a mere female head, of the size of life, on the door of the sagrario, I believe, of the last and favorite altar on the left hand.

Perhaps we ought to notice the dress of the Dominicans before leaving. I premise that all the priests here wear robes reaching to their feet, with or without pantaloons, just as they please. The hats of the clergy have an enormous brim, and rolled up at the sides, and are so large that they pay $1 60 duty, while a layman's hat pays but eighty cents.

The reverend character to which I here introduce my reader is not a priest, but an eminent statesman, and, as these lines go to press, a candidate for the presidency. No other man did more to bring about the Revolution of 1851 than Mariano Ospina; but when the government wished suitably to recompense

HABIT OF THE JESUITS.

his services, he was nowhere to be found. His modesty led him to shrink from the public gaze, and, when he would change his quarters one night, the keen eye of some friend who was very anxious to meet him recognized him in the habit of the Order of Jesuits, his big rosary hanging down, so convenient if he should happen to want to pray. As a substitute for street lamps, he carries the inseparable companion of a Bogotano's night excursions. So here we have Don Mariano, taken from a grave Granadan caricature, to serve us as a model of the dress of regulars or monks. That of the Dominicans—rivals to the Jesuits in our hate—consists of a white flannel habit under a black one. Each order has its peculiar habitos.

The dress of the seculars—priests that are not monks—is radically different from the regulars. They wear no habitos. Their innermost visible dress is short, and has sleeves: it is called chaqueta. Over this comes the sotana, without sleeves, extending down to the heels like female dress, only scanty, not containing more than three *breadths*, as the ladies say. Over this, in all weathers, they wear a cloak—manteo—with or without a hood. The dress is alike ungraceful and inconvenient.

Before leaving Santo Domingo, look at that lady dressed in white flannel. She is called a Beata—a blessed one. She is a devotee that confesses daily, takes a sort of pastoral oversight of every family in which she can get a footing, aids some favorite priest in getting masses to say, and, in a word, is a professional busy-body. Beatas are represented in a Bogotá paper to be rarely handsome or young, mostly married, and a nuisance

N

generally in every house but their own, a place they do not infest much.

We now proceed to the Cathedral. It is an old building, having been founded 15th of March, 1572. It is said to be the design of a native artist, and, to judge of his work, we must know his limiting circumstances. What the building lacks in point of proportion is height. The proposition of the German householder in New York, that "ground is cheap up in the air," may not always be true in a country subject to earthquakes. Let us suppose, then, that he dared not add the other ten or twenty feet that the building needs: he must disguise the deficiency. In the façade, the altozono does this to a considerable extent, and, to make up the rest, the towers were run up even too high for their strength, as it seems, for they now bear in their upper works the marks of the great earthquake. But why not diminish the area down to due proportions? This would not do, for the room was really wanted for processions, and to hold the immense crowds that must get in, even though they can not see.

Now, as you enter, you find right before you an immense box, so to speak, some twenty feet high, thirty feet square, and open at the top. This is called the coro—choir. The walls on three sides are four feet thick; and the other side, toward the altar, is an open grating of iron. In the thickness of the wall is a spiral staircase, and on top are two organs, and space for hired musicians and hired male singers.

The institution within this box is a mystery to me. The *personnel* of it seems to be a dozen or so of a higher class of priests, called canónigos, a word that I believe is translated prebendaries, and a few boys—minoristas—dressed in red flannel, and some kind of white girl-clothes of cotton or linen reaching down to the waist. You may find this concern in full blast every Sunday at about 3 P.M.; but, after watching them carefully, you may not know more about them than what I now tell you. Each has his own seat, partitioned off from the rest by arms, as in the Fulton ferry-boats, and the seat rises on hinges. These seats may have been, in English, *stalls*, and to take possession of them, to be *installed*. The seats run around three sides of the room, and in two rows, one above the other. The centre stall in the upper row was always vacant. This, I suppose, belonged to Archbishop Mosquera, as the one on the right of it was occupied by Dr. Herran, then the Provisor, and now Archbishop. I conjecture that the service has degenerated down from singing, as they were reading aloud in a drawling manner, now one at a time and now all together, but always unintelligibly, in which respect they resemble some of the able choristers of the North.

My mind runs back to my theory. I imagine that, when a coro was first built, it was filled with the sweetest male singers that could be found in the land, regardless of expense, that it might be a model of sacred music to the whole people, and a joy to all those who could treat themselves to a visit to the Cathedral. If that be true, never was there a case of more complete perversion of original designs. If I might doubt my senses, and think that the horrible din was to holier ears delightful music, still the fact remains that I have never seen an audience of even one beside myself. And yet this establishment cost the province of Mariquita $1148 80 annually for the salaries of the chapter, as these canónigos are called, or $1669, including all their share of the expenses of the Cathedral. And the nearest point of the province is more than two days' journey from the Cathedral!

A man showed me a picture, hanging on the side of the choir, that he considered miraculous, or nearly so. "You see that horse," says he. "Now stand full in front of him, then to the left, then to the right, and the horse's head will follow you as you go."

"Do I understand you, then," said I, "that you should expect to get so far round to the right as to see the left side of the head and neck?"

"Como no?"—"Why not?"

"Well, I should regard it as a decided miracle if you could get so far round as to see the side of the head the artist had not painted, or cease to see the side that he had painted."

"Quien sabe, señor?"

Once in front of the choir you see more of the building. Vast and lofty pillars, with gilded capitals, support the roof. Projections inward from the side walls furnish a large number of alcoves or chapels, each with its altar, and confessionals are scattered around with a profusion that seems to imply that once they were more demanded than in these degenerate times. In fact, the whole establishment, if worked one day to the utmost, must be capable of delivering a small army from Purgatory; but it is mostly locked, and, when opened, is generally as quiet as a Saratoga hotel in February.

The space from the steps of the choir to those of the high altar is more liberally seated than in any other church. Here alone are several seats, one behind another, provided for the "Seminario conciliar," theological school, as inscriptions indicate, besides the line of seats running up the centre. The great altar itself is a detached lofty pile, rising far toward the roof, and helping to mask the vast extent of the Cathedral. To one of the pillars, between the choir and the altar, is the pulpit, exquisitely carved and gilded. It has a sounding-board over it, of the antique New England pattern.

Behind the altar is still a very considerable space, enough for a small church. The immense area of the Cathedral is thus broken up, so that at no point can the eye measure it. And so far is it from the possibility of a united audience, so many the obstructions that cut off the view, that I knew of one case where a young couple, under the influence of a waltz played by the hired musicians on the top of the choir, during the services of an evening in Holy Week yielded to the temptation and danced.

Between two sacristías of vast proportions is yet another chapel of considerable pretensions to beauty. The contents of the sacristías must be costly, although, as a church, the Cathedral is poor—quite poor compared with Santo Domingo. But so many performers must dress in these green-rooms with a great variety of habits (and these paramentos, as well as the ornamentos of the altar, must vary in color according to the day), that the number and cost of them must be very great.

Now let us go to the church that I like best, San Agustin, and it shall be the last. We keep along south in the same street in which we have been all this chapter, till we cross the Bridge of San Agustin. On our right now lies a ragged place, like a fractional vacant lot, called the Plazuela of San Agustin, and on this fronts the convent. I once heard here some really tolerable singing, and tried to get in, but all the doors were locked. I have often visited it since, always disappointed in the music, but otherwise pleased.

The high altar, like that of the Cathedral, stands clear, so that processions can march all round it. But you must not imagine there is any dignity or splendor in these processions. A part of this consists of six poles, always held awry, to the tops of which is attached a piece of silk as large as the cover of a Rockaway wagon, but no attempts are made to keep it stretched out smooth. Under this walks a priest with the custodia, and as the procession marches round, all the kneeling multitude turn round toward it like sunflowers, so that when the procession has performed a revolution round the altar, they have revolved once around their axes. I was complimented here once with the offer of the first candle in a procession, a candle a yard long, but I felt constrained to decline the honor. I was struck in seeing a monk, at the close of that procession, extinguish his light by putting the lighted wick against the pavement, exactly as we see it in allegorical pictures.

There are here two or three capillas quite removed from the body of the church, one of which would make a nice little church by itself, only that its principal door comes out of the main church.

I wish to call your attention to two pictures here, which have interested me more than any others in Bogotá, not so much on account of the superiority of the execution as the design. In one, on the back of the high altar, our Savior awaits the preparation of his cross. He has been maltreated terribly, and from his side a large piece of skin is gone, laying bare the ribs. An executioner, having occasion to use both hands, holds a large spike in his teeth: he is stooping down, and looks up at you, and the want of two teeth from the vigorous set he shows gives him an air of ferocity that makes you shudder. The only other figure is the Virgin, overwhelmed with grief, but much younger than her son. But the cross itself interests me. *It is not a new one*, but an old thing, once handsome, painted green, but cracked by the sun, bruised by rough usage, and polluted with the stains of numerous executions.

The other picture is on the right-hand side of the altar, and is interesting from the subject—the marriage of Joseph and Mary. Joseph, contrary to the practice of Italian artists, is young, does not look like having had children by a previous marriage, nor on the verge of imbecility. The Virgin here, as every where, is always young. I know not whether the Church claims perpetual youth for her, but certain it is that if any painter dared to make her decrepit and wrinkled in her last days, the Inquisition would burn him, if it could.

I have found considerable courtesy in this convent, and would prefer a visit here to any other. Luther was an Agustinian. But I have not time to take you over the convent. On the next block south, on the left hand, is the parish church of Santa Barbara, who is always represented as in the act of having her throat cut. The church is quite small, but has a picture of great reputation for efficacy. All these nine churches and convents are on one street, and there stand two more at its two extremities at the edge of the city—the Convent of San Diego at the north, and Las Cruzes at the south.

We will visit but the chapel of a single nunnery. I have never tried to get into the interior of any of them. I should have no difficulty in getting permission, but I should not have found enough of interest to pay. We will, for variety's sake, turn one block down the San Agustin, cross on a log, and go toward the lower side of the Plaza. The first building on our left as we go south is the Quartel—barracks—of San Agustin. On the next block, on the left, is quite a good front to a public boy's school. I was passing here one Sabbath, and, finding there were boys in there, I hoped to find a Sabbath-school. Vain hope! it was only a rehearsal of an examination that was soon to come off. On the corner of the next block, on the right, stands the Observatory. Now the spacious, never-to-be-finished capitol is on our right for a whole block, and we come to the Plaza at the corner diagonally opposite the Cathedral. We turn down west, having on our right first the Casa Consistorial, then the prison opposite the cabinet offices, and then the next two blocks on our right are devoted to the immense convent of La Concepcion, which occupies two blocks in the heart of the city.

A bird's-eye view of Bogotá would surprise you with the number of churches and the size of the convents. Many of the convents have already been taken from the Church, and converted to some purpose more useful to the descendants of those whose money built them, such as schools, hospitals, etc., but the space occupied by the remainder is enormous, and they are said to own about half the real estate of Bogotá.

The number of monks and nuns can not be great, for, in the 32 Granadan convents there are but 697 persons, exclusive of 469 servants and 97 pupils. All of these could find space enough in a single convent of this city. Jolly times they must have had of it till Archbishop Mosquera took away the nuns' horses, abolished their theatres, forbade their masquerading in male attire, and allowed even to the aged and infirm but *two* servants each. Even now their sufferings can not be excessive, for in Santa Inés there are 73 servants and but 46 other inmates. Nuns are never suffered to leave their convents, nor have I ever heard of any recent charges of their violating their vows.

In the middle of the wall of La Concepcion, on the right hand, begins that of Santa Inés on the left. This was the first church in Bogotá that I entered. It was Sunday, and I had Don Fulano's little boy for a guide. Amid all the other profanations of the Sabbath around me, I was not surprised to hear a hand-organ, and instinctively looked round for the *monkey*. I had forgotten where I was. The hand-organ proved to be a church organ, and the accompaniment was mass in a nunnery. But the singing was horrible. In no other nunnery is there any choir, and here the music is all by nuns, who only can learn of each other, and have little motive to learn. It was as bad as the fighting of cats.

Two stories of the nunnery are grated off from the body of the church. The lower part of the church has two gratings of iron, four feet apart, extending all across the end opposite the altar. Behind the gratings is a curtain. Above is a grating of broad slats of wood, along all the one side and the end of the church. Not much can be seen of those within.

The walls of the church of Santa Inés are covered with a series of pictures, representing scenes from her life, in all of which she is accompanied by a lamb that seems never to grow bigger.

In the first picture the lamb is looking on to see the future saint take that first washing which we of the coarser sex seldom are permitted to witness. A maid is carrying something to drink in a tea-cup (set, as always here, on a plate instead of a saucer) to the newly-delivered. She is lying in a sort of berth or bunk —cuja—quite inappropriate, professional men think, to her situation.

The sacristy is to appearance in the body of the convent, but it is supposed to have no other door than that which leads into the church. A confessional, placed so that the priest's right ear is close by a perforated tin plate in the wall, is a necessary part of the furniture of a convent.

The sacristan of a convent is sometimes, if not always, a man. I have seen the keys of the outer door drawn up into an upper window of the convent after closing at night, as if thus to show that all communication with the world was cut off.

Now this is all I know about nunneries. Farther investigations pay neither for making nor reciting. There is little or no beauty about them. Youth and intelligence must be very scarce in institutions so obsolete, now happily verging to extinction.

CHAPTER XV.

PÁRAMO AND POLITICS.

Dancing.—Mules, Bulls, and Horses.—Quesada, the Conqueror.—Bolívar and Santander.—Colombia: its Rise, History, and Disruption.—One or two Rebellions.—Heroic and frail Woman.—Hail.

AND now you must be tired of churches. I have been for these long months. I will defer to another time the remainder of the tedious details of dull ceremonies, which must not, however, be omitted in a faithful picture of a country in which they were once regarded as of the highest importance. Let us rusticate a while, and take a series of trips around the capital.

Bogotá, being situated at the western foot of a mountain range, is half surrounded with mountain and half with plain. My visits have chiefly been to the mountains. I will take these up in the order of the points visited, beginning at the north. I take first, then, the expedition of December 1st, 1852—the longest, the most disagreeable and unprofitable of them all. I wished to see a páramo—a region too cold for cultivation. I set out very early in the morning, mounted on a fine horse, kindly lent me by our minister, Mr. King, and accompanied by Dr. Hoyos and Señor Triana, of the Chorographic Commission. We went along the Alameda, which, after passing San Diego (*c*), becomes merely a macadamized road, leading toward the salt-mines of Cipaquirá, the emerald-mines of Muzo, and, more than all, toward the fane of the miraculous and miracle-working picture of Chiquinquirá.

We leave this convent a little to the right, and the two cemeteries twice as far to the left, and the road bends slightly to the west. Next we cross a brisk little stream—the Rio Arzopispo—and soon come to a collection of houses, called Chapinero. Just beyond, I picked some flowers from a black cherry-tree—Cerasus Capollin—so like our own native black cherry that I should not know but by comparison that it is not C. Virginiana. As I have never seen it except on road-sides just out of Bogotá, it may well be an introduced tree, and, for the same reason, I have never been able to judge of its fruit. It is here called cerezo. This and a willow—sance, Salix—are the only trees growing, even by cultivation, on the plain of Bogotá, or near the city on the mountains.

On the left is a hacienda, to which, at a later period, I walked with Mr. Green, to see something of a political festival to celebrate the accession of the Liberals to power on the famous 7th of March, 1849. We staid but a short time, and left before the affair was fully under way, as our worthy representative soon tired of the affair. We saw some dancing worth notice. In a small room near the entrance there was a fiddle or clarinet playing, in anticipation of the military band yet to arrive. Two or three females, not of the highest class, were present, and ten times as many of their peers of the other sex. Two of them stood up to waltz. In two minutes a second man stepped in and took the place of the first, without breaking the time. A third and a fourth succeeded, till, the girl becoming tired, her place was supplied by another in the same way. How long the waltz lasted uninterrupted I can not say, as we came off. If the musicians had relieved each other in the same way, there is no saying when the time would have varied or the step ceased. In nothing is the Granadino more indefatigable than in dancing, either by night, or, as in this instance, by day.

A few miles farther on we turned off to the right, and took leave of the road, the second in New Granada, though a little out of repair. Keeping closer to the base of the mountain, at length we climb it. This, like chopping off a man's head, can be said in three words, but the performance is no trifling matter. We were mounted on horses unused to climbing. On our way up we were overtaken by a loaded bull from Bogotá. We were amused to see how little he made of climbing where our fine animals were put to their utmost. For the very worst of roads they are surer of foot than a mule, but can not supersede them on any other. Mules are quicker, and will, I think, carry a much heavier load. A mule costs much more than a horse. They are surer of foot, but I suspect they can not endure more. The fact is, that the mule will not let you abuse him as a horse will. A horse, to escape the lash or the spur, will exert himself till he will never see another day of health; but when the mule can do no more without injury to his constitution, he is as conscientious as a politician: urge him as you will, he will do no violence to that sacred trust. Hence mules are a semi-barbarous institution, as cargueros are a barbarous one; and as cargueros have successfully opposed the opening of mule-roads in some instances, so the Spanish institution of mules has opposed itself to wheel-roads, and in one instance, in the mother country, even to the opening of a railroad when completed!

The bull left us, but we were rising rapidly. How the vast plain stretched itself out beneath us! Sheets of water covered as much of it as at any time of the year, for the rainy season was nearly past. Off against us stood Funza, said to have been the capital of the Muiscas, the most powerful nation in New Granada, when, in March, 1537, the indefatigable Gonzalo Jiménes de Quesada, whose name for heroism should stand with those of Cortés and Pizarro, and for moral worth (small praise) above them both, first saw this plain. He had left Santa Marta nearly a year before with more than 800 men. After struggling with the wilderness, storms, starvation, and disease for more than 9 months, he had risen from the banks of the Opon with only 170 men left. These had *brought* with them (in some places literally carried bodily!) 62 horses; and with these he made his way to this vast plain beneath us, conquered the Muiscas, and other Chihcha nations, without receiving any re-enforcements. Quesada survived the various dangers of wars, conspiracies, and law, and died of leprosy in Mariquita, beyond Honda, 10th February, 1579, at the advanced age of nearly 80.

We rise higher, and vegetation is ever changing. Here I noticed for the first time a peculiar and beautiful shrub of the Tiliate order, the Vallea stipularis, with its copious pink blossoms and pretty leaves, larger and thinner than shrubs at this altitude often indulge in, not unlike those of the poplar. A still more beautiful Ericate shrub, the Befaria resinosa, bears here the name of pega-pega, from its sticky blossoms, an inch long, growing in dense clusters, of a rich rose-color of all shades, from the deepest to the most delicate. Here only did I find them with so little varnish as to be readily detached from the paper in drying.

At length we ceased to ascend. At the top we found a hilly country rather than a plain, and on a distant hill saw a *tree*. We descended to a hacienda, consisting of three mud cottages. The largest was in the form of two sides of a square, and had three habitable but very small rooms, apparently for the occupancy of one man, not very nice, but, judging from his chapel, particularly pious.

The other houses were at a little distance, and were a house for a dependant, and a kitchen. From the gentleman's bed-room a bell-pull extends to the other house, a contrivance almost unknown in this country—the first bell I have seen, in fact, large or small, except those in churches. We left our horses in one of the vacant rooms, and sallied out for plants. We were soon driven in by a storm, for the páramo had *got angry*, as they say here.

We were kept wet and cold a long time at the house, while they were preparing some chocolate for us at the kitchen, on the strength of a friendship between the proprietor and Dr. Hoyos. I walked up and down two of the rooms to gain heat. It was actually hailing without, the nearest approximation to snow ever ventured on here.

Dr. Hoyos and Triana are on opposite sides in politics, and we may as well listen to them a little. I kept no notes, but if I have exaggerated any the opinions of the Liberales, as they fell from the enthusiastic young botanist in employ of government, it must be under the influence of the still more enthusiastic young poet and jefe político of Ambalema, José María Samper (Agudelo), whose "Apuntamientos" is the fairest specimen of republicanism "run into the ground" I ever saw.

As for the pious Dr. Hoyos, once an attendant on the pious and eminent priest and botanist, Mútis, his sentiments represent those of the few pious men of the nation, the extreme right of the Conservadores. As Samper may be regarded as the type of the youngest of *Young Granada*, speaking through Triana, so may Don Mariano Ospina, not inaptly clothed in Jesuit robes, on page 193, be the oracle of respectable fogyism, as represented below by the mature-minded, slow, almost regressive Hoyos.

Below us, on the plain, was a hacienda of ex-President Santander's. Taking that for our text, we make *Triana* observe:

To that man New Granada owes more than she ever has or ever will to any other.

Dr. Hoyos. We owe much to Santander indeed, but had it not been for Bolívar, we should have had no chance to owe any thing to Santander or to any other patriot. Without a man like Bolívar, a general equal to Napoleon, and a statesman equal to Washington, our distracted country would have contended in vain, not so much against the courage as against the numbers, ferocity, and brutality of the Goths of the mother country (metropolí).

T. I can agree with you only in what relates to Bolívar's military talents. As a statesman, the Vice-president Santander, residing in Bogotá while the Libertador was at the head of the army, directed judiciously, except when the impetuous warrior dictated some decree from the camp to throw into confusion the sagest provisions of the "Man of the Laws." And small merit was it to deliver us from a transatlantic tyrant, to rule us himself as a dictator in Bogotá!

H. What Bolívar did was a necessity forced upon him by

the confusion and political ignorance of the country. For eleven years, from the glorious 20th of July, 1810, to the Congress of Cúcuta in 1821, we were without a form of government. Bolívar was elected President, and Santander Vice-president under that Constitution, but the liberty of the country was yet to achieve. The changes introduced into our condition by that Constitution were too great and too violent. We had no experience in self-government, for which we have even to go to the English language for a name; every thing had been left to executive power, and now the executive was too weak.

T. It was rather too strong than too weak. The executive is the only dangerous element of government, the only department that has ever turned despot. Instead of the changes being too great and too sudden, they were too timid and too few to meet the wants of the case. Not a rag of the old system of tyranny ought to have been left for a day. The authors of that cowardly Constitution were afraid of their own shadows. They had no confidence in the power of democratic institutions, and therefore dared not install the true republic. Instead of freeing all the slaves at once, it meanly ordains the freedom at 18 of all thereafter born, leaving the others to be ransomed by the slow operation of a fund. Capital punishment, the connection between Church and state, the exemption of the clergy and military from civil courts, and, indeed, the army itself, is inconsistent with republicanism. So are all monopolies, all limitations of the right of suffrage, all restrictions on the liberty of the press, imprisonment for debt, and, in a word, every particle of the institutions handed down to us by our tyrants.

H. And you would have all changed at once?

T. Certainly; it was the only course that could have given the country rest.

H. Now, to my mind, such a beginning would have been clearly impossible. And the restlessness of political enthusiasts, that let themselves loose upon the government, both from the forum and the press, with plans and language alike extravagant (to say nothing of revolutionary schemes), was just what necessitated more severity in administration, and more restraint on the press. Bolívar's work was not to administer a free government, but to prepare a liberated people for liberty. He would have steadily advanced to that end, had not turbulent spirits, like Dr. Francisco Soto and Dr. Vicente Azuero, been perpetually thwarting every measure of preparation.

T. What preparation, *nor* what dead baby ?* Do you call re-establishing convents that had been abolished; strengthening the power of the priests, that had been destroyed by their adhesion to the cause of tyrants; issuing arbitrary decrees to abrogate contracts fairly made (that for the navigation of the Magdalena, for instance); placing restrictions on the schools, and delivering them over to the priesthood bound hand and foot —do you call that the work of preparation for freedom?

H. We shall never agree on questions as to priests and schools. I know that I am in a hopeless minority, but I have right on my side, as you must confess, or avow yourself no Christian. But, apart from this, Bolívar opposed himself, not to the will of the people, but to the ravings of political lunatics. Elected by the Convention of Cúcuta, he was re-elected by the people in 1825, after these acts of regression, as you call them. But demagogues who sought office, not the good of the people, beset his course, till, in 1827, he resigns. His resignation is not accepted, and, as a last resort, he again appeals to the people in the Convention of Ocaña.

T. I wonder that you dare allude to the Convention of 1828. A candid history of the years 1827 and 1828 would fully bear out Samper's remark, that the liberators of a country ought to meet with any other reward than a share in its subsequent government. General Páez had risen in rebellion against Colombia on the 30th April, 1826, from motives of sheer ambition, and with no other pretense even. Bolívar visits him, concocts plans with him, manifests open friendship for him, and then returns to Bogotá and resigns the presidency. His tools, who were in majority in the Congress of 1827, refuse to accept his resignation, and call the Convention of Ocaña for the express purpose of adding to his power. Meanwhile, what is going on at Guayaquil? The Intendant there is Tomas Cipriano Mosquera, the proudest, if not the richest man in New Granada,

* ¿ Qué preparacion ni qué niño muerto? The *ne plus ultra* of uselessness with a Spaniard is a dead baby, or sometimes calabashes—¿ Qué preparacion ni qué calabazas?

the head of the royal family of New Granada, for he now is ex-president, brother of an ex-president, father-in-law of an ex-president, and brother of an archbishop [since deceased].

H. And all of them worthy of the highest posts they ever filled.

T. Well, our Chevalier Bayard, "sans peur et sans reproche," as you call Mosquera, proclaims Bolívar dictator.

H. A masterly step, by which Mosquera had nothing to gain, and on which hung the last hope of the integrity of the nation, which hope had two fatal obstacles to contend with: the transcendental chimeras of you Liberales, and the ambition of a hundred intriguers for high offices, including twenty who wanted to be president. But go on.

T. Well, the Convention meets March 2d, 1828, the blackest year of Colombian history.

H. You may well say that. But go on.

T. Bolívar is in the minority. He locates himself, with 3000 troops, at Bucaramanga, as near Ocaña as he dares come. There, after trying in vain to intimidate the majority, he induces a minority of twenty to secede on the 10th June, and leave them without a quorum; and then, three days after, on the 13th June, Pedro Alcántara Herran, who married into the royal family, calls an assembly in Bogotá, and again proclaims Bolívar dictator, as his father-in-law had done the year before in Guayaquil.

H. And for the same reasons, and better. But go on.

T. The Liberator and Enslaver accepts the post. On the 27th of August of this same 1828 he issues his organic decree, virtually abolishing the Constitution of 1821.

H. And in September?

T. In September, but for the interposition of a prostitute lodged in the palace, he would have met the reward of his deeds.

H. You admit, then, that the conspirators of 1828 had decided to assassinate him who had sacrificed all his property, endured starvation and the cold of the páramos with the common soldiers, and risked his life in a hundred battles for the freedom of his country?

T. When a benefactor, turned tyrant, is protected by such

men as the Mosqueras and the Herranes, and by that unfailing foe to liberty, a standing army, there is on cheaper or better remedy—no other in this case. What is necessary is right.*

H. And who was the head of this conspiracy?

T. There was no head. Seven young men of Bogotá presided each over his section.

H. Youths who had never seen a battle, and knew the use of no other weapon than a poniard. But Santander?

T. There is no doubt but that the Vice-president, robbed of his office a few weeks before by a tyrannical decree, and who, on the dictator's death, would be the constitutional President, knew something of what was going on; but he had no direct part in the conspiracy, and was condemned to death without any evidence of complicity. You, Señor Norte Americano, have seen the *autos* of the trial in Colonel Pineda's collection of pamphlets, have you not?

I. I saw them, and the commutation of the sentence from death to banishment in Bolívar's own hand-writing, but I did not examine them farther.

H. And now let me tell you how it was: Bolívar's dictatorship was in accordance with the wishes of all lovers of stability, but was contrary to the theories of certain young students of Jeremías Béntam, and in the way of hundreds of projects of personal ambition. All these pointed to Bolívar's death as the cutting of a Gordian knot, but the final result could have been nothing but terrific anarchy. Santander and Bolívar were different by nature, and could not work together in such tempestuous scenes. We will hope that the Vice-president would have kept himself free from such a stain on his character had he not felt himself injured by the decree of the 27th August, 1828. The conspiracy extended even to Popayan, and doubtless embraced both López and Obando, but it became so nearly discovered that the mine had to be sprung almost at an hour's notice, at midnight between 25th and 26th September, 1828. The assassins, covered with blood, are already at the palace door, and the guards are already overpowered by the sword and dagger, when the Liberator first learns his danger. He resolves to die

* See Samper's Apuntamientos, pp. 102–106.

a Roman death, and proceeds, unarmed, to meet his murderers. But Manuela Sáenz—

T. Has ever any president, since the bachelor Bolívar, kept a mistress in the very palace?

H. Our best presidents have had their failings as men. The heroism of this woman (to be classed only with Rahab) has changed the whole face of our history, and saved us from one civil war more. She detains Bolívar—directs him to the easternmost window, the last in the Palace as you go up toward the theatre. He drops from it, only eight or nine feet, into the clear street, goes up to the corner, turns south to the River San Agustin, and hides under the bridge two blocks above the Bridge of San Agustin.

I. And Manuela?

H. The woman, who has never thought of dressing, meets the assassins on the stairs, dares them to kill her, and declares that otherwise they can come no farther. They are past her; the stains of bloody hands are on her white robes, but she is otherwise uninjured, and the Liberator is safe. And while he lives there is no hope of the success of the conspiracy. A few of the leaders paid the penalty of their lives, and others were banished. Santander himself continued in banishment till, in 1832, he was elected President.

I. What became of Bolívar?

H. He returned that day to the palace. One unfortunate attempt more was made against his power in Antioquia, where poor José María Córdova, who had fought at Bolívar's side, high in rank though still a boy, was stretched on the bloody field of Santuario. This fatal day was in the year 1828. General O'Leary, now British embassador in Bogotá [since dead], commanded the Dictator's troops on that occasion.

Bolívar was superseded in 1830 by Joaquin Mosquera, the last President of Colombia. True, Tomas Cipriano was his brother, and a good president, his bitterest and most ambitious enemies being judges: he was none the worse for being of good family. A new Constitution was at the same time adopted; but Páez in Venezuela, and Flórez in Ecuador, secured the rejection of both President and Constitution, and a bloodless and complete dismemberment of Colombia was effected in 1831.

Bolívar, when relieved from office, retired to Cartagena. The man who had encountered more perils than any other of his generation died a natural death, at San Pedro, near Santa Marta, on 17th December, 1830; and he died poor, after so long possession of supreme power.

We may suppose the discussion to have reached this point, when the arrival of something warm from the kitchen gave a new turn to things. I do not introduce this as a fair specimen of the conflicting accounts from which the traveler has to form his opinions, for the statements I have given could have hardly been expected to occur unmixed with falsehoods, believed or not believed by the narrator, and exaggerations which it would be difficult to pare down to proper dimensions; but by giving these details, I may escape coming to a conclusion in a doubtful matter.

Of the precise nature of the something warm I can say nothing. I think I have recollected enough for one day, so you will excuse my stating its name, composition, or how it tasted. This over, and followed by some dulce from the cojinetes of the pious conservador, we began to turn our thoughts homeward.

I have not yet spoken of my zamarras. Don Fulano thought it not respectable for me to ride out without zamarras, so he lent me his. They are a sort of overalls, or imperfect pantaloons of hide—I should judge, in this instance, of bull's hide. Certain it is that, once in them, I was as helpless as a modern knight in ancient armor. It took two to extract me from them and encase me in them; to mount, I had to climb on a bench; and when I dismounted, it seemed as if the saddle was sticking to me. It was months before I repeated the experiment, and then with a more pliable pair. Zamarras are exhibited in the figures of the Orejon, the Carguero and Babe, and the Vaquero. In the last they are of the skin of the *tigre*, called jaguar in other Spanish countries, which I suppose to be the Felis discolor, the most formidable animal of the New World, but fortunately rather rare, and cowardly.

Once fairly stuck upon my horse, I had time to look again at the weather. The ground was white with hail, but now it neither hailed nor rained. *Facilis descensus* was not written on the side of a wet mountain. Before the rain the descent would have been difficult, now it was absolutely dangerous. Both my friends' horses fell with them during the trip, but we escaped unhurt. In some places, after again reaching the plain, we found *five inches of hail!* In a fit of absence of mind, it seemed natural enough to me. I forgot that to-day is here reckoned the first day of *summer*, or, as we would call it, of the dry season. The terms seem equally inapplicable to-day. This crop of hailstones is counted a blessing, and is eagerly treasured up for ice creams.

Indeed, the plain had been visited by no ordinary storm. Roads were turned into rivers. Encumbered as were our hands, to say nothing of my zamarras, it was no easy task to pick our way. Triana suggested that our horses might profit by the advice to Virgil's ram, *Non bene ripæ creditur;* which, I affirm, coincides with the idea of Horace, that the Ibis is safest in the middle: "*In medio tutissimus ibis;*" while the conservador, with a caution habitual to his creed, suggests that, if we follow the advice of such heathen, we may have occasion to cry, *De profundis clamavi.* However, we reached home, before dinner of necessity, but near night, not very richly rewarded for our journey except by the good we derived from each other's company.

CHAPTER XVI.

MONTSERRATE AND THE BOQUERON.

Aqueduct.—Bathing Excursion.—Houses not Homes.—Quinta of Bolívar.—Hill Difficulty, and a Way of doubtful Holiness. — Chapel. — Perpetual Snow. — Some nice Plants. — A cold Region and its Inhabitants. — The Boqueron. — Leñeras.—Scarcity of Wood.

In the last chapter I mentioned passing the Rio Arzobispo—Archbishop River—which bursts down from the mountains just beyond the northern limits of our Plan on page 153, and hurries down into the plain to join the Bogotá.

One day I wished to bathe. The most attentive friend I had in Bogotá, who could never do too much for me, conducted me here. We were to start at ten, but he was occupied till twelve. In fact, it is almost impossible to set out at a fixed time here. We proceeded along the Alameda till we came to the convent of San Diego (*c* in the Plan), when we began obliquely to ascend the foot of the mountain. We soon struck the aqueduct that supplies our part of Bogotá. It is a sort of drain a foot wide, with the water six inches deep. Most of the way it is covered, but not so as to protect it from surface wash.

It had recently rained, and the water at the pila was of a rich brown color, but where it entered the head of the aqueduct through a small strainer it was perfectly clear. I did not like very well to know that the dirt I drink had been so recently incorporated with my chocolate.

We followed the acequia to its origin, and the river upward from this point. Soon the climbing became arduous, and at two (our dinner hour at home) we stood together at a fine fall of twenty feet into a pretty little basin. I began to make preparations for a bath, but my guide and physician assured me that the water was too cold and I too warm.

The barrier before us seemed insuperable. We passed it, however, at the risk of our necks, to another fall and basin very similar to the lower, and just above it. We came near being imprisoned here by a shower making absolutely impassable the dangerous path we had climbed.

High above us on the cliff was a man throwing down sticks and roots for fuel. They fell to a spot near the path by which we had been coming up here, but before we had passed the place where his projectiles struck, he had completed his load, descended with an unbroken neck, drawn his ropes out from a hiding-place where we had seen them, bound the fagots on his shoulders, and gone to sell them.

Our descent was not so easy. We could not tell why we came there, as, though the lower falls yielded us a large number of plants, and some very rare ones, a Vaccinium among the rest, there was nothing new that we wanted after passing the first point where our bones were in danger. Farther down was an Aroid plant in flower that I must have. We could not reach it. We looked about for a stick to pull it down with. Absurd idea! every stick big enough to strike a mule with has long since been carried to town and sold for fuel. But I must have it; so I mounted Dr. Pacho on my shoulders, as he was the lighter and I the stronger. He could barely reach it, but after several good pulls down came it, he, and I in a heap together. Farther on, we passed the proper place without even discussing the proposition of bathing, as night was now approaching. I returned loaded with rare plants.

On the banks of the river, below where we first came upon it, was the smallest human habitation I ever have seen or expect ever to see. It was so small that I could not have lain straight in it except diagonally, and its breadth and height were less than the length. I have seen poorer houses, however, for it was tight, and had a door that would fasten, and was fastened: it was a house, and not a hovel. But a house is not always a home. I know not, indeed, that there is really a home except among the northern races of Europe. I know of no word nearer to it than casa—house—in Spanish, and have not once found it a loved place, as home is with us, in all my wanderings. The perennial absence of fires for warmth may have something to do with it. In this respect our poorest cabin stands as far above the richest residences in Bogotá as they excel the little kennel against the eaves of which I was leaning, looking over the ridge-pole as some sad thoughts passed through my mind.

The next visit in geographical order was Montserrate, the chapel-crowned peak that hangs over the north end of the city. Señor Triana, the young conservador and botanist, was here my companion. The time of day he selected was before breakfast, and being, perhaps, the most prompt man in New Granada, he called for me at daylight. I went at once, to the astonishment of the servants, and to the great scandal of my hosts when they found that I had gone out without my chocolate. I carried with me, however, the materials necessary for that beverage, and a small tin pail in which to boil it.

If the reader will turn to the Plan of Bogotá on page 153, he will see in the northeast corner the quinta, or country-seat of Bolívar, marked there with the letter *d*. We threaded our way through the city to the point where a dotted line along the San Francisco leaves the city, and runs up to the quinta. This dotted line is a path along the bank, with a range of miserable huts, like the negro quarters on a Southern plantation, extending along the north side for some distance. We soon turned out of this toward the north, and then rose so high as to overlook the little patch of fruit-trees, inclosed by high walls, that, with the house within, was once a magnificent present from the Liberator to Pepe Paris, a worthy patriot since dead, who erected the statue of Bolívar that adorns the Plaza. It is said that when Pepe was feasting there one day with Bolívar and other friends, one of them had the audacity to drink to Bolívar that he might become King of Colombia. Pepe gave the next toast. It was, "Bolívar: if he ever become king, may his blood flow like this wine!" dashing it with the word to the floor. All was silent: Bolívar sprang up, caught Paris in his arms, and embraced him.

Soon from steep walking we came to climbing. Here the various paths became contracted into one that went up in zigzags. It was amazingly worn, being sunk into the earth in some places to the depth of many feet by the travel of three centuries upon the same spot. Had it been a road of daily use for business, it would not have surprised me; but that a road, traveled only for pleasure or devotion (often for both at once), should have become so deeply worn in the steep face of a mountain, seemed incredible. Some of these cuts—here called callejones—look like deep ditches worn into the ground by the action of water, so that you can not see out as you pass them.

As we rose, the plain opened out beneath us, and the city displayed itself as in a map. It is any thing but a beautiful sight, for you see but little except tiled roofs, and the ugly towers of churches, that look all the uglier when you look down upon them instead of seeing them from below.

Now we come to several little niches, called eremitas—hermitages. They have nothing in them but a little cross in each. The larger ones might shelter a couple of persons from the weather, and here, possibly, other objects than Our Lady may be worshiped sometimes.

At a distance of ten or twelve miles, the Chapel of Our Lady of Montserrate appears to be about two thirds the way up the hill, while from the city beneath it seems perched on the highest pinnacle. Neither view is correct: there is land adjoining the chapel 50 or 100 feet higher, but the higher tops seen over it from the distant plain are much farther off. The altitude of the church is little more than 1800 feet above the city. Observers differ as to whether it is more or less than two miles above the sea. The thermometer stands here from 49° to 52°.

Arrived at the top, we found a group of buildings, consisting of a church and residences for priest and sacristan, the last of whom resides there with a disgusting family and a pack of very noisy dogs. The key, I was told, had been carried down to the city that morning by a boy. It was a lie, no doubt. Two sides of the pile could be seen from the plain, and these were beautifully whitewashed. All around, out-doors, were the remains of fires, and other evidences of field-feasts. Of the brands of our predecessors we made a reluctant fire to boil some water, brought from a spring a little below, for our chocolate. After all, it cost more than it was worth in precious time, for, though the air was rather keen, we had provided against it by extra dress.

While this was doing, we went up to a platform with a parapet around it, and looked off. The prospect here well repays the toil. First, there is the city beneath your feet. You could see the houses and all their courts, the rivers with their few bridges, the convents and men in the Plaza dwarfed to insects. Beyond lies the plain, covered in spots with water, which has been increasing ever since the rains began. Then there are hills rising like islands, and the irregular coast-line of the rim of the basin. But beyond, my eye caught an object which is never seen without interest. It was a peak and a long plain at its base. Both are covered with perpetual snow. They are the Peak of Tolima and the Páramo of Ruiz. They lie 90 miles, air line, to the west, five days' journey beyond the Magdalena. The clouds soon shut out the sight, and I have never seen it since.

I dare not trust myself to speak of the plants that I found here. Some I saw on the before-mentioned trips, and some even in ascending to the plain of Bogotá. Most of the plants I speak of at this altitude are scraggy shrubs, with small stiff leaves. Few, indeed, are as high as my head, and I know not that there was an annual herb among the whole.

Smallest leaves of all have the Aragoas. There are but two species in the world, and there is no other genus much like them. Both these species are confined to these heights near Bogotá, one being common—A. cupressina—and the other very rare, so that I at length despaired finding it, and my friends here had never seen it. They look like young spruces or cedars when out of flower. The flowers are small, white, and anomalous. They are regular and four-parted, but are referred to the irregular five-parted Scrophulariate family.*

A splendid vine, the very queen of the composite family, is dedicated to the honor of Mútis, the old priest who corresponded with Linnæus, who came from Spain somewhere about 1760, was for a long time in pay of the government as botanist, originated the Observatory in Bogotá, and died there 11th September, 1808, at the age of 77. Well for him that he was not a younger man, and living in 1816, for the Goth Morillo would have shot him as a learned man had he been true to his country. As it was, he only sent his writings to be buried in the archives of Madrid, inaccessible to botanists till they are nearly useless. Cáldas charges him of withholding information, and even of purposely leaving his writings in a condition to be of little service to any other than himself. The Mutisias belong to the rare Bilabiate division of Composite plants. They have long heads of splendid scarlet blossoms in an involucre, that might serve for a model of a porte-bouquet.

The Thibaudias are numerous at cold altitudes. One I saw here with an eatable but rather insipid berry, called uva cimarrona—wild grape. It is an Ericate bush, with thick, long corollas, that look as if carved out of red coral. These thick flowers have a pleasant sour taste.

Here, too, I saw the characteristic plant of the páramos—the frailejon. Various species of Espeletia besides E. Frailexon are so called. They have yellow composite flowers, like elecampane, and trunks like gigantic mullein-stalks, in some places six feet high and four inches in diameter, and without branches. The frailejon yields a stiff kind of turpentine, that is brought to market in a sort of bottle, made by folding the leaves of the plant. These leaves are 8 or 10 inches long, tomentose and white like those of the mullein. They serve sometimes to save

* In the Nov. Gen. et Spec. of Humboldt and Bonpland there is a plate bearing the name of A. juniperina. The branch is identical with that representing A. cupressina, but the anatomical details are different and not true.

the traveler from death by cold when he is caught in the páramo by night or storm, without any refuge from the cold except by burying himself in these leaves. Fire is not thought of. There is no fuel.

The only other plant I shall mention is the chusquea, a grass that might be regarded almost as a climber. Its hard woody stem is brought in bundles into Bogotá, to be used in the construction of the roofs and sides of cheap houses. It is the Chusquea scandens.

We entered the buildings attached to the church. They seemed a convent on a small scale, uninhabited, indeed, but in good order. Not so the kitchen. It seems to be the daily and nightly habitation of a large family, human and canine. The former seemed to care very little for us, but the latter manifested a great interest in our legs, but evidently were afraid of the consequences of yielding to their impulses. In the church there is said to be a miracle-working copy of a miracle-working picture of Our Lady of Montserrate in Spain; but this could work nothing for heretics, of course, nor for Liberales, who, in fact, are little better.

The kitchen faces the north, and from the parapet there the ground descends rapidly to the garden and the spring, in a little amphitheatre scooped in the mountain. We passed round west and north of this. On a little plot of grass near the kitchen the family were spreading out a large supply of priestly vestments—albas, casullas, capas pluviales, ornamentos, parmentos, cíngulas, estolas, frontales, etc., etc., etc. Now, good reader, do not look for these things in the glossary, for I hardly know them one from another, and you do not wish to.

We walked along to the north, nearly to the head of the Archbishop River. First we rose a hill higher than the top of the church. Then descending, we walked a long way on the top of the ridge, having on our right a gentle descent, and again beyond higher mountains, nearly twice as high in reality as the place where we are. On our left was almost a precipice extending to the plain beneath. All this distance we met scarce a plant that grew on the plain beneath, or on the mountain's base.

Southward of the church the ground descends gradually for some distance. I was shown a spot here where it is affirmed that the ground is warm. I think the word ought to be used with some qualification, for I doubt whether a thermometer buried there would ever rise to 60° before the final conflagration. Imagination works wonders—indeed it works most of the wonders that I have yet examined here.

I saw growing here a gentian, a veritable Gentiana, five inches high, sometimes blue, and sometimes entirely white. And another familiar genus, the Lupinus, I found represented by a huge plant as high as my head, near the church ; but I am forgetting my promise a little while back. Well, I will just mention one more, which closely resembles our common house-leek or live-forever. I suppose it to be Sedum bicolor.

A little southward of the "warm ground" the land descends rapidly toward a huge gulf, the Boqueron, through which rushes the San Francisco River, with a road creeping along its side. We descended to a peak, called the Macaw's Bill, which looks up the basin of the San Francisco, a space of moderately hilly country, dotted with cottages and small fields cleared of bushes.

But I must not dismiss it so. From the head of the Boqueron, which might easily be spanned by a suspension bridge 1000 feet above the river, the ground rises in every direction. The west side of this amphitheatre is the wall through which the San Francisco breaks at the Boqueron, and on the two sides of which once stood the chapels of Montserrate and Guadalupe. The first we have just left ; the other, which stood at a greater elevation, is a pile of ruins that we have yet to visit. The eastern border of this habitable slope is the páramo of Choachí. We might make the circuit of all this slope, occupied perhaps by 50 wood-selling families in huts and hovels, by traveling about 20 miles, without descending at any time to a spot as low as where we now stand. Our track would be nearly a circle.

All the space within it seems at first to be a forest, into which settlers have moved for the first time only a month ago, and have just cleared spots large enough to build on. But it would need but a single tree to dispel the illusion. In all that space there is not perhaps a trunk three inches in diameter, or a bough 20 feet above the ground. All is bushes—stunted, gnarled shrubs, that make a walk there a terrible monotony. We know no English name for any useful plant that will grow there, except potatoes and barley. Not even these are cultivated, and how and why people live there is an inexplicable mystery. With every desirable climate in the world within two days' journey of them, and land to be had any where for the asking, why do they live here?

As I must give a reason, I will venture on two. These people must live near Bogotá. The same necessity that keeps some 20,000 wretches in New-York, who must starve every winter, and live by their wits all summer, because they can not endure the terrible solitudes of a country town, compels these poor creatures to live where they can visit Bogotá every few days. They would live on the plain, but there the ground is all taken up by large proprietors, who can grow rich by raising wheat or cattle, but who could make nothing by raising so cheap and useless product as *men*. These weeds of the animal creation are suffered to grow, like other weeds, where the ground is not susceptible of cultivation. And these poor people are indeed weeds—"creation's blot, creation's blank," not figuring either among producers or consumers. Had they not immortal souls, were they not susceptible of religion, education, and civilization, it were a pity some measures could not be taken to exterminate them, for I know of no creature in the animal kingdom that enjoys less and suffers more.

The other reason why these poor creatures do not migrate to warmer lands is that they dislike high thermometers and barometers. An atmospheric pressure of 30 inches of mercury is intolerable to their lungs. They can not persuade themselves that the air is not charged with some deleterious substance. It seems to differ from pure air just as a viscid liquid does from water. Neither would they be capable of enduring the heat and light of a New England summer without being cared for like polar bears. I would not attempt to summer one of them in New-York without the aid of darkened rooms and ice-houses.

From the Macaw's Bill we climbed up and returned by the road we came, for descent here was out of the question. Indeed, we hardly dared throw stones into the Boqueron lest they should fall on the head of some luckless traveler in the road beneath, where they seemed to be moving like ants. In fact, there was no danger, for our projectiles, urged horizontally with our utmost force, seemed to turn like a boomerang, and to strike almost under our feet.

Never had I been so laden with floral treasures as when I returned to Bogotá. I had picked a small-flowered Alstrœmeria, the vine of which had grown into a loop, through which I put my arm. In this way it seemed as if dropping out of my mammoth bouquet. As I was passing down by San Juan de Dios, a little girl thought she had better secure the prize that otherwise must fall to the ground, and laid hold of it from behind, not thinking that I should feel it as it took leave of me. I turned round, and evidently surprised her by the specimen I gave her of my attainments in Castilian, for she fled precipitately.

I made an attempt with Señor Triana afterward to pass the Boqueron on horseback. Passing up out of town, we left Bolívar's country-seat (*d*) and the river (*e*) on the left, and on the right two grist-mills, an extinct paper-mill, and a manufactory of crude quinine (*g*). Our road rose rapidly till the mountain shut us in, and the Church of Montserrate, high on our left, disappeared from view. Patches of the cliffs were red with Begonias unexcelled by any ever seen by Hogg or Dunlap. The Odontoglossum, with its bushel of yellow orchid flowers, here and there perched itself just out of human reach. At length came a pass too narrow for a path, and we had to climb a point of rock on the south side. Such a getting up stairs on back of horse or mule I never did see. At length my friend's horse came to flat rebellion, and turned round as if to fall upon my head. My horse revolted also. Perhaps their heads were dizzy. At length I passed the recusant, who proceeded to scramble up to the top.

No sooner were we up than again we had to descend. When the water is not very high indeed, the poor market-people follow the stream to avoid this cruel ascent and descent over stairs built of round stones, forever wet.

A curious bush that we found in fruit here cost me immense trouble. At first I could find only fruit, a globe of the size of a plum, with a pair of green horns. Long after I found the pistillate flowers, but as it is diœcious, I never could find the other sex. It proves to be Styloceras laurifolium, which is badly represented as to its fruit in Humboldt and Bonpland's *Nov. Gen.*

We were now in the wildest part of the gulf. Nothing was visible but rock and sky, with the brawling stream rushing through the chasm. Here it began to rain. My health would not permit me to be wet with impunity, and we turned and retreated.

Against the rock where we turned I saw a poor woman leaning to rest. She had in her hand a long peon's staff, and on her shoulders a bundle, nearly as large as herself, composed of small sticks. This is a common sight. In this way Bogotá is supplied with fuel. Little coal is used. All the wood is sold in bundles (not weighed, however, as in Paris), whether brought on backs of women or mules, or in carts. A little below I met a little girl, not twelve years old, loaded in this way. Her scant dress, her naked feet, and the cold, tempted me to pay her a dime for her load and throw it into the river. She would only have fished it out to sell again. To ameliorate the condition of the poor needs wisdom more than money.

How long has this vicinity been woodless? Probably the Indians stripped it early of its wood, and it has never had a chance to grow again in all the centuries since. In my opinion, the slopes toward the plain might be nearly adequate to supply the demand for wood and timber, could it only have a chance to grow. I do not see that the land here has owners, nor would any one be enriched by it in this generation if the timber were preserved. And this would be impossible without sentinels night and day.

It is worthy of remark that, wherever I have passed the boundary of the plain, all the slopes toward it have been stripped of trees; but soon after you begin to descend from it, and particularly after the first steep descent, the country is well wooded. The hills there have been stripped of wood to meet the demands of the Sabana: this may always have been prairie.

CHAPTER XVII.

THE PRISON, THE HOSPITAL, THE GRAVE.

Guadalupe.—Discomfited Saint.—Boqueron and bathing Girls.—Miracle-working Image.—Fuel-girl and Babe.—Powder-mill and Magazine.—Soldiers.—Cemeteries.—Day of Mourning.—Potter's-fields.—Gallinazo.—Hospital.—Doctors and Apothecaries.—Provincial Prison.

My kind friend, Dr. Pacho, who showed me where to swim, but not when to swim, proposed one day, as I was recovering from my sickness, to which I have alluded already, that we should make a short excursion the next day. Though still somewhat weak, I consented.

I breakfasted early, and we were soon above the city, at a place called Agua Nueva, where a dotted line is seen on the Plan, passing from the east end of the street that runs up past the Cathedral: this is now a good road leading to the Boqueron. This road we crossed, and I soon found we were rising higher and higher, directly in the rear of the north part of the city, and just south of the Boqueron.

We came to the foundations of a church on a shoulder of the hill. The origin is said to be in the fact that, when the fane above was ruined by an earthquake, its sacred image was thrown down here, many hundred feet below, but that the next night it returned to the ruins above. They then attempted to rebuild the chapel down here, but the design fell through, and the poor image was at length compelled to content itself with quarters in the Church of San Juan de Dios in the city below, from whence it has not since tried to escape.

Up went the tortuous ascent, but in many places the path was sunk into deep callejones. We still ascended till we could see over Montserrate—could see the horizon beyond—nay, even look down on the plain as it stretched off to the north of it. We came at length to the ruins of the upper church, in its day more splendid than that of Montserrate. This is the chapel of Our Lady of Guadalupe.

Mounting these walls, I found myself higher than I ever had been before—11,039 feet. I placed Mount Washington, in my imagination, with its foot at the level of the sea beneath me, and found its top so low as scarce to be discernible.

From this point my friend, who never lost an opportunity of getting into trouble, suggested a descent toward the northeast, from which we could reach the city by passing through the Boqueron. In fact, he thought this the easiest way to return home. We were soon committed, and too far down to retreat. The whole side was densely covered with bushes, and without a path. But gravity will do wonders when one trusts himself to it, and, strange to say, we reached the bottom, by good fortune and good management, bringing our clothes with us. Another task remained: it was to pass the Boqueron without wetting my feet, as at this time, when I was not acclimated, such a course would have inevitably brought on a relapse. The wild magnificence of the scene is unsurpassed by any thing I recollect. For more than a mile the walls were too steep to scale, and the bottom too narrow for a wagon-road.

Through this narrow gorge much of the supplies of Bogotá pass on the shoulders of men and women and the backs of oxen. Wood, charcoal, wheat, fowls, turpentine of frailejon in bottles made of leaves, and even plantains from the warmer regions beyond the mountains, come pouring down at all hours of the day, and particularly early Friday morning.

Narrowly escaping a complete ducking in my efforts to save my feet, I had crossed and recrossed the stream till but one more crossing remained at the outlet of the Boqueron. Here a new obstacle met me. To pass where the road did was clearly impossible; above was unscalable rock. Below was a narrow path close beside the water, where a group of bathing girls held possession. The whiteness of their skin showed them of no plebeian caste; indeed, I learned they were headed by a schoolmistress. How these naiads lived in the freezing current, where I dared not dip my foot, was to me a mystery; but there they were. I must get round them as best I could. I did so, and at length below passed the stream, and gained the mouth of the Boqueron. Now came the rain. It rains every afternoon in the middle of the rainy season, but I was slow to find it out, and my kind friends generally managed to be caught in it.

We took refuge in a venta. Passing through a little tienda, where market-people are apt to leave too much money and take too much chicha, we entered a desolate, empty sala, and seated ourselves on the cold poyo of adobe—a brick bench running around the room. Here we watched to see it rain. Across the patio were two other mean mud huts. The posts of the corredor were of the rough, curious stems of tree-ferns — palo bobo.

I saw here a stupendous earth-worm — yes, an angle-worm, almost big enough to "bob for whale" with. But there is no need of hyperbole; it was about two thirds of an inch in diameter, and eight or ten inches long.

About 3 the rain ceased, and the doctor, finding I had had as much exercise and fasting as was good for a convalescent, agreed with me that it might be time to get home to our dinners.

I made a somewhat similar expedition a few days after, only I left the height of Guadalupe at my left. I passed first, on the base of the mountain, a church called Egypt (*p* on the Plan), whether from darkness or bondage, or both, I know not, but in either sense more churches than one might with propriety bear the name. Leaving the outskirts of the city behind me, by rising still higher we reach the little Church of La Peña — of Our Lady of the Cliff—with its miraculous image of Joseph, Mary, the infant Savior, and an angel bearing the custodia, in which they keep the consecrated wafer or hostia. This is the most venerated image I have ever seen. It was found by an Indian on an almost inaccessible peak above, carved out in the living rock, from which its base was not detached. With immense labor the piece was detached, lowered with ropes from its native crag, and here a temple was built for it. They covered the divine workmanship all over with paint, put showy dresses on the figures, and put the group in the camarin, where it continues to work miracles, as are attested by wax models of arms, legs, eyes, etc., and pictures of various catastrophes, out of which those who called on La Señora de la Peña for help came out alive.

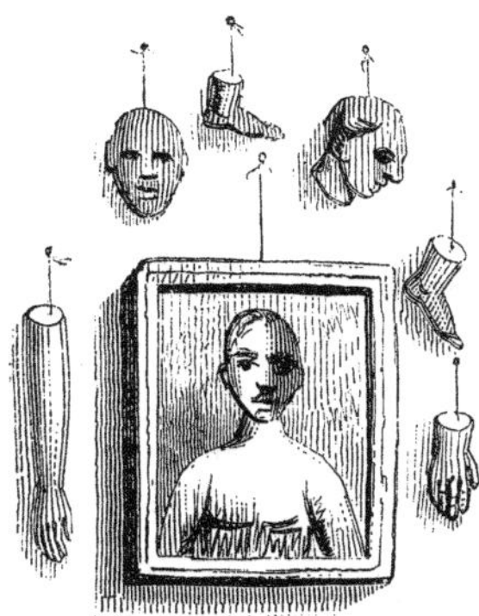
VOTIVE OFFERINGS.

We borrow the annexed diagram to show how the wax figures would look were they not crowded together, covering each other; and the style of execution is fairly emulated by the engraver. The pictures were in the same style, or poorer, and exhibited a great variety of haps and mishaps. One lady, for instance, was riding up to Montserrate, and her horse turned a somerset down the bank with her. Through the intervention of this stone image, she was not killed. Another was crossing an exposed place during a bull-feast in the Plazuela of San Victorino. The bull tumbled her over, and a comical sight she was, according to the picture; but, thanks to La Peña, she lived through it.

From here our course was southwest. A steep ascent, a mountain swamp, and a well-worn path over the ridge brought us in sight of two miserable little fields, and a hut covered with grass. Here we saw a man, his wife, and two little children preparing loads of wood for the city. A descent directly south brought us to a road, paved in some places, running along the banks of the Fucha. I turned and went from the city on this road.

As I was going up a steep pitch, I met a sight which I shall not soon forget. It was a young girl, apparently fifteen, but doubtless older. She had on her back a large load of wood, but was descending the steep road with a quick, elastic step: in her right hand was the long staff they always carry, and on her left arm her babe, unconsciously drawing its nourishment from the living fountain. Ah, woman, how varied but universal are thy wrongs! The father of this innocent may have been some country priest, living in coarse luxury, with nothing to tax the energies of his mind—neither cares, responsibilities, nor duties beyond the performance of prescribed ceremonies at prescribed times—nothing, in short, to do but "to draw nutrition, propagate, and rot." She, living possibly in a mud hut, seven feet long, six feet wide, and five feet from the eaves to the ground, contrives to eke out a subsistence for herself and babe by picking up a load of sticks near her kennel, carrying them and her babe from seven to twelve miles, and selling her load for three half dimes.

Near here I gathered the fruit of a curious shrub, the Coriaria. The flowers had been very small—scarcely noticeable, indeed, except for their number, and for apparently growing on the leaves; but when the time came for it to go out of flower, the petals, instead of falling, took to *growing*. They became so distended with bright red juice as to appear almost black, and to have crowded each other out of shape, and into angular masses, hiding entirely the little capsule, and appearing like a berry. I found here, too, for the first time in South America, a mistletoe growing on a bush.

The road from here to Bogotá does not closely follow the River Fucha, but rises over a shoulder of the mountain at a considerable height, while the river enters the plain through a gorge. Here I found a gigantic figure painted on a sloping rock in the river, as if wading across it, with a child on his shoulders, and using a palm for a staff. It was Saint Christopher (*Christ-bearer*), of whose history, unfortunately, I know no more than is shown by the etymology of his name. I wonder if his mother gave him that name in infancy, and if, when grown to more than man's stature, he had the honor to carry once or repeatedly the infant Savior on his shoulders. But it is useless to ask.

Just below here I took my first bath in the chilly climate of Bogotá. I was in the water but an instant, and "bathed like a cat," Dr. Bayon said; but the dip cost me that sickness of a fortnight. How the "hard inhabitant" can enjoy himself in the wintry stream—how even little children are, as I have seen them, copiously and deliberately bathed, is to me amazing.

My visits to the plains have been fewer and less interesting. One was to a spot a little below this. We passed through fields with walls of unburnt brick and roof of tile—the gateways also roofed. A more hateful fence to the hunter or the botanist can not be found. He will not think of scaling it, and, perhaps, when he needs a gate, none is to be found. We passed the southern borders of the city, and came to a mill, where wheat is bought and converted into a flour equal to our second or third rate. As a tropical voyage damages our superfine flour, it does not shame theirs when it gets here.

On the same canal which comes from the Fucha stood the national powder-mill: government has since abandoned it, and the *Serrería* is to be sold. Examined from an eminence, it appeared to be an orderly, well-conducted establishment, but I did not enter it.

On the very banks of the Fucha stands the magazine, under a guard of soldiers. It is a solitary building, with a piazza, surrounded by a high wall, part of which has been carried away by the floods. The soldiers were asleep, and I had entered the inclosure before I knew it was *guarded*. In the piazza hung a soldier's babe in a hammock, and near stood their guns. Their cooking was done by building a fire in the piazza against the walls of the magazine. We found the mother of the babe near the desolate concern.

A little way from here I saw a body of troops washing clothes in the river within a line of sentinels. They had a few women engaged with them. The fewness surprised me, for when an army is on march there are more women than men. I have been repeatedly assured of this, and that the commanders expedite their march, and aid them across the rivers with the greatest attention. Soldiers here are smaller than other people. I am not tall, but I can look over the heads of a long line of troops, and see the top of every cap. I was first struck with the diminutive stature of the natives in a dense crowd in a church. It was new to me, who had been so often buried in crowds, to find my head projecting over the upper surface of one. I have sometimes been mortified by the rowdy conduct of the offscouring of the States in Spanish countries; but when I see such troops, I do not wonder they are tempted to pitch into them, just for a little fun. One of the officers I saw was of unmixed African blood.

I beg leave to introduce to the reader two specimens of this unfortunate and not very reputable class. The taller of the two is one of the President's Lancers, and the other one of the infantry. The dress of both resembles that of Northern troops, except that the feet are partially covered with alpargates, figured and described on page 236. Imagine the taller of these rather

FOOT-SOLDIER AND LANCER.

short, and no more impudent than a cavalry soldier is apt to be: might not some of the chivalrous sons of the Union be tempted to make him "know his place?"

The country around the Fucha is not exactly flat, but intermediate between plain and mountain. All west of here is entirely level, and at this season of the year much of the ground is covered with water. It differs from Western prairies in that they have depressed edges, the boundaries being streams at a much lower level. Here the boundaries are hills, and the stream in the interior is at the surface of the plain. In both, the centre is apt to be wettest.

In the plain west of the northern end of the city is the principal cemetery (*a*), the pride of Bogotá. It is an ellipse of about an acre, surrounded by a high wall, with a chapel at the farther end. Thus much I could see from the mountains. My visit there happened to be just after All Saints, 2d November, the season when, in several successive Mondays, they do up the mourning for the year. I passed and met numerous groups of mourners, gayly laughing and chatting as they tripped to or from the house appointed for all the living.

The theory of rural cemeteries is not understood in New Granada. Romantic situations are not sought, and great extent is not desired. It may be desirable that some monuments be perpetuated, but the bones themselves are not a sacred deposit, so it matters not how full the ground may be while there is room on the surface. Hence the Granadan cemetery or Panteon is condensed, and most of the bodies are placed in the oven-like bóvedas. The wall of the Cemetery of Bogotá is made up of bóvedas. These "narrow houses" are placed side by side, in three or four tiers, extending around the vast ellipse, except that the space opposite the entrance is occupied by a chapel, without which a cemetery is not complete. The roof that covers the bóvedas extends over a walk before them, where the visitor is protected from the weather, as he contemplates paintings and inscriptions, on tin plate, in water-colors or oil, or chiseled in marble, and beautiful rose-colored fine sandstone that would never bear frost. Many remain as they were left when the aperture was closed on the inhabitant, and the name and date were written in the fresh mortar with a stick.

A series of masses were going on, with the humane intention of rescuing the deceased from an unpleasant situation, in which some of them must now have been for long months. While the chapel was full of worshipers, another group were going from grave to grave, with one or two priests, singing a little, and sprinkling a little water on each grave. The price of a bóveda is $8, which gives a right for ten years, when the bones are drawn forth without farther expense to either the purses or the feelings of the survivors. A grave in the ground is cheaper, and the body is left till the ground is wanted again. A perpetual right in the ground can be secured, but not in a bóveda.

I had left the ground, when I met a bier on the shoulders of four men, who were walking at a brisk pace, and shaking from side to side a body of which I could see the clasped hands and naked face. The body was that of an aged female, dressed in white flannel. Arrived at the grave, it was full of water. Here was a pause: some were for thrusting the body down into the water, others for dipping it out; but some men who were digging an adjoining grave gave it up to the necessities of the case, and awkwardly, and with offensive exposure of the person, the body was laid in it. Then a boy caught up a huge lump of mud and pitched it down. It struck the body with a sullen sound, made the whole corpse quiver, tore aside part of the clothes, and disclosed the face and one little hand of a babe a few months old that had been concealed there! I was horrified, but stood my ground. Clod after clod fell on their naked faces, until, little by little, the shocking scene passed from view.

While these bodies were being buried like those of brutes, a dozen priests were within the consecrated grounds, but came not near the scene. I turned away sick at heart, but with a stronger desire to live to reach my native land than ever I felt before.

The burial-place of the poor is down in the damp plain west of the city. The Bogotanos hoped I should not see it, for it is truly a horrible place. The fence leading to it was of *wood*—sticks tied to poles with thongs of raw hide; but the fence of the cemetery was of tapias and tile. Within were bones scattered over the ground, and even a skull or two, and that unclean bird, the gallinazo or chulo (Vultur Jota), nearly allied to our turkey-buzzard, was perched on the wall, desiring to defile his beak with the flesh of Christians, which I hope he could not reach, though he could smell it. This creature usually finds its upper limit before reaching the height of this plain, but Bogotá seems to be an exception, as it is warm considering its altitude. We see large numbers of them walking over the waste places, seeking food, or opening out their sooty wings on a roof, where their peculiar position leads people to say that they are praying in cross, as they do at La Tercera. The king of the vultures, rey de los gallinazos—Vultur papa, the Vulture pope—is a different bird, and not gregarious, like the gallinazo. When he comes to their feast, they, either from respect, or possibly from mere prudence, leave the whole to him till his majesty pleases to eat no more. On the whole, I do not think the gallinazo, though a graceless loafer, is so uncleanly as our turkey-buzzard—Vultur Aura—whose every feather disgusts, and when he has gorged so that he can not escape, is not ashamed to spew out his obscene repast on his captor.

Half way up to the ledge above the city, near a brick-kiln, where they burn their bricks with brush smaller than hazel-bushes, is a place where they bury suicides, and sometimes, it is said, malefactors. They are buried like beasts, and their memory perishes with them. Still, the good woman, whose rancho stands near the spot, dares not venture out-doors at night, as if the miserable walls that can not keep out the air could protect her from ghosts. I will add, now that my theme has taken so grave a turn, that the use of coffins is a new and growing practice here, but as yet they are very expensive. The poor are carried to their last resort by four prisoners from the Presidio, attended by soldiers with loaded muskets. The introduction of bóvedas would, I think, be a benefit to our own cemeteries.

From the *grave* to the *doctor* is to go back but a single step, and yet I mean no disrespect to the profession, or to Dr. Merizalde, to make it and him the subject of my next remarks. A more estimable or modest man I do not know than this pious and venerable physician. His library is to me the most interesting private library I have seen in this country, and it is worthy of a more extended notice than I can give of it. It contains many very rare books, some of which have here been reposing for two centuries, while the other copies of them have been exposed to various casualties in Europe—have been flooded over and lost among the offspring of a prolific press, or worn out by too much use. To such dangers a book is no longer exposed when it has found a refuge here; and I know of no more promising a field for a hunter of rare books than in the old libraries of New Granada.

Dr. Merizalde is the principal physician of the Hospital. I met him there once at the early hour which he devotes to this labor of love. The good old man had quite a number of students in his train, and went from bed to bed with the tenderness of a father. I was surprised at the number of patients I saw with a cake in their hand, but at length I noticed on the doctor's arm a blue cotton handkerchief, tied at the four corners, that must have held near a peck at first, from which they had been dexterously transferred to the beds of patients without attracting any notice.

The Hospital is an old convent of the Hospital Brethren of St. John-of-God—San Juan de Dios. It was put into their hands at its erection as the best thing that then could be done; but the monastic history of Bogotá has been terrible. The only order ever here that was not a humbug and a scandal was the Jesuits. Say what we will of them now, I can not doubt that they were faithful at that time, and the first banishment of them from this country was an unwise and cruel step, dictated by any thing else than a regard for religion. But the monks of San Juan de Dios settled the question of how few patients they could take in, and still enjoy their spacious convent and fat larder. Government found itself at length compelled to suppress the order, and put the Hospital under charge of the gobernacion of the province. I think, however, it receives nothing from the provincial treasury.

The Hospital is not in good order: the rooms are old, the bricks of the floor are traversed by several crevices in each, that form so many secure depositories of dirt, some of which may perhaps date from the last century. Every thing seemed to have been badly contrived, and needed a thorough reform. This would require funds which there is no probability of their soon receiving. The kitchen was dirty and inefficient, without any large vessels for wholesale cookery, or any labor-saving arrangements. It seemed as if the cooking for each separate patient may have been carried on independently of the others, and every thing looked more as if the whole affair was there only temporarily. So, too, of the dispensatory: it was in the most shocking condition, and never can be any better without a radical reform. It gives the impression, too, that the medicines themselves must be the worst of their kind, when every thing about them bears evidence of so much neglect.

As to the diseases, they can not be the same here as with us. There is little or no consumption: I do not recollect of even a single case. Dysentery reigns prime minister in the court of Death. I tried in vain to get at the statistics of the matter, but there were none at hand, and can only express an opinion that about one third of the deaths, if not one half, are ultimately from this disease. I was surprised at the small number of insane patients. Dismal indeed is their condition, and I think few recoveries could occur here. Syphilitic patients are not admitted. Many that apply from other diseases must be refused; and Dr. Merizalde assured me that, were the hospital empty and opened for this disease alone, it would be filled in a day!

Of course, the old monastery is not without its pictures illustrative of the life of its patron saint. Here we see two devils tossing him back and forth to each other. I saw the hanging-scene described by Steuart, but our recollections differ widely: instead of a monk hanging a heretic, it seemed rather to me that the devil was strangling a man either with a rope or his tail, and that the saint delivers the victim. It is not very important which is right, only I would put this most charitable construction on the matter; but if I am wrong, so much the worse for the devil.

Speaking of pictures, I saw one that, I confess, surprised me a little, hanging at the door of the church at a great fiesta. Pictures are frequently loaned on such occasions, and any face, male or female, is at once received as a saint. The one in question, however, was not in a shape to give much scope to charity: it was the priest Abelard making love to Heloisa. I mentioned the matter at home, and a guest present showed that she was better posted up in that old love-affair than was creditable to her, in my opinion.

I can not say that I think the medical school or the faculty stand very high in general. Probably one half of the population never pay a fee—dying is cheaper. Dr. Cheyne, a Scotch gentleman who married here long since, and one or two natives who have studied in Paris, are the only ones on whom I could venture to rely. Fortunately, I never stood in need of them. The people here are said to be very averse to large fees. Out of cities a man can not live by practice, so it seems to me, as there is not the tenth of the whole population that ever receive any medical assistance from the day of their birth till their death, both inclusive.

There are four or five apothecaries' shops here. They appear as good as need be: not as showy as our best, but really in good condition and well served. I knew best that of Dr. Lombana. If a prescription were written with the weights here used, I would have no fear but that it would be properly put up. The safest way would be to write the prescription in granos of $\frac{77}{100}$ of a grain: a useful fact to remember, if we could only be sure of it. But the diversity of languages on earth is hardly more perplexing than the diversity of weights and measures, and here they are little sure of them, for their own have been changed so often. Now the legal standard is that of the French. It ought to be universal.

You are struck with the medicines here as being the same as at home. There are no druggists here. Even the ipecacuanha, if not the sarsarparilla, are brought from Europe or the United States. The pharmacopœia is the old Spanish one, but most of the medical books read here are French. Indeed, a man who reads no other language than Spanish ought never to pass for an educated physician.

From the Hospital it is natural to go to the Prison. I would wish to be excused from this task; but as the jefe politíco offered to accompany me in person, and as a prison is always a proper place to tell the truth of, I could not excuse myself. The provincial prison is in the same block with the Halls of Congress, and distant not 200 feet from the chair of the President of the Senate. The entrance is on the street that runs down from the south side of the square. A guard of soldiers is always at the door. The prison within is very small and dirty at least, if not excessively so. It has not a whole patio to itself, but only a part of one, built in by a high brick wall, with a corredor running round two sides only. Here I saw still some debtors, though on recent notes there is now no liability to prison. One room was used as a chapel, having a meanly furnished altar, but at the same time it served as dormitory. This building is the nightly resort of a detachment of presidarios, that are employed during the day as scavengers, and in the burial of the poor, etc., always under the watch of soldiers.

The prisons can hardly be alleged as a reproach to the government. True, they are horrible, with the single exception of the Casa de Reclusion at Guaduas, but the authorities can not remedy the matter, though they would. The government is poor. It can not maintain suitable officers, nor can it furnish new buildings; and with crowded rooms and low salaries, not Howard himself, were he alive, could keep a prison from being what that of Bogotá emphatically is—a nuisance.

CHAPTER XVIII.

THE VALLEY OF THE ORINOCO.

Hydrography.—Páramo of Choachí.—Cordillera of Bogotá and the Provinces on its Summit. — Eastern Wilderness. — Thermal Springs. — Indian Reserves. — Fortunate Priest.—His cunning Penitent.—Cordage Plant.—Laguna Grande. —Hid Treasures.—Murder of the Chibcha King.—Señor Quevedo.—Bolívar. — Joaquin Mosquera.— Rafael Urdaneta.— Domingo Caicedo.— José María Obando.—Francisco de Paulo Santander.—Six Administrations and three Rebellions.—Murder and Mystery.—Sucre, Sardá, and Mariano Paris.—Une.— Páramo of Cruz Verde.—Rare Plants.

I HAD seen plantains and oranges descending to Bogotá by the steep roads that lead from the páramos. They do not grow there. Beyond there must be a warmer place, and I wished to see it. They told me I must go to Ubaque. To Ubaque I resolved to go. But where could that be? In the basin of the Orinoco? I thought it hardly possible, and I asked a military gentleman. He assured me that its streams were tributaries to the Bogotá. But he spoke of cane and plantains there, and when I suggested that water could not flow from a cane-field up to this cold plain, he admitted the difficulty.

Bogotá is on the very edge of the basin of the Orinoco. The hydrographic notions of the country have not been very exact, and much space that is supposed to be drained by the Magdalena, in reality sends its waters to the Orinoco. Most maps show the Bogotá Chain, or Eastern Cordillera, as a well-marked, straight ridge, running northeast. Mosquera's map puts Bogotá half way between this ridge and the Magdalena, or even nearer the river. Tanner's map of Colombia, of 1829, the best yet extant, puts Lake Tota and the battle-field of Boyocá far west of the ridge. I had to close up his outlet of Lake Tota into the Sogamoso, and open with my pen a new one, the Upía, from the opposite end of the lake, and over a high mountain ridge into the Meta, and Orinoco. The map of Acosta, the best Granadan geographer that ever lived till Codazzi took that place, shows that same error. Lastly, another map puts Bogotá entirely east of the Andes, in the plains of the Orinoco!

In all my previous expeditions I wore boots. I now introduced my foot to a new *chaussure*, the alpargate or alpargata. Imagine a mat made of braided string of the exact size of the sole of the foot. The braid is first coiled in the proper shape, and then sewed by a long needle passing through the whole width from side to side. A woven cap is sewed on at the toe, although the very tip is left open, so that the extremity of the great toe is visible. At the heel a strap is fastened, so as to come up behind, and be held in place by a showy woven string that ties in front of the ankle. In the figure it is worn slipper-fashion, and to the practiced eye looks strange, with the leg of the pantaloons in such close proximity.

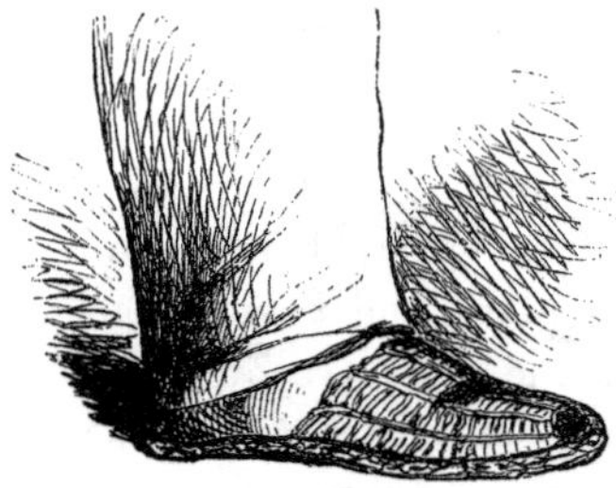
ALPARGATE OR ALPARGATA.

The alpargate is the best possible defense for the foot in walking. It yields to the motions of the foot, lets it *take hold of the ground*, and does not heat it. Were I ever to walk for my life, I should, if possible, walk in alpargatas. The price in Bogotá is fifteen cents a pair, but in the Cauca they are both dearer and poorer. Still, I can not do without them. It is a significant circumstance, too, that I often find no pair large enough. I am not in the habit of looking much at feet, but all testimony goes to the point that this is a land of beautiful feet, and that, I suppose, means small feet. If so, the best proof that I can allege is to say that I never yet found one alpargate too large for me, although I can wear most gentlemen's slippers that I have had occasion to try.

There are two other routes to Ubaque, but, as I like to take a circuit, we will, by your leave, go by Choachí. So first we pass the Boqueron, in which we have already spent much time, and pass through the amphitheatre we saw from Montserrate. A small venta stands just out of the Boqueron, and, as we turn and look back, you agree with me that highway never penetrated a more rugged defile. Were it within one hundred miles of New York instead of two miles from Bogotá, it would be much frequented. Many ladies here have never passed it. Sublimity is at a discount here: there is too much of it.

We rise continually by deep-worn roads, sometimes steep, but for considerable spaces nearly level. We left the San Francisco at the mouth of the Boqueron; indeed, it is formed there by streams coming in from all directions. What a lonely road! It seems as if it were through a country that had been rejected, and very properly, as unfit for human residence. Now our path breaks into a dozen, and all bad; now they concentrate in a callejon so narrow as to render it difficult to let a poor woman pass you with a huge load of charcoal on her shoulders covered with frailejon leaves.

We rise continually. We mark our progress by the mountains behind us, and particularly the Church of Montserrate. Now its top is seen no longer against the blue sky, but against the blue ridge on the opposite side of the plain. Now the frailejon becomes abundant, and vegetation assumes a more gloomy hue. Guadalupe, too, sinks, and the whole ridge that frowns over Bogotá, with its head covered in angry clouds while we have pleasant weather below, has now subsided so as to allow us to see the plain over its highest peak, and far, far beyond, if clouds hide it not, the Quindio. And yet we rise.

The last steep is gained, and before us what would be called rolling prairie stretches off miles to the east. At the beginning of this stands the first house on the road since we left the venta of the Boqueron—and such a miserable house! A small inclosure here was devoted to potatoes or arracachas, but besides naught seemed to encourage the hopes of man. Siberia must be a paradise in comparison. Long and desolate was my journey over the páramo of Choachí. And yet it scarcely deserves the name of páramo: it is too low and too warm. There were a number of houses, too; but I am told that in bad weather the inhabitants must keep within doors.

Why is this plain colder than those of Africa? The sun strikes it as fairly. The air, nearly twice as rare, can not carry off the heat so fast. I confess that I know of no reason except that the surface is farther removed from the molten interior of our planet, the chief source of our heat, which is aided less by the sun than we are apt to suppose.

The under surface of our Northern snows melts in the spring, and the ground thaws before the rays of the sun reach it. The streams that descend from perpetual snows are, I suspect, supplied from its under surface.

Still, it is to be expected that the temperature of even the lowest places in this country should be less than that justly due to their elevation, or, if you please, to the thickness of the crust on which they stand. Every breeze that fans the nook of Vijes from the west has left, not 20 minutes before, altitudes where you would shiver. If from the east, it may have been warming some two hours, and if from the south, much longer; but even from the north, we can scarce get a puff that has not been playing around some peak that frost visits every night. Hence, if a man wants a specimen of the torrid zone, he can not find it in New Granada, and there must be many plants that could not live here except in hot-houses. Hence, too, a Granadan never has heard of a warm night.

But this talk, though good for dog-days with my readers, is too cool a theme for the páramo of Choachí. Let us hasten on. There are some peaks above us that I should like to climb, but want of time and prudence alike forbid. If the páramo should *get angry*, "ponerse bravo," we should have fine times and fine fare in one of these desolate, fireless, windowless huts, even could we reach one. How still it is! No birds come here. Insects have here no home. The very streams do not gurgle as they do below. This must be due to the rarity of the atmosphere. I drank of their waters at a natural bridge of a large flat stone, under which flowed a small mill-stream, a tributary to the Orinoco. In an hour from Bogotá we cross the "divide," though I had great difficulty to even learn the name for a hydrographic basin—*hoyo*—for intelligent men never had thought of one.

In one of these hollows I passed a singular bush—any bush is singular here—but this had leaves as large as apple-leaves, white underneath, and of a pungent taste. It is the well-known Winter's bark—Drymis Winteri. It is not much used as a medicine. It is called canelo, thus confounding it with cinnamon, which it might serve to adulterate, though it has only the pungency to excess, while the agreeable flavor is entirely wanting.

We approach the eastern edge of the páramo. I am amazed at the width of the mountain summit, and consider it the type of the whole Bogotá chain. Entire provinces sit on the top of it, side by side, north of here, for in Vélez, Socorro, Tunja, Tundama, and Pamplona, few important towns lie on either side down in the region of the cane.

And this mountain top is the garden of New Granada and of all South America. Nowhere in America, except in some few of the United States, is there so dense a population as swarms in this sea of hills. They lack but the proper education to make them one of the best races on earth. The Socorranos are proverbially enterprising, and all of the inhabitants of the cold lands are constitutionally industrious.

Nature has here been prodigal of her mineral wealth. Just north of the great Sabana are the mines of rock salt at Cipaquirá. A little farther on are the iron mines of Pacho. The emeralds of the world come from Muzo and Somondoco. North of Muzo is the copper mine of Moniquirá, and, lastly—to say nothing of tin, lead, and sulphur, none of which are systematically extracted—the gold deposits of the vicinity of Piedecuesta. But the most valuable of all mineral deposits is coal, and this, though perhaps less abundant than in England or Pennsylvania, is practically inexhaustible in the present condition of the nation.

I look forward from the very eastern edge, where little crosses, erected in gratitude by those who had lived to toil up the steep ascent, stand thick around my feet; or perchance some may be those of persons anxious about their descent, who prayed to reach the bottom with unbroken bones. If any expect here to see THE PLAINS, the boundless prairies of the Orinoco, he will be disappointed. You may consider them and the Magdalena to lie at about equal distances from here; and so you see before you a depth that the eye can not measure, and beyond it the mountains rising again, head over head, and you know not by sight that you have passed the summit-level of the Cordillera.

How are these mountains occupied? What are their names?

What towns are at their base? The mountains are unnamed, and useless to man. A few horrible paths thread past their base, but they are unknown to the traveler. The Orinoco and Amazon drain nearly one half of New Granada, but of its 2,243,730 souls in the census of 1851, only 51,072 are ascribed to this region, besides that of some cold lands usually supposed to be drained into the Magdalena. Of these, 28,873 are in the cantones of San Martin and Cáqueza, in the province of Bogotá—the empire province, that extends from the Magdalena to the Orinoco; 18,523 to the province of Casanare, and 3676 to the vast territories of San Martin and Mocoa, between which the law has not marked out the limits.

And in all this vast space there are but seven post-offices. Here, then, we have a future world, the very edge of which only is occupied with a few civilized Indians. Cáqueza, a good day's journey from Bogotá (25 miles), is as far in as people often penetrate. All this side is sparse settlement; all beyond is effectively wilderness.

RIDING IN A SILLON.

While pausing as if for a plunge, let us take a survey of a party just emerging from the depths beneath us, who have been stopping to adjust their dress to the climate on which they are entering. The principal figure, which a casual observer might regard as a heap of something carelessly laid on a mule, would, after unwrapping it like a mummy, be found to have for its nucleus a respectable and somewhat elegant lady of Bogotá, though not at present in a condition for athletic exercises. Hence she has been condemned to make this expedition in a sillon—a conveyance by no means so secure, except when a lady is clumsy, as the Turkish, or even the European.

Her feet, you see, are on the contrary side from that which they occupy when she uses the side-saddle. The sillon is richly ornamented with red morocco and silver, and is so cushioned as to be quite easy to the rider when going at the pace of an ox, but not probably as comfortable to the beast as a saddle. Behind follows her husband, bearing her first-born in his arms. The figure on foot puzzles me most. Clearly he is no Indian, and his hat is that of a gentleman; but the load he bears, the pantaloons rolled up, and the alpargatas, indicate that for once he is taking resolutely a position to which he is not used. My solution is not a very charitable one, and it may not be true. It is this: they are a party that have been down to Choachí, or, perhaps, to Ubaque, to *templar*, which I translate *thaw out*. They have been gambling there, and have lost. They went down on four hired mules, with a carguero for the child, and come back as we see them, because they have need to retrench. One saddle and part of their luggage—equipaje—has been left for another opportunity—perhaps in pawn. This explains all we see.

A descent of a hundred feet brings a material change of vegetation. Here I came upon a splendid plant, that at first looked something like the trumpet-honeysuckle, with scarlet flowers three inches long. It proved to be an earth-growing Loranthus, a bush eight feet high. I afterward found, just east of the Boqueron, a smaller species—L. Mutisii—with flowers six inches long; and I have seen another terrestrial species, with much smaller yellow flowers. A splendid Melastomate bush grows down here too, and farther down some tall trees of that Order tantalized me with flowers for which I sighed in vain. This species has been published by Karsten and Triana as Codazzia rosea. Here, too, I incautiously seized on a large, handsome yellow flower, a Loasa, that stung like a wasp.

Just before entering the woods, I stopped at a venta with some peasants that I had fallen in with. They opened a wallet and took out some provisions, and proceeded to lunch. One of them ventured to urge on me a delicate morsel, a piece of roasted crisp rind of pork, but I declined, assuring him that I was not in the least hungry.

At the bottom I found a hot sulphur-spring. A stream ran from it into a little bathing-house, where also was led in a stream of cold water, so as to reduce the temperature till it could be endured. A considerable quantity of gas escaped from the spring, which I supposed to be carbonic acid. I had not even a thermometer with me, and can only say that it seems quite probable that the spring is hot enough to boil an egg in time. It is strange that this spring is not more known and resorted to as a watering-place; but the Bogotanos love cold bathing, and would rather ice their water than heat it.

On the Plain of Bogotá are also thermal springs worthy of examination, but I did not even hear of them till too late to visit them. Those of Tabio, some twenty miles north of Bogotá, have a temperature of 114°, while a stream flows near them with a temperature of 53°. There are also others at Suba, ten or fifteen miles north of the capital.

From the spring, which was a little below the road, I proceeded south to Choachí. This is a tolerable village, standing on a level spot on the side hill, but a mile or more from the roaring stream that flowed along the base. Both sides of this river are thickly settled with Indians. I have not seen so much cultivation in all this country, and the scene delighted me inexpressibly. The district of Choachí contains 4691 inhabitants; Ubaque, a little farther on, 3399; while on the other side of the stream, the district of Fómeque contains 6645. The amount of white blood in all this multitude is quite small.

The land here has been kept in the hands of the Indians by a benevolent provision of the law, restraining them from selling except according to certain provisions; but, with the advancing

BOGOTANOS AT CHOACHI

ideas of liberty, it is seen that it is undemocratic to restrain thus a man's liberty. The matter is now with the provincial Legislatures, and in some provinces these reserves—resguardas—can be sold only at auction, and in others, any man that can persuade one of these thoughtless aborigines to sell to him can buy at any price, however small. It grieves me to hear that large numbers have sold. Among the most diligent buyers of resguardas is the Cura of Choachí, who is now the owner of land that once was occupied by a score of families.

I was talking with one of his flock, and mischievously asked what kind of a mistress the priest kept, and the simpleton, without any apparent surprise at the question, told me that she was very pretty. And yet, I think, it is of this place that they tell me of a 'cute trick at the confessional. An Indian was going to confess, and his unlawful companion accompanied him as far as a certain *cross*, where he desired her to await his return. So our priest, who disliked concubinage, as it diminished his marriage-fees, asks him,

"Are you married?"

"No, señor."

"Do you live with a woman?"

"I *have* lived with one, señor, but I have left her as far back as the cross."

Now by *The Cross* the priest understood their festival of 3d May, which had elapsed so long that he thought proper to let bygones be bygones, and José got off with quite a light penance. The matter being squared up to mutual satisfaction, he returned to "the cross," rejoined his companion, and they went home.

Choachí is by no means a pretty place. The houses are all of one story, and thatched; and if any of them are casas claustradas, still they appear more like four huts placed corner to corner than a regular house. The Plaza is small, and I think I would much prefer to reside on the opposite slope. Still, the vicinity of the thermal spring, and other causes, make it something of a watering-place. On the opposite page is exhibited the most successful imitation of European costumes and customs that I have ever heard of. That all these six figures, clad in imported articles exclusively, could have ever been met in one day, exceeds my belief. With such care has every thing national been banished, that I am tempted to think that they themselves have been imported to order packed in sawdust.

To me there is much more interest in the two remaining figures. The Indian woman, who is selling Granadillas to them, is seated behind an empty cage to sell fowls from. Her way of wearing her mantellina, hanging loosely down her back, shows her a reinosa or uplander. The term New Kingdom of Granada did not at first include the coasts, and a kingdom-man is now used as the opposite of calentano, or inhabitant of the Tierra Caliente. But the person that interests me most is that boy on his way from Fómeque to Bogotá. He too carries fowls, and some other articles for sale, protected by a goat-skin, also for sale. He has taken off his hat to say *Sacramento del altar* to the grand folks, who are too busy scrutinizing the Granadillas even to see him.

He wears under his hat a handerchief bound on his head. A heavy ruana and a camisa protect part of his body. Then comes a pair of scant zamarras, that have perhaps some pantaloons under them still more scant, while his ankles and insteps must take all risks that offer themselves. The sole only of the foot is protected by the albarca of hide, far inferior to the alpargate except in mud. It is not often so well secured as here we see it. Generally a toe is thrust through a loop made for it, and it is slightly fastened at the heel.

At Choachí I left the main road, and ascended among the fields until it was again quite cold. Here I was under the necessity of asking the way at a rancho. It consisted of two roofs and a gable, while the end toward the north was open as door and window. Quite a number of happy-looking Indian girls seemed to be at work within. They were employed on the fibre of Fourcroya, a plant too important to be passed by. It is frequently called aloe and century plant. But the century plant is not an Alöe, but Agave Americana, while this plant is neither Alöe nor Agave. Like the Agave, the Fourcroya is a slow-growing plant, with leaves three or four feet long, five inches wide, and half an inch thick. After vegetating in this way for years, it shoots up a flower-stem ten or twenty feet high, generally sheds from it abortive flowers and bulbs, and then dies.

This plant is called magué, cabuya, and fique. The pith of

the huge flower-stem, often six inches in diameter, is used as tinder after the ends of the fibres have been once scorched. From the leaves is extracted a fibre resembling that which is called *Manilla-grass.* The long leaves are split, and two hard sticks, held close together on opposite sides of a piece, scrape away the epidermis and parenchyma, leaving nothing but the strong white fibres of the length of the leaf. No other apparatus is used in the manufacture. It is twisted into cords and ropes, knit into bags (guambías, mochilas, and talegas), or braided into alpargate stuff. It might, were articles of commerce needed, supply a large quantity from dry knolls, useless otherwise except for pasture. I suspect that it could be nearly prepared for use by simply passing it once through a close pair of iron rollers.

The Fourcroya is an Amarillate plant. The finer and more costly fibre, called pita, is said to be from a Bromeliate plant, of which I never have seen the working of the leaf, nor yet the flower; and from the leaves of the prince of the Bromeliate family, the pine-apple, a still finer fibre is now found in our Northern cities in the form of most costly handkerchiefs.

Well, these poor Indian girls, on the shoulder of the mountain, separated from Bogotá only by a few miles of steep rock and páramo, were twisting cabuya in that low, miserable rancho. They were evidently alarmed at the sudden appearance of a foreigner at the mouth of their den, and were quite relieved when I informed them that I wanted to know the direction of Laguna Grande, nothing more. True, they suffer far less outrage from the Spaniards than they would from the more brutal outlaws of the Anglo-Saxon race, but they are less protected by law there than they would be in those Northern States where the testimony of an Indian is received in courts. Poor race! In Dante's Hell they should be employed in the exclusive work of torturing conquerors and legislators.

I had risen to the foot of the ledge that has the earthy land above Bogotá on the west side, the páramo on its broad top, and cultivable slopes extending on the east side far down to the river below me. I followed along still south till directly before me was an abrupt descent to a basin nearly filled with many acres of water, black, still, and cold as death. Lake

Avernus in summer must be smiling in comparison, but in a bleak Italian December they must be as like as twins. No summer ever smiles on Laguna Grande. A perennial autumn, with its alternate sun, mist, and storm, have reigned here from the day of creation till now. It has a fringe of bushes, with quaking marsh within, and a centre that is said to be unfathomable. No singing-bird has ever discovered this retreat, and, but for the chill-loving disposition of these Andine Highlanders, the Reinosos, man never would have found it.

What a fine place for traditions! I mentally exclaimed. Was there ever a place more apropos to spirits and genii, or to hidden treasures? So full of this idea was I that my first question to some friends I met below was, "Are there no hidden treasures at the bottom of that pond?"

"They say that there is wealth incalculable there, Señor," was the reply. "It is said that, on an annual festival, the Zipa, or chief, went out to the centre of Laguna Grande in a boat, wearing a rich array of gold and emeralds, and during the ceremonies he took them off one by one, and dropped them into the water."

"And has there been no attempt to recover them?"

"It has often been projected, but never attempted."

But, besides the treasures thus thrown in for glory, there is equal probability of others thrown there for spite. In 1538 or 1539 died, near Bogotá, Zaquesazipa, last Zipa of the Muiscas, "with extraordinary fevers—calenturas." These calenturas—burnings—are supposed to have referred to the applications of heated horse-shoes to his feet, and other similar torments, by Quesada the Conqueror, Hernan Pérez his brother, Suárez (Rendon), and García (Zorro). The object was to make him tell what had become of the treasures of his cousin Tisquesusa, whose kingdom he had usurped when Quesada murdered him. These treasures never have been recovered, if they ever existed, and, if thrown to utter destruction, were most probably buried beneath these black, still waters; but this is not probable, for hiding-places on land may answer the utmost desires of concealment.

Now, as I am writing, it occurs to me, for the first time, to inquire whether this deep hole be the crater of a volcano. It is on a side hill that might be called steep. North and west of the laguna the ground rises as steep as a man can easily climb. To the east the ground rises slightly for a few rods to a height of not more than ten feet, I should judge, above the level of the water, and then falls rapidly. I can think of no possible theory to account for its origin except this, but I did not notice any evidence there of any other than a sandstone formation.

Two or three huts of Indians, who keep some rather cross dogs, stand near the lake. Want of time, and the expectation of a future return to the pond prevented my observing with the care I now wish I had used.

A steep, long walk brought me down to Ubaque. It is quite a collection of poor houses just above the upper limit of the cane. It is one of the watering-places of Bogotá. Though inferior to many others, it is perhaps the most accessible. I confess I would rather go down to where the cane-boiling furnaces are smoking in the valley below, for here it is yet much too cold to suit me. The Plaza occupies nearly all the level ground there is, and the houses on the one side are crowded against the hill, and the ground descends steep behind those on the other. A noisy torrent, cold enough to make one's teeth chatter in half a minute, tears down to the river below, and makes a deliciously cool bath, which the Bogotanos enjoy for half an hour at a time. I was glad to get out of it in the least possible time, and would as lief be buried naked in a snow-bank as to venture in it again.

I here became the guest of an excellent family of Venezolanos, the Quevedos. Señor Quevedo is an officer of the War of Independence, living in Bogotá on his savings, his half-pay, or by his musical talents. I am sorry to come to such a conclusion, but I am led to regard this and another Venezolano family, that of Colonel Codazzi, as the two most interesting I have found in Bogotá. It is perhaps because I understand them best, or they know best how to make me at home. I think, too, that there are few ladies in New Granada better educated than some in these two families.

Señor Quevedo is an enthusiastic admirer of Bolívar. I am happy to come to nearly the same conclusions with himself in the main, but I would like to know more than I can well ascertain about his concessions to the priesthood. I can not consider him, however, as actuated by a base love of power. And when Joaquin Mosquera was elected to his place, I do not regard it as a wise step, and fear that there may be meaning in the hint of Samper, that the "youth—juventud (*b'hoys?*)—of Bogotá" had more to do with the matter of superseding Bolívar than they ought. We may well suppose that the old hero sighed at leaving the reins in hands all too weak to hold them.

I can not think that Bolívar had any thing to do with the revolution in which Urdaneta, after the battle of Santuario at Puente Grande, September, 1830, drove out the feeble administration. Rafael Urdaneta, a good subaltern general, was never called to be the supreme head of a nation, and his rebellion was an immense mischief, without other motive that I can guess than personal ambition. Little good did it do him or his faction, as in nine months, 15th May, 1831, he was as easily driven out as his predecessor.

What became of Joaquin? He seems to have had enough of the executive, and in the short space from the retirement of Bolívar, we find the supreme power in the hands of President Mosquera till September, 1830; Dictator Urdaneta till the 15th of May, 1831; Vice-president Domingo Caicedo till December, 1831; Obando till March, 1833, when the Convention that formed the first Constitution of New Granada by itself, in 1832, made Santander, then an exile for his share in the conspiracy of 1828, the first President of the new republic.

Santander was a good president. So I believe from the charges against him by Samper, all of which I think redound to his credit. Especially would I commend to future governments his energy with the Sardá conspirators. Sardá had no other motives than ambition or fanaticism. Many of the conspirators were seized, and Sardá and Mariano Paris, who escaped, were *outlawed*, a proceeding that might be with advantage introduced at the North, were we not so tender with criminals. I, for one, think they deserve no more protection than our other citizens. Paris was caught and shot, under plea that he was likely to escape. Sardá was assassinated at night, in a house where he was hid, by José Ortiz, a lieutenant in the army, who was not openly rewarded nor brought to trial. Sixteen of the others were executed. This was in 1833, and six years seem to have passed without another conspiracy. Had Obando and López been treated in the same way, perhaps Herran, Mosquera, and Arboleda never would have been found in arms against their own country.

But as there are few active men in New Granada that have not been at some time engaged in a revolution, they have become exceedingly tender on that point. It is now settled that neither death nor the penitentiary are to be the penalty for rebellion any more, but only banishment, without confiscation of goods, till politics change. But the latest improvement proposed is this, that when an officer is banished for turning his arms against the authority he has sworn to support, *his pay should be continued to him!*

Now this is all nonsense. Take every general, and of other officers all who have commanded detachments at five hours' distance from a superior; hang one and shoot the rest. Cashier for cowardice all other officers. Imprison with hard labor all the LL.D.'s and priests (the latter for life) clearly proved in it, and the next revolution will be the last.

José Ignacio Márquez, LL. D., who was elected President by Congress on 4th March, 1837, was also, I believe, a good president. He is charged with not being rabid enough, and with having taken no steps toward Red Republicanism. It is said also that, being elected Vice-president for four years from March, 1835, it was unconstitutional to make a president of him.

The rebellion of 1839 began in Pasto, in consequence of the suppression of some convents, a fact that indicates that the Márquez administration was not entirely inert. Pasto is said to be the most elevated valley in the world, and, if not the most beautiful, is perhaps the most rebellious. The Pastusos are ignorant and very Christian. Their nearest market is by carrying potatoes, etc., over horrible roads, on their backs, seven days' march to Barbacoas. But when they are so fortunate as to be invaded, the camp of the enemy is the best home market they can ever have, to say nothing of the privilege of robbing travelers between Bogotá and Quito. Thus, with them, peace and prosperity never come together.

Samper maintains that the Márquez administration wished

the rebellion to become as serious as possible. This I regard as simply absurd.

Another cause of the revolution was Obando. General Sucre, marshal of Ayacucho, was shot in the woods of the Berruecos, in Pasto, in open day, on the 4th June, 1830, in the time of Bolívar. The mystery of that affair probably never will be solved. It may have been only the work of his wife and her paramour, General Isidoro Barriga. But the deed was rumored in Bogotá soon after poor Sucre started from there, and was anticipated in Popayan as he passed there; and a picket of cavalry, sent, it is supposed, by General Juan José Florez, afterward president of Ecuador, and lastly pirate, is said to have come from Ecuador secretly, traveling by night, and to have returned after his death. Lastly, Colonel Apolinar Morillo, once a robber and afterward a tool of Obando's, was arrested for the crime, convicted, confessed it, said Obando ordered the act, and was executed.

Thus rumor knew it beforehand; causes sufficient for the *secret* commission of the crime are known; a public cause from a quarter opposite the rumor is found; scores of men, that knew of the deed before and after it was done, confess to dozens of priests; and, lastly, the very man who did the deed tells us all about it, and how Obando, and perhaps López, instigated him, Sarria, and Erazo to it; and yet the truth never will be known!

I give here a strange and incredible story, that will show better than a dozen pages of dissertation the difficulty of unraveling political mazes here. Archbishop Herran was said to have been Morillo's confessor before his execution. His sister-in-law, daughter of General Mosquera and wife of General Herran (then a mere girl), is said to have visited the criminal frequently (probably an unfounded lie). He was convicted by perjury, and promised pardon if he would confess the deed and avow Obando's agency in it. This he was to do on the shooting-bench (banquillo), and be pardoned there. He went there, accompanied by the prelate, told his lie, received the last rites of the Church, the confessor stepped away, and instead of the pardon came the dread word, Fire! and Morillo spoke no more. And there is many a brain here so fevered with political hate as to believe all this, and to believe it without evidence.

All *political* offenses up to June, 1830, were included in an amnesty of the Constitutional Convention in 1832. Besides, it was a crime against the laws of Colombia, and New Granada had no right to punish it when Colombia ceased to exist. So, when Obando was summoned to trial in 1839, Samper regards it as a persecution, because Obando had been Santander's preferred candidate for president after him, and was now mentioned again for the next canvass. He complained of unfairness in trial. He fled. He returned to take up arms against his country in the wilds of Pasto and Popayan, where half his life had been spent in scenes of blood.

Ambition, federalism, and minor discontents made the matter worse in 1840. So many governors turned traitors that the revolution has been called El Revolucion de los Gobernadores. It is difficult to count the battles that were fought, the blood and treasure spent. But for the talents and energy of Mosquera, then Minister of War, and General Herran, the debility of Márquez would have yielded to the combination of adverse circumstances; but the party in power triumphed at Culebrera on 28th October, 1840, almost on the very spot, at Puente Grande, where Joaquin Mosquera lost his power ten years before. The action of Tescua, near Pamplona, 1st April, 1841, and some skirmishes on the coast, were the last of this unhappy rebellion.

Of course, the life-sparing Samper, who would not have an outlaw killed to prevent a battle, makes a great outcry at the severity visited on the leaders of the rebellion. Mosquera and Herran had never then been rebels themselves, and took more lives than they would again. I can not say I think them too many, if only well chosen, which Samper, of course, thinks they were not.

Now my worthy Venezolano host must not be held responsible for all these sentiments as I give them. I have not implicitly followed his views, though I know of no man's that are safer; I have made much subsequent inquiry upon them, and have conversed with Obando himself on the assassination of Sucre. About that I am completely puzzled.

I wished very much to visit Fómeque. Its white church, its apparently scant village, and its hundreds of well-tilled little farms, more in number than I had seen before in all New Granada, were a temptation to me almost beyond my power of resistance. But I had made no preparations for such a journey, so I reluctantly abandoned all hope of seeing Fómeque and Cáqueza, and at early dawn took a cup of chocolate and set out on my return.

We crossed the stream that runs south of the town, and ascended through a wide gorge to Pueblo Viejo, a neighborhood of scattered houses, that I suspect bears the legal name of Distrito of Une. At the last of these houses, the most western farm in the valley of the Orinoco, I stopped to breakfast. The materials for this meal had been brought from Ubaque, but some exchanges were made with the three interesting proprietresses of the house, who, now a little in years, were carrying on their neat farm by hiring. I left them really with regret, and beg the reader, if he ever go from Cruz Verde to Pueblo Viejo, to turn off to the first house a little south of the road that he finds on cultivable ground.

Soon I was toiling up the steep ascent, and in the far east other hills were rising from behind those that at Ubaque served as a background to the farms of Fómeque. Here I met a barberry—a real barberry—but not sour, and, in fact, uneatable. I doubt not that it was Berberis glauca. I had been long wondering why none of this genus were to be found. I found another as I descended toward the west, and still another, all that I have ever seen in New Granada, just before the last descent to Bogotá. This first one had the leaves very white beneath, and here too I was struck with the general color of the woods. They were gray. Lichens on the bark, the foliage, the flowers on the trees, all seemed to contribute to the most peculiar and the lightest shade of color I ever saw in a landscape densely filled with vegetable life. I had noticed this in descending from the páramo of Choachí, but in a less degree. In descending to Fusagasugá I noticed it more strongly than any where else.

Just at the foot of the last arduous ascent I found that I had lost or left my knife. It was some miles back that I had last used it. It was impossible to designate to my attendant where I had probably left it, nor could I rely on getting another. No alternative was left me but to retrace my steps for even the chance of finding it (I had met several persons), but I succeeded. It was a dear purchase, though this long space, which yielded little to man but charcoal, was nearly level. I thus passed two or three miserable lonely houses, almost without cultivation around them, three times in three hours.

Now came the last dire ascent of half a mile, much of it as steep as the stairs in Bunker Hill Monument. Now we come to the top, where the ground is thickly planted with crosses. They stand at the top of every such steep in this part of New Granada, and are often your first notice of a horrible descent. The air up here is dreadfully chill, though the sun shines bright. With a mist and a fierce wind in the face, this páramo of Cruz Verde is really dangerous, though but a little way across.

In a marsh on the páramo I found two little flowers, neither an inch high. I set about gathering them, and desired my servant to aid me, but the poor fellow was so cruelly treated by the wind and cold that he soon gave in, and sat down in the warmest place he could find. I did not blame him for not relishing entering the mud with wet fingers and feet, with the wintry blast howling round him, for such insignificant weeds, of which a hundred—an hour's work—would not weigh an ounce. I picked here, too, some Lycopodiums, and what I thought might be Selago among them. It was destined to astonish me when I found it to be Alchemilla nivalis, a Rosate plant! It was but a single specimen and out of flower. As Aragoa abietina grows just west of the páramo, it well deserves a day from the botanist.

A little while after leaving the páramo, a chasquí overtook us. He was a runner, a bearer of dispatches from some official at the east, perhaps to the governor in Bogotá. He had left or passed Ubaque late in the morning, and was now pressing on, so that, had we not quickened our steps to four miles or more an hour, he would have passed us easily. These chasquíes used to serve without pay, if they do not still, and an appointment to this "onerous office" was sometimes an intimation of some official to his enemy that he had not forgotten him. At length I fell upon some plant I must collect, and the chasquí, who delayed not a step, disappeared at a turn of the road.

I stepped into a miserable cottage to screen me from the wind while I put my plants into paper. From the shape of my package, they supposed that I had *saints* (pictures) for sale. A few cheap colored lithographs of "Mary," and "Ellen," "Rose," &c., would be invaluable presents to this poor people. They lead a miserable life, being many of them wood-sellers. They do not cultivate much, probably because it takes some months before they gain any thing from their labor, and they know not how to look forward so long.

Sometimes the ground was slippery for rods with water; in places, the road was the bed of a brook, and we crossed some rivulets on round stones. Now the ground at our left assumes the appearance of a steep valley, where these waters gather and descend to the plain, which bursts upon our sight just here. This is the Rio Fucha, which below serves as a bathing-place to the Bogotanos and Bogotanas, where it is seen on the Plan of Bogotá at *m*.

The sun is fast descending, and so are we; he beyond the Quindio mountains, and we to Las Cruces, the southern church in Bogotá. We have passed over unnoticed the last part of the way, for we have seen it in a previous chapter. And now, good reader, you, as well as I, would willingly rest.

CHAPTER XIX.

CONGRESS, CONSTITUTIONS, INSTITUTIONS, AND WEATHER.

Congress Halls.—Opening of Congress.—Audience.—Constitutions of 1843 and 1853.—Defect of the latter.—Finances.—Descentralizacion.—Mint.—Mails. —Provincial Schools.—Colegio Militar.—Observatory.—Cáldas.—Hoyo del Aire. — Schools and Studies. — Manufactories. — The dependent Classes. — Weather, Temperature, etc., of Bogotá.

CONGRESS meets as soon as the festivities of Christmas and New Year are over. The plan of the ceremonies is nearly based on our own. I had the pleasure of witnessing the opening on one occasion. The heads of departments (ministros), who have a voice in the House, have seats there, and were present. The message was ready printed, and, at the proper time, when each house had chosen its president, and the message had been read, copies of it were distributed to the members. One little peculiarity of their ceremonies is to place the military of the capital (generally some hundreds of troops) at the disposal of the presidents of the two houses.

The halls are one enormous room, nearly divided into two by a partition. The western end, farthest from the front, is for the Senate. A gallery runs round the whole except the western end, and the space not under the gallery is railed off for the use of the members. Speaking places (tribunos), like pulpits, are provided, but not used except in set speeches. The north gallery, the east, and the east half of the south is open to all, and also the space beneath, so that the Chamber of Representatives is surrounded on three sides by the spectators. But the south of the Senate is reserved, and over the President's chair there is no gallery, so that the Senate is exposed to observation only on the north side. Ladies with tickets, foreign ministers, and some officials have access to the reserved gallery, which extends a little way into the House of Representatives.

The spectators are called the barra. Their conduct is outrageous, often disturbing the proceedings with cries and insults against some of the members, and always with impunity. It would be a happy thing for the nation if a new capital could be selected west of Cipaquirá or Muzo, where there could not be a large city. If that is impossible, the English system must be resorted to of admitting to the House only by ticket. I saw little of Congress, for the very reason that it was disagreeable—perhaps it is undemocratic to avow it—to mingle with such a rabble. One member, I was told, could not speak without being taunted with a petty theft he had once been charged with.

I may as well speak here of the Constitution. That of 1843 was so long a document that I never had a chance to read it; it is, in fact, a treatise on politics. For changes, it was requisite that one Congress should pass them, and that another, chosen certain months after their publication, should confirm them. Congress made an entirely new Constitution in 1851, and, I believe, a very good one. It was not before 1853 that it could be sanctioned. That Congress made so many changes in it that it might be called an entirely new one; but they voted that it was the old one, and that it was constitutionally adopted. No man, as I know, in the whole nation disputed its validity, and most hailed it as the advent of "the true republic"—a thing that seems to all of them like a millennium, always at hand, but, alas! never yet seen.

The crowning defect of the Constitution of 1853 is that the executive is too weak. It has no veto. An objected bill has but to pass both houses a second time. The patronage of the executive is very limited, and no power is left it that could have been taken from it.

The next most fatal defect is that the two houses of Congress are not a sufficient check upon each other. Six persons are voted for on the same ballot for Congress. The highest six are elected: the first is Senador; the second and third, Diputados; the fourth, Senador suplente; fifth and sixth, Diputados suplentes. All hold their office for but one year. If the two houses disagree on a bill, they meet together as one, and the majority carries every thing. Here is no element of stability. The most astounding changes are ventured on with little hesitation, and every thing can be as easily reversed next year. Three times has the entire system of weights and measures been changed: that of the French has now been adopted for the second time. Important changes in the number of provinces are made continually; new ones are erected, and then again suppressed. Each new whim of the nation will carry in a Congress that scorns to look to its predecessors for wisdom. Though there is a party called Conservador, the conservative spirit is entirely unknown in all the nation, so I have no hopes of any stability under the new Constitution of 1853.

The highest story of the great house in which Congress meets has the Treasury offices at the northern end. The Ministro de Hacienda, its head, Señor José María Plata, is a good man, but he has a terrible task. The treasury is in a state of perennial bankruptcy—all the effect of bad legislation and revolutions. The last remedy of this was DESCENTRALIZACION. It was a happy idea of assigning to the provinces a small part of the revenues and a large part of the expenses for them to manage just as they could. This measure was called for because the nation is opposed to all indirect taxation, and direct taxation by national officers is nearly impossible in such a country.

Of indirect taxes the first important one abolished was the alcabala, or a percentage on all sales. The last was the monopoly of tobacco. Those now remaining are salt, spirits, stamps, peaje or toll, and customs. Spirits, and peaje, and the old ecclesiastical taxes of tithes and first-fruits, have been passed over to the provinces; most of them have abolished the excise on spirits and ecclesiastical taxes.

Señor Plata has been in correspondence with me on coinage. We find that the silver real is a little heavier than the new dime, while the gold condor is somewhat lighter than the double eagle. He at length decided to recommend the slight changes necessary to make our coins identical. The silver is now identical with that of France, and is a tender for all sums. Consequently, the gold is bought and sold at varying prices.

The Secretary of Finance (Hacienda) has the charge of the whole matter of mails. *A priori*, I should expect this to be the worst managed post of the whole administration. To my admiration, it is the best. It is far more wisely adapted to their condition than ours is to us at the North, and is not susceptible of any radical improvement. Despite of barbarism and barbarous roads, there are comparatively few irregularities, and the losses very few, and all borne by government. The department not only supports itself, but yields a revenue.

Most of the mails are weekly each way: the rest are twenty-six a year. The offices are few, not over 150. The mode of conveyance is left at the option of the contractor, but in many places the mail must always be carried on men's shoulders. On better roads, mules carry cubical trunks, called balijas. They are covered with (tanned) leather. Cargas are not to exceed 220 pounds. Correristas may not carry things to traffic in, and their bundles are searched to prevent it. The Indian is born a commercial traveler, for within a few hours of him many things may vary 50 or 100 per cent. in price. Hence this needful precaution.

The hours of arrival and leaving every office are fixed by decree, and each post-master—Administrador de Correos—must state the hour on the way-bill, and actually see him off. Their regulations to secure suitable correristas are different from ours. Theirs permit a negro to carry the mail, but would take it from a drunken man, and imprison him. Ours are satisfied if he is a white man, and it matters less if he be drunk or sober. Indeed, I doubt if nine tenths of their carriers would not be prohibited by the laws of our glorious Union from serving in that capacity, and yet, incomprehensibly enough (I am ashamed to admit it), their department is served far better than ours.

When I came up the Magdalena there were two steam-boat companies on the river. In the Santa Marta Company the nation has an interest, but it was too poor to buy one in the other. A system of canoes and bogas for mails is provided on the river independent of both, but when the Santa Marta boats overtake a mail, they must take it in. The others, in self-defense, are obliged to refuse to do so. We left one behind us so in the Barranquilla, but it afterward passed us as easily when we were in the champan. The nation has the power to require all boats to take a mail at a fixed price, or even gratis, if it chooses. It would do a real service to the country should it require fixed starting days for at least one weekly steamer each way, and forbid any irregular steamer from starting just in advance of the packets. The uncertainty of meeting boats is a great obstacle to travel here.

One important peculiarity of the mail system here is what are called encomiendas. We have no bank-notes, and if we remit, it must be in coin. Gold dust, emeralds, sample cards, etc., are sent in this way, and once, I believe, I saw even a saddle-tree thus mailed. I once sent a horse by mail—a live horse! Its head was securely tied to the tail of the mail-horse at the beginning and end of the journey: I know not which horse carried the balijas the most. I had a ruana once sent by encomienda from Bogotá to Cartago. It is supposed to have left Bogotá at 2 P.M. of Wednesday by mule, and Ibagué at 10 A.M. of Saturday by a human carrier—carguero—and to have arrived at Cartago at 6 P.M. of Tuesday. Travelers rarely pass this space in less than a fortnight.

The identical coin committed to encomienda is paid out. Bills of exchange, drafts, etc., are unknown. No fear of loss is entertained. Not one mail-robbery per year occurs. A peon, wretchedly poor, carries it through a wilderness where it is 126 hours from office to office (Popayan to Pasto); an Indian takes it 125 hours' journey to the next office (Pasto to Mocoa): both know that their heavy load is mostly money, but they neither think of robbing or being robbed. Never mind: they are barbarians, and their very color would be a legal bar in our happier land to their being placed in such temptations. We ought to send them missionaries to Christianize them.

The rates of postage are high, and that is more excusable in a country where so few write letters. A letter from one place to another in the same province pays ten cents per half ounce; beyond the bounds of the province it is fifteen. Books under four ounces, newspapers, seeds, and grafts go free. The rates for encomiendas vary according to value and distance.

One word of advice as to foreign mails. There is nominally a mail connection at Panamá between the United States and New Granada, and you can pay through. Do no such thing, unless you wish to lose both money and letter, as I have done. To get letters to New Granada, get them on board some ship that will touch at a Granadan port, and let them be mailed there. To get them from here, arrange with some consul. That model of a consul, Mr. Sánchez, of Cartagena, is full of good works of this kind toward entire strangers. I have been under similar obligations to an unknown consul at Panamá; but trust not the United States mail at Panamá unless in the last extremity. I would sooner trust the cook of a schooner bound to Santa Marta, Sabanilla, or Cartagena.

Granadan travelers are often embarrassed by the importance of Christian names—nombres—and the little account made of surnames—apellidos. Women do not change their surname when they marry, but may connect the husband's to it by a *de:* thus, when Señor Barriga married Dolores Fuertes, she became Dolores Fuertes de Barriga. Their son José may write his name simply José Barriga, or José Barriga Fuertes, or José Barriga y Fuertes. I prefer José Barriga (Fuertes).

In the letter-list the Christian names are arranged in alphabetical order, and Honorable John Smith must seek his name under the letter H, John Smith, Esq., under J, and Mr. Smith, under M and S. Had he forewarned all his correspondents to direct to Juan Smith invariably, he would have saved both himself and the officials much trouble. Directed to Don Juan el Inglés, they would be surer of reaching him than by any possible direction in a United States post-office.

The gobernacion of the province of Bogotá is in the opposite end of the Casa Consistorial. The Gobernador, Pedro Gutiérrez (Lee), is an intelligent, efficient official. His mother's name seems to have been English. Padre Gutiérrez, his father, is the excellent Cura of Las Nieves.

Among other favors due to the governor was an introduction to the Colegio de la Merced. The reader will be glad to accompany me there, as we shall find no other like it. It is in the extinct and spacious convent of the Capuchins, at the beginning of the Alameda, just north of the Plaza de San Victorino. I knocked at the door, and it was opened by the porteress, who usually sits on the floor of the locutory sewing. She informed me that the order was not sufficient for my admission, but that it must be taken to a gentleman who is authorized to admit. I begged, however, to see the directress, and she conducted me to the locutory.

The room is divided lengthwise by a fence, and the door by which pupils entered to see their visitors was the other side of it. It was much too low to separate lovers, and too high by far for the convenience of mammas that call to see their daughters. The directora entered, however, by the door from the hall. I begged her to excuse informalities, and admit me without delaying me, and she cheerfully did so.

I have often wished to get a fair insight into the colegios for boys, and have never got farther than the public halls. I despair ever seeing any thing of the internal life and domestic arrangements of these institutions. Here I was taken by surprise: I was shown every thing. I was asked into every room —parlors, halls, dormitory, teachers' apartments, chapel, bathroom, refectory, garden, and kitchen.

An interesting sight it was. Not a room but had some curious peculiarity, but all arranged with the best intentions. The whole was neat, but nothing elegant. Drawing and needlework were taught to excess, but vocal music not at all. Their rigid discipline allows no girl to go into the streets, and allows access to parents with some difficulty. The pupils were at their drawing lessons. They appeared cheerful and pretty. I volunteered some suggestions, among which were to get the garden cultivated, to fix the chimney in the kitchen so that it could be used, to pray less, and sing some. All of this, and my sincere commendations of the school, were very kindly received by the lady whose politeness and cordiality made this one of my most delightful calls in the country.

The Colegio del Rosario is just two hundred years old, having been founded in 1653 by Archbishop Torres. It is in the third block north of the Cathedral. I entered it from the house of the vice-director, on the north side of the block. Here I saw a very old library, with few or no new books, some very old portraits, and one or two halls. Students were walking to and fro in the corridors, repeating aloud the lessons they were to recite. They were an intelligent body of students, but very young. I heard a class reciting English to a teacher who could barely speak it a little. It was "as good as a play" to hear them make mistakes, and especially to hear him correct them. Ours is a terribly hard language for them to articulate.

I visited repeatedly the Colegio Militar. It is in the second block south of the Plaza, with the entrance on the east side. The school appears in a highly creditable condition as to mathematics, and some examinations that I witnessed there are worthy of all praise. The library is modern, and good for its extent, which is not great.

I became acquainted with a French professor there, named Bergeron, who is something of an enthusiast. He desired to call on me with some mesmeric subjects, by whom he would convince me of the truth of clairvoyance. He came, and failed. He is a believer in hidden treasures, of course, and satisfied himself, by aid of clairvoyance or otherwise, that an immense quantity lay open to view in the Hoyo del Aire. This is a terrific chasm, with perpendicular walls, like the shaft of a mine. It lies 14 miles north-northeast of Vélez, and five miles southeast of Paz. It is on a side hill, so that while the upper side is 387 feet deep, the lower side is but 247. As the hole is nearly circular, its oblique mouth must be elliptical, so that while its least diameter is 285 feet, the longer is 367, and the circumference is 884 feet. These dimensions I take from the estimates of Colonel Codazzi. As the breadth of this well is just about equal to its depth, there is no want of light or vegetation. In fact, the sides are thickly matted with plants, and at the bottom grow respectable trees.

Here lay Professor Bergeron's treasures, if there be any truth in mesmerism. They had been thrown in by the Indians, in their desperation, to keep them from the covetous grasp of the Conquerors, and he must have them. So, before leaving Bogotá, he prepared ropes, windlass, and a sort of balloon car, capable of holding two. He did not exactly like the idea of going down there alone. He selected for his companion a worthy priest, Padre Cuervo, who cared less about gold than natural curiosities and Indian relics—a very rare taste in a Granadino. He consented to share the danger, the professor taking entirely to himself the expense and the profits.

But when they came there the Frenchman stood aghast. He was a mathematician, knew the depth in metres, and had provided the requisite quantity of rope. But he had not provided the requisite quantity of courage, for it was an enormous hole to look at. Even from the lower side, 247 feet is a great way to swing down in a basket. So the Padre Cuervo might go down first; and he did; and he wrote an encouraging letter and sent up to his patron, but he could not venture down. In fact, he doubted whether there were any treasure down in such a hole, after all.

The good priest was in his glory down there—alone in his glory. He found a stream running out, and followed it for a long way under-ground—a dismal region, peopled with that mysterious bird, the guácharo. This is often supposed to be a species of Caprimulgus; but Padre Cuervo says that he satisfied himself that it lives on nuts, which it brings by night from quite a distance. It would, indeed, be difficult to procure, within the few fastnesses in which they are known to live, a sufficiency of insects for their immense population. I now recollect but two other places where the guácharo is known to live: in the famous cave in Venezuela mentioned by Humboldt, and at the Bridge of Pandi, where I saw them and their nests, but in a retreat far more difficult of access than this. The name of this remarkable bird is Steatornis Caripensis.

Bergeron was a little disappointed with the results of this expedition, but the good-natured priest, though not a little elated with his success, had the consideration not to publish his account of the expedition till the professor had returned to France.

Professor Bergeron accompanied me to the Observatory, which

is in the rear of the Colegio Militar. It is the oldest in the New World. It is at the lowest latitude and the highest altitude of any in the world, and yet even astronomers know little of it. A good account of it is found in the Semanario Granadino, page 44, of the Paris edition of 1849. I extract some particulars from it. It was commenced by Mútis 24th May, 1802, and finished 20th August, 1803. It is an octagonal tower, 24.6 feet of internal diameter, and 51 feet high. It has two stories, the upper of which is 24 feet high, and has in the ceiling an opening to let a ray of the sun at noon fall on a meridional line on the floor below. A smaller tower, clinging to the southwest side of it, and rising 16 feet above it, contains the staircase and a small observer's room. It was furnished with good instruments at that date, such as the Graham clock used by Condamine, seven Dollond telescopes (no grand one), and an 18-inch quadrant of Bird. The clock and the quadrant, and some other instruments, are still in the museum, but many of the instruments have been destroyed in one of the civil wars by soldiers, who took the Observatory to be a fortress, from some images of cannon that the fancy of the architect chose to put upon the upper story.

A pluviometer in the garden adjoining was all the apparatus near; the building was absolutely empty. Why will not science again take possession of this favored post, and remodel it according to the present state of observation? No habitable spot has a more brilliant sky or a rarer atmosphere. The financial condition of the nation forbids them even to think of improving it, but there is nothing that they would not willingly do to aid others in enriching science by means of it.

It would be injustice to leave this memorable spot without recounting briefly the history of the first and only astronomer who ever resided in it.

Francisco José de Cáldas (Tenorio) was born in Popayan in 1771, finished a course of law studies in Bogotá in 1793, entered on mercantile pursuits, and failed. He then gave way to his natural bent, made him instruments as he could, such as telescope, quadrant, &c. An attempt to mend a broken thermometer, and construct a new scale by boiling water, at Popayan, gave him, in 1799 or 1800, the idea of ascertaining altitudes by the variation of the boiling-point, an invention which has not been duly credited to him in books. In 1802 he became a member of the Botanical Expedition under Mútis. In 1806, Cáldas became the first astronomer in the Observatory of Bogotá. The previous years had been spent in perfecting the geography and botany of his country. On the 3d January, 1808, he commenced a scientific weekly journal, El Semanario Granadino, which continued for two years. It was republished in Paris in 1849, edited by Colonel Joaquin Acosta, and improved by the suppression of some temporary matter.

And now began the long and terrible War of Independence, and Cáldas left his observatory and his science, first to edit a revolutionary paper, then to serve as the chief of a company of engineers. In 1813, '14, and '15, we find him in Antioquia, planning fortifications, casting cannon, making powder, teaching engineering, and serving the revolution by every faculty. In 1815 he returned again to his old work of inciting rebellion through the press at Bogotá; but when the Spanish General Latorre entered Bogotá, 6th May, 1816, Cáldas fled to Popayan, where, after the battle of Tambo, on 29th June, 1816, he was seized, and condemned to die. Now he turned to supplicate the butcher Morillo, not for himself, but for science. He asked only that he might live in the closest prison, on the hardest fare, with a chain on his ankle, till he had arranged his papers for publication. In vain. The Vandal wished to destroy them more than him. In the Pacificador, in Colonel Pineda's collection, we read: "Oct. 29th, Dr. Francisco Cáldas, Engineer General and Brigadier General in the rebel army, was shot in the back, and his property confiscated." He was only 45.

Thus died, nobly and honorably, the wisest and perhaps the best man that South America has ever produced—the Granadan Franklin—for he resembled Franklin in many respects, only he was more highly honored; for he not only risked his life for his country in the field, but died for her on the banquillo. Other scientific men, not so eminent, shared his fate. Among them were the botanist Lozano, and the chemist José María Cabal. Indeed, so terrible was the cruelty of this wretch, that, in looking over the portraits in a gallery of the Colegio del Rosario, it appeared as if one half had been murdered in cold blood, and of the remainder, some had died in battle, some had been sought in vain for slaughter, and one who had been caught was *spared*, thus fixing a sort of stigma on his reputation, as if he was not worth butchering.

With sad and angry feelings I turned from the garden, overgrown with weeds, into the paved patio of the Colegio Militar. And here I am reminded of a later occurrence, which I think illustrates the fanatical hatred of the Gólgotas to the army and all concerned with it. Our own West Point has to run an annual gauntlet, though we have no Congressmen that aim at the entire abolition of the army. Here those who are entirely opposed to the army, added to those who wish to weaken and embarrass the present administration, are never much short of a majority. Well, it seems that one day some one mingled with the dulce of the dinner a quantity of tartar emetic so large that it could hardly have been sold innocently by any druggist in the interior. No life was lost, but a terrible scene was the consequence. One student only had not partaken of it, and, from the customs of the country, no one would be likely to take a double quantity of dulce. The whole city was in alarm, for there is no respectable family but has some friends in the Colegio. The President had a son there. All were at once removed to the houses of parents and friends, and the scanty medical knowledge of the city was all put in requisition. The author of the deed, who, we hope, knew not the danger of it, never was discovered.

In the by-laws of the Colegio Militar I find a peculiar and significant regulation about sickness: "Cases of serious sickness shall be removed to the officers' ward of the Military Hospital, and treated at the public expense; but if the disease proves to be 'el gálico,' the patient shall be removed to the wards of common soldiers, and after his return to the Colegio he shall not leave the premises unaccompanied by an officer of the school for one year."

There is, or rather was, another national colegio here, that of San Bartolomé. The embarrassments of the treasury have led to its relinquishment. It was not needed, as the Colegio del Rosario is a provincial establishment. Another establishment is the Semanario Conciliar, a school for the training of priests.

I am under the impression that the locality, if not the apparatus of this, has been rather unfairly seized upon by government, in the belief that it was useless to community. It seems to me that there is no present lack of priests, unless it be among the Indians, where, indeed, a large number of good missionaries could find enough to do.

Some attempts are made to encourage the sciences, and a good laboratory has been established here at the expense of the nation. I attempted to visit it, but could find no time at once convenient to myself and those who had charge of it. M. Lewy came out from Paris to teach here, but he became discouraged and returned. Public taste does not run to material facts.

Greek and Hebrew are, I believe, unknown here. I know of no works in Spanish to facilitate the study of either; nor have I met a single book in or on either of these languages in the country, unless it be in the rare library of Dr. Merizalde. In the same way, agriculture, mining, geology, practical mechanics, are yet to have their beginnings as studies.

I visited two common schools, one of each sex. That for girls is the poorest girls' school I have seen, while that for boys was not much better, poorer than any other girls' school, but about equal to the average of boys' schools. The pedagogic profession is not respectable in New Granada. It would be well to require from candidates for certain offices that they shall have taught an entire year in the same common school. Should this be required before gaining a doctor's degree, for instance, quite a different class of talent would be called into these schools.

In the southeast corner of the city, or just out of it, is one establishment, however, that does credit to Granadan perseverance and talent. It is the pottery of Don Nicolas Leiva. To understand the difficulties he has contended with, you must know something of native character, and especially its aversion to steady labor. In entire provinces you can not find one man who has *ever* wrought faithfully all the working days of an entire month; and yet this pottery would do credit to the United States. Among the uncommon articles made here are porcelain mortars and pestles, and those Venetian shades that exhibit soft and delicate figures by transmitted light. In one of these Señor Leiva had achieved a very good likeness of himself. I am under particular obligations to the attentive and persevering proprietor.

The glass enterprise had a much more natural termination. Of all bipeds, perhaps the most unmanageable is the glass-blower. To succeed here, a glass manufactory would need special laws, giving the director all power short of life or death for the space of ten years after the enlistment of the operative. But so limited is the demand for glass, that it would be better not attempt to make it here again for a few hundred years to come.

The cotton factory and the paper-mill, the quinine works and the foundry, have all failed. I attribute most of the failures to the same cause—the want of suitable operatives. Even now vast quantities of rags—a perfect mine of them—are to be seen on the borders of the San Francisco. The quinine works manufactured only the crude alkaloid, which the European manufacturers are said to have finally decided not to buy, lest it should ruin some parts of their own business; so the San Francisco, as it hurries down from the Boqueron, can find nothing to do but turn two common grist-mills, which, though they never grind maize, would not, in the North, be thought suitable for wheat.

The key to all this is a want of education in the masses. They are tolerant of hunger: of comforts they know nothing, and desire none. Their morals can sink no lower, and their religion can raise them no higher. Their beau ideal is to escape hunger, to keep dry from the rain, and to be free from labor and care. They pay no taxes, beg when they can, and earn nothing except in case of extreme emergency, but in such case they will submit to any thing. Once they had the Hospicio fitted up as a work-house, but such a thing can only be kept up so long as some man shall make it his hobby: it is all run down, and is become a beggars' nest. Even prostitution would not be likely to be a gainful course, wars have carried off so many of the one sex, and the low masses of the other are so abject. Poor Bogotá!

With some remarks on the weather, I now take my leave of the capital, to return but once, on a special occasion. Mosquera supposes that the city is 8655.5 feet above the level of the sea. Quite possibly it is rather higher. I would put the lowest point on the plain, at the marshes, at 8650 feet. The latitude was estimated by Cáldas at 4° 36′ 12″, and the longitude at 60° 32′ 14″ west of the Isle of Leon, equal, it is supposed, to 74° 14′ 15″ west of Greenwich. Boussingault estimates the mean temperature at 58°; Cáldas supposed it higher, and so have most others; but I think with Mosquera that 59° is nearly right. January and June seem to be the coldest months. The wettest months are called spring and fall months in the United States. The barometer and thermometer have both quite a narrow range. One terrible morning at sunrise the thermometer is said to have been down to 44.6°. This was the 9th of May, 1834, and the witness is Colonel Acosta. Judge the domestic comforts on that morning of families that have never warmed themselves by a fire; and I really believe no man ever learned to do so in New Granada except in the house of some foreigner. I never knew of artificial warmth in any other house than that of Madama Carrol. On another occasion I heard of it down to 46.4°; but such events are as rare as earthquakes. So, too, the thermometer has been up to 68° in the shade, 26th of February, 1808, the hottest day on record. The natural range ought to be put at from 55°, the very lowest, up to 66°. Persons used to this like it; but, if you are too cold, just step out into the sun, and you are sure to suffer with the heat.

As to moisture, Bogotá has essentially a dry climate. They use pepper-boxes for salt, and, in ordinary weather, without difficulty; while at Honda salt needs to be spread with a knife, as butter is at the North; but for all this, there are sufficiently numerous rainy days here in the course of a year. It is difficult to know the precise number, as some would count it a shower when the rain did not wet the entire surface of a flat stone, while others would not unless it really rained so as to detain a person in-doors. I count very small showers as such in the first six months, when I estimate the rainy days of each month as follows: January, 8; February, 9; March, 20; April, 18; May, 20; June, 10; July, 3; August, 4; September, 5; October, 6; November, 8; December, 10. This makes 121 days in the year in each of which it rains some, or almost exactly one day in three; and yet, I think, in the last half of the year, all the lesser rains were omitted. Still, the rainy days must be less than half the whole. Now how many of these are respectable showers? About one in five of the first six months, and nearly half the others. In 1808 there were ten days in the first six months in each of which there fell from two thirds of an inch to an inch and three fourths. I can find no good data for an estimate of the quantity of rain that falls annually, but, from a careful use of those I have, I make the quantity very near fifty English inches, probably a little less.

As to the time of day that rain falls, it is rarely in the morning. All through the rainy season you make your calculations with as much security as in the finest climates in the world, only you take it for granted that it will rain in the afternoon. Thunder is moderate in quantity, and of rather inferior quality, being quite tame compared with our best specimens in the Northern States, and perfectly contemptible beside the ordinary run in the Southern States. To match that, you must go to Chocó. With thunder often comes hail, and rarely in immense quantities. I think half the hail I ever saw fell in one day on the plain of Bogotá. It is no meteorological mystery that heavy falls of hail are always succeeded by ice-cream parties, and that these never occur at any other time.

Frost, I imagine, visits the top of Guadalupe frequently, but on the plain it is rare. It requires a succession of cloudy days and clear nights. I have noticed things bitten by it once only. It has far greater power here in a still night from the rarity of the air. The sky assumes a deep blue unknown to lower regions, and all the dense clouds lie lower down. I have been able to read by moonlight even when I could not see in what part of the sky the moon was. From the same reason, the wind has less power. As it weighs only about two thirds as much per cubic foot, the momentum is proportionably less in a gale of the same velocity. It is curious to see the air escape from a bottle corked at a lower altitude. In short, the difference strikes you in various ways, as the temperature of boiling water (195°), and its action on food, on cooking, and, above all, on the lungs of persons who have been born here, and can never live contentedly below.

CHAPTER XX.

THE FALLS OF TEQUENDAMA.

Leaving Bogotá.—Mule-hunting.—Soacha.—Agriculture at Tequendama.—Course of the River.—Description of the Falls.—Comparison of Cataracts.—Photographic View.—Mist Theory.—Tree-ferns.—Haciendas of Cincha and Tequendama.—Saw-mill and Quinine Factory.—Sabbath Reading.

Two months had my trunks rested quietly in Bogotá, while their owner became acclimated, and learned something of the ways of the Andine world. I now determined to visit the two most stupendous works of nature in this region, the Falls (Salto) of Tequendama and the Bridge of Pandi. Most visitors at the falls spend only an hour there. They ride there from Bogotá, and return the same day; or leave Bogotá in the afternoon, spend an uncomfortable night in the village of Soacha, or are guests at the hacienda of Canoas, take a picnic breakfast at the falls, and then return. This last is generally a good plan, but I wished to spend more time there, and therefore availed myself of the permission of Señor Manuel Umaña to make the hacienda of Tequendama my home for a few days.

Now came the inevitable trouble of the Andine traveler—to find cattle. I was not aware that a good carriage-road ran to the very head of the falls, and that a return coal-cart might be found in which my trunks could be deposited without that careful packing and equalizing necessary in mule-travel. After I had lost one day in trying to find mules, the kind Señora Tomasa engaged two carga mules, a saddle-horse, and a peon from Soacha. They came, of course, later than promised, and, after taking leave of my disinterestedly kind friends, I was soon alone on the vast Sabana, leaving my cargas and peon to follow.

Two months' daily rain had made less difference than I had expected. The color had improved, but was not as beautiful as our spring spreads over fields long covered with snow. The road was a carriage-road, but not so remarkably good as that toward Honda. As I journeyed south, the hills were never far distant on my left. A mile or two south of the city, a young gentleman, whom I had never seen before, overtook me on the road, and continued some way past his destination to a substantial bridge across the Fucha, when he took a polite leave and returned.

Three hours' easy riding brought me to Soacha, famous for the bones of carnivorous elephants once exhumed here. It is a small, scattered village, in a district of 2918 inhabitants. My mules were owned here, and I stopped a moment and paid for them. Leaving Soacha, I found myself on an arm of the plain, having on my right two ridges of hill. Between them, rising mist marked the falls. Disregarding this, I had still to pursue my way to the south, till, after a mile or two, I entered the great gate of the plantation, and took a course more consonant with my wishes.

Several small plows, without mould-boards, such as you find in the Bible Dictionary, were scratching up the rich black soil, and some men were laying a stone wall, substantial enough for the foundation of a house. Before me was the mansion, now deserted of the family; and hid in a hollow by its side were a saw-mill, the houses of some dependent families, and a quinine factory.

The director, M. Louis Godin, an intelligent French chemist, was domiciled, I was told, with a countrywoman of mine. I found her of pure African blood, and a very favorable specimen of her race. She bore in youth the name of Joanna Jackson, and thirteen years ago had a mother living in Haverstraw, to whom she said she would gladly send a hundred or two of dollars if she knew she was living. She said that when she left the people were talking of voting for General Jackson and Mr. Van Buren, but she conjectures the general must be dead by this time. In the interim she has been over Ireland, England, Germany, and Russia, as a servant, and is now a lady in New Granada, and has her white servant. Of the two persons who can make quinine on a large scale in New Granada, she is one.

At length my baggage arrived, and the large parlor of the mansion was thrown open to its reception. The patio of the house is very large, and the buildings are of but one story on three sides, while there is a second story in front, nearly all of which is occupied by the sala or parlor. The room contained four sofas, a dozen chairs, and three tables. A comfortable mat bed was thrown on the floor, in a corner, and, after taking a child's toy-mug full of chocolate, with bread and sweetmeats for my dinner, I was left to repose.

After an early cup of chocolate in the morning I sallied forth. To understand my course, you must understand that of the river. It had been creeping along the plain at my right, altogether unsuspected by me, till I reached the hacienda. There I found it entering a narrow gorge of the basin rim of the plain of Bogotá, where a quarter of a mile of dam would again convert the plain, as it has been in former ages, into a lake as large as Lake Champlain. It had approached the gorge by a course for many miles of almost exactly south (south 7° W.). Here the little mill-stream, coming from the arm of the plain, mingles its dark waters with the yellow tide of the Bogotá, and they at that instant enter the gorge. Now is heard, for the first time in its course, the murmuring of the Bogotá. With its character it changes its course. For half a mile it flows almost west (S. 78° W.). Again it makes another turn, and for perhaps 2½ miles N.W. (N. 36° W.). Here, as it enters the forest, it takes another turn almost north (17° W.), so that, after doubling the hill, it flows almost in the contrary direction to that it had in the plain.

At the gorge it has already fallen below the surface of the plain, perhaps 30 feet, and seems to have been struggling vainly with its destiny, for a straight line of a mile cuts its bed eight times. The road I took along its bank rises over the first point of the hill, giving a fine view of the plain; then we descend to where the river, after a moment's respite, is again roaring and plunging at our right. Ah, poor river! that yesterday flowed softly between banks of green, now chafing with rugged cliffs and huge boulders, hasten on to thy doom.

Our road is still a carriage-road. We open gates and pass bars till we lose sight of the river as we enter the forest. The road now explains itself. In the ledge on the left is a stratum of coal nearly two feet thick and of good quality, on this side of the river. Still nothing is seen of the cataract till we are even past it, when the river is seen pouring down into a gulf that yawns among the trees. It is near us; but to descend is no small task. Take your machete, and proceed with caution. Avoid five things: do not cut in such a direction that, when your machete has cut a vine, it shall terminate its course in your thigh; neither let your left hand intervene between the blow and the object; do not fall upon your machete, nor against a stick that you have just sharpened by an oblique cut, neither cut a bent shrub when it can retort the compliment by knocking you over in straightening. The Spanish term for this labor is *romper monte* (to break thicket).

But the snakes! the deadly snakes of South America! I had not thus far seen a live one, and but one dead one. With nothing on my feet but alpargates, I therefore fearlessly ventured on. I made my own road, as the guide I reluctantly received from Dr. Umaña knew not the way, and it was easier to make a new path than find the old one.

At length we are upon the brink of an immense chasm, and we will pause to describe it. Writers tell us it has the appearance of a work of art. We gather from their descriptions that it is like an immense dry dock, the bottom of which is seldom visible from the top; open at the lower end, while down the perpendicular side of the upper rushes a river. Now you must be informed that the descriptions are made from the opposite bank, where a *public* road leads down to the brink. From that side a front view is impossible; for the fall is not at the end, but at a corner of the parallelogram, and to them only the side adjacent is accessible. The fall is too nearly in a line with their side, which runs N. 19° W., while across the fall is N. 27° E., a difference of direction of only 46 degrees, or about half a right angle. Further, because their side is straight they imagine ours to be, but a *side* view of ours shows great indentations and projections. Neither are the sides parallel, for they approach at the lower end, not only optically, but really. The bottom, too, is clearly visible, all except where the fall strikes, where it is covered, of course, with a perpetual mist. On their side an inclined plane of debris extends, in some places, two thirds the height. On ours there is a shelf beneath us, on which you see some tree-ferns growing. On their side they think the debris extends up but a little way, and our ledge they scarcely see; hence it appears much more regular there than here. The strata here dip four or five degrees to the south, and as the walls are probably at right angles to them, theirs must overhang a little: hence more debris on that side, as fragments are more liable to fall.

But notice one peculiarity of the Salto, which gives it its character, and adds to and subtracts from its beauty. The fall is not a *clear* fall. The water falls smoothly for 27 feet 8 inches, and here, striking on a ledge, the sheet is dashed almost into foam, and accomplishes the remainder of its journey more like spray hurled downward by irregular violence than a fluid under the influence of gravitation. Its irregular and constantly varying outline reminds us of a column of smoke or steam, but as this motion is violent and angular, while that is slow and graceful, a comparison between them can only be justified for want of a better. Cones of spray here and there seem to shoot out suddenly in advance of a falling mass, but are soon overtaken and absorbed by the body from which they sprung. These cones must be masses of water not yet broken up, that are carried by their momentum out of the body of spray that falls more slowly. Here the resistance of the air breaks them up into drops, and they are lost in the mass to which they are now assimilated.

A rainbow hangs over the falls when the position of the sun permits. It is varying every instant; for where now it is brightest, an instant hence there may be no mist, or there may be a mass of water too irregular to form a rainbow. The point where these observations are best made is a sort of table rock just at the brink of the water. Another rock overhangs it, covered with Thibaudias, ferns, and orchid plants, making almost a grotto for the observer.

We must not forget that this is now just the close of winter, and consequently, in the three months of summer which follow, the stream, now too small in volume for the mighty proportions of the gulf, must grow smaller and smaller. One observer gravely declares that the whole is dissipated in mist before reaching the bottom.

Of the depth you can judge nothing. It does not look much, if any, deeper than Niagara, but it is almost exactly three times as deep. It is difficult either to see or hear a stone fall to the bottom; but, throw it as you will, it seems to come in toward the ledge as it descends, and is in a fair way to strike exactly beneath your feet. The reason for this optical illusion is well known. The course of the stone soon becomes parallel with the perpendicular wall, and as both recede from you, the principle of foreshortening seems to bring them almost together.

Various estimates of the depth have been formed, some extending even to "half a league." Other estimates in order of time are as follows:

Mútis (barometer)	698	Cáldas (dropping)	602
Ezquiaqui (measure)	724	Gros (measure)	479.425
Humboldt's MSS. (dropping)	581	Cuervo "	417.3
" Published account	600		

The measure of Baron Gros appears to be unquestionably accurate. Acosta gives the same altitude to the Great Pyramid; and as Niagara is said to be 160 feet, Tequendama lacks less than a foot of being three times as deep. The bottom of the chasm is a hundred or two feet lower than the foot of the fall.

The pre-eminence in depth, then, over every other cataract in this hemisphere does not *tell*. It can not be compared to Niagara. You do not here hear the awful sub-bass of Niagara. The noise is even less than that of many smaller cataracts, on account of the quantity of air carried down with the water. In fact, I think most of the roar is from the first leap of only 28 feet. If Niagara has a rival in the world, it must be the Falls of the Missouri, of which I have seen no good account. It seems a little curious that Europe should monopolize all the *high* falls. Norway, Sweden, Switzerland, and the Pyrenees alone seem to boast of higher falls than Tequendama; but of their six perhaps two only exceed this in sublimity—Lulea in Sweden, 600 feet, and Ruckon Foss, Norway, 800 feet. But where, in this competition of cataracts, is Asia, with the highest mountains of the world? Has she *no* cataracts? Obviously plains, not mountains, must furnish the great cataracts. Tequendama is the daughter of the Plain of Bogotá; and if Asia has none equal to it, it must be because her elevated steppes are almost rainless deserts.

The chasm of Tequendama was not made by the present falls. Most rivers emerge from the mist of a fall in a pool of unfathomable depth. The first you see of the Bogotá, it is running down an inclined plane of debris; but, in some other geological era, a mightier stream, occupying the whole breadth of the chasm, may have made excavations, which the present is but filling up with stones from above.

Tequendama wants the *power* of Niagara. The river *might* be forded a little above. Human effort might arrest its course, and bid the cataract cease for a while. Were there ground near on which a manufacturing city could be built, the whole could be drawn off and let down over a series of breast-wheels, as at Paterson.

The *mist* of Tequendama has started some philosophical speculations in my mind. The people say that it often spreads in a dense fog over the surrounding country. This fog begins in the morning, at from 9 to 11. Is there more fog here than at Bogotá? A day-fog would diminish the mean temperature of a place; a night-fog would raise it. The temperature here, then, ought to be lower than elsewhere at the same level. I found it, by the water of a mine, about 54°, but I would like to see it confirmed. Now, although Bogotá is 850 feet higher, its temperature is given four degrees higher. This indicates a confirmation of my suspicions. In passing four times in sight of the Fall Mountains, I have always seen the mist either hovering among them, or pouring from them to overspread a few square miles of adjoining country. Now we must remember that this country has no fogs like ours, but bears clouds and mountain mists in tropical profusion. This small body of water contrives to manufacture a hundred-fold more mist than Niagara, at a lower altitude. The mist is begun *mechanically;* of this there can be no doubt. Is it not propagated meteorologically? Has not one particle of mist the power of generating another in a favorable atmosphere? Here is a grave question. The quantity of mist *generated* directly by the falls seems very small; that *proceeding* from them varies at different hours of the day, and often streams off 5 or 10 miles. Possibly all that the weather has to do with this mist is to absorb it at some hours and not at others. Meteorology, as a science, is yet in its infancy. New Granada offers a wide field for the study of some phases of it, which are to be observed nowhere in the whole world except among the Andes.

I could look out from where I stood to beyond the outlet of the chasm, and see the hills there. Down one of those hills I saw a zigzag path, apparently well trodden, that seemed to have no other object than to reach the water below the falls. I then thought that the people above must come down there to wash or to cross the river. I noted well its position, for I hoped to cross to the right bank at some future time, gain the top of the hill, and there descend.

As I could not do that, I made a long expedition down the left side of the chasm, to see if I could descend at the end there. I dare not guess how many hours I spent in this toilsome march. I went, at my first trial, half way to the farthest point I could see at the top of the precipice. Here I found that an apparatus had been constructed to lower persons down to the shelf below to seek for hidden treasures. I learned next day that it would take many days to get round by that way to the lower level, as no path existed, and every rod, and nearly every yard, must be cut with the machete.

But I was much mistaken about that zigzag path. To reach that hill-top from the opposite side of the stream, you would have first to descend to the level of the river and go up that path. It is part of the highway from Soacha to Tena that here dips down to the level of the Bogotá just to rise again in half a mile.

Fifty-three weeks after I stood on that same point of hill from which the road comes down, and there caught my first distant view of the lonely fall. I could see but about 50 feet of the upper part, and the noise was hardly audible. The great parallelogram, as it is described, opened toward me, but a point of hill shut out of sight most of the abyss within. It seemed to me that I had reached the outmost verge of the inhabited world, and there, just beyond it, surrounded by dense and untrodden woods, was this gloomy rather than magnificent cascade.

I have said that the plain of Bogotá was bordered on the west by a range of low hills, which, on their western slope, become precipitous, and often absolute precipices at a certain height. This is the height of the summit of the chasm down which the Bogotá here leaps. Now draw in your imagination a line on the exact level of the top of the falls, as far south as Nieva, and as far north as Cipaquirá. It might strike one or two Indian villages, but, if not, every mile would be wilderness almost untrodden. Let us begin at the north, and explore, in the imagination, this cornice of the mountain. All the way on your left, to the eastward, you have woody hills, the summits of which are at first but a few hundred feet above your line, and separate you from the inhabited plain. West of you, on your right, is at first precipice, with a few gaps. In the distance, to the west, you see Villeta, more than 5000 feet (nearly a mile) below you, with its cocoa-trees and cane-fields. You next cross the road by which we ascended to Bogotá, and find the Aserradero about 100 feet above you. Then, as you cross the road from Mesa to Bogotá, you see in the distance La Mesa on a detached table more than 3000 feet below you, but still near the upper limit of cane and oranges. Next we pass the head of the falls, and see nothing but tangled wilderness till we cross the road descending to Fusagasugá. That town afterward appears on a slope of the mountain a little higher than La Mesa. Here all east of you is wild mountain and desolate plains. Next you pass the fearful chasm over which Nature has thrown the Bridge of Pandi, and, by traversing still 100 miles (air line) of wilderness in a southwesterly direction, you see at length the tawny Magdalena at Neiva, 7500 feet below you. In all this vast space you have crossed three roads and two rivers that have broken through from the east. You may have passed, besides, two Indian villages and some Indian trails, and nothing more of the works of man. Is not this wilderness indeed?

The portal of this wild is the yawning chasm of Tequendama. I descended to it, accompanied by the governor of the then province of Tequendama, and an attendant bearing ropes, etc. We had gained this point early by traveling in the dark before day. We were resolved to penetrate up the bank of the river to the very foot of the falls. It was impossible, and, I think, can hardly be ever possible when the river is too high to be forded. First on the one side and then on the other, the stream dashes against cliffs that hardly can be scaled. Were we camped on this spot for a few days, I would hope, even at this stage of water, to reach the spot. It is said also to have been reached from the cliff above, on this right bank, by a dry path, but difficult in the extreme. To this we could find no guide.

[From a Photograph by Crowther.]

FALLS OF TEQUENDAMA.

We ascended toward Canoas and Soacha, and the ascent seemed interminable. We at length reached the very top of the ridge that hems in the Sabana, which we did not see. Following south along the ridge, we came to the road that leads from Soacha over a bridge, past the Hacienda of Canoas, to the Salto, and also to some coal mines. An enormous descent is before you, and good judgment, good directions, or a guide is necessary to keep you from losing your way. I believe you should leave the coal mines on your right, and keep the road that cost the least. At length you reach a clear spot, where the mule-road ends, and where so many parties have breakfasted as to leave to the place an abundance of chicken-bones and the name Almorzadero. To this spot coal is brought up stairs by cargueros, and by another steep flight you descend to the falls as best you may.

The main position on this right side is close at the head of the fall, as is the only one known on the left bank. There is another on the brink, called El Balcon, to which there is a tolerable path, and where stands a tree bearing the name of the *discoverer* of the spot. At this point was taken the only good photographic representation of the falls that I know of. It was by Mr. George Crowther, then engaged in commercial operations in Bogotá, and an amateur photographer. The engraving on the opposite page was drawn on wood by Mr. Thwaites.

No art can do justice to Niagara, and still less to Tequendama. Landscapes spread horizontally: the eye can not measure depths when it sees them—how much less when they are represented on a plane surface; still, you have here an accurate delineation of the falls, if you only view it properly. The axis of the camera was depressed in taking it, and the eye should fall on it with like obliquity. As I hold the plate vertically some inches below my eye, I see the summit of the cataract on a level with where I stood, but it is very doubtful if any one who has not seen the Salto can get this view of it.

I advise you, therefore, to imagine the view taken from the summit of the debris about one third of the way down. About half the fall is visible then, but not a front view of it. Now, if you can look at it till the upper leap appears to be nearly thirty feet high, then the abyss will open before you in its true proportions; if not, I fear that those human figures, which are in reality far too large, will do little toward a perfect measurement of it. That tree-fern, if it had really stood where the artist has put it, would have escaped notice in the picture, so distant is what seems to be the immediate foreground. Still I am more than satisfied with the picture, although it does not accomplish impossibilities. No attempt to take a photographic view from below is likely to be made. On the right bank, no spot above could be better than that selected by the artist. On the other side far better points of view might be found, but they can only be reached by the machete, as probably not a trace remains after a year of such paths as I cut, if not trodden. To reach the exact front requires but a few minutes' cutting after leaving the mine on the left side. The best possible point of view is from a jutting crag that here extends some way into the parallelogram, as the chasm is said to be.

It is curious to read the exaggerated accounts of the place. We are told that such is the deafening roar that the boldest hardly dare approach within a hundred yards of the brink. A perpendicular fall could hardly make less noise than here, and I think we do not even hear the water that strikes the bottom. Ezquiaqui says that the falling mass has excavated a hollow of 108 feet in depth in the inclined plane of rocks on which it strikes. This could not be easily ascertained. I have understood from others that there is quite a place behind the falling water, where persons have been without difficulty. I do not rely on the statement, as it does not seem probable. The water is not a falling sheet, but a mixture of water and air, that must bring down with it a far greater rush of wind than that of the Cave of Æolus at Niagara.

I myself have been deceived as to the climate at the bottom. True, a few miles below are cane-fields, but in these few miles the bed of the stream makes a trifling descent—say of considerably over half a mile—in addition to the perpendicular fall. But "we see palm-trees down on the shelf, and these do not grow except in Tierra Caliente." These "palms" are tree-ferns, as any botanist can tell at a glance, and above are as fine specimens of tree-ferns as you will see any where. And a most interesting object they are to a botanist, though by no means so beautiful as the palm, seldom exceeding twelve feet in height, with a rough, shaggy trunk, crowned with a large number of horizontal fronds very uniform and precise in their shape. Drawings of the tree-ferns are not, however, apt to do them justice. The crowns of those at Tequendama are far heavier, and the fronds far more uniform in size and direction, than in the example seen in the plate. The trunks are generally of about half the height there seen, with hundreds of fronds as long and heavy as the longest there given. They seem to delight in this precise altitude, and, indeed, not only were these the first I ever saw, but nearly all that I have seen since are near here, at the beginning of the descent to Fusagasugá. In these two localities I have seen quite a number of species of different genera, though all alike in habit, and undistinguishable except by close observation. It is a little curious that Humboldt seems to have found but a single fern in all the bounds of New Granada. They are very abundant and varied, both in the valley of the Cauca and in the neighborhood of Bogotá.

Tequendama is one of the richest localities of plants that I have ever seen. The woods are damp, while most land at this altitude is dry. On four of the five days I have spent here, I have literally loaded myself with rich specimens. For some I have had to reach far over the abyss, in a position in which caution is instinctive. But there is much here that I can not get, and some plants in fruit to which, I fear, I shall not soon get a clew. Here grows the granadillo, of which I saw a dead trunk, but could not identify a living tree. If it is not the Bucida capitata, I can not tell what it is: it is almost impossible to identify woods that you see worked here. I can not tell this from rose-wood by any recollections that I have.

Before leaving the falls, I suggest some facilities that should be provided for visiting them. A visit should be made early in the day. The nearest place where you can be sure of spending the night is Soacha, and you may not be comfortable there; and yet it would cost little to make visits here quite pleasant. The locks ought to be taken off the gates, and the wagon-road on the left bank thrown open to the public. A cottage with two rooms, and a shed for cooking, ought to be erected near the falls. A foot-bridge, or even a mule-bridge, should be thrown over the river a few rods above the fall. A mule-road should be made into the hollow below the falls, and from there up the chasm to the foot of the fall. Thus a cottage, a bridge, and a mile of mule-road are all that is needed to make the summit and foot of the falls alike accessible to persons from Bogotá and La Mesa.

The left bank belongs to the hacienda of Cincha, the property of a brother of Señor Umaña. The house is the nearest to the Salto. I had no introduction to the proprietor, but met with a dependant who occupies part of his house, whose conduct toward me was much more like a gentleman than a peasant. The superintendent of Cincha, Señor Abadía, appeared quite the reverse.

The hacienda of Tequendama is much farther—two miles—from the falls, but far more valuable, and better situated on the last nook in the plain. The saw-mill was a curiosity. It had a large breast-wheel, which, with its gearings, cost as much as the entire mill need to have done. It ran very slowly indeed, and did rather poor work. The quinine factory had been a grist-mill. Some part of the apparatus was quite costly; the rest very coarse, but sufficient. The director, M. Louis Godin, was a true Frenchman, kind, cordial, and active. His lady, who "could not be married to him for want of her certificate of baptism," was a good specimen of the Dutch negress. I am not ashamed to confess that I enjoyed her society very much, and I afterward took considerable pains to see her again. Even had I no worthier motive for appreciating her, the specimens of northern cookery she exhibited would have been very attractive to one who had been deprived of it so long. The quinine made here is not esteemed in Bogotá, but I am satisfied that it is skillfully made and pure, and, while there may be worse, there can be none better. The bark is pulverized entirely by hand, and comes from places in the mountains south of here, as nearly as I could ascertain. Every man keeps his own *quina secrets.*

On Sunday Señor Umaña came and paid off his laborers for the week. They must have been nearly a hundred in number. His counting-room contained two articles that surprised me. One was a coach, apparently in good order, that could be run to Bogotá any day, but which, I think, from force of habit, stands idle year after year. The other was Pope's Essay on Man, in

English. Such an unexpected addition to my religious literature was not to be neglected, so I took it up to the parlor, and read it through with great pleasure and profit.

CHAPTER XXI.

BALLS AND BULLS.

Cibaté.—Priest traveling.—Spinning.—Yoking Cattle.—President traveling.—Perpetual Rain.—Riding à la Turque advocated.—Carguero and Babe.—Sleeping in slippery Places.—Unnecessary Ascent.—Balls.—Bull-feasts.—Open Prison.—A Walk.—Rich Gardens, unfortunate Statesman, and frail Poetess.—Snails' Eggs.—Masquerades and April-fools.—Gambling.—Dr. Blagborne's Family.—Little Alice.

I LIKE to start early in the week. The Scacha mule-owner had promised to have beasts ready. We agreed on the price. I was abundantly satisfied with six dimes per beast from Bogotá to Tequendama, and unfortunately told the owner so. He demanded eight dimes from there to Fusagasugá. As I thought it reasonable, he added that he must count the peon as a beast, making thirty-two dimes instead of twenty-four. To this I assented, and he feared his generosity would be his ruin; so, when I sent for the beasts, instead of sending them, he sent word he must have ten dimes. He made me lose a day, but he, in turn, lost his bargain. I returned no answer, and when, the day after, he sent his peon and mules, another was loading my baggage for the trip.

Traveling south, I have had all the time at my left that chain of the Andes at the foot of which lies Bogotá. The western rim of the Basin of Bogotá might be considered as another and much lower ridge, which, having diverged from the other, has again approached it so as to leave room for a road, and handsome farms on each side of it. Nearly all the houses stood back at the foot of the hills. This arm of the plain proved longer than I expected. I found its end at Cibaté, where, however, there is no village.

At Cibaté I parted company with a priest—a fine, pleasant fellow—who had been settled at Pandi, but was now without charge. He invited me here to take some refreshment with him, to which I was not inclined. He was quite inquisitive about the United States, and wished to know if it would be long before the immigrant Catholics would be so far able to outvote the Protestants as to establish their religion by law.

PRIEST ON A JOURNEY.

I can not vouch that the above portrait was taken from this worthy subject, but it will do very well for him. His face is bound up to protect it from the dry wind and the intense light, one or both of which sometimes destroy the skin, and often chap the lips. Before him, on his saddle, is tied his bayeton, his defense from rain by day, and his blanket at night. His legs are defended by zamarras of dog-skin, and his hat by a funda, or case, made of oiled cotton—hule—or oiled silk. I judge his to be cotton, for it is of a dull red or brown.

Behind comes his peon with an enormous dog-whip—perrero—of which the handle is the toughest wood known here, if not to man. It is called guayacan, and is quite probably a Guaiacum. I have never been able to find it growing, nor get a stick of it entirely free from knots and crooks. It never seems to attain a diameter of more than an inch. The horse has evidently been making some trouble by following his nose off among the bushes, where he should not go, and is now taking the back track and also the consequences. On his back is a huge bag, called by the Moorish word almofrez, or, more properly, vaca—cow. The hide of a cow would be insufficient to make the bag, nor would the entire animal be sufficient to fill it. I have seen them as large as the largest feather-bed.

From Cibaté I rose till I had a fine view of the plain, of which we must now take a long farewell. Nothing but the cold makes it a glad one to me. As I left the hacienda, I saw the leaves of various plants nipped with frost, a rare occurrence, indeed, but one that may happen any month in the year, not only under the mist of Tequendama, but all over the plain. I confess I am anxious to reach a more genial clime.

As I passed along, I saw a woman going from one house to another, spinning cotton as she went. There are many species of Gossypium growing in Tierra Caliente, but those that are most resorted to, I can not say cultivated, are large shrubs, with quite a scanty fibre. The apparatus for spinning is a stick, with a potato or other weight stuck on the lower end. It has this superiority over all others, that it needs no machines for picking and carding, is the cheapest and most portable in the world, and is not liable to get out of repair. Further, to spin street-yarn must here be rather a meritorious act.

Near the very top of the hill I saw a man yoking oxen. One had been caught with the lazo and tied to a post, and the yoke tied to his head. The other was dragged to the spot *vi et armis*, and his horns securely tied to the same straight stick called a yoke. They could not move their heads a particle, nor look behind them; but when angry, they could look daggers at each other with one eye apiece. They are said to make a queer use of the yoke in some parts of the country upon the páramos. They have a long yoke with an ox at each end.

When they catch cattle for slaughter, they hold the victim down by keeping his heels stretched out behind till the centre of the yoke is brought over his head. He is raised on his fore feet, as horses (not cows) rise, while his heels are held fast till his head is secured to the yoke immovably. They are then released, and his new acquaintances show him the way home in style. There is no love lost between them on the way, but the recruit's volition is of very little consequence.

I now lost sight of the plain, and of my little peon and his three little mules, for he took a spare one in case of accident. He came in next morning. I descended, rose and descended. The road might still be called a carriage-road, but of the worst description. Here I met the President's Lancers, who have been tagging after him during a fortnight's relaxation at Fusagasugá. Soon after came the President, accompanied by an officer. I exchanged a few words with him, and farther on met his baggage, with a lancer or two.

Soon the road grew worse than any I had yet seen, though nature had thrown no difficulties in the way. I thought a company of sappers would have been more useful to the President than lancers.

Here I came again to the gray woods. The effect on the landscape was that of an immense quantity of Spanish moss, or of Usnea barbata at the North, but the cause lay in no one thing. Then came the tree-ferns, and some huge stalks of what I guess to be achipulla, the root of which is eaten by bears and men. I have never seen the growing plant, which is eight or ten feet high, but I think it is Amaryllidate or Liliate.

The road now grew damp, nay, absolutely wet. I had passed the Boca del Monte—the mouth of the woods. Then came a clear open space, made for or by the resting of travelers. In solitary roads these are called contaderos, or counting-places, because here they count their company, to see that no essential individual, quadruped or biped, is missing.

At the contadero a large assemblage of little crosses announced that I stood at the summit of no common ascent. Whether it was because I erected no cross I know not, but the descent seemed to me interminable. Here, it is said, no man passes without being rained on. Whether this means that it rains there all the time, or only when it catches a man worth wetting, I know not. I received this time the fewest possible drops to make good the assertion. I have passed there four times since, and have had no farther occasion to complain of neglect. Once, indeed, I caught it essentially. I had slept little the night before. It rained monotonously. The road, which ordinarily seems like riding down the Bunker Hill Monument after some earthquake had displaced half the steps, was worse than usual. The poor mule, who had the responsible task of bringing me down to the bottom, to warmth, and to sunshine, was tasked to the utmost.

I was not labeled "*keep dry*," but only "*with care*," and while he was doing his whole duty I fell asleep. His back was generally at an angle of 45° with the horizon; mine had subsided into so many curves as would bring my shoulders nearest the saddle. How long I slept, or of what I dreamed, I have no idea; but I waked to find that my encauchado had slipped forward, so that a stream from my hat was running through the head-hole and down my back to the saddle.

Descending, still descending, like riding down an interminable Bunker Hill Monument or a Trinity steeple as high as *Jack's bean*. Here I met women riding *à la Turque*, or, more directly speaking, astride. Near Bogotá this is not practiced much. Not one woman in five does it, and those who claim to be ladies *par excellence* will not own that they ever do it except in the roughest roads. But it does not appear to me ungraceful, still less disgraceful. You see no more of the rider's ankle than she chooses; she is less exposed to awkward accidents, and is delivered from those really dangerous riding-dresses of civilization. She does not ride with her chest twisted, and has her animal more at command. In fact, the bifurcate construction of man is his charter of supremacy over the brute race.

Infancy must not be trusted to the risks of a horseman's arms here. A more secure conveyance is exhibited in the plate on the following page. This worthy descendant of the Muiscas, that has taken off his hat to you, says, "Sacramento del altar." The whole phrase, if he ever said it, would mean, "Praised be the holy sacrament of the altar!" Your answer should be, "Para siempre"—"Forever." Perhaps you assent to the efficacy of the mass in this response.

CARGUERO AND BABE.

He carries a box, with pieces of hoop nailed on to support a cover and curtain of cloth. The whole thing was extemporized in half an hour. Within is a babe, an unconscious traveler, whose mother is half an hour behind, for she rides a quadruped.

Descending, still descending. But "it is a long lane that has no turning," and, however illimitable moral descent may be, physical downhill generally stops at the least when it has reached the ocean level. Once I caught a view, through a gap of trees, of the mountain beyond, and of the distant plain. I was in a deep shade of trees and clouds; the distant scene lay in bright sunshine, but covered with a mantle of that blue scarcely ever seen except upon mountains. No painter would have dared to color it as I saw it. It looked like heaven.

Descending, still descending. At last the descent became more reasonable, such as a carriage-road would delight in, and I rejoiced over my task as accomplished. In this frame of mind I caught sight of a respectable mountain in front of me. I was about on a level with its summit, and it was too obvious that I must go to the foot. Again I began to ride down stairs, determined that my patience should not fail again till I had reached the very bottom. At the foot of the mountain opposite me I reached a stream, and in a spirit of leisure and thankfulness ate some hard-boiled eggs, which the kind and provident Joanna had put into the pockets of the saddle, and then slowly set forward. Three disagreeable surprises now came upon me in succession: that I had yet an immense descent to make; that I had to climb the opposite mountain before descending; and that night was to overtake me in the mountain.

This ascent was entirely unnecessary. A shorter road could be made around the mountain than over it. The Spaniards had an aversion to roads on the sides of mountains. This unnecessary ascent was so great that it would be a prominent event in an overland journey from Boston to Oregon. It is not equaled by that of Mount Holyoke—if, indeed, by that to Catskill Mountain House.

I reached the top just after sunset, and again the short tropical twilight revealed the plain in indescribable loveliness. A vexatious but whimsical affair diminished by an hour or more the length of my night ride. I had been very tender of my little horse—a weakness to which I confess I am subject, because "the merciful man is merciful to his beast." I had more than once attempted to lead mine, but he elongated his mortal frame as if consenting that his nose might reach Fusagasugá that night, provided I would allow his body till next day to overtake it. And he held back, giving me the labor of partly transporting him, till my strength and my patience were both exhausted.

Just at dark the idea occurred of driving him. I fixed the bridle securely to the saddle, cut a switch, and placed myself in the rear. The plan worked admirably. We got along better than at any time since we had left the plain. It soon occurred to me to see if I could catch him again, and I found my pony liked the new arrangement so well that he meant it should be a permanent one. Nay, he even proposed quitting the highway entirely for the fields and woods. This I prevented by some active steps. When I quickened my pace, the way pony marveled over the huge rocks was edifying. I had wet one foot, and, I fear, lost some of my patience, when, by a sudden motion, I seized a rein and brought him to.

If the reader supposes I rode at the same delicate pace the rest of the way, he knows little of human nature. The merciful man does not treat all beasts alike, and, had not the rider been under obligations to be merciful to his own neck, this particular beast would have suffered some.

At Fusagasugá I found the Church in full blast with explosive rockets, whirligigs, and other fireworks letting off outside, for it was the eve of some saint. I rode past all this, and in the bosom of an English family, entire strangers to me, I found satisfaction enough in one hour to repay me for the day's ride.

By daylight, the plain, instead of paradisiac alluvium, proved to be diluvium, or drift of rather a diabolic kind, for it was thickly strewn, in some places almost paved, with huge stones. Nor was it horizontal, but descended rapidly toward the River Fusagasugá, which lay at the foot of a ridge of the mountain, and ran west. The plain lay between this ridge and the one next interior or southeast of it, and might itself be considered as one of the many spurs sent down by the latter ridge, all terminating at the base of the former.

Fusagasugá is an ugly-looking town, lying at the upper end of the plain, adjoining the mountain, as all Spanish towns generally are. With one exception, there are no houses but mud cottages. I can not solve the politico-economical problem of the existence of the town, as there are not visitors enough to aid it essentially, and there is not industry enough to support it. These puzzles are driving me to the conclusion that the Granadino earns little and spends little, and, rather than work, will endure the ills of poverty. Nearly every house in Fusagasugá is a tienda, a regular tavern minus lodging-rooms. The rooms are two, besides, perhaps, a kitchen in the rear. One is the store, in which the customers are admitted only just within the door; the other a parlor, scantily furnished. The floors are mostly of earth.

I spent most of the holidays at Fusagasugá, but saw little to interest me in the village. I absented myself from the pleasant family long enough to see a part of three balls, held in the parlors of friends. They were solemn affairs, both the dancing and the sitting still. The ladies sat by themselves, and, with the children, filled nearly all the seats. The music was from two clarinets and a tamborine, for the "Brighton of Bogotá" can not boast a fiddler. Very little beauty was present, and a decided amount of ugliness. The morals of the place are said to be in so happy a state that there is not a female in the place whose character is such as to exclude her from these reunions, to which neither invitations nor partners are requisite.

The figures are not always well understood, and very few went through them manifesting any other motive than a sense of duty. In solemnity and gravity, however, they do not exceed the upper classes in New-York, who deem enthusiastic dancing vulgar.

One of the balls had a supper of hot roast meat and turkey, with quantities of pies seasoned with garlic, and dishes flavored with lime-juice and capsicum. The ladies ate first. One gentleman, in helping the ladies, helped himself also. He had in his hand a double joint of turkey. When a piece was nearly cut off, he would offer it to a lady, who would take it in her fingers. When his own piece was nearly off, for want of another hand, he took it in his teeth, and then went on with grave impartiality to help the next. A lady wanted drink. A gentleman held a cup to her lips, and, as she drank, made the noise nurses make when inviting babes to drink. In all this there was a vein of humor, in strong contrast with the general solemnity of the performances.

I learn that the gentleman distributing the morsels of turkey is an illegitimate son of President Santander. I had seen, in the Cemetery of Bogotá, a monument to "the legitimate son of Santander," but did not think at the time that the spiteful epitaph meant to insinuate that he had illegitimate children also; but unexpectedly I saw here the living monument to a fact that does not tend much to diminish the respect with which Granadinos look on the "Man of the Laws," claimed by many to be the greatest man ever born on Granadan soil. The young man bears his father's name. I last met him here in the Valley of the Cauca, with five others, having in their charge an immensely valuable assortment of Church trappings of every description, which they were exposing for sale in every place between Bogotá and Quito.

The Christmas ball was at its height when the church bells rattled out the time for cock-mass. All parties went to church re-enforced by the ascetic part of community, so as to make a respectable congregation. The same musicians went into the choir with their clarinets and tamborines, and gave us the same or similar tunes. The priest had in his lap a doll or image of a boy, which a large number crowded round to kiss. Then came a procession as far as the church door and back to the altar. A long mass followed, and all parties, sleepy enough, went home and to bed.

Sabbath brought no intermission either to billiards or balls. I regretted not going on Sunday evening, just for a moment only, to see the Cura officiating as "Ensign (patron) of the Ball," a fact of which he assured me himself afterward. This is also the market-day of Fusagasugá. Such an annoyance can never be understood by description. But if one could see, as I did, the ladylike daughters of my host patiently engaged for an hour, or even two, in a repulsive duty that could not be delegated to servants nor adjourned to another day, you would feel that the nuisance is beyond Christian endurance.

The mass and market occurred together, of course. I would not uncover at the elevation of the hostia, and generally was out of the market at that time, so as not to offend the faithful. Once, indeed, while I was with one of the ladies in market, we were caught by a procession which came out of the church and went round the square. I did not remove my hat. Fortunately, no fanatic who would dare interfere saw me. Many are in favor of prohibiting all processions out of church.

Christmas is the season of bull-fights at Fusagasugá, an amusement forbidden at Bogotá, on account of the sacrifice of human life with which it is frequently attended there. They were busy inclosing the square in front of the church with a pole fence on Sunday. I had determined to witness this sport, notwithstanding the cruelty of it. Both the sport and the cruelty I found were entirely imaginary, for the accompanying sketch is rather an idealization than a fair specimen. This bull in the picture happens to be uncommonly fierce, and not to exhibit that

THE BULL-FEAST.

spirit of meekness that I generally have observed in animals occupying his position. After one or two irresolute pushes at his tormentors, who invariably dodge him, he often becomes so obstinately quiet that he will even let you throw fire-crackers under his feet without deigning to respond, except by a look of sullen contempt. The toreador does not now bear the name matador, for he no longer kills, though he sometimes is killed, but always by accident. He bears no weapon, but often has his ruana in his hand, which he manages to throw over the bull's eyes, and then there is the fun of seeing him get it off without tearing it, perhaps. You will not fail to notice that the tips of the bull's horns have been sawed off.

But our bull in the engraving seems to be thoroughly roused. While prostrate and held by lazos, a belt was put around his body, and that chap, with a spur on his naked heel, sprung upon him as they let him up. That man in a heavy bayeton has got a lesson. He will, in future, take care not to encounter the foe when neither in a condition to fight or fly. Indeed, I can not say but that he does the latter as it is, but he seeks no safety in that flight. Now he is after the cachaco. Oh, if he could only get one horn into that hated coat, the amusement of the crowd of ruana-wearers would be complete!

I have seen bull-fights, as we call them in English, till I am tired of them. It would be better to call them bull-feasts, as a translation of the Spanish expression of fiesta de toros. The only thing objectionable about them is the waste of time, and the danger to which the toreadores expose themselves. Most of the toreadores are graziers, who need to understand how to conduct in the presence of a bull. I know of a lad of 16, who had a bull fastened to the horn of his saddle, when his girth came loose, and the bull pulled him and his saddle off the horse. In such a case, if you can foil the bull with your ruana a little, he will turn his attention to some other pursuit more agreeable to you, if not better for him. At any rate, the bull has the safest game of the two, though not the most agreeable.

I visited the cantonal prison in Fusagasugá with more indignation than any other I ever saw. We came to the door, and saw quite a number of men inside, who invited us to walk in, and we did. "Where is the Alcaide?" asked my friend.

"He is out in the street, Señor."

"And leaves you here without locking you in?"

"What would be the use of locking us in, where we can get out when we please? We could dig through the walls, or break the rods of the window; and the fence between the yard in the rear and the woods beyond would not stop a hog."

"Why, then, do you not escape?"

"It is against the law, Señor."

"Evidently this is wrong," said I to my friend. "A man who can be kept in this mud shell ought to be at large on parole. It is a cruel mockery to shut a man up by law in a room, and leave the doors open."

Most of these men had been charged with the theft of a quantity of cinchona bark. Had they been guilty, they would have run away. So this prison is a test as infallible as that for witchcraft used to be. Tie the accused in a sack, and throw her into a pond: if she drown, it will be a sign she was innocent. Commit a man to the prison of Fusagasugá, and if he does not run away, you may be sure he ought never to have been arrested.

All through these forests east of us are cinchona trees. It is very difficult to ascertain any thing of the trade, for all the land that bears cinchona is private property, and the gatherers—quinquineros—often find it to their advantage to take the bark to a man who does not own the land. Even the legitimate trade is kept as secret as possible. The consequence is, that I have seen the flowers of but two cinchonas, and of both the bark is worthless. All my efforts have only once enabled me to see a small tree of a good kind.

At the lower end of the plain is a hacienda called Novero. It has an extensive patio, and most of the family rooms are arranged around it on the ground floor; but there is a second story of a single room, and the roof extends over a considerable space outside of the room, making a delightful walk in the open air. Never was there a more beautiful climate than that of Fusagasugá. Twice have I celebrated New Year's here by bathing in a stream of delightful temperature, and thinking of snow at home. It is just at the upper limits, or rather above the convenient culture of cane, plantains, and oranges, and for these I would submit to a slight increase of heat.

This I found at the Chocho, a hacienda of the late Don Diego Gómez, three miles southwest of Fusagasugá, on the banks of the Fusagasugá. Four walks that I took down there will remain for a long time as very sunny spots in my memory. They were almost enough to make one forget home for a time. I went in different company on the different visits, and if the fair pedestrians ever read the paragraph which commends their prowess in a six-miles' walk, I hope they will forgive this allusion to "the memory of past joys pleasant and mournful to the soul."

The picture will not soon fade from my mind. The oak-crowned mountain, that rises above Fusagasugá on the east, sends down a stream that, by its convenience, determined the location of the town. Descending still, it enters a tangled hollow, called the Magué, from some fine Fourcroyas that grow there. Farther down, clearings are made in this thicket, and some cane-patches squeezed in, not for sugar, but for feed. Thus it hurries down to the Fusagasugá at right angles to the river, and to the long, straight hill beyond it, where stands the miserable little town of Tibacui—miserable, at least, for its drunken priest, who goes from the correction of the stocks to the altar, and from the altar, on Sundays, to Fusagasugá to gamble and drink. I saw him once ride past me on the Sabbath drunk, as my companions said, but I had not noticed it.

Fusagasugá stands chiefly on the right bank of the little brook, but the road to Tibacui and Mesa (distant 39 miles scant—but 17 hours) crosses the stream on a narrow bridge just below, and follows down the left bank. For half a mile the road is fenced out like country lanes at the North, but innocent of wheels. You pass several cottages on the left, among them one that belonged to General O'Leary, the British minister. The lane ends with a gate as you enter the estate of Novero, and pass down the green slope, leaving the buildings some way to your left. Long and sweet was the path down this sunny slope till we came to some tuna (Opuntia) plants, with ripe red fruit as large as a small pear, and beset with fascicles of spines exactly like those of our prickly-pear at home. The fruit has neither sweet nor acid enough to make it very good, but it can be eaten, and therefore must be. A dozen of them, when freed from the terrible microscopic spines, are not worth one good orange from Fulton Market, and the removal of the spines is no trifling task; but, as the fruit must be eaten, it must be done. My epicureanism was rewarded with one persistent little spine in my palate, that defied all my efforts at extraction, till I had vowed never to pick and shave another tuna for myself or for any girl living.

Another fact was impressed on me. I had adopted the plebeian chaussure, alpargates; and, as one of the long spines of a fallen tuna stem made its way between the braids, and penetrated deep into my sole, I was convinced that, excellent as alpargates are for ordinary walking, they are a poor defense against thorns. Farther on I saw another plant, that was remarkable for sending down a bunch of flowers on a peduncle as large as a pack-thread, and six feet long. The flowers are followed by pods covered with a velvet of microscopic barbed spines, and containing large, round, flat seeds. It is one of several species of Mucuna, called here pica-pica, and, from the form of the seeds, ox-eye—ojo de buey. They may all be called cowhage.

The path descends much more slowly than the stream till it reaches a point of the hill where it must almost leap off. You involuntarily pause here to feast your eyes. You trace the straight course of the Fusagasugá, running at the base of that long hill opposite to us, without a gap or a spur for 15 or 20 miles. On the right the valley rises gently till it reaches the woods that cover the steep ascent to the Sabana, while far away to the left you see an opening where it empties into the Suma Paz just before reaching the Plains of the Magdalena. I think it was on the banks of the Fusagasugá that I ate my eggs in my descent, and that a carriage-road might strike it high up near where it issues from the woods. The distance to Bogotá would be about the same, 25 miles, but the time might be reduced from eleven hours down to six.

At the foot of the hill is a bridge across the brook, and another over the Fusagasugá, and then a little below is the Hacienda of the Chocho, so called from a species of Erythinia, a small tree with beautiful scarlet flowers. Señor Gómez might have been an eminent statesman. He had enough learning and talent for it, and, it seems, too much interest and patriotism. He was charged with a complicity with that attempt to assassinate Bolívar that failed on the 26th September, 1828. His trial for it was unsatisfactory to both prosecution and defense, and the sentence worthy of a dictator. "Forasmuch as nothing appears against Diego Gómez, he is condemned to three years' surveillance at Turbaco."

"I am splitting my brains," says Don Diego to the officer who was carrying him to Turbaco, "to find out the logic of that sentence, *Forasmuch as* nothing appears against me, *therefore* I am condemned," &c.

"Never you trouble your brains," replied the official; "the nation never will be ruined for want of logic! (This is literally true, for Bacon never has supplanted Aristotle here.)

Three years brought great changes. He left his lady, Señora Josefa Acevedo de Gómez, an estimable poet, worthy of the companionship of Mrs. Hemans and Mrs. Sigourney; he found her the mother of a babe conceived in his absence. They separated. He became a sot. She retired to a home in the edge of the vast Andine forest, a few hours from here, where she pours out the bitterness of her soul in touching strains, demanding of Death why he takes the happy and the hopeful, and overlooks her. (See Acevedo, in the Parnaso Granadino.) Their estimable daughter married beneath her family, it was said, and, though her husband is a worthy man, she was not permitted to bring him to the Chocho. I write these things more freely, as in these few days news has reached me that the unhappy husband and father has left this world. The son-in-law proves a worthy successor of Señor Gómez in the particular in which I esteemed him most—the cultivation of fruit.

I have said that gardens are unknown in New Granada. At the Chocho are three, all with high walls, and padlocks on the gates. Without these, fruit can not be cultivated. These gardens contain nothing but perennials, chiefly trees, for monocarpous plants can not be kept up where all labor is spasmodic. As all other mammals are kept out by hedge, gate, and padlock, the most formidable foe that invades the premises is the bat. They come in myriads of myriads, and, of course, in the night. Human weapons are as powerless against them as against locusts. The pomarosa is their first choice. It is a Myrtate fruit, perhaps Eugenia Jambos, of the size of a small peach, and with a slight flavor of wintergreen. Between bats and children, I never expect to see a ripe one. In default of this, they even attack the mango—Mangifera Indica. This fruit, of the shape and size of a pear, but with the large end attached to the stem, is a decided favorite in the tropics, though I can not forget how it has been described as a mixture of tow and turpentine. You must learn to overlook these two ingredients, which are never entirely absent, but not always prominent.

Another fruit that I saw here for the first time is the madroño, Theobroma arborescens. It is built on the plan of the cacao, but, as it is no larger than a plum, it has but two or three large seeds, and a scant pleasant pulp that scarce pays the trouble of eating. It is from a fine, handsome tree. Of oranges there was no end to the variety. Dr. Gómez had some slips of red currant that he was anxious to make live. He had several date-palms growing, but they were not old enough to be sure of their sex. Some fruit-trees I have seen nowhere else, and therefore pass them unmentioned and undescribed, for what is common must take the precedence of what is rare.

These gardens are famous for snails, Bulimus oblongus, that are as large as a goose-egg, and themselves lay eggs as large as those of sparrows. By the kindness of the family I secured quite a number of them, in the faint hope that they may reach the seaboard.

The festivals still continued: the 28th of December is the Innocents' day, or the commemoration of the children slaughtered by Herod. Persons take the liberty of acting in some respects like children in honor of the day, particularly in what we would call April-fooling. When a person is victimized, he is told to consider himself an Innocent—"téngase por Inocente." The same idea runs through some satirical poetry. One, for instance, devotes a stanza to our friend López. In English and Spanish it might run thus:

El que por ser Presidente Creyó así gozar del mando, Y es juguete de algun bando Téngase por Inocente.	Let him who thought the land to rule When he became a President, But finds himself a party's tool, Regard himself an Innocent.

I shall not to describe the grotesque masquerades that held possession of the streets by day and partially at night. The Yankees can beat them when they try; but the masquerade ball of the evening did not deserve the name. A man who had sewed some bands of white on the seams of his clothes, or a lady who had dressed her hair in calico, was considered to be in masquerade. It is noteworthy that this, which I intend shall be the last ball I ever attend in my life, was held in the very same house where I attended my first, and from which I went to cock-mass 369 days before. They are essentially dull and tedious, and even the first did not pay me for the trouble by gratifying any curiosity, and all since have been visited only from a sense of duty to my readers, to see with my own eyes what I describe.

It was Saturday night, and I fell into conversation with the priest, who never fails to attend.

"Do you not need to be preparing for the Sabbath?" I asked him.

"I am preparing for it," he replied.

"How! Do you call this preparing?"

"Why, the mass on fiestas is much later than on other days, and I should be very hungry were I not to eat just before midnight, as it is forbidden to say mass after eating."

"And if there be no ball?"

"Then I go to the billiard saloon, which is always open."

"But if you swallow a single mouthful after midnight?"

"I take care about that, for I have a good watch—a rare article in this country, you know; but if I should find I had done so, I would not consecrate the hostia I consumed at that mass."

"I understand: you would say, in place of the words of consecration, *Panis es, et panis manebis*—bread thou art, and bread thou shalt continue to be. But would that mass have any efficacy for those that heard it?"

"None at all. But I would not say those words; they are a mockery. I might say even the precise words of consecration with the special intention of *not* consecrating, and it would not be consecrated."

Quite a group had now gathered round us, for it was in the

interval between two sets, and I changed from Spanish into Latin, and proceeded: "I wish to ask you one more question. Do your canons, like those of Moses, require abstinence from women, as well as from food, previous to officiating?"

"The canons require that at all times, and therefore contain no special injunction on this point. An infringement does not invalidate the mass."

"Then, an hour hence, unchastity would be a less sin than the eating of a cracker?"

But it was too evident that our Latin was understood by the by-standers, from the close analogy of the Spanish, and I could press the good priest no farther.

Street gambling of various kinds, by the light of flaring tallow candles, helped to add to the liveliness of the nights. Most of these games appear peculiar. A favorite game was called lotería. I could look over the heads of all the company that surrounded the little table, where each of a definite number of players had staked his cuartillo, and had a card with a series of pictures on it. The pictures were in different order on every card. The same pictures, on blocks, were in the dealer's bag. He puts in his hand and draws out one, and calls out, in a loud, drawling tone, "Chulo chupando tripo"—"Gallinazo eating entrail." Each player lays a grain of maize on his copy of that interesting picture. The dealer lays down the block and draws another, always using several words in proclaiming it. At length a lucky fellow cries out "Loteria!" He has four grains in a row. The dealer ascertains that the four corresponding blocks have been drawn, gives him all the cuartillos except one, and makes up a new game.

I can not think the remark of a traveler (Duane) correct, that the Bogotanos come to these places to gamble because they are ashamed to do it in Bogotá. I fear it can not be denied to be a national vice, too common to excite shame. They come here to enjoy themselves, and gamble because they enjoy the occupation.

I must leave Fusagasugá, but I should do too much violence to myself were I to do so without mention of the family to whom I owe more than I can ever repay. Dr. Joseph Blagborne came out from Great Britain in the service of the Santa

Ana Mining Company, which he left on account of a difference with the resident agent, I believe. He practiced medicine a while in Bogotá, but, when he became a citizen of New Granada, he received a beautiful piece of ground two hours from here, and is bringing it into cultivation. He is beloved, but not appreciated here. They know him to be benevolent and kind, considerate of the feelings of the poorest, but they do not suspect how much of thorough, real education there is sheltered in that cottage; they understand the gentleman, but not the scholar.

But he is not alone. Mrs. Blagborne and six interesting daughters, as thoroughly English as if they had been born in the Fast-anchored Isle or in Boston, make the weary traveler forget for a while that seas roll between himself and any land of homes. You would little suspect that they had some of them never seen a school, or a master, or a modern school-book. In the cultivation of their minds, his little garden at home, and that beautiful Eden guaranteed to him by the most liberal, if it be not the strongest nor richest government on earth, Dr. Blagborne finds that pleasure which gayer scenes and the rounds of fashionable folly can never afford.

Dear little Alice! what a sunbeam you have been across my path! How happy have been the hours we have spent in the thickets where heat and cold are alike unknown, where your quick eye hunted out for me the delicate fern, the minute passion-flower, and the well-hidden bird's-nest. And when a rare mistletoe hung provokingly just out of my reach, don't you remember how the forty inches of your little form, added to the height of my shoulders, just brought the fragile boughs of the parasite within the reach of your fingers and my herbarium? And now I am not ashamed to say that of all the inhabitants of this half continent I love you best.

CHAPTER XXII.

THE BRIDGE OF PANDI.

Hacienda del Retiro.—Slow Horse.—Probable Origin of the Bridge.—Humble Posada.—Bad Priests.—The Bridge.—Cemetery of Pandi.—District Prison. —A warm Walk and cold Ride.—Dull Horse and fragile Sticks.—Problem of Achilles and the Tortoise exemplified.

On my way from Fusagasugá to Pandi, I made a visit with Dr. Blagborne to his Haciendo del Retiro. It is a few miles south of Fusagasugá, and off the road to Pandi. It is a cove scooped out of the mountains, a beautiful gentle slope, but so shut in by abrupt and broken ground that ten rods of fence effectually protect a thousand acres from invasion. Bananas still grow abundantly here, where the tall, hollow stems of Cecropia peltata have fallen to make room for them. The yuca must stand here near its upper limit, but the potato and arracacha are in their perfection. The ground rises steadily to the east, covered with huge trees, that must include precious cabinet-woods, as well as an unknown quantity of cinchona. To the west the scene is different. You now look entirely over the hill beyond the Fusagasugá, and, when the weather is clear, the awful peak of snowy Tolima stands disclosed. But of the nearer world it is only a little that can be seen from here, and of human labors Dr. Blagborne can say, as he stands here, " I am monarch of all I survey."

I engaged, as guide and companion to Pandi, a hair-brained young fellow, an employé of the gobernacion at Bogotá, as he tells me. He regretted not having gone in his military coat, to show me how the people would take him for a recruiting officer, and fly to the woods. He mounted himself on an animal that had two faults: he was both lazy and lame, if not even worn out —destroncado. My own beast, thanks to a fair friend, a much better judge of horse-flesh than I, who kindly secured it for me, was as good as need be. We made an early start—that is, we were off before ten, and were soon on the edge of the inclined plane of Fusagasugá, where it is cut off by a large stream coming down from the hills.

Pandi is west of south of Fusagasugá, distant from 25 to 30 miles, over spurs of the left-hand mountain, while that on the other side of the Fusagasugá is uniform in its general direction, and with few projections. Each valley the road passes is sure to have a stream running to the right, where they unite with each other as they flow westward.

But now, from the summit of a ridge, we can look over a low spot in the left-hand mountain into an immense valley beyond, lying between that and a still inner range. Examine that spot, and it appears as if a large gap had been broken in the mountain, as by a blow from this side. What remains has the same slope on this side as the rest of the mountain, but on the other side the descent is steep and precipitous. The summit ridge there must be rather sharp.

But the basin within, where does it discharge its waters? Not to the north of this, I am certain, or I must have seen the pass, and crossed the stream between here and Bogotá. To the east? No, the eastern ridge here is still higher. To the south? That does not seem impossible, but if not so, no outlet is visible from here. If there be no southern outlet, the whole must once have been a mountain lake perhaps thousands of feet deep. Over this sharp ridge would be a good outlet for it, and if it be of the horizontal sandstone we often meet here, it might wear down rapidly. It might be cut down hundreds of feet, and even so deep as to drain the lake without increasing in width.

But can you see any evidence of the existence of such a stream? Not in the least, although a long space of the mountain side lies clear in view. Such a narrow channel, and so deep as this would be, must be exposed to land-slides. Such rocks as reach the bottom must share the fate of the original rock there, be pulverized and carried down. But suppose a mass of rocks should slide down too large to descend the narrow chasm? This might well be, and then we should have a *Natural Bridge.* Let us see.

But I was not destined to see that day. José's horse fairly gave out, and I mounted him on mine, and pursued my way on foot much more comfortably and rapidly. While daylight lasted I enjoyed myself. Among other bushes, I noticed a Euphorbia of poplar-like leaves, called, on account of its very poisonous nature, by the same name as the manchinael-tree—manzanilla. I think it is E. cotinifolia.

Each hill was lower than the preceding, and, thus descending, I reached Pandi at about 8 at night, and found posada at the house of the alcalde. It is a tienda, with a third room adjoining the parlor. A miniature chicken and a very clean wooden spoon (no knife or fork) were set on for my dinner, and for my bed was placed an ox-hide, afterward exchanged for a borrowed hammock. I asked for a chair to be put in the piazza, as this place is lower than Fusagasugá, and the night was warm. They had no chair, so they put out a bench, ten feet long, with no back to it.

Pandi has a church, but, at present, no cura. They sent away their last for various reasons; among others, chasing one of his flock with a knife when he was drunk. The people of Pandi were once cursed with the present incumbent of Tibacui. It is a great defect of the Romish system that it has no way of disposing of a bad priest. It can convert him to no other purpose, as we do a razor that will not shave. It can not kill him, as we do a horse with a broken leg. It can only maintain him as a gentleman at large, or make a missionary of him.

But the bridge. Well, morning has come, and, having taken a cup of chocolate, we will set off. The distance is a mile or more, in the same direction as yesterday, crossing in the way another stream, running, like all the others, to our right. The bridge itself, and the narrow chasm that it blocks over rather than spans, is sometimes passed without seeing it. This narnow cañon, as Frémont would call it, is said to be 300 feet deep, with perpendicular walls. Its general width appears to be from sixteen to twenty feet. I do not regard it as impossible that a human leap might clear the gulf. The structure is, as I intimated, in horizontal sandstone. The direction of the stream was N. by W., or 13 degrees west of north. Doubtless the bridge was the work of a land-slide, and so extensive must it have been that it has left four or five rods of the chasm covered over. Travelers tell you of how many stones the *arch* is composed. I should place no reliance on any such statement, had not Humboldt seemed to confirm it.

You are told that the lowest bridge is made by three enormous stones, that were falling simultaneously, and caught in the form of an arch there, the middle one being largest and highest.

Baron Gros, who has spent more time here than any other intelligent man, regards this lower bridge as a single cubical stone, too large to enter the chasm. Let us call it a stone of forty feet by forty-six; the northern end, down stream, much the lowest. Exact observations can only be made from beneath, for it is covered with vegetation so as to resemble part of an ordinary dry ravine. I am inclined to think there must be more than one stone, for near the middle of it is a hole two feet in diameter, through which we threw large stones down into the water.

Ascending to the upper edge of the lower bridge, you creep under an enormous flat stone, resting on the banks on both sides, and entirely free from the lower bridge. This enormous flat stone makes the second bridge, which may have been separated from that beneath it by earth at the epoch in which the whole mass descended together. This earth has since disappeared, leaving the stone, with its ends resting on the opposite sides of the chasm, while the rest of the slide descended partly into it. So we have a bridge over a bridge. It extends a little farther up stream, so as to cover the upper edge of the lower bridge.

On this broad stone lies a large quantity of earth, put there, I conjecture, to make a roadway, but this being found too low, a wooden bridge was built above of poles, covered with earth, as usual, and, what is unusual, protected by railings. One of these is necessary, for the broad stone and the wooden bridge are at the very upper edge of the land-slide, so that from the upper side of the bridge you can lean over the railing, and look perpendicularly down to the roaring river beneath. The Suma Paz would be a large stream if flowing in an ordinary channel through a plain—smaller than the Hudson, Connecticut, or Delaware, but as large as the Housatonic, Mohawk, or Merrimack. Humboldt supposes that here, swift as it is—a perfect horizontal cataract—it is about twenty feet deep. I have examined the river below, and think it quite probable.

I did not go below, thanks to my horse and other detentions, which rendered it impossible. Were the bed of the river but passable, a descent would amply repay all trouble; but, besides the fearful *suspense*, with 300 feet of water beneath you, you would find it impossible to pass from spot to spot, even on the same side of the stream. It is a task for a samphire gatherer.

On the shelves of the rocks, a little above the water (perhaps more than half way up), I saw the nests of the guácharo in great abundance. These nests appeared to be cones of dried mud, but even the little Dollond telescope I carried would give me but imperfect data by such a vertical view. On throwing stones down, the birds were aroused in immense numbers. I can not learn that a specimen has ever been procured from this spot, and it may not be the guácharo. It is supposed to be as large as a crow.

The bridge is at an altitude considerably below Pandi, for the thermometer at 10 o'clock was near 80°, higher than I have seen it since leaving Honda.

On my return from the bridge, I visited the most desolate cemetery I ever saw. It was an ellipse, that had been inclosed by a thatch shed, now broken down in some places, so that, as well as the chapel, it furnishes to cattle a shelter from the sun. There are no bóvedas—no monuments: every grave is trampled down by cattle, and the area is filled with long grass, and all as neglected as the tombs of Idumea.

On my return to Pandi, after using again the wooden spoon, I visited the District Prison. I spoke before of the eight national prisons of three kinds, and the thirty-one provincial prisons, which, however, contained (August 31st, 1851) but forty-three prisoners. The system requires also 99 canton prisons and 756 district and hamlet prisons, making a total of 894 of these benevolent institutions for a population of 2,243,730, or a prison for every 2510 souls. That of Pandi occupies the two ends of the Alcaldía. Of course, they never shut up a man in these card-houses: it would be ridiculous. They lay down a hide for him to lie on, and *put one leg in the stocks.* This would seem no joke to an American who had not yet had his trial, especially if, with this slight impediment to his marketing and cooking, it was still to be done at his expense, or not at all. The treatment of different prisons is different. In

Bogotá they feed the poor, but not sufficiently. The rules of the different provinces are different in this respect, nor can I, by any possibility, come at any general statement of them. I think in this province (for the canton of Fusagasugá was then in a province of Tequendama, since reunited with Bogotá) they give them water, and nothing more.

I started on my return about 11, leaving José, my horse, and my gun to follow soon after. So they did, that veracious individual informs me; but I waited for him at various points of the road, and when, unfortunately, I came to the other horse, my course was slower still. I wore out all the riding-sticks I could find. I begged a boy that overtook me on foot to cut me some tough ones, but they wore out like asparagus sprouts. I finally got tired of whipping, and, I suspect, the poor brute tired of being whipped. I at last required no more of him than that he should keep stepping, and with a moderate use of sticks as long as they lasted, I contrived to keep him up to the minimum of continuous motion.

It was quite warm when I left Pandi at 11 A.M. I started in my coolest trim, leaving all superfluous clothing for José to bring on. Now, as the sun was descending and I rising, the cold began to penetrate to my bones, but I had no way to keep warm but by my attentions to my horse. As José had also my money, I was under no temptations to extravagance, even had I been willing to delay for food.

Long after dark, I arrived at a bridge that I had noticed before as over quite a stream, and so long, so narrow, so high, and so slender as to make one's flesh creep. I have had to ride horses blind of one eye over such bridges, but that is dangerous: they always take such one-sided views of things. Of course these narrow bridges have no railings, for if they had, the baggage-mules could not go between them, as they would be too near together. I had no difficulty in keeping my terrapin on the narrow way over the trembling fabric till, after a long, long while, I no longer felt the ground sway under his reluctant steps.

I arrived in Fusagasugá between 9 and 10, having lost about half a mile for want of a guide. José arrived 10 minutes later. He "started about half an hour after me, came on smoothly and rapidly," and to this day "it is a mystery to him why he did not overtake me."

CHAPTER XXIII.

IBAGUÉ.

Sugar-mill.—Boqueron.—Ferry over the Suma Paz.—Melgar.—Immersion.—Custard by a Chemist.—A Ford.—Inquisitiveness.—Equivocal Generation.—Crossing the Magdalena.—Strait and narrow Way.—Espinal.—Live Snake.—Late Breakfast.—Conscience at a Ferry.—Ibagué.—Schools, Books, and Studies.—The Priest and the Cock-pit.—Extreme Unction, Coffin, and Grave.—Provincial Paper.—Blockhead Legislators.—Taxation.—Legislative Asses nearer Home.

Beasts are not dear at Fusagasugá when the right persons look for them. I paid to Pandi, two days, 60 and 80 cents; to Bogotá, for a week's absence, $1 20; and to Ibagué, five days' journey and back empty, $4 each. Ibagué lies on the western verge of the valley of the Magdalena, about 75 miles, air line, west of Fusagasugá. To reach it I must descend to within about 700 feet of the sea-level, and pass through the *torrid zone.* What sufferings I must endure from heat! What anacondas and boas, jaguars and pumas, I must kill or run away from! What perils from rattlesnakes, robbers, scorpions, centipedes, and other creatures of that ilk, I must encounter! I resolved to encounter all these perils on foot—yes, absolutely on foot, contrary to the advice of every friend I could consult. All urged me to abandon the idea. I was to be seized by fever; killed by heat; used up by fatigue, and exterminated generally. We shall see.

I took an early start from Fusagasugá on Tuesday, 11th January, with two good baggage-mules and a good peon. Said good peon failed to come in season, and my start was early only comparatively speaking; that is, I rose at 4, and left a little after 10. I had provided myself with bread and chocolate for five days, and a good-sized fowl—dear little Alice's purchase. Some meat was sent me, but it looked so green and smelled so strong that I sent it back, preferring to take my chance.

My first day's journey was on that inclined plane on the upper eastern end of which Fusagasugá stands. On my right I had the River Fusagasugá, and beyond, a chain of mountains almost without spurs. On my left was a stream formed by the union of all the streams I passed on my way to Pandi, all of which I then supposed flowed separately into the Fusagasugá. Beyond this, on the south, was a continual succession of spurs of the eastern branch of the Andes.

This plane is broken across in one place by a deep depression, from which you rise to La Puerta, the hacienda of Don Lucas Escobar. I had been before at his trapiche or sugar-mill, one of the best in the land. I know of but three that go by water. That at Cuni may be better than this. Señor Escobar's rollers are of iron, horizontal, and three in number. They are turned by an overshot wheel, and the juice runs directly down into the kettles, where it is boiled by the waste cane—basajo.

All the cane is brought on the backs of mules, and the number of mules so employed is considerable, as the field is enormous. The chimney is built at a distance from the house, and is very tall. The horizontal flue dries the fuel. Don Lucas takes the Correo de Ultramar, published in Paris. It is so rare to find a man who takes a paper here that the fact is worth mentioning.

The house at La Puerta stands on a very pretty table of land, at the foot of which, toward the Fusagasugá, lie the cane-fields and mill. It is not a pretty house, but rather a collection of huts. The plain on which it stands slopes to the west. It is very uniform in character, grassy, stony, and bosky. The whole day appeared like a walk for pleasure in a park, only the steady, gradual descent seemed too good to last—too much like the broad and easy road we are taught to shun.

My downward way had an unexpected termination, like many another. The path entered a clump of trees, and in a single rod I found myself almost surrounded by an abyss. I was on a point of land which had narrowed imperceptibly, till before me lay the Boqueron. This gorge appeared from Fusagasugá like a narrow plain between two hills, for the spot where I now stood seemed a part of it. Now it lay beneath me, a narrow, crooked chasm, just admitting a river to pass it.

I descended, crossed the united streams from the mountain spurs by a bridge of poles, and in a few rods farther came to the

Suma Paz itself, and waited at the ferry for my mules. I suppose this ferry is two or three leagues below the Natural Bridge. The stream itself is not so mild as to merit the name of Perfect Peace, which it borrows from the awful mountain height in which it rises. Here, perhaps, is the only spot above its junction with the Fusagasugá where it would admit a boat. I found it here quite rapid, broad, and over my head. Just below, after receiving the stream I crossed, it unites with the Fusagasugá, and below the junction bears both names. It preserves rather the direction of the Fusagasugá, but the Suma Paz furnishes much the larger body of water. As a whole, the junction of these three rivers resembles Harper's Ferry, perhaps the most romantic spot in the United States.

A Granadan ferry is a serious event in a day's journey. The mules are to be unloaded and compelled to swim, and this is said to fatigue them very much. The baggage is to be placed in a canoe and ferried across; all is again to be adjusted to the backs of the beasts. The more beasts, of course, the worse the detention. Now it fortunately came just at night, and the reloading was but partial. The fare is generally so high as to be something of an object to the treasury, to which it falls. Here it was a half dime for each person and mule-load.

We slept better for having the ferry behind us. There were two houses on the bank, and Roque selected the largest. My chicken and chocolate were placed on the fire as soon as the mules were put at ease, and I finished my dinner before dark. I had cut some candles into three pieces; one of these I now lighted, and read till I was sleepy, slung my hammock, and found myself more comfortable in it than I could have been in any bed in New York. Various hides were laid down on the earthen floor for the beds of the family and my peon. This is the bed of the Granadan peasant, and he sleeps on it in the clothes he wore in the day, and with no other devotions than crossing himself. Their practice of smoking in bed is very disagreeable to me.

I rose at daylight, my chocolate was made at once, and while the mules were loading I set out. As I intimated, I had to rise out of the gulf where I slept. This was pleasant enough for me, but a horrible thing for the poor mules.

At length I reached a point where I must take a last look at Fusagasugá. Beneath me lay the junctions of the three rivers, and the narrow channel by which they made their way to Magdalena. Beyond lay the sloping plain on which I journeyed yesterday, and at the farther end the mountains which formed the abutment to the plain of Bogotá. Far to the right I could just distinguish the walls of the basin from which the Suma Paz passes by its deep channel beneath the Bridge of Pandi.

On the left, the long, straight mountain, that formed the right bank of the Fusagasugá, had assumed a singular aspect. It was naked of vegetation, and black, and almost as regular as the roof of a house; but it was divided into large irregular patches by means of vivid green of uniform width, and apparently consisting of grass without bushes. The rock was of a basaltic color, but I believe it is old red sandstone, judging at a distance.

I turned. My view was limited by other mountain spurs, but I could see that the mountain opposite here receded from the river, leaving space for a plain of great height and width, as green and apparently as perfect as any lawn. Beyond, all was shut in with hills, as was also all this side the river, except a little valley of palms and tree-ferns.

In a corner of this valley was hidden a cottage at which I was to breakfast. Here I found two or three disgusting women; one making cigars with one hand, and holding a babe to the breast with the other. On the earth floor were two little girls about beginning to walk; one covered with dirt, the other with dirt and rags. Fortunately, I needed nothing from the house, and, after finishing my fowl with the aid of the two little monkeys, I went on my way.

A few ups and downs, and turns, opened to my view the broad, torrid valley of the Magdalena, varied by mountains, woods, meadows, and streams. I can not attempt to describe it. I can only say it was "wondrous fair." To this lower level we were now to descend just as the day was waxing warm. Now came the test. The *mula* that bore my trunks acted as if she was possessed. All along she had been in the practice of running on ahead, and when she had gained enough she would lie down, putting the peon to the trouble of adjusting her carga each time. Now she raced on, and we had enough to do to keep up with her. The streams we passed were numerous, several compelling me to denude my feet to wade across. At every stream I lost ground. The heat was increasing. At length the beast slackened her pace, and I entered Melgar ahead of her.

Melgar is one of those market towns whose existence is a nut for politico-economists. Imagine, in the middle of an uncultivated plain, a large town of mud and thatch, with a church, chapel, and public square, without a trace of industry. I begin to believe the story of two 'cute chaps, who, shut up in a room together, *swapped jackets* back and forth till each had gained five dollars. I was desirous that Melgar should gain something by me, but I sought meat, eggs, and fruit in vain. I ate here an orange, but it was so poor I ate it only out of politeness.

My mule recovered her spirits in the pause at Melgar. She trotted on till she came to a large stream, running, as all the others run, toward the river on my right. She crossed the stream, and quietly lay down on her left side, just in the edge of the water. My Endlicher, a twenty-dollar book, and the dried plants of the last month, were the chief sufferers. It was a long time before we came to a suitable place to stop, but we arrived at 4 P.M. at a very clean house, where I removed the encerado from the trunk, and exposed the wet contents to the setting sun.

I had bought eight eggs for half a dime before reaching this house. I sent a quarter dime to another place, and the messenger returned with a totuma of milk, and the promise of a like quantity in the morning. I had sugar with me, and, much to the interest of the family, I made a custard in my smaller kettle, which I put in the next larger, filled with water. A bath in the stream, in which my trunks had been dipped above, consumed the rest of the day. I found my custard creditable to a chemist, and my hammock all that a hammock should be.

The master of this family has several peons in his employ, but himself goes without clothing from his hips upward. I remarked to him that he certainly bore one mark of a Christian, a broad cross of thick black hair along the mesian line and diaphragm.

We started late in the morning on account of a violent rain all night, which ceased about 7, but rendered a stream ahead impassable. Having made another custard and taken my chocolate, I set forward. Near the stream I stopped at a house, breakfasted on my custard, opened my trunks to dry their contents. The quick eye of a woman who stopped there discovered an unusual stock of desirables, and she came to me asking a present to remember me by. She was one of the last Granadinas that I would care to remember, or be remembered by, but I judged it best to comply, so I gave her a *shell* of an abundant species, which had lost its operculum, telling her that at home such a shell would be treasured up with much care. This is the first application for a present I have received.

The water fell slowly, and I gave four men three dimes to carry my cargas across. The current was so violent that I could not stand in it, but they carried every thing across securely, and at dark I reached the banks of the Magdalena.

The road of this afternoon was diversified by winding round the bases of mountains. Two plants here interested me. One was of the Cinchonate Order, and had a sprig of small inconspicuous flowers, except that the lower flowers of the raceme had each one lobe of the calyx enormously elongated, and colored bright crimson. I suppose it to be Calycophyllum coccineum. I have seen it four times in all, but never have been able to save decent specimens of it. Those that I have I begged from the ornaments of a torch carried one night in honor of Santa Barbara. The other was a Dalechambia, of the Euphorbiate Order, and had what appeared a flower of two red rose leaves. Within was a large gland, with some staminate flowers on one side of it, and pistillate flowers on the other.

I passed a bank where a cow was eating clay, apparently pure and destitute of any saline taste. The bank had been eaten quite away.

I passed the village of Fusagasugá Ferry, so called because the road down the Magdalena there crosses the Suma Paz. I kept on my course without stopping, Roque being half an hour behind. I had got twenty rods from the last house, when a body of men came running after me, calling to me to stop. I asked the reason, but received no answer till they came quite up to me, when a respectable-looking gentleman, feeling called upon to answer, said that they feared that I would lose my way. I replied that I had no fears on that head, and offered to go on, when they opened on me a volley of questions, which would have convinced me, had I doubted, that curiosity is the peculiarity of no sex or nation. In short, the object of this expedition was to solve a problem that perhaps had never occurred to any member of it before—where a stranger *on foot* could have come from or be going to all alone. I gratified them in this, together with my business, aims, and prospects.

I stopped for the night at a nice-looking house, where the peon had to destroy $10 worth of cactus (Dunlap's estimation) to make the gateway wide enough for my cargas. The nice-looking house was occupied by two unmarried ladies and their babies. A hideous goîtred servant had hers (I think its father must have been blind, but you may judge for yourself) slung in a hammock in the room where I slept, and she herself slept on the floor.

GIRL WITH GOÎTRE.

Here I found that my bread, sugar, and chocolate had been immersed in the stream we passed. I dined on bread and chocolate only, with a little sausage. My sleep was a little disturbed by two of the babies, which cried in turns, and, after an early chocolate, we repaired to the bank of the Magdalena.

The river here is about as broad as the Hudson at Albany, and much more rapid. The canoe could not take all my baggage at once, and the delay was so great that it was about ten when we left the ferry. After this delay I was not in a humor to be fooled with. We were to travel in good earnest, and, if the sun scorched or the rain poured, so much the worse.

And the sun did scorch. We were traveling south up the river, having it on our left, and before us a limitless prairie, intersected by a few small streams of milk-warm water. The road down to one of these was so narrow that the mula contrived to fasten her two trunks in the banks, so that to advance or recede was impossible. I turned back, and found that Roque had released her, leaving the load in the form of a rustic arch across the road. While reloading, the macho went on and hid himself. We were making up lost time, and the sun was doing its best to keep us warm, when we entered Espinal at about 1 or 2 P.M. This is one of the prettiest and neatest towns I have seen in New Granada, and its shops were of a superior order. But how came it posted here, upon the naked, parched, and shadeless plain?

Making no delay in Espinal, we went on our burning way. It was the 14th of January, and if all my friends managed to keep as warm as I that day, great must be the virtues of anthracite. In fact, I began to fear that I should kill or cripple my beasts; and at length, meeting cargas that had left Ibagué that morning, I judged the surest way of reaching my journey's end the next (Saturday) night was to relent a little.

The heat of this day reminds me to speak of my dress. I doubt if I could have performed the journey with any boots or shoes to be found in New York. The alpargata, which I have already described, can not be surpassed in such service. My body was just covered with a single thickness of blue twilled cotton—the form of the dress almost exactly resembling the juvenile dress in which I gloried in my second year. To this was added nothing more than a belt and my hat.

A traveler makes a funny story out of a robbery he suffered in the plains of Mexico. An attempt to rob me would have been a better joke, for they left him with more than they could have found on me, especially as it devolved on Roque to carry my money and settle my bills. Except my hat, compass, knife, belt, and spectacles, the value of what I wore, when new, was $1 20.

I had begun my breakfast for to-day last night in good season. I had bought some eggs at noon when waiting for the water to fall, and at night beat them up with sugar. I found milk at the ferryman's after crossing this morning (a remarkable occurrence), and had just cooked my custard, when the peon was ready to start. I waited for the first good spot after I left Melgar, and breakfasted at 4 P.M. A large custard is not very nice after carrying all day tied on a mule's back under a vertical sun, but my appetite was good, and it passed for a late breakfast, but better than none. Late as it was, it was twenty-eight hours before dinner.

After breakfast I saw the first living snake I have met in this country, and as it is a *good sign* to kill the first snake seen every year, I did so. Before singing any pæans over my victory, I may as well give the dimensions of my foe. It was about six inches long, and a little thicker than a knitting-needle; I put it into my spirit-lamp to preserve it.

At dark I arrived at the River Coello. Here I found a tall man, naked except a handkerchief about his loins, standing on a stone in front of a house, talking with the proprietress. He offered to take my cargas across the stream on his shoulders. He appeared as nearly drunk as I ever saw a Granadino, and without answering him I went down to the river. He followed me, and as I saw there a good canoe, I let him pass. When the peon came up he found that there was no authorized ferryman. I explained to him that this did not forbid the owner of the boat passing us gratis, or, if no other way occurred, I would seize on the boat and ferry myself. But it was now night, and there was no denying that he and his mules were terribly tired, so we returned to the house.

Here I found a deaf and dumb girl, the first of this class I have met. I have before noticed the scarcity of lunatics; both of these classes will probably increase, the latter certainly, with increased cultivation of intellect. They were much surprised to hear of the education of the deaf and dumb.

Here I saw a sick babe, and I thought that those who are fond of a fling against the medical profession might read a lesson from the case. Among the lower people it appears as if the dangerous sickness of a child causes little anxiety, and its loss little grief; its burial is certainly a scene of rejoicing. It goes merrily to the grave with rites entirely peculiar, and bearing the name of a little angel.

I desired nothing after my four o'clock breakfast but chocolate and bread. Having repeated the same in the morning, as I could buy nothing here, I set forward with no breakfast in prospect till I reached Ibagué. A young man at the house, to save me from the crime of seizing on the boat, offered to ferry across my cargas for triple the price the law would allow a ferryman, and I permitted the peon to accede. I crossed in the boat, while Roque undertook to pass the horses below. He found it too deep, and I had to swim down and bring them across, with him clinging to the tail of the hindermost. He could not swim. So, after paying a triple ferriage across the river, I had to swim it twice.

The Plain of Espinal is bounded on the west by steep mountains of horizontal sandstone, with the Coello at their base. As we entered an indentation of the plain, it became stony and a little elevated. This was just as the sun lost its power last night. As it sunk behind the mountains, we descended to the level of the river, and ascended its right bank in a romantic glen. After crossing the river this morning, we rose to a narrow plain in the mountains where lies the scattered pueblo of Coello. Again I descended, reascended, enormously, as it appears, though to me it seemed much less than it really must have been.

Here I found a vast plain in the mountains, stony, in some places almost paved, dry, and scant in grass. It resembles that of Fusagasugá, but is more level, and is surrounded by mountains of entirely different geological character. It is bounded on the south by the Coello, which thus skirts two immense prairies, but shows itself to the traveler only in a broken valley between the two.

I stopped at a venta, where I could get neither milk, bread, meat, nor fruits. Eggs and salt I refused, and pressed on. Here my peon begged permission to fall behind an hour or so and rest his beasts. I consented, added a thin coat to my scanty clothing, entered an arm of the plain between two stoneless mountains, and discovered Ibagué at 4 P.M., cooped up in a little elevated plain between two spurs of the central Cordillera of the Andes. The town lies between the right bank of the Chiapala and the left bank of the Combeima, which here unites with the Coello. The Coello is here called the San Juan, and still above the Toche.

The expenses of this trip are rather a curiosity:

Two beasts and peon	$12 00	Eggs	$0 10
Bread	50	Milk	5
Chocolate	11	Guarapo	11
Fowl	20	Lodging and incidentals	00
Ferriages of self and cargas	85	Total	$13 97
Candles	5		

Excluding what would come under the term of fare in the United States, all that I could conveniently spend in four days was $1 12, and none of this was at places where I spent the nights. The peon paid the bill of the mules at the stopping-places, and provided for himself according to his fancy. He is bound to pay his own ferriage; and if the beasts are aided by the boats in swimming, he pays also for that, but the owner of the cargas pays the ferriage of them.

Although in these five days I saw no floor but earth, and but few tables (those not spread, except with my coarse utensils), no beds but dried hides, neither teacup, tumbler, metal spoon, looking-glass, newspaper, book, or pamphlet, it was one of the most delightful trips I have ever taken. When I found before me an ascent, I rejoiced. It promised me prospect and coolness. When I came to a descent, I rejoiced. It led to new trees and a purling brook. When I came to a plain, I wished I had a horse, to fly more quickly over it, but it would only have been to wait the longer for the mules. Had I been taken lame or sick, a horse could easily have been procured at any stage of the journey. And now I have proved my power of walking in the tropics, though I had been repeatedly assured I should find it impossible to walk.

I arrived in Ibagué on the afternoon of Saturday. Unluckily for the gentleman to whom I had a letter, I caught him in town, where he keeps in his house a dependant, a servant, and his little son, who attends school. He resides, with the rest of his family, in the country. Had his family been living in town, perhaps he would have been glad of company; had he been on his plantation, he would have escaped entirely. He could have kept me in his house, but it would have been only so much trouble and expense to be passed to the account of disinterested benevolence. Room in his house would have cost him nothing, had I sought my meals elsewhere, but that was not to be thought of; so he sent his son in different directions with little success. Ibagué has experienced two or three severe fires in as many years, and scarce a house has been rebuilt. In the midst of the search, an acquaintance passed the window. "Man," he called out, "do you know of a vacant house?" "No," he replied. "Will you have the goodness to look for one for my friend?"

"Why not, man?" was his cheerful reply. By the time the weary beasts arrived, the task was accomplished, the eating-place found, and all I had to do was to direct the unloading of my mules, and go to dinner about 8 P.M.

I fancied myself master of a large, deserted house. In a suite of three small rooms I found a bedstead of the usual construction—an ox-hide stretched like a drum-head on a square frame. This was all the furniture of the three rooms. The middle one had a door, the others windows, differing from doors only in having a grating to prevent entrance when open. Here I put my baggage, and slung my hammock in the parlor. I retired, sole inhabitant as I supposed, leaving the doors open for Roque. In the night I heard a tramping and clanking like that of a German ghost dragging his chain. It was not a ghost, but a man who arrived from the country, and was making his way, jingling his spurs at every step, to an adjoining apartment.

Daylight showed that some rooms were used as a carpenter's shop, and others by the proprietress (who kept a grocery) for preparing chocolate, baking bread, etc. Two or three fat hogs passed from the front door to the back yard when it pleased their fancy; the midnight comer's horse had the zaguan for his stable, with similar liberty of ingress and egress. The very hens flew out of the parlor windows when any thing in the plaza invited them. All was liberty, except for a fighting-cock who was tied to a stone in the patio.

Where I ate, several others also ate their solitary and sometimes scanty meal. They were young gentlemen, employed in offices in town. Of these chaotic meals I desire to retain no remembrance farther than that they cost me exactly 4 dimes per day. Latterly there were added to our number two others, destined to be my fellow-travelers all next week.

Sunday is market-day in Ibagué; but the market is scantier than that of Fusagasugá, a town of half the size. Besides the market, the other institutions of the Sabbath are two masses, a cock-pit, and billiard-saloon.

The limits of authority are very vague here, but the priest seems to have no protection from the lowest. The priest of Ibagué preached a sermon on the Sabbath that the governor did not like. He wrote him a letter about it. About the 1st of

January, 1852, the priest of Ambalema received eight dimes of a young woman whose child he baptized; the jefe político wrote to him to return the money. If a priest wishes to absent himself for four days, the governor ordains that he shall apply for leave to the alcalde of his parish. Thus the poor priest has three civil masters (four including the President), with an ecclesiastical head besides. The worst of it is, he receives contradictory orders, and is punished for disobedience of either.

Two interesting documents were read by the priest in the church at the Sabbath mass, both of which he kindly gave me. One was the *Allocutio* of Pius IX. on the affairs of New Granada, censuring the action of the government under Mosquera as well as López, and pronouncing certain unchristian laws null and void. The other was a circular enjoining faithfulness to religious duties during the approaching Lent. This last interested me chiefly for the signature, of which the annexed is a facsimile:

Domingo Antonio Riaño.

This flourish is called a rúbrica, and is the essential part of the signature. In a document of many leaves, every one ought to bear the rúbrica, but the last only requires the name and surname, and these may be, as in this instance, printed. In Bulls for eating meat, I have seen both name and rúbrica applied by a stamp. The rúbrica must have had its origin in the mark affixed by those who could not write their name, but it is now an additional security against forgery. Few are so complicated as the specimen above, but some much more so. They are placed under the name as well as after it, and no Granadino is satisfied with a plain signature and nothing more.

The public schools of Ibagué are the Provincial College, a boys' school, and a girls' school. I visited the latter on the third day of its session. It was the most pleasant sight I have seen in New Granada. The school had been burned out. It was now in a clean, new house. The girls were all seated on the floor in clean dresses, and as still and orderly as could be desired. Sewing and praying are two important branches in the female schools here. Fortunately, they were engaged in the former. Lately, theology has received a severe check in this province. The gobernacion has banished from all the schools the catechism of Father Astete, the longest, dullest, and most orthodox of all the school catechisms. There are not less than three others in the schools, but these are forbidden every day but Saturday. Some in these schools learn to pray, but not to read.

The girls in this school were all young—none, perhaps, as old as twelve. All were learning to read, but scarcely any two had the same book. They were as diverse in their topics as would be Baxter's "Saint's Rest," Gunn's "Domestic Medicine," "Report on the Tariff," Doddridge's "Rise and Progress," and Morgan's "Masonry Revealed." In one thing they all agreed: they were uninteresting to children, with perhaps one exception, a book written for the amusement of adults. A scandalous attack on the banished archbishop has been circulated by the government, and, it is said, used in schools as a reading-book. I do not doubt it, nor that the still more impudent attack on the government by the Pope will be found in the same schools. Such of the Spanish narratives of the Tract Society as do not attack the religion of this country would do good service. One of them, "Theophilus and Sophia," was read with much interest in a school in Bogotá. There is here a great want of children's books, and an absolute destitution of school reading-books.

Nor have they any good geography. In the colegio here it is not permitted to study geography till after algebra and geometry. I have a good test question: Where is Patagonia? Those who know are not surprised at my ignorance, as it is in South America, of which they suppose me profoundly ignorant. But in general I get, even from educated men, the conjecture that it is somewhere in Europe. One of the most intelligent of my acquaintances was talking to me of our Fishery Question, and I was unable to convince him that a British squadron was not stationed in Greenland. At this moment he thinks me badly posted up in this matter.

Their arithmetics are a phenomenon for the psychologist to explain. I should not dare to write a critique on one of them, for it could not be regarded otherwise than as an exaggeration or a caricature. Their slates were all destroyed in the fire, and there are no others for sale nearer than Bogotá.

The teacher was a pleasant-looking woman, with two children, a club-footed little boy of four or five, and a saucy girl of two. She has a husband, too (not a matter of course), Secretary of the Jefe Político, I think with a salary of $192.

I attended an examination of the Colegio Provincial, but my efforts to get an idea of the ordinary routine were in vain. One feature I think objectionable: the province paid the board of some of the pupils, while others, too poor to pay tuition, were refused admission. The school edifices were much more spacious than necessary, but not in good order.

The duties of curate here are discharged by a vicar, with a nominal salary of $480, and an assistant, at $240. The vicar I found a pleasant man, anxious to render himself agreeable. I called on him on Sabbath afternoon to return a book that he had lent me. I found him dining al fresco. I had dined, but ate a piece of an ear of roasted maize and some sweetmeats. He then invited me to go with him to the cock-fight. I did not consent, but went out with him. We were informed that the fight was over, and I went in with him. He was received as a boon companion, and immediately set himself to work to get up another fight for my *gratification*. This I thought was carrying politeness a little too far, but in vain were my protestations. I began to tremble for the result, for I would rather suffer any thing than be the cause of so much cruelty to two noble birds like one that I saw dead at my feet. But the reverend father's exhortations did not appear to have as much effect as when in the pulpit in the morning, and, to my great relief, I escaped without witnessing a cock-fight.

I was another time at the vicar's house, when he was called upon to administer the sacraments to a dying person. I begged permission to be present. "With pleasure," said he, "if you will only have the goodness, as a favor to me, to walk uncovered when I am carrying the Holiest." "Oh, as to that," I replied, throwing my hat in a chair, "do not be uneasy; the night is warm. I will leave my hat here." But neither proving too much nor conceding too much satisfies; so I had to take my hat, and enter a tienda till the Great Umbrella was at a sufficient distance.

Then, Peter-like, I followed afar off, till I came to a crowd kneeling before a small house. As I entered I took off my hat, of course. The small room had been temporarily divided by a curtain. Behind it was a neat little chapel, with a bed in it. This conversion of half a dingy cabin into a beautiful niche of a chapel, with crucifixes, saints, candles, and flowers, had obviously been the result of attentions and loans from the neighbors. Here the priest was hard at his work. The confession and absolution were all over, and he was praying like a locomotive. You can easily tell when a priest is using Latin, which occurs only once or twice a year. He reads only about eighty words to the minute. But the moment he strikes into a much-used place, he gallops off at the rate of 200, or even more. After reeling off thus what would cost me an hour to utter, he opened a small metallic snuff-box, broke off a piece of a wafer, and put it into the patient's mouth. More rapid Latin. Then he took a bottle of oil; into this he dipped a silver wire, and, taking into his hand a piece of cotton, he applied the oil with one hand, and wiped it off with the other. He applied it to the ears, eyes, nose, mouth, thumbs, and toes. All this was done in the most expeditious manner, and with a nonchalance that implied that the poor fellow was used to dying. The moment that the dying man had received the consolations of religion, the good priest and his sacristan gathered up their traps and were off. That night the carpenter was busy making a queer-shaped box. It was a coffin for the dying, made, one would fancy, from a misunderstood description of those used at the North. One of those who were keeping the carpenter in good company and good spirits was the father of the dying. The cemetery of Ibagué was beautiful 50 years ago, but is now in disgusting disorder. It is finely situated on a point of the plain that overlooks the Combeima, but is overgrown with weeds and bushes, and the tombs are neglected and dilapidated. Here they laid that strange-shaped coffin next day, for the young man was dead. The priest did not come.

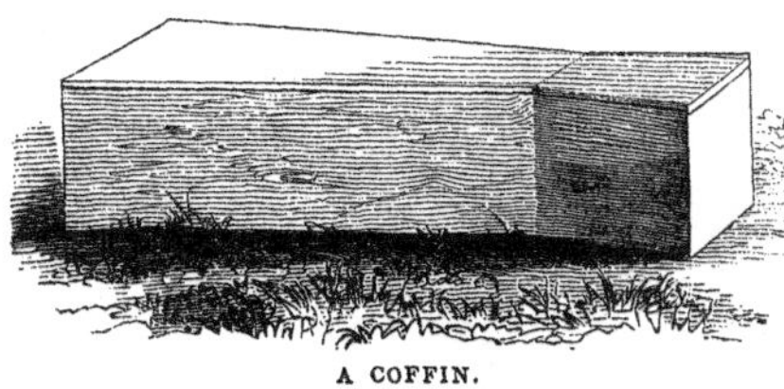

A COFFIN.

Ibagué is a peon town. Its foreign revenue has been chiefly

from cargueros, who carried men across the Quindio Mountains, over a road too bad for mules. The road is now improved, so that, in the dry season, mules can pass quite comfortably; but there is now increased travel, and cargueros, servants, mail-carriers (on foot), and chasquíes are, perhaps, more in demand than ever. It bears the same relation to the Quindio that Independence does to the Rocky Mountains, except that it is impossible so to make arrangements as to avoid paying tribute to it. Ibagué is the fourth town in the province in population, and in wealth the fifth, sixth, or seventh.

In Ibagué fruit is attainable, and often cheap enough. I bought oranges at the rate of 72 for a dime. The plain is long, and the scattered cottages on it present a beautiful appearance, especially when the children are playing in the moonlight. Water is accessible; but we prefer quoting from La Imprenta of May, 1852: "The water comes to Ibagué from the sides of Tolima by a canal which passes through the principal street that crosses the town. At every square this canal has a deep opening, in which the incautious traveler, who does not understand geography, might breathe his last; but this is not the worst: the water-carriers, and especially the female members of this profession, descend to the bottom of these wells for water, and, having performed such ablutions as suit their fancy, go their way. How clean must the water be when it comes upon the table?"

Another interesting chapter of Ibagué life is the niguas. Nigua is the Spanish for *Pulex penetrans*—the penetrating flea, jigger, chigger, or chigoe. This is a microscopic flea, about as large as the head or one joint of the leg of our well-known bosom companion. In like manner, she chooses her habitation in out-houses, houses where the cruel mop comes not, and the dire effects of water are unknown. There she hops about, like other damsels, seeking a settlement for life, till, by good fortune, she lights upon a human leg, or, still better, foot. She makes her way to a toe, and then her fortune is almost secured. She penetrates beneath the skin (not under the nail) by means that the microscope has not revealed to me. There, like the invalid in the Mammoth Cave, she enjoys an unchanging and agreeable temperature. She is never destined to know what hunger is; her day of prosperity is come.

Prosperity in the nigua, as in the human race, works wonderful changes. The agile damsel of yesterday will be to-morrow a shocking obesity: so changed, in fact, that I absolutely failed to convince a naturalist friend of the identity. Place around the human waist a thousand yards of cotton sheeting between the skin and the flesh, and you would have an idea of the dislodged nigua that I have now beneath my microscope, with a white spherical body as large as a small pea, with head and arms of the original color and size, invisible to the naked eye. She is full of eggs, but it is past my conjecture where their father is. Every nigua that enters a toe becomes a mother in a few days, if left alone. They may be, like the leech, unisexual, or, as in the case of the soft-shelled turtles of Southern rivers, the male may pass for another species.

The farther history of the nigua, happily, I am unable to give from personal experience. The young are enterprising settlers, and soon remove to a suitable distance from their native spot, and, in their turn, find themselves blessed with a numerous family of daughters ready to obey the great organic law of nature.

The annals of Natural History tell us of a martyr who tried to carry a family of niguas across the Atlantic in his foot. They increased beyond his calculation—beyond his power of extermination. His leg, upon his arrival, was soon added to the collection of a surgeon as a unique specimen of great value.

Where there are niguas, *à fortiori*, there are fleas. To see both in perfection, I am recommended to visit the ancient town of Popayan. It is said that when you see a man who can catch fleas by instinct, you may be sure he is from Popayan. If you see him put his hand into his clothes and draw forth a backbiter from exactly between the shoulder blades, you may be sure he is a Popayanejo. You draw the same inference from his having lost a few toes, or even toe-tails. Popayan is the paradise of fleas. Turn an ungreased horse loose in a yard, and in half an hour he is frantic. In vain the inhabitants bathe two or three times a day: the plague knows no longer intermission than till their backs are dry. In going to bed at night, you mount a table, toss from you one article of dress after another, whip yourself thoroughly with your shirt, throw it in one direction, and rush for a high-hung hammock in the opposite. I tell the tale as it was told to me, for my desire to visit Popayan has much abated within a few days.

It is added that the niguas are, if possible, a more serious evil than the fleas there, even destroying life. The victim dies covered, or, rather, filled with one colony of niguas, from the extremities of the toes to the extremities of the fingers.

This is a long introduction to a very short story. One day that week I had three niguas taken from my toes, the next four, and the next five. As I needed my feet for another use on Monday, I was a little anxious at first, but I soon reduced the number to an average of less than two per day.

This was the first grand onset of the nigua, and some will call it a just penalty for the vulgarity of wearing alpargatas. Perhaps so, for I had but one nigua in all the time that I wore boots, while, in general, I have since had one or two a week. The last general attack was at Honda, and it was equal to the first, only that I had become able to extract them myself.

This is by no means a painful task, and there is a positive gratification in it. It is akin to the satisfaction of a good sneeze. The irritation of the presence of the insect occasions an itching, which is relieved at once as soon as the skillful operation is commenced. A pin, needle, or knife-point is used as a probe; an opening is made in the cuticle, and, by a skillful circular motion, the cutis is pressed away from the nigua on all sides, and then the whole body is extracted, without breaking, if possible. It is only in case of great personal neglect that limbs, and even lives, are lost. Numbers of lives have been lost so in hospitals. The old doctrine of applying the remedy to the instrument that inflicted the wound is not believed in here, but it would be efficacious: the nigua and the mop can not coexist.

Ibagué is the capital of the province of Mariquita, not by virtue of size, commercial importance, or central position, but in consequence of its climate. With a good bed, this would be perfect. Humboldt says of it, *Nihil quietius, nihil muscosius, nihil amœnius.* I agree with him, save only that I found not a single moss in Ibagué. It is cooler than its altitude requires in consequence of its proximity to the Quindio range, and particularly to the perpetual snow of Tolima, to the cold páramo of Ruiz, and the Mesa de Hervéo.

The Governor of Mariquita receives $1440, the jefes políticos of Ambalema and Honda $320; the other three, $240 each. To this add secretaries and stationery, and the expense of governing 86,985 people, exclusive of alcaldes and president, is $5835, an item of government patronage unknown to our system, and derived from their old monarchical customs. The new Constitution attempts a reformation here. The gobernador and alcaldes are to be elected by the people, and the office of jefe político is suppressed.

I found the gobernacion of the province in the house of the governor, a young man of unassuming appearance, who rejoices in the name of Uricoechéa. He was unusually busy, making arrangements for a body of troops which went from Bogotá to Pasto in October, while the republic of Ecuador expelled the Jesuits, and now, finding no farther use for their services, were to be quartered a while in Ibagué.

The governor made me a present of a file of *La Imprenta*, now named *Voz de Tolima*, the government paper of the province, and the only one, I think, in the province. It is about the size of two folio leaves, and is published once a fortnight. Like all the papers of New Granada, Northern readers would pronounce it insufferably dull, but to me it is full of interest. The cost to the government this year is $1626; and though at first I regarded the measure as foolish, I am well satisfied that it is a good one. It is divided into official and non-official parts. In the former I find the ordinances of the Cámara, the decrees of the governor, law cases, and important decisions, circulars to the jefes políticos, and reports from them, examinations of schools, advertisements of runaway prisoners, and even the public documents of districts, when of sufficient interest. The non-official part contains every thing else except news.

I passed the Provincial Prison many times a day, seldom without their calling to me from the windows, limosna—alms. At length I began to answer, "No tengo limones—I have no lemons or limes." At last, one day, I put some limes into my pocket, and when they assailed me with "limosna," I gave them to the fellow, saying, "Aquí teneis tus limoncitas—here are your limes." They gave me up. The prison was indeed a bad one.

I saw the Cámara in session. It has a strong Conservador majority, while the gobernador is, of course, a Liberal. What I saw here teaches me not to translate the word *Conservador* by *Conservative:* there are no Conservatives in New Granada except fanatic Papists. All the rest deserve the name of Destructives, and might be classed into Red Republicans and Redder Republicans; and the Redder men may belong to either party, but, except the Gólgotas, the reddest I know of are the Conservadores of the province of Mariquita.

This assertion is too important in its general bearings to leave it unsupported with facts. I find in the Imprenta eight vetoes of Uricoechea in twenty-two days. In four cases the bill was passed over the veto, which can always be done by a majority of the one Chamber, the most facile of all legislation except by an absolute monarchy, and worse even than that. I examined these eight cases, and in all I am confident that the gobernador (who seemed too young for his office) was right, and the Cámara wrong. One of them deprived the jefes políticos, who are compelled to serve and to reside at the Cabecera de Canton, of their salaries. They tried to change the name of the province to Marquetá, derived from the Marqueton Indians, who once resided there. Mariquita is a diminutive of Mary. The Supreme Court decided that a province could not change its name.

But my strongest facts relate to taxes. Direct taxes were unknown. They voted not only to introduce them, but to rely wholly on them at the first experiment. The excise on spirits was rented out for some years to come, at a good sum, to a man who had unfortunately introduced some ill-judged and costly apparatus that probably would not pay. From the monopoly the province suffered no other inconvenience but that vagabonds must work more or drink less. Well, the Cámara ordered the contract to be rescinded without the contractor's assent, preferring to have cheaper rum and less revenue. But the new system, which was invented, not copied (for this is the way with all republics), would not work at all. Next year came another radical change. All direct taxes were repealed, and the whole revenues needed for two years, and for the indemnification of the spirit contractor, were to be raised at once from a tax on the exportation of tobacco. This threw all the burdens of the province on the largest town, Ambalema, the great tobacco mart of New Granada. The utmost they could hope to effect by this would be to drive away the tobacco trade to other provinces, and reduce the population of Ambalema from 9731 to less than 5000. But new difficulties beset them. At the lowest corner of the province, on the Magdalena, stands Nare. Under the new order of things, no tobacco is *exported*, and Nare takes it all. It seems that the Nareños, men, women, and children, smoke more than their own weight of tobacco daily! The last achievement of the Conservadores that has reached me is a sumptuary law limiting Nare as to the amount of tobacco it should consume, in order that some might be left for exportation.

I wish I had done with this matter, but, as the hope of all parties here seems to be the abolition of all indirect taxes, I must tell my reader what a *progressive tax* is. Their theory is philosophical. Taxes are to be paid out of income, and he that has no income can pay no tax. No more can he whose income shall be insufficient for his wants. Property is not taxed. A poll-tax is feudalism, barbarism, and slavery. A man needs a certain sum—say $100 a year—to live on. He that has less than that can pay no tax. If his income be between $100 and $400, he can spare 5 per cent. of it very well; should it be between $400 and $2000, he can conveniently spare 15 per cent. of it; and if it exceeded $10,000 a year, he could easily spare half of it. This is progressive taxation, only I have copied the figures of no one scheme.

This scheme is designed, you see, for the special protection of vagabonds. The thriftless and improvident shall be exempt from all burdens to government. Nay, were there but one citizen in the province of the wealth of an English duke, they might exempt all incomes of less than $100,000 a year from taxation, and make him alone bear the expense of government. Such was the scheme recommended by the editor in the "Voz de Tolima," the organ of a Conservador gobernacion; and I saw a similar one recommended by a gobernador of Bogotá—a Liberal.

But, insecure as the property of citizens must be under this species of legislation, that of foreigners is not attacked in this way. True, the province had the same constitutional right to raise its revenue on the silver mines instead of the tobacco, but they well knew that such a step would have brought a British fleet before Cartagena, and therefore it was not to be thought of.

Another consequence of this theory is, that vast amounts of property in the hands of the wealthy escape taxation. Broad leagues of land are held by wealthy families, waiting for another generation to buy and settle them. As they produce nothing, they are not subject to taxation. The addition of a *horizontal* tax of one cent an acre on land, and a poll-tax of a dollar, would relieve all the embarrassments of the treasury, and the last would be a benefit to the taxed, but it would be an outrage on *theory*.

I speak these things with reluctance. They are the fruit of speculations drawn almost entirely from French books and Granadinos' brains, wholly uncontaminated by any contact with realities. Do you wonder at their stupidity in not copying our system of taxation? Then why does not New York city enjoy the benefits of a postal system like that of Berlin or London? Why have we never enacted or even examined the Bankrupt-law of England, while in some states solvent men are ruined every year by grab-laws? Why have we still poorer mint-laws than England adopted in 1816? Because legislators love the rachitic offspring of their own brain too well to adopt the fairest and healthiest progeny of any other.

Ibagué is surrounded with beautiful scenery, whether you stand and look about you or take rides and walks. I do not often ride on my small excursions. I made a trip to Tolima, however, subject to the encumbrance of as uncomfortable a mule for a botanist as ever I saw. It was not, I am sorry to say, the Peak of Tolima that I visited, but only an Indian town a little way up the Combeima. This volcanic peak, that has thrown its pumice around Ibagué, is said to be only three leagues from it, but the way is so bad that a visit there costs five days. I had time to spare for such a trip, and it could not have been better employed; but the damage to my locomotive powers made me abandon all ideas of crystallized sulphur, rare plants, and volcanic action; so I only went up to the Indian town that does much to supply the market of Ibagué.

I followed the plain up a long way, and then descended to the lower grounds of the Combeima by a steep, zigzag, paved road. The agricultural spirit of the Indians has filled this valley with little properties and little cottages, and I gladly followed the river up to a ford that I was not willing to cross without necessity. What with rain, and mud, and the obstinacy of the mule, the trip did not pay.

I bathed in all these rivers, but the best place was found by going down the Combeima, and crossing by a frail foot-bridge, a little above its junction with the Coello, to that stream. They are of about equal size. The Chiapalo is much smaller, but warmer and nearer.

I do not like the Ibagueños. I have not found so unsociable a people in the whole country. Except the attentions that my letter of introduction compelled, and the official courtesies of the gobernador, neither of which were scanted at all, the only attentions I received were from the priest. I am sorry for this, for there seems nothing wanting to Ibagué but good society, or even the ordinary amount of Granadan hospitality and sociability.

In leaving, I had my first and last difficulty about a bill. My house-rent was made $1 60 by charging to me all the vacant rooms that were accessible to me. I decided to pay only for what I had used. Not a symptom of accommodation did her ladyship show all the time my packing was going on, till it seemed to me that I should either leave without paying, or have some experience of the Granadan Code of Procedure, which I was not unwilling to try. Five minutes before starting, however, the terms were reduced to eight dimes. I gave her a dollar, for I thought the experiment was worth the balance. It was the most quiet quarrel I ever had, for not an unkind word was uttered in the whole of it.

CHAPTER XXIV.

THE BACK TRACK.

A Crash Towel.—Excellent Family.—A Granadan Ghost.—Piedras.—How to extinguish a Cigar.—Rio Seco.—Drowning in Dry River.—Neme and Bitumen.—Sulphur Water and something stronger.—Granadan drunk and noisy.—Tocaima.—Sky-roofed Prison.—Fall of Horses.—Juntas de Apulo.—Muddy Rivers and muddy Roads.—Anapoima.—Mesa.—Road round a Hill.—Presidio.—Hospital.—Surveillance.—Volcan.—School Examination.—Tertulia.—Expedition to Tequendama.—The Laggards.—Tena.—A cool Drink.—A Fast.—Affectionate Reception.

I AM on the back track this morning. I am on horseback, and entangled in with others, so that I am no longer the independent man that I was when on foot, and happy with only three bestias—two quadrupeds and a biped—I crossed the Tierra Caliente before. Our baggage is off some time since, under the charge of a thief, who has already been helping me transact some of my business. He employed a woman to do some washing for me. He assured me that the articles were all safely returned; but I missed a towel—my only crash towel.

Towels here are generally made of plain cotton cloth, and, though often embroidered with red, are not what our wet hands demand. This crash was a new article to her, and seemed cheap enough to be stolen, and dense enough to be highly desirable, so the affair was determined on. It so happened that we ate for a day or two at the house where the washer-woman harbored. Our horses were at the doors, all bills settled, and we ready to mount, when I had the washer-woman called in, and told her that I wanted my towel. It cost me great trouble to make her understand that it was not a night-shirt, a pocket-handkerchief, a ruana that I wanted. The word toalla is not used here, and she could not understand its equivalents. Then she went to her box, and drew forth article after article. She had got the box half emptied; I stood patiently looking on, till out came the towel; she seemed much pleased to find something that I would like, and gave it to me with an air of satisfaction that really looked like generosity. I felt like rewarding her with a dime or two, but refrained, and thanked her cordially, tied the towel round my waist, wished her good-day, sprung into the saddle, and was soon out of town.

I was soon after on the same plain from which I had entered Ibagué, but on a different side of it. In coming, I had been within a mile or two of the Coello; I now took a more southerly course, near the Chipalo. Few were the houses on the road, but the other side of the river was very beautiful to me, presenting a constant succession of houses and farms. Probably the land is easier to work there than on this stony plain.

I soon had another pleasant surprise. We turned into a little side path an hour or two from Ibagué, and I was suddenly introduced to the pleasant family of Dr. Pereira. It was remarkable for the degree of education to which the younger members had attained; I greatly regretted not having met them sooner. One of the sons, Dr. Nicolas Pereira (Gamba), has published a poem on Don Angel Lei. The author condemns it as faulty and extravagant, and he is right. He intends to rewrite it.

I should have spoken of Don Anjel, and also of that sleepy convent of San Diego in Bogotá. His body was buried there about 1820, the last interment that there has been in the chapel of the convent. Lei was an officer in the guard of the Viceroy before he turned monk. He had engaged himself to Luisa Sandoval, one of the belles of the day in Bogotá, who died. It is possible that her death wrought his conversion, but the tale runs in various ways, all different from that. I receive it that he was sitting by the side of Luisa at a bull-feast, when he became fascinated with a new face, irresistible to him. At Sandoval's he was dull that evening, and left early. In the street he met the unknown, who took his arm with an air of innocence rather than boldness. They walked in various directions, and at last crossed over the Bridge of San Francisco, went one block north, and turned down under the bridge between the two convents, and entered a splendid house, brilliantly lighted. They saw no living soul. With an infantile affection, she led him from room to room. At the earliest dawn he roused himself from a bed of guilt and shame, and hastened to the palace to his morning duties. He had left his watch and sword hung on two ornamental hooks at the bed's head. After breakfast he sought the house of the unknown, and found it an old ruin! He ventured up the broken stair, and over perilous floors, till, where the bed should have been, he saw his watch and sword suspended from two rusty spikes; but the floor was so broken that they were inaccessible. He left them, hastened away, and became a monk.

Others say that, on his way home from the spectral house, he met a spectral procession bearing the body of Luisa; others again, that he found his watch and sword hanging on two human bones projecting from the walls of the cemetery; others still, that he awoke that morning with a skeleton in his arms. Where there are monks there will be fables. But ghosts and fairies seem to all to be of Northern origin. The scarcity of them, or their absence from Southern Europe, needs to be inquired into. I asked the Spanish of ghost, and they thought that alma bendita—blessed soul—came nearest to it. This supernatural girl they called an hada.

Dr. Gamba has the best floor that I have seen in New Granada. It is of some calcareous cement, that unites the two excellences of being hard and not inclined to crack. As no wooden floors are to be thought of, it is quite desirable that something that can be kept clean, as rammed earth can not, and that shall be more agreeable than bricks, should be found for this use. I fear, however, that, in most places, lime will be found beyond the means of the peasantry, but with good roads bitumen would be attainable over the whole country.

With young Pereira's Anjel Lei in my pocket, we were soon on the plain again. We went northeast toward a high, detached hill, behind which lay Piedras. A detached range of steep hills ran due north, separating this inclined plane from the lower horizontal plains on the banks of the Magdalena. This range we approached obliquely. The whole plain might be called piedras—stones—only there is said to be, at a place called Cuatro Esquinas, an intermission of them; but if so, I passed it unnoticed.

It was dark when we struck into the gorge between the hills, crossing quite a stream twice. It was the Opía; and we were finally on the left bank of it, but on ground much higher than its bed. We had some difficulty in finding posada, but at length we joined ourselves to some others, bound also to Bogotá, and secured a sala to ourselves. It was rather warm, especially after the cold nights of Ibagué. Water was scarce with us, and, thirsty and tired, I was glad to get into my hammock. Most of our party slept in the piazza till a night-rain drove them in. Then I had almost to fight with a cigar, that I could not endure in-doors in so crowded a room. It was only as I was about to employ all the water that we had left in extinguishing it where it shone, that, to save this waste of water, the smoker abandoned his cigar. Next day it turned out that the annoyance was from an impudent servant, and I was sorry I had not thrown the water without the warning, for it is a breach of all decorum for a servant to smoke in the presence of superiors. He was only carrying out the familiar Spanish proverb that "in the dark all cats are gray."

Next day I went to a steep hillock, just out of town, for plants, and was struck with the movements of two black birds with long tails. They were following the motions of a hog. They kept on the ground a yard from him, one on each side, and following him as faithfully as his shadow. This they did for a long time. I conjectured that they were picking up fleas that left him.

Piedras stands on a table of land an hour or two from the Magdalena. It consists of thatch houses mostly, or, properly, huts. On the Plaza resides a character that I had a strong desire to see when it was too late. He was described to me as a man of great wealth, sense, liberality, and eccentricity. After leaving, I was shown a distant hill, crowned with what I should have taken for a German castle, but they told me it was built as the last resting-place for his family. Much of his liberality is said to be in secret.

We had a long descent to the ferry of Opía, so called because it is at the mouth of that river, and there we were detained some hours. Here I noticed a sand-bank washing away at the rate of some inches per minute. The baggage of an incautious traveler might easily be swept off so. I would have been glad to spend a part of this long interval in bathing, but a wholesome fear of the raia—a ray-fish, with a formidable sting—detained me. As we rose from the river on the east side, I found abundant specimens of Melocactus, or Mammillaria, a plant I have seen nowhere else out of green-houses. A dense patch of it would be impassable.

At length we came out to cultivated grounds. Here we found the most luxuriant feed I have ever seen in all my travels. The price was a cuartillo per beast for a night. We were on the banks of the infamous Rio Seco. Its name is a stupendous lie: instead of being dry, it was as full as it could hold. I found a friend of a friend waiting for it to fall. He had waited till he was tired, had examined the river, and, much against my wishes, they all decided to advance after we had been there an hour.

I stood and trembled on the bank, while some precious collections found their way across dry, as I then supposed; but, unfortunately, when the evil was past remedy, I found the damage was serious. To be ready for emergencies, I had disencumbered myself of clothing before my cargas entered the river. I then left my horse in care of a servant, and walked across, as I do not like entanglement in any difficulty. A rare and interesting tree overhung the bank where I came out, and I was eagerly stripping it of its flowers, when I heard some one coolly remark, "That boy will drown." I turned round, and saw a boy of about twelve rapidly washing down stream, and none were moving. I plunged in, and brought him out, scarce able to stand from fatigue and fright. Catholics, I think, are less impressed with the loss of life, as, the sooner one dies, the less they are apt to suffer in Purgatory.

We followed up the left bank of Rio Seco till dark, when we reached a good posada at Neme. *Neme* means *bitumen*, of which there are copious deposits in some parts of New Granada. I saw traces of it north of Ibagué, but none here. At Méndez, a little above Honda, there are immense deposits of it. A patch or two of sidewalk, and a little of floor, in Bogotá, are the only instances of its use that I have seen. Here we met a large company of travelers bound west, and our two parties had a good time generally. In this I could not share, on account of the labor my plants demanded, and the exhaustion caused, I verily believe, by the anxiety I had while my treasures were braving the fury of that infamous Dry River.

In the morning, instead of keeping the left-hand road, that had half a dozen or a dozen more crossings of Rio Seco to make, we took another. We were rising a little out of the Seco valley, when we stopped more to commemorate our fast than to break it. In fact, things were looking a little like famine. We ate some roasted bananas, so insipid as to seem innutritious. The inhabitants of the little hut strip off a certain kind of bark for tying bundles of tobacco and cigars. They had nothing that they could sell us. Farther on I collected a most singular fruit of a tree or vine that I snatched at in riding past. I mistook the follicles for floral leaves until better informed. Soon I came to a large stream of sulphur-water, that diffused its odors for a great distance. Hasty as was my exploration of this, it was an hour before I overtook my company again.

We had risen over an immense ridge, and had descended again into the valley of the Bogotá, when I overtook them at a place where spirits and guarapo were sold. A mixture of the two was passed round and pronounced excellent. I stopped but a few moments, and hurried on, that I might have more time to loiter. In an hour they overtook me, and the friend of my friend was "roaring drunk." He raced, shouted, reeled, till he seemed past recovery—caught his predecessor's beast by the tail, and cut more antics in one half hour than usually occur in New Granadá between one earthquake and the next. It is contrary to nature here to be otherwise than stupid and quiet in drink. I am assured that he drank but moderately, but I have always had a prejudice against moderate drinking of intoxicating liquors. Especially I wish to see no more experiments of thirsty men on guarapo and rum mixed together. By the time we had entered Tocaima he had subsided into a quiet gentleman again.

Purgatory has been called the Tocaima of the future world. I must say it is warm at Tocaima, especially considering its elevation. No warmer spot is known for a hundred miles. It was midday when we arrived, and Tocaima was doing its prettiest. We waited an hour or two. Tocaima looks like a decayed town. I went out to explore, and saw a roofless house with barred windows. This pen was the prison. I think there was shelter from rain in some part of it. Opposite this was a ruined convent.

As soon as the heat would permit we proceeded, and at length reached the banks of the Bogotá. It was swollen, and of a hideous blackness, rolling mud as fluid as water. Its waters pass over decomposing shales and carboniferous strata. If Rio Sucio is nastier than this, I hope never to see it. I find we have not taken the best road for a tourist. There is a hill of enormous height, called the Volador, hereabouts, and the riding-beasts might have been got over there, by favoring them a little, in less time. As we followed up the Bogotá, one horse gave out entirely, and was sold. Several of us took to our feet. I was walking along leisurely, when three beasts before me turned into an open gate, and went up a steep path through a pasture. I followed, caught the rear one, and mounted. The others reached a closed gate at the top, and followed a fence along in the same direction that the road went below. I followed, and just was reaching out my hand to seize the bridle of one, when I saw them both slowly sink before my eyes in a thicket of bushes. I gave the alarm to the owner, and urged him to go with me and get help at a house at the top of the hill. He believed there was no danger; it was now dark; the posada of Juntas was just around the hill; he would send back a baquiano (one acquainted with the spot) from there. So we went on. We passed a land-slide—derrumbe—at a risk of ourselves sliding down into the dirty river, and soon arrived at the best posada I have seen in all the land.

The landlord (posadero) assured us that there was no such hole as I thought I saw, and that a servant would doubtless find the horses quietly feeding there. He went, and did not find them. Next morning a peon was sent toward Tocaima for them, and was gone some hours. Breakfast was over, and my friend learned that the pasture was bounded on one side by a cliff nearly perpendicular. Half way down that cliff, in plain sight of their fellows at the door of the posada, stood the two horses within musket-shot of us. How they got there alive, or how they were to be taken down or up except piecemeal, was more than I could tell. I was glad to see the owner shed tears. But in half an hour the truants were down, making a hearty breakfast, and I was off.

This place has something of a historical interest. In May,

1851, the Dictator Urdaneta found himself with a veteran army to support him, and an almost unanimous nation against him. His friend, García Delrio, met General López, since President, and made a treaty with him, which resulted in the re-establishment of Vice-president Caicedo in the supreme power. When the Congress refused to permit to Urdaneta's friends the advantages promised in that treaty, Caicedo retired from office, and Congress appointed General Obando in his place.

Juntas means junction. Here the dirty Apulo meets the dirty Bogotá. At this posada money can procure, for man and beast, all that travelers need. Rings are placed in the wall (as I learned in the morning) for hanging hammocks. The hanging of mine is often quite a task, and was so here. The posadero is a Socorrano. Socorro is the Yankeedom of New Granada. Here I passed a wooden bridge, eight feet wide, roofed with zinc, over the Apulo, and rose at once to a great height on a tongue of land between it and the Bogotá, though a much better road might be made nearer the Bogotá without rising. Here the road was abominable from steepness and from mud. There are two grades of muddy road. One is almohadillado, or pillowed. It has ridges running across the road, about two feet from crest to crest. These are of hard, slippery earth, and the mule steps over them, putting his feet down into deep mud holes between. These ridges lie like pillows (almohadillos), with mud holes between. They have been called mule-ladders in English. A man can walk on them, but if he slips he goes in deep. Some horses, lightly estimating the value of their riders' necks, *will* walk on them, in spite of your fears.

On almohadillado you can make more than a mile an hour, at the worst; but it may degenerate into an atascadero, that is, the ridges may be reduced to uniform mud of indefinite depth. The holes in almohadillado can be no deeper than the length of a mule's legs. An atascadero, when it becomes impassable to the strongest beast, grows no deeper. That is a consolation. Neither almohadillado nor an atascadero can exist where the steepness of the road exceeds 45°. The place of both is there supplied by a resbaladero, or sliding-place. Some magnificent specimens of resbaladero are said to be a rod long, steep as the roof of a house, and as smooth as an otter-slide. I have never seen fair specimens of this.

By the time the reader has mastered in sound and sense these three slippery and sticky Spanish words, he may imagine me to have contended with the realities, to have met an immense drove of mules carrying masses of salt in coarse nets on their way from Cipaquirá to Popayan, nearly 300 miles, and to have descended into an enormous hollow. Here I took a nice bath, and was again high up the hill at a venta when the first of my party overtook me. We toiled on, and did not all unite till we had reached Anapoima.

A nice place is Anapoima. It has a good posada for the rich, a free tambo for the poor, and a venta for both. We fared sumptuously here. The enterprising proprietor has, among other things, a blacksmith's shop and an English smith, and back of his house, down toward the Bogotá, here in sight beneath you, but out of hearing, a cane-field, no doubt, and a cane-mill. I particularly noticed a vine in his patio. I see no reason why it should not do well here, only the grape will not succeed well without care.

Here I mounted again, and we soon were on our way. A more pleasant road than I had lately seen ran along a ridge till it began to ascend another steep hill. At the left there was a private residence so surprisingly like a convent—chapel, bell-tower, and all—as to deceive a practiced eye. The road up the hill itself was paved, but the moment you reach the top you strike a straight macadamized street running a mile or two up a gentle grade. It is the principal street of the town of LA MESA DE JUAN DIAS. This *mesa* is a plain or table-land, bounded by abrupt descents in every direction. The principal street runs near the northern edge, where beneath flows the Apulo. The task of descending to it is very severe. South of the town are fields. These, too, end abruptly by an even steeper descent to the Bogotá. The table was once connected by a ridge with the grand ascent to the plain of Bogotá, but that ridge too has sunk far below the table, and in the depression stands the town of Tena.

It seems as if Mesa ought to be without water. In fact, rain water is used to a considerable extent, but there is quite a spring just south of the town, where washerwomen congregate. It is one of the highest spots in which oranges grow.

I had no thermometer with me, but I have a strong suspicion that the temperature is put too high by Cáldas, 72.5°. Mosquera gives it even three degrees higher. I think it must be near 70°. The difficulty of access to bathing-places seems to be the chief objection to Mesa as a place to go from Bogotá to change climate. It is free from the clouds of Guaduas, and the climate to me is delightful.

We found a delightful and pleasant home in the family, not merely the *house*, of Señor Juan Triana, now no more. Don Juan spoke English enough for all necessary purposes, and his amiable lady was a well-educated Granadina. Her name is Manuela Caicedo: she was born in Chocó, or in the Cauca. Her table, spread in the patio under an awning, was the best that I have seen in New Granada.

At her table I met the Gobernador, Justo Briceño. The three cantons of Mesa, Fusagasugá, and Tocaima then constituted the province of Tequendama, and Mesa was the capital. A more efficient officer than Briceño could not be found. He was first appointed by the President, and, at the change of Constitution, elected by the people. He was particularly interested in highways, and needs nothing more than the practical knowledge of a northern teamster to make him all that could be desired. We passed, on the road to Tena, a piece of new road that ran round a hill. It was clear that the old road on the ridge could be mended for less than the new, shorter, level road would cost, and they called him crazy for encountering the extra expense. I went over the hill from curiosity. The ascent and descent were prodigious, as bad as the worst in some New England counties. The mule-ladders were beautifully developed. And the distance was double. I wish New Granada had more crazy roadmakers.

The fine road through the streets of Mesa is at the cost of the nation. The province is not obliged to spend a dollar on it, but it might exact toll of all that pass over it. Every carga of molasses that enters Bogotá from here pays a toll at Puente Grande to the province of Bogotá. Briceño sees the impolicy and injustice of such impositions. He is extending this good road up to the plains of Bogotá. It is not intended for a wheel-road, and, I fear, will, in some places, be too steep.

A detachment of the Presidio is making the road. I saw one company near Tena, and another a little east of La Mesa. The troops that guard them are part of the regular army, and are under the command of the governor. The prisoners sleep in an ordinary cottage, and, by day and night, have no other wall around them than lead. They beg of the passers-by on every occasion. Señor Triana was contractor for furnishing the presidio with food and drink. They drink large quantities of guarapo. We drank the same at the table.

The Hospital of the province and that of the presidio were one and the same. It is an ordinary cottage of two or three rooms and a kitchen. Things there could not well be worse. In the kitchen were no conveniences for cooking. The floors are infested with niguas, so that they destroy life. Half the cases here were large superficial ulcers. The governor is sure that they are not made on purpose, but I must doubt.

I was in the Gobernacion one day, when a man came in, who, addressing the secretary, Señor Guzman, said,

"I am here, Señor."

"Very well; where have you been?"

"I have been at work on the estate of Don Fulano."

"Will you continue there?"

"I shall for the present."

"Very well; come again this day two weeks."

The secretary had opened a book and made a record of the interview.

"Who was that?" I asked.

"It is a man condemned to a certain period of prison and another of surveillance—vigilancia. His imprisonment has expired, but he can not pass certain bounds, and we must see him regularly, and know where he is and what he does."

"What trouble to you and him! We have not in the English language such a word even as surveillance. We use the French. Had he been at the North, he might perhaps have been let off on condition of never coming again where he is known."

The secretary stared. "And do you think a rogue does less damage where he is unknown?"

"No, I can not say that; but then the evil that he does will not harm us."

"Ah! that indeed," and the good official shrugged his shoulders, as if to say, "That plan is good enough for heretics."

I went to the provincial prison to see a noted presidario of good family, Francisco Morales. He had entered into a plan with a doctor and a judge. They had poisoned a priest of Bogotá, held a coroner's inquest on his body, administered his estate, and robbed it. The robbery only could be proved, and Pacho Morales, as he is called, was condemned to the Presidio. He has worried poor Briceño terribly. He asks whether any arrangement could be made at our best prisons to accommodate so refractory a fellow. He has not succeeded in getting a stroke of work out of him yet.

Once he commenced abusive and seditious declamations. A trumpeter was stationed by him, and commanded to blow every time he tried to speak. He chained him to a post, and has punished him to the last extent he dare, and now Pacho shams sickness. I wish I were his doctor a little while. I found him with his window toward the street stopped up (a great grievance), and a sentinel in sight of him continually. He was quite penitent, as he would have me think, and asked me for a Bible. Don Justo is fearing that he will make his escape.

One day I crossed the Apulo to see a *volcan* on the opposite slope, on the road to Anolaima. An immense descent brought me to the river, eight inches deep, and charged with black mud. A similar height was to be gained on the north bank. Here I found a scene of transcendent interest—a glacial motion of hot stones and earth. I took off my alpargatas, lest I should be betrayed to a place too hot to escape from. I could walk over most places. A pale smoke was issuing from some spots. The glow of fire is seen from some such places in the night. The slide was five or ten rods wide, and was advancing into a thicket of trees, overwhelming them at the rate of two or three feet a day. The sides of the *fire-glacier*, so to speak, were smooth, and grooved with the masses that had traveled down. The steepness was about that of steep carriage-roads. I suppose the sliding is due to the spontaneous ignition of pyrites in the depths below, and the slow combustion of coal. Such phenomena are said to be more active in wet weather, which furnishes water to the pyrites.

When it shall have advanced a dozen or two rods more, it will reach a small pond that must have had some similar origin. It is not deep, for I waded in some way; but they tell me that there is a treasure in the centre, in a large cauldron (funda), with another cauldron reversed over it. They can not get off the cover. So said some peasant women living near, who urged me to take some refreshment with them, and were the more earnest when I told them that I had no money with me. The spot was not two miles air line from Mesa, but I found my trip a very fatiguing but interesting day's walk.

These phenomena are frequent, and I am coming to the conclusion that all the rough, irregular valleys west of the Sabana, and, perhaps, on all the western slope of the Cordillera de Bogotá, are the work of similar decomposition. Signs of this must be sought by a man of more leisure than I have been.

I attended an examination of the public boys' school. The same faults I had noticed before were too plain here; all was rote, and no thought. I picked out the smartest boy, and when he went to the black-board, I handed to the gobernador the sum of "the hare and the greyhound." The hare starts eighty varas before the hound, and runs twenty varas a minute, while the hound runs twenty-five. Señor Briceño said no boy in school could do it. It passed from my hands to my neighbor's, and then the master asked for it. He left the examination in the hands of the committee, and bent all his energies on the sum. In ten minutes he had an answer, but it was wrong.

I attended a tertulia, or evening visit, in La Mesa. I hope I wrong no one in saying I thought it tedious and stupid. The ladies, who were pretty in the main, took possession of a corner of the room that just held them, and maintained it. The gentlemen formed a line, from one end of theirs to the other, through the middle of the room, but so that each person spoke only to his next neighbors. No general conversation went on, and none across the circle. A couple of ladies went out a few moments, and I exhorted the Governor, who was apt for such encounters, to interpose his person in the vacancy, and break their phalanx for the evening. He attempted to do so, but the ladies, returning, claimed their places in such a manner that he had to yield. I attempted to engage a lady in conversation, when I found myself at one end of our line, but I could get nothing but commonplaces (the Spanish is poor in monosyllables), and gave up, in fear of being regarded as impudent or ill-mannered for conversing with a lady.

From Mesa I started for the Falls of Tequendama. We had in company Governor Briceño, and two young men who had never seen the Salto. A servant and sumpter mule completed the train. We started late, of course. Briceño and I went on slowly to Tena, five or six miles, and then we waited for the rest hour after hour. They arrived about sunset, and we went on by the light of a full moon to pass the night at a hacienda. We lost our way, and had a horrible time. The road was hardly fit for quadrupeds, even by daylight. We began to feel the want of our dinner. My horse fell down a bank. How he got out, or why I went not down, I could not see, for it was dark. At length we came to where a torrent tumbled over a pile of stones; whether it was in the road or out, we knew not, but we could not pass it. We turned back, and, after an hour more of dismal wanderings, we came to the Hacienda of Saragoza, and stopped there.

Our beasts were scarcely put up or turned loose when the owner came from Bogotá, and we got up quite a dinner, and by elëven we were taking a nap. This lasted till three, and then we were on our way, with a baquiano to guide us. He led us to and over the pile of stones—a perilous task in the dark, and thus on. Early in the morning we passed the ruins of San Antonio. It was a town of which the site had been carried off by a volcan or fire-slide. The whole face of the country had changed, and all we could see of the ruins was a bit of the corner of the church, half a mile, it is said, from where it was built. A rugged, naked valley occupies the place of the plain on which San Antonio stood.

A little farther on we paused to take something, I really can not tell what. Then one of the laggers called out to the guide, "Baquiano, be spry now; a real if you will run." On we started: in ten rods we came to a house and a pretty girl, and the two worthies must stop and ask her some questions. We followed on with the guide up a long hill, and past some scattered houses, and an Indian settlement called Curzio. But our laggards came not, and we had no alternative but slowly to advance. Meanwhile, we asked repeatedly for a guide to the foot of the falls, but in vain: all assured us that no man could reach the spot. About nine we reached a point whence the falls were visible. It was the hill top at the head of the zig-zag path mentioned on page 279, and our course to the falls is described in the succeeding pages.

It was the middle of the afternoon when, returning from the head of the fall, we again reached this spot, and there we saw our two truant friends, who were now enjoying their first and last view of Tequendama. This glimpse of the upper part of the falls at a distance was all the reward they had for a ride of three days. When they left the pretty girl (how long they stopped they did not say), they mistook their road from that very spot. They did not discover their mistake till they were in sight of the Sabana. Here they hired an Indian girl to guide them, and they had caught their first glimpse of the falls, and the last, perhaps, for their lives, just as it was time to return to Saragoza, where we had left all our bedding, etc.

We stopped at the first cottage to do what we could to appease our hunger. I soon left them there, and started on foot, reviewing deliberately and carefully the scene of the catastrophe of San Antonio. At dark I was near Saragoza, and, for the third time, threaded in darkness a trail through the woods that lay between the house and the little footpath that they called highway. Our kind host bade a servant wash my feet, and ordered dinner. Before it was ready the party arrived, two of them rather crestfallen. Their delays had spoiled the whole expedition, and they had reaped a corresponding part of its benefits. Don Justo had visited the Salto repeatedly, and appreciates it as much as any Granadino I know.

Our host brought bitter complaints from Bogotá of sacrilegious laws. From the priests had been taken away the monopoly of marriage, and even the right to marry, as each marriage had to be acknowledged before the District Judge. I tried to make him see that the judge did no more than give the certificate, which the priest gave before when he was a civil officer; but he insisted that it were better to leave their children to the consequences of legal illegitimacy than to receive a certificate of marriage from unconsecrated hands.

On the morrow we had one of the earliest Granadan breakfasts I have ever eaten, and we were on our way soon after nine, and in due time drew up in the patio of the antique *great-house* of Tena.

Tena would be a fine place to rusticate, only it has no society and no market. It is warm, and has plenty of water. It stands on the ridge that extends from Mesa to the base of the plain, and has the land sloping off rapidly down to the heads of the Apulo on the north, and the banks of the Bogotá on the south. From here the road rises rapidly to the plain at Barro Blanco.

I took a good bath just after leaving, the last I could *enjoy* before descending again, however many I might *endure*. I climbed on foot, or rather walked up, for the steepest kind of a carriage-road reaches nearly up—as far as the presidio has worked. It might be made, with good engineering, a carriage-road all the way; but as no carriage ever went up a hill in New Granada except on men's shoulders, it will not probably be located where such a thing will be possible. Already enough has been spent on it to have built from Bogotá to the Magdalena a road as good as ordinary mountain-roads in the States.

The last part of the ascent was an old road of stairs and quingos. It was a real scramble, and I arrived at the venta of Barro Blanco heated and thirsty. There I met with a new beverage—guaruz. It may be an abbreviation of agua de arroz—rice-water—and seems to be a chicha in which rice has been substituted for maize. It was opaque, but white, instead of a dirty yellow like chicha. To imitate it, I would take a mixture of rice flour, brown sugar, or panela, and water, and let it begin to ferment till a slight taste of carbonic acid was perceptible. But the coolness made it the most exquisite beverage I ever tasted, and I took a second draught. I paid dear for it, for I was in absolute danger. I had on my thinnest clothes, was as hot as Tocaima, the barometer at 22 inches, the thermometer at 65°, and I with a mass of ice, as it seemed, in my stomach. I sprang to my saddle for my bayeton, but it was packed away, and I had nothing to shelter me. Then I started to see if I could gain heat by running. In so rare an atmosphere this was impossible, only I escaped dying.

Z

After two or three miles I mounted, shivering still, and put on my encauchado as a defense from the cold, and thus endured it till night. The road lay for a long distance among the hills that skirt the plain and at their base. We crossed arms of the plain, and were again among hills. The road seemed to be avoiding water, that covered large parts of the Sabana. We at length entered on plain, bridge, causeway, and good macadamized road, all at the same time, and took a straight line for Cuatro Esquinas. There, on a road once traversed before, we proceeded till we reached the Hacienda of Quito. Here a cold, polite reception, chocolate (no dinner), and beds awaited us after our fatigues since breakfast. We breakfasted next morning at 11, after a virtual fast of 26 hours or more, with an appetite sharpened by a ride past Culabrera, over Santuario and Puente Grande, and through Fontibon.

The joy of Don Fulano's servants at my reappearance at the door was extravagant. One of them, the biggest, if not the dirtiest, tried to give me a hug, but she could not do it unless I stooped down on my mule, and, as I would not understand her movements, she contented herself with shaking hands. The fat Señora and her dry little Quiteño husband saluted me in the same foreign style. It *was* good to get back, after all.

CHAPTER XXV.

CROSSING THE QUINDIO MOUNTAINS.

The Party.—Early Start.—Late Dinner.—Sulphur Mine.—Hot Springs.—The Presidio.—An Accident.—Cold Night.—I love my Neighbor, and she loves hers.—Twice-told Tale.—Boquía.—Balsa.—Ranchos.—Cartago.—Ball.—Prisoner set free.—The Drama in open Air.

PRESTO! I am in Ibagué again. Was last chapter a dream? Was there a ghost in it? Yes, it must be: here I am, in my hammock, in a large sala in Ibagué. Four gentlemen are spread out, two on tables and two on the floor. The crying of a babe has awakened me, and a woman's voice, from the room where it is, calls Antonia! Antonia! Antonia appears to be a black girl sleeping just outside of her mistress's door, and sleeping to some purpose, if, indeed, she be not dead.

Yes, it is even so. We are to start for the Quindio this morning, for, Sunday being market-day, all our purchases and those of the peons are made, and we are to have an early start. An early start means to rise at dawn, or earlier, and get off at ten. We did not do so well as this, for we were finally off just about eleven.

The company consists of five gentlemen, two ladies, three children, four servant-maids, eleven peons, twenty-five horses and mules, and one dog. Our train was a long one—the ladies on side-saddles, the other girls astride, two little boys in a chair, one baby in a pine box, two vacant chairs for the ladies, one man with a box on his shoulders, two led horses, and an uncertain number of baggage mules. The gentlemen, of course, were mounted, except myself, who resolved to try the passage on foot. So we filed down the bluff to the banks of the Combeima, which we crossed on an ancient substantial bridge. Here, then, I stood at the very foot of the Quindio mountains, the middle range of the Andes.

Quindio is not received as the name of the chain, but of this particular crossing-place. Chains of mountains here have no name. I have called the eastern chain the Bogotá Range; this will always be known as the Quindio, while the western has been called the Cáldas Range, but the name is not received. It is a little curious that Humboldt mistook the name of this mountain, and always wrote it Quindiu. I am not aware that any Granadan ever wrote it so.

I have reserved to this spot some remarks that perhaps I ought to have made earlier. The mountains about me are unique, so far as I ever have heard. They are remarkable as having at their feet a wide plain, sloping down toward the river from a great height above it, and not alluvial. This inclined plane is separated from the horizontal, alluvial plains of the river by a chain of steep but not high hills, that I take to be sandstone.

But the strangest thing of all is in the structure of the mountain itself. As I stand here on the brink of the Combeima, at the very base of Tolima, you might imagine crags jutting out over my head, or precipices, from the base of which the road must gain the summit as it can. It is not so. Not a particle of rock is visible. In all my wanderings in and around this chain, I have seen ledge but twice, if, indeed, more than once. Slopes there may be so steep that a fall from them would be fatal, and some of great height, almost perpendicular, but in them I see no rock at all. I can only regard it rationally as some rock entirely disintegrated, and perhaps I must call it granite, as where the road cuts through it I see no trace of stratification.

Our order of march was generally the cargueros, the girls, the gentlemen and ladies, and lastly the baggage. My own place was at my option, as I could out-travel them all, and needed to take no other precaution than not to over-travel the baggage at night. I kept generally in advance.

Most of the road at the eastern end was newly made, but on the same old route as 200 years ago. A detachment of the presidio were then engaged on it. And in all these days there was no diverging path, and not a house off the road, so there could be no possibility of losing my way. I had added to my thin walking-dress a ruana, rather to make it appear less nude than for comfort. When I became lonely, had questions to ask, or found something curious, I would wait till some of the party came up. The whole distance is called eighty-seven miles, but it would make a great difference whether you reckoned the slopes or only their bases. It would be more useful to estimate a journey by the height ascended and descended, as the horizontal distance matters little in comparison.

We ascended incessantly for some hours to and past Palmilla. This is not a village, but only a house or two. Then came a long farewell to cultivation, a long descent, and then, toward night, some land as varying as an ordinary road among, but not over, mountains. We had intended to sleep at El Moral, but we started too late.

A little before dark we reached Las Tapias. This consists of a house and kitchen, certainly not without occupants, but, in the confusion of peons and servants, I could not distinguish them. The baggage was behind. Only two mats, which came on a led horse, gave us a place to sit, without entering the dark, windowless cabin. We had nearly lost our hopes of our baggage when it arrived, and the girls set about getting dinner. The arrieros erected a tent over a huge pile of trunks and packages. These tents are generally erected in the centre of the road, or, rather, the narrow road is in the centre of the tent. The tent-poles are sought on the spot. The cloth of the tent is the property of the gentleman, who is the chief of our party by all consideration, as he is husband of one of the ladies. The other is an unmarried sister of his wife. I call him Señor.

At 10 a mat had been spread in the house, a table-cloth spread on it, and a comfortless, ill-prepared dinner was seasoned with cheerfulness, kindness, and hunger into a real feast. I had, however, one ground of complaint that none but the servants could remedy, and they would not. Besides paying my scot—escote—for the marketing, I had bought an extra supply of chocolate of my own; but the guarichas would always make me wait till the last for my chocolate, and then add water to it, so that, though I imbibed more fluid, I received no more nourishment. I found all contention on this point useless.

Supper over, an enormous almofrez was produced: out of it came a good bed, as large as a double bed ought to be, together with a mattress, hammocks, blankets, night-shirts, and dresses, an infinity of articles. Three hammocks were hung; a gentleman placed his bed under the three, at right angles with them, so that if any cord broke, he might be sure to share in the misfortune. The mattress was placed on a wide wooden bench made to sleep on, and the large bed occupied the place of our table on the floor.

At 4 we rose, stowed all the bedding into the Trojan horse, that seemed always to have room for more, and, with the addition of my bed, was no fuller than before. The combined industry of four girls got us a breakfast about 7, and, after much delay, we started long before the mules were ready. We descended still more, to a stream, a tributary of the Coello, which, I think, was in sight on our left. Then we rose to El Moral. This is but a single house, though marked on the maps.

From here was another uninterrupted ascent for some hours. In this time I had left all my company behind, and had passed Buenavista and an interesting spot called Azufral. Unfortunately, I had no notice of it till too late. It is an excavation for extracting sulphur. The altitude is given at 6470 feet, and the temperature is estimated at 61°, while in the excavations the thermometer rises to 118°, according to Humboldt. No man can breathe there, for the air is 95 per cent. carbonic acid, and 2 per cent. of the remainder is hydrosulphuric acid. Of course, such galleries can be carried to no depth.

Near this spot is a contadero, or clear plot, the highest spot of the day's journey, that bears the name of Agua Caliente—hot water—from a hot spring near there. The spot may be said to be at the base of Tolima. I have not been able to hunt up the spring itself, which is, however, some little distance from the road. Had preceding travelers mentioned the spring and the Azufral, I should probably have seen both, for I was far indeed ahead of my party.

I employed part of this leisure in a way that makes me shudder as I write. I found a little palm between 10 and 20 feet in height and nearly 3 inches in diameter. It is quite abundant about here. I wished to bring down one to examine the fruit. I cut upon it, at a convenient height, with my heavy machete, slanting downward, till the sharpened end of the trunk suddenly slid off the stump, and, impelled by the weight of its fruit, entered the ground like a crowbar. Its weight was very great, and it struck close to my foot, that was protected only by an alpargate! Had the position of my foot been a little different, it would have been pinned to the ground.

In these altitudes I was surprised with rain. I preferred rather to be wet than to turn back for my encauchado, so I walked on.

Now I was descending. The road was wet, but stony, for the formation seems to be different here from other parts of the road. If, indeed, it be trachyte, I found little to indicate it. The descent was steep, and at length continuous.

My breakfast had been very slight, and my dinner last night had not left a surplus in my animal treasury, and before reaching the summit my appetite became clamorous. Its appeals were useless. I had passed but one house, Buenavista, since passing El Moral, and I had nothing to expect short of Toche, the present locality of the presidio, which lay in a valley far beneath me.

The road presented a solitude unequaled by any thing I had ever seen on a traveled road, if, indeed, that can be called solitude which is filled with the voices of birds. Among the rest were turkeys, and a beautiful toucan of a brilliant green. The cry of one species of this bird is rendered by "*Dios te vé!*"—"God sees thee!" I picked up the cast skin of a snake on the way.

At length my eyes were greeted by smoke that gracefully curled, but not around green elms. I hastened down the steep hills, slippery with the rain, and reached a roaring river (the Coello) at the bottom, where was a fire, but neither house nor human being. The road ran up the left bank of the river till it came to a place where a land-slide had carried it into the river. The remedy for this was new, beautiful, singular, and original. A Yankee would have built a water-wall to confine the river to its place, and taken earth from the steep hill to fill in. To favor this plan, the river is full of boulders here of all sizes, while elsewhere no rock is to be had. Instead of this, the engineer made a zigzag up a hill that we would regard as all but impracticable. This road ascended half or two thirds the height of West Hoboken Hill, and then, without a yard of level ground, it descended again to the level of the river. It was broad and beautifully cut, as in a pleasure-ground, but, unfortunately, will soon be destroyed by the weather. And this is the most important change in the site of the road that has been made, perhaps, for two centuries!

Just as I began to climb the hill, I met a beggar with a knife in his belt. To enforce his claim, he informed me that he was a presidario. Had he assured me that he had murdered his mother I could have given him nothing—my money was behind. At the very foot of this descent, two rods from the road and ten feet from the river, is a small mound occupied by a hot spring. Any traveler will readily find it by this description. It appeared to be throwing up an enormous quantity of water, which, had I been in a hurry, I should describe as passing off by a subterranean channel. In fact, I believe it threw out no more water than could have been dipped out with a coffee-cup, but with it an immense quantity of carbonic acid gas, and that with much force. The spring was 8 feet long, 3½ wide, and 6 feet deep. I got in, and judged its specific gravity rather greater than sea-water, but I may have been deceived by the upward tendency of the gas discharged beneath me. The temperature was 90°. The mound was evidently oxide of iron, that had been thrown off by the spring, as is also some salt of lime, probably carbonate, that incrusts twigs around there. The gas that came off seemed almost entirely carbonic acid, but traces of sulphur were noticeable. The gas issued evidently from that end of the basin nearest the river, and it bore the body of the bather perceptibly toward the other end.

On the right hand (north) of the road, 20 or 30 rods up stream, was a smaller spring, 6 inches in diameter and 6 feet deep. Little gas escaped. Less exposed to the air, its temperature should be higher. I made it 91°. That at Agua Caliente is said to be far greater.

I had still nearly a mile to walk up the river over a very wet plain, which, but for the drains, would deserve the name of swamp. In the ditches here I saw the first and only conferva I have seen in the country. Near the upper end I saw a field fenced in, which, however, appeared not yet to be ready for cultivation. Then I crossed the Coello on a covered bridge just above the mouth of the Tochecito. In the fork of the two rivers is a dry plain, covered thickly with large boulders, so as to be difficult to ride over. Here stands Toche.

I arrived about 12, and my first idea was to supply the deficiencies of my breakfast. I called for bread, butter, chocolate, fruit, guarapo, and eggs, but could only obtain the latter, and at the rate of eight for a dime. I ordered four eggs boiled, and, by the time they were done, they had found two bits of dry bread. A board in a corner served for a table, the handle of a spoon for a spoon, a chair turned down for a seat. While eating, they assured me that the officers here used panela and water for chocolate, and liked it. They could furnish me the same, and I tried it.

Before 2 our party began to come in, but all the beasts were not in till about 3. It was decided that we could not go on to Gallego; this gave us a dinner by day, and afforded me an opportunity to observe the community in which we were to spend the night. Toche, I think, was one house before the presidio was stationed here. That has been enlarged, two others put up, and a dozen little huts. The huts are for men on parole. They are called francos, and are not, like the guardados, kept all the time within shot. The franco that I met today was a messenger that had been dispatched to Ibagué. It is unwise for them to try to run away, but they often do.

At night the presidarios were marched down the zigzag that we have to climb to-morrow. They were drawn up in a line, the roll called, and their rations given them. These are meal, or maize, or rice, and salt, and an immensity of panela, a quarter of a pound per diem. Most of the prisoners are on parole, and sleep in the huts; the others are thrust into one of the houses, and kept under guard. There are twenty-five soldiers, more or less. One of them marched a prisoner up to us who wished to beg. He had the additional merit of a large chain from his waist to his ankle, showing him to be one of the worst of the presidio. Even this did not avail him: we left him to the mercy of the President, whose only pardons seem to have been of prisoners who had risked their lives in the service of cholera hospitals on the Isthmus.

Altogether, the prisoners are well treated here, and, to a poor man, it is worse to wait his trial a week in Bogotá or Ibagué than to serve a month here; and to any man, a week here is better than to wait his trial a single night in the prison (stocks) of Pandi.

We were here the guests of the warden, to whom all the gentlemen of the party were personally known except myself. He gave up to us his entire apartment, quartering himself for the night abroad.

In arrangements for the night, I saw a specimen of that disregard of the comfort of others that even personal friends are said to be liable to show in traveling. The instance was slight —the premature seizing on a sleeping-place by the youngest LL.D. It only merits mention from the extreme rarity of the occurrence. For myself, I had an excellent night's rest in my hammock in the surgeon's room.

I had looked up from Toche to the road above with amazement, and an incredulity that would not believe my eyes. It appeared rather to be a work of fortification than a road. Zigzags, as steep as an armed soldier could ascend without climbing, seemed to run to points that nearly overhung the place where we stood. The lines and turns were as sharp as if carved in stone or built of brick. But no one could think it a road, for it aimed evidently at the highest peaks, and not at any pass that a road should seek.

INSCRIPTIONS ON STONES NEAR TOCHE.

But it was a road, and our road. Up we went, till, in three or four miles, I had risen more than in any other road of the same length in my life. And up there a new wonder met my incredulous eyes—two flat stones, with inscriptions, which show that this road is more than two hundred years old. They were copied by Señor Raphael Pombo, who kindly executed for me the annexed drawings. I read the first, "Por aqui paszó (for pasó) *Francisco* de Peñaranda, a 24 de Agosto, 1641."—Here passed Francisco de Peñaranda, 24th August, 1641. The second is broken, and I can not satisfy myself of the surname; neither can I learn what member of the ancient and noble family of Peñaranda was here at that day.

Now all this outrageous ascent is unnecessary. Our day's journey follows up the Tochecito. We keep mostly far above it, but probably only from Spanish or Indian aversion to roads on side-hill. And yet all quingo road is effectively side-hill road, for on one side is bank, and on the other steep descent.

I stopped to see some presidarios work, and to talk with the officer of the guard, when a new sight met my eyes: for the first time I saw one human being bearing another as a beast of burden. We were at the end of the labors of the presidio, and in advance were bad portions of road that the two ladies

SILLEROS IN THE QUINDIO.

were thus to pass. The accompanying sketch represents rather scenery of the next day in the first great de[illegible] the valley of the Cauca, but it here serves to illustrate [illegible] have now to describe.

The sillero is not an extremely athletic man. He is nude from the waist up, and his pantaloons are rolled up at the bottom as far as possible, especially in muddy weather. A rude chair (silla) of guadua, with a piece of white cotton cloth put over to keep off such rain and sun as it may, is all the apparatus. This is secured to the sillero's body by two belts crossing over the chest, and another passing over the forehead. The rider must keep absolutely still. If the sillero slip or stumble, any motion, however slight, of the rider, will insure a fall. It is, therefore, much easier to ride asleep than awake, and far safer. At the time I saw them first, the way was so terribly steep that I could not but think that a Northern lady would walk to rest her horse. There is sometimes the same feeling here. A lady told me that she refused to submit to it at first, but her condition forbade all idea of an alternative, and when compelled to yield, she did so with many tears. Colonel Hamilton, a British minister, arrived in Ibagué barefoot, with his feet bleeding, accompanied by two silleros, whom he paid liberally, but never used. Our two ladies took it more naturally. La Señora was already asleep, and Señorita, her sister, was reading.

A prodigious descent and a slight rise brought us to Gallego. We had hoped to pass the previous night there, but when I saw the spot I was glad we did not. It was an open tambo, a mere roof set on posts, without a particle of lateral shelter, or one element of comfort. Gloomy enough was the scene, for it was an immense wilderness of the wax-palm (Ceroxylon andicola). The tall and slender stems (represented as far too low in Humboldt's *Nova Genera*) were rising thick in every direction. The cylindrical trunks were from 12 to 15 inches in diameter, as straight as the shaft of a column, and terminated at the summit, say 50 feet high, by a tuft of huge leaves. The trunk, which, like all palms, is destitute of bark, is coated with a considerable film of wax, or, rather, it is believed, resin. It might be made a profitable business to collect and sell this, as much of the wax used in the churches is imported, and sells here at an extravagant price, nearly $3 per pound, when in the form of candles.

In nine months from the time we were seated there, eating dulce and drinking water, the scene was much changed. The presidio had been there, and left the tambo inclosed with walls, and had added two little huts and a shed. A man was still living in one of the huts when, as a slow, bitterly cold rain made the dismal scene tenfold more dismal, at nightfall, wounded and bleeding, I contrived to get off my horse at the tambo. My last meal had been before starting, on the morning of the day before, though chocolate and a little bread had sufficed to keep me alive. Of even this support I was partly deprived, for that morning I had incautiously bitten into a berry so intensely nauseous as to cause me to vomit up the little I had swallowed an hour before. I had thought it to be Passiflorate, but it proved to be Cucurbitate.

I was coming from the west, and, just before reaching the highest point of the Quindio, a shower came on. I mounted chiefly to keep my saddle dry. Both hands were filled with plants, that I had gathered even as I rode along in the rain, and over all was my encauchado, which is quite an impediment in an emergency. I was mounted on a rather tall and awkward horse, and the road was of the steepest. The rain had just ceased, and we were on the very last ascent. In ten minutes we were to leave the valley of the Cauca, when my horse fell. It was not necessary for me to dismount, but he would rise more easily. I attempted to land outside the path in a tuft of bushes, but, when too late, saw that I was stepping off a steep bank into the top of a thicket of shrubs.

I caught at the saddle. My horse was rising. I pulled him over. For an instant I saw the huge creature, whose feet were uppermost, directly above me. How I was not crushed under him I never shall know. To my surprise, I saw the horse roll down below me. He found himself in the road again where he had been a minute before, for he had fallen from one quingo to the next. I looked: my saddle was unbroken, my bag of oranges safe, the package of plants that I carried undamaged. Only the last gathered were crushed, and them I abandoned. I climbed up again, and then found a wound on my leg. I dared not mount, lest I should faint from pain. I abandoned my encauchado and horse to a servant, and walked in agony for half an hour. This was about noon, and now at night I stood in the rain at the tambo of Gallego. There is no level spot here large enough to hold two huts. The one in which I spent the night was about fifteen feet higher than the tambo, and distant about twenty feet horizontally. The steep paths were full of slippery mud, so that it was scarce possible to walk without falling.

Fortunately, the man that lived in this solitude had killed a black bear, and sold us some of the meat. The servants had nothing to spoil it with, and, in spite of the pain and the blood still trickling down my leg, I made a delicious dinner about 8. I then, with great difficulty, got some water to wash the wound, tied a silk handkerchief on it, put my dearly-earned plants in paper, slung my hammock, and by 10 I was asleep. Eight-and-forty hours after the accident I was in Ibagué, had taken off the handkerchief, procured some warm water, and was washing the bits of gravel out of the festering wound. Had I unfortunately broken a thigh, I could not have reached assistance, either by advancing or receding, in less than a week.

But this was all in the future, while we sat on the ground an hour eating marmalade and drinking the water, so deliciously cool then and so chilly thereafter. At another place, a contadero, I saw a monument like a tomb-stone, that must have been brought there at immense cost, on which I could read but one word, the revered name *Cáldas.* It turns out to be erected in honor of a mass celebrated there by Bishop somebody some centuries since, as I am informed by *a* Señor Cáldas, whose name suggested to me the lamented Granadan sage. He was waiting here to rest, and inscribed his name for want of something better to do.

Farther on we passed an abundance of fine drinking-places, from which the water flowed into the Tochecito, on our left; then came a great descent to the river. All the way down grows a cucurbitate vine with an elastic fruit. At length we are down to the bottom, and I feel sure that up to this point a road from Toche could have been built with less distance, no descent, no blasting, and level enough for carriages. Probably it would cost less than government will spend on the road during this visit of the presidio. We cross to the right bank of the Tochecito, here a small mill-stream, and commence our grand ascent. I relieved the tedium of the way by translating Longfellow's Excelsior into Spanish, and getting explained to me the difference between *la bandera*—the banner—and *lavandera*—a washerwoman—by a gentleman who knows no difference between the sound of *b* and *v*. He made me comprehend by the time he got well out of breath. I am afraid I hardly acted fairly.

Nearly at the top was the tambo of Yerba Buena, so called from an abundance of peppermint—Mentha piperita—that grows there and in many other places. We halted early at Volcancito, a tambo inclosed by upright poles, then the best in the whole mountain. The roof let in some light, the walls admitted the wind freely, and the floor was of loose dirt. It was early, and I gloried in Volcancito, gathering Fuchsias of different species, Begonias, and other tropical plants, together with an Epilobium, that reminded me of home.

I had a different idea of the climate of Volcancito in the morning. About sunset the cold began to sting my feet, and I had to change my alpargatas for stockings and slippers—my only alternative, for we open no trunks this week. In washing my feet I found water too cold for me, for the first time in South America. I immediately began to dress for bed, putting on first flannels of the thickest description, then a night-shirt, a woolen hunting-shirt, and over all a thick hunting-coat. I risked my nether half, in which the blood had been circulating well since leaving Ibagué, in a pair of flannel drawers and corduroy pantaloons.

These were my *extraordinary* preparations. I began my ordinary ones soon after dinner. I had studied in Ibagué, where they have cold nights, the art of sleeping warm in a hammock, and, as it is not understood even here, I will communicate it. I took my two thick blankets by one end, holding them up together, and lowered them to a mat on the floor. Then I laid them across the foot of the hammock, and, with assistance (for it was very high), threw myself into it. Next I drew the blankets out of their folds and over me by the end I held before. Next I brought the edges of the blankets within the hammock. So far every body knows, but as yet I have nothing beneath me but a thickness of cotton; my rear must be better defended. Here comes my secret. I draw myself up from the centre of the hammock, where I am to sleep, toward the head. Then I put the edges of the blanket beneath me, so that they pass each other, beginning at the feet and ending at the shoulders, where the process is very difficult, but is aided by gradually sliding down the hammock to the point of equilibrium. Now only remains the delicate task of placing myself diagonally in the hammock, so that the head and feet are less elevated. All these operations, be it remembered, are to be performed as on a slack-rope.

All were suffering with the cold. It was a time for Mark Tapley to be jolly in. I called on Señor for a tale, and he complied. He told one which gave me a new idea of a language in which there are no indecent words, or, if there be, it is past any conjecture what they would represent. Fortunately for me, the character of all the parties present was beyond suspicion, so I was only surprised, not alarmed, at a tale that in England would date back to the days of Charles II.

But there is another puzzle about that tale, either ethnological or psychological. It must be that I have heard a variation of it before, and that in English, and before I was ten years old. How shall I ascertain? Can any member of the Percy Society inform me if there is a tale of past centuries about two people spending a night in a tree, and throwing down a table, or a door that would serve for one, on the heads of some robbers that were dividing their booty below? If so, childish tales have an older date and a wider range than I could have thought possible, and this foolish one must be known all over Western Europe and both Americas.

Unfortunately, I had succeeded too well with my hammock. A generous glow at length pervaded my frame, and my heart began to expand, and inquire into the state of those around me. Señorita was very cold, and had no prospect of sleeping all night. I asked myself, "Can I spare my thinnest blanket?" My expanded heart answered, "For a lady, an amiable young lady whom I esteem, and who is suffering with cold more intense than ever she has known, I can." But I found that, like the last feather that broke the camel's back, this blanket was necessary to break the power of the cold. I passed a sleepless night. I tried a new manœuvre; I put myself on my right side, on the right edge of the hammock, bringing the rest over me for a cover.

Thus I resembled a huge follicle, or, zoologically speaking, a bivalve, holding my shell shut with my hands, a knee, and my head, which rested on the inflexed edge of my upper valve. This failed, and, when too late to sleep, I added my blanket and hammock to the covering of one of the cold would-be sleepers on the floor, and crawled in by his side to thaw.

In the morning I found Señorita's shawl on the bed of the young LL.D., that lay at the foot of hers. She too had a heart, and, in a moment when her left hand knew not what her right hand did, she had lent it before she received my blanket. A hearty laugh followed this discovery, and to this day the mention of Volcancito seems to make a peculiar impression on the young lady.

Short and unsatisfactory was the breakfast we made before leaving Volcancito. We were near the edge of the Páramo, and even here the ground is sometimes covered with snow for nearly a week at once. A peculiar visitation sometimes overtakes the traveler at these altitudes. Without suffering intensely with the cold, he suddenly loses his strength, then his life. This is *emparamarse*, an occurrence that had nearly proved fatal to one of my friends, and which I have had occasion once or twice to guard against. But now we had nothing to fear, and I even resumed my scant walking-dress, and had a delightful day. We crossed an abundance of cool streams, all flowing to our left. On the banks of one of them I found a magnificent Equisetum, 5 or 6 feet high. I lost it by trusting to the assurance that others as large could be found in the plains of the Cauca, and from the great difficulty of saving specimens on this solitary road. We reached in an hour or two the dividing ridge, and kept it for some time.

Here the road became bad as we descended, though nothing in comparison to those frightful semi-subterranean ditches through which Cochran rode and the fat Hamilton walked for long distances, without elevating the head up to the level of the ground. These trenches (callejones) sometimes lay along our road like buffalo-traps (mule-traps), and sometimes opened upon it like the mouth of a deserted mine. Had either of these travelers been given to exaggeration, they would not have attempted it in describing these callejones.

This was the scene of my catastrophe on a later trip. Here too is laid the scene of a tale, that well may be true, of a Spanish official who, having a right to compel the service of unpaid silleros, rode one with a pair of those horrid mule spurs. The poor Indian, goaded past endurance, threw his brute of a rider down a steep, where he was killed by the fall, and then fled to the woods and never returned.

The ladies, who had been in their chairs only a little in the latter part of the steep ascent from Toche, now took them for a good part of the day. Señora slept, Señorita read, and the sillero went on as if his chair was empty. None seemed to feel that there were any necks at stake.

At 2 we reached Barcinal, the first house since leaving Toche, the sixth in seventy-two hours. Here was a family of Antioqueños, who supplied us with masamorra, made of cracked maize, boiled and eaten with milk. This is a favorite dish in that secluded province. I like the Antioqueños and the Antioqueñas, and I like their caps, but I think I should not like the too frequent recurrence of masamorra.

Between Barcinal and Toche there is no good place to pass the night, and yet they are more than a day's journey apart. The best remedy is a better road, and one could be made that would bring one through even in bad weather. Had we proceeded to Gallego the second night, we might have reached Barcinal on the following, and saved the martyrdom of Volcancito.

A steep, rough road led from Barcinal down to Boquía, on the banks of the Quindio. Boquía is the head of a district in the province of Cauca. It has some tolerable houses, a good posada, the beginnings of a church, a wheat-mill that I saw in actual operation, and a covered bridge over a branch of the Quindio. Provisions might sometimes be bought here.

After fording the Quindio, quite a large mill-stream, nearly two feet deep, we found a broad and beautiful ascent, followed by another that put the ladies in their chairs, and brought us to El Roble (The Oak). We stopped here early, and just in season to avoid a brisk shower, which surprised the arrieros before their tent was completed. El Roble is not so high as Volcancito. We passed the night more like Christians, eating at a table, sleeping in a house, and Señorita even had a bed-room to herself nominally, but she could not be secure from intrusion.

We left El Roble on Friday morning. A gentle descent of about three miles brought us to another Antioqueño family, at Portachuela, a pleasant place to stop. Here I found out what arrepas are, and discover that I have avoided them in New England under the name of Johnny-cake, and in Illinois as hoe-cake, pone, and corn-dodgers.

We stopped again at a contadero, called Lagunetas, and dispatched peons to bring us drink. I suppose that, as the name implies, they found it in "mud-holes," or "little ponds." In going west, it is well to drink here, or to carry on water from Portachuela.

From here on I found the roads slippery with rain, and almohadillado, i. e., full of "mule-ladders," between the rounds of which the animal puts his feet into a deep mud-hole. I put my feet there too by misfortune, and one time my knee, to the no small detriment of my personal appearance. I soon lost sight of my company. I found no water to drink all day, but found a drink of milk on the way. Here I was overtaken by a man going from Boquía to Cartago in a day and a half; for us it is more than two days, if not three. He had a corner of his ruana pinned up into a pocket, from which projected the head of a live chicken, a present to a lady in Cartago.

About 2 I arrived at La Balsa (The Raft). I had promised myself a good swim in the river, but found there was no river here. I am totally at a loss for the origin of the name. I scarcely found water enough to wash the mud off my feet. Here I waited an hour or two for the company, and when they arrived it was decided to go no further.

La Balsa is the first place that deserves a name since leaving Ibagué. The population of the district is stated at 199, and that of Boquía 198, but both are scattered over more than 100 square miles each. I know of no reason for a town here, but it is very convenient to us. I now made a grand discovery, and that was that I liked plantains cooked. So rarely are they cooked really ripe, that I knew not the taste of a ripe one. Here is the first place that I have seen them abundant. They take them to Cartago to sell. A large raceme of green ones was given to one of the led horses for his dinner.

Here we dined on the floor, and, in consequence of a rain coming on just after we stopped, I got no plants. We made the acquaintance, more lasting than profitable, with the zancudo, which I found, on examination, is no more nor less than the musquito. In all my trip from Honda here I do not know that I have seen any, and here they were so few that I only heard one or two.

Saturday morning found me a little anxious about the end of our journey, especially as it had begun to rain. I put on my encauchado, and, though I could have had a horse the whole day, kept my feet. Señora's sillero could not do as much; he spilled his precious charge four times in the morning. I happened to be talking with her at the time of the first fall, and continued with her till she again took the saddle.

One comical picture might have been witnessed had there only been a spectator to laugh. The chair was broken, and must be mended. He stood his burden upon a huge log, three feet in diameter. It must be sheltered, and the only possible shelter was one end of my encauchado, but it served well its purpose.

The Señorita, more fortunate, had not a fall in crossing the mountain. I saw one place where the foot of her sillero had slipped a yard; but she is less timorous than her sister, and seems to have kept from starting. Two silleros fell with the Señora.

At Piedra de Moler, which signifies either grindstone or millstone, is a ferry across the La Vieja, into which the Quindio empties some way above. Here we paid a peaje or tax of 80 cents each to the province of Cauca. It can not be called toll, for it is not expended on the highways. With the exception of a little piece of territory that lies west of the Cauca, where a road that runs up and down the river may belong to the province, all the road in the province is national, but it is very rare for either nation or province to spend any thing on it. I recollect in the space of nine months only the building of a single foot-bridge, and am sure I have seen no other labor or money expended on the highway.

This time we did not allow the ferry to delay us much. We stopped to see the beasts swim across—an interesting sight—

went to the ferryman's house to eat some eggs and roasted plantains, and came on, leaving our baggage to follow in two detachments.

The rain had ceased, but threatened, so that I thought prudent to retain my defenses. An immense hill only remained to ascend and descend, for Cartago is on the bank of the river we passed.

Ascending the hill, I saw the Bihai (Heliconia Bihai), a Cannate herb, that supplied leaves for shelter to travelers before tambos were built. The leaves are of that characteristic Scitaminate form shown in our gardens by the Indian-shot (Canna), and in pictures by those of the plantain and banana. They are from one to two feet long, whitish beneath, and are hung by a notch in the petiole to horizontal strings passing over the poles that make the roof of a rancho. Each peon and carguero was bound to carry his quota of these from this place going eastward, and the traveler might have to sleep nearly a fortnight under a thatch thus transported.

From the top we had the first good view of the Valley of the Cauca. It was not level, but rolling, as they say at the West. Its vivid green contrasted beautifully with the dry plains of Ibagué and Espinal. I can scarcely believe that there can be a more beautiful scene than that where the plain breaks in upon the view. Around you still is the rugged scenery of the mountain, while in the blue distance are the Cáldas mountains, which I fear I shall never cross. It would be more beautiful still were the Cauca visible; but, as its right bank is lined with uninterrupted swamp and forest, it is not to be seen but by penetrating to it. We had obtained a single glimpse of the valley the day before, not long after leaving Lagunetas, but it was only through a narrow opening of the trees.

Soon after coming in full sight of the plain the duties of the silleros ceased. At the first pool below, they put themselves in their best trim to make their appearance in Cartago. Camisas were drawn forth from some safe storage, and hats and ruanas, added to the simple costume of the mountains, made them into ordinary peasants.

At length we reached the plain, but when we made the change from primitive formation to the alluvial I can not tell. I doubt even if the line is capable of being determined, so strongly do the soils of the two resemble each other.

The expense of the trip I can not tell exactly. The cost of beasts was 52 dimes each, including peon service; the subsistence may have been half that sum, but we kept no separate accounts. Our expenses will be found rather below the average cost of crossing the Quindio, unless the losses from petty thefts are to be reckoned in. My chief loss was a hatchet having two chisels deposited in a cavity of the handle, a towel (not that crash one), and, of course, as much rope as they could easily lay their hands on.

We arrived in good season on Saturday, but our baggage did not get in till too late for mass the next day. Cartago is a town of about the size of Ibagué, but much lower and warmer. But still I suffered little with the heat here or with the cold there. For a man who is under the necessity of corporal labor in the sun, the climate of Ibagué is much to be preferred to that of this part of the Valley of the Cauca. My lowest altitude in the valley has been 2880 feet, and the highest temperature in the shade was 85°, at La Paila, 11th June, 1853, at 4 P.M. Even this is tolerable. The hottest I have seen in the sun was 127°. This I have seen exceeded in New York city. For the rest, my observations in the valley may be seen in the Appendix.

Cartago has much more of tile and less of thatch than Ibagué. The place is old, but not entirely finished, for I saw one house of tapias still going up. They put together a frame, with sides of strong plank, shovel in earth, and beat it down. Bars that hold the frame together leave holes through the wall, but these can be stopped. The work is rather slow, but as no frost ever attacks these walls, they are as good as brick, and in an earthquake even better. By whitewashing occasionally, they are as beautiful at a distance as marble, and much cheaper.

I searched the churches for any thing of note, and found only a Saint George—San Jorje (pronounced hoar-hay)—mounted over one of the altars, with his dragon beneath his horse's feet, of course. This saint is rather rare in this country.

Cartago stands on the La Vieja, but opposite the town is a large grassy island, with a small and safe arm on this side, and a stream beyond that would be navigable for a small steam-boat. It is two or three miles from the banks of the Cauca, as, indeed, are all the towns. This little branch is a favorite bathing-place, and Sunday is a favorite day, so I found the little stream swarming with all ages, both sexes, and a variety of costumes and colors. The stream was now so high that a girl of twelve or fourteen had just been rescued from drowning, they said. I saw her adjusting her hair very composedly, and the danger, if it had been real, seemed to have made no impression.

On a subsequent day I visited the jail. It is like any other house. One chap was making pictures, or paintings, he called them, of such a desperate character that I think he ought not to be turned loose without formally forswearing the brush—I will not say pencil. Another held undisturbed possession of the front sala and the adjoining bed-rooms. His windows opened out on pleasant balconies, in view of the plaza mayor. One of his frequent visitors proposed to the alcaide to put a ladder up to one of the balconies, and save himself the trouble of letting him in and out.

The girls' school seemed to be in a remarkably fine condition. The patio was full of flowers, better cultivated than any where else probably in the whole province. The children seemed more lively and cheerful than ordinary; the result of zeal, I think, in the teacher, who seemed more than usually qualified for the task. Give her books, and her pupils would become ladies. I went to looking over their reading-books, and found one reading-lesson of so singular a nature that I could not resist my desire to possess it, so I went home and tore in two a number of *El Dia*, a Jesuit newspaper. I selected a half which had a long string of verses, beginning, "I, the President, am an Ass, and my master, Faction, rides me." This I gave her for a reading-lesson in exchange for hers, which was a small electioneering hand-bill, containing all the names of the candidates of both parties, with a foot-note to each, praising those of one party, and bringing scandalous charges against the others. A picture of the Goddess of Silence in the room is the work of Señor Santibañas, one of the best native artists now extant: small praise, I allow.

I called at his studio, and saw there some clam-shells, a thing so rare that I have known no others in all New Granada. He directed me to a pond where I found two species alive. The pond had no outlet, and the bottom is quite muddy, but it is still resorted to for bathing by some who do not like the brisk, clear water of the river. One of these species* is said to have been also picked up on the pebbly banks of the Paila River, 30 miles south of here. I can not now think it lived there.

I attended in Cartago the best ball that I saw in all the country. I can not deny that it was dull, but the participants appeared quite like gentlemen and ladies. Still, there was a restraint and stiffness in the affair that we do not see in our best society at the North, and which I should not expect in a Southern race. One event of the evening struck me too strongly to be easily forgotten. A young gentleman entered the room about 8, radiant with smiles of satisfaction: he was cordially received, and entered into the dancing with great spirit. I found that he had lain all the week in jail for debt. It was only since dark that he had gained his liberty, and he did not seem at all mortified at the occurrence.

Imprisonment is abolished for debts contracted since a certain date, but the old laws were even too severe. No amount of security would suffice to liberate the debtor against the will of the creditor—nothing but the money. The creditor is to allow the prisoner a real a day for subsistence.

They had just had a grand time in Cartago before my arrival. The Plaza had been fenced in for bulls. The favorite game of *Horned monkey* (Cachimona), in which dice are used and coins change owners, had disappointed some and elated others. But the only thing of interest that I lost was some open air plays on a stage of guaduas, that was still standing in a corner of a plazuela, in an angle made by a church and the sacristia. I must content myself with the account of this from an article in the "Neo Granadino" by an eye-witness, who had left Cartago just as I arrived:

"It was announced as something extra that there would be two plays acted. But let no one imagine (although it might be reasonably expected) that they were to be minor pieces, farces

* Since writing the above, I have learned that by Lea this shell of ambiguous habitat has been named Anodonta Holtonis. The other was Mycetopus siliquoides.

of one act, or comedies adapted to the taste of the multitude, for whom the dramatic compliment was designed. They had the knack to hit upon two grand dramatic spectacles, in which all the performers, even to the prompter, commit suicide. They abounded in places, histories, passions, customs, catastrophes, courts, cardinals, princes, and executioners, whose names the *amateur* performers could not pronounce. And they were to be acted on a scaffold erected in a corner of a public square, for the benefit of all those who could afford the price of standing bareheaded half a night in the open air.

"After a long delay, and clamorous calls for the rising of the modest cloth that played the part of curtain, it rose. Then rose, too, the laugh of the spectators, who protested and resisted accepting as Lord Chambeland, Duque de Norfold, and Sir Grammer, the three worthy citizens who topsyturvically (*alrevesadamente*) pronounced these names, and applied them to each other. These English noblemen were dressed in the masquerade of private theatricals.

"But the uproar reached its height when Henry VIII.* appeared. On his head was a crown, that he had to hold with one hand lest it should fall when he moved. His dress, modern in the extreme, showed that the capricious monarch was very prophetic in the matter of fashions. He spoke, addressing himself rather to the masses than to his interlocutor. He told of Edward, of Malcolm, of William the Conqueror, of William Rufus, of Edgar, of his successor David, father of Steven—of the Empress Matilda, of Catharine Howard, and of other names and other things, all well known, of course, both in the theatres of Paris and on the 'boards' (guaduas) of Cartago.

"Now some began to grow desperate, drowning the voice of the actors, and exciting obstreperous laughter in the audience. In one of the most pathetic passages they shifted a scene, or, rather, the cloth that served for one, and many cried out at once that the *door* is *fawling*—que se *quee* la puerta. A child began to cry, and from more than one voice was heard the rude order to give that baby the teat—(*ubre*, not *pecho*). Then stones began

* It is easy to foresee that the Reformation was not to be highly exalted in this drama; but the Romish Church are not to blame for making the most they can out of old *Bluebeard.*

to fly. Dr. Galindo was hit near us, and we retired well pleased, you may guess, with the *atraso** of that sovereign mob, who observed so much decorum and quiet in the presence of all the authorities, civil and military, who (I had forgotten to state it) were present."

CHAPTER XXVI.

A CAUCAN FAMILY.

Scheme for Revealing and Concealing.—Introduction to the Family.—House in Cartago.—Bad Ear-ache and Ball.—How to go to Bed.—Water-boys.—Fleas. —Horsemanship.—Using a Hacienda as an Inn.—A Peasant Liar.—La Cabana.—An ugly Hole in the Dark.

My good reader, I am going to take you into my confidence so far as to tell you what I have been doing in the whole day since I translated the paragraph above. I have made out a *key*, changing the name and residence of nearly every person that I am hereinafter to mention. If you will take my book in hand, and come into the Cauca to track me out, you will find every brook, hill, and hole as I am now to lay them down. So, too, in general, as to the houses, the descriptions shall be very exact, only in three or four cases I may *move* them for special reasons.

But the characters that I shall draw shall be as faithful as I am capable of making them. In one or two cases a conjecture shall be suppressed, but no ascertained fact withholden that would throw light on human nature. No character shall be a composition, or taken from two or more individuals; and, however much the scene of an occurrence may be varied, the characters in it shall be real, and generally shall bear the same name throughout.

And now we will go out on the plain, and meet the first party that we judge worth our study, as they may be coming in from the country. As we stand by the pond, in which live the shellfish mentioned a few pages back, we see a party approaching.

* Atraso is the reverse of progreso — progress — an idea almost worshiped by the Granadinos. Unfortunately, of the presence of this Messiah of theirs we find too little evidence, but their desire for it is earnest and universal.

They suit my purpose, for I know them well. The portly, intelligent gentleman that leads the van is Señor Eladio Vargas (Murgueitio), a well-educated gentleman, who is returning from his hacienda, on the banks of the Tuluá, to his home in Cartago. He has studied in Lleras' Colegio in Bogotá, as have all the best-educated gentlemen of my acquaintance; and, like many of them, he is a violent political enemy of his preceptor, and you must make allowance for all he says of him. We always have to make allowance for some things even in our best friends, and I must confess my fear that Don Eladio does not always stop with exaggeration even.

In the house of a respectable merchant in Bogotá he found his wife, Señora Susana Pinzon de Vargas, an amiable, not over-energetic lady, with whom he is riding, and to whom he is very attentive and truly kind. I am able to say that the Spanish race make far superior husbands to the French, nor do I know that, in this respect, they are excelled in the world. Doña Susana learned what she knows chiefly by being immured in the school of the widow of President Santander. She is not, however, greatly inclined to books. She is, at least, respectful to the Church, and wears a carnelian cross, the gift of a pope to a bishop, who was her uncle. She is just now intensely suffering with ear-ache, and to this is added the fatigue of a journey 50 miles from the banks of the Tuluá.

With her comes her sister, Señorita Manuela Pinzon. Educated with Susana by the care of the Señora de Santander, she is perhaps more literary, and in body and mind more active than she. As to her personal appearance, the reader must judge for himself. But in the figure opposite you see her in the dress in which she took a fancy to be pictured, and in which she has been wont to display herself and her horsemanship in the Alameda of Bogotá. You would see, on her approach to Cartago, the same horse, bridle, saddle, and face; but in dress all is changed, except the ruana, and possibly the hat. An ordinary walking-dress is the basis of her costume. A handkerchief, thrown over her head, is kept in place by a fine ruana, lined with silk on the under side, and a hat, perhaps a small one, of jipijapa, like an ordinary boy's hat, tied under her chin.

Señora Manuela is of a cheerful and lively turn of mind, not

FASHIONABLE RIDING-DRESS.

so pious as her sister, but still a faithful attendant at the mass on days when absence is sin—on the fasts and feasts. She can talk rapidly and much, but she says little that would interest those who knew none of her acquaintances. And yet her stock of information is considerably above that of ladies in general, for she has read a number of novels of Dumas and Sue—translated into Spanish, of course, for very few ladies here read French.

But the most decided character of the group is yet to be mentioned. It is the gentleman's sister, Señorita Elodia Várgas. She has a character of her own, as well as a face easily remembered. Of a stronger make than most ladies, and with a varied life, she has been alike at home in the Cauca, Bogotá, and Chocó. There I think she was born, to rule over a hundred slaves, that washed gold for her father, ate plantains and fish, and went almost naked. They are free, and the family revenues are reduced indeed; for the gold-washings can not be prosecuted by whites in Chocó, and free negroes will not work when they desire nothing that gold can bring. Hence only one fourth as much gold is obtained as before 1852. So the old place in Chocó has gone to ruin, Señor Várgas is dead, and the family must live on what the ill-managed Hacienda of La Ribera can yield.

But all this seems to make little difference with Elodia Várgas (Murgueitio). Dignified, calm, and pious, she seems to be above such changes. She is a faithful observer of all the ordinances of her Church. She is in many respects the head of the family, and her strong will is law to the members of the family as well as the servants. They lack firmness—she has enough; and her judgment proves the best in the end.

Just as we re-entered Cartago we passed one of the numerous bridges that cross the brooks and ditches which are plenty in the plain around. The old wooden structure had given way, and let in a gentleman's carga mule. A part of the load had been a live Guinea-pig, brought for some days from up the river, which, when on the threshold of a new home, had thus finished its mortal journey. We crossed the ditch—brook I ought to call it, I suppose—without being much bespattered, and in a moment more were in the Plaza, and, entering a porton, soon found ourselves in the patio of a casa alta.

As we filed up the stairs, at the head there was another file to meet us. Don Eladio found himself first in the arms of his widowed mother, Doña Ana Murgueitio de Várgas, a woman of nearly sixty, something like her daughter Elodia, though hardly as dignified as she will be at her mother's age. I wish it were more common for old women to be pretty here, but that can not be without education. But of really *old* women there can not be many in the country. I can not think now of an octogenarian of either sex.

Next in order came a pretty girl of about seventeen—Mercedes. Of her parentage or relations I know little, except that Eladio whispered to me, at the first opportunity, "She is the daughter of a white man." I should think her mother, too, might have been as white as his.

With two more embracings Eladio's salutations were finished. These were with a venerable negro cook, and another servant, a few shades lighter, and a little cleaner in dress. In all these huggings I had no part. The first half of them, or even less, would have pleased me as well as the whole; indeed, I was contented with the matter as it was.

The house had originally been one of magnificent dimensions. It occupied three sides of a square, and covered ground enough for a large hotel. But it had been inherited by two children, who proceeded to run a wall through the middle, with a porton on each side, and in the same way the front and back patios were divided. Evidences of diminished magnificence in this way are visible over all the towns of the Cauca, but in this case it was an advantage; for, had the furniture of the family been scattered over double the space, it would have cost them much unnecessary walking to go from article to article.

In addition to the interior corredor, we have balconies overlooking the Plaza, and an exterior corredor on the side that overlooks a church patio filled with a dense mass of weeds. This corredor is our dining-room, and a pleasant one. The kitchen is still farther from the street, a large, desolate room, without a table or chair, and, withal, somewhat dilapidated in its walls. The tinajera, the forge-like cooking-place, and the grinding-stone, are all that the room contains. The transit from the sala to the dining corredor can not be made without passing through the principal dormitory of the family or through this kitchen. The road by the dormitory, even had it been the longer, would be better to travel in going to dinner.

One article of furniture surprised me. It was a spacious and elegant iron bedstead from Europe, with a wide, thick, and soft hair mattress, that might have made a bed for the President, had he been a Conservador and their guest. As it is, it seems rather an article of curiosity, for I do not know that it has ever yet been covered with sheets, unless it be to keep the dust off; nor is it of any use except to show what Sybarites the Temperate Zone harbors. How we all sleep here is more than I can say. The ground floor in the rear is a stable, and in front it is rented to a family. The servants sleep in the kitchen, or on the floor of the principal dormitory. I assign the smaller dormitory to the queenly, pious Elodia, sprightly Manuela, and Mercedes, the white man's daughter. And Eladio, his mother, wife, two children, and their nurse, with the two other servants, could find plenty of room in the large dormitory. My inseparable friend, the hammock, hangs in the sala, a luxury by day and a necessity at night.

But Susana Pinzon de Vargas has the ear-ache. She is distracted with it. It is worse after dinner. She can hardly sit still long enough to nurse her babe. And a ball is coming off to-night. It is not a hacienda ball, such as we are yet to see, but a town ball, such as we saw in the last chapter, from which it seems that neither the sick nor those in prison can be spared; for Susana went not distracted as I feared, but, needing some distraction in her agony, went to the ball, and, as I could not attend this evening, I saw her no more till morning.

In the morning she was no better, and the doctor was called. He prescribed cupping, and the barber was accordingly sent for. He produced a scarificator, and Doña Susana was surprised that so ingenious a piece of mechanism should have strayed beyond the walls of the Inquisition. But the proposition of trying its multiplied knives on her was simply absurd. And, indeed, scarification in any form, however proper for others, could never be permitted on her. The physician was gone, and when Eladio proposed, as a compromise, that she be bled in the arm, she assented, glad to be thus rid of the barber, and he assented, glad thus to gain his fee and be off.

An accidental discovery here looks worse than it is: let no lady faint over it or scream audibly. I happened in the dormitory one morning before Señor Vargas had risen. He was late, for the Señorita Manuela Pinzon, his sprightly sister-in-law, was already dressed and conversing with him when he began to rise. He sat up in bed stark naked, except so far as covered by the bed-clothes, for, like Jaques Couche-tout-nu in the Wandering Jew, he denudes himself entirely when he goes to bed. I do not know whether this custom prevails out of the Cauca: I should not have discovered it if it had.

I can not tell what people do in Cartago. It is a quiet place for one in its position. It stands where four great ways of commerce meet. Above is a grazing country, that yields horses, mules, beef, and pork. Beef is cheaper on the vast plains of the East, in Casanare, for instance, but there they have no demand for it. Below Cartago is the gold country of Antioquia, including also part of the province of Cauca, where little food is raised. Rough, steep, and rocky, it looks to the plains above for its beef and pork, horses and mules. I estimate this digging population at 249,822, most of whom eat some beef and pork, and use some beasts of burden. West of here is the gold-washing, fish-eating province of Chocó, with a population of 43,639. Enough of these see beef and lard once a year, or oftener, to make the population dependent on the pastures above Cartago a quarter of a million.

Some horses and mules are driven over the Quindio, but no beef. Dried beef is sold for this journey. Most of the salt used in the upper Cauca comes over the Quindio, and a large part of the imported goods. Most of the hides of animals raised here are put to uses unknown at the North, as mats, beds, baskets, trunks, packing-boxes, chairs, cordage, harness, fence, doors, and other uses too numerous to mention; so there is no hide trade. A tobacco trade is springing up. The cinchona of the province of Popayan passes through Cartago, and over the Quindio, to avoid the risks of Buenaventura. Tobacco makes its exit in both directions. Cacao is raised above, and sent through here to the mines. Rice might be. Indigo might be exported.

You would expect merchants here with advertisements out in all directions of "Highest cash price paid for cacao;" "Beef wanted;" "Wanted 100 mules;" "Northern goods given for indigo;" "Coffee received in the smallest quantities for silks and hardware." No such thing. Probably no merchant in Cartago ever spent a dollar in advertising. Barter is unknown to me, if even the word is found in Spanish. *Trueque*, the nearest word, would hardly suggest the idea.

Commerce has three stages of existence. First is naked cash, without bills, barter, or credit. It is sure—sure as the march of a snail. Next comes barter, mixed, of course, with what cash there may be in a region. For this the Cauca commerce seems waiting. Lastly comes the *fast* system of cash, bills of credit, bank-notes, exchange, double-entry, shaving, great fortunes, and splendid bankruptcies for half a million. The light of this millennium is yet to dawn here.

With all this, I am surprised to see so little in the streets of

WATER-BOY AT CARTAGO.

Cartago. The most active doings I see are the movements of the water-boys. They are mounted on a mule, a horse, or the ruins of either, while yet the vital spark remains. To the four corners of the saw-horse that serves as a saddle are hung four tarras of guadua. The imp to whose mercy the quadruped is abandoned rides deep enough into the arm of the La Vieja to dip up his water without dismounting. He ought to dip it up only on the upper side of the horse, with no other water-boy above him, nor any groom washing down horses, nor any bathers, but you can not make such a scapegrace careful. His mind is all bent on running races with water-boys as wretchedly mounted as himself. Now he is stopped by a woman that offers him a cigar if he will hang on her two tarras, and return them to her full. He asks no consent of his beast or his employer. So a water-boy knows no want of cigars.

I can not take leave of Cartago without mentioning the most numerous, and by far the most active part of its population. The flea is a beautiful object when secured in balsam between two plates of glass for the microscope. Trained to drag a chain or draw a carriage, as these little hexapods are said to have been, they are worthy of the attention of the curious. And organize them into an army, and the sharp, slender claws, so beautifully exhibited in the microscope, show themselves admirable for clinging to you, and the curious lancet is a most perfect instrument for perforating the human cuticle.

But to all these good qualities there are two drawbacks. One is his nullibiquity—*nirgendheit* our German cousins would call it—his *no-where-ness* "when you put your finger on him;" and the other is the hardness of his cuirass. It would take me till night to tell you of all the adventures which have taught me the extent of these qualities. One time I will "put my finger on him" really. I crush him, ruin him, pulverize him, and take up my finger to feast my eyes on his mangled carcass, when lo! he bounds off eight hundred times his length, and I can almost imagine a tiny derisive laugh at the idea of his getting a broken leg or a sprained ankle so easily. I can find another more easily than catch him again.

Another time I wet my finger before I put it on him: he shall not fool me so. I rub him till I have broken every bone in his body, and almost the bones of my finger besides. I stop and deliberate whether I will let him up yet. No; I will make assurance doubly sure by giving him one more crushing. Then I take my finger off, and lo, "he isn't there!" Of course I look foolish. But no mortal can stave off his fate when his time comes; so I find recorded in my diary, "Paila, 9 July, 1853. Had a capital day. Dreamed of home last night; had recent beef for dinner; got a new plant, caught a butterfly, and *killed a flea*." The flea that died that day met, doubtless, an accidental death; but my last visit to Cartago initiated me into the art of flea-catching by incessant practice. I killed dozens of them. It was almost worth a journey there. Once I went down the La Vieja and bathed. I turned my clothes inside out, and with unpitying eye saw no less than six ejected, far from any house, to take the chances of the weather; and all the way home I was the sole tenant of my vestments.

But we must leave Cartago. Don Eladio and his wife, her sister, and the children, are to start for Tuluá. His kindness mounted me on an easy horse and a safe one, for he considers me a babe in horsemanship. What he would say to one whose equestrian education had been finished on a Yankee farm, without any farther lessons at the South and West, I can not tell. There ought to be no better horsemen in the world than those of the Cauca, but you would never observe the fact. The Caucano is not proud of his horsemanship. He makes no display, and I do not know of any one who has any reputation as a horseman, or wishes any. They ride as if by instinct and of course. Still, I think we have some greatly exaggerated accounts of Spanish-American horsemanship.

We soon passed rock in situ—not in a mountain, not in a high hill. The road had once passed over a steep knoll, 15 feet high. Travel had cut it down to a level with the plain for a space of 10 feet in width.

The sides and bottom of this cut are horizontal strata of sandstone. Farther up I found strata of infusorial earth in it. It is so soft and so white that it is used as chalk, and both are called tiza. The best I saw was 10 or 15 miles above Cartago, where I picked out a specimen from the bank for my friends at home.*

I can not say enough of the country over which we swiftly sweep in a large and gay troop. Bosques, knolls, green glades, gentle slopes, hill-sides, and small plains came along in an ever-varying succession. Only the brooks were mute. They had neither velocity nor pebbles to give them voice. They added no beauty where they alone could have added any.

At Saragoza, a small village, some who had mounted to accompany us took leave and turned back. Just there I saw the first and last live specimen of the sloth, here called Perico lijero (swift Perico). It may be the Acheus Aï. Aï is a natural interjection expressive of pain, and is given to the animal on account of his doleful cries. He was as large as a middle-sized dog, and clung to the stick to which he was tied, and by which his possessor bore him on his shoulder. They live back downward, in a state of perpetual suspense that would be quite dis-

* It was lost.

agreeable to ordinary animals. They are no more helpless on the ground than a lamb would be in a tree. Specimens of mammals are so scarce here that the traveler should never presume on future opportunities. Much to my regret, I had to leave this.

At dark I discovered the head of the column entering the gate of Señor Pedro Sánchez, a few miles north of Obando. It stands somewhat out of the way, on a pleasant knoll. I did not suppose at the time that he had any better business than keeping a sort of tavern, by giving his rooms up to travelers. I have since learned not to judge men by their furniture. The family left the sala to our sole occupancy. The spirit of delay, that guides all travelers' movements here, made our morning start to hang off till 3 P.M. For this we made up by a dinner between 9 and 10. My short, rapid ride fatigued me exceedingly, more so than the hardest day's walk.

While waiting in the piazza for dinner, they diverted me with the babe-carrier by setting him to lying. He was a thick-set Chocó negro of about 40 or 45, whose comical ways of pacifying the babe on his back, when it worried, had diverted me much more than did the lies he now told, which had no other merit than their size and coolness. Among the rest, he said he was engaged to a beautiful princess in Europe, and was going on soon to claim his bride. He appeared fully satisfied when he found he had earned from me the surname of Pedro el Embustero (Pedro the Liar).

We were obliged to supply our own water, and that delayed us considerably. The peon that went after it had with him another to dispel his fears, light his way, or drive off the wild beasts with a bright-flaming brand that resembled pitch-pine, but was called ciprés. Neither this nor cedro are coniferous trees. The latter may be Amyris or Cedrela. Of the former I could obtain leaves only.

It was a pleasant January evening as we sat out there in the piazza, neither too warm nor too cold, till our dinner was ready, and then I was soon hung up in my hammock, and the others spread round miscellaneously, and all asleep on tables, poyo, and floor. We decided to rise at two, take chocolate immediately, and start at three. No such plan is ever executed. We left at half past four, but without our chocolate. It was still quite dark when we were finding our way southward, not without difficulty, for most of the road was unfenced, and paths led in every direction. At daybreak we summoned up a family in Obando (formerly Naranjo), who kept a sort of venta, and would sell some aguardiente to those of us who needed.

We then proceeded. We left Pedro el Embustero with his babe to make up in diligence what he lacked in fleetness. Nature has provided the young with means to keep pace with the dam, but I know of no means to prevent a babe on negro-back being an impediment to the journey of the mother mounted on a good horse. Of this we felt the full force to-day. The servants and baggage left us behind.

Here we passed the Rio de los Micos on a respectable uncovered bridge, the only bridge, in fact, capable of bearing the weight of a horse in all this region. I pass no bridge unmentioned.

At Victoria we called for breakfast just as the people were coming out from mass in a church not far from us. The town, if town there be, is small, and, it seems, could spare us nothing to eat. A mile or two farther on, and half a mile off our road, we were more fortunate. It cost us, however, two hours and a half, and as we left it was getting rather warm to travel in the sun.

I saw here my first níspero, the fruit of Achras Sapota, but having no resemblance to the zapote, a Matisia. The níspero is of the size of a tolerable peach, with a number of quite large seeds. It is a comfortable fruit to eat, but there is a gummy milk in the skin that repels, and very little in the flavor to invite a Northern palate. The zapote is just the reverse. It is as large as a good-sized apple, and has a thick buff rind, with a reddish-yellow pulp within. It is a little fibrous, but of a pleasant flavor. It breaks open readily, and discloses a huge seed within, not unknown to us of the North on account of its beautiful, smooth, chestnut-colored back, with a rougher, whitish hilum occupying the whole under surface. The pulp is generally eaten away from the rind, which is at last thrown away. Neither is a first-class fruit.

I am sorry we must leave our party so soon, but I have a call to make at La Cabaña, a hacienda west of the road a few miles above Victoria. With earnest adieus to Susana and Manuela Pinzon, and a real reluctance in separating me from Señor Vargas, and other gentlemen to whom I could not well introduce the reader, as we may not meet them again except as strangers, I rein off to the right, and soon a hillock intervenes between me and the cavalcade. I pursue a westward course for a surprising distance. I have considered our road as lying between the Cauca and mountain forests, that have been unoccupied since the extermination of the Indians. So it is in theory; but this belt of pasturage, which is often not a mile wide between the forest of the Cauca and that of the Quindio, may extend far into either.

Finally, I wind round a marsh surrounded by hillocks, one of which is crowned by the buildings that bear the modest name of The Cabin. Dr. Guevara meets me at the door, and his wife, Señora Monzon, is happy to meet one who knows her father. It is supposed that the name once was Monson, and that her ancestry is partly English. The house seems an accidental combination of three straggling buildings, which seem to mark out, if not inclose, a patio. In one respect, it is the most admirably situated hacienda in the Cauca. It is on the innermost knoll, overlooking a broad and beautiful pasture that extends almost to the very banks of the river. We can not see the tawny flood that we saw last as we passed its mouth on the Magdalena, but it is here hid from view by but a narrow skirt of woods, and the hills of the other banda are quite near us.

But there is one drawback—the water. Most houses stand near a brook. All towns must. I know of no well, nor any name for one in New Granada. I know of but two springs (at Mesa and Libraida) which are used. La Cabaña is the only hacienda that I know to be supplied directly from the Cauca. Their tinajera contains seven huge tinajas. A troop of negro women go to the river every morning, and bring water on their heads to fill the one emptied the preceding day. It stands a week to settle, and is then fit to drink. This may not seem like drinking from a deep well or a spring that is cool all summer, nor yet like drinking iced Croton water, but such luxuries can not be known here. The Cauca water is as good, perhaps, as any in the world, and may be compared to water at St. Louis without ice. Elsewhere I have only drunk it at ferries, mud and all.

La Cabaña has another attraction. It has a study, a room really devoted to reading and writing. Dr. Guevara's library must amount to over 100 volumes, all in Spanish and French. He takes also the Correo de Ultramar, as does also a gentleman in Cartago. It is encouraging to meet these signs of a literary taste.

I gained the highway at a point above where we left it. I went south of La Cabaña half a mile, crossed a brook called Rio Hondo, in a deep ravine, from which the ascent was the ugliest I have ever seen yet. Then I wound around bosques and knolls for a mile more to the road. One night afterward I retraced these steps after dark, and dark it was when I arrived at the brink of the ravine, hoping, bad as it must be, that it was the very same spot where I had risked my neck in daylight before. Conceive what the descent must be in the dark. Suffice it, I never yet have broken my neck. It has not often been in so much danger as there. Arrived at the other bank, I found the bars at the top converted into an impregnable fence, not to be passed by a horse without destroying a great deal of human labor. I looked above and below, then tied my horse, and finished my journey on foot. Señor Guevara sent a servant, who brought in my horse by a circuit of some miles. The bars had been fenced up in consequence of the carelessness of passers, who left them open and allowed his cattle to stray.

CHAPTER XXVII.

ROLDANILLO AND LAW.

A Gentleman Liar.—Pleasant Family.—A nice Swim.—Over the Cauca.—Rich Family and few Comforts.—La Mona.—Sabbath Eve.—Roldanillo.—Good Priest.—Select School.—Church Organ.—Law.—Superiority of our System.—Incredulous Priest.—Civil Suits.—A queer Fruit.—Swimming the Cauca.

DON ELADIO VARGAS and I had been riding from Cartago to Saragoza when we fell in with Belisario Cabal. He is a young LL.D., who lives I know not how, unless it be by his interest in the Hacienda of Chaqueral. Law pays little or nothing here. I was, as usual, trying to extract from him any information that he might possess about the resources and elements of wealth of the country. He stated that he had great hopes of vanilla. I remarked to him that any export worth a dollar or more a pound would be likely to be able to bear the costs of getting to the ocean; but no cheap ones, at present. He said that he had 10,000 plants of vanilla already set out, and hoped yet to increase the quantity. I was glad; hoped they *would* succeed; should be very happy to see them; I had seen none but spontaneous vanilla plants. He hoped I would call at Chaqueral some time when he was at home. After more talk of the same sort we arrived at Saragoza, and Belisario went on.

I had better now speak of vanilla, although hardly in place here. It is not the Tonqua bean, but a long pod of a similar flavor. It is no bean at all, but is filled with very minute seeds. It is an orchid plant. The best species seems to be Vanilla aromatica, but some other species have some of the peculiar flavor, or rather odor, but perhaps in a less degree. I can not tell whether the Vanilla aromatica grows here. I think it does, from the appearance of the fruit in size, shape, and odor, but have no description to compare the plant with. Most orchids grow on trees, pseudo-parasites, not drawing any nourishment from the tree, as does the mistletoe, here a very common plant. The genus Vanilla consists of thick-leaved vines, that cling to the bark of trees, but have their roots in the ground. They grow in deep woods, and, as orchids are apt to do, very sparsely. You are by no means sure of finding two specimens of the same species on the same acre or in the same day. I have spent hours and hours in hunting vanilla flowers, but never found but two. The cultivation of such a plant would be very peculiar, but might be a mine of wealth should it succeed.

When Belisario had gone on, Eladio told me that all he had been telling me was a string of lies.

I stopped, and looked hard in his face. Couldn't I understand Spanish?

"He has not a single root of vanilla in cultivation," said he. "It is all lies."

So, when I had proceeded up from La Cabaña to Las Lajas —*Flat Stones*—River, I turned off to the east toward Chaqueral, not to see a vanilla plantation, but a liar. A gentleman liar would be less of a curiosity now; but my readers will excuse me—I was green then, and believed what gentlemen told me. A man needs to be a year in a country before he can begin the study of the character of its inhabitants to advantage. I wanted to see how Belisario would look, what he would say, when I insisted on seeing his vanilla plantation.

Leaving to my right a house on a pretty knoll, on the right bank of the Rio de Las Lajas, I passed through a hill by one of those hoof-worn cuts so common on the Cauca, even on plantation roads. I entered on a plain beyond, or the valley of a brook. Here I met young Belisario, who was very glad to see me. He was going up to Libraida on business, but he would turn back and introduce me to his aunt and cousin (that noun was feminine—prima), and would be back to a late dinner. In fact, he does not live at the hacienda, but at Buga, where he attends to his business. It was fortunate that I found him near home.

So we turned round, and proceeded in toward the mountains by an unending series of knolls, plains, cuts, and little precipices of 6 to 10 feet. We bent northward, too, till I began to think that he was leading me by a roundabout way to Victoria, and that there was not even a Chaqueral, an aunt, or a prima, any more than a vanilla-field. At length we saw the house of a tenant, a field for fattening cattle, and then the house. It was a mere cottage, on the top of a steep knoll, not far from the right bank of that troublesome Rio Hondo that I found south of La Cabaña.

The house was a cottage of three rooms. Along the front ran a corredor, and before it was a fence half down the hill, with an entrance gate. Behind was a smooth, well-swept area, that might be called a patio; but there were no buildings around it except a shed to cook under, in place of the kitchen that had been burned down.

Of course, the central room we entered was the sala. On the north end (left hand) was the family-room (very small), and on the opposite end was a room for Belisario, or, in his absence, for Don Modesto Gamba, his uncle. Opposite the front door was the back door, that opened out on a diminutive piazza or corredor, with two small closets, or pantries, at the ends. Such were the reduced halls of the vanilla planter. Don Modesto seemed to be a sort of partner or tenant of the young lawyer. He was now out, probably at work with his own hands. Doña Paz Cabal de Gamba was sitting at a table, making cigars. The prima, Isabel Gamba (Cabal), was sitting by the door on the floor, making a gown. Her cousin introduced me, and wished me a pleasant time till his return.

All hopes of vanilla being postponed till after dinner (most probably at night), I began to make the best of circumstances. I was evidently not unknown to them, though I had never heard of them. Isabel was about 18, and wore the peasant-dress, which suited her very well. If there is some negro blood in her veins, it is not perceptible. The gown she was making was for herself—she dresses, then, sometimes as a lady. A novel, translated from the French, lay on the table. She loved reading, but never had any education. Cousin Belisario lent her books. Her brother, a student in Bogotá, had given her some.

Here, then, was an intermediate link between the aristocracy and the peasantry of the country. She belonged rather to the latter by birth, but, although she had never been educated, she had contrived to pick up enough to make her really quite attractive, as more than one aristocratic Caucano would acknowledge, if he dared speak his mind. My own opinion, at this distance of time and place, is this, that she is just the most agreeable native lady that I have found in all New Granada. Her father and mother are plain, good people, that seem quite contented with their girl, and hope the best for their absent son.

All their domestic help consisted of two little black mute girls of perhaps 8 and 10. They are not idiots, and are very lively, can hear as well as any body, understand all you say, but do not speak more than a syllable or two. I have watched them closely, and even studied them, as in many points they resembled those remarkable dwarfs exhibited in the United States as "Aztec children," the remains of an extinct race. I had busied myself with those "Aztecs," and had fortunately discovered, by a letter from Granada, their history, and that they were dwarfed specimens of a mixed race of ordinary size. The little mutes at Chaqueral scarcely differed from them except in size. They were lively, active, cheerful, ready to do any thing that their strength permitted, but could not be made to speak a word.

I spent the day very pleasantly reading and talking, with one or two strolls along the margin of the stream. In one of our chats Isabel looked up from her work, and asked me if I had any children.

"I never was married," I replied.

"Belisario told me that you was a bachelor, but I thought quite probably you might have children nevertheless."

"Were I so unscrupulous as to be a father before marriage, I should be enough so to deny it also. Were I suspected of such a thing, I have not a friend that would not close his doors against me. Such persons are not admitted into the society that I frequent."

I did not tell her of the upper-ten-dom of New York, where only poor and vulgar debauchees are rejected, perhaps for the reason that follows:

"Were we to be so particular here," says Doña Paz, "we should have to live without society."

They thought with me that it was a great misfortune that things were so, but she did not know that their religion had any thing to do with the laxity of their morals. I had been before asked in the same way about my children by a gentleman who had already invited me to an intimacy with his amiable family.

At night Belisario returned from Libraida, and his uncle from his work, and we three sat down, I at the head, and they at the side of the coarse, long, substantial table. I had the post of honor there in the arm-chair; they sat on the poyo. Isabel stood and looked on, to see that we wanted nothing. After we were through, the dishes were removed to the ground at the back corredor, where she and her mother sat down and ate.

On another occasion, when they had with them Belisario's sister, Virginia Cabal (pronounced Virr-hin′-yah), and the gentlemen were both away, I protested that I was not used to eating alone, and they must eat with me. Two more plates were put on, and the young ladies sat down, but they refused to eat. They conversed till I was through, and then dined with Doña Paz on the ground in the corredor. I think the custom of the women eating apart from the "lords of creation," and on the floor, is giving way a little. The best families in the Cauca do not practice it.

In the morning, the first topic was Vanilla. The plantation was too distant to visit, but we would go and see some spontaneous specimens. Don Modesto accompanied us. We passed up the stream some way, and he showed me a plant climbing quite high on a tree. It was another species of Vanilla, and not V. aromatica, as was clear from the fruit, which was shorter than the true pod, and not triangular, but flat, and more than an inch broad. I judged the pod to be bicarpellary.

But the cultivation of the precious plant was so important that I would grudge no time to see it with my own eyes; so after breakfast we mounted, and went inward toward the mountain. We went in farther than I have ever since seen any occupied land, except near Tuluá. We came to a pasture that is shut in mostly by a ravine and a stout fence; beyond this we entered the woods, so that there was nothing but a forest between us and the neighborhood of the Magdalena. Here he showed me three plants of a vanilla that he assured me he had planted. I examined them, and pronounced them likely to live. I happened to know that we had already passed over his line into the property of another man. I thought it inhuman to carry my vanilla-hunt any farther, and "was fully satisfied."

We looked at another spot where he thinks the water brackish. Salt is very high here, being brought a little over 300 miles on the backs of mules. It is only given to fatting cattle. Chaqueral is a hacienda for fatting bulls. They are bought for 6 to 8 dollars each at the age of 3 to 4 years, subjected to the requisite surgery, and with six months of Guinea-grass and salt are ready for slaughter. There are but two cultivated grasses here, Guinea-grass and Pará. These pastures only are fenced. Brackish water here would be a fortune. I have often helped hunt for it, but I have never been sure that any contained chloride of sodium.

On our return, we found that a gentleman from the next hacienda had called. I saw him here often at other times. He plays cards there with the ladies, makes himself agreeable, and, as he is a bachelor, he may yet make Miss Isabel happy. I call him Don Justo, without troubling the reader with a surname.

Belisario Cabal "is a taxidermist. He set up and presented to the National Museum of Bogotá many, if not most of the ornithological specimens there." I suggested that they would be more appreciated by the New York Lyceum—a worthy institution, that, at the expense of a few excellent business-men and literary gentlemen, has gathered quite a museum, which they keep open to the public gratuitously whenever they have funds to procure chambers for the invaluable collection. He promises to send them some birds. When he does, if yet this book survive to another edition, I hereby promise to remove all my vanilla from Chaqueral to some other place, and say nothing about the cultivated plants.

I went once to Chaqueral on purpose for a swim with the ladies. There is a deep spot—charco—in a stream (I shall not tell you where it is), that is so long that it is called el Credo—the Creed. The Creed, I believe, is the longest office in the rosary, and the extraordinary length of this deep, still water gave it the name. It is, in fact, a dozen rods long, with an average depth of three feet, and an almost uniform width of five or six. It is embowered in deep woods, and bathed with the coolest air of a perpetual summer. Were man born only to swim, his Eden would have been here.

To our party for the Credo, besides Señora Cabal, Isabel, and

Virginia, was added Don Justo, a lady who was first married about three years since, and her daughter, a simple, not very captivating girl of about 16.

As we were riding there, Isabel asks if my horse can not pace. I think so, though now on an easy trot. She advises me to draw in the reins and whip him up. A pace results, but she decides that it is not spontaneous, but learned. Afterward she asks me if I did not speak last night of having come on a horse. Doubtless I did, since I rode neither mule, donkey, nor bull. She informs me that it is a mare, and that she is with foal. I mentally conclude that I never would try to cheat her in a horse-trade.

Our horses are at length tied to trees near the Credo. Justo has brought with him no bathing-dress but a handkerchief. As he sees me differently provided, he decides not to go in at all. The mothers likewise do not go in. The Señoritas appear in long robes, open a little on the back, but quite as appropriate as any thing not "Bloomer" can be. The stranger-girl can not swim. Justo and the mothers, seated on the rock, chat and watch us. We spatter them a little.

I was dressed before the others left the water. I was talking with Virginia as she was combing her hair preparatory to dressing. At length Justo calls me to him, while I am sitting there with my back to her. He kindly tells me it is not pleasant to a lady to have a gentleman so near her when dressing. So we stand there talking with our faces toward her, and not four rods off, till she and the others are ready to ride. Truly etiquette is mystery.

It is with great reluctance that I leave the family of Señor Gamba. But, before I go, Isabel must show me her garden. A space twenty feet by eight is inclosed with slats of guaduas seven feet long, placed on end. Four of them are loose, so that they can be partly taken out, and make a hole large enough for a sheep to walk through. Here we creep in. The most interesting article I find is five stalks of wheat thirty inches high. I think she will get five heads of wheat in harvest-time, but not of a very good quality. This experiment proves nothing. This is poor from other circumstances than a climate naturally unfavorable. A large crop might fail from reasons that may not affect this. It is said that wheat has grown in places of this altitude, till pests, animal or vegetable, incapable of existing in colder places, had so multiplied upon it as to render it unprofitable. But I am spending a great while in so very small a garden.

We return to Las Lajas, and go straight across the road to the river. Dry land approaches nearer the river here than in any other place I know of. A shout to a sugar-mill opposite, and the use of a friend's name, brings over a canoe for a gratuitous ferriage. We wish to visit the Hacienda of La Vega. Here we see the Cauca at the lowest point I have ever seen it below the mouth. I have never seen it except at ferries and at Vijes, so completely is it protected by morasses. It may here be from a quarter to half a mile wide, and identical in appearance with the upper Magdalena and the Missouri, a river of dilute mud.

Three plants fixed my attention in a short walk above the ferry. Here alone I have seen the yuca in blossom. It was nearly three feet high, with a spreading top, and rather pretty, smooth leaves. Next was the almendron, Attalea amygdalina—a palm with scarce any stem, so that its head seemed to rest on the ground. In the centre of a great crown of leaves was a mass of fruits, a spatha crowded with nuts. The kernel resembles the almond very much, only it is firmer in the texture, and I did not perceive any taste of Prussic acid. Next I came into a thicket of jiraca. The leaves are sold off the ground from this thicket, so as to be a profitable article of cultivation.

I can not tell how I came to the cane-mill of La Vega, so I will tell you whom I found there. First, there was the owner, Don Ramon González, his wife, Rita Pinto de González, her sister, Reyes Pinto, and too many little ones to count. They have come down here for a campaign of making dulces of various kinds, particularly alfandoque. They tell me they are all through, and I have come in very good season, as in an hour they would have started home.

My horse has barely rested from his fatiguing swim when we mount—that is, as many of us as there are animals for. Each horse carries an adult and a child, and when the horses are all occupied, there remain on foot only the proprietor, his wife, and their babe. Said babe was naked when I came upon them, but in compliment to me, I suppose, they put on her a thin calico dress. I am much surprised that they, in particular, should be left on foot, but they tell me that it is not far that they have to walk—about a mile, in fact.

My share of the burden was little Dolores, a girl of five. They generally called her La Mona—the monkey—so that for a long time I knew her by no other name. Even now I am not sure that I have it right. The little creature had been in perpetual motion, and, once on horseback, dropped immediately asleep.

We at length come to the road from Cartago to Roldanillo, and then to a house. It belongs to Don Ramon, but he lives two miles farther on. This house is the residence of his wife's father, Señor Pinto, her sister Reyes, and several little children that I have not counted. Reyes is unmarried, and these children are all accidental.

The house consists of two cottages, with a space between them for a patio. It is dusk, and we sit there in preference. Nothing is said about dinner, probably because it would be idle conversation, there being nothing whereon any speculation could be based, nor in which it would result. I assure you such things are forgotten here with very little inconvenience. It is all a notion that two good meals a day at least are essential to health and happiness. Many are the days that I have taken nothing after breakfast but a single small cup of thick chocolate, a ripe, roasted plantain, a saucer of molasses, brown sugar, or preserves, and then a drink of water, and have done very well. So I did this evening, sitting on a pile of jipijapa leaves, which I preferred to the bare ground, in company with the two ladies and their various children, legitimate and otherwise.

Don Ramon had gone to La Vega, and brought back with him a bundle of letters for me. It will illustrate the result of a combination of all sorts of obstacles to the free transit of letters to state that I then learned the death of a sister that I supposed was in usual health. She had been dead 363 days.

Señor González and family went early next morning to La Vega. I should describe it as two cabins standing in a sheepfold. The front yard was, in fact, occupied by a considerable flock of sheep, and the corredor served them for hovel. No attempt was made to keep it clean, for it would be useless unless other lodgings were assigned to the sheep. Within was an absence of comfort that was very striking in a man of so much foresight, intelligence, and wealth as Don Ramon. He is an invaluable officer in the district, a clear-sighted, enterprising man. His business is prosperous, and he has as much money as he can well invest. He is no miser, but spends freely whenever he has occasion.

Yet, besides his kitchen, his whole house is three small rooms with earth floors. The sala is 12 feet square. It has a poyo running all round, two heavy, coarse arm-chairs, that belonged to his grandfather, General González, and an immovable table, made by fastening a board 30 inches long and 18 wide on the tops of four stakes driven into the ground. It is conveniently located in a corner, so that the poyo may serve as seat at one side and one end. Hence two chairs are all that are needed, and he has no more in the house. His bed-room is 12 feet by 7. Two shelves, 7 feet by 4, and 2 feet from the ground, are the beds. In the remaining four feet hangs a frame in which the babe sleeps. She can thus be swung by the occupants of either bed. The opposite room contains saddles, boxes, etc., and is a general receptacle for things not in immediate use.

The oldest girl, Mercedes, comes home from school at Roldanillo. She is about eight, and Elena, who comes with us from the sugar-works, six. So they have four children, all girls. Mercedes is a cordial, sociable child. I wished to hear her read, but there was nothing in the house for her to read. They have a house in Roldanillo, and all their books are there. Elena is shy, strong-tempered, and unfriendly. La Mona, on the other hand, becomes my friend at once—is never so happy as when in the hammock with me. The sala has that conveniency always swinging, a seat by day, my bed at night. Ordinary guests sleep on the poyo, or on a hide on the floor, for he has not a table large enough to sleep on.

As I have an F in my name, it is supposed, of course, that it is Francisco. It is quite a relief for me to have a name that every body can pronounce—a luxury, in fact. I wish I had borrowed a good name before I left home to use here. As I am hunting flowers with the children, I injudiciously mention that I do not like the name of Mercedes, as it is plural—mercies. Mercedes does not like the name of Francisco. She is nonsuited by being informed that my name is not Francisco, and is eager to learn what it is, in order not to like that. She will never find out. Still, she likes me and I her, but we do not like each other's names.

Our little table is large enough. There are but two to eat at it. Rita and the children eat on the floor of the back corredor. I miss something at these meals, and more than the cookery is at fault.

The want of fruit is a great privation. Practically, fruit here reduces itself to ripe plantains, bananas, and oranges. Ripe plantains are a necessity to me. I meet bananas about once a month, and have eaten as many as ten at once. Not half the oranges are fit to eat. Though the best oranges in the world can be raised here, I do not know of a good orange-tree between here and Ibagué. Don Ramon owns four houses and some thousands of acres of the best land on the face of the earth, on which nine tenths of the fruits of the world would grow, and I do not know that he has a single tree, bush, vine, or herb that yields an eatable fruit except the staff of life, the plantain. Does the reader protest that I am not keeping probability in view? I answer, that, were I making up a character, it should be more *natural* to the Anglo-Saxon, but I must put down things as I find them.

Let us now look at the town residence of Don Ramon González. The village of Roldanillo stands in a nook of the Cáldas chain, or Western Cordillera, below the mouths of the La Paila and Las Cañas, and above that of Lajas, Hondo, and Micos rivers, all of which come in from the east, and are variously and incorrectly laid down on the maps. Rio Frio comes out of the western mountains, and empties into the Cauca above the village. The census tables, which give the population of districts only, give a clew to the comparative size of villages. With rare exceptions, the more populous a district, the larger its village. Thus, Roldanillo district, with a population of 4800, must have at its "head"—cabeza (which is also the cabecera (capital) of the Canton of Roldanillo)—a population of some 4000. Here we may expect physicians, schools, balls, and respectable festivals. It is not strange, then, that the González children were all born here, are to be educated here, are to dance here, and to spend their money here.

Indeed, we would in charity hope that here is their residence, and that it is only occasionally that they occupy for a few weeks the mud cottages of La Vega. It is not so—can not be so. Don Ramon has no faithful mayordomo — overseer — as may sometimes be found east of the Quindio. He must see with his own eyes, and be present constantly, or every thing stops and goes wrong. Still, the town house is much more respectable in size, material, and furniture. It is large enough, if not with rooms enough. It has but five rooms indeed, including kitchen and stable; but all these are spacious, and all, except the stable, in the upper story of an adobe house. The bedsteads and table are movable, and as elegant as might be expected from the hands of a rough carpenter in a land where the lathe is unknown.

In fact, the only approximation to a lathe I have seen here is a contrivance to make an object revolve three or four times in one direction, and as many in the contrary.

Don Ramon has also a chest of books here. I think one volume has been added in his own day, the Colmena Española—Spanish Hive. It appears to be a translation of the Penny Magazine, and, were copies plenty, would have done a good work for the rising race. I did not see any book that I thought had been purchased by his father, but previous generations appear to have been much better patrons of the bookseller. Thus all the books had passed the minimum point, and age now only adds to their value.

On the Sabbath I drew from this treasury a Latin work on Jewish antiquities, which, if compiled from the knowledge and traditions of the Jews in Spain, ought to have a peculiar interest at this day. There was a rope-dancer to exhibit that evening, and, as all the rest of the family wished to go, La Mona was hired to stay with me and a servant by the loan of a pair of side-combs that belonged to Mercedes. They were of tortoise shell, ornamented with bugles. Imagine me, then, seated at the table, with a tallow-candle in the candlestick, bending over the old parchment-bound Latin volume, and resolved to have a Sabbath evening to myself. La Mona was rightly named: in mischief she closely approximated the more quiet of the monkey tribe. When the coast is clear, the first thing she does is to strip herself as naked as any other monkey—except the side-combs. Then she climbs up on the table, and seats herself near my book. Next, she takes out her combs, picks all the bugles off them, gets some into the cracks in the table, and buries others in the tallow that runs down into the base of the candlestick. The servant has no authority over her. Rarely does the mother try to exercise any, though the child is not often so completely let loose. Next, she must play with the candle. When she had aided my lucubrations over Jewish antiquities about an hour, I grew tired, and told her if she took my candle again I would blow it out. A moment after we were in total darkness. The servant offered to go to the neighbors' and light the candle, but I told her to let it be. "Come to me, Monkey," I said, and the little thing snuggled down into my arms, and in five minutes more was fast asleep. I rolled her in a cloth and laid her on a bedstead.

At 11 the family returned, bringing their chairs with them. On all such occasions the spectators must find their own seats, and it is so even in the theatre of Bogotá. Thus closed my Sabbath in the family of Ramon González.

One day a boy came in from the street bringing up my little Greek Testament. La Mona had thrown it off the balcony. I had to tie a string to it and hang it up on a high nail, as if to put it out of the reach of ants. I did not wish her to play with my tooth-brush, and hid it behind a little doll tied into a rocking-chair, placed on a high antique chest of drawers. The spiteful, shy Elena discovered my hiding-place, and proclaimed that Francisco (Fran-thees′-co) had put his little brush in the chair of the baby-god! What I had taken for a plaything was, then, an object of religious regard, if not of worship.

Elena was mischievous too. I was sitting reading at a balcony one day, when she brought forward a book I had borrowed, and threatened to throw it down into the street. I told her if she did I would strike her. She did not believe it. La Mona, too, had brought another book, and at the same instant both threw them down. I boxed their ears. A great outcry was the result. Elena ran off screaming, and never came near me again that day nor the next. La Mona threw herself into my lap, and sobbed for a long time, and would not leave me for an hour.

Filial irreverence runs wild in New Granada. I have seen a girl of 8, the daughter of a most respectable and high-spirited mother, strike her and call her the vilest names known in any language, and that with impunity. I am not prepared to assert that family discipline is known at all here. Less would be needed than with us, by far. As it is less called for, it is not so strange that it is in almost entire disuse.

I visited the boys' school at Roldanillo, but saw nothing worthy of remark. I saw also a select school for girls. Select it was, for the number was only five. In intellectual advantages this was no way superior to the average of public girls' schools, if even so good; but the pupils were more out of the way of learning bad language. The teacher was the sister and housekeeper of Priest Elias Guerrero, the most amiable member of the clergy I have seen here. He is without the charge of any church. I could not but feel sad to think of so affectionate a brother that could never be a husband; so intelligent and worthy a man exposed to the sins that are (humanly speaking) inseparable from forced celibacy.

I staid a night at the house of Padre Elias. He had to say mass the next morning. I proposed to accompany him. He assented, only requesting me, if my conscience did not permit me to kneel in mass, to stand where my nonconformity could not be seen; so I stood in the sacristy. The church is quite a large, desolate concern, not over rich in pictures and statues; but it has an organ. I went up to try it. A man tried to blow it, but it would take two men to do it; and you could find no two pipes in harmony in it; such a shrieking, growling, squalling, and squealing as it made was almost diabolic.

After breakfast Señor Guerrero went to work examining a peculiar book, that had been made by adding leaf after leaf of stamped paper to a nucleus of two or three sheets with which it had begun. It was a criminal trial—proceso. A man had been charged with some crime, and had been denounced. The denunciation was page 1. Page 2 stated that he was not guilty. Page 3 was from the juez letradro del circuito — the circuit judge—ordering the judge of the first instance to take the evidence of A, B, C, and D. These made up documents 4, 5, 6, and 7. No. 8 was from the accused, demanding that some one be assigned as his counsel, as he was too poor to employ a doctor of laws. No. 9 was from the judge of the first instance, ordering Reverend Elias Guerrero to defend the accused. In No. 10 my friend had asked that B and C be re-examined on certain points, and E and F examined; 11, 12, 13, 14 contained the results of these examinations, which he was sewing on previous to passing the concretion over to the personero, or prosecuting attorney of the province of Buenaventura.

If it shall seem to the personero that the case is made up, he will demand, in No. 15, an interview at a proper time between the juez letradro, the accused, his defender, six jurors—jurados (*sworn men*)—and himself, in which these documents will all be read, and the case argued. We may then hope that No. 16 will contain the vote of a majority of the jury, and No. 17 the sentence of the judge.

Such is the outline of the French, Spanish, and Granadan process, as it seems to me. It is much more dangerous to men of bad character than our blessed English system, which yields a more perfect protection to the criminal than any other ever invented. I tried to describe our process to him, but I fear that he did not believe all I said.

"In the first place, we catch the accused."

"But if you can not catch him, what then?"

"Why, of course, then we do not try him."

"Why not?"

"He might not have a fair trial if he were not present."

"Well, give him fair notice, then, and if he thinks it better to be present, let him come. Do you never catch men that you find you have no occasion for? And would it not have been better if they had been tried before sending off to a distance to bring them home, if they did not want to come?"

"That may be; but it is contrary to our theory (founded on an old law-book, I believe, called Madre Vidrio—Mother Glass) that the man must be first caught and then tried. Next after catching him is to bail him."

"But suppose he has stolen $100,000?"

"Then we demand security in the sum of $40,000 or less. Excessive bail is unconstitutional; and a bail of as great an amount as he has stolen would be more than he could get, therefore it would be excessive."

"But if he gives his bail $40,000 of the stolen money, and then runs away?"

"Then the bail moves heaven and earth to have the security reduced to $5000, which he pays into the treasury, and gains $35,000 by the operation."

"And the man who was robbed?"

"Why, he revenges himself by having the thief arrested again, if he can catch him."

"If?"

"But, generally, he will not run away. The danger of conviction is not so great as to justify it; for 12 men must be unanimous in his conviction, and they must walk together without stumbling over a path bristling with law-points planted by skillful counsel. Acquitting men has been reduced with us to a science. A man can make but fair wages at getting others condemned, but he may even get $10,000 at a single job for getting a man clear."

"Caramba!"

"A celebrated advocate, Henry Clay, is said never once in his life to have failed in clearing his man, even when charged with murder. Consider what a fool a man would be in spending $40,000 in bail, and risk being caught again, when he could retain Henry Clay for one quarter of that sum, and, after being acquitted, live respectably among his old neighbors, and die happy in the house where he was born."

"Verdad!"

"But the Boston people have carried the matter farthest. Once Boston had a bad name for hard usage of criminals. People of other states were horrified by the hanging of a man of good family for murder, when they could see beautiful chances of getting him clear that were idly suffered to pass. Since then they have made their jurors judges of law as well as of fact, and the consequence is that their juries hang on the slightest cause."

"Hang the accused?"

"No, indeed. They are unable to agree, and are discharged. A new trial is ordered. Not a word of the old trial will answer. All the witnesses must be heard again, and if a material one should die, or happen to become an engineer on a Russian railroad, the trial must go on without him, and the accused be acquitted."

"Well, your Union must be a paradise for malefactors. I no longer wonder at the desperadoes that keep our isthmus in a perpetual terror."

"Yes; but I have not told you all. The denouncer is sometimes called on to give bail as well as the denounced. For instance, a mate of a ship maltreats a sailor. Jack complains, and is locked up as a witness. The mate gives bail. The hot season comes on—hotter than in Tocaima. For fifteen long hours in a day the sun beats on the prison where the witness is shut up, but the mate is not ready for trial. He is drinking ice-water, and at some genteel employment on shore. After the trial, the witness, who has been shut up six months, is set at large, and the criminal is condemned to be shut up in a better cell six weeks."

"Vaya! you are joking—usted se chancea."

"Not at all. I had my overcoat stolen, and, in a moment of consummate folly, I told the police. Fortunately, the thief never was discovered. Had he been caught, the time I should have been compelled to spend hanging about a court-room would have been worth to me more than two overcoats."

I can not give the rest of our conversation. I own that I utterly failed to make the priest understand the superiority of our system to theirs: such is prejudice. The most degraded of our population at home can see it at once.

Their civil suits have much more resemblance to those of the New Code of New York and other States than to our criminal processes. The demanda is handed by the plaintiff to the judge, and by him served on the respondent. There are three classes of cases, one below $16, and one above $200; and the lower the class, the more expeditious the process.

The questions of delay must first be adjusted, and then it is decided whether there are facts at issue. Only in this last is there a delay in the decision. The evidence is taken by the judge, and is secret, though each party is made acquainted with all applications for evidence made by the other. When the term of proving has expired, either party can demand publication of proofs, and each then sees the evidence collected for the other. Then the parties are heard, and the judge decides the case.

In cases of less than $16 there is no appeal. In sums of over $200 the case may go up to the supreme court of the nation, but the appeal must be based on nullity of the previous sentence, or notorious injustice.

As a whole, promptness before accuracy seems to be the motto in their civil causes. They have a notion that a man might as well lose a just cause at the end of a week as gain it at the close of the next century, when all the parties are dead, and the costs have eaten up all the property of plaintiff and defendant. Our happier system prefers that a case be kept up till the close of the millennium rather than it be decided irrevocably wrong.

It was at this priest's table that I learned to eat the Avocado pear, Alligator pear, Persea gratissima, here known as aguacate, and in Bogotá as la cura, *feminine* (but *el* cura, *masculine*, is the parish priest). This fruit was more difficult to master than any other I ever met with except the tomato. I now discovered that when I had in my mouth a piece of meat already masticated, a particle of aguacate made a very nice sauce to it. The moment I began to understand it as a vegetable gravy, I had little difficulty; at length I relished it with a little salt only. Now it is, perhaps, the only fruit that is absolutely unreplaceable at the North.

Roldanillo has a cocoanut-tree too. The nuts are sold at a dime each at the foot of the tree. Cocoanuts would grow well any where in this part of the Valley of the Cauca, but they have never been planted. You can not expect a good supply of fruit in a new country, and this has not been settled much over 300 years by the white race.

From Roldanillo I had arranged to go to Libraida or Zarzal, directly across the river. I parted with the good priest with no little regret, and bade a final adieu to La Mona with still more. I had taken leave of them all, and was already at the head of the stairs in the corredor, when the dear little monkey caught me by the leg, and declared that I must not go. She is an exception to Granadan children, for there are few of them that I think know much what it is to love or be loved. I have met no other like her, and she seems rather of a Northern race.

For some distance the road to the river has a spur of mountains on the right. A road at length turns up the river toward Cali, and you, as you leave it, enter the low, rich bottom-lands, little, if any, above high-water mark. It is now the dry season, but the road is not free from mud. In company with me was a gentleman and a dependant, who served as companion and servant. We had to wait for him for some time, and lost our way once before turning down to the ferry.

My friend and I determined to swim the river, leaving the attendant and horses to cross by the boat. The horses swam faster than we did, and well it was for us. They had not touched shore when my friend was shouting for help. It was, indeed, quite a swim, the longest I have ever taken except in the Mississippi. I judge it between a quarter and half a mile. It is said to fatigue horses more than a day's journey. If so, men can swim better than horses, for I felt no effects from my exertions, and my friend was also near the shore when the boat picked him up.

To reach the solid, dry ground of the eastern banda was one of the worst rides I ever saw. The very bank was dry, but soon the road plunged into a morass, where it broke into numerous paths, all, however, so deep with mud as to cover a large part of the body of the horse. I consider the mud a more serious obstacle than the river; what it would be in the wet season I dare not conjecture. At length it became drier; some grass became visible in glades between the trees, and at last we reached the little village of Libraida.

CHAPTER XXVIII.

GRAZIER LIFE.

Libraida.—Priest.—Partial Hospitality.—Impediment to Church-going.—Noon-day-ball.—The Priest's Partner.—Utility of Hurrahs.—Dinner.—Duck-pulling.—Beheading Cocks.—A Spring.—A Ride with Company.—La Paila.—Mortmain and ecclesiastical Incumbrances.—Herding.—The Lazo.—Colt-breaking.—Breeding of Colts and Mules.—The Bull-fishery.—Bull-driving.

ENTERING Libraida, I rode at once to the house of the priest. I had seen him before, and often since, but this time he was away from home. The first time I called on him was at noon of a warm day, the 1st of February. I was in company with my friends of Tuluá, Don Eladio Vargas, his wife, and her sister. Padre Duran is their friend, and I was indebted to them for an introduction.

Introduction, strictly speaking, there was none. He saw at once that I was a foreigner, and I was soon informed that he was a priest. He brought forward aguardiente. Eladio drank, the ladies tasted, or pretended to, and I declined with thanks. Then cake, made of yuca-root, was offered *to the ladies only*, and they ate. I had seen this partiality in offering refreshments once only before. Next came a coal in a spoon, and a handful of cigars. Susana and Manuela do not smoke unless secretly; they took the cigars, but declined the fire.

At a later call there I found him teaching a boys' school, and at the close he went to baptize a child in the church. It is one of the poorest I have seen, having but two altars, and a miserable apology for a pulpit (never used, I think), and a floor of earth. I was about to enter, when an unsuspected obstacle prevented. I had on a pair of zamarras, and they can never cross the threshold of a church. I wondered at that, as it was the only *Christian* thing I had on, every thread of my clothing being heretic, as well as the body within them. But so it was; all might come in but them. Smoking in church is in violation of the same principle.

But now I find the priest at Uña-gato (cat-claw), the name of a bush with formidable hooked spines, that thus gives its name to a neighborhood in this district. I unexpectedly met an acquaintance going there, and no wonder; for to-day, 29th June, is the day of St. Peter and St. Paul, and the Uñagateños are celebrating the day. Our course was south, and our road lay between the highway and the river. But it always seems as if you were in the highway, and that the little cleared land in sight of you was all that lay between the river forest and that of the mountains. A succession of glades and bosques, and a stream or two, brought us to a knoll or ridge, much nearer the river than ridges usually are, and perhaps not a mile from it. Here were two or three cabins of peasantry, and in one of them we found the ball.

Just as I entered, the priest was dancing with the prettiest girl that I have seen in these parts. So thought others, for one suggèsted, "Viva the Cura's partner!" and in return came a scattering volley of vivas. Cheering simultaneously with three hurrahs, or three times three, is unknown here. It is a pity. I think a great deal of the efficiency of an Anglo-Saxon mob depends on lusty simultaneous cheering, hence we are unequaled in this democratic branch of our government by any nation on earth. A bochinche, of persons ten times more highly excited, has none of the deep power of a mob that has drunk plentifully, and feels its strength and unanimity in the thunder of three cheers.

But I wander. "The Cura's partner" was dressed as a lady, as were five or six others. The rest of the fair sex were in camisa and enaguas only. The room was densely filled, and it was as an act of courtesy that I gained admission. Judge my surprise when I saw the pious and queenly Elodia Vargas there. She is on a visit in the district. I shall not speak of the dancing, as we shall see it again, and more at leisure.

Soon we were notified that dinner was ready. We moved to another house. Under the piazza of this, a narrow, long table had been set, so that the ladies, sitting next the house on a barbacoa, or immovable bench of guadua, were in the shade, while we of the tougher sex sat under a vertical sun, but little incommoded with the heat. We had an awkward dinner. The meats were abundant, the plates sufficient, but the sum of the knives, spoons, and forks exceeded the guests at the table by but one or two. The ladies refused to eat with their fingers. To me had fallen both a knife and a fork. Where much is given much is required. I spent the whole dinner cutting meat into mouthfuls, of which few indeed fell to my own share.

A second table was filled with musicians, and some second-rate characters, while the mass of the festive crowd either fasted or ate at the kitchen. What we call music consisted essentially of two drums and a clarinet. They played while we ate. While they ate we sat in the house, and I tried to make conversation with the pretty lady, but with indifferent success.

Now the priest, who seems to be Master of Revels *ex officio*, calls out, "Bring the cock and dig the pot." A hole was dug in the turf, and an unfortunate cock interred therein up to his ears. But the hole is too shallow; he rises up with the earth on his shoulders, and the hole must be dug deeper. Even at last he was kept in by wedging the turf about him, so that he could not get up. Meanwhile, a still more unfortunate Muscovy duck was suspended by his feet over one of those deep cuts common in these roads. The mode of suspension was very imperfect: two poles of guadua set in the ground had a strong hide rope—guasca—passed over their tops, and poor Muscovy was fastened in the middle: the two poles were steadied by two men. The ladies came out and seated themselves on the bank to witness the sport. The men on horseback passed under the duck at full speed, and endeavored to wrench off its head. I left them to their amusement a little while, and on my return the duck was dead. Every attempt to pull off the head only filled the hands with blood and feathers, and the invincible duck was left for the cock.

According to the rules, a lady was to be blindfolded, to take a machete, and, if possible, cut off the poor bird's head in three blows. The curate, who seemed to take this diversion under his special patronage, selected for executioner the most respectable and pious young lady of the company, our queenly Elodia. With much reluctance she consented to be blindfolded, took the machete, went one step toward the cock, stopped, and removed the handkerchief. The curate's partner in the last waltz was next applied to with much urgency, but resisted. Finally, it was voted to blindfold a man. No sooner had he begun to step than all called out, "You are going wrong! More to the right! More to the left! Strike where you are! Go two steps farther!" And all this at once, and twenty times repeated. Confounded by this "advice gratis," he gave three sweeping strokes wide of the mark. "There goes his head!" cry half a dozen, and the executioner removes his bandage amid shouts of derision, and sees the cock's head projecting unharmed between his feet. A second followed; but my curiosity was gratified, or, rather, my endurance exhausted, and I left the ground in search of plants. As I mounted my horse to return, the remains of the second cock were passed over the fence to the kitchen.

The priest, the ladies, and several gentlemen returned at the same time to Libraida. There had been another decollation, and another party larger than ours was already on horseback. We commenced riding round among the diluvial hills that diversify the uninclosed ground around the village, shouting "Viva San Pedro!" The priest called out to me that I did not shout. Thus appealed to, I ventured, in English, one good "Hurrah for Saint Peter!" which drew a roar of merriment from the company. Soon after we halted at a sort of tavern, where the priest had arranged to treat the company to milk punch.

A little northeast of the town is a spring, just west of the road that comes in from Cartago. It furnishes water to the village, which, unlike all others, is not on a stream. I really know of no other spring in all the valley of the Cauca. In dry seasons the streams diminish as they come down from the mountains, and in rainy times all their accessions are from superficial water. I have no reason to doubt but that wells would yield water were they dug, but at present there is no need of any.

I took a peep at the prison here only because some of my young Conservador friends were shut up there in 1851, when just too old to be whipped by their mothers, for taking up arms against the government.

A little before 5 I left for the Hacienda of La Paila. As the gentlefolks could not think of leaving without dancing all night, I contented myself with the guidance and company of one or two wearers of camisa and enaguas that could not conveniently be away from home till morning. The road is a little difficult to find, from the fact that Libraida does not stand on the real highway, but west of it, and it was some miles before we seemed to have got fairly into it. The open ground, or mixture of glade and bosque is not continuous, but in many places the forest of the mountain unites with that of the river. In these spots a place for a road was anciently cleared, a dozen rods wide, and it is now grown up to grass, and will never bear another tree. But the road does not at this day always follow these openings, which may lead you upon an impassable morass, or a river with no road down the bank. Villages are just as likely to be built off the former road, like Libraida, as on it. The travel leaves the theoretical road and makes ways for itself. As no labor is expended on the road, and the land is not fenced, no man knows what precise spot is the legal property of the nation as highway.

We found some mud. Here I noticed a large, beautiful orchid flower growing very frequently on trees. It was white and pink. It is here called lily — azucena — and is a Cattleya. Strangely enough, I found on knolls here a terrestrial orchid, with a stem seven feet high, of a totally different section of the Order, but with a flower so like this Cattleya in size, shape, and color, that, remove the tip of the column from a flower, and I could not tell from which plant it had been taken, while the pollen, leaves, and whole habit of the plants were as different as possible. The terrestrial plant was Sobralia. This shows that the pollen of orchids furnishes a prime characteristic.

At Las Cañas River I found the guadua in flower. It is strange that a plant so common should flower so rarely. Mútis, who spent his life on the botany of the country, never found it. Cáldas found it once or twice. I can not learn that any other botanist has found it but myself. I gathered a large quantity. Rio de Las Cañas is almost always fordable. It is apt to keep about a foot deep—say a good mill-stream.

Farther on I came among low hills, and in half a mile farther found a *tree Passiflora*. It was a slender tree, but I had to stand erect on my horse to cut off the lowest limb. I afterward found another species that is a bush, and there may be yet other passion-flowers that are not vines.

This hilly land lasted more than a mile, and then came an open plain, of which we skirted the eastern edge. It is called El Medio. We shall return to it presently. Again we come to a piece of woods, at the farther edge of which flows the largest stream we have passed since leaving Cartago. It is Rio de la Paila. A slender bridge of guadua has since been thrown over it for footmen. With some little risk, I crossed diagonally up stream. Horses do not swim much with their riders here.

A guadua bridge is best built where a large tree has limbs overhanging the stream. The butts of many large, long, slender guaduas, laid side by side, are secured to either shore with the stems reaching upward over the river. Others are, if necessary, spliced upon these, till the tops of the opposite sets can be bent down and interwoven into an arch, which the architect may imitate with advantage. Of course, the centre is much narrower and thinner than the ends, because the guaduas taper upward. A floor of transverse slats of guadua is tied upon the arch, a railing may be added, and the structure made firmer by vines, which tie the bridge to the branches above. Thus the whole bridge is nothing but grass stems tied together by woody vines —bejucos. The structure requires neither auger, chisel, saw, nor nail.

Beyond the river the road bears to the west, to avoid some very high hills. We proceeded to the base of the first of these, and found ourselves at the ancient Hacienda de la Paila. The chief attraction to me is the mistress of it. I had met the Señora Emilia (pronounced Amelia) at Chaqueral. She is, I believe, some relative of Doña Paz, if not, in fact, a sister. I recollect that at the time I met also another lady of mature age there, and we were conversing about the wives and families of clergymen in the United States. None of them could conceive how a clergyman could induce a reputable lady to marry him. Indeed, they hardly thought it decent to defend the idea of a married clergy. I spoke of the Cura of Banco, who has several children born every year, and asked them whether it would not be better that he should be permitted to have one good, decent wife, and a family that should be a model of what a family ought to be. The stranger lady would prefer the Cura of Banco as he is; for his sacraments are efficacious now, wicked as he is, whereas, if married, those who trusted to them would be lost. Señora Emilia thought somewhat differently, and some things she said raised her at once to a high place in my esteem.

Emilia Barriga has been married twice. When Emilia Barriga de Sanmartin, she bore two children, José Sanmartin (Barriga), or Chepe, and José María, called, for shortness, Pepe. She then married Mr. Modest Slack—Don Modesto Flojo—and had a lot of daughters—six, I believe—and has now an infant son. Sanmartin owned, or rather held, the Hacienda of La Paila, of which more anon. Señor Flojo and the younger children have not much property. But little difference is seen between them. They are all smart and quite amiable children, and the oldest Sanmartin is not yet sixteen.

The hacienda extends from Las Cañas River to the River Murillo, which formerly bounded the provinces of Antioquia and Popayan. The width there is seven miles. The length, from the Cauca to the summit of the Quindio, may be 30 miles, and the whole can not contain less than 500 square miles, and may well be a thousand. During the good old regime of tyranny, when prosperity was the lot of the rich, and unrequited labor that of the poor, the hacienda is said to have boasted 36,000 cows and 800 mares; now the mares are greatly reduced in number, and the cows can not be a tithe of what they were. Two hundred years ago a dying Sanmartin bequeathed this property to the souls in Purgatory, and, until lately, it has been in dead hands, "manos muertas," from which, I suppose, comes the French word mortmain. It was fixed that the stewardship of the land should descend, on nearly the same principles that a crown does, from his eldest son downward. None of his descendants, as a steward—mayordomo—had power to sell or divide. Nor was it a mere honor. The estate was to yield so many masses per annum at $1 60 each, and all that the property yielded over this was the steward's. This excess of revenue became at length so great, that the stipulated sum to go for masses came to be considered as a sort of tax, and the steward as the owner, subject only to this irrevocable annual payment.

This arrangement was designed to keep this estate, as large as a county, perpetually undivided and in the hands of one man. Republicanism might protest against the arrangement, but it would be sacrilege to change it.

But I have not told all. A previous Sanmartin, the grandfather of him that deeded this domain to the use of the toasted inmates of Purgatory and for the benefit of the priests, pledged it and incumbered it with ten masses a year for the same benevolent object. The person who was to receive the $16 per annum was the capellan, and the incumbrance was a capellanía. These words have the same basis as chaplain and chaplaincy, but the meaning is quite different. If the capellan has too many masses to say, he may hire another to say them, and if he can hire them for less than $16, he may put the balance in his pocket. Nay, the capellan need not be a priest, and a capellanía is a piece of property as well as a stewardship. And the Sanmartin who originated the mayorazgo, as the right of stewardship is called, settled on his other son a capellanía of $160, which has come somehow into the hands of my friend Ramon González.

Land that is charged with a capellanía can not be sold, even if not in dead hands, without the consent of the capellan. Many estates have in this way been incumbered with six capellanías, and a division, or even a sale of it, becomes almost impossible. Is there no remedy? Did the Sanmartines of the 17th century exceed their rights in thus fixing impediments to the alienation or division of the property by their heirs? Much can be said on both sides, and I suppose much has been said in some lawbooks that I never shall read. I am inclined, for one, to think the work should be undone in some way, that society may not be blocked up till the end of time by a superstitious provision in a will of the 17th century.

So, too, thinks the democratic—ultra-democratic—government of New Granada. Hence the law for abolishing mayorazgos, and the law for redeeming capellanías and other perpetual charges—censos they are called. Cursed laws they are; cursed by the pope, cursed by the archbishop, cursed by the bishops and other clergy, cursed by fanatical old women of both sexes and all ages that believe that Christ gave this fair country to Peter, Peter to the pope, and the pope to the archbishop and bishops of New Granada, and that man was made for the Church, and not the Church for man.

This bold step, denounced by Pius IX. in his allocution of 27th September, 1852, was taken by the López administration. It was the offspring of republican ideas, and of necessity, and would meet my full approbation had it no other application. New mayorazgos had long since been prohibited, and now all existing ones were cut off at a blow. All censos can be transferred from a piece of real estate to government by paying to the treasury eight times its annual product. All this estate, then, must belong to Chepe Sanmartin, who was steward of it, though a minor of twelve years of age when this law made him owner. Were the capellanias redeemed, it would be held under no other limitations than ordinary real estate of minor heirs.

But I am assured that the law has abounded in mischievous results. Hospitals and schools must share the fate of nunneries and collections of greasy monks, for all are called pious foundations. Perpetual ground-rents ought to be redeemable in some way, and if no other could be found, in this; but it is asserted that ordinary loans of money on bond and mortgage are thus convertible into demands on a bankrupt national treasury. This, if true, is infamous indeed.

I beg the learned not to laugh at, nor the unlearned to undervalue, my essay on tenures. It has cost me immense study, and even as I write it is with a feeling of uncertainty as to some of the facts. Doubtless there are in Blackstone law-terms that I might have introduced had I known them; but I have written this for American *laymen*, as the lawyers call us, the uninitiated.

It was not unintentionally that I coined the surname Flojo (*slack*) for Don Modesto, the second husband of Emilia Barriga. Perhaps, in this land of slackness, a slacker man lives not. Hence the estate is all run down, the cows run wild, the tenants run lawless, and, but for two circumstances, the family would have run to ruin. A special love for a big saddle-bottle, which he has affectionately named La Pechona (*the full-breasted*), and which he loves to suck a little too well, and a general love for dogs, hunting, and idleness, seem the most striking characteristics of the man whom the good Emilia made the stepfather of Chepe and Pepe.

The two things that saved the family from ruin are, first, the energy of Emilia herself, and that of a young cousin of hers, a decided character. Damian Caicedo, LL.D., is of mixed blood and low origin. At 16 he could not read his mother tongue. A fortunate accident disabled him for severe physical labor, and he at once began an education that he completed amid every kind of self-denial and privation. He is just taking hold of the affairs of his slack relative, and, if I mistake not, will yet make his own fortune in mending those of his friends.

I could not expect all the conveniences that I might desire in this family, but there were other things to make amends for all deficiencies. I enjoyed myself; I taught the children—an agreeable task for me. And for the Lady Emilia herself I have a real esteem; if but one of my Catholic acquaintances should get to heaven, I think it will be she.

"If you were only a Christian," she said to me one day, "I think you would be most like a saint of any man I ever saw."

"Were I a 'Christian,' instead of a heretic as I am, I should be like other Christians, for it is their religion that makes them what they are."

"No, it is not. Those who are wicked among us sin in defiance of the teachings of the Church. And all need forgiveness, but it can come to none except in the way God has appointed."

"But he did not enjoin that the intervention of a fellow-sinner is necessary to make the pardon of God available."

"And how dare you deny it?"

"Listen, for it is a fact that I am going to tell you. When I was a little boy of six, like your little Sara, I gained access to my mother's sugar-jar, and carried off a lump as large as a lime. After I had eaten it, my conscience smote me. I did not fear detection, but the anger of God. So I went off behind a knoll, and kneeled down in a large hole, where a rock had been dug out of the ground, and confessed my sin to God, and prayed for forgiveness. Do you think that God forgave me?"

"Ah! you ought to talk with a priest, and not with an ignorant woman like me."

She wants my little Testament very much, and I am sorry I can not spare it. But my Bible is too heavy to carry with me when I leave my trunks, and I must deny her. [I mailed it to her from Cartagena. The postage was five cents, because its weight exceeded four ounces.]

Damian's sister came here on a visit while I was here, and with her came a mulatto lady to teach the children. There is nothing interesting about either. The females eat at the table after we leave it. I have managed to eat with them once or twice, but they prefer that I should be at the first table.

The house, as usual, contains no inner doors, though there may be said to be two rooms and a passage. Two beds are located in the passage, and the inner room, that serves us much for sitting-room and study by day, is the principal dormitory at night. My hammock requires more space. I attach one cord to the roof in the inner room, and the other passes out at the top of the outer door, and is fastened to a post of the piazza; so I occupy the whole house, though bodily I sleep alone in the outer room, or sala.

The children's beds were mere rugs to lie on, and a blanket apiece to wrap themselves in like a cocoon. The motherly Clementina, the oldest girl, wound up the little boy with her. Of course, they denude themselves utterly before wrapping up. I had the impudence to ask the children if the young ladies did the same, and they said yes.

I can not pretend to conjecture the number of houses on the estate. They are scattered from the road to the river, but there are none far east of the road. A line of houses skirts that large plain north of the La Paila called the Medio. The inhabitants there are mostly white. There is a group on the south bank of the river, half a mile below the ford; the inhabitants of these have a good deal of negro blood in their veins. On the south end of the road, across the estate, there are no houses. These families of herdsmen, of every color, have been a great study for me.

The chief exports of this tract are young bulls, young horses, and hogs. The latter are raised by the inhabitants of the river forest, the others by the family. Some of the tenants owe personal service for rent. This is generally rendered on Friday and Saturday, and most of it performed on horseback. The others pay a ground-rent of from $1 60 to $3 20 per annum. All have their estancias, or fields, in the forest. They contain from half an acre to two acres, inclosed by an elliptical or circular fence of split guaduas. Those who live in the open land have often quite a distance to go to their fields, but, as they work only occasionally, it makes little difference.

Cacao-orchards—cacaguales—are also found in the forest, but they are not numerous. People have hardly forethought enough to plant any thing that will be so slow in yielding returns. The platanal yields ripe fruit in about a year, and may be kept up indefinitely; but when the fence is thoroughly rotted down, they prefer beginning in a new place. In all the dry forest toward the river, these inclosures are scattered within short distances of each other, like plums in a pudding. Sometimes two adjoin each other; others almost touch or lie in sight of each other. Cane is also raised, but in small quantities, only for horse-feed, aguardiente, sirup, and a very little panela.

A few bags are made from cabuya, and one man braids jipi-japa hats; but nothing probably is made and sold off the hacienda, and all articles of clothing are imported, not excepting alpargates even.

But the grazing interest demands our more particular notice. I will attempt its description, premising that the estate contains three distinct herds of mares and three of cows, in three pastures or ranges—the Medio, the Central, and the Guavito. The central pasture is separated from the Medio by the La Paila, and from Guavito only by broken ground running from the eastern forest to the western. I will describe the rodeo, or herding, of a Friday at Guavito, the larger of the three pastures.

On Friday morning an unusual sound strikes my ear on awaking. It is the step of many horses approaching the corral, or inclosure, near the house. All hands must have been on the move for some time, for they are mounted, driving in the horses of the central pasture. One object of this muster is to catch animals for the grand campaign of the day at Guavito.

We will not go down to this, but, while breakfast is preparing, let us examine the horses we are to mount immediately after. The horses themselves are the most obedient and well-broken I have ever seen. The slightest intimation of the bridle will guide them. They will patiently gratify your whim of flower-gathering, even at the expense of running their head into a thorn-bush. You may stand on the back of many of them, leaving the reins at your feet, or, throwing the reins over the high pommel of the saddle, leave them for some time. Their gait is generally very easy. They are not large, nor is much regard had to parentage.

The bridle was made here. They would not like to trust to a bit made abroad. The Caucan bit is a formidable affair. The reins are attached to one end of a lever of the first kind; the fulcrum is in the horse's mouth, against the lower jaw, and far back the other end of the lever is ready to press against the palate, and force open the mouth. If he attempt to hinder this operation by holding fast the apparatus with his teeth, they only seize upon two hollow cylinders, within which the bit plays freely. One stout chain passes within the mouth, near the fulcrum; another, under the jaw, counteracts this, and, as the mouth is forced upon, they gripe the jaw beyond endurance. Still a third chain unites the points to which the reins are attached. The reins and headstall are of raw-hide, twisted or braided, according as fancy or economy dictates. The reins would resist a strain of half a ton. A broad piece, often ornamented, passes across the forehead, which may be slipped down over the eyes if you wish to leave the horse without hitching. Finally, the reins, after uniting at a point convenient for the hand, separate again into two long thongs, which may be used to tie the horse, or as a whip.

The saddle is a study for an anatomist. The cojinetes are a cover over the whole, made of a leather resembling buckskin. It is often padded and embroidered with silk. It has two huge pockets, each capable of containing a pair of shoes, or $200 in silver. Removing the cojinetes, we come to a surface of hard leather—the coraza. This takes off: under it you see three straps of raw-hide passing over the saddle in three distinct directions, and uniting in a ring on each side. The girth consists of twisted raw-hide, passing several times from the ring on the off side to another ring. It is adjusted by passing a thong four times between this last ring and the one on the near side. This thong is drawn tight enough, and tied in a peculiar knot. Under the girth-straps is yet a third cover, which takes off, and leaves the saddle a skeleton of wood and iron, padded on the under side. Across the middle of this skeleton—saddle-tree (fuste)—passes a strong strap, fastened in the centre by a string of leather passing many times through the strap and the saddle-tree, sewing them together. Both ends of the strap are pierced with holes to buckle on the stirrups. The stirrup-leathers are imported. The best stirrups are the slipper-form of brass or wood: common stirrups (de aro) are used, or even a stick of wood supported by two strings. The crupper is like ours; but, besides this, the vaquero's saddle should have an arretranca to enable the horse to hold back without straining the girth. Beneath the saddle, and to protect it and the horse, is placed a sudadero: it is a mat of rushes, a rug, or, at worst, an old sack folded. It would have saved me some labor had I been told by my books that in New Granada a high-pommeled saddle and an arm-chair are *silla;* a low-pommeled saddle, a side-saddle, and a fresh-water turtle are *galápago;* a common chair, *taburete;* easy-chair, *poltrona;* ottoman and stool, *cojin;* sofa, *sofá;* lounge without a back, *canapé;* bench with a back, *escaño;* bench without a back, *banco.* Saddle, bridle, sudadero, stirrups, and halter (jáquima), constitute a *montura.* A traveler here ought always to own his montura, and watch it well. Horses, cows, and goats will eat his sudadero, and dogs will eat all the rest but the tanned leather, wood, and iron; of these last, including the contents of the cojinetes, the peons will rob him; his clothes are victimized by the washwomen, and his skin by musquitoes, fleas, and niguas. Happy is he if he can save his bones and his conscience (particularly the latter) undamaged, and, leaving his cash and much of his flesh, return to his native land with his credit and his constitution.

But where am I running to? In the first place, breakfast is ready; secondly, I have no right to complain, for my *belt is too small for me;* only the more respectable insects have drunk my blood, and I have found the rogues fewer and smaller here than at home. But to horse! to horse!

Off with your slippers; put on a pair of alpargates, and draw on a pair of zamarras; buckle the huge spurs securely to your heels; take your guasca (rope of hide, with lazo or noose at the end); tie it under the right flap of your saddle, with a peculiar knot which Pepe will show you; tie your halter in the same way on this side, and mount. You will find vaqueros worse mounted, without cojinetes or halter, without zamarras or alpargates, the spur fastened to the naked heel, and the pantaloons rolled up to keep them from the mud. More than one you will see with nothing on but hat, ruana, pants, and spurs; their feet stuck into stirrups carved out of wood, or merely resting on a bit of wood suspended from the saddle by a forked thong.

THE VAQUERO.

As we approach the corral of Guavito, the "mares" (for they speak only of them in the pastures) are driven in before us. Other vaqueros come in from below, bringing with them the mares from that direction. They enter the corral together, their feet pattering on the ground like rain on a roof. The corral has an inner yard, to which the mares run directly. A man on horseback guards the entrance. Others are not mounted to their mind, and proceed to catch fresh horses.

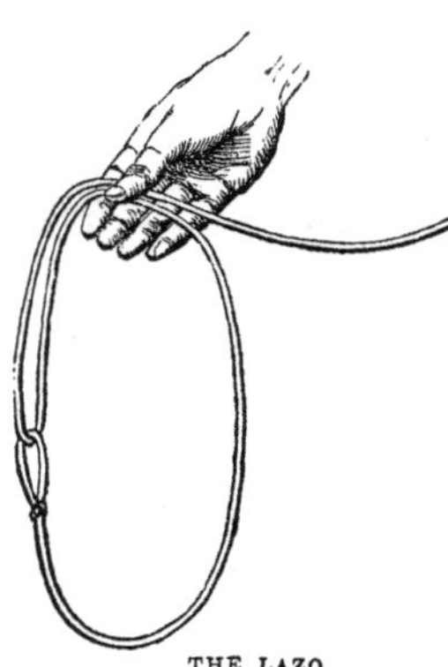
THE LAZO.

This is generally done on foot. The vaquero takes the guasca coiled up in his left hand, and the lazo (noose) in the right. The running knot (llave—key) is not at his hand, but at a third of a circle from it, when the lazo is opened out into a circle, as in the adjoining diagram, where the longer diameter of the ellipse should be regarded as four feet, and not estimated from the size of the hand. He has it already in his hand, has singled out the animal he will catch, and is waiting a moving of the herd. The instant he finds his prey approaching, he commences whirling the lazo round his head in such a way as to keep the noose spread until the propitious moment comes to let go. He then pays out the guasca with the left hand, letting it run through the right till the time to hold it fast.

I think the idea we have of skill in the use of the lazo is exaggerated. Even in the corral it is well to catch five horses at ten throws. One assured me that 100 throws would catch 80 or 90 horses. The next six throws caught but one. Still, the noose and the lash, the bow and the gun, are the four instruments by which man holds his title to rule over the animal world.

The moment a broken horse finds his head is your aim, he tries to mingle it with others, and holds it particularly near the fence. As you approach he at length starts and runs with all his might for the other side of the corral. You throw the noose as he is going from you. The moment it touches his neck he stops short. He is as tame as a girl caught in blind-man's-buff. A colt, on the other hand, when he finds you are aiming at him, is wrought to desperation. When caught, he runs and chokes himself in the noose; he flounces and throws himself on the ground, but all in vain. The hand of man, ever a terror to him, must approach his throat before his stertorous breathing, like that of a man in a fit, can be relieved.

The horses are shut in with bars—*trancas*—of guadua, and we sally forth in long procession for cows. The tame band are near in the open plain. With a long circuit we get ready to slip between them and the forest. "Examine girths," says Cristóbal, who has command. Every head is bent down. Some dismount. "All ready!" The head of the column dashes forward at a gallop, and soon a line of some 30 horsemen, at distances from 3 to 10 rods apart, extends between the herd and their wonted refuge. We advance, and the cows, with a general lowing, proceed peaceably but rapidly in the desired direction.

Suddenly a cow, with head erect, and tail horizontal and rigid, breaks our line at full gallop for the thicket. Two horsemen start in pursuit, and she soon finds a noose about her head. When she has run the length the guasca permits, her head can go no farther, and her body is unwilling to stop. She falls, and is not disposed to rise. One vaquero approaches, carefully keeping out of the circle of which the tightened guasca is the radius and his companion the centre. Whirling the end of his own guasca round and round suddenly, he brings it down like a slung-shot upon the poor rebel, and she starts to her feet. Still she will not move one step. He raises his foot, and drags his cruel spur along her back. She darts forward, and the horse of her leader, the moment he feels the guasca slacken, starts on, keeping one eye upon the movements of the cow. After zigzagging and floundering a while, she waxes wroth, and assumes the aggressive upon her leader. Now she finds the other lazo about her horns, and each horseman keeps her from reaching the other. I have heard of a cow becoming so enraged as to drop down dead on the spot. Bulls are never so utterly furious.

Meanwhile, the herd, lowing and running, enter the corral, and move round and round like a whirlpool filled with horns. Last comes the captive; but how shall we liberate her? He that takes a wolf by the ears should always consider first how he will fare when he quits his hold. To loose a cow takes more time than to catch her. A third man throws his noose so that it lays partly on her back and partly on the ground behind her. If she does not move of her own accord, he catches her by the tail and pulls. Either in yielding or resisting, she steps both feet over the guasca. It might then be drawn tight around the middle of her body. Instead of this, it is slipped off behind, and tightened about her heels, which are pulled back, and, with a slight push or pull, she falls. She is now helpless. I have seen a horse drag a cow in this manner by the heels into or out of a yard. Her head is safely approached, the lazos removed from it, and the horseman remounts. The slackened guasca permits her to bring her feet forward, and in separating them she opens the lazo. She springs upon her feet, reflects a second, makes a dash at a horseman, who eludes her. Shaking her horns, as if blaspheming in her heart, she runs off to the herd, who are thus taught that the way of transgressors is hard.

The outer corral has two entrances: a horseman is stationed at one, and a ruana on a stake at the other, and we start off for the wilder herd. Our way is riverward, over beautiful valley land, sprinkled with clumps of trees and thorny bushes of acacia. Silence! We steal along at a walk, curving our course around an unseen centre. Now Cristobal starts forward at a gallop, with his head bent down to the horse's mane. We follow, and the herd find us shouting between them and their refuge. A few desperadoes plunge with a crash into the thorny thicket behind us, the rest gallop in the opposite direction. A bushy ravine extends across our course near the corral. Instead of crossing it, almost the whole herd pass our ranks, and disappear toward the river—all but now and then one arrested by the lazo in her flight. Those who have not thus caught a prize beat the bushes, dislodge an animal, and catch him as he runs. In this way we secure at least a delegation from the wild herd; we will hope to do better next time.

Now begins the business of the day. What calf has not his ear-mark? What youngster of two months has not his little brand on his cheek? What yearling not branded for life on his side? A lazo on his head, another on his heels. A fire is burning by the division fence, and the irons are hot. Here is a calf with a sack of morbid growth. A spatula of wood is whittled out with a machete; fifty maggots of all sizes are dislodged from the cavity, and it is filled with the first dry, soft, absorbent substance at hand.

A young bull is caught who is not to be trifled with. The guasca is thrown over a forked post—horca—and in vain he tries to approach his captor; every movement brings him nearer the fatal fork till his head touches it. His heels are secured as before. Look out for him when he is let loose! But in five months' constant exposure, I have known but one horse gored by a bull. The cows are at length released, and rush lowing from the corral.

Now comes the turn of the horses. They are subject to many more infirmities than the cows, are of more value per head, and, besides, are to be trained. Hence they are reviewed much oftener and more carefully. Owing to this, they are not so wild.

This life would not be without its perils were not the vaquero so tough. He is riding at full gallop, and his horse puts his foot into a deep hole covered with grass. He comes to the ground as from a rail-car. He picks up his guasca, and, if his cow has not got clear, off he starts again in the chase. His girth breaks when he has a bull tied to the pommel of his saddle. He manages to escape unharmed. I have known but one serious accident, the dislocation of a shoulder-joint.

Both horse and rider enjoy the sport highly. It is severe sport for the horse, who will injure himself before showing any sign of flagging.

A curious scene closes the rodeo. A vaquero catches a wild colt which he is to break. He manages, amid his struggles, to exchange the guasca for a halter, and binds the infuriate youngster securely to the tail of his horse, who goes homeward from the corral with the meek resignation of a deacon who has a dissipated son.

I have not seen the process of breaking. The young reprobate, unlike his biped prototype, grows more and more tractable, and at length leads submissively. He is then led in the same way when mounted, and feeling that his head is not his own, he does not try to defend his right to his back. The horse with which the colt is placed in such intimate relations is called his godfather—padrino. Beating and brutality are no part of the system.

The gait of the pupil is carefully attended to. In some cases the fore foot (hand) is tied to the corresponding hind foot by a cord shorter than the natural step would render agreeable. In other cases the feet are loaded with bags of sand or shot to make him raise them better. He is made to walk round in circles of small radius, or in double circles like a figure 8. Trotting is not in request, as there are no carriage-horses.

The father of colts is a polygamist. He has his family—atajada—under so much subjection as to keep them from mingling with those of his neighbors. When they have all been mingled up in the recojida, as the assemblage in the corral is called, as they go forth he calls them about him, and, if any one shows a disposition to straggle, he goes after her, and administers as much correction as the case demands with his teeth. The padrotes seldom fight with each other, though I can not imagine that they have come to their present good understanding without some boxing in days past. I saw, indeed, but one horse-fight, and the originator of that was a traveler's horse, that had got out into the pasture, and was ignorant or regardless of the compacts, truces, and treaties then and there in force.

Individually, these animals are by no means so respectable as they ought to be in a grazing community. More than half of them could be bought at $25 each, and one good Northern horse would buy forty of them. But scientific breeding would require more care than any man here is disposed to bestow. These animals are not exempt from the menial service of the saddle, and, with one temporary exception, I have found them as manageable as any other. Ladies ride them through herds of horses without inconvenience.

A gentleman once told me that he was an ounce of gold richer that morning than he expected, and asked me, as a Yankee, to guess how. I told him that a mare, from which he had expected a colt, had given him a mule. I was right. The value attached to this hybrid race encourages the disgusting practice of breeding them, which was forbidden under the Mosaic dispensation. The ass is a privileged animal on the plantation. A blow inflicted on his sleek hide would be felt keenly by his owner. He goes where he pleases. When he comes to the house, he walks through the dining-room toward the kitchen to see if there is any corn or salt for him. If there is, he has it without stint. There are two of them at La Paila. With a meek and placid countenance, they go about from pasture to pasture, and you meet one of them now at the Medio and now at Guavito. They are friends; and I knew them once to perform a duet in the very dining-room, as they were returning from a regale at the kitchen door. Think of that, ye dilettanti! who magnify a feline serenade in open air, under your closed windows, to the event of the night. What would you say of two asses trumpeting at once in the house?

To forward the views of these *priests*, as I loved to call them, to the scandal of the faithful and amusement of the irreverent, some of the heads of families—padrotes—are subjected to a cruel operation. An incision is made in the urethra, that cuts off all hope of progeny. The victim is called a retajado. It is remarkable that the asses keep on friendly terms with these unfortunates, while with others they have furious battles. From some such encounter one of our meek friars came out with an injured ear, which will never revolve again "with motion dull upon the pivot of his skull," but this particular "long left ear" must hang down forever from the effects of a padrote's teeth.

One night, at dusk, I was delighted to see Don Ramon González ride up, accompanied with three men, who slept all night in the corredor. Early next morning, they and all the disposable force about the house disappeared on horseback. Before breakfast they came in, one by one and two by two, each arrival accompanied by a young bull. Some men were so strongly mounted, and their captive so tractable (*tractable* is from *traho, to draw*), that one horseman alone could draw in a bull. Generally, it needed a second man to add propulsion to the attraction of the first. In the case of the furious and indignant, a second guasca was requisite to secure the captor from the assault of his prize. All these couplets and triplets tended toward the central corral, where half a dozen prisoners were stalking about in ill humor while we breakfasted.

As we came out from breakfast the vaqueros were assembled in full force. Dinner was deferred, and the bull-fishery was continued till dark. Some evil-minded fellows rendered the ordinary mode of loosing a bull unsafe. A noble horse was gored at night, and died next day. Two different expedients for loosing them were now adopted. One was to draw the animal up to the fence, after he had entered the corral, by the united strength of many men tugging at the guasca. One stands with only the fence between him and the frantic creature's horns. He takes hold of the lazo, and as the guasca is suddenly slackened, he opens it, and Bos Taurus walks off.

The other mode is more ingenious and easier. The bull is thrown down by a noose on his heels at the very entrance of the corral. A guasca is attached to the lasso about his horns, so that it can be pulled open at will. He is headed straight to the entrance, and his heels let go. He bounds in, of course, and a pull on the newly-applied guasca (contra-guasca) releases him, or, if both get entangled in his horns, he in time shakes them off.

By night of the second day they had 31 prisoners. These, at $6 40 each, more than pay Don Ramon's capellanía; the rest he pays for in five-franc pieces. As they are destined to the slaughter within the year, there is no need of branding and counter-branding them. To counter-brand is to repeat the brand; for the repetition of a brand, like a second negative in English, cancels the first. Early the next morning the horsemen are in the corral stirring them up. There is a great variety of disposition among them. All are hungry, it is true, and utterly disgusted with their present condition. With a few exceptions, there is little fight in them. Horsemen multiply in the corral as the bulls grow tamer. Now they surround them, condense them, and seem to knead them up into a ball.

After breakfast I too mounted. Some horsemen from the Medio, and others from Don Ramon's, are continuing the kneading process, and shouting "Toma! toma!" Toma means *take it*, and is the call to a dog or other domesticated animal when you offer him food. Hence it is the voice used to call an animal. I do not know as the bulls regarded the word in any very inviting sense.

Now the bars are opened wide and for the last time. Half a dozen horsemen are within, and the rest are drawn up in two lines, forming a lane toward the banks of the Rio Paila. With some difficulty the yard is evacuated, and the bulls stand in a lane of horsemen. As they advance toward the opening in front of them, we advance, calling "Toma! toma!" We proceeded very slowly. One made his escape. Three vaqueros were after him. Soon he was sprawling on the ground in advance of us, held by his heels, and it was not till the rest were with him that he could get up. Several escapes and recaptures of this sort delayed us, till Don Ramon decided to pacify a particularly refractory fellow that was bent on mischief. He had him by the heels, and the other guasca had been removed. He dismounted from his horse, and stood before the bull, and rubbed Cayenne pepper in his eyes. All this while his intelligent horse stood bracing backward, holding the guasca tight, it being tied to the saddle. Had he stepped forward two paces and let the bull loose, maddened by the Cayenne, the result might have been tragic; but the horse knew his duty and did it. Our hollow square at first consisted of 65 horsemen, one at least of whom was a little afraid of horns. A good knowledge of bovine ethics is necessary to the safety of your horse in such a neighborhood. As the cavalcade proceeded, one after another could be spared from it, and in the end only a few of our men proceeded with Don Ramon's.

CHAPTER XXIX.

GRAZIER SPORTS.

Cara-perro and Grass-climbing.—Virgin Forest.—Manifest Destiny.—Ciénega de Burro.—A Burial.—Rogacion.—Niguas in Church.—Neglect of the Sick. —Rejoicing over the Dead.—Distilling.—Election.—What is in a Name?—San Juan.—Bride's Dress.—A Swim.—Murillo.—Overo.—Buga-la-Grande.—Woods in the Night.—Advantage of a Guide.

A SERIES of knolls overhang the house at La Paila. They show rock in but one place, but are steep and almost precipitous. Their sides are well wooded for hundreds of feet, but the tops are covered with grass. The highest of these is called Cara-perro—dog-head. It is supposed to resemble in shape a dog's head, and the summit is the tip of the nose. I dare not assert that its height exceeds the diameter of the base, but to reach the summit cost me the most formidable climbing I ever executed. Such hills are common here, and flank the road on the east all the way up the valley; but Cara-perro is the highest for many leagues around, and I know of none higher that can be seen from the settlements.

I was told there was a cave on the side of Cara-perro, and I was desirous of visiting it. Said cave was merely a cropping out of horizontal strata of sandstone, of which the upper, with the superincumbent earth, slightly overhung the lower. Such is the Caucan idea of a cave. In many other places the steepness far exceeds that of any artificial terrace. Some of these knolls are climbed by steps cut in them, and in places climbing would be out of the question.

For this trip I had selected a fiesta, a day in which they regard it a sin to do ordinary work, but are ready for any extraordinary job, as risking their necks on a grassy slope or in a deer-hunt. Two gentlemen went with me, and one of the concertados (men hired by the year), and the carpenter of the hacienda. This carpenter is a character. He bears the name of Pio Quinto, but he rather disgraces it, for the chief characteristics of the vagabond seem to be a dislike for work, a love of strong drink, geometry, religious books, and loose women.

Our first precaution was to take a calabaza full of cane-juice, here called chicha, but in the valley of the Magdalena, guarapo. His Holiness took this in charge, from a natural affection for liquids having even the smallest trace of alcohol. We dipped into the woods at the base of the hill; then rising, we came to where it was necessary to cut our way with machetes. From here we emerged upon a grassy ridge, which terminated like a buttress against the steep knoll.

Here we were obliged to use our hands, holding to the grass. The passage of each one made the ascent of the succeeding more difficult. I paused to take breath and look at Pio V. I found him directly beneath my feet, perspiring profusely, and trembling like a leaf. He had the consolation of knowing that if I lost my hold, I should carry him with me to a distance below that it was not very agreeable to fathom with the eye. I do not like climbing grass as well as rock. If rock really is fast it stays fast, but to have only the strength of a grass root between one and perdition is enough to make him shiver.

From the summit the concertado had to descend and bring up the calabaza, which the carpenter was obliged to abandon. Meanwhile, around us opened a prospect of great interest and beauty. The western chain, along the base of which flows the Cauca, stretches from south to north in almost a straight line, and rising at a single leap to the greatest height between us and the Pacific. Not an inch of the Cauca is visible; so distant and so straight is it that the trees hide it entirely. This forest appears interminable above and below, and we forget the broad pasture plains between it and the mountains, and the innumerable cultivated patches and houses which it hides.

But to the eastward we turn with more interest. The River La Paila, whose waters are visible at our feet, has its course marked out by the foliage of the guadua, greener than any other, and more graceful than can be conceived. In less than a league above there is a spot destitute of trees. All such are called llano—plain—whether they be flat or hilly; and all land covered with thicket is called *monte* if but a few miles through, and *montaña* if more. This was a pasture, where, in the war of 1851, were concealed successfully all the horses of the plantation.

Still farther in, on the banks of the Buga-la-Grande, are seen the pastures of San Miguel, where the rebels of 1841 discovered the hiding-place of the horses. These two pastures are but specks in the vast landscape of fertile valley beyond valley, untrodden by man since the extermination of the dense Indian population whom the Spaniards found peacefully enjoying this country.

Was the sum of human happiness increased by their subjugation? Was their paganism supplanted by a religion more moral or less bloody? What has become of them all? How is it that I have not seen a single Indian in all this valley? Who will recount to us the innocent loves that have passed beneath the perpetual shade of those trees on the distant mountain-side where murmur the head-waters of the La Paila? Who next will visit the long-deserted spot? Of what race and nation will be the woodman whose axe will one day sound there, prostrating trees that have grown three hundred years within the sight of the white man, but where his foot has never trod?

Questions who can answer? With a strong desire of penetrating this region, a desire which perhaps no one yet born will see realized, we turned to descend by a route less steep than the ascent. Even this led over the top of a lower knoll scarcely to be descended, for always descents are more difficult than ascents. An uninterrupted inclined plane inspires a fear much like that which we feel on the brink of a sheer precipice, and perhaps even greater, when our standing on it is not perfectly secure, as it generally is at the summit of a precipice.

In the meditative mood inspired by those eastward glances, I stood on the shoulder of the hill. Some Fourcroyas had there thrown up their tall flower-stems 20 feet high, and their summits were white with blossoms. These seldom perfect their fruit; but there was sprinkled among them an abundance of bulbs, ready to take root on their fall. I had left my machete at the house, and I attacked a huge stem, five inches in diameter with my patient pocket-knife. Slowly cutting thus, my thoughts reverted to the signification of my employment — a Yankee whittling down a century-plant—so small an end after so patient a growth. Then I thought of Mexico, and that "manifest destiny" which neither fortifications nor protocols can resist—no, nor yet the best interests of both nations avert.

Southwest from us I saw on this excursion a sheet of water that they told me was the Ciénega de Burro. I had seen a water-lily from it which was different from any I had seen before, and determined to visit the spot; so I marked a place where the pastures approached it nearest, and took the bearings. I was told that it was impossible for me to penetrate there alone, but I have lost more than I have gained by guides thus far, and set off without.

I penetrated the forest to a considerable distance before I found a path that ran in a suitable direction. At one time, as I stood on some rich black earth, I felt my feet sting, and saw that the ground was covered in all directions with large tiger-ants, that were fastening their envenomed jaws in my feet wherever the alpargatas left them exposed. I ran some rods, and stopped still in the midst of them. Again I ran to a clear spot, and was able to dislodge my tormentors. No harm came from their bites.

At length I came to open water surrounded by quaking marsh. From the nature of the marsh I expected one of those "bottomless ponds" I have sometimes found in New England, but I was mistaken. The water was nowhere more than three feet deep. I found here a Sagittaria, which looks to me like my old acquaintance S. variabilis. The Nymphæa I spoke of was abundant, and of other rare plants a bountiful harvest.

A second visit here cost me great labor with little fruit. I cut half an hour in a thicket of Mimosa, advancing in all that time less than a rod. I then abandoned my work, and made a wide circuit round the obstacle. This time I found my horse had slipped his tether and escaped to his native pasture, the Medio, and I had to walk all the way home, and return next day for my montura.

Near the house are various holes rich in water-plants and germs of future musquitoes. They were excavated for brick-earth, and are some of them carpeted over with the beautiful pale-green Pistia Stratiotes, and in others grow Limnocharis, Hydrocleis, Heteranthera, a Nymphæa, and other interesting plants. In still another marsh grew Pontederia azurea. This and Stratiotes were common enough on the coast, but here they strangely reappear together after an interval of hundreds of miles. Is the water brackish here? It may be slightly, though I have not satisfied myself of the fact. Two days' journey in toward the Quindio, however, are the famous salt-springs of Burila. They belong to the hacienda, and, by an ancient royal prerogative, I am told that they have the right to make salt there without paying tax to government. It is strange they do not, as the salt used here comes from beyond Bogotá, and can not be cheap.

The salt of Burila contains iodine. Hence the use of it as a condiment cures goître. I attempted to penetrate there, but my plan failed. I am told that plantains grow there, and the Phytelephas, so the land must rise very slowly, as we can also see from Cara-perro. On one occasion, a gentleman and some peons profess to have penetrated two days farther, and to have turned back for want of water. Even at this distance from the river, the wild lime (Citrus Limetta), supposed to be an introduced tree, is found growing wild. What an amount of valuable land lies waste here! No one lives at Burila, for they would be lonely in there. It is better to be poor than to be doomed to a solitary life, where fiestas and dancing can not come; so they bring salt from Cipaquirá, live in villages, dance, and are poor.

In damp ground, and near the Paila, I found an Aroid plant of long leaves, with a juice acrid to blistering, and an atrocious odor, like that of its congener of the North, the skunk cabbage. This abomination, known as runcho, bears the name of Dieffenbachia. Alas! poor Dieffenbach. Did he think that Schott hit the mark when he honored him with the name of the most disgusting plant in all New Granada?

I made an attempt to descend the Paila to the Cauca, or rather to follow a road down. I went on for miles (it seemed) through crooked paths, past estancias, where herds of swine are called to eat green plantains by the side of the fence. Passing dangerous quagmires, I would come to the hut of some hog-raiser, who rarely comes out to grass. I became tired of riding over such horrid paths, left my horse at a group of huts called Frisolar (bean-patch), and still went on. At Caracolí I found some better houses, but learned that the distance from the Cauca was yet too great for me to accomplish and be out of the boundless contiguity of quagmire before night.

At the Medio my attention was particularly called to a large solitary tree called Guazimo, probably Guazuma tormentosa. I was wondering whether a full catalogue of its epiphytes would not amount to a hundred species. It seems to me quite probable. Here and there hang down cords of a Cactate plant, Rhipsalis, called here disciplina. There a Bromeliate, Pitcairnia, shoots out a spike clothed with bracts, the upper ones of which are scarlet, like the tipping of a trooper's feather. Numerous Orchids, of course, there are, some of which were brought down for me by the lazo, and one or two species of Tillandsia.

At a house near the bridge I found a bread-fruit growing. It is Artocarpus incisa, with a leaf similar to that in the South Seas, but the fruit is a little smaller and full of large seeds, while in the islands it is generally seedless. It is valued here for the seeds, which are called chestnuts. No one had tasted the baked pulp. Here a circumstance occurred that gave rise to a hearty laugh all round. I was talking with a couple of women that I suppose are grandmothers. They wore the camisa as low as the most fashionable ball-dress, and as loose as are any of their habits. Well, on the very edge of the camisa of one of them I spied a large caterpillar, crawling where he was in momentary danger of falling in. I wished to remove the intruder without alarming her, but, as I put my hand toward her, she mistook its aim. Her virtue was alarmed; she gave a start and a scream, and consummated the catastrophe. I could make no answer but to laugh heartily, and tell her to take it out herself then.

From the superior whiteness of the inhabitants of the Medio, the balls here are rather attractive to the Paileños. I went to one myself, which I found, as usual, stupid. I must, however, give some account of it. There were no seats, or not enough, for the women, so they sat on the ground at the sides of the room. Men stood in two groups just within the doors, and some also were permitted farther in. Cakes and aguardiente were for sale in the corredor. Another table, more convenient to the damsels within, has on it in a bottle a fluid that bears the familiar name of a friend of mine, Miss Taylor. They spell the word *mistela*, translate it *mixture*, or, in this particular case, *cordial*. The staple of the dances was waltzes and the bambuco. Generally the floor was filled with waltzers. One couple I saw that were not over eight years of age, managing to skip about so that none of their seniors should tread on them.

The bambuco I have not yet described, although it was performed for my instruction at Fusagasugá. One couple need the whole floor in the bambuco. It is decided that *he* is to dance it. Then they wonder who *she* will be. He bows to *her*. She borrows a pocket-handkerchief (mine, perhaps), and steps out. She moves to the music, but *ad libitum* as to the direction, and he follows her motions as faithfully as a mirror. If she moves east, he dances west; when she goes north, he goes south; when she turns a little, he turns as much, and in the contrary direction. Thus they advance, recede, turn side to side, or even entirely round; so they dance without ever touching each other, till she becomes tired, drops a courtesy, and sits down. He thinks he has acquitted himself extremely well; his carelessly turning up his ruana, to show the brighter colors of the under side, is not bad. But his chef-d'œuvre was that kick of the dog, without losing either time or place. The quadruped, surprised and indignant, looks round, and, could he speak English, would ask, "Why I?" But his partner appears unconscious of this achievement; not that she is insensible to it, but it is beneath the solemnity of the occasion for her to be betrayed into a smile.

Her mamma, a coarse Bogotana, with a cigar in her mouth and a turban on her head, really thinks that Solitud is not so bad a dancer; so, too, thinks the young occupant of the house, and he is a judge, for he is an artist. We saw him first, you recollect, in the jail at Cartago, but he has forgotten that little circumstance, and we will not remind him of it. I see that two of his productions now grace the walls. The San Cristoval will do; but that hunting-scene is magnificent. For music, we must content ourselves with a bandola (banjo) and pandarete (tambourine), the noisy alfandoque held over the performer's head in the

THE BAMBUCO.

extreme left, and a noisier drum, which, though not seen in the sketch, is heard all over the Medio.

The torbellino or whirlwind is another dance after the bambuco plan, only, as the name implies, more violent in its action. I saw at this ball the queerest couple I have seen yet. A little girl of under ten was called out—sacada—to dance the bambuco with the tallest vaquero of the hacienda. To see her little body directing the movements of the whole of his reminds one of a battle between a king-bird and a crow.

On the south side of the river, in the edge of the woods, lives Sánchez el Manco—the one-handed. He is the most thrifty tenant on the estate, and has horses, cows, swine, and rather extensive fields, including a cacagual, or cacao-orchard. Now and then he sends me word that he has a raceme of bananas ripening, and then he is sure of a call from me. His children are the prettiest in all this pasture, and he likes my approbation of his proceedings. One day he wished to present me with a fowl. I told him I would prefer a single leg of it, and he invited me and Don Damian to come down next Thursday at 2. On Thursday it rained, but we did not mind that. Soon we were dry in his house, and our horses and saddles safe in the porch. We sat with him an hour and a half, had a pleasant call, and then we went home without saying or hearing a word about dinner.

Sánchez has with him a lad that is suffering from inflammation of the eyes. They say he must go blind. I tell them no. If they will send him up to the house daily for a week, I will make them better in that time. I give them to understand that medicine as well as advice shall be gratuitous. They promise to send him, because they can not decently avoid promising. They never sent him, and, as I left La Paila, the light of day was closing on the poor boy forever.

I am reminded of another thing here that surprised me not a little. I noticed a deep hole in the door-yard of Sánchez. I asked why he dug it there. He said that it was done by money-diggers. They thought they had ascertained that there was a treasure concealed there, and begged leave to dig it out. The one-handed consented, on condition that they would fill up the hole. They dug, and, finding nothing, they were so disappointed that they went off and left the hole open, saying that they had worked enough for nothing. When a boy, I had seen holes dug for Kidd's treasures 100 miles from tide-water. There is nothing new under the sun.

This side of Sánchez el Manco lives Timotea, who gains an honest penny by making palm-leaf hats, and sudaderos or saddle-mats of rushes. I engaged a sudadero of her for two dimes. I went at the appointed time, and it was not done. I went again, and she had finished it and sold it. She promised me another. I went for it, and, as I asked why she had not done it, I was whittling a fruit with my penknife. She had not finished it for the want of two pieces of hide to protect the rushes from being worn by the girth. "Can not find two bits of hide?" said I; "here are two." So saying, I picked up a piece of hide on which a girl had been sitting to braid, cut off a projecting corner, and cut it in two. Timotea was surprised. She evidently had not thought of that: it ruined the seat. The next time I called my sudadero was ready.

In one of these houses I saw a corpse. It was that of a man. It was decently extended on the earth floor, with a sort of robe on, with a girdle of new rope of cabuya (Fourcroya). Several candles were burning around, being stuck into masses of mud, shaped so as to answer for candlesticks. A large number of persons were gathered around, quiet and thoughtful. One was saying a string of Paternosters and Ave Marias in Spanish. I was there when they carried him out on a bier made on the spot by tying slats of guadua together with bejuco. The burial-ground is not far from there. It is in a desolate condition, and the fence has entirely fallen. The grave was five feet deep, of ample width, but shorter than the body. An extension, or place for the head, was dug in at the southern end, so that when the body was properly placed in its last resting-place, it occupied the whole grave, and in filling it no earth would be thrown into the face. It was altogether as respectable a burial as you would find in the same class in life in a Western state. All the religious ceremonies (simply prayers of laymen) were finished before the burial began.

Deaths had been frequent, and particularly in this family. It was decided to be an epidemic, and the remedy was concluded to be a procession in honor of Santa Barbara—a rogacion to her.

She is the patroness of the little chapel at La Paila. I had visited said chapel once before, when, one Sunday, the piously-disposed went in there to pray. Short work we had of it, for our orisons were scarce begun when the service was adjourned. The cause was that the niguas had taken possession of the holy place, and were concentrating on the defenseless girls their myriad hosts. I washed half a dozen off my legs on coming out. Now, however, it had been sprinkled and swept till it would do to worship in very well.

The priest came in the evening, bringing with him his wafers, a chalice wrapped in a cloth and tied under his arm, and a vial of wine with a paper stopper. During the mass the next morning a poor fellow was attacked with epilepsy in the church. They took him into the sacristy, and, to recover him, they concluded to apply wine to his nostrils. The wine in the bottle is unconsecrated; so they turn the vial up till the paper stopper is saturated, and rub it on the nostrils and lips of the patient, and then put it back into the vial. After the consecration came the procession, on a very humble scale, with an image borrowed for the occasion. The hostia must be carried under an umbrella for want of a canopy, and in default of a better I lent them mine. It was whole when I closed it last, many months before, in Bogotá; now I find it broken, no one knows when, where, or how. After the ceremonies were over, I found a cork that I could spare, and whittled it down to fit the vial of wine, and threw away the wad of paper.

The wife of Martin, who lives just at our gate, is dead. He takes on like one distracted. She died, they say, of worms, a very common complaint here, where nearly every pair of jaws is a cane-mill. They kindly sent her medicine from the house, but it was not administered, because they had no molasses to give it in.

I was called to see a sick child, three years old, between the house and the river. It had worms, and was quite sick. The mother wrung her hands, and cried, "Oh dear! what can mother do for her poor little nigger girl?" Negrita is a favorite term of endearment here, even for white children. I inquired what they gave, and found it was worm-seed herb (Chenipodium anthelminticum), which grew in the door-yard. They gave it in aguardiente. I directed the doses to be increased in size and frequency, and given in molasses. I hunted up a cowhage pod for them. I also advised the discontinuance of verdolaga, which is nothing but that inert weed purslane (Portulacca oleracea), so common in the United States, on which they were relying, and told them to come next day and I would give some calomel. Hearing nothing from them, I went, two days after, and they had not complied with any of my directions, as they thought the child "too weak to bear medicine!" One morning, soon after, I said, "There was a ball last night?" "No, Señor." "But I heard a drum—was there no dancing?" "Yes, Señor, there was dancing, but not at a ball. That little girl died last night, and they were rejoicing over the little angel (angelito)."

I never saw this strange ceremony, for they preferred I should not. The little thing was tied into a chair, and put on a kind of shelf, like an image for worship, high enough up to leave the whole room for dancing; and there parents and friends had danced most or all the night. The anticipation of this merry-making tends, I think, to mitigate the dread of losing a child. The ground of the rejoicing (which is also an ordinance of the Episcopal Church of the United States and England) is, that the child has gone to Limbo, and not Purgatory, and will suffer no more.

If those who doubt which kills most, disease or the doctor, would only go with me to the benches and floors where lie stretched the miserable sick poor in the Valley of the Cauca, they would return with quite a different idea of the healing art.

All the ill-bred children here fear me or my spectacles, I know not which. This is particularly the case with two little girls, of five and three, that live between the house and the river. They are fat, very black, and always naked. I met their mother coming up from the river with a large múcura of water on her head. As soon as the children saw me coming, they clung to her clothes so that she could not walk. After I had passed and they began to go on again—the little ones fearfully looking back at me—I turned as if to walk back. Instantly they bellowed, and clung to their mother. Before she had time to look round with the heavy load on her head, I was again innocently walking toward the river. I repeated my trick again with the same success, and then, thinking it "too bad," I left them.

I stopped to watch the motions of another black rascal, a boy of about ten, who was victimizing a pig. He had a lazo of bejuco—vine. The pig had been found in a pen, and noosed there. The boy was still in the pen, but the pig had run out through a hole two feet square, that served as a door. If the boy should stoop to go through the same hole, the pig would drag him off in the stooping posture. And should he climb over, the pig would run off with his lazo before he got down; so he wound his bejuco around a stake beside the hole, which held his pig till he had got out. Then came a grotesque attempt at riding, with a fall every two rods; but as he clung to the bejuco, his steed could not escape him, and so I left them.

Across the river is a little establishment that is occupied, sometimes for weeks together, by Mother Antonia, an authoritative old beldame, very useful on the place. When corn is to be planted, or when so near ripe that monkeys and parrots begin to steal it, she lives there, and keeps one or two boys with her. I found her in possession of two species of quadruped poultry I should call them, only they were kept for their flesh and not their eggs. The larger is called guatin, and may be Dasyprocta Acuschy. It is as large as a cat, and its gait is a succession of leaps, like a rabbit's. There was but one of these, and that finally ran away, pursued by dogs. The other animal, Curí, was of the size of a very young puppy of the mastiff breed. I suppose it to be an Anæma, and, if it be not the Guinea-pig, I have forgotten the difference. Both are raised for food at the head of the Cauca. The Curíes keep in joints of guadua prepared for their refuge, and eat plantain leaves and fruits. They are nice pets.

I went once to visit Bernabé, the district judge. He is a negro, with a mulatto wife, Dolores, and two or three children, that seem a little lighter than she is. I may be deceived, but, again, perhaps Bernabé may be. The judge can not read. He lives on the base of a knoll overlooking the pasture of Guavito, and his house is supplied by a small brook that flows down a ravine, and is often almost dry, or with no running water. There always happens in the beds of these brooks to be some water in the charcos or holes, and as you advance toward the source you find a very little running in the channel. Cattle understand this, and, when impelled by thirst, follow a dry brook *up* till they come to water.

I found Dolores in the kitchen, and she sent a little girl to tell me she could not leave it just then. I went out for the sake of seeing a Caucana fairly busy. She was distilling aguardiente. A large tinaja, A, was standing on tulpas (three stones), in the middle of the floor, with a fire under it. It contained some fermented cane-juice. The condenser was a brass pan or kettle (paila), B, that covered the mouth of the tinaja. Under this condenser was a peculiar earthen plate, C, called an obispo—bishop—so constructed as to receive the drops that fell from the under surface of the kettle, and permit them to run off in the tube D. This tube is a mere reed. To prevent the free escape of steam, a lock of cotton was put in the mouth of it. To keep the condensing kettle cool was Dolores' present occupation. She dipped it full of water from a trough, and then dipped it out again into the trough, and thus continued filling and emptying it incessantly, while the drops of the dearly-earned fluid fell deliberately into a junk bottle placed beneath.

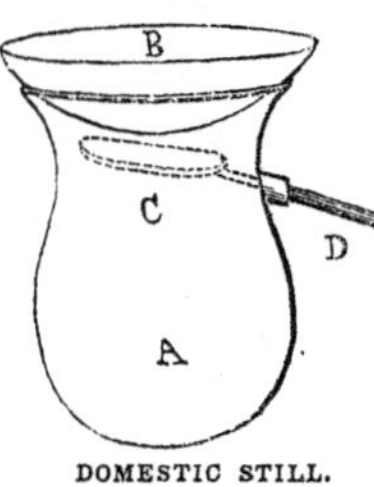

DOMESTIC STILL.

I went up into the woods for plants, and on my return found Dolores released, and selling their sirup—melado. I asked her at what price she sold it, and she did not understand me. They have no liquid measures in use here ; so I asked her how much that tarra held which she was using for a measure, and she told me it held a half dime. Spirits are sold by the bottle at a dime a bottle. The bottles vary much in size, but they are chiefly wine bottles.

We went down to the house—a clean and lofty sala, with an inner room adjoining, and one porch converted into a room that serves at once for entry and bed-room, with a thoroughfare through it. A hammock constantly swings in the centre of the sala ; a little table of guadua is immovably placed in one corner. On this I found now displayed all their table furniture—two plates, a knife and fork. Some fried fish, from the Ciénega de

Burro, and a roasted plantain, were set on, and I was bound to have a lunch. I did not enjoy the fish so much as I did the plantain, but I ate it resolutely. It was kindly meant. The last time I saw Dolores she gave me $3 20 to buy some medicine for her, which I have duly sent her. It was a quack medicine, and my conjectures as to its use would not be much to her credit; but we must make all allowance, and hope the best of her. Two of her little girls are at the Overo, further south, boarding and going to school.

I went back to Libraida, the head of the district, to see an election. A series of them, four days apart, and about six in number, were coming off. It was under a new law, which was exceedingly rigid in securing the rights of the citizen to a secret vote. The elections must fall on different days of the week, and of course only one of them on the Sabbath. All votes in the same province must be of the same precise size, about six inches square. Three officers sit in a room, and no man can come in except electors, one at a time, with a ballot once folded between the thumb and index of the right hand. The loss of either of these organs disfranchises him. He holds it out horizontally; an officer takes it, unfolds it face downward, drops it into a box, and the voter goes out at the back door, where no persons are permitted to remain, and jumps over the fence in the rear. The counting was a great ceremony. The declarer held the ballot aloft in both hands, so that all around could see both sides of it, and then read it while others recorded it.

I saved a copy of the Christian names in the check-list as a curiosity. The most frequent name was José-Maria (Pepe), of which there were 19 voters in a list of 324. Next most popular was Joaquin, 17. Then followed José, 13; Pedro, 12; Francisco (Pacho), 10; José-Antonio and Manuel, 9 each; Antonio and Juan, 8 each; Manuel-José, 7; Vicente, 6; Dionisio, Ramon, and Sántos, 5; Domingo, Felipe, Isidoro, Juan-Antonio, Julian, Mariano, Miguel, Tomas, Torribio, and Santiago, 4 each. The following eleven names were repeated three times: Agustin, Antonio-María, Benito, Bonifacio, Eugenio, Eusebio, Fernando, Ignacio, Juan-Agustin, Luis, and Nicolas. There were two each of the following twenty names: Alejo, Anselmo, Carlos, Elias, Emigidio, Esteban, Felix, Hermengildo, Ildefonso, Jacinto, Juan-de-Dios, Juan-José, Luis-Antonio, Martin, Manuel-Antonio, Pascual, Pedro-José, Salvador, Tiburcio, and Timoteo. Seventy-eight had no tocuyo among the voters. Their names were Adolpho, Alonso, Ambrosio, Anacleto, Anastasio, Andres, Angel, Angel-María, Apolinar, Atanasio, Bartolomé, Bautista, Benancio, Bernabé, Bernadino, Blas, Camilo, Cancio, Cayetano, Ciriaco, Claudio, Cristóbal, Damian, Damoso, Enrique, Evaristo, Exequiel, Facundo, Fermin, Fulgencio, Hilario, Jesus, Joaquin-Antonio, José-Abad, José-Bárbaro, José-Bernardo, José-Eulofio, José-Fortunato, José-Manuel, Juan-de-la-Cruz, Juan-María, Juan-Nepomuceno, Justo, Leandro, Lino, Lucio, Manuel-Ascensio, Manuel-Eleaterio, Manuel-Esteban, Manuel-Sántos, Marcelo, Marcos, Melchor, Paulino, Pedro-Antonio, Pedro-Esteban, Pedro-Fermin, Pedro-Valencio, Pio-Quinto, Primitivo, Quinterio, Rafael, Raimundo, Ramon-Nonato, Roso, Ruperto, Segundo, Servando, Silvestre, Simon, Sinforoso, Teodor, Traton, Valentin, Valerio, Victor, and Victorino.

Now all the gentlemen aforesaid, and not a few minors—menores de edad—have been anticipating the advent of Sanwhán, or, as they spell it, San Juan. It is not the saint, however, but the day they seem to expect as eagerly as any schoolboy his holidays. For many weeks I have heard of the approaching San Juan as a great time, like the Fourth of July with us. While Edge, the pyrotechnist, has been busy in Jersey City with his dangerous playthings (edge-tools are always dangerous playthings), Luis, sitting under his shed, has been making cohetes or rockets. He makes a strong case of goat-skin, and puts in it a tea-spoon full of blasting-powder. One end of this is attached to the top of a hollow stem of a woody grass chusquea filled with a mixture of pulverized powder and charcoal. Both are tied to a small stick, the straighter and lighter the better, but the first that comes to hand will answer.

The eventful day was Friday, 24th June; but these events love to be anticipated. On Tuesday a couple went to Libraida to be married. Their return on Wednesday noon was celebrated and announced by a sufficient number of these rocket-crackers described above. This was also the signal for the commencement of a day ball in a cottage near the gate. In the course of the afternoon I went down, and came back with a description of the dress of the bride, put on, of course, after marriage, for nothing but sombre colors are allowed in church. I give it for the benefit of any who may have occasion to adopt it for the same important ceremony.

The hair was short all over the head, but, being as crisp as wool, retained without difficulty a side-comb of gold and some artificial flowers on each side, and a complete garland behind. The ear-rings were of gold, quite original in their pattern, reminding me of the top of a steeple, the ball being represented by a stone of the size of a cherry. On the neck was, first, a chain of gold going twice around; second, a string of pearl beads; third, another gold chain. The camisa was of fine white muslin; sleeves of another muslin, shot with red, reaching below the elbow; collar of the same, two fingers broad, falls down from the top, which is so low in the neck that it hangs off one shoulder, but, per contra, probably does not extend half way to the feet; enaguas of de laine, slate color, with two flounces. A belt of material resembling that of gentlemen's braces passes twice round the waist and tucks in. Below this, the skirt sags in front three inches. In the mouth, a cigar; on the hands, four gold rings with emeralds; on the feet, nothing, with pantalettes of the same.

The ball, after lasting some sixteen hours without intermission, closed early on Thursday morning. After a ball or other fatigue a swim is very refreshing. My affairs brought me accidentally in contact with a swimming party this morning. It consisted of the whitest and handsomest girls of the Medio, the young men of the "house," and vaqueros. I believe I have described the bathing dress of gentlemen and ladies. I will repeat, however, that the men wear a pocket-handkerchief—never more nor less. The girls wore less than ladies do, only a skirt and a handkerchief tied around the neck at top, and confined at the bottom by the skirt. I fancy they profess not to go in at the same place, but in two places, say five rods apart; but they do not fail to invade each other's bounds. The women use a profusion of soap.

As the parties were about entering the water, the mother of some of them, and grandmother of the younger ones, who had staid behind to get a child asleep, came riding down to the river at a full gallop, shouting "Whoop! San Juan!" This cry from young and old, male and female, became familiar to my ears before night. Their road back was the same I was going. Most of the men were on horseback, and the females on foot. It so happened that the cavalcade rode on each side of the pedestrians, assuming the form described above in the process of cattle-driving. This, when perceived, amused them not a little, and they rode on, calling "Toma! Toma!"

After my return home it was announced that a party of Sanjuaneros was approaching the house. Demetrio loaded the gun, and Mother Antonia hastened to place cake and aguardiente on a table in the corredor. The party advanced with whoopings and rockets, to which Demetrio responded, setting fire with the wad to the thatch of the cane-mill. In the party I counted twenty-six females, every one of them astride (to be specific) of a horse, a mare, or a gelding. Without dismounting, the wine-glass of raw spirit, without sugar or water, passed the whole cavalcade. The men drained it, the women only sipped. They went as they came, on the gallop. I joined the party some time after at the lower cottages. Many had flags made of a handkerchief, and adorned with ribbons. All the women wore shawls on their heads under their hats and ruanas.

I found them galloping back and forth on the vast plain, without more aim than bees seem to have when they swarm. One would snatch another's flag and run; others start in pursuit; others follow to see the sport. The rest go so as not to be left alone. In three minutes the whole party are halted in a spot half a mile from where they started. Pio V. had in his hands the remains of an unfortunate hen that had been snatched from some twenty hands, having lost in these struggles much of its feathers, its life, and, I believe, its head. It was not a very pretty plaything—neither wholesome to the eye nor nice to the hand. A cock had been beheaded according to the rules on page 414 a little before I joined the party.

Arches were erected in front of two houses, ornamented with cloth, etc., and fruits, as plantains, slices of a huge species of Citrus (called cidra), and a pineapple. Under the arch you find a bench and a table, with aguardiente for sale. Now you find them all gathered before a house. Fulgencio, ex-judge of the district, has bought a bottle of spirits there, which must pass from mouth to mouth till it is empty. Owing to the time lost in pouring into a glass, a bottle is drunk in less time without one, and, what is surprising, is emptied by fewer persons.

This was followed by a race between two horses, in which the stakes were from a dime or two to perhaps three dollars. My conclusion from all this is, that the beloved disciple was fond of horse-racing, dram-drinking, shouting, and gunpowder; but perhaps it is John the Baptist that is to answer to these charges.

The day itself, Friday, differed in nothing from its víspera or eve, only perhaps the assemblage was more numerous. Without doubt, on both days all the saddles and bridles were in requisition, but the horses and riders were not all the same as yesterday, and perhaps more were *in pelo* (without saddle), and with halters for bridles.

Saturday brought no remission, unless it be that the cohetes had been nearly all let off. Toward night there was a bull-feast in the front yard, but quite a different affair from those of a higher grade, as at Fusagasugá. Young bulls are selected, and yet, upon the whole, I had rather be the bull than the toreador. He is led into the middle of the yard with a guasca on his horns. He is thrown down by hand, not by a lazo on his heels. A noose is then put on his heels, and that on his head taken off. On his release he dashes at the horsemen, and they avoid him. They provoke him by riding up to him, and he makes another pass at them. A footman approaches with a ruana in his hand; the bull springs at him, and he leaps upon the fence. The bull shows no perseverance, but runs on as though he had not thought of his adversary. Another dexterously leaves his ruana on the head of the bull. If other measures fail, the toreador escapes danger by lying down. When, at length, the bull becomes tired of the sport, and no longer resents the insults he receives, the gate opens, and he runs off to the pasture from which he was taken. Even women were on horseback in the inclosure; but at one time I saw a "speck" of danger. Fulgencio attempted to avoid the bull by leaping on the fence, but, being "half-scratched," or "a little warm" (*medio rasgado, un poco caliente, en pea, teniendo perico, en polvo,* etc.), was not as active as usual, and lay at the animal's feet, if not at his mercy. Where should a bull begin on a district judge that can not read nor write? Not at the head nor the heart. Imitating awkwardly the process of rolling up a piece of cloth to lay on the shelf, the bull began in the middle; but, after a poke or two, the simultaneous attack of other toreadores made him desist.

Leaving the bull-feast, I went to the Medio. Here the company passed me. The most natural comparison would be with a party of Pawnees in gala dress; but I thought first of the Bacchantes, the excesses of whom are probably exaggerated in the accounts given us. Stationary writers are tempted to exaggerate in order to say something extraordinary: travelers have no motive to exaggeration; their only difficulty and their wisest aim is to make their readers comprehend and believe things as they really are. Those women who have two shawls use the red on these occasions, and wear the blue on their head in church. Most ruanas also have red in them. As women wear the same hats with men, and on horseback wear the same ruanas and sit in the same way, at a distance it is impossible to tell a woman from a man.

Matea, "whose husband was killed in the wars" (very lately, I should judge, from the age of her youngest child), excited my attention by her hard riding and perfect *abandon*. Do not imagine her a widow in black. All the black she wore was placed by nature in the cellules of the cutis, and as for the fathers of her children—*quien sabe?*

Jacinto, nearly our best horseman, on our return fell into the river from his horse, which stood perfectly still till he mounted again, benefited, no doubt, by having taken a little water with his spirits.

On Sunday again there was horse-racing, and we had another bull-feast. I have not spoken of the balls, though there has probably been one every night. It is really amazing to me to see so much drinking, so little drunkenness, and no fighting, especially in a people where drunkenness is not very disreputable, and where they have a civil war every ten years.

San Juan being past, we move up the river. We enter the pasture of Guavito. Down on our left is the corral, and on our right the house of the black judge Bernabé and Dolores the distiller stands on a commanding knoll. Now the forests approach each other, and have the appearance of having in ancient years been cut through with the axe. One or two mud-holes have rather a profound look. Then comes the River of Murillo, the southern boundary of La Paila, of the canton of Cartago, and once of the province of Antioquia. It is a small stream in which the water barely runs in dry seasons.

On the left, after passing the river, are the houses of the Hacienda of Murillo. We can not stop to study the family at the principal house. I only mention that here I saw a female monkey chained up: these unlucky and disgusting prisoners are almost always of the other sex. Here, too, I saw a cat, an animal about as rare here as parrots at the North. This and the last I saw were both blind of an eye. I can not tell why the climate disagrees with this cosmopolite animal.

My stay was mostly at a smaller house, the guest of Don Manuel. He is a wandering character, who seems to have lodged here as he drifted about. He has seen many and queer things, especially in Barbacoas and Chocó, where he has been for gold, little of which seems to adhere to him. He is quite communicative, especially when drunk, for he will get almost as drunk as an American. In one of these confidential moods he assured me that the servant, Catalina, whom I was teaching to read, was his own daughter; had been his servant from childhood, but knew not her parentage. The great trouble with him is that I never know when to believe him, drunk or sober; and yet, withal, he is a very intelligent man, with more than an ordinary share of learning.

Catalina was now housekeeper. Another Manuel—a great rogue, as Don Manuel said, made up the force of this bachelor's hall. Don Manuel has had a wife, but I know not where she is, and also has respectable daughters somewhere. Catalina is about seventeen; not a bad-looking girl, but rather too fond of the priests, her protector thinks. She seems willing to learn, if it will do any body any good to teach her; but when I reproached him for leaving "his daughter" in ignorance, he said that he would willingly have taken pains with her had she wished to learn.

Don Manuel delighted in Chocó stories of snakes and secret

remedies for their bites and for hydrophobia; of ants whose bite was mortal; of creatures that are insects at one part of their life, but then their feet take root, their backs bud and produce stalks of flowers, the seeds of which are again walking animals. And he tells what he himself has seen and knows till you persuade yourself that he believes in every word he says. My own opinion, duly considered and mathematically expressed, is, that the moral momentum of the man, found by multiplying the accuracy of his observation by the fidelity of his narrative, and deducting for the resistance of forgetfulness, is not sufficient to overcome my incredulity; or algebraically expressed, $o \times n - f = m < b$.

One of his best stories is of an attempt to cure leprosy with the bite of a venomous serpent—the equis. I expected that heroic treatment would succeed *in his hands*, but the venom appeared unproductive of good or harm. This particular equis had been caught in a lazo, and housed in a calabasa. Don Manuel discovered, to his astonishment, that he had a control over the beast, which would come out of, and return to his "house" at his command, as if it understood Spanish. He believed that a great many negroes and Indians in that serpentiferous Chocó have antidotes and prophylactics for the most deadly venom. He tells of a Chocóano that had a tame coral snake, the pet of the whole family, till, in a fatal hour, she brought forth a brood of young ones, that, ere he knew of their birth or they their duty, had mortally bitten one of his children. But it is not fair to repeat these stories while I refuse to endorse them. They are, however, but a natural production of the Pacific coast. Still I must admit that I had to believe some of his toughest stories in the end, and more of them may be true than I now think.

Once for all, let me say that I have little confidence in snake remedies. The most positive statements in respect to them are often entirely false. It is a general impression that the venom of serpents of different species differs more in power than in nature. This is very doubtful. Sensibility to poison certainly varies in different species. A bite of a rattlesnake that would kill a horse would only make a man deadly sick (with fright perhaps), and would not harm a hog.

A spontaneous recovery from a snake-bite gives reputation to an inert remedy. Besides the Mikania Guaco, of which I have never seen the flower, and Aristolochia anguicida, also called guaco, there are many other plants that have the same name and the same reputation. All have two distinct colors in the leaf, as has the rattlesnake-leaf of the States—Goodyera pubescens. Many rely on the cotyledons of Simaba Cedron, called cedron in New Granada. Besides extraction of poison, and the immediate severing of the bitten limb, I know of no surer way than to combat the symptoms as they appear.

Leaving the broad plains of Murillo to the west, you advance to the Overo. Overo means egg-tree, and has its name from a tree that bears a fruit in shape resembling an egg. Overo has an unfinished church—or chapel I suppose it is, for it is in the district of Buga-la-Grande. You pass a small stream, in a very large bed, having every appearance of being subject to violent freshets, and beyond you come to the Portazuela, the residence of the amiable Dr. Quintero.

Dr. Quintero is a bachelor of 32, but has living with him his widowed mother and three amiable sisters—the youngest about 13. Here I had the pleasure of eating with the family again, "as heretics do." One little thing, the first time I ate here, took me by surprise. It was after a late dinner, between eight and nine. Of course, chocolate followed immediately on the conclusion of the meal. I had finished my cup, and it had disappeared, when, to my surprise, I found *another* was prepared for me. I must be known, then, by my reputation of drinking two cups of chocolate at a sitting.

Dr. Quintero has a medical library, and practices physic. He reads, however, neither English, French, nor German. In this case, his library can consist only of old books and text-books, for none of the current medical literature in this century flows in Latin or Spanish channels. I have seen no other doctor's office, study, or library since I left Fusagasugá, although there doubtless is one or more practicing in Ibagué, and I saw the one that called to cure the ear-ache in Cartago.

Dr. Quintero does not pretend to live by his profession. I think none but an avaricious man (and he is not) could practice here without a loss even. He owns the hacienda, or uncultivated area, it may be called, of Sartinajal, farther up, and off the road to the east. He has also pastures and a herd of mares near his house. So it seems as if he learned his profession as a matter of respectability—a proper mode of employing his youthful years. And was he not right? Shall a man be thought crazy because he prefers respectability to wealth? I am ashamed to think what Dr. Quintero would say of our candidates for medical honors when he came to fathom their motives for embracing the profession, and found them all, rich and poor, instigated by the universal mania for wealth.

I was charmed with the first appearance of the ladies here, but found them, as it seems to me, too timid to serve one for company. They appeared most at home, secluded with their needles, in their inner apartment. I invaded their sewing-room, hoping to make myself at home there too, but my experiment was not successful. An acquaintance with them must be the work of time.

We see in the Cauca no *casas claustradas*, or complete houses, containing a court in the middle, except in paved towns. I know of none between Cartago and Tuluá. So, when I speak of Dr. Quintero's kitchen, I mean a separate building used for that purpose. Dr. Quintero's kitchen has a chimney. The design of this is to give draught to a kind of furnace or brick stove, with openings on top to set earthen kettles in. Had it been three feet higher it would have passed out of the roof, and delivered the kitchen from smoke, but they had not thought of that.

On leaving here the little sister made me a present of a cord made of horsehair, to bind my bundle of paper to dry plants in. The advantage of it is that it does not injure by exposure to wet, nor can dogs eat it. These exemptions make hair ropes—cerdas—invaluable for tethering horses, a practice quite necessary here. The best of these which I ever saw was also a present to me from Dr. Quintero, quite a number of horses having been despoiled of their flowing honors on my account one morning while I was there. The small cord I have lost. Of all little thefts I have suffered here, this grieves me most.

The mud-holes—atascaderos—of the Cauca Valley are formidable to pleasure-travelers, as they are continually marring the comforts of the journey. Many of them are watercourses over which there are the remains of a bridge; but if any of them are passable they are at once forgotten, while the sloughs to be crossed make you remember them a long while. One of these, oddly enough, occupies Dr. Quintero's gateway, like a sort of moat, so that all footmen have to climb the fence, for you could not walk through the gate without wading in mud more than a foot deep. A formidable specimen of the same occurs half a mile south of his house, in the road. I crossed it by jumping my horse into it, and then following it up some way till I found a place where it was possible to jump out.

Soon we came to a magnificent stream, larger than the Paila, but smaller than the Rio de la Vieja. The farther we go up south, the more merry the streams are. Pebbly bottoms and rippling currents were all the country lacked below to make its beauty perfect. This stream, *el* Buga-*la*-grande, once rose so suddenly that, though my baggage went over easily two hours before me, when I came to it, having ladies in company, all thoughts of passing it that day were abandoned. We went down the river to a hacienda and passed the night, and crossed at a place much below early the next morning. That night I slept (as far as sleep was possible) without my hammock. We were on our way by sunrise, threading lanes in a settlement west of the road. Here we passed a country school in full operation at about eight in the morning. The scholars were to go home to breakfast at about ten.

North of this river were a large number of scattering houses and a church. Here is the head of the district of Buga-la-Grande. This place is memorable to me for its oranges, at once plenty and excellent. For the second time in my life have I really found oranges in abundance. Dr. Quintero had a good supply to spare for his guests, but here there were more than were needed. My feast here will not be forgotten, though two dimes would give one as much in New York market; but we do not enjoy them so.

A few miles farther on we came to the stream and hacienda of Sabaletas—the Minnows—the residence of Sr. Vergara. At the cane-mill here I drank a mixture of fermented guarapo (here called chicha) and boiling cane-juice, already quite sweet. I found it delicious, and, in spite of all warnings, drank of it very freely. To the surprise of all, I escaped unharmed, while they looked for nothing less than a fit of colic.

I came upon this family one night after they had all gone to bed. The sala has hammock-loops in it, and, in consequence of this convenience, in three minutes after the bridle was off my horse, the candle was again extinguished, and I was comfortably reposing in my hammock.

Señora de Vergara is a Venezolana. I find that I peculiarly like all the emigrants from Venezuela that I have yet seen. Perhaps they know the heart of a stranger, being themselves far from home, though among their own race. The daughters seemed very well educated, and were quite pleasant company. I had with me a dilatory Granadino, who liked to chat with them, but he must be in Tuluá that night. They urged us warmly to stay, and, when we constantly refused, the lady said, "If you will go, you have not a moment to lose. The upper end of the road is not fit to travel in the night, and you will now be caught before you can reach town." She almost drove us from the house. I was very much delighted at the time, and still more when I became convinced that her energy was all that saved me from sleeping in the woods that night.

It was sunset when we parted, and I had three miles yet to go to reach La Ribera, the home of the Várgas family, to which I introduced the reader at Cartago. Much of the way was woods, and all of it was mere path, without a regular road. My horse had never been there; but I had been over part of the road four times, and part of it but once, and then with company. Starlight in a tropical forest, far from any house, is nothing to trifle about, especially after you have seen the peasantry skinning a leon. This animal (probably Felis concolor, puma, painter, and panther) appears to range from Canada to Patagonia. The individual which I saw was killed in the forest of the river. It seemed little inferior in strength to his African namesake. The tigre (Felis onca, jaguar, ounce, catamount—if, indeed, these animals are the same all over the continent) is weaker, more agile, and more cruel, as is generally supposed.

I had for my consolation the fact that deaths from wild beasts, venomous serpents, mad dogs, and lightning are very rare among mankind. True, there might be more from serpents and wild beasts, were it the custom to be roaming about in deep woods in the night. My horse could see the path though I could not. I could still see enough to keep my general direction, and all accidents were in our favor, so we came through safe.

I found it once a day's journey from La Ribera to Dr. Quintero's, thanks to the marvelous efficacy of having a guide. Said guide was Lorenzo, the body-guard to Señor Flojo of La Paila. I had assured Señor F. that we should get home by night. "No, you will not," says he; "you will sleep at Portazuela." "I shall certainly be home." "You certainly will not," says the good Emilia. But I had not counted on the benefits of having a guide.

Lorenzo contrived to get ahead of me at one place before we reached the highway. Soon I detected him leading me off a little to the right. "You are out of the road," I shouted. "I know the way," he answered. Soon it was obvious that we were not approaching the highway. I reined in. "This is the best way for us," said he; "I have an errand at Sartinajal." I love to see new road; there was no real necessity of my calling at Sabaletas, so I gave in.

Five minutes after, I happened to look at my arm; the shirt sleeve that covered it seemed to be made of strainer-cloth. "I have not my own shirt on," I exclaimed. "Yes, Señor, you have," said the confident Lorenzo. "But I tell you I know! Look!" and I raised my hand, not to strike him, but to put him down more surely by ocular demonstration. "Indeed it is yours, Señor. The fact is, that a cow ate a sleeve out of it, and the Lady Emilia put in another of cloth, as like it as she could get." I looked at the other sleeve; it was a "fact truth." Guides do know some things.

They were glad to see me at Sartinajal. The woman turned out to be Lorenzo's mother. The house was a mere hut, and no white people lived there, or perhaps ever had. I must get off and go in, indeed I must. The saddles were taken off, and the horses tethered. I must look at the country, for I was farther from the river than any other house stands that I have seen. There is little or no timber growing about here. The country was rolling, and most of it much higher than the bottom of the valley. It seemed a boundless pasture, ready to be occupied if there were any one to herd and care for the stock. From here, too, I could see the distant pasture of San Miguel, which I had seen from the top of Cara-perro. It was now many miles to the northeast.

It was not time to go yet, indeed it was not. I must eat something. No matter if I was not hungry, I must eat out of compliment. I suspect that the dog Lorenzo had brought with him a couple of ripe plantains to roast for me here, as the surest bait to catch a Yankee. After eating, I must not go yet. There was something drying that his mother must iron and send to Dr. Quintero's. Now the cat was out. It was very true that I should not see La Paila that night. The dry pasture furnished me nothing to study. I had exhausted my occupations and my patience.

We left Sartinajal at nearly 5. In a mile or two we came to the Buga-la-grande, and followed down the river, crossing its bed five or seven times. Had the river been higher, we must have taken a longer road. We crossed it last at dusk, just as it began to rain. Soon I could not see the ground. I could still make out Lorenzo's form before me. When that disappeared, I asked him to throw up his dingy ruana, that I might see his shirt. Said shirt was not very white, and at last night shut that in, and I could not see my horse's ears. I had strained my eyes till my head ached as if it was splitting, and that ugly ravine was to be crossed. I shut my eyes but opened my ears. Now a jump downward, and my horse is in the ditch. Much I feared that we should fall backward or sidewise in scrambling out. All's well that ends well. At 15 minutes past 8 I was safe under the hospitable roof of Dr. Quintero, and resting my aching head on the table. I breakfasted next morning at Murillo, and at 1 P.M. was at La Paila, blessing my stars that I did not often have a guide.

CHAPTER XXX.

THE GRAZIER AT HOME.

House-building of Guadua, Mud, and Thatch.—Plan of House.—Servants.—Ablutions.—Breakfast.—The Dairy.—Dinner.—A Sabbath.—Baptism.—Marriage.—Dinner and Ball.—Drinking without Drunkenness.—The Bundi.—Carrying home the Girls.—A Love Affair.—Lay Baptism.—Lying.—A Week's Sickness.—Diet.—Monkey and Fowl.—Slaughter of Beef.—Turtles.—Agriculture.—Prices.—Fertility and Poverty: Abundance and Hunger.

I WISH to give a more accurate picture of domestic life among the first families in the Cauca. For this I have selected the Várgas family, as I wish strictly to avoid entering the domain of fiction by combining the occurrences of two or more families. I write this in the earnest hope that no reader will recognize the originals, or, if unfortunately it should be otherwise, that the discoverer will be so good as never to make known their name or residence to any inhabitant of South America.

It will be recollected that when I introduced Señor Eladio Várgas to the reader, I mentioned that, in the times of slavery, they were wealthy. Besides this estate of La Ribera, and their mines in Chocó, that now yield not a dollar, they have two haciendas in this valley, though there is a lawsuit with an adverse claimant to one of them. La Ribera alone could support them handsomely were it well managed, but their chief desire seems to be to keep things along here, and to spend in Cartago all they can scrape from this estate, while I doubt whether the others yield any thing at all.

I hardly can guess what was the theory on which the house was arranged with regard to the highway. It faces nearly to the north, stretching from east to west 137 feet. It is covered with thatch of Carludovica, here called iraca, and, when on the roof, paja. The ground inclines slightly, so that while the west end is some two feet above its surface, the opposite extremity is a hole dug as much into it. Still the floor is not quite level. Said floor is of brick in the finished rooms and corredores, and of earth in the others. The walls are, like those of ordinary cottages, entirely of three materials—guadua, bejuco (vine), and mud. Posts of guadua were placed erect on the ground at distances of a few feet; slats of guadua are tied to them both within and without; all the space between them is filled with mud; then the whole is plastered over with mud for mortar; part has been whitewashed with lime, and it is intended at some future day, when they can get lime enough, to give the whole a second coat.

Lime is hard to get. It is an ugly thing to carry in sacks on mule-back. I know of but two lime-kilns in all the Valley of the Cauca—one at Vijes, the other five miles above. These are not worked much, for the demand is so small, and transportation so difficult; so plastering and bricklaying is all done with mud, and even whitewash is a luxury for want of wheels.

In theory the house is 115 feet by 19, and divided into 8 rooms, each 19 feet from north to south, but of various widths. But the roof projects so far over as to cover a corredor 7 feet wide. Seven more rooms are constructed all around the house on this corredor. Besides these, in the rear are two more houses, one adjoining, and the other a little removed from the principal house. All this is made clear by the following diagram:

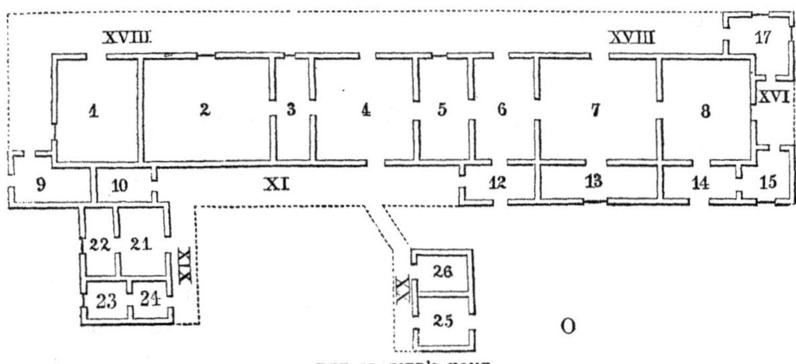

THE GRAZIER'S HOME.

Here the corredores are numbered in Roman, and the rooms in Arabic. The principal corredor, XVIII., extends nearly half way round the house. Just outside of it is a trench made by stamping of horses, the wallowing of a few hogs belonging to the servants, and the occasional visits of horned cattle, etc.

This, in the rainy season, furnishes an admirable supply of musquitoes. On account of them, as it is not healthy to sleep under a musquito net in the house, I hung my hammock in this corredor in front of room 2. I afterward occupied No. 9, which was rather extravagantly furnished with a large, coarse table on trestles, two bedsteads, which served me only for tables, shelves, book-case, etc., etc., and one chair. My hammock swung from corner to corner, so far as the re-entering angle would permit. My table stood before the window, which was a grated opening two feet square, with a shutter. I had also a large table for day use outside the door in the corredor, but I could not leave things there in the night, because the goats used to jump up on the table to sleep.

No. 1 was bachelor's hall. It was 15 feet by 19, matted, had a door and a window, and 3 bedsteads. Gentlemen travelers sometimes slept here, and more or less of the males of the family. No. 2, 21 feet by 19, was the female room. Don Eladio, his wife, and their sisters, occupy it when they are here. His mother rarely, if ever, comes. It had a window down to the floor, and a door opening into No. 3, a narrow room 7 feet by 19, occupied by either sex according to convenience. This has a window, and is a thoroughfare from the women's room to the sala, No. 4. This last is 19 feet square, has doors in all its four sides, with shutters to all of them. I mention this because most inside doors here are mere door-ways, and, if closed at all, it is with a curtain. The size of the remaining rooms is 6, 11, 20, and 14 feet by 19: No. 5 only is entirely completed, and possession of it is disputed, as it were, between the youngest son Carlos and a hired man or two.

If we pass out the back door of the sala into the corredor XI., we at once enter on the domain of a small army of female servants. A brick bench (poyo) runs along the wall, about 20 inches high and 24 broad. East of the door this serves for a forge for minor cookery, as chocolate-making, etc. Next the door, on both sides, it is used for seats. The next portion is used for a dresser for dishes, etc., by day, all of which must be carried in at night for fear of the goats. The west end is built into a tinajera, pierced for three tinajas, with a space under them where pans may be placed to catch what water exudes through the unglazed earthen vessels. Near this, too, is the grinding-stone, with a place under it to put fire to heat the stone when chocolate is to be ground. It ought to be a little over 100° F. Again, in the extreme south end of corredor XIX., a continuation of this, are two large kettles of cast brass (pailas), each a section of a sphere, set in an arch. They are used for making sweetmeats on a large scale, and for other extraordinary operations, as soap-making.

Over all this space Pilar reigns supreme. She is a mulatto woman of about 20 or 25. Her mother is the negress who rules in the Várgas kitchen in Cartago. As to her father, it is a matter that defies my conjecture. She directs affairs, sets the table, waits on it, sews, teaches three little black girls to read, using the corredor as a school-room, and is, in fact, the most efficient person of either sex on the whole place, and does more work than any two of them.

Pilar, the little girls, and one or two of the adults, sleep in No. 10, separated from my room only by a partition so thin that I can hear them at their prayers occasionally of an evening after the family have all gone to bed. The rest of them sleep in 23 and 24, or in the kitchen, or wherever they take a fancy. Rooms 21 and 22 are store-rooms or pantries; 25 is the kitchen; and 26 combines, I think, a kitchen, store-room, and sleeping-room for the old cook. In the centre of the kitchen, 25, is an arch about 8 feet long, pierced for several earthen kettles, with a stump of a chimney about as high as a man's head. An oven, O, a few rods east of the kitchen, under a small roof of its own, completes the conveniences of the house of La Ribera. The kitchen is infested with negro children, dogs, and smoke, and, if seen detached from every thing else, would resemble the abode of a family of savages, or, rather, of a small tribe of them. It can become no dirtier—can be made no cleaner.

Here lies Roso, a little boy of whose parentage I know nothing, if parents he ever had, stark naked, rolling in the dirt. There again is a babe (naked, of course) with a piece of meat in his fist. He is the offspring of Escolastica, a black of about 17. Older than Roso is Cristina, who generally wears an enaguas, often rent from top to bottom, or with a breadth worn out of it, but never clean. Isabel, older still, and always naked down to the hips, wears enaguas. Two girls, still older, but under 10, sometimes add to this a mantellina or blue woolen shawl. Pilar would be glad to keep dogs' noses and children's fingers out of the dishes preparing for us, but the others care nothing about it, provided they do not take so much as to be missed, and her authority is faintly felt in the kitchen.

A desolate shed of a chapel serves us for worship, as we are too far from the Church of San Vicente. It is without pictures, images, pulpit, seats, or floor, and has but one confessional and one altar. In the sacristía are some vestments for ordinary service, some cheap implements for mass, a respectable old missal, and a complete set of wooden toys for the amusement of the infant Savior (Niño Dios—Boy-God), when they make a pesebre—manger—at Christmas.

A blacksmith's shop, and shed that will hold two horses; a cane-mill, that is never used; the foundations of one building, never to be completed, and the ruins of another, that fell down in the last revolution before being roofed, make the sum total of buildings.

There is no garden, and no fruit-trees that are of any use, except a single second-rate orange-tree. Three other fruit-trees yield nothing that is not stolen before it is ripe. Such is La Ribera. Let us now see how a day passes there.

We are not early risers at *the house*, as the family residence is denominated by the cottagers; but, as the hour of six approaches, also approaches the sun to the horizon, and would be visible soon after but for the clouds, that render a rising or setting sun a thing unknown here. As rises the sun rises also Pilar, the "mistress of keys," crosses herself, and, I conjecture, dresses herself—perhaps washes her hands and face. She sets herself to sweeping the back corredor, the sala, and front corredor, a task hardly worthy of the chief housekeeper when perchance goats or cows may have made the front corredor their dormitory. Escolastica rises from a hide laid on the ground, leaving sprawling naked there the son of (she says) Dionisio, and, without any dressing or washing, sets herself about something that bears the semblance of work. Three negritas, naked from the waist upward, one with her skirt rent in three from top to bottom, come and place themselves astride the wall of the corredor—*pretil*—to see if any body passes in the distant highway. This mode of sitting appears more agreeable to the negras than in a chair: Escolastica and others older find it convenient at times. Estefana, the cook, rakes open the kitchen fire, and lights her cigar; or, if the fire is out, strikes a light with flint and steel as readily as you would put on your coat. Her tinder is the huge pith of the Fourcroya—maguey.

Roso, the negrito, the happy possessor of his nudity and not a thread more in the world, comes from his nest, and, without any fear of wearing out his clothes or blacking his skin, sits down on the floor to play. Joaquina leaves her lair, and sits down till milking-time. Josefa rises and walks about. The men-servants make their appearance from various nooks where they have passed the night. Manuel goes to his smithy, that he may not be seen about the house idle.

Manuel Estevan, Dionisio, some shades lighter, and Jacinto, many shades darker, also take their seats on the pretil, a bench, and my table, and appear to be busy with a part of a saddle, a bridle, and a halter. Aureliano, Cosme, and Gregorio, three white boys, who, under the name of servants, contrive to escape with half the work one boy ought to do, post themselves in the corredor to watch the operations of three dogs. Volcan and Enamorado, led by Folía, selected, at 5 o'clock, one of the milch cows for their amusement, and they have worried the poor thing ever since; but they are all cowards, and dare not bite her. Ramon, a larger boy, neither whiter nor blacker than the other two, creeps, as if with sore toes, to the *inclosed* pasture—potrero—and drives several horses into a yard; throws a lazo over an old white horse, which is too lazy or too well bred to run, and goes off to an estancia to look for plantains for breakfast.

Carlos Várgas, the youngest of the gentlemen, catches another with more difficulty but more dexterity, and calls Jacinto from his busy idleness to saddle it, and also another for himself. They start off together to the open pasture, and will return at breakfast-time or a little after. They go to see if any thing has happened there. Toledo (this is his surname), the horse-breaker, has tied each "hand" of a colt to the corresponding foot, and is riding him round and round in a very small circle in the sugar-mill. Pepe Gómez, a relative living in the family, has ridden off to the cacagual, or chocolate-orchard, to see if any cacao needs gathering, and to see if the hogs have broken in. Pepe and Antonio come forth from No. 1 or No. 2, as the case may be, and, without attending at present to their ablutions, sit down in the corredor to read a Spanish translation of a French novel, published as a sort of extra by the Correo de Ultramar in Paris. I have not particularly introduced these younger brothers of Don Eladio. Of Pepe I will only say that he is worth any two of his brothers in business, energy, and reliability, and only inferior to the pious and dignified Eladio. Antonio, who is but 17, has quite an active turn of mind, that loves to exercise itself in horse-racing, dancing, cock-fighting, in the administration of baptism and medicine, and other useful offices.

Prompt washing is not the custom here, and I have been led gradually to defer my ablutions till near breakfast-time. I have gone to the tinajera, and found there a bowl and water, but no dipper nor servant; half an hour after I would find a dipper, but no bowl; and the next time all that I wanted except water, for now the tinajas are all empty. Soap is sometimes imported —that made here is black and pasty. In all cases it is dear. Ashes are not sold, nor is soap-making a trade; neither are the berries of the Sapindus (chambimbi) of as much use as might be expected. They are abundant, being uneatable by animals, and about half an inch in diameter.

Now that I have marshaled my *dramatis personæ*, do not imagine that I am going to follow them all through the day. I will only say farther of their color that Pilar and Josefa are mulattoes (the former good-looking and intelligent), and the rest of the females of pure African blood, except a babe three eighths, perhaps, white. In number I make 23, and of the family there are enough in Cartago to swell the total to about 40.

Now there passes out of the front door a procession of five women and girls, carrying on their heads an earthen jar, a round calabash, a long calabash, a tarro of guadua of two joints, and a green jar in form of a double cone. Those who can not carry their vessels mouth upward have served themselves with an orange for a cork. They go to the river for water.

Joaquina makes her appearance in the corredor with a jar on her head, and in her hands a hair rope and two totumas. The cows have been kept from their imprisoned "sons" all night, not without some lowing and bleating. Gregorio admits one of them. Her delighted offspring rushes to the maternal bosom, but alas! only to find a halter on his nose, the middle of which ties his head to her "arm," while the end is employed in tying her heels securely together. Both generations are in the milker's power, and, with a totuma in her left hand, she proceeds with her right to rob him, before his face and eyes, of the last drop that pays the trouble of extraction.

Mother and son are permitted to pass the day together in the potrero, and two of the boys shut up the calves at night. As they perform this service on horseback, it is not always done with the fewest steps possible. After milking 14 cows, the old lady puts her jar, with about four or five gallons of milk, on her head, and returns to the store-room, 21. Part of the milk she boils. Often a part is taken for our morning chocolate. In the rest she rinses a pound of tripe, and adds lime-juice and too much salt. The coagulated milk, when drained of whey, is cheese; of course, this can not be kept like ours.

Cosme is set to cut up (*picar*) sugar-cane for a horse that is tied in the corredor of the sugar-mill. He borrows a machete of an older servant, who, like a soldier or ancient knight, wears it always in his sheath. The pieces must not exceed two inches in length, and ought not to include the whole of any of the hard nodes in the same piece. Aureliano, who has been presented with a machete for his own, is sent to an estancia to feed in the same manner a horse tied there to fatten. He is kept there to save the trouble of carrying cane. His stable is a thicket of plantains, to one of which—an *herb* 8 inches in diameter and 12 feet high—he is tied. He takes him to the river to wash and water him, an operation that costs an hour, for the rogue of a rider must take time to swim, and, as he finds two or three amphibious negritos to help him, it can not be done in less. He can whip any of them, and even whipped Ramon the other day, who is much older and bigger than himself; he is the pertest little scamp in the hacienda, and Gregorio and Cosme have to "stand round" when he is by.

But breakfast is ready. Some dried beef—*tasajo*—has been boiled in water to make a soup—*sopa*—thickened with cakes of maize, or with plantains roasted and crushed. The meat, reduced to a form resembling oakum, has been fried. It is so dry that, if laid on a sheet of letter-paper instead of a plate, it possibly might neither wet nor grease it. It is rather insipid. The borders of the platter are covered with slices of plantain, fried. When perfectly ripe they are delicious; a little earlier they are insipid and hard; green, they do not fry them. Generally, a roasted plantain is found by each plate. Entirely ripe, they are very good; a little short, they are mealy and insipid; green, they are hard and (to me) uneatable. Unfortunately, the peasantry and the servants generally eat up the ripe ones, and leave us with green ones. But there is another dish; and of this you must take the testimony of an enemy, for I detest it. It is called sancocho, and is the staple of both meals, and with the peasantry generally the only dish except roasted plantains. For this dish, take any quantity of tasajo (that which did not spoil in drying is best), with or without bones, fat or lean; put it in an earthen pot—*olla*—with a pailful or less of water; add shreds of green plantain, and, if you have them, pieces of squash and yuca-root (Manihot utilissima). Potatoes, turnips, carrots, parsnips, onions, and beets would be admissible, but the first can not grow here, and the others are universally neglected. Sweet potatoes—batatas—inferior to ours, so that I doubt their identity, are sometimes added, and tomatoes. This mixture is then boiled. The bogas eat it with spoons of totuma from the shields of tortoises; the peasantry from broken ollas and totumas with spoons of wood or totuma; the respectable familes eat it with heavy ancient spoons of massive silver from soup-plates of the old "willow pattern" of our early days. A fried egg or two, or as many as there are covers, may be found on the table. If boiled, they are eaten with salt only. As you are closing your meal, a small cup of thick chocolate is set upon your plate, or offered you on another plate. Saucers are seldom used as such. Your chocolate contains about two cubic inches of cacao and brown sugar—*panela*—ground together on a warm stone.

The tables are not well attended here, considering the disposable force of a family. More than half this charge may fall upon the *ama de llaves*—"mistress of the keys." I ought to add that breakfast concludes with water. Two or three tumblers, or silver cups, are brought in on a tray. They are successively filled from small tin cups till all have satisfied their thirst. Then, if a priest be present, but never otherwise, the "Lord's Prayer" and some others are said by way of returning thanks.

It is now about half past 10. How, or when, or where the servants have breakfasted I know not, only that it is not together, nor at a table, nor with knives and forks. Things wear as quiet an aspect after breakfast as before. Viviana has caught every hen that has shown a disposition to lay, and shut them up to secure the eggs. The negritas now set themselves down in the corredor of the store-room to sew, under the direction of Josefa, or to read, taught by Pilar. Private instruction here is no better than the schools; and a mulata, a slave 18 months ago, just able to read, is no better than the public teachers, nor much worse. The first book is the "Cartilla." It contains the alphabet, and *abs*, and some prayers. This is followed by the "Citologia," no more interesting to youth. I have looked at every book in which children learn to read, and have not yet found a child who had any thing to read that could interest him. An old law-book; "Artillery Tactics;" the "Theory of Human Liberty and Constitutional Rights," a Protestant tract—any thing that is not damaged by being worn out, or missed if lost, is good enough for a reading-book.

More horses are now saddled, and all the young gentlemen —including the three adult servant gentlemen, who neither dig, nor chop, nor go afoot—are scouring over the plains; but whether they are looking after stock, or chatting with the peasant-girls and projecting another ball, is more than I can tell. Nor can I tell much better what the women are doing—not making the beds, nor washing the windows, nor sweeping the floors, nor making puddings nor pies. The patter of quick footsteps would indicate a cataclysm or a frolic. The voice of cheerful song here never comes from one whose hands are busy. They are not brewing, and it can hardly be possible that they are baking, although they have two or three forms of cake made of the starch of yuca (not the Yucca of botanists); but these are rare. One of them, the suspiro—sigh—greatly resembles that Northern confectionery called a sugar kiss, in being filled with minute air-cells, only a "sigh" is larger than a "kiss," and not so sweet. Another kind of cake, almojávana, almost exactly resembles sponge cake. You can hardly persuade yourself that it contains no flour.

One by one the men drop in. The long table is again covered with a cloth. Pilar carries in dishes from the back corredor, and, carefully wiping them, puts them on the table. It is noticeable that there is never a knife or spoon too much on the table, but not always enough. The entire absence of teaspoons is remarkable. All their spoons are a little larger than our dessert spoons, but contain more silver than our largest. All the excess of silver and other table furniture must be kept carefully locked up, for servants are very careless here. The store-room, too, must never be left open, and the fruit-orchard ought to be always under lock.

The dinner begins, as the breakfast did, with soup. The everlasting sancocho is sure to be present; but in addition to, or in place of the meat-oakum, perhaps you may find a guisado, much like baked beef. It is often very tender, and, I think, superior to our ordinary New York cooking. After the meat comes a teacup or small bowl of boiled milk, eaten generally with roasted plantains; to this succeeds sliced brown sugar (panela), sirup, or sirup and milk boiled together, or some other sweetmeats. The varieties of these, from squash to fig, are innumerable. With these and with chocolate, they never fail to mingle their extemporaneous cheese; or, if this be wanting to their chocolate, they substitute its principal ingredient—salt. After the dulce comes water, served as in the morning. During a meal they rarely or never drink, unless it be wine or aguardiente.

The sun is now hastening toward the hills that separate us from the Pacific, and finally enters the immovable belt of cloud that surrounds the horizon.

The almanac does not give the time of rising or setting of the sun, for there is not much difference at different seasons of the year, and it would be useless to calculate it when it could not be used for regulating clocks, if they had them; but clocks and almanacs are alike scarce. The almanac is only to show the day of the month, the saint of the day, and the rising of the moon. The moon exerts an imaginary but important influence upon agriculture here. They salt cattle and kill trees in the decrease of the moon—el menguante. They plant trees in el creciente—the increase of the moon; and I know of none who doubt its influence. I have found no evidence of it any more than that the pupils of cats' eyes indicate the state of the tides, as some believe. They pay no heed to the sign of the zodiac in which the moon happens to be.

The calves are now shut up. Escolastica goes out and collects weeds (Sida—escoba) for a new broom. The negritas set themselves to playing at marbles with corozos, the seed of a thorny palm, in the front corredor. A peasant from a little distance comes to the house. Five dogs bounce out upon him; the peon coolly draws his machete; Volcan, more zealous than prudent, receives on his "hand" a machetazo, which, for a day or two to come, will make him put down three and carry one. A boy brings in three eggs tied in a cloth to exchange for a candle, both bearing the value of a cuartillo. Ramon brings in a load of cane on a horse. The pack-saddle has two horns—one before, the other behind. To each of these is hung a hook on each side, and on two of these hooks rests the cane. He tells me his load has not slidden off the hooks more than once in coming. All the cane for the cane-mill is carried in this way or on human heads. A horse draws four guaduas at a time (six if seasoned) with one pair of hooks, the other ends resting on the ground. If a single guadua is wanted, it is tied to the horse's tail; the boy mounts his back, and rides home in triumph. Sometimes a man on horseback draws a guadua for a quarter of a mile only with a lazo.

It begins to grow dark. The cattle and horses approach the houses. The wildest stay near the cabins in the edge of the forest; the tamer come to those at the foot of the hills. The goats come down from the hills or in from the plain, and would get into our very beds if we would let them. These precautions look as if the "lions," "tigers," and "bears" of which they speak (humble imitations at best) were dangerous; but, after examining all the stories I have heard, I can not certainly learn that they ever did any harm, except by frightening people. A cricket—chillador—in a corner of the room makes a distracting noise, incredible to one who has not heard it, and we are compelled to kill him. The wind, which blew from the sea all the morning, is now blowing seaward, bringing from the woods an ample delegation of musquitoes. Viviana comes from the kitchen with a furnace of fire on her head. She sets it in the corredor, and with chips, cobs of maize, and fragments of guadua, makes a smoke to drive away the musquitoes. The family sit on a bench, some heavy arm-chairs, and the pretil or railing of the corredor. Antonio has his guitar. Jacinto has his tiple in the back corredor, where the women are smoking. Two negritas are waltzing "on the sly" in the dining-room.

At length a lighted candle is placed on the dining-table. A negro comes to have a demand written; for such things the family good-naturedly find time, and paper, and pens, and ink, and law. Pepe Gómez brings in the writing-case and makes out the document. Pepe is reading aloud in the "Piquillo Aliaga" by Scribe. Toledo and others are listening, and at every surprising passage they exclaim "Caramba!"

Pilar carries the dishes to the inner closet, leaving behind two knives, and a definite number of cups, spoons, saucers, and plates, and two tumblers. She spreads the table-cloth, puts on the plates, a knife, a piece of "cheese," and the spoons. Some green plantains, fried, and then flattened between two stones, come in. Next enter three cups of chocolate on a plate. Each of these is set on a plate by itself. The rest are brought in in the same way. A plate or bowl of *dulce* is set on the table, and the saucers to eat it from. Last comes the water; and the tumblers are filled and refilled, some drinking from the tin cups, till all are satisfied. This ends the eating and drinking for the day. This arrangement is seldom varied from, except by omissions. Rarely is there the addition of a cup of strong, clear coffee, without milk, but with considerable sugar. This is taken at rising. Granadans do not take chocolate or coffee before rising, as travelers say some people do.

It is now nine. The men soon retire for the night to beds and benches, which pass into each other, as the naturalist says, by imperceptible gradations. Then is heard the voice of the women in praying the Rosary, a sound easily recognized after hearing it once. To this succeeds the furious crying of Cristina, who fell asleep on the floor somewhere. They have hunted her up, and are carrying her to the room No. 10. She squalls half an hour, and after that nothing more is heard except the hum of musquitoes, the fighting of dogs, the bleating of calves and maternal responses, and, worse than all, the diabolic noises of the goats.

Another day has passed without making any more change in the Valley of the Cauca than on the face of the ocean. And so have passed generations. If some Rip Van Winkle should wake from a sleep of two centuries, the only thing to surprise him would be the dawn of civil and religious liberty.

I can not better continue my picture of this family than by faithfully noting the actual events of a single Sabbath. On Saturday night the bells of the chapel rung a little—just enough to say that there would be mass in the morning. The good Cura leaves San Vicente occasionally for a day, and comes and spends the Sabbath with us; and well he might, for more than half his salary comes from this hacienda. I went to church in the morning, as I always do when I have the opportunity. Well, in the first place, we had one baptism and two fractions: that is, two of the babes had received just enough baptism to save them from hell had they died before this time, but not enough for decency.

The priest met the unbaptized at the door of mercy, or side door of the church. One assistant held a little plain wooden cross, and another a lighted candle. After the prayers he put salt in the babe's mouth, and went to the font, an excavated stone, on a pedestal, with a hole for the water to run off. Here awaited the other two babes. One was held on the *left* arm. "Put the head *there*," said the priest. The woman turned herself, so as to bring the head to the required spot; the feet of the babe were more out of their place than ever. An exclamation of impatience from the fasting Cura led an assistant to aid in placing the babe on the right arm. First he put spittle on the ears and nostrils of each; then he completed them one by one. He took from his portable baptism-box a silver vial, with a rod passed through the silver-capped cork, and some cotton. With the rod he made a cross on the breast of each, and another between the shoulders, and wiped the oil off again with the cotton. The dress of one tried the Cura's patience again. He exclaimed, amid his prayers, "Better bring your babe naked than with a dress tight at the neck." I held it away with two fingers as well as I could. Then the babe's head was held over the font, face downward, and holy water was poured from the little silver *teapot* on the crown of the head. Another cross was made on the crown of the head with the oily rod, the head covered for a moment with a white cloth, and the task was done. These prayers would occupy a Protestant clergyman about two hours, but our curate dispatched them very soon. If he skipped a word, or pronounced it wrong, he left it for next time.

He went back to the vestry, put on different robes, and, again accompanied by the cross and candle, met a marriage party at the door of mercy. These were more awkward than the mothers. First, the groomsman, who happened to be the husband of the bridesmaid, placed himself next the bride. Then the bridegroom tried to insinuate himself between the bride and bridesmaid, apparently intending to be married to one of them at least. When the parties were placed aright, the priest read them a long address, telling them, among other things, that it was their duty to endeavor to raise up heirs, not so much to their goods as to their religion, their faith, and their virtue. The bride, though never married before, need not excite his anxiety on that point. Not only were two of her children witnesses of the ceremony, but, besides, she was visibly in a state which is here designated by the word *embarazada*. I am aware that this detracts materially from the poetry of my picture, but I can not help it; the sole merit of my sketch is its fidelity. I must add, then, that the older of her two children appeared to be three fourths black, and the younger three fourths white. The mother was a mulata, the other three adults of pure African blood. All were barefoot; the females wore that plain dress which alone is permitted to rich or poor in church—the head covered with a shawl, the body with a dark-colored skirt (saya).

The address through, the priest directed them to join their right hands. This was accomplished after much delay. When the priest asked the bride if she was willing to have this man for her husband, she made no answer. He repeated the question; no answer. "Say yes or no," exclaimed the priest; she said "yes." Two rings were taken from the small silver tray used in the mass. The priest put one on the finger of the bridegroom, and the latter put the other on the little finger of the bride. It was large enough for her thumb, and she instantly removed it to another finger. Then the priest took eight or ten reals, half francs, and dimes, from the tray, put them in the hands of the bridegroom, and he in those of the bride. In the course of the subsequent prayers the fasting priest fairly lost his patience at their awkwardness, as might be seen by the angry tones and snappish accent he gave his Latin. Then he stopped short off, and administered a rebuke in plain Castilian.

These prayers over, their hands still joined, the priest passed the band—estola—of his robe round the man's wrist, and led the pair, followed by the other pair, to the altar. They knelt, and mass commenced. Two golden chains, united by a ribbon, were put on their necks. Two yards of white cloth, with a fringe, was spread over her head and his shoulders. Regularly, they ought to have partaken of the Eucharist. I afterward asked the priest why they did not; he informed me that the bride's situation did not admit of the delay and fasting that were necessary to prepare them for that sacrament.

Mass over, every one is at liberty to amuse himself as he pleases, for Sunday is a holiday, and it is a sin to work more than two hours, but no sin to play. At night I found that an extraordinary activity had prevailed in the kitchen; fresh pork and chicken appeared on the dinner-table, and a bottle of aguardiente. At the head sat the Cura, and a vacant space opposite me was at length filled by the four who had figured so conspicuously in the morning. I was not prepared for this. If I must eat with negroes, I will do it with a good grace, but I could well have spared the company of an "*embarazada*" bride. During the dinner we had the music of two octave flutes and a drum.

This was ominous of the evening; in short, bad as was the weather, we had a ball. When I went for my chocolate, I found the good Cura, with his gown tucked up, dancing the bambuco with unusual grace with one of the nymphs of the pastures. As I was making my retreat, young Carlos, about 16, was waltzing with an aged manumitted slave that had been his nurse, and that of all his brothers and sisters before him. Later in the night was a scene yet more curious, as I am told. The pretty little Mercedes, of 17, the white man's daughter, waltzed with the negro blacksmith, Miguel. He appears over 70, is very tall, very grim, and is the most pious man on the plantation. It must have been a sight. I tried to persuade her to it again at a day ball, but she would consent only on the condition that I should first waltz with her. She even dismounted for this purpose, after being ready to start for home; others seconded her proposition so eagerly that I could only get off by protesting that the Presbyterian Church did not permit dancing.

In the morning, when a crevice of my window-shutter let in unquestionable evidence of day, I arose to see the last of the ball. In the front piazza, where the goats usually sleep, was a woman established with aguardiente and cakes for sale. She had brought a demijohn half full, of which remained a bottleful. She had sold to the amount of $11 20, and would have sold more had I been willing the night before to lend money to those who had none of their own to spend.

I entered the sala, and there I saw a sight that Christy would give $500 or $1000 to see. The dance was the bundi, a Chocó dance. Two couples, very black, and past the summer of life, had the floor. The four were slowly revolving about the room in a large circle, while each couple alternately rushed toward the centre, and receded as the other advanced. This is the *theory*, but the *manner* defies me. The man commences his centripetal movement as if he had "*broken loose*," and you feel a fear that his partner will be demolished in a collision. And then the ad libitum steps of his retreat! But the music! One was drumming with his fingers, the other thumping a bench with a broomstick with all his might, and both, with others, were singing "Ai ke le le" obstreperously. So furious was the fun, that I thought every minute some one would have to give in or drop dead. Set after set danced the bundi, and the last to leave the floor was our cook, an aged negress, who, having been busy in the kitchen all day, wore a camisa that had seen eight days' service in a kitchen without a chimney, and, further, had two holes worn in it just where it should be whole.

Such orgies in the States would have presented a different result. The supply of rum would have been exhausted if any less than a barrel, for probably there was not an individual over six years old that did not drink. How many fights would there have been? How many in the morning would have been unable to walk? But here I saw only two (one a boy) who gave indications of having been drinking. I see that I am among a people of a different race, just as our Indians are a different race from ourselves in respect to alcohol.

I must not forget to add that the bride kept up all night, and in the morning I saw her sitting watching the dancers with the gold chains still about her neck. One of her children had his head in her lap, the other was sitting by her side smoking a cigar. Saturday night she was up all night at a ball. To-night is another ball, and probably to-morrow night another. This is not all. She has her fasts to go through, and to commune, before the marriage will be so complete as to permit them to sleep together. I wonder how she lives through it all!

I urged the priest to have his mass in the morning, immediately on the cessation of the dancing, before the dancers went home; but he told me that, the day not being a fiesta, the people were not under obligation to hear mass, and it would be better to have it at the usual hour; so most of them dispersed before mass.

A little before mass I saw the young gentlemen of the family on horseback. Each had before him, on his high-pommeled saddle, a nymph of the dance, who had come on foot the night before. His arm was round her waist, and, that both parties might be equally sure of her safety, her arm was also around his neck. She sat sidewise. It happened, by accident no doubt, that this good fortune fell to just the youngest and handsomest of the bewitching brunettes of the whole company.

In the mass he had the communion to administer to a man. In the act of administering it, he discovered a negress, or, rather, a negrita, who, instead of being on her knees as a Christian should be in the presence of the body of Christ, was sitting on the ground. He paused at once, and called out, "On your knees! on your knees! One would take you for a Protestant!" and on he went with his prayer or formula, leaving me, hopeless Protestant, on my feet close to him.

A few days afterward, the pretty Mercedes, who danced with the tall, grim old negro Miguel, received some letters from Quilichao, where she had been at boarding-school. She offered them to me to read. The first was from a schoolmate, and began, "Mi querida negra"—"My dear negress." I was astonished. She *was* "a white man's daughter," then; but whose? and what negress was her mother? She can not be darker than a quadroon. As I write, I am infested with the idea that she is a very near relative to Don Eladio. The other letter was from her teacher, and contained this expression: "I hope, my dear negress, that you are enjoying your visit at La Ribera." Such terms of endearment are not new to me, but I select this case as unusually authentic.

I have witnessed some queer bathing-scenes in the Tuluá. True, they are not so outrageous as at Honda; but here I am able to guarantee the entire respectability of the parties. One company was Don Eladio, his wife, her sister, and two of his brothers. Here I first saw ladies that I esteem swim with gentlemen dressed only in a silk pocket-handkerchief. They seemed to enjoy these promiscuous swims very much, but still I fancied I could see it checkered with a half-acknowledged concession of some impropriety in them.

I became the owner of a horse while in this family, and it happened to be the first animal I ever owned. The purchase was not a matter of my choice, and the possession of him was no advantage to me, but a continual vexation, which the few dollars advance at which I sold him did not compensate at all. I gained, however, a valuable experience in the care of him. He was broken in before coming into my hands, but quite young. I named him Aliaga. I took possession of him on my birthday, which he duly celebrated by knocking me down with his "hands" for my impertinence in interfering with two flourishing colonies of ticks—garrapatas—in his ears. He sprained both my wrists; not so much, however, but that at that time I was able to convince him of the impropriety of his proceedings, to finish greasing his ears, and ride him into the river to wash him. From that day I was almost helpless, and it was a month before my wrists became entirely well.

Aliaga was a terrible fellow to lazo. He was too fleet for

that. He hated a blow from a heavy guasca as he would from a whip, and not without reason, I fancy. I never knew him to be thus caught in the open plain but once, and then after a chase nearly as fatiguing as a day's journey. I own that I was somewhat surprised—others were amazed—when I found I could go up to him in a herd to which he had escaped by breaking his bounds, and put a halter on him. None of them had ever witnessed such a feat. We had some good times together. On the whole, it would have been better for me to have secured a good attendant on my arrival at Bogotá, and a horse of my own as soon as I arrived in this valley, where they are cheap. This plan would have saved more than it would cost.

Toledo, the horse-breaker, must have led an eventful life. He is a Socorrano—one of the Yankees of South America. A quarrel, he says, with a man superior to him in influence caused him unjustly to be thrown into the Presidio. I am myself inclined to think that many worse men never get in. He came here, then, low in character, and deformed with a large goître, which is here considered to be as great a disgrace as any other kind of personal ugliness, though I am told that in some secluded spots in the country, north of Bogotá, it is thought rather respectable to have a good coto, or goître. Toledo's has entirely disappeared by the use of the iodiferous salt of Burila.

Toledo goes among the families about here some. He proposed to take me with him to a place to test the merits of a sort of combination of plantain and meat, yet unknown to me. The time set run by without his saying any thing farther on the subject. I reminded him of it, and he set another time, and yet a third, with the same result. We never went. I ventured to advise him one day to marry, and named to him a rather pretty Caucana that I thought would be equally benefited by the alliance. With some hesitation, he acknowledged that he was just then thinking of marrying another. He did not think his choice superior; but, in fact, there were other circumstances to be taken into account. To be plain, her father was very angry with him, and threatened to kill him if he did not marry her. Indeed, the old man was raving, so that the daughter could not live at home. On learning the facts, I told him that I thought her father had reason to be angry, and I was glad to see him care so much about the poor girl's reputation. I advised him to marry her, but, when I came to see her, my heart almost failed me. She was as ugly as a monkey.

One day Escolastica came to me to learn what day it was. I told her it was Tuesday. That was not what she wanted, but to know what the saint of the day was. I told her that we had no saints but God in the States, and wanted to know why she needed to know. She said that a child had been born near by, and was not likely to live, so Antonio was going to baptize it when they ascertained the saint for whom it was to be named. I wished to see it done, but they had "concluded not to have it done *then*." It was done later, without my knowledge.

I saw Antonio one day cruelly beating a poor fighting-cock that he had kept tied by one leg for some weeks. He had given the fattened bird an opportunity of fighting, and it refused. He boxed its head till it hung down, and all around said it was dead. He carried it off, and when he returned he said it had recovered. I was told that this was not true, and it was confirmed at our dinner by the remains of the cock.

I remarked to Antonio one day a difference between English and French fictions. In the latter, all the best characters lie sometimes, while those in ours never do.

"Therein," said he, "their fictions are more true to nature, for we all meet with occasions in which we have to lie."

Don Eladio himself once was speaking to me of the oppression that he, a Conservador, suffered from the Liberal officers of the district. He stated the amount of his taxes, and I was convinced that it was unjust. I mentioned this to an eminent Liberal, who told me I did wrong in believing men's assertions so implicitly. He urged me to see the tax-list with my own eyes. I ascertained afterward that Señor Várgas had overstated the sum by some 60 per cent.

While in this family, and when the ladies were all at Cartago, I had an attack of fever, which served to remind me of the blessing that my otherwise uniform good health has been to me.

I was sleeping in the corredor on Tuesday night as usual, sufficiently protected from the weather and the musquitoes by my musquito-bar, when I was taken with a fever. In the morning I did not leave my hammock till I decided to take an emetic. Now if a hammock is convenient in such a case I have yet something to learn. After long delay, a traveling cot was put together in the room No. 9, and I sat up, using a bedstead as a table. I opened a box of medicines, a box of those rascally apothecaries' weights, and Cox's "Companion to the Medicine-chest." While yet I had sense enough to do it, I had decided on a mixture of tartar emetic and ipecacuanha. Now I gazed at the book, then at the weights, then at the table of weights. I selected weights, balanced them with medicine, forced myself to review and re-review weights, weight-table, prescription, and labels, so that it took me more than half an hour to be sure that I should not commit a fatal error. Pilar brought me a bowl of warm water, set a tray by my bedside, and left me to my fate.

At night my hammock was again hung for me, and I spent the night in the corredor. On Thursday morning Pepe contrived to hang my hammock in the room No. 9. At first this was thought impossible, on account of the re-entering angle. Here I lay, mostly dozing and insensible. Once I came to myself enough to see that it was dark. I recollect once I was in the sala, driven probably by thirst. I slept or was delirious till 3 in the morning, when I came to consciousness. There was a ball in the sala.

For three long hours I lay there, hoping that some one might look in upon me, but in vain. At 6 my thirst became intolerable, and I went again to the sala. The ball was at its height. The waltzing knew no intermission. The floor was all the time full, and, whenever a couple got tired, another was ready to take their place. The musicians were relieved in the same way. Here I waited till I was dizzy. It was a long time before I could obtain any thing. I hoped to get some warm drink, but was told that it would be impossible when all the servants were busy dancing. I had to content myself with a drink of cold water.

Dr. Quintero was sent for. He came on Friday afternoon, but I was already some better. I had contrived to rouse myself long enough to prescribe, weigh out, and take a dose of calomel and rhubarb, but with little or no advantage. As I now surrendered my case into the doctor's hands, he desired to know the doses I had taken, but I could not tell him. I neither knew the size of his granos nor he the size of our grains. I told him that about 7500 of our grains would make one of their ordinary libras, or pounds, but this did not enable him to reduce their weights of medicine to ours. I believe that 100 of their grains are about equal to 77 of ours. Dr. Quintero gave me at first two doses of sal soda and lime-juice, and, for the next day, a mixture (I suppose) of decoction of cinchona and Epsom salts. He steadily refused any compensation for his long ride and his services.

On Monday I was better, though since 3 o'clock Friday morning I had not slept at all. My chief occupation on Sunday had been to try to go to sleep, and I kept quietly at it all the night, and, though unsuccessful, was quite comfortable. Now I began to think of eating again; but what should I eat? Neither butter, flour, meal, potatoes, rice, nor any substitute for any of these was to be had. For meat, I sent a man out to shoot me a monkey. He shot one, but he clung to the tree, and would not fall. The next day I succeeded in buying a fowl, by paying what I should consider a fair price for an acre of land—40 cents. At one cabin they found a spoonful of rice, and at another about as much meal, so that I made a dinner. When my fowl was finished, I declared myself well, and took hold of tasajo again.

In cookery, there is no effort made to develop the resources of the land. Tomatoes grow here without culture after once seeding the ground, but they never are cooked. Indeed, I suspect that, as they run wild, they become poisonous. I ate some from a yard, where the house had been burned and the grounds abandoned, and was attacked with a severe burning in my throat in consequence.

I suffered much here from the want of ripe plantains and from the character of the beef. I think my weight varied progressively with the age of the beef. It was too bad, but I always rejoiced when I saw two horsemen come up to the house with their lazos upon a cow between them. The fatal fork—horca—was out before my window. One would throw his guasca over it, and at every movement of the poor cow, which was generally very angry, he would lessen the distance between her and the horca; the distance, like that between us and the grave, is never to be increased. When the victim's head is at length within twenty inches of the fatal post, the other horseman dismounts and throws her. The lazos are released from her horns, and a stout hide rope—rejo—binds her head thoroughly to the post, and she is suffered to rise.

This is in the afternoon. She stands there all night, and all the dogs in the place know that she dies ere sunrise. They assemble, and Felix comes, and one or two assistants. The jugular vein is opened while she is yet standing by a sudden dextrous thrust. The dogs crowd under, and lap the warm blood as it flows and smears them over. The poor brute falls, is unbound, and dragged away from the stake. Twenty dogs sit on their haunches, in a circle of fifteen feet radius, with their faces all toward the centre where the butchers work. The skin is at length spread on the ground, with the rest of the animal on it. With busy knives they now cut off some masses for the consumption of to-day and to-morrow, and cut the rest up into strings. The mass rapidly diminishes, till on the skin there remains nothing but viscera and bones. These, too, are then borne off to the kitchens of the family and the peasantry, and the skin is pegged down to the ground and left. The gallinazos that have been perching round now fly down upon it, walk all over it, and, if any particles of meat have been left adhering which their bills can remove, they eat them.

The strings of beef are carried into the corredor XIX., and laid on a piece of dry hide kept for that purpose. A detachment of dogs follow the first load that is brought in, through the sala, of course. They watch and steal if they can, while it is rolled in salt, and hung on poles that are kept always ready, between corredores XIX. and XX. The gallinazos seldom venture here to steal it. The disgust with which unpracticed eyes regard these festoons of tasajo finally wears away.

For a day or two after the "day of slaughter" (spoken of in the Bible as a day of feasting, James, v., 5) I ate scarce any thing but meat. Then, as the fare deteriorated, I lapsed almost into sheer vegetarianism. Once or twice I resorted to the oily eggs of turtles, which needed no butter to make them into an omelet. These the cook seasoned by guess, for not a servant would taste them. The prejudice against turtle-eggs is unknown on the Magdalena, where the bogas feast on them in their season, and passengers do not disdain them when they can get them. The Caucan turtle does not differ perceptibly from the snapping-turtle of New England—Testudo serpentaria. The eggs are spheres of an inch in diameter, without a shell. I saw a single terrapin, apparently an Emys, at La Paila; but it was a novelty to all who saw it, so rare are they.

When able to be out again I went to see them clear up land to plant. The chief implements are the machete and a tool shaped like a spade, with a straight stick for a handle. It is lighter than a spade, and with a smaller blade than a shovel. They call it a pala; I would translate it *push-hoe*. Axes are not much used here. They are long and narrow, and without what we call the head or poll. Of course they are very inefficient, but it would be quite difficult to introduce our more costly and heavier axe.

They aim at planting just at the commencement of a rainy spell. In fact, they plant maize about twice a year. It takes about four months to ripen. I saw likewise here a plantain-field lately set out, the only new one I have seen. Sprouts broken from the base of an old stem are here set at proper distances, say a rod or more, apart. Cane is set in the same way, but much closer together. A little attention should be given to the corn and plantains at first, that it run not up to bushes again, but plowing is unknown. There is a yoke of cattle belonging to the family. They haul guadua and timber, if any be wanted. There is a cart and a water-cart, but I know not that either has ever been used.

I can give no market-price for maize, rice, or any like substance. They are sold by the palito or box-full. The size of the palito differs one half. I should guess maize to be about from 10 to 60 cents per bushel. I put dried cow beef at a dime per pound—called equal to 3 pounds fresh, but really a little less, unless very thoroughly dried. Fresh meat is sold at 90 cents per arroba, legally equal to 27.5592125 pounds avoirdupois, or $3 27 per cwt., free of bone. Hogs, unfattened, may be put at $3 20 each; young bulls at $8; unbroken colts, $13; broken, $20.

But the most villainous animals ever called domestic are goats. The goat is able to take care of himself. He goes up to the naked tops of the knolls every morning, comes down at night, bleats around the house, and makes himself hateful in every possible way. Goats climb into the oven, and jump up on the grinding-stone and lick off the chocolate. At night, no sooner are the doors all shut than they invade the corredor, jump up to roost on the pretil or on the table, and, when I hung my hammock there, would entangle themselves in my musquito-net, and were an unutterable abomination to me. I often thought that the distinction between sheep and goats in the Bible was well put. Sheep are rarer because they need care, but they seem to be healthy here.

They say that the tobacco of this region is as good as that of Havana. I do not rely upon that opinion. I do not believe that better coffee can be raised than in some parts of this valley. The cacao-tree is said to be indigenous to the Cauca. Indigo might be raised here in any quantity, and cochineal. Both these articles will pay transportation, but they require too much labor and care to suit the disposition of the Caucanos.

What more could Nature do for this people, or what has she withholden from them? What production of any zone would be unattainable to patient industry, if they knew of such a virtue? But their valley seems to be enriched with the greatest fertility and the finest climate in the world only to show the miraculous power of idleness and unthrift to keep a land poor. Here the family have sometimes omitted their dinner just because there was nothing to eat in the house. Maize, cacao, and rice, when out of season, can hardly be had for love or money; so this valley, a very Eden by nature, is filled with hunger and poverty from Popayan to Antioquia.

CHAPTER XXXI.

THE PASTURES IN THE FOREST.

Sudden Start.—Wardrobe for the Woods.—Plan and Company.—Barleycorn Boldness.—Night in Woods and Rain.—Departed Spirits.—El Chorro.—Thermometer broken.—A Country all aslant.—Las Playas.—Rancho of Century-plant.—Substitute for Cords.—Jicaramata.—Guavito.—Threat of Famine.—Sabbath-day's Journey.—Routed by Hunger.—Snakes.—Treasure-hunting.

I HAD been to Chaqueral to see Isabel Gómez as much as any thing. I was returning to La Paila, where I was then stopping, when at the river of Las Cañas I met my host, Señor Modesto Flojo, accompanied by Dr. Quintero. I was surprised to learn that they were in pursuit of me. A project had been hatched up to hunt for cinchona in the forests, high up the River Tuluá. It was now Friday afternoon, and it was proposed to reach Portazuela that night, and La Ribera next day, in time to make all necessary arrangements so as to take to the woods early on Sunday morning. To this I would not assent, but agreed to the plan, with two modifications. We were to leave La Ribera on Monday, and not to travel the succeeding Sabbath; and paper must be taken for me to collect plants in.

All this was assented to. I had an hour at La Paila to arrange matters for a week's sojourn in the forest. I took a fatigue-dress, hunting-shirt, hammock, flannel night-dress, encauchado, bayeton, a little Greek Testament, a needle-book, pocket-compass, thermometer, machete, pocket-knife, comb, and a ream or two of printing-paper. All this, except the paper, I accommodated about my saddle. The object of the expedition was a secret. Some of the party had mules at pasture that they wished to see; the others went with them to have a hunt.

After leaving La Paila, we stopped in Guavito at the house of Bernabé, the negro judge, who was skinning a goat; then, again, at Murillo, and at 7 P.M. were seated at a comfortable dinner at Dr. Quintero's table at Portazuela. There was other company there, and the house was full. My hammock was ingeniously hung by passing the ropes over the tops of two opposite doors from the sala into inner rooms, and tying to them two cobs of maize, so that they could not draw through. My weight rendered the opening of the doors impossible till I rose.

In the morning, the thongs of raw hide to tie my hammock over the pockets of my cojinetes had disappeared. Dr. Quintero charged the theft upon the dogs of a guest. "My dogs do not eat rejo," said their owner. Dr. Quintero, who happened to be cutting raw hide at the instant, threw a strip to one of the accused, which pleaded guilty by swallowing it instantly; not a word was said.

After breakfast we all went to La Ribera. Here they told me that they had again concluded to start on Sunday morning. "Very well," I said; "leave me a guide, and I will come on after you on Monday." Finding me firm, they concluded to have a hunt on Sunday, and start as agreed; so I rested, according to the commandment, and the party, some of whom had slept in Tuluá, met and killed a deer. Damian, the young lawyer, whose energy makes amends for Don Modesto's slackness, had joined them, and had pledged himself to eat the hides and hoofs of all the deer they killed that day. They were so pleased with their success that they excused him from the task. The mode of hunting is to post themselves in ambush near where deer are likely to pass when pursued, and wait while the thicket is beaten with dogs and peons.

At night our company was complete, and at daylight in the morning we were on our way. There were in all 11 of us, viz., Don Modesto Flojo, commander-in-chief; Damian Caicedo, his wife's nephew; Miguel and Manuel Vicente, two brothers-in-law; Pepe and Chepe Sanmartin, his sons-in-law—two smart lads, though but 15 and 13; Dr. Quintero; a Señor Tascon; Miguel (a guide); and Lorenzo, Don Modesto's concertado, and my famous guide on another occasion.

We had barely started, when Don Modesto and Tascon turned back, and we advanced more slowly to give them a chance of rejoining. We wound our way along the side of an enormous hill, called the Picazo, at a very high elevation, but far below the summit. A few miles farther brought us to the end of the grass—llano—at Las Minas. Here we stopped and made a delicious breakfast on yesterday's venison. We had not dismounted ere Don Modesto and Tascon came in, bringing with them the object of their solicitude, La Pechona. She, as well as they, was in spirits, or, rather, a pint and a half of spirits were in her. Hidden in the cojinetes of Tascon and Manuel Vicente were two of her frail sisters, whose company greatly animated the day's ride.

From Las Minas our route for several miles was upward, till we came to oak trees. We had a road from which I did not see any other diverge that did not enter it again. With every obstacle the spirits of Señor Flojo seemed to rise. Now and then his shout would ring through the woods, "Don't you flinch, my dears, for here go I!" I had been unwilling to expose my Aliaga to the hardships of the journey, and had left him in charge of Dr. Quintero's sisters, and was mounted on a fine young mare of Don Modesto's. He seemed very unwilling that I should favor her, but I persisted in dismounting whenever a thick tree or such obstacle lay in the road *up hill.* Once or twice, at an ugly spot, he would call out, "Whoever dismounts here shall not pass again for a man till he has been searched." I dismounted all the same.

High up among the oaks we stopped at a contadero to rest. The day was delightful. Up we went again, and soon came to trouble. Even this road had its callejones. The sumpter mule was walking above a deep one that was too narrow for her load to pass in it, and she fell in. They loosened her load, and dragged her off it by the tail down to a spot where they could set her on her feet. Then they got her and the load out of the callejon, changed her for Manuel Vicente's mule, and we went on.

We straggled very much. We halted at another contadero, where we attained the greatest altitude for the day, and I went back on foot to see if the boys and Tascon were not lost. Then came an unintermitted descent for an hour or more. A roaring stream was heard at the bottom. It was Rio San Marcos, a branch of the Tuluá, which we crossed, and at 4 we came to the Tuluá at Platanal. Here is the first we have seen of the Tuluá, which, even up here, would be a pretty good stream to ford. Apparently it rattles over a stony bed almost till it reaches the very Cauca, without becoming quiet as do the streams farther north.

A council was held, and it was decided to go no farther. We had dinner to get, and dispositions for night to make. Platanal is an open spot a few rods square, on the right bank of the Tuluá. I had some plants to put in paper, and among them a bush Passiflora. I lost the most beautiful Inga to-day I ever saw growing wild. Here I discovered that they had failed to bring, as they promised, some ground maize. For vegetables they had green plantains, and I made a miserable dinner. Two men went back and built a fence across the road to keep the mules from returning. This is generally done of nights, even when traveling in the highway, where there are no pastures or pens.

The weather was threatening. Some united together and made a tent of their bayetones, sleeping under it almost without bed or clothing. Stems of caña brava, a grass as large and straight as fishing-poles, served very well for a frame-work. Don Modesto and others slept wrapped in their bayetones under the open sky. All wore their day-clothes. I hung my hammock between two trees, and passed another rope between them over my hammock, and on this hung my encauchado, so that the edges of it were lower than my hammock. Beneath me I put my saddle, paper, and day-clothes. I had sewed up the head-hole in my bayeton, and used it for a blanket. I went to sleep looking up into the gloomy sky, but was soon waked up by Dr. Quintero, who told me I must not expose my head to irradiation; so I drew it in under my roof.

I woke at sunrise, and it was raining. As yet I was dry, but how should I dress? A knotty question. The tent offered a solution. I reached under my hammock, and got my hat and my clothes. I then sprang out, and ran "between the drops" to the tent, and dressed there. Meanwhile a cup of chocolate was brought me—a small silver cup, that would hold half a gill. I had stipulated for a silver-rimmed cocoanut-shell for my allowance, but this morning they could not make enough in the rain. Tascon, Manuel Vicente, and Miguel the peon came in with the horses, and brought with them a venomous snake that they had killed.

Died in the night La Pechona and both her sisters; cause, rapid consumption, aggravated by the rain in the night. They yielded up the last drop of their spirit about daybreak. Don

Modesto is a sincere mourner, and Tascon disconsolate. While we were preparing to mount, the bereaved attended to the obsequies of all that remained of the dear departed. They wrote not even *resurgam* on their monument, lest their resurrection might occur before our return here.

The bereavement had a wonderful effect on Don Modesto. The daring, jubilant leader of yesterday was no more. No more we heard the cry, "Don't flinch, my dears, for here go I;" now it would mean, "Wherever I go a child can ride." We soon had an ugly brook to cross. Dr. Quintero had to go back to help him down the bank. We were still on the right bank of the Tuluá; some time after passing this branch of it we came out to clear land again. We gathered on a jutting knoll, and looked down on our camp of last night. The rain had ceased, and the sun was coming out. The Tuluá here seemed to bend its course more to the northward; it came down from the east between steep grass-covered hills. Above us were the heights of Tiemble-cul.

I would not think of riding my little mare up there. I tried to drive her, but, as I was in advance of the party, she would not go. I led her a while, but it was so slippery that I feared falling under her feet. I finally exchanged her for a gun, and after an amazing climb I was at the top of Tiemble-cul. You could see from here the settlements in a place between Tuluá and Buga. It seemed an hour before the party came in sight. I managed to finish drying my clothes in the sun first, but had hard work to keep warm the while.

Level and descending ground now brought us through a small piece of woods to El Chorro. Here was a house, kept at present by a boy named Ursulo. Our luxuries here were a roof, milk, and arracachas. I cooked some rice, made sirup from panela, and ate. I dried my hammock, and dried all my paper over a fire, and obtained many new plants. We staid all day, and they tried to kill a deer. Down nearer the river the hill-sides were covered with paths of the tapir, here called danta. We had no hopes of shooting one of them, as they remain hid all day, and the river was too far below us to permit our thinking of descending. Chorro means a rill or torrent. A cold stream rolled down the hill-side a few rods beyond the house, which yielded us the water we needed. The house is on comparatively a level spot; that is, a cask might stand safely near it without any danger of its rolling down to the Tuluá. Back of it the ground rose up to an unknown height. Part of the slope was covered with wax-palm (Ceroxylon) and a thicket of other plants.

Before dark we were informed that somebody was coming. It was like picking up a boat at sea. We all came out of the house. It was Don Antonio Besero, with two peons. He owns mules farther up at Las Playas, and had come to-day from Las Minas, where he camped last night. The peons built a fire out doors. Within, we had a candle-end and a pack of cards.

Before breakfast, on Wednesday, I went up to the palms. On my return I found my thermometer broken, an irreparable loss, as it needed comparing with a standard thermometer. No one knew how it happened. Don Modesto took the death of La Pechona no harder than I the loss of my thermometer. I ate no breakfast. But we must march. We went up the river, but also receded from it, going obliquely up an immense additional ascent. We met some bulls that we wished farther off, or on ground better for sport.

At length our path lay along an immense inclined plane that seemed terminated by the sky above and the river below. So steep was the hill, and so narrow the path, that they would not suffer me to ride for a long way; so we all walked, leading our horses. In this position we halted with a snake in front of us, which was shot as a matter of precaution. I could neither carry him on nor examine him for fangs, so we all voted him venomous, and left him. At length we had to descend two thirds of the way to the river. I think it took us an hour of steep zigzag; then we came to a brook, and we all halted. Granadinos rarely drink without first taking dulce. A piece of panela was produced, and cut with a machete into inch cubes, or larger pieces. A totuma was taken from a peon's hat, rinsed, and passed round with water from the chilly rill.

Again we were on the still worse slope of almost a precipice, but not yet dangerous, so I kept my saddle. In one place I found it necessary to pause to adjust my hat in so critical a place that a peon told me afterward that he "prayed the holy

Virgin that I might not fall." Here we saw several giant vultures sailing through the air. I ask the name, and they tell me it is the buitre. I ask if it is not the condor, and they know no such bird. I can hardly doubt but it is Vultur Gryphus, the largest bird that flies. His wings are remarkable; they have several feathers projecting beyond the rest like extended fingers. The scenery that passes under his eye is, like himself, gloomy, solitary, and gigantic. Cows, horses, and mules have nothing to fear from him while well and able to offer resistance, but calves and colts, when very young, are blinded and destroyed.

We continued descending till the rain threatened to pour in upon us. We held a council in a rocky ravine, and voted to camp, but Don Antonio finally persuaded us to advance to Las Playas, where we crossed the Tuluá, here about two feet deep. Here we built, *on Don Antonio's land*, a rancho of the leaves of Fourcroya (pita, cabuya), the best thing we could find, although the leaves are very heavy, being 3 or 4 feet long, 5 inches wide, and nearly an inch thick. Each leaf has a notch cut in it, to hang it across a horizontal pole, or bejuco, or cord of fique, passing along the slender rafters. The plant grows here in abundant quantities, so that this region may yet export from it a cordage like Manilla. Fique is another name for its fibre.

While the camp was building another venomous snake was killed, of which I saved the head. I hung my hammock under the rancho, leaving room enough for the rest of them beneath me. We remained all Thursday at Las Playas. They hunted, but killed nothing but a pava—Penelope—not so large as a common fowl, and two small birds. Here I found an Agave, I think, much more like the century-plant of Mexico than the Fourcroya is. From my seeing it in but one place among the settlements, I infer that it is indigenous; still they call it Cabuya de Mejico. Don Antonio has a great horror of heresy, so that our debates on religious points served to make the time pass where, for want of house and candle-ends, the other game (cards) could not be played so well.

I asked him whether the Virgin could be in two places at once. He thought it possible. In a thousand places? He thought not. If a thousand persons were talking to her at once, could she hear them all, and know every thing that every one did? He thought not; but why all these questions? "For this reason," I replied: "God is omniscient and omnipresent; therefore, if all the world were praying to Him at once, he would be with them all, and know every thing that they said, thought, and felt; but if too many prayed to the Virgin at once, I feared that some of them would lose their trouble; therefore I thought it most prudent to pray to God in the first instance." Before Besero had finished his answer, I fear I was so far asleep as to assent to it.

On Friday morning the others were driven to make inroads on the rice, which had thus far been reserved to me. They tried the experiment of frying dry rice in lard, of which they had brought a bladderful, just as Scotch snuff is elsewhere put up. Dry rice fries harder and harder, if any thing. When they abandoned it, I added water, tore the two small birds in bits, and made a stew for the starving dogs. Hunters do not think raw meat agrees with dogs until they become accustomed to it.

After breakfast we recrossed to the north bank of the Tuluá, and pursued our way up to Jicaramata. We camped early, but in a place where Fourcroya is too scarce to build a good rancho. I had to clear a spot to hang my hammock between two trees. Each day the process of drying paper by a fire built for the purpose is becoming a more severe task, but upon this depends all my hope of bringing out my plants. Here a deer was shot. It was probably Cervus Peronei, similar to C. Virginiana, but considerably smaller. We made it last us two meals, and gave the dogs nothing but the viscera, the bones, and, lastly, the skin. We had salt, and I cooked my own dinner on a spit, and found it delicious. I salted another piece, and plastered it against a tree, out of dogs' reach: this was my breakfast. I am so far driven by necessity that I now claim my share of the cheese they take with the chocolate. I think, in a day or two, I could eat green plantains, or even sancocho.

On Saturday, Dr. Quintero, Dr. Damian Caicedo, Miguel and Manuel Vicente, and a peon, went with me to Guavito, the innermost pasture. The continual slopes toward the river, which hitherto have rarely allowed an acre of level ground in a square mile, seem to have so far intermitted, that from Jicaramata up the land is as level as in ordinary rough New England towns. Here we passed a spot that might make a fine farm after draining off one or two pools—lagunetas. But, at the ordinary rate of South American progress, it must yet be a thousand years before a wheel-road will be made here.

A thick wood intervened between here and our *Ultima Thule*, Guavito. We had great difficulty in finding the almost obsolete path to this pasture, which, distant as it is from human habitation, is probably only two thirds up to the dividing ridge between the Cauca and the Magdalena. Guavito seems to be left to grow over without burning off. These pastures are valuable, because mules brought up here have surer feet and harder hoofs. This of Guavito is of less value, as beasts of prey infest it more. Still farther up we can see the naked summits of hills far above us, apparently destitute of rock as is the ground where we are. Those, however, are páramo, and not, like these, kept open by fire. Wild cows are said to live there unowned.

Here we held a council. Miguel and Manuel Vicente built a rancho in the woods; Quintero, Damian, and I hunted for cinchona; and the peon went back for the rest of the party, who had staid behind to hunt. After some hours in the woods between Guavito and Jicaramata, we went back to meet the others. We met part of them half way, bringing part of the things. Don Modesto was sick, and would go no farther. Tascon and Lorenzo, the peon, were to stay with him. We all agreed to turn back, and came hungry to a camp where there was little to eat.

A new council was held, and the state of our larder was such that I advised without scruple a retreat on Sunday morning to El Chorro. I stipulated, however, that a peon should bring on my horse, etc., and allow me to spend the day on foot and alone. This night the rancho, which had been enlarged, admitted my hammock, and my encauchado was made part of the roof of it.

Sunday I spent alone, but not in a state of physical rest. I enjoyed the day better than many others. Only once the party behind me lost their way, and I had to direct them, from an opposite hill, by shouts and signs, till they at length reached a path. I was so lightly clad that I feared, also, some danger of being emparamado, or benumbed; but I tripped rapidly over the coldest part of the way. I arrived before 5 at El Chorro, and found Besero and his peones there. The others came in soon after, having abandoned one saddle-beast, which was brought home some weeks after, as I have been told.

On Monday morning we ate every thing except a little chocolate and perhaps some dried beef. The fried arracachas seemed exquisite to a famishing man. They tasted like potatoes sliced raw and fried. I never have tasted them so cooked except when starving, but I judge they might be good even to a pampered palate. I was off by 8. We had intended to start at sunrise, but, after making the best arrangements possible, every thing fell through, and the last of the party did not leave till 9. The roads were horrible, for it had rained. At Tiemble-cul I dismounted, and walked to Platanal. I rode to Rio San Marcos, and thence walked to within a league of Las Minas. In the ascent from San Marcos, Pepe's horse gave out, was left, and probably eaten up that night. The young rider proved a smart walker, and held out bravely. He rode my horse some, now one of the freshest of the lot.

All day we never united: we were routed. In the end, the dismounted Pepe, with Dr. Quintero and Tascon, came out ahead. Next came Don Modesto, Chepe, and myself. We passed the Picazo at dark, and before 8 we were at La Ribera. The remainder came in an hour after us. Those who accompanied the baggage-mule had the worst of it. Her load was but empty dishes, an empty saddle or two, and things that riders found their horses too weak to carry, but they say she fell about twenty times. Four silver cups, that ought to have staid at home, came in ruined. Amid all this, however, La Pechona was not forgotten; the three bottles came in unscathed. Such was the end of the expedition to Jicaramata.

I made another excursion, hoping to reach the oaks east of Las Minas by passing El Yesal, the gypsum place. In this I failed, and the fruit of the expedition was a fine equis or x-snake, so called because he seems marked over with that letter. He was a little less than three feet long, has formidable fangs, and a formidable reputation. As I could find no better place for so dangerous a trophy, I was obliged to tie the head to my hat-band. A negro spied it on my way home, and wished to buy it to make medicine of. He offered me $3 20 for it. [The New York Lyceum has it.]

I must not forget to add an incident that occurred at La Paila with the head from Las Playas. I was at work barefoot in my room; the wind blew the head off the table, and I trod on it. I raised my foot, and found the head hanging to it by one of the fangs, and the other broken off, whether in my foot I know not. Fortunately, my first terror at being bitten by a venomous snake had long been past, and though ever after I feared the possibility of a bite more than before, the terror consequent on a bite, I hope, will never be so great again. I never even mentioned this accident to the family.

Speaking of snakes, the account they give of one here is really a little the most horrible story, I think, ever invented. It ties its tail firmly round a bush, and you are not apt to see it till you are within its reach. So long as you stand there you are unharmed, but the moment you try to fly, quick as lightning the miscreant whips his venomous, hooked, and horribly strong fangs into you. Of course I do not believe a word of it.

I made one other excursion in the vicinity of Tuluá. This was in quest of a silver mine, of which there is an old tradition, back of the Tablazo, east of the town of Tuluá. To reach this from La Ribera I passed through the town of Tuluá. It stands south of the River Tuluá, and so you cross that rather violent river on a high, long, narrow bridge with no railings. It consists of hewed beams laid side by side from shore to shore, sometimes with earth laid on them. When one of them breaks the others are crowded together, so that the width of this bridge is variable. At its widest some will never ride across it, though narrow bridges are generally safe in the daytime, if your horse be not blind of one eye.

Of the town of Tuluá I know little. I have been six times through it, but never dismounted in it. It is a paved town, the cabecera of a canton, and the distrito has a population of 4352. The Tablazo is an elevated grassy plain, not so high as the Picazo opposite to it, but of many hundred acres. The deep dell back of it may contain silver, but to me the boulders look much like those any where else. I had a pleasant day, however, but paid for it in a terrible time for getting home in the dark and rain. There is here, as elsewhere, a great deal of credulity in relation to mines and treasures; and, in this respect, it is a misfortune for a country really to contain, as this does, much hidden treasure, and also, as there are here, rich mines of gold and silver unexplored. I do not count that of Tablazo among them.

CHAPTER XXXII.

BUGA AND PALMIRA.

Rice-fields.—Mud-holes.—San Pedro.—Buga.—Another Horse Story.—Zonza, the Beautiful.—Rio Guaves.—Cerrito.—Church.—Care of Toes in School.—Herran Administration.—Constitution of 1843.—Mosquera Administration.—Water-mill for Cane.—Poor rich Family.—Irish Gentleman and Granadan Wife.—How to spoil a Dinner.—Palmira.—Full Jail.—Arithmetic.—A Fast.—LL.D.'s turned Traders.—Cockroach Story.—Mud, Palms, and Indigenous Cacao.—Ferry.

UP the river we go again. It was nearly dark when we left Tuluá for San Pedro. I have since passed that road again in the night, and all that these two transits would enable me to say is, that the crossings of muddy streams make it terrible in the dark. They are, some of them, if not indeed most of them, artificial water-courses—acequias—made for irrigation, and to convey water to houses. The proprietors of acequias are, of course, bound by law to bridge them, but they do it so rarely that I do not now recollect more than one or two that have a bridge which can be passed. If we rode rhinoceroses or hippopotami it would be different; but to be bespattered by your neighbors, to bespatter them, to bespatter yourself, and, worst of all, to fear being absolutely ingulfed by the criminal negligence of rich landholders, is trying to patience.

Passing by daylight over this road made a different impression. There were other things besides the mud-fords to notice, for the country is really beautiful; and, say your worst of the mud, I have never lost a horse in it, which circumstance convinces me that I have dreaded it too much. Here I saw an arrozal or rice-field, the only one I ever saw, so rare is the culture of rice in South America. This piece was small, but the structure of it surprised me not a little. It was an absolute plane, inclining slightly to the west. On the upper side was an acequia, that sent over the field a sheet of water about one eighth of an inch thick, that formed no channels and covered all the ground. A ditch was made at the lower end to receive the water again and carry it off.

Opposite the little town of San Pedro is a hacienda, to which my mind runs back with delight. I am sorry I have not had better opportunities to become acquainted with the peculiarly amiable family that occupy it. Here, as at La Ribera, the ladies sat at the table with us. Our dining-room was the back corredor; my bedroom was the other, with my hammock extended from a window-grating to a pillar of the roof. A curious screen separated the dining-room from one of the nicest gardens in all the country. I did not at once discover that it was a thick matting of a Passiflora with a very small flower. There are several such species here. This formed a dense curtain, capable of shutting out the sun and admitting the air—a perennial veil of leaf and flower.

Directly under the eaves of the house ran a cheerful rill in a channel of burned bricks. Water for the table was dipped up at the upper end. The plates, as taken from the table, were set in it farther down. Most operations which are done in dishes and pails of water in our kitchens are here done in the acequia, if there be one. There seemed to be a mystery about this acequia, for I could not tell where this water could come from. The house was west of the road, and the water must cross it; but, apparently, the house stands *higher* than any point of the road that I could see. I have spoken already of the acequeros' skill, the results of which here puzzle me.

In the morning we were astonished with a breakfast at six! It is little short of a miracle, being, perhaps, two hours earlier than any other I ever heard of in all the land. The family can be no ordinary people certainly. Here I filled a bag with oranges, which were as abundant and as good as man could desire. They have also cocoanut-trees, which, if they do not yet bear, are majestic ornaments, and keep up a very pretty music in the night-breeze by the rustle of their leaflets. They need twelve years here to grow in.

We were off earlier than most families could have sent us away with chocolate only. A little above, I saw some trees rather taller and more slender than most apple-trees. I thought at first they were deformed by dozens of hornets' nests. I looked again, and really the supposed nests were the fruit. It was the guanábana (Anona muricata), called in Jamaica sour-sop. The flesh is firm, slightly fibrous, so as to eat beautifully with a fork. Elegance of eating is a high recommendation to a fruit. However delicious the flavor, you can not enjoy a fruit that smears fingers and face, clogs the teeth, or keeps you on the alert to separate eatable from uneatable. The guanábana is as large as the largest pine-apple, slightly acid, and not quite sweet enough, and with no aromatic flavor. The pulp separates in morsels, and is free from the rind and seeds. Two other Anonas are to be mentioned. The A. Chirimolia, the chirimoya, is smaller, of less regular shape, more fragile rind and tender pulp than the guanábana. It is by many reckoned the best fruit in the world, and by others rejected in disgust. Its flavor is almost exactly that of its congener of the Valley of the Mississippi, the Anona or Asimina triloba, there called papaw. The Anona squamosa is of the size of a large apple, much like the chirimoya in physical constitution, but inferior in flavor. They call it anon. The guanábana, which I prefer, is undervalued here, just as our Northern papaw is abandoned to negroes and opossums.

After picking from a guanábana all I wanted, dropping seeds along the road for a mile, and eating with my fingers without unfitting them to handle white satin, I threw away the rest. Soon after ordinary breakfast-time, we were rattling, in a long single file, over the pavements of Buga, the capital of the province of Cauca. After turning various corners, the head of the column rode into a house, and we all followed. We dismounted in the patio, and soon were seated in a parlor more civilized than usual. I received no introductions, but the conversation showed that I was known to them. In explanation, I was told that one of the young LL.D.'s with whom I crossed the mountain was a cousin to them. Some dulce and water were served, but no cigars offered. Per contra, they had some curious articles of *vertu*, images, etc., made of tobacco: they were exposed to the inconvenience of needing to be moistened with aguardiente from time to time. I always knew that tobacco and rum were allies. On the table were books, and a portfolio of drawings, and guitar music. All these looked strange to me, so long had I forgotten them.

Buga is on the right bank of the Piedras River, a broad, shallow stream, over which they think of throwing a foot-bridge of guadua. It has less volume than the Buga-la-Grande and the Tuluá, and nearly the same as the Paila. A vacant space of stony ground here separates the town from the river bank. The shore is lined with washerwomen and garments spread out to dry. Yankees complain of the mode of washing here, but with little justice, I suspect. Steuart describes them as "thumping and squeezing their linen upon the broad smooth stones, making the collar and wrist buttons *rain down like hail* into the stream." True, they wash without tubs and kettles, and do not scald their clothes; but I do not know that they injure them, and, when a man tells about buttons *hailing* down, I am inclined to think he exaggerates. They do not know our way of rubbing, nor do I know that it is better. If a man must have his clothes washed as they were in his mother's kitchen, let him do it with his own hands.

Just out of Buga, toward the river, I noticed a beautiful bush, with large red flowers, bright green leaves, and sharp thorns, as I found to my cost. It proved to be a cactate flower, and was probably a Pereskia, a leafy Genus in that leafless Order. A few miles farther south are three or four houses, mere huts. We will select one of them, on the west and lower side of the road, and take seats and rest in the piazza while I tell you a story.

I swam a horse across the Cauca above here, between Vijes and Cerrito once, and before the horse reached Cerrito he appeared tired out. There I spent two days, and the animal fared well. The next day I came down here, less than fifteen miles. Some miles above the poor horse flagged. I thought he could not possibly be tired till I had punished him with a severity that makes me ache now. He so far gave out that I was obliged to dismount and drive him. The poor fellow knew that his home was forty miles below, and probably despaired living to reach it again; so when he came to a narrow lane (you see fences are more common here than below), he suddenly turned into it, and tried to run away. Poor fellow, he could not run; a cripple could have overtaken him. I brought him back, but did not strike him for trying to run.

So I came to this house, and the occupant was in the yard. I asked him what ailed my horse. He said, He is destroncado. The word means maimed, but he meant exhausted—not tired, but used up as if by a typhoid fever. He took him in; we unsaddled him. He went and brought some cane. I drew my machete, which was tied to the saddle under the flap, and cut up the cane. He could still eat. Then I walked to Buga to get advice, and a horse if I could. They told me I could probably get him to San Pedro next day by going most of the way on foot, and very slowly. I dined at Buga. At dark I was back. I cut up all the cane the horse would eat. I retired, hanging my hammock in the little room that served as bedroom for the man, his wife, and their children.

In the morning I cut more cane. They told me to wait till after breakfast, and let him eat. I breakfasted on fried eggs and fried plantains, with a good cup of chocolate. When I offered to pay them, they refused; I protested, and the woman consented to take half a dime to pay for the eggs she bought for me at the house opposite. I urged, but the utmost they would receive was a dime. Bless them!

I mounted my horse at the Piedras, and rode through the back streets of Buga. I passed a place where they had killed a cow, and were pinning the hide to the ground. On the fence were half a dozen gallinazos, waiting for a chance to pick up a morsel of meat; then they looked at my horse, and, by a wicked leer, seemed to insinuate that I was trying to cheat them. Somehow I felt guilty, for they looked at poor Rozinante with the eye of a gratified connoisseur. I could have knocked them off the fence with a good will.

"Step by step goes a great ways," says a Spanish proverb. San Pedro, prompt hospitality, sympathy, and a fresh horse, were before me. And I was not disappointed, although I do not even know the name of the good people who live there. I sent the horse they kindly loaned me back from La Paila by *mail.* Weeks afterward, I was riding home from the Medio, when Pepe Sanmartin overtook me, and asked me "if I knew what horse I was riding." I told him I did not. "Well," said he, "it is the caballo destroncado."

We left Buga about 11. By 1 we had crossed the Zonza, a small river, with a few houses south of it. Here the sun became intolerable; and had the day been as long as in northern summers, it would have been nearly as severe. We stopped at a venta, where a billiard-table occupied the sala. I went back to the river to swim. The water then, about 2 P.M., was at nearly 100° F. It had a strange effect on coming out. I was dressing myself in the shade, and I found it too cold. I had to step into the sun to warm myself. I started a little before the others, and stopped to see them building a church with adobe. In all New Granada I have seen no new church in the process of construction except at Zonza and Overo. All the others are either finished or abandoned. I rode on, and stopped on a gentle rise to wait for the company. Never have I seen, and never expect to see, in this mortal world, another place so beautiful. The ground was gently swelling; clumps of trees were scattered here and there in every direction. The Quindio range in the east terminated in plains at some miles distant, and the river-forest, too, had retired far from the road.

Nestled in the distant hills we could see the buildings of a hacienda that bore the appropriate name of Paradise Vale—Val Paraiso—just high enough to make a perceptible difference in climate. Much of the land about here is irrigated, and, therefore, of perennial greenness. With ordinary diligence, three crops of maize, and four of many things, could be raised here. Few things besides wheat, potatoes, spices, and maple-sugar could not be raised here. Bolivar, too, was struck with the beauty of this place as he passed through. He asked its name. He was told Zonza (an imbecile, *fem.*). "What brutality," said the Liberator, "to give so unworthy a name to the fairest spot in the Italy of the New World!"

Soon we came to more muddy crossings of acequias—some bad, and others worse; and I was told that all of them, for many miles, were derived from the Rio Guaves. Then we came to the river itself, and it was different from all the rest. The beds of all the other streams are from 8 to 20 feet below the banks. This could not be more than 4; and yet it rippled away over a pebbly bottom as pure, as happy, and as noisy as childhood ought to be. Farther on we left to our right the direct road to Cali, which leans toward the Cauca for some miles, then turns square down to it through a muddy lane of forest some miles long, and terrible in the rainy season.

Before sunset we were at Cerrito, the only regularly laid out town (with a Plaza) this side of Cartago, except the paved towns and Libraida. In the centre of the Plaza stands a ceiba (Bombax Ceiba), the most glorious shade-tree I ever set my eyes on; in size it is equal to a large elm, in shape a little more regular, the trunk almost smooth enough to varnish, and the thick green leaves already varnished. Just east of it is the church, of which the adjoining figure is a faithful delineation, kindly furnished me by the artist-traveler, Mr. Church.

CHURCH AT CERRITO.

The front door, the bell-tower, the higher roof at the farther end over the principal altar, and the wing, which is the sacristia, are a fair illustration of the usual arrangement in churches in New Granada. Very few indeed have the sacristía on the other side, or behind the altar. The mercy-door is, of course, on the side hidden from view, for, as you enter the front door, it is nearly always at or near the middle of the left-hand side.

I visited the boys' school here for less than five minutes one day. I do not always learn as much that is new by a longer visit. It is conducted on the Lancasterian principle, as are all the public schools here. Monitors were at this moment passing around, examining the toes of the boys, cutting their nails, and extracting the niguas. This is a part of the regular business of Saturday afternoon, and wisely enjoined, so neglected are too many of these children at home.

Here we turned at a right angle to the east, passed the mercy-door of the church, and, as we left the village, entered the estate of Aurora, the property of Señor Miguel Cabal, late gobernador of the adjoining province of Buenaventura. We were soon seated at a plain, prompt dinner. I found our host a man of unusual intelligence, and, what is more, of a candor that leads me to rely more on his statements than on those of any other one man in all New Granada. He is a Liberal, and, therefore, I thought it a good time to get information on the Conservador presidents Herran and Mosquera. I rely upon little here that does not come in the way of admissions, and sometimes very reluctant ones.

The successor of President Márquez was to be elected by Congress in 1841. It could not have been a quiet time, for the minority, it is said, attempted to break up Congress by a want of a quorum. All of them that could be caught were put in prison till enough were obtained for the purpose. One still was wanting to make a quorum when they were brought into the hall for the election of president; that one lacking of a quorum was supplied by the corpse of a member who had died. A majority of this whole number, of living and dead, of free agents and prisoners, gave their votes for General Pedro Alcántara Herran. So says Samper, *Apuntamientos*, p. 345; but I am almost driven by all farther inquiries to the reluctant and terrible conclusion that this whole story is an unfounded falsehood, if not a shameless lie!

General Herran is son-in-law and companion in arms to his successor, General Mosquera. Their campaigns together had been chiefly against rebels on this side of the Quindio, and here were their warmest friends and bitterest enemies.

Herran is not a great man; but, after examining what his

worst enemies say, I conclude that he made a good president. His worst act was calling back the Jesuits, who had been unjustly expelled by Carlos III, by a decree of 18th Oct., 1767. Up to 1740, never were men more faithful and true to the interests of humanity, as they understood them, than the Jesuits in New Granada. Then they were forbidden to extend their operations, and their restless spirit could find no other vent than in increasing their wealth and power. They were becoming more powerful than the King and the Viceroy, but had shown no disposition to abuse that power. They were expelled for not being as inefficient, as useless, and as wicked as all the world around them. As they went forth at night, lest a tumult should arise among their converts, and on foot, leaving their immense wealth the spoil to the crown, civilization wept. Half-civilized Indians threw away their clothes, left their villages to decay and their fields to become thickets again, and went to hunting and fishing. Many of these missionaries died of want before they found a refuge in Italy and England.

This law never was repealed, but in 1842 Congress authorized the government to invite *missionaries* from Europe to come and civilize the Indians. Herran has a brother high in ecclesiastical rank. All churches and all safe governments are conservative. By some unhappy fatality, the President was induced to consent to a return of the Jesuits, who had been growing more wicked and dangerous every year since their expulsion. They came and settled in Bogotá and other large places, already overstocked with idle and inefficient priests, and did their best to make themselves useful and necessary to the Church. We shall hear of them farther on.

The course of the Herran administration was a general, slow, safe reform. He and his chief friends were slaveholders, and yet slavery was verging toward a sure extinction. None now born were slaves for life. He systematized instruction and repressed vagrancy. The laws were all compiled. But one of the most admirable of his works was a penal code—a systematic classification of crimes and punishments, such as is perhaps unknown in the English language. Another long essay issued during this administration I have never read, nor will I venture to criticise, except for its length and its inappropriateness. It is called the "Constitution of 1843," the second of New Granada. I think it must have fewer positive faults than its more democratic successor of 1853.

Herran was succeeded by his father-in-law, General Tomas Cipriano Mosquera. More aristocratic in his feelings than his predecessor, perhaps with more talent, and certainly with no less patriotism, Mosquera was unquestionably a good president, and, in my opinion, the best New Granada has ever had, and as good as the best we have had since New Granada was a nation. They charge him with great cruelties in suppressing previous civil wars. It may be so; but he would have been accused of severity had he been only a little too lenient. A Conservative, his whole administration was a series of cautious changes for the better. A brother to the archbishop, he brought on himself the censures of the Pope by abridging the privileges of the clergy. A slaveholder, he still was true to the principle of gradual extirpation of slavery. Immensely rich, he labored to bring about a change in the system of taxation that would be of special benefit to the poor. He did his utmost to benefit intercommunication by land and water, and his liberality in the concessions to the Panamá Railroad should teach our nation to respect his name and the character of his country that has ever supported them.

"Why, then," I asked of Señor Cabal, "did your party oppose the administration of Mosquera?"

"It was just a piece of ambition and desire for office," said he.

Samper, the craziest of Red Republican theorists, explains it in these words: "Parties have sometimes incomprehensible aberrations." While he condemns much in Mosquera that I approve, he admits that his party ought to have voted for him. These are his words: "Judging by appearances, skillfully got up to produce a complete hallucination, in an evil hour they decided on the disastrous General Borrero."

Señor Cabal has an interesting library, and takes the "Correo de Ultramar." He has a garden, and good orange-trees. He has a cane-mill and a *distillery*. I purposely avoided visiting the last, out of friendship to the estimable owner. His cane-mill is a sugar-factory, which is rarely the case here. As it must be 20 miles from the nearest waterfall (100 quite probably, for rockless countries can have none), and half a mile from the Cerrito at a point lower than his mill, I would have thought it a piece of insanity for him to attempt to introduce water-power. But he has succeeded, thanks to the cheapness of labor, and the miraculous skill of Granadan acequeros. Even when accomplished it looks absurd.

After breakfast, horses were brought out for a ride. There is a young person in the family, of the middle class, between lady and peasant. In aiding her to mount, as she put her foot in my hand I discovered that it was *bare*. I could not easily overcome my prejudice that human skin is less nice to touch than the tanned hide of an ox. The governor was the last to mount. As he did so, his horse started, threw him, and dislocated both his wrists. I rode off, and in a few moments returned with a doctor; but surgical cases are so rare here that much skill is not to be expected. My residence in South America has brought to my knowledge but one more dislocation (of the humerus—set by the horse-breaker Toledo), and nothing else worse than bruises and scratches, of which mine in the Quindio (p. 366) was perhaps the very worst. Unfortunately, therefore, the dislocation was not properly reduced, and, weeks afterward, the reduction was performed in Cali.

La Señora de Cabal had three pairs of birds of different species. Far the most interesting of these were two little parrots, about the size of canaries, unable to talk, indeed, but the most intelligent birds I ever saw. Mr. Jenney, of Honda, kindly made me a present of a pair of the same species. I suffered every thing for them. I carried them on foot ten miles in a box, cared for them all the way down the Magdalena, and in the terrible ride of night and day from Calamar to Cartagena (65 miles of *such* roads, in 26 hours), I carried their cage hung round my neck. Bruised and shaken as they were, they would cling to the wires to get a chance to look into my face, and I never spoke to my horse but they answered me. At Cartagena this rough life was over; but at the very sea-side one died and the other was lost. Never have I mourned for any of the brute creation as for these poor little parrots.

Near here I once made an instructive visit. It was a reunion of nearly all our company over the Quindio at the house of one of them. He met us on horseback soon after entering on the estate, and cordially embraced me without stopping our horses. We arrived about 5. As good a dinner as could be prepared on so short a notice was served at 9, and all the very large and interesting family sat down with us. We left the next morning at 8, without even chocolate. This, I am told, was caused by the inefficiency of servants since the liberation of the slaves. Five years ago we might have breakfasted at this hour. Servants have no motive to work where a sparse population occupy a fertile soil in a climate of perpetual autumn. We breakfasted, with two or three wooden spoons, at a dirty, wayside venta on what we could pick up.

A little to the right of the main road to Palmira I was told there was an Englishman named Birr′-ni. He was said not to treat his wife very well as to clothing and family comforts, but such was my desire to see one of our race that I decided to call. Mr. Byrne proved to be an Irish gentleman and a Catholic, an ex-consul of Great Britain. His wife is a fortunate woman in the respects named: I know of not another in the Cauca that need not envy her. She is a Granadina, and speaks no English in the hearing of strangers, but appears like one of our race. His two oldest children, a boy and girl, are evidently English, though they can not speak a word of our language yet. If ever a poor home-sick traveler comes here, who can not talk any Spanish, how would he be tantalized by the company of such a lady and such children!

Where government pays a foreign resident a sufficient sum to maintain a family, it ought to select one of our own race and religion, and require him to take with him a family of the same. But consuls are either inadequately paid, good business men, living by commerce and kind by instinct, or, if they are amply salaried, you find them rewarded politicians, bent on laying up something to indemnify themselves for outlays in past elections. Hence I would sooner give a friend an introduction to the family of Mr. Byrne, foreign as it is in every thing but sympathy, than to a minister sent abroad by a political triumph.

I committed one act of consummate folly at Mr. Byrne's. While there was preparing such a dinner as I shall not find again this side of the Quindio, I went into the sugar-house and ate so freely of fragrant, warm sugar as to actually unfit me for eating any thing else. Here I saw molasses drained from the sugar absolutely thrown away. It is called miel de purga, and these sirup-eaters are too dainty to touch it.

Mr. Byrne is a flourishing farmer. While other foreign sojourners here have made it their study "how to buy cheap and sell dear," he has been ever ready to buy human labor when it was in the market, and so bestows it on his broad domain as to add to its permanent value. This is too slow a way to get rich to suit most who go abroad in search of wealth, but such a man is a benefactor to the country. I know not that an experimental farm would do more for it. His buildings are in excellent condition, and the house is painted. This is so extraordinary a thing that I know of no word better to express it in Spanish than to say it is varnished. I can not now recollect a square inch of paint either on buildings or other articles in all this valley, except a varnish applied to totumas and other articles in Pasto, which is supposed to be a sort of resin or gum of unknown trees brought from the distant head-waters of the Amazon. This is usually colored red with arnotto, warmed, and applied mechanically in a thin film without reducing it to a liquid.

I tore myself away from the Byrnes with a regret that none but a sojourner in a strange land can know. I met him and his boy twice afterward, but we were both journeying, and could exchange but a few words; but I shall long remember them. For a little while still our road lay up the Cerrito, which is only a good mill-stream. Farther on we pass the hacienda of a Señor Isaacs, an Antillan Jew turned Catholic, married to a Catholic wife, and the father of quite a family of active children. I am but slightly acquainted with them, and have never been at the hacienda.

We stopped a while at a venta on the banks of the Sabaletas, a larger stream, over which there is a bridge of guadua. It requires some courage to venture across this frail fabric, although some of them are said to be strong enough to bear a mule. A sprightly girl here seemed greatly to attract the fancy of my companion, who wished her to go home with him and live with his wife, but why, or in what capacity, I could not guess. She promised to go at a future time, but my conjecture was that they did not mean any thing, or that either supposed the other in earnest.

We had passed below here a robber, as they said, in custody of two armed men, all on foot. They were on their way to Buga. It is quite common to go armed here, either with a pistol or sword, but it is entirely useless. The chief reason why no more robberies are committed is, that they are not eager for money, and, therefore, lack a motive. I have never wished myself armed, or protected by the arms of another, for a single moment.

Palmira stands on the banks of a miserable muddy brook. Why it stands there I can not guess. It is the cabecera of the southern canton of the province of Cauca, and a district of 10,055, which makes it the tenth town in New Granada in population. As it so happens that *all the large towns*, except Bogotá, are unknown to us at home, I will name them: 1, Bogotá, 29,649; 2, Socorro, 15,015; 3, Piedecuesta, 14,841; 4, Medellin, 13,755; 5, Cali, 11,848; 6, Sanjil, 11,528; 7, Vélez, 11,178; 8, Valle,* 10,544; 9, Sonson, 10,244; 10, Palmira, 10,055; 11, Puente Nacional, 10,018; 12, Bucaramanga, 10,008; next comes Cartagena, 9896. Tamalameque, which is found on all good maps, contains a population of 726, scattered over the whole district.

I know of no place of the size of Palmira that excels it in the population of its jail. To this bad pre-eminence I think the administration of López brought it by giving it wicked rulers; but of that we shall see more presently. The jail is miserably insecure. It is of unburnt brick, and the windows open on the street.

The only public institution which I visited besides was the boys' school. I was then making my investigations on the amount of arithmetic learned in the common schools. Here I proposed this sum: A boy bought a cage for 12 cuartillos, paid 5 for having it mended, and sold it for 19: how much did he

* Valle, Valle de Jesus, or Jesus-María, is a town in the canton of Vélez (the most populous in New Granada), some 20 miles southwest of the town of Vélez. It is of no importance except as the centre of a dense population, chiefly of Indians. It has no post-office, and scarcely has a name of its own.

gain or lose? It was given to the best boy in a large school, but he could not do it.

My host here, Doctor Z., was a lawyer who had turned merchant, as is quite common. I saw another LL.D. here sell a string of glass beads to a mulata to put on her babe. Dr. Z. has little reverence for the priests. He told me a tough story of one of them. He was a negligent priest, who was called suddenly to administer the last sacraments to two dying persons. At the bedside of the first he opened his wafer-box, and behold! an intruding cockroach had eaten all but the least particle of the hostia. According to the doctors, all consecrated wafers must be eaten by a Christian. What the cockroach had swallowed must be no exception. He judged the moribund to be so far gone as to be unconscious, and so, taking the prisoner in his fingers, he asked, "Have you faith to believe that what I now present to you is the body of God?" "The body of God!" cries the poor fellow, opening wide his glazing eyes; "it is a cockroach!"

I was invited to dine with a family here. It was a Friday in Lent, and I had to do without meat. This is the only instance in all my Granadan experience where the lady would not allow any meat on her table. I have seen one lady and one child fast, but no more, except this family. The priests are supposed to fast.

The space is very broad here between the foot of the hills and the river. Below, large estates extended from the river to the mountains, or to the edge of occupied land. Here, above, fenced fields are much more common, and there may be several farms, one east of the other; but, generally, the river-forest here is much wider than below; in some cases nearly 10 miles wide. On leaving Palmira we turn almost due west. Our southward journey in this volume is virtually at an end.

Between here and the river lies some of the worst road in the world on account of mud. The distance between Palmira and Cali is given as 18 or 19 miles, but it is as far as a horse ought to travel in a day. At one place we had to unsaddle our horses and walk across a slough on logs, holding them by the halter lest they drown. Its desperate character might at once be known by seeing Pontederia azurea growing there.

Then came a palm forest of a thousand acres. Our course would lay around the fallen stems with a monotonous plash of horses' hoofs. I saw here some cacao-trees which I was assured were indigenous. I so believe them, for I think no mortal would live here to cultivate them.

Good news! we are at the ferry at last! Our saddles are in the boat, we hold our horses by the bridle, and set loose from the shore. A few rods diagonal paddling of man and beast, and we scramble up the west bank of the Cauca. We have left the province of Cauca for that of Buenaventura.

CHAPTER XXXIII.

CALI AND VIJES.

Cali.—Church built of old Clothes.—A Priest making Jews.—Rare Flower and miraculous Image.—North American in the Hospital.—Schools.—Weaving.—Sounds familiar.—Funeral.—Celebration of a Party Triumph.—Election of López.—A Turn northward.—A fine Bridge.—Yumbo.—Copper cheaper than Iron.—San Marcos.—Route to the Pacific.—Copper Mine.—Gold Mining and Washing.—Comb Manufactory.—Maladministration in the Cauca.—Lands in common.—Our Priest: his Eloquence and Morals.—Visit to a Hermit.—Heroic Eating.—Espinal.—Bolivia.—Pretty Child.—Locating Road.—Fence of Cornstalks.—Railroad to the Pacific.—Defective Government.—Constitution of 1853.—Finances.—Protection of Vagabonds.—The Granadinos are a moral People.

We are on the left bank of the Cauca, and about 4 miles east of Cali. For some distance the land is liable to be overflowed, but at length we come to soil that is capable of cultivation. There are one or two haciendas near the road. At length we see before us an immense compact grove, with palms rising here and there above the rest of the foliage, and, above all, some steeples, and the bodies of two churches, one of them crowned with a fine dome. That grove covers Cali.

A nearer view does not belie the pleasing prospect at a distance. It stands on the right bank of Cali River, on dry, open ground, half a mile perhaps from the foot of the western or Cáldas chain of the Andes. It may be regarded as the sea-port of the Cauca Valley. It is the capital of the province of Buenaventura, and, while that port has but 1986 inhabitants, Cali, the fifth town in New Granada, has 11,848. It is one of those old towns that I love to meet with, where most of the architecture is solid, and few indeed of the roofs are thatched. It has a sufficient supply of suppressed convents for hospital, colegio, and other public uses, and one still in operation, a Franciscan convent of monks, besides a beateria, or place for the special devotions of females.

This convent of San Francisco is probably the richest west of the Quindio. Its church is exceeded in size only by the Cathedral of Bogotá and the church at Chiquinquirá. It is really the finest church I have seen here. They say it was built of *old clothes*. From some notion of the people, they love to be buried in the robes of a Franciscan friar. An old robe is preferred to a new one, and some say the older the better; so a friar can not afford to keep his clothes till they get shabby. A man not acquainted with this custom became alarmed once for the extinction of the order. Every day or two he met a Franciscan going to his last home. On discovering his mistake, he wondered if the devil could be cheated as he was.

At a high mass here I was surprised by hearing a priest that could really sing; it was a great treat. I was so much interested in him that I sought an introduction to him, and called on him. He proved to be an *Italian*. He had refrained from making music a special study, he assured me, because he was desirous of preaching, and if he became a chorister it would interfere with his bent. I never heard him preach, but urged that he could not render a better service to religion than by rendering the musical parts of it endurable. He told me he was also engaged in image-making, and showed me some *Jews* that he was making for the processions of Holy Week. I told him that I thought a priest's time better spent in making Christians out of pagans than making Jews out of gypsum. He asked me to dine with him, but I deferred it till another occasion. When I next visited Cali he had moved to another convent.

San Pedro is a parish church of Cali, but is not equal, in either size or splendor, to San Francisco. It glories in a suite of large, *new* pictures, apparently all by the hand of the same artist, and a very industrious one. I am wicked enough to like new paintings, and, though this artist will never equal Vásquez, I looked them over with great satisfaction.

They had a great procession here, in which some image of the Virgin went from her home through a large number of the streets and back home again. Great preparations were made at some of the places it was to pass, to ornament the houses by hanging out calico, and whatever they thought ornamental. After the procession was over I was permitted to see Our Lady of the Queremal. Quereme is the name of a fragrant flower that is not known to grow in but one place in the world, and that is west of Cali. It is the Thibaudia Quereme, and the place where it grows is the Queremal. It is sold in the market of Cali whenever it is in flower. Well, in that famous place was found an image, all carved out of stone by supernatural means. This was brought to Cali, as if there had been an error in its first collocation. It has been covered with paint and clothes, and set up in a camarin to be worshiped. I went up into the camarin and examined it.

Farther south, on the very borders of Equador, is an image supernaturally painted on a perpendicular ledge of rock. With immense labor, the art of man has been able to construct a chapel to protect it and adore it in. None of these, however, can near approach in fame the oldest of these cheats, the old daub of Chiquinquirá.

I learned that there was a North American in the hospital here, so I felt I must call upon him. He was a negro from Boston. The nature of his affliction did not greatly prejudice me in his favor. I found his situation very comfortable there; as good, in fact, as in most of our hospitals at the North. The hospital is spacious and well conducted. I found he needed nothing but some aid in finding employment after his discharge.

I visited the colegio. It was, perhaps, my most profitable visit to a school. I introduced myself to the sub-director, who seemed anxious to enlighten me in their modes of teaching. I was curious to hear his boys conjugate a Latin verb. Our faulty way is to accentuate the termination in all cases. Most teachers consider it inevitable. So our boys say, Amabámm, amabáss, amabátt. Here they said amábam, amábas, amábat. But the most intolerable curse of our Latin schools is the stupidity of teaching a false pronunciation that makes a man a barbarian wherever English is not spoken; that is where he needs Latin most. Fortunately for me, I had for years used the Continental pronunciation which is laid down in the best of our systems of teaching Latin, Bullions'.

From Latin I set them to parsing Spanish, and got them on that untranslatable phrase, Qué tal le ha ido a usted (what so to him has it gone to your majesty), which means *how have you been.* The boy was puzzled; the sub-director was helping him out, when the director entered. Then sprung up an earnest debate between the two. The sub-director supposed an ellipsis of several words—less than twenty, I think. The director maintained that the phrase was no more capable of analysis and the application of syntax to its components than a compound interjection. I withheld my opinion through pretended modesty, in reality because it agreed with that of the inferior. Most of my readers will be likely to adhere to the director's notion that it is *unparsable*, and so we will leave it.

My chief objection to the system of education in this colegio is, that it is too speculative, and undervalues practical knowledge, as geography and chemistry; and too ambitious, having too much of calculus, and too little of arithmetic. Every thing is attempted, and, therefore, little is mastered.

I visited the primary girls' school. It occupied the whole of a *casa claustrada*—a quite needless amount of space. It was a well-ordered school. I set myself to guess the proportion of African and European blood in the school, and think it was about one third African, with no visible intermixture of Indian. They sang, but only as a devotional exercise. They had a little printed collection of hymns. No two hymns could be sung to the same tune: long metre, common, and short, are unknown here. This would be an inconvenience in attempting to introduce the necessary Protestant hymns, and of theirs there is none that the Protestant could use except the Trisagio, or hymn to the Trinity, which is not, after all, worth much either as to words or music. I expressed a wish to obtain their hymnbook, which they assured me I could do at the *gobernacion.* "We have enough to spare here," added the directora; "but, as they are receipted for, it is impossible for us to give away or lose one without being held accountable." When a teacher resigns, a clerk of the gobernador comes, counts all the property of the school, and gives it over to the successor, taking a receipt.

I saw a loom in Cali. It is the only one I have seen. A rude affair it was, far inferior to any of our old hand-looms. There are no arts that need introducing here more than spinning and weaving. Spinning must precede weaving, which can not flourish while spinning is done in the antique mode, and spinning-wheels are unknown. Had half the expense spent in introducing factory machinery into New Granada been spent on domestic machinery, a new era would have dawned here. Neither spinning nor weaving have been introduced into New Granada by Europeans, though possibly this loom may have been patterned after those of Spain. The manta, or native cotton cloth, made from an indigenous shrub, was one of the riches of the aborigines before the conquest, and the mode of spinning can not have improved any since that day.

I am sorry to say that I heard one sound in Cali that reminded me of home. I am ashamed to tell what it was, but as a faithful, conscientious traveler I have no alternative. It was a man quarreling with (I suppose) his wife. For how many months has this been an unknown sound to my ears! I heard two women quarreling in Bogotá, and came near seeing a quarrel of two bogas on the Magdalena; but these men are of a degraded race and mixed blood, ignorant and half civilized, wear machetes to cut bushes, and not a bowie-knife to fight with, and do not even whip their wives.

There is a hospital for lepers here. I was anxious to visit it, but my friends protested; so much would they dread the introduction of elephantiasis into their families, to gratify my curiosity. I can not think the disease so contagious as they imagine, for I do not hear of those who live with lepers contracting it.

I attended the funeral of a General Borrero—not, as I then supposed, the candidate for President in 1847. He was a member of La Tercera, the third order of St. Francis, and accordingly was buried as a monk. "When the devil was sick, the devil a monk would be." His body lay, the night before the funeral, in a chapel of the convent. The next day they sung the mass of the defunct, with the accompaniment of the best musicians and vocalists that could be hired in Cali.

Then marched forth a long procession through the streets, with hats off, and candles thirty inches long and two in diameter, dropping wax in the street. They went to a small church, or chapel, at the northern extremity of Cali, adjoining the old cemetery. Here some farther singing and praying was performed, and the procession proceeded eastward, out of town and over the plain, to the new cemetery, where as yet no chapel has been built. I did not enter the cemetery with the procession, nor see the body deposited in its last resting-place, owing to a little accident in leaping one of the stagnant brooks that cut the plain in every direction; I had landed in a soft spot, and covered myself with rich black mud nearly up to my knees. When I had got it washed off, and had entered the cemetery, the body was already placed in a brick bóveda, or oven, about three feet high, and they were building up the mouth. Burnt bricks are always used for this work.

One other great affair came off here, the celebration of the triumph of the Liberales, on 7th March, 1849, when President López was elected president. The affair was official, and, frankly to speak my sentiments, therefore in bad taste. Especially it was adding insult to injury to require the Franciscan monks to celebrate an event that grieved the heart of every fanatic.

The celebration began, of course, with the vesper of the day, on Sunday night; this was by an illumination. As there is no window-breaking mob here, and no windows to be broken, the affair suffered in brilliancy accordingly. In the Plaza there were but thirty-one lights, and most of these were in the balconies of government offices.

On Monday there was a grand mass in San Francisco. Artillery and infantry were drawn up in front of the church. At the proper time, when all the bells rang, the drums also beat, and the rattle of musketry and the thunder of cannon added wings to the devotion of the dense crowd that filled the vast and beautiful church. Soldiers on parade do not kneel or remove caps at mass.

From my Conservador friend, Don Eladio Várgas, and the

amiable botanist, Señor José María Triana, of the Comision Coregrafica, whom I unexpectedly met here together, I had most of my information about that memorable day.

"The day they celebrate," says Don Eladio, "was one of the saddest in the annals of New Granada, not more in its consequences than in itself. It was the triumph of the poniards of a Bogotá mob over the representatives of the people. They were besieged in the Church of Santo Domingo, where the session was held, and elected López only to escape assassination."

"What assassination nor what squashes (calabazas)?" says Pepe Triana. "Who but your idol Mosquera had the command of the military in Bogotá at the time? I myself was one of that mob, as you call us. I know not one of us that was armed. The only arms I saw there were a pair of pistols, which were handed to Dr. Ospina, Mosquera's evil genius; nor do I know of others, except that two Conservador representatives, Neira and Pardo the pious, intimated that they were prepared to sell their lives as dearly as possible. And I know that the military preparations were complete. The night before, the cannon were loaded with grape. All the horses of the cavalry had their saddles on all night, and, at the time, all the troops were drawn up at the barracks with guns loaded with ball. Lines of trumpeters, disguised in citizens' dress, extended from Santo Domingo to all the barracks. Within, of course, the trumpeter that always attends the sessions of Congress was present in his uniform. What danger could threaten Congress with these preparations?"

V. "I do not deny your account of the preparations: it was the President's duty to make them. But you dare not deny that Congress was threatened. This I will prove beyond contradiction from the 'Apuntamientos' of Samper. First he says that 'because López had more votes in the popular election than Cuervo and Gori together, the democratic party rightly considered that this circumstance authorized them to demand his election—lo autorizaba para *exijirla!*' page 444. Next, page 446, 'At each ballot which contained the name of General López, there arose in the auditory an exclamation of joy and enthusiasm like the strophe of a triumphal hymn: a vague and sudden murmur, which expressed disgust, was the echo to the name of

Dr. Cuervo.' And again, 'When, at the third ballot, the choice was limited to two candidates, and Cuervo had 43 votes, López 41, and the rest were blank, some of the barra thought Cuervo was elected, and a prolonged murmur, like the distant roar of the tempest, resounded under the dome of the temple.' Those blank votes are said to have been cast by way of experiment, to see whether they could elect Cuervo and be safe."

T. "Still there was no mob and no menace, for then Congress ordered the church to be cleared. All went out quietly into the bitter cold rain, and waited in the open street while the last decisive ballot was taken. And that infamous vote of Mariano Ospina 'for José Hilario López, in order that Congress be not assassinated,' was the beginning of the calumny that you are now trying to keep alive."

Now what can an impartial traveler make out of a discussion like this? My conclusion is that the will of the nation was executed in the election of López; that Congress was not free in the election, and that there was danger in resisting the will of the populace; that they yielded to it partly through cowardice, and partly because their conscience convicted them of the wrong they wished to do in defeating the will of the nation; and, lastly, that the pressure exerted upon them amounted only to implied threats, which probably never would have been executed. And I think that Samper throws some light on this question in his remarks on the election of Joaquin Mosquera in 1830, when the "youth of Bogotá succeeded in inspiring the Convention with confidence." This draws one to the conclusion that the elections are not always free. The conduct of President Mosquera was admirable through the whole of it, and especially when, at the close, he promptly went to the residence of López to congratulate him on his election.

An accidental circumstance led me to call on Dr. Manuel María Mollarino. I supposed him at the time to be an M.D., but, judging from his library, I infer that he is (as are most of the doctors here) an LL.D. I little foresaw then that the supreme power was so soon to be placed in his hands as Vice-president. He is an intelligent gentleman, and speaks very good English; better, I think, than any one I have met who has not resided in an English country, or, as Vice-president Obaldía, on the Isthmus. He is a Conservador, but not of an ultra stamp, and, had he any power in his hands, would use it well; but the President is too much like a head clerk to sign papers.

There are some fine walks about Cali, but none better than up to the Church of San Nicolas, on a high knoll that overlooks the whole city. Leaving this on my left, and descending toward the river, I followed up its right bank. I passed the aqueduct which supplies Cali with water at a place where it was carried over a hollow. I was surprised that it was not larger, although I believe it is larger than any in Bogotá; its external dimensions are only about thirty inches square. Farther up it is an open acequia. I could not believe my eyes here, for it seemed that the acequia descended toward the river, while the water was flowing in it quite rapidly from the river. I had to stop and examine before I could convince myself of the optical illusion.

Farther up, I ended my southward progress where the road to Buenaventura crosses the river. An immense pile of bales of tobacco, incased in hide, were here waiting either for the mules to rest or for others to be hired. I am now in latitude 3° 25′ north, and perhaps nearer the equator than I shall ever be again. But no differences of latitude are felt here. Like the length of days near the solstice, where a week makes not so much variation as a single day at the equinoxes, the seven degrees I have traversed in these pages make but an imperceptible difference, while that of the two degrees between New York and Boston is very considerable.

There are interesting coal mines and beds of lignite near Cali that deserve the attention of the traveler, and some things here that might richly reward the mineralogist, but I did not learn of them in season to visit them.

I left Cali in company with Señor Triana and Señor Monzon, director of some mining operations which we wished to visit at Vijes. We crossed the Cali over a brick bridge, the longest and best bridge, as well as the last, that I have seen in all New Granada. It is wide enough for a carriage to pass, and consists of seven arches. You would forget where you are while looking at the bridge; but look above at the washerwomen that line the bank, or the swimming boys and swimming girls below, and you will see that you are in New Granada yet.

Another stream is to be passed, and you are fairly on the way. I saw on a shed or hut as I left a singular roof of guadua. It was made of stems split in two. One set was placed like open troughs, side by side, running straight down from the ridge-pole to the eaves. Over the adjacent edges of these were reversed an equal number of others, that prevented the rain from getting in between them.

Under a large tree by the wayside we found a man resting, who begged of us. He gave as a reason for giving him alms that he was a convict recently liberated from presidio. Farther on, as we were going south, on our left hand, Señor Monzon showed us a natural picture, an Ecce Homo. Like the Old Man of the Mountain, in the White Hills of New Hampshire, the resemblance appears in but one point; but, unlike that, it requires considerable imagination to see it at all: I utterly failed.

Here we come to the most terrible quagmire that I have ever seen out of the Quindio, except, perhaps, on some of the roads to the bank of the Cauca. I crossed it once in the dark, and, in all my travels, I have suffered no more from fear. Deliver me from the quagmires, and I will meet cheerfully the precipices, fierce bulls, robbers, and serpents.

I stopped that night at the Hacienda of Arroyo-hondo, a benighted stranger. I met that ready hospitality that never fails a gentleman in any house or cottage in a land where negatives are almost unknown; "in the sweet land of *sí*," as one calls it. Here I saw perhaps the oldest cane-mill that goes by water-power in the country. The rollers were of copper, brought from the south, or else extracted from a mine near Vijes. They are upright, and the water-wheel is a tub-wheel. It is not well contrived, and never before have I found copper cheaper than iron.

A mile or two to our left is the town of Yumbo. Still farther north is a hacienda at the foot of the mountain, where there is a lime-kiln. The only other in the Valley of the Cauca is, as I have said, at Vijes, a little farther down. A curious bird here attracted my attention. It was a species of swallow, a variety of Hirundo rufa, it is said, that has two long tail-feathers projecting like the divergent blades of a pair of scissors, hence called tijareta. Another of the wading tribe is here found, always on dry ground, picking up snails or other helpless animals with its long, curved bill. From its cry it is called cocli, and is supposed to be a Scopus. Another bird, looking much like a hawk, has quite similar habits. It is often seen perched on the back of a cow, particularly if she be lying down. It is supposed to free cattle from insects that infest them, and is therefore called garropatero. It may be Crotophaga Piririgua.

The hills, and therefore the road, are approaching the river. We are here on the principal road from Cali to Buga, and also to Roldanillo on this side, till here the two roads part, and the one directs itself to a ferry, and the other to a spur of the hill, over which it climbs. I left them both and turned to a hacienda in a nook of the hills, called San Marcos. Here I found a pleasant family, and, by a trip up a small stream, gained some interesting information.

I went up about three miles. I rose steadily, but not rapidly. No extraordinary skill would be here needed to make a tolerable wagon-road. Here I found solid rock every where, which much reminded me of the mica-slate regions of Vermont. Veins of quartz were abundant, and often auriferous. There were some small waterfalls, the first of even six inches that I had seen in the Valley of the Cauca. At length I came to where a ridge of earth seemed to stretch across the valley. I stood on it, and west of me extended the Valley of the Dagua, that empties into the Pacific at Buenaventura. I can hardly believe that there can be any easier way for a wagon-road from Bogotá to the Pacific than this. The port is almost exactly west of where I stand, and it can not be twenty miles to tidewater.

Returning to San Marcos, they gave me the first fruit of the pitajaya that I ever saw; I mean the yellow pitajaya, for the red one is not worth eating. The true Cereus Pitajaya of Jacquin is said to be a maritime species, with the fruit scarlet without and white within, while this excellent fruit is yellow, both rind and pulp. I call it one of the best fruits of the tropics. I have never seen the expanded flower of any species of Cereus here. They open at night.

Riding under a tall Capparidate tree, I began to rise a rocky spur of the Cáldas chain. Soon on my right were some old diggings, from whence is said to have come all the copper of the bells of the convent of San Francisco in Cali. In a few rods of it are more recent excavations for gold, now arrested, I am told, by a lawsuit. The spur reaches down to the very river bank, and then bends down the river as if to meet another spur sent off a few miles below. Between is a large plain, mostly shut in by steep hills, which, however, do not prevent it from having a water-front on the muddy Cauca of a mile or so. This is the Plain of Vijes, where our story had its beginning, and where it is soon to reach its end.

A steep descent brought me to the small village of mud and thatch where Señores Monzon and Triana were awaiting me, and also dinner at the hospitable board of the former. Señor Miguel Cáldas lives opposite, in far the best house in town. He has had a comb manufactory here, the machinery of which he has just sold to some gentlemen in Cerrito, opposite here, in the eastern Banda. Combs ought to be a profitable manufacture where horns bear only a nominal price; but no factories can flourish here till there are more necessities and fewer holidays. The combs were carelessly made, and the utmost a Caucan establishment can aim at now is to supply the local demand, which is chiefly for side-combs, and perhaps a few dressing-combs. They are by no means so important an ornament as at the North.

Minas should be translated deposits rather than mines. The works of Señor Caicedo, under the directions of Señor Monzon, are rather explorations than mines. There are two veins opened in half a mile of the Plaza, and a mill constructing for grinding and amalgamation. It does not look to me as if it would work. There are some gold-washers here—a queer race. They have a chief who is paid for doing nothing but to manage them and keep them at work. They wash in an ox-horn flattened out. It requires a great deal of skill to separate microscopic particles of gold from the heavy ferruginous sand, and bring it to sight, when it is said *pintarse*—to paint itself. Their operations here do not pay. All the hope of Vijes is in the quartz, which, I should judge, might be valuable when properly wrought.

Señor Cáldas is a highly intelligent man, but perhaps the most violent Conservador I have met with; and not without reason. At the last election he was accused of *treason*, and a gang, I might say, of soldiers were sent down to arrest him, and he was dragged off to Cali. The only reason why he has not committed treason was for the want of any chance to succeed. The idea was simply absurd.

I have reserved till now the mention of a sight that met my eyes frequently between Buga and Palmira. I saw many fields that had once been fenced, of which the fence was destroyed. I think I have known a mile, I might say miles together, destroyed. They tell me that a thousand men have been employed in this work of devastation at once. I applied to the authorities for an explanation of the matter, but for a long time received none, but then received too much. I never was able to read it all.

"No man can dispute or explain away," says Señor Cáldas, "the chief facts. Your own eyes, Señor, have seen the devastation of once flourishing properties; but that is little. The men who did it called themselves Perreristas. Perrero means a dog-whip, the heaviest whip known here, with handle of guayacan and lash of raw-hide. The owners of these fields were whipped with them whenever they caught them. Many suffered this ignominy. Many left their property to ruin, and lived in the large towns in poverty and want, and not even then in safety. Houses, too, were damaged, as the Señor has also seen. Women were violated. And all this was done by the secret orders of President López and his more infamous successor Obando."

"I can not deny the crimes," replies Triana; "but there are extenuating circumstances that you do not mention; and as to their origin, I can not agree with you in attributing them to even the gobernadores, and still less to the President. There has always been a ferocity in the politics on this side of the Quindio. More blood has been shed in this valley than in all the rest of the republic. Pasto has always been an active or dormant volcano. The property of this central part of the valley has been all in the hands of rich holders of slaves and mines in the Chocó. They have had no sympathy with the poor. They have been the owners of a large part of the inhabitants of this valley also, till the law made them loose their grasp on the 1st of January, 1852."

"But what has the liberation of slaves in 1852 to do with this matter of 1849 and '50?"

"The liberation, little; the anticipation of a premature liberation, much. Even in Bogotá, never had there been such political fury as characterized the period after the presidential election of 1849, when the excitement ought to have become quiet. The press, the pulpit, and the Jesuits were all busy. Schoolboys formed political societies; young ladies, at their windows, frowned on gentlemen whose politics they did not like, and even women of mature age joined in societies for the extermination of democracy as an enemy to religion. Such were the societies of the Boy-God—Nino Dios. All this was before the López administration had done good or evil."

"Were these schoolboys all Conservadores? Was there no Sociedad Democratica, no Escuela Republicana?"

"There must be defense where there is attack. The administration must free itself of its most dangerous enemies, the Jesuits, and how? Congress was in session, but, before any law relative to them could have passed both houses, even had the Senado been willing to support the administration, their machinations would have broken out into a rebellion from Cúcuta to Túquerres; so, while the 'Gaceta Oficial' was preparing, as usual, the daring decree in the 'Gaceta Oficial Extra' of 18th May, 1851, was printed elsewhere, and suddenly the whole fraternity were put on the march at a day's warning, and with no opportunity to spring their mine."

"But what has all this to do with the Cauca?"

"Simply that here Conservadores and oppressors were the same, and that their fury prompted to deeds that provoked the oppressed beyond endurance. I quote Samper's 'Apuntamientos,' page 533: 'The oligarchy denied to the commonalty the unoccupied land, denied them wood, and the fields and waters that they could use, and must have in order to live. They imprisoned them for debt; they insulted them with a contempt that concealed the fear they had of them; they vilified them in speeches, and slandered them by the press; they denied the dependent man his rights, whipped and martyrized him if he were slave, despised him if he were free, oppressed him with monopolies, brutified him with superstition, and charged on him as a crime the popular victory of the 7th of March.'"

"Gammon. The fact was that the land and many of the inhabitants were owned by the rich, but the lower classes had full opportunities to buy their liberty and land. They did not choose to. To do this they must be industrious and economical, two things they hated. They heard that it was preached in Bogotá that 'property is robbery;' and here is the explanation of the whole. These poor people were instigated to carry out this new gospel and bring on the millennium of barbarism."

"And López directed these outrages?"

"That I most seriously believe, but I do not expect to convince you. I fully believe that two sets of directions were sent to Cali to our Gobernador Mercado, one to publish and another to act by: one to suppress outrage, and the other to encourage it. But I do know, and you can not deny, that Antonio Mateus, then jefe político of the canton de Palmira, and at this accursed moment Gobernador of Cauca—"

"By the free vote of a majority of the citizens of the province."

"Ay, if you will have it so. Do you doubt that he himself, while jefe político, headed bands of perreristas? Do you doubt that he stood looking on while twelve of his bandits in succession outraged a respectable lady in open day in the Plaza of Candelaria?"

"I can not justify any wrong, however much provoked, nor am I going to say that I think Mateus an honest man; but how can I tell what to believe when Conservador malice spares not even the dead? Have you seen the poetry on the death of Carlos Gómez, gobernador of Cauca? While his poor widow is overwhelmed with her affliction, the Conservadores are singing,

"'Earth has one bandit less,
And hell one devil more.'"

"Well, if it was not his complicity, it was at least his inefficiency that brought all this ruin on so many haciendas, and impoverished the provincia he was sent to govern. Samper himself admits as much while defending the López administration as best he may. He says, 'Governor Mercado has been to Governor Gómez as Buenaventura was to Cauca, as small faults are to crime.' And when the mob assassinated Pinto and Morales in Cartago, on 19th June, 1851, the very best that could be said of the gobernador would be that he was near the spot, and took no part either in killing or saving them; and the appointment of Mateus by Obando as governor of Cauca, even had he been innocent, was an outrage, since so many regarded him as a monster. He first appointed Wenceslao Caravajal, a Liberal, it is true, but a fair man. Did the Conservadores oppose his plans?"

"No, they spoke well of him."

"Well, Señor Holton, did not you witness the panic that spread over the province when he was superseded by Mateus?"

"I must say," I replied, "that I regretted that step of Obando's. If he be a good man, even the heads of government judge him ill. I asked a member of the cabinet the reason of this appointment, and he told me it was Obando's own act, opposed strongly by all the cabinet, but persisted in with such earnestness because Mateus had done Obando some personal service, that finally they yielded out of respect to the President. I regard it as the worst act, perhaps the only bad act of Obando's administration."

"Now, Señor Norteamericano," continued Cáldas, "I have heard you speak of insurrection as in all cases a crime, and condemn that of 1851. Had you been here then, what advice would you have given these men on the other side of the Cauca when their fences were destroyed, their wives and daughters outraged under the very eyes of the officers of the law, and their backs exposed to the infamy of the lash? Would you advise patient submission or rebellion?"

"It was a hard case," I replied; "and I never felt so much like justifying Mosquera, Herran, and Arboleda as at this moment. But did insurrection remedy the evil?"

"No; nor do I know of any remedy but to migrate to a country that has a reliable government. Do you think the United States could be prevailed on to make this region a part of their territory?"

"Such a step would be highly inexpedient for us. Now we have a compact territory, so that when once the Atlantic and Pacific are united by railroad, no power can attack any part of our country so easily as we could defend it. But add to our territory the Sandwich Islands, Panamá, or Cuba, or this valley, and it would be giving bonds to other nations to keep the peace with them. To desire it would be as if a man wished his nose longer than his arm, so that his assailant could pull it when too far off to be struck for his offense. The addition of any island or detached territory would be a curse to us which no imaginary advantages would repay."

"Then I see but one remedy. If this continue, we must kill and dry beef enough for the journey, kill all our other cows for the gallinazos, and all the horses we do not need on our journey, burn all our houses, and leave our fields to the Red Republicans to fight over; for with such a government no man of property can live."

Now I honestly believe that there is at least a shadow of justice in his views. What with Samper's theory, and that "blind faith in principles" that he admires so, and with the utter absence of all desire of property in the masses, the majority is the most dangerous tyrant this nation can have. But I will return to this subject after speaking of some things about here.

One strange peculiarity of Vijes is that the lands here are common property. Some man in times past owned all this plain, and, of the hills adjoining, a quantity unknown to me: from their steepness and aridity it would seem the less the better. When he died it fell to his heirs without division. Some may have sold half their share, and in this way there are more than a hundred owners of this property. There are many cases of this kind in New Granada, and laws to regulate the improvement of the soil and other questions that must arise under this cumbrous co-proprietorship. It will be a very difficult thing to bring about a division. At present no one wishes it, for large parts of this fertile plain are yet untilled, and there are considerable parts of it which I have not, in these many days, explored either on horseback or afoot. It includes one or two detached hills in it. All the rest is level and fertile.

The population of the district is 1160, most of whom live in the village, and nearly all of them near it on the plain.

Once in the memory of man this people attempted a new church. They fairly began it and stopped. The Cura, I believe, has not yet given up all hope of getting them at work on it again, but I see little prospect of it. He is the best preacher

I have heard in New Granada, where preaching is so rare, and preaching talent still rarer. At the time I heard him he was holding a protracted meeting, as we should say, that is, preaching every evening for more than a week, preparatory to the separation of Church and State. If it makes every priest work as hard as he did, the new arrangement will keep them from eating so much of the bread of idleness.

Perhaps earlier it would have kept him from other evils also, for they say that in his leisure he got so attached to a damsel here that his conduct became scandalous for even a priest. Finally, the authorities went to the parents of the *Curita*, as they called her, coining a feminine diminutive from cura, and told them that the girl could have employment as a servant in the beateria of Cali, and if she would not take up with that she should have a place in prison as a vagabond. So much care for the morals of a priest I have nowhere else seen, nor do I see the use in it, for they tell me that it would be necessary to send off six or eight girls more before they could get his morals up to the standard of decency. I ventured to joke his profession on account of this notorious weakness. He did not deny the impeachment, but only replied, "Somos hombres"—"we are men."

Here I met with quite a familiar tropical plant for the first time, Curcus purgans, called friar's cathartic—purga de fraile. I suspect its spread over the globe as a weed has been aided by its convenience as a purgative without any other forethought than to drop a seed into the ground. I met with another interesting natural production here. I believe it was a veritable equis, perhaps the most venomous snake we have. He was nearly three feet long, and, as I was without weapon or boots, I let him alone. I think there can be little danger of a bite through a boot even of the thinnest leather. The softness of leather would be worse than thinness, as I think two thicknesses of stiff buckram would be almost a perfect protection.

There is a hermit living in the hills near here. He is said to be over eighty, though he is quite smart and active. Old people are not numerous in New Granada. I have seen very few indeed; and the revered class of genuine hermits I thought had died out in past centuries; but, finding so much of past centuries living about me, I resolved to see the "venerable man" with my own eyes.

In the simplicity of my heart, I chose the sacred hours of the Sabbath for this pious pilgrimage, and was soon following up the north branch of the brook of Vijes, among the ledges from which it comes. How far I went I can not say. The path had become a little dimmer, but showed no disposition to die out or bifurcate, so I went on. Just as I was on the point of giving up, I saw a platanal, put, one would think, at the upper limit of the plantain. Still I saw no house, and went on; upward, if not heavenward, was my way, till I turned a point of rock and came in sight of the hut.

Three furious dogs came instantly bounding out at me. I confess I was surprised, for when one visits a hermit, he does not, as ever I heard, go armed against the hermit's dogs. Next came the hermit's boy running out after the dogs, and calling to them to come back. So I got safe to the house, where I found not only the hermit, but the hermit's woman and the hermit's family. I must say that in all this my feelings underwent something of a revulsion. A hermit ought to live in a cave, or, if there be none, at least in a hut constructed of the leafy boughs of trees; but here was a mud cottage, as dirty as any other, and just like the poorest on the plain below. It faced, indeed, a little brook that ran down the hill, and at a convenient distance was a pretty miniature cascade, a rill that fell into it.

I looked at the family, counted them, and estimated the mixture of blood in their veins. There was a daughter and two sons. The two oldest might be his, but the younger seemed to have met with some accident that threw a greater proportion of African blood into his veins. The hermit's woman was about forty, half his own age. She had been engaged in weaving a ruana. The loom was a square frame, of the width and half the length of a ruana, say three feet wide and two feet high. Threads of warp had been wound round and round it, as on a reel, the color being changed so as to produce the requisite stripes. The woof had been simply inserted by sheer industry, without any apparatus to separate the threads of the warp, and, of course, without a proper shuttle. When the web is thus completed, it is an endless piece, and if sewed up at one side would make a seamless sack. Instead of this, it is cut open, and an opening cut in the centre; it is bound at the "raw edges," and becomes a ruana.

I solicitously assured the family that I had breakfasted, had taken chocolate, that I needed nothing more. All would not do. Even a Granadino, after a long walk like this, could "repeat." The chocolate was brought me, with that abominable cheese already crumbed into it with the matron's own fingers. I resolved to make an effort, and I did. One thing made a greater effort necessary. I do not wish to make a hero of myself in swallowing a single cup of cheese and chocolate, but I will tell you just how it was. Right in front of the cottage, where I sat on the poyo by the door (for I did not go in), was a pole covered with strings of beef that had just begun to dry. I asked the hermit why his beef looked so black, and particularly why, at this altitude, it smelt so strong. He told me that the cow had been killed by falling from a precipice. The darkness of the flesh, he assured me, was in consequence of the blood in it, which also increased the tendency to putrefaction, and aggravated the circumstance of his not having found the animal immediately after the accident. So I fished out the cheese with my spoon, and ate it, thankful that it was not beef, and sipped my chocolate, asking no questions for conscience' sake.

The old man had been a lego, layman, or servant at the Franciscan convent at Cali. When lime was wanting to build their beautiful church, he came out to Vijes and burned lime for them till the edifice was completed, "In consideration of which services," says a document he showed me, already some twenty-five years old, "he shall have the privilege of being buried as a Franciscan monk when he dies." And now I am fully resigned that eremitism die with him from off the face of the earth before I see any thing more of it.

I made a much more pleasant excursion to Espinal in the next nook below Vijes. About a mile from the town I began to climb the spur that bounds this plain on the north. I had a beautiful view at the top, and then descended to a long, narrow plain, pinched in between the mountain and the river. Then came another hill, from the top of which I could look down on the plain of Espinal. I found afterward that at this stage of water it is easier to get past the bases of these hills on the banks of the Cauca, by which course, on my return, I saved my horse much severe climbing. After reaching the plain, I passed a plantation of guadua; a profitable investment of money, and a good use of that rare characteristic here, forethought. Never before have I met with this grass—here a necessary of life—except growing spontaneously.

Espinal and Vijes may have been alike in their origin. All the difference between them may depend on the entailment of Espinal, which kept it unpopulated, and the property of a single heir, while undivided fractions of the Vijes land gave rise to a village, filled with heirs of the original proprietor, and assignees of those heirs, and heirs of those assignees, and so on.

I had intended to strike into the Cáldas Cordillera here, to join some friends that were gold-hunting there, but the family at Espinal assured me that their provisions were exhausted, and that they must return to-night, so I awaited them.

Espinal has a splendid cañaveral, or cane-field, that has been in good bearing for some twenty years, costing them nothing but the fencing the while. They were meditating a water-mill for the cane. In examining the stream, I fell in with an interesting vine, Aristolochia reticulata. The flower is small; the fruit of the size of a medium cucumber, but when ripe it dehisces into an elegant basket six inches in diameter. Another splendid species, A. ringens, called saragoza, which I found at Cartago and La Ribera, has a much larger flower. The history of a single flower shows how the botanist has occasionally to fight with circumstances. I picked the only flower I could find or had ever seen—a superb affair—on Saturday P.M., at Ribera. On Tuesday night I lost the flower at Chorro, two days from settlements. On Wednesday I threw away the leaves at Las Playas. On Monday morning I found the flower at El Chorro, and brought it home. On Tuesday I secured new leaves. During the week the ants stole the flower, and, as I could not get another, I again threw away the leaves.

The history of a shell will illustrate also the chances a specimen may run. I brought the shell in question to Ribera from beyond El Chorro. The ants run away with it. After I left, it was found and sent after me to La Paila. I left it there, and it was sent to me in Cartago. There, in my hurry, it was left again. On my third night in the Quindiò the mailman overtook me. Carefully drawing a small packet from his carriel (pocket slung by a belt), he unrolled it, and behold, that same shell!

The difficulties I have had in hanging my hammock in the house are well illustrated by the mode of doing it at Espinal. The beams were too close to the ceiling to permit the rope being thrown over. No ladder was to be had. I placed the table under a beam, set an arm-chair on the table, and a second arm-chair on the *arms* of the first, and then, standing on the arms of the second, I accomplished my purpose. To climb in, I put the table under the hammock, and a chair on the table.

One more expedition remains for me. It is to Bolivia, the hacienda of Señor Cáldas, to see his family, and to examine the approaches to the Pacific. I had seen a drove of cattle go up the brook toward the lime-kiln. I was told they were going to Panamá to feed the laborers on the railroad. A gentleman offered himself as a guide, and we started one day on the same route. The wheel-road (for there was once a lime-cart at Vijes) soon changed to a bridle-road, and that to a path, and that to a goat-track, and still our course was upward on the rocky slope of a hill. A forest crowned the summit, but seemed not to venture far down the side. Fire must once have destroyed the lower and drier woods: it was probably kindled to secure pasturage.

Thus we toiled up for an hour or two. Then we stopped to drink at the stream. Here I noticed a knoll over the right bank of the brook, which we had been following up, though always far above it, and on the hillside on the left bank. There were cattle on that knoll, and I wondered how they got up there. I asked my guide, and he said, "We shall see;" so we climbed the knoll, for there lay our road. We did not ride up, for that would have been cruel, had it been possible even. On its top we saw another knoll like it, and nearly as high above it. This must be ascended in the same way; and then we mounted, and entered the woods.

The woods were damp, and the road wet. Interesting trees overhung our path. Among the most interesting of these were a Lecythis, with dark crimson flowers, and for a fruit a five-celled woody *box* of more than two inches diameter. It was a small tree. A magnificent Melastomate tree, with large roseate flowers, and a Gesneriate herb, with bright scarlet spots on the under sides of the leaves, are also found here. We at length came out on the clear land—llano—of the Pacific slope, and in sight of Bolivia, and at nearly the same altitude. To reach it we had to descend nearly a mile, cross a ravine, and reascend.

Señor Cáldas is constructing a new road from his house through the woods, by which much of the steepness and distance can be avoided, as well as this last ascent and descent. He took me to see it. The first day I changed a considerable piece of the road through the woods, escaping a cruel steep, such as all men who have ever driven a carriage instinctively dread. The next day we went over his summit, and I found that all this way we had much lower ground on the right of us, so on the third day we changed this also. We then reviewed the whole through the woods, and I had the satisfaction of seeing a route practicable to carriages traced from his house to within sight of the Cauca. But here I gave up. Vijes lay at our feet at an angle of depression as steep as the roof of a house. To build a carriage-road down would require the resources of a Napoleon; a mule-path was all he had hoped.

I was exceedingly pleased with La Señora de Cáldas and the children, two pretty girls, the eldest of whom had red cheeks and intelligent eyes. She is by far the prettiest child I have seen in South America, if not, in fact, the only really pretty child of native origin. Like others here, however, she was not as affectionate as are our children. They are unused to any other caresses than permission to kiss a parent's hand, the only kissing I have seen here.

I met here also Señora Susana Pinzon de Várgas, and her sister, the fair Manuela Pinzon. They had come up to the cold for the benefit of Susana's babe. I can not conceive how any one can want so cold weather, for I suffered severely here. I was without bayeton, hammock, or night-flannel. I slept on the poyo of the sala with such little covering and bedding as the family could spare. This kept me from dying, although the thermometer was at 56°, and the house had never had a fire in it. Manuela and another young lady slept in a sort of separate house; Susana, being a matron, or for the convenience of the babe, slept in the family-room. Manuela complained also of sleeping cold. I suggested that she and her companion sleep within the same cover. She thought two persons could not learn to sleep in this way, and was surprised to hear that people at the North did not do themselves up into separate *cocoons* to sleep.

Here is the coldest place where I have seen plantains grow. Potatoes, of course, grow finely. At the table of Señor Cáldas I tried, for the first time in my life, an Aroid corm or "root," which may be Arum esculentum, a native of Africa. It is here called rascadera, because, I imagine, its acrid juice irritates the skin. In the Sandwich Islands it is the staff of life, and called taro; in Louisiana the negroes eat it under the name of potaño (Sp.), tannier (Fr.). I found it quite palatable. Señor Cáldas is quite a gardener, but a large part of his garden is devoted to pinks. His coffee looked the best of any I have seen, and must differ greatly in flavor from that of the plains below.

The acequia that irrigates his garden and supplies his kitchen supplies a bath too. This is a deep square vat in the open garden, simply dug in the ground and nothing more. The idea of an immersion at this temperature was enough to make me shiver. He once attempted to drown an ant-hill in his garden by means of this acequia. It swallowed all the stream readily, but produced no results. The laborers went on shearing pieces from leaves as before. They were not to be drowned. What became of the water? This mystery was solved by seeing, a quarter of a mile down the hill, all the water of the acequia gush out of the ground at a drain his enemies had prepared for any such contingency. He then set two peons to dig for the mother-ant, a misshapen being more than two inches long, incapable of locomotion, whose whole faculties seem concentrated in the work of reproduction. They dug for two days, and probably killed her unawares, for after they gave up the ants were effectually subdued.

In the garden I saw one of those curious Indian graves called a guaca. They are worthy of a more complete investigation than I have been able to give them, for they differ from every thing I have seen or heard of. Some are simple square pits excavated in the ground, covered over first with logs and then with earth. Others have side excavations in them, and very often small passages running from one to another. Bones and relics are found in them, of course, but I find very few of them in the hands of people here. They are diligently hunted for gold. A man who has a passion for this (and it very naturally becomes a mental infirmity) is called a guaquero.

As the guadua does not grow up here nor yet caña brava, nor chusquea, Señor Cáldas has been perplexed for fencing materials. A Western settler, with axe, maul, and wedges, would soon show him how rails were made, but such things are unknown in New Granada. As a substitute, he has chosen stalks of maize. They are secured erect, somewhat after the manner of picket fence, and answer well. Here alone have I seen strawberries cultivated, but it was not the season for them. The species here, as at Bogotá, is Fragaria vesca, the same as ours.

Señor Cáldas thinks, under peculiar circumstances, the Pacific Ocean is visible from near the house at sunset. I doubt it. We took a long ride in order to get a good view of the valley of this branch of the Dagua. I examined well the ground from where I had explored in my trip up from San Marcos, which spot was fully in sight of here, but far below us. We could see a hill above Juntas, as I was told. I have no doubt remaining that a good carriage-road can be built from the fertile plains of the Cauca to the tide-waters of the Pacific, so that the teamster may drink of the muddy Cauca in the morning, and at night taste the brackish waters of the Pacific.

Can a railroad be put here? As a physical question of grades and curves, I answer, I have little doubt of it. Will it pay? That is a serious question. I answer, not at once; and never while the government is what it is. That the time will come when the Cauca will be connected with the Pacific, and the Magdalena by railroad, I strongly hope; but there are great difficulties in the way.

The most formidable physical difficulty is in the unhealthy nature of the Pacific coast. It is a net-work of muddy creeks and islands, as bad, perhaps, as the west coast of Africa. If a town could be located west of it all, it might be healthy, and from such a point cultivation might spread to the east. Bad as

Buenaventura is, its business must increase with the growth of Panamá, Oregon, and California. Could the Cauca have peace, and I now hope it will, the productions and trade must also be stimulated from this source. Here I stand, not three days from Panamá, and the valley behind me has held a population equal to all that New Granada now has. Even west of me are fertile and healthy lands not occupied. The population of the whole canton that lies on the Pacific is 3338. The belt of malaria must be broken—it *shall* be.

But there is a moral difficulty. This people love to dance, but they hate to work. How will you induce them? With gold? The line of the road may run through the richest gold deposit of the world. How can you *hire* cutting and filling done where the earth contains an ounce to the bushel? Hunger can not urge them, nor cold, nor nakedness; and among the rights most sedulously guarded by the theories of the ultra-republican is the right to be a vagabond. These theorists are in favor of exempting the improvident and indolent from all burdens. He buys no land, and often pays no rent. He votes, and pays no taxes. The nation is bent on repealing, as soon as they are able, every tax that now yields any thing. They have abolished tithes, of which it cost four fifths to collect the remainder. Excise on spirits and tobacco have gone. Salt and stamps must go. The vagabond gives no notes and eschews law, so he pays no stamp-tax. He must eat salt, and here he pays a tax of a cent or two a year. The plan for the future is to assess all taxes on incomes that exceed a certain amount. This will let him clear. A poll-tax is a barbarism. So little does he use of foreign goods, that, even while the impost system remains, almost nothing is exacted from him under it. The gross revenue of the nation is less than half a dollar a head, and this by loading the wealth of the nation as heavily as it can bear, while unthrift and indolence go scot free.

Again, there is no stability in the government. I do not now speak of revolutions, for the last two were unsuccessful, and I think we have seen the last of them; but the *theory* of their government is against stability. Whether there ever was a worse Constitution than the present I know not. Its adoption was an infamous lie of the Obando administration, to which the nation assented. The Liberal Congress of 1851 made a Constitution which the Congress of 1853 had a right to adopt or reject. It did neither: it altered it till it lost its identity, then voted that it was the same, and adopted it. Then the nation shouted for joy, and cried, "At last the true republic has come!"

The executive is shorn of its powers. Both houses are chosen on the same ticket, and their deliberating in two chambers is a farce, for the absolute majority of the whole Congress voting in joint meeting carries every point against the will, it may be, of all the Senate, and in spite of any executive veto.

And changes the most stupendous, such as it would take twenty years to bring about in England, are the work of a single week, perhaps. In England, neither the size, shape, nor number of the counties has changed within a century. If there has been a year without a variation of the provinces of New Granada, I am not aware of it. It would be harder to abolish the troy pound in England than to overthrow twice the whole metrical system of New Granada.

What will be the end of these things? I conjecture bankruptcy. The expenditures are double the revenue; but they are not to be so when their plans are *perfected!* I see no remedy but to plunge back into the barbarian darkness of the United States, or even beyond them. But to restore poll-taxes, imprisonment for debt, passports, and vagrancy laws, ordaining that the labor of man shall build roads, bridges, school-houses, ay, and prisons too, even though he have no wish to travel, learn, nor yet to be imprisoned, would be enough to make a theorist like Samper rave; and I fear it will not be done till they have suffered greater calamities than they have felt since the Spaniard left their shores.

Such conclusions grieve me, for I love the Granadan race. These pages testify to an uninterrupted series of kind acts of them toward me—kindness that I can never repay. I can hardly mention a single reasonable request of mine neglected—not one refused. Even many unreasonable ones, as I afterward knew them to be, were granted, often at an inconvenience that I greatly regretted. The authorities, too, have been as kind as private individuals. All sorts of documents have been furnished me, even by offices that had to send to Bogotá to replace those spared me. Nothing has been withholden me that a traveler could ask.

I have not made them the returns I would have wished. I would have gladly pointed them more directly to a purer religion that can remedy the evils they are struggling with; but while I could profess to be a communicant of a Protestant church, circumstances rendered it unadvisable to do more. And now, in enlisting the sympathies of our own people, I am doing what I can.

To tell the truth of them, I have been obliged to speak of their faults and deficiencies. But, after all, I here boldly declare the Granadinos a highly moral people. I speak not of the Scotch and English standard of morality; that is not fair. They are of a religion highly adverse in its institutions to the laws of chastity, and in this they must be compared with Catholic countries. Now grant that the proportion of illegitimate births be 33 per cent., and I think it must be less, then it is the same as that of Paris. In Brussels it is 35 per cent.; in Munich, 48; in Vienna, 51; and, I believe, in sacred Rome, far worse. Suppose, then, that New Granada is as defective as Paris, the most moral of these cities. You must recollect that, when Paris was yet a great city, unmarried priests, corrupt monks, and unrestrained civil and military officers were forming a new code of decency and morality for simple, half-naked Indian converts and subjects. What marvel if it be as loose as that of Paris?

Again, as to the crimes against life, I suppose, in all the nation, there are not a fifth as many murders as in New York city alone! Probably a single year in California has witnessed as many murders as have been perpetrated in New Granada, among two millions and a quarter of all races, since it has had its place among nations. I have more than once had to blush for the ruffianism of the scum of our nation, like which nothing can be found in the very worst population of New Granada. But again to figures. I can not estimate the murders in New Granada at more than 3 per million per annum. The *commitments* for murder in England are 4 per million; in Belgium, 18; Ireland, 19; Sardinia, 20; France, 34; Austria, 36; Lombardy, 46; Tuscany, 56; Bavaria, 68; Sicily, 90; the dominion of the Pope, 113; and Naples, 174.

Say I not well, then, that the Granadinos deserve a high place among the nations of the earth in point of moral character? And we, especially, owe them our respect and esteem. The conduct of the government at Bogotá in relation to our Isthmus transit has always been more than generous—it has been noble; and to us they look for examples of government—to us for their closest allies in trade. And, lastly, we two, of all the nations of the earth, are without any established church, granting equal rights to all men of all creeds. Long may we remain so, but not long alone. VIVA, PUES, VIVA LA NUEVA GRANADA!

CHAPTER XXXIV.

SUPPLEMENTARY.

Date of Crucifixion.—Lent.—The purple Curtain.—Blessing Palm-leaves.—Ass in Church.—Pasos.—Nazarenos.—La Reseña.—White Curtain rent.—A speaking Trumpet.—Lamentations.—Monumentos.—Good Friday.—Great Curtain Rent on Saturday.—Paschal Sunday.—Resurrection Scene.—*Cui Bono?*—A Revolution possible.—A Murder.—Bochinche of Good Friday.—Coup d'etat.—Scenes at the Palace.—Constitution abolished.—Invasion of Honda and Mesa.—American Legation stormed.—Battle of Cipaquirá.—Affairs of the Cauca.—Surprise at Guaduas.—Scaling Tequendama with Cannon.—Battle of Boza.—Storming of Bogotá.—Fall of Melo.—The next President.

MY task is done. It has not been as well done as I wish, but it is done faithfully and conscientiously. I have told you all I have seen with a patience and a faithful minuteness, only restrained by the fear of being tedious beyond endurance. I have reserved for this supplementary chapter only events on and since Palm Sunday, April 9th, 1854, including chiefly Holy Week at Bogotá, and the Revolution of 1854.

The Jews began their year with the first appearance of the new moon after the vernal equinox. The 14th day of the year (at full moon, of course) was the Passover. Our Savior was crucified on the 15th day of their year, on the day after the full moon. All this is known, and not left to conjecture, as is the anniversary of Christ's birth, which was most probably in the warmer part of the year, when shepherds spent the night in the open air.

The Romish and English Churches ordain the annual celebration of the death of Christ. They call the Friday nearest the Passover Holy Friday or Good Friday, and make it the anniversary of the Crucifixion.

A period beginning forty-four days before is Lent—Cuaresma. It begins on Wednesday, and that day is called Ash Wednesday, because priests put ashes on the foreheads of as many as apply, which some contrive to keep on for several days. Lent contains forty fasting days, and every Friday and the last Thursday are rigid fasts. No marriages are allowed in Lent. Sunday before Good Friday is called Palm Sunday, the week succeeding is called Passion Week, and the Sabbath closing the whole is called the Paschal Sunday. Palm Sunday is adopted as the anniversary of Christ's entry into Jerusalem, in order to make the festival begin and end with a Sunday, as is most convenient for celebrations. From Good Friday, the time of the Ascension of our Lord (40 days) and the Pentecost (50 days) are reckoned. Those days which thus depend on the moon, and vary, therefore, as to month and day, are called *Movable Feasts.*

The splendors of Rome are not to be expected in a city of 40,000, even though it has borne for 300 years the title of City of the Holy Faith—Santa Fé. So poor is the Church here, and so indolent the priesthood, that the most to be expected is caricature and puerile imitation.

Christmas and Corpus Christi are greater days with the Bogotanos—Corpus particularly—than any one of the eight days of Holy Week, which still is, as it ought to be, the greatest festival of the year. All the week before, the busy note of preparation is heard. Images must be taken down, cleaned, repaired, and mustered. So the chief altar of every church is veiled with a large purple curtain, which hangs immovable till rent on Holy Saturday.

The more enlightened here appear ashamed of the performances, and seemed desirous that some of them should escape my notice and my irreverent pen ; and, as there is but one centre of attraction at once, you must know not only what to look for, but where it is. I had nearly lost the principal piece in Palm Sunday for want of due notice, and the family were evidently little pleased that I had got wind of it.

I went to San Francisco at 8. With a condescension that

all here show to strangers, I was permitted to insinuate myself into an immense crowd, and took my stand on one of the lines of benches extending from the front door to the high altar.

On the elevated platform of that altar, in a dense crowd of boys of from 10 to 15 years of age, were several priests, chanting a blessing on some 20 palm-leaves, cut, braided, trimmed, and some of them ornamented with flowers. The crowd thickens, some noise ensues, and the priests have to push violently, but good-humor prevails.

Now an image is descending around one edge of the purple curtain. Preceded by the palm-leaves, it is advancing toward the door. It is on the back of a live ass. I should call it the figure of a young woman, dressed in purple, with long auburn hair (not of Spanish origin) on its shoulders in profuse curls. On the head is a golden glory, with rays diverging in three directions. It has no beard. It rides astride, with a monk on each side to hold it on. An ass-colt, as large as a small calf, follows, so crowded upon by boys that I hardly saw it. Preceded by the palm-leaves, and accompanied by singing monks, the image turned and went out of the mercy door, which opens into a patio of the convent. From there it entered the street, and came to the front door of the church, which was shut. After singing within and without, the door opened, and the image passed up to the sacristía.

I followed. Some stout monks unloaded the ass as they would take off a forked log, pushing the garments aside very irreverently, and lugged the heavy image off up into the camarin, and locked the door.

A stout Philadelphian outside had something thrown at his hat for not taking it off to the procession, but nothing farther was done, and he kept on his hat.

At 4 P.M. I saw another procession. On a stage—anda—was placed a figure of Christ on the Cross, and two female figures, with long hair and rich velvet dresses, but not well got up. They are said to represent the Virgin and the Apostle John. A figure or a group, with the stage that holds it, is called a *paso*. This, which I call paso No. 2, was borne by 14 men. They had black bags on their heads, with holes cut to see out of. The bags are called capirotes, and the wearers Nazarenos. They wore a tunic of glazed black cotton, tied round the waist with a rope of cabuya. The rope passed round and round, making a white belt sometimes six inches wide. On their shoulders they wore pañolones or shawls borrowed of their female friends. A white piece of cotton for a handkerchief, tucked under the girdle, or a monstrous string of beads (never smaller than that seen peeping from beneath the Jesuit's dress on page 193), a cushion on the shoulder, and alpargatas on the feet, complete the equipment of the Nazareno. Each had a crutch in his hand, on which to rest the paso at pauses.

The paso was preceded by boys bearing a cross and ciriales, and by three boys ringing hand-bells. The last wore cucuruchos. These are conical black caps, thirty inches high, covering the face, and with holes for the eyes. After the paso came a band of music, and a disk borne by the alférez, the proud man that had paid for the wax burned in the procession. Two peons bore the candle-box, a sort of hand-barrow painted brown. The gentlemen who made up the procession were headed by the Cura of Las Nieves, Padre Gutiérrez, father to the present gobernador of the province. In the bareheaded crowd, of both sexes and all conditions, that surrounded the procession, I was surprised and sorry to see a respectable American gentleman.

The procession entered several churches, and prayers were said. On its return home to Las Nieves an Ave was said for the founder of the church, "should he still chance to be in Purgatory," after a terrible roasting of near three hundred years.

On Monday, P.M., a much larger procession set out from Las Nieves with three candle-boxes, several bands of music, and eight pasos, viz.:

No. 3. A black cross, with a strip of white cloth on the arms, and flowers at the foot.

No. 4. The Good Shepherd: the Savior, a lamb on his shoulders, its feet tied with a cord, the ends of which were held by two stout angels, in form of women with wings.

No. 5. The Last Supper: Savior and disciples in vestments for mass, looking like an omnibus with thirteen priests inside, one of them drunk. This was John, copied from Da Vinci, with his head inclined as no one holds it in *riding*. It was in very bad taste, and took thirty Nazarenos to carry it.

No. 6. Scourging: hands tied to a pillar thirty inches high; face not indicative of suffering; body naked to the waist, and the back one mass of raw dried flesh. Two Roman soldiers, with noses terribly aquiline, and upraised scourge, not in the attitude of striking. The soldiers are called Judíos—Jews.

No. 7. Savior, richly dressed, fallen under his cross: two soldiers, and a boy with hammer and nails, evidently as light as cork, in a basket on his shoulder.

No. 8. The Nailing to the Cross, it is said: it could not be well seen from any possible position.

No. 2. As yesterday.

No. 9. Dolores: an isosceles triangle of gorgeous cloth, lace, and spangles. Angle at the apex from 30° to 40°. On the triangle is a beautiful head, with flowing hair. On the breast of the figure a silver heart, transfixed with a silver sword.

TUESDAY MORNING.—LA RESEÑA AT THE CATHEDRAL.

This was preceded by the novelty of three priests saying three masses at the same altar—a temporary one in the back of the building—while a grand mass was performing at a temporary altar before the purple curtain of the high altar. Next came music from hired performers in the orchestra on top of the choir, and from the canónigos in the choir.

Part of the chapter slowly advanced toward the altar. Each canónigo wore on his head a hood that would hold a bushel. In addition to their usual robes of white muslin over black, they wore black gowns, open in front, with trains 3 or 4 yards long. Dr. Herran, the head of the Granadan Church, provisor then and archbishop now, was at their head, with an enormous silk banner, 2 yards by 3. It was black, and had a plain red cross in the centre. He ascended the platform, and they stood in a row at the foot of its stairs, on which a clean cloth had been spread.

He waved his banner for a long time, while solemn music came from the orchestra. He managed tolerably well to keep his train extended in all his movements. Twice he folded his banner and rested it against the altar, while he knelt at its foot. As he was waving it for a third time, a thundering crash from the choir started me. It was made by throwing down the hinged seats in the stalls, or by the stamp of the feet of musicians on loose boards. At that instant the canónigos had fallen prostrate on the steps, and all you saw was six gigantic figures, extending from the third step of the altar back some 20 feet. The red cross still waved over them; all else seemed lifeless. Long after, they arose; six train-bearers gathered up their robes, and they retired to the choir.

This was the only performance in the whole week, or that I have ever seen in a Catholic church, that ever made any solemn impression on me. All else was puerile, and, when not painfully unfitting, ridiculous. More music succeeded, and a triplet of masses at that temporary back altar, the only ornamented place in the Cathedral.

Tuesday, P.M., was another procession, much like that of Monday, with seven pasos, viz.:

No. 10. A plain cross, much like No. 3.

No. 11. Child with lamb on his shoulders.

No. 12. Christ with the Doctors. A boy of five standing in a chair; three men.

No. 13. Christ and the Cyrenean. Divine face bruised; rich dress unruffled; Cyrenean scantily dressed, with turban on, not touching the cross; soldier before them blowing a trumpet.

No. 14. Scourging. Two soldiers, one with a spike made of half-inch iron between his *lips*.

No. 15. Crucifixion. Three figures nearly nude: that in the centre nailed to a cross, the others tied. From the wounded side of the centre figure a blue and a white ribbon (blood and water) proceed to two cups in the hands of little angels in the front of the anda. The side figures have a wound on each leg. Two Marys, and a John, who was like a woman, except a chin smooth shaven.

No. 16. Dolores: inferior to No. 9. Two little angels held her hands. Troops, music, and other accompaniments as usual. Cucuruchos worn by little boys of 7 or 8.

On Wednesday, A.M., Reseña repeated at the Cathedral. It was preceded by a new and imposing ceremony. A white curtain was drawn in front of the platform of the high altar, with much space between that and the larger purple one that covers the altar from roof to floor. A protracted mass was celebrating, when suddenly a colossal fire-cracker exploded, and the vail was rent, and displayed a crucified figure of the size of life; then succeeded the Reseña as yesterday.

Wednesday, P.M., was the greatest piece of charlatanry except the ass in church. Accordingly, the church of San Agustin, where it came off, was densely filled. By a politeness in which I find the Agustinians to excel all others, I had a comfortable seat on the platform. A young monk preached on the contumely which Christ suffered. When he spoke of his condemnation, he said, "Listen to his sentence." Thereupon a voice, hidden in the roof, began speaking through a speaking-trumpet the words, "I, Pontius Pilate, Governor of Judea," etc., etc., in Spanish, of course, prolonging his vowels, and pausing every eight or ten syllables for breath; and it was to hear this that the vast crowd were thronging, treading on each other, pushing, steaming, and corrupting the air; but in all the crowd there was, I think, but one person voluntarily pushing or molesting others; except in his neighborhood, all was still and orderly.

After much delay, the pasos for a procession were got through the crowd and mustered in the street. The pasos were,

No. 17. A cross, nearly like No. 3.

No. 18. The Seizure: Judas kissing; a soldier with a pair of blacksmith's tongs entangled in the long hair of the Savior; Malchus on his back, his ear yet whole; a wrathful apostle over him with a machete.

No. 19. The Mockery: one soldier tearing the Savior's hair, another standing behind him with a very knotty club, copied from the Spanish playing-cards.

No. 20. St. Veronica holding by two corners the handkerchief with which she had wiped the Lord's face; three very bad portraits of the sacred face on the handkerchief.

No. 13. With the addition of a smoking-cap to the head of the Cyrenean in place of the turban.

No. 21. Crucifixion: much like 15, except the thieves were absent, and the white and blue ribbons terminated in apothecaries' minim glasses.

No. 22. Dolores: the extreme tail of her dress twisted and curled up. On the very tip stood a funny little angel in black, with a black feather in his cap.

No. 23. A shaving or splinter of the very cross in a custodia, placed in a silver shrine borne by *canónigos*. Three companies of soldiers bore candles in the procession, and General Melo was alférez, and bore the estandarte that signified that he had supplied the wax.

On Wednesday night Lamentations were sung at the Cathedral by the orchestra, and the Tinieblas by the chapter. A row of candles were extinguished one by one during the tinieblas or shadows. Six tall candles at the altar were constructed to go out spontaneously, and those in the choir or orchestra were also extinguished, but there was still burning enough to see a little. The music reminded me of the Æolian harp, and also of the howling of dogs at midnight. It was, on the whole, the most agreeable part of a tedious performance.

About 9 commenced the Miserere. The hired musicians sung this by a single candle, so placed as to illuminate only the book. This music is good, but is, I think, overrated. Zingarelli's Miserere, in our "Mozart Collection," is far superior to it. As many seemed to have gone to see the lights put out as to hear the music. I was very tired before I left.

HOLY THURSDAY.—This is indeed a great day. No wafer can be consecrated at the mass on Good Friday, so at the mass to-day two wafers are consecrated, and the one for to-morrow is kept in great parade, generally at a side altar, tricked out in all manner of finery. It is called a monumento. Every body visits the monumentos. I was at it all day and all the evening, and visited eighteen of them. They took the form of pasteboard edifices, grottoes, staircases, etc. The edifice at Santa Inés had a fine dome on top, and filled the whole end of the church. At night it blazed with 170 candles: it had no images. Many others were really pretty.

The wafer of the Cathedral is kept under a guard of four soldiers, like the corpse of a general. It is placed with great pomp in a silver chest locked with a golden key. The keeping of this key is the highest honor. This year it fell to President Obando. The keeper of the key wears it on his neck by a golden chain, and delivers it up at Friday's mass with great ceremony. On one occasion they say that the key-keeper went to Tunja in the interim, committed a murder, and returned in season to deliver up the key in person. The distance he must have traveled was 211 miles: it is 74 hours travel for the mail! The distance is not exaggerated, but the story may be false.

Up to the consecration in the mass to-day the bells have been in a continual state of excitement, knowing no rest except at night. Now, saving that the Cathedral clock still strikes the hours, all are silent, even to the hand-bells at the altar. In the place of bells are used *matracas*, somewhat like, if not identical with, the watchman's rattle.

In the afternoon occurred at the Cathedral the washing of the feet of twelve poor men by Dr. Herran, but this I did not see for want of due notice.

Another procession set out from La Vera Cruz, one of the chapels in the monastery of San Francisco. Though it had but five pasos, the character of the persons who followed them made it the most interesting procession of the week. The pasos were,

No. 24. A cross, much like No. 3.

No. 25. The Garden: the Lord kneeling among the flowers before a bush of the most splendid terrestrial mistletoe, Loranthus Mutisii, with a little angel in the top of the bush. N.B. Mútis always had the most beautiful species in the genus named after him. I ached to get hold of these scarlet flowers, six inches long, for I had then never found more of that species than a single mangled flower in the street.

No. 26. Bearing the Cross: single figure, half size.

No. 27. Christ at the Pillar: he has turned his back to it, his hands still being tied to it. It is, as always, thirty inches high. Peter is kneeling before his Lord.

No. 28. The Sentence: Savior; Pilate; two soldiers; table; modern writing implements; sentence, written on paper in Spanish; water-pitcher.

Here followed the merchants, with candles and music preceding their image of the Savior (No. 29), *not* made up of money-bags, with small gold coins for eyes.

Next, the students of the Colegio of Santo Tomas, in barretes —clerical caps—gowns, and the broad white collar of their school. Following them was (No. 30) their heavy, beautiful bronze crucifix.

Lastly and chiefly came the LADIES OF BOGOTÁ, in black hair, eyes ditto, and black lace veils on their heads, preceding their paso (No. 31), the Virgin. I never had imagined that there was so much beauty in Bogotá.

The military closed the procession.

Good Friday is a commemoration of the most memorable day in the history of our globe—the *Fourth of July* of the universe; but probably we shall never be certain of the precise day of the year on which it occurred, as we do not certainly know the exact year. Even if we knew it, ought human additions be made to divine ordinances for celebrating the great event? I expected for to-day solemn appeals to the senses; that, in the Cathedral, dirges, darkness, and dumb show should prevail "from the sixth to the ninth hour." Unfortunately, the Church differs from me; "so much the worse for the Church."

The morning mass has three attractions: first, the officiating priest and his two assistants prostrate themselves at the altar, and lie there covered up with a purple cloth for some time; secondly, the adoration of the Cross, which is laid before the altar on a cushion, with a money-dish at its side. After the priests, many of the most respectable citizens go up two and two, kneel three times, kiss the cross, put money in the dish, and retire. Thirdly, the taking the wafer from the monumento. President Obando did not appear this morning, and the key was on the neck of the dean of the chapter. The mass is earlier than usual, with the consecration and other parts omitted, and no extra mass is allowed this day.

It was expected by some that the Cathedral services would include a series of sermons through the three hours of agony, but, since the re-expulsion of the Jesuits, it is difficult to find preachers enough. I found the *property-men*, as a theatre-goer would call them, hard at work. When they were through, and the vast edifice moderately full, the canónigo Saavedra, a bitter enemy of the late lamented Archbishop Mosquera, began a sermon, which I could make nothing of on account of distance and noise. Twice he sharply rebuked the crowd, which at length became so dense as to fix every component of it immovably.

The whole stage was covered, mostly with boys. Two ladders projected above the level of their heads, and also the cucuruchos of various boys. As it was nearly a yard from "the pivot of the skull" to the top of the cucurucho, its point exaggerated the motions of the unseen head of the wearer in a very ludicrous manner.

At length the two ladders were applied to a cross planted in the platform, having on it a figure slightly under size. Two priests ascended: one passed a cloth round the body, the other drew out the nails. They lowered the body, carried it to the feet of an image of the Virgin, and then laid it in a splendid sarcophagus, all silver and tortoise-shell, of the shape and size of a bathing-tub, and filled with costly pillows. The sermon was done, and the vast Cathedral relieved of its crowd. I escaped to open air, and placed myself in wait for the procession in the Calle Real.

Paso 32 was a simple cross, much like No. 3.

No. 33 was a representation of the holy winding-sheet, which retains the figure of a human body on it, and, strangely enough, is yet in existence! The representation was stretched on a frame like a screen. The figure was visible on both sides, and was too naked to be decent, and too dirty to be ornamental.

No. 34. St. John the Evangelist.

No. 35. Mary Magdalene.

No. 36. The Sarcophagus, with Joseph of Arimathea and Nicodemus at the head and foot. It was followed by the large black flag, with crimson cross, used in the Reseña.

No. 37. Our Lady of the Solitude, by far the most costly image in Bogotá. The figures on the dress are said to be wrought in real diamonds and other precious stones. Six little angels in black lace surrounded the principal figure.

These all went to La Vera Cruz, where the sarcophagus was taken from the anda and deposited there. They started on their return, when the programme was broken in upon by the first bochinche—riot—which was a precursor of scenes yet to follow, and in connection with which it will be described. Some think that there was a design to despoil Soledad of her jewels in the melee. I do not believe it. She and all the rest escaped safe to the Cathedral, except Joseph of Arimathea and Nicodemus, who took refuge in San Francisco.

I omit for the present the incongruous events of the afternoon. The Lamentations were to be succeeded by a sermon from a Dominican friar, who had the reputation of being long-winded. I went, and found the front door of the Cathedral closed for fear of the mob. Unfortunately, I found the mercy-door open, and entered very late, but soon enough. The sermon commenced at nine. The subject was "the Sorrows of Our Lady of the Solitude after the death of Christ." I had secured a seat facing the pulpit. The odor of unwashed skins, or, perhaps, of ill-conditioned ulcers, made it almost untenable; and at last, finding that the fleas had converted the floor where the women sat into a mart of human blood, and unwilling myself to be a martyr to them, I went home.

Gloria Mass was Saturday, at 8 A.M. Numerous ceremonies of annual occurrence were performed. Fire was struck with flint and steel, and the huge Paschal candle, with five lumps of incense sticking to it, was lighted. Holy oil and holy water were consecrated. The priests lay down again as yesterday, and were covered up a long while. They then went to the sacristía, and came back in white vestments.

As the mass proceeded the purple veil was torn asunder, and, an instant after, the huge fire-cracker went off again, having hung fire a little; the hand-bell at the altar broke loose, and rang as if it would never stop; the bells of all sizes, whole and cracked, from this tower and all others, joined in; and well did they make amends for two days' silence. Now the people began to disperse; soon the mass closed, and I went home, glad that there were no more ceremonies to be observed to-day.

Paschal Sunday.—Long before light I was in the streets, prompted by a spirit of diligence rather than of curiosity. Already at Santo Domingo were women kneeling before the door, which was not to be opened for an hour. It had rained in the night, and the morning air was damp and raw. At Vera Cruz I found lights within, the doors barred, and a large crowd about them. At 4 they were opened.

At the altar was a splendid scene. There was the tortoise-shell crib, with a figure standing in it much larger than the one put in on Friday. It had a red flag in the left hand, and the right pointed upward. At each side was a figure of a soldier, tumbled back and propped up, but not in the attitude of a falling man. I heard mass, went home, and to bed again.

At 8 I was again in the street, when a Virgin (paso 38) went to meet the figure in the sarcophagus (No. 39). A man went before firing rocket-crackers—cohetes—and a large silver double cross—cruz alta—which had opened every procession muffled, was now disclosed. The streets were fuller than ever. I thought it useless to try to enter the Cathedral, but made the attempt. To my surprise, I found little difficulty, thanks to the innate politeness of the meanest Granadino. I even succeeded in reaching my favorite post on top of the choir in front of the orchestra. Here I faithfully sat the great mass out, but saw nothing particularly interesting to record.

On leaving, I asked a priest where I could hear a sermon. He told me he thought none would be preached that day in all Bogotá. I learned afterward that there would be one in the convent of Santo Domingo at night. I went, and found a good seat. From this I was driven by the odor of my next neighbor. I could find no other, would not stand, and came away. Thus ended my Holy Week.

As to the effects on my own mind, the most striking is utter fatigue and disappointment. There were a few good faces in the figures; a very few were quite good; but true attitudes, that did not set the laws of gravity and the principles of anatomy at defiance, were rare indeed; and had there been even a masterpiece of art, it would quite probably have escaped notice. So to degrade sacred subjects must have a terrible effect on those who make a trade of it.

But, suppose all to be arranged in the highest style of art, would it promote the cause of piety of heart? I think not. There are some really good *crucifixions;* they impress the beholder, but they lose their force in time, and only blunt the feelings to the more ordinary impressions from meditation. As to the merit of these performances, I have on my side the judgment of all the enlightened Granadinos. There is a general desire among them to forbid by law all religious processions in the streets. But as to the theological question of the permission of such appeals to the senses, I should differ from them; but I can not here discuss the question.

I return now to Friday night and its bochinche. Nobody knew its origin. It was near the bridge, convent, and barracks of San Francisco, but south of them all. It may well have been an insult offered in a dining-saloon to an officer by some hot-headed theorist schoolboy, or the reverse. The lower class sided rather with the military. Stones flew. Well-dressed gentlemen ran. I went to see what was the matter, but could see nothing. The governor, Pedro Gutiérrez (Lee), was soon on the ground. He called for a file of soldiers to station across the street, just south of the bridge. I saw them mustered, and marched out from the barracks.

The street was now full, and mostly of young artisans and loafers. I observed the conduct of the gobernador narrowly, and thought it highly judicious. He did not proceed harshly, but coaxingly, often jokingly. Thus he traversed the dense crowd from the bridge to the Cathedral. The armed police—guardia de policia—were out in the Plaza, but did not act. No arrests were made, and all was quiet.

In the last chapter I stated that I thought we had had our last Granadan revolution. I must now say why I retained my opinion after what I saw on Holy Friday. In the first place, authority had triumphed in the last two revolutions. Second, the liberation of the Church removed one strong motive for rousing fanaticism to arms. So I counted for nothing all the talk I had heard from the beginning of March to the middle of April, because it was clear to me that any attempt made at this time would fail.

I did not take into account, as I should, first, that there was little risk in failing. Almost all the eminent men in the nation had been rebels in 1841 or in 1851. By the very law, treason is not a capital crime, even when it ends in bloodshed. Second, I did not reflect that a civil war might therefore be enkindled merely to gratify present revenge without hope of ultimate success.

The government itself was desperate. It had yielded to Red Republican (Gólgota) theories too far. These speculators had adopted the belief that universal suffrage and a free constitution were a remedy for all human evils. They had, as their expositor Samper says, "*a blind faith in principles.*" They had made their changes too rapidly, and were bent on trying all kinds of experiments; and especially they had a fanatical hatred to a standing army. That of New Granada did, in fact, strike me rather as a nuisance, but it was small and diminishing, and all attempts at a militia had failed.

General Melo, the commander of the cavalry in Bogotá, seemed to have become particularly obnoxious to the Gólgotas. They hated him. An ex-gobernador said to me one day, "Melo's troop rode furiously past me just now; they had as lief ride over one as not. If I had had a pistol, I would have fired after them."

Melo was charged with murdering a corporal, named Ramon Quiros, in December, 1853. His dying statement, as he lay in the military hospital a day or two after his wound, was that he was stabbed in the street by a person unknown. Half Bogotá believe that Quiros died with a lie in his mouth to save his murderer. They say that he went out of the barracks by night with his uniform covered with a ruana contrary to rule, and returned stupefied with drink. Melo reproved him; he answered insolently, and Melo was fool enough to run him through; and then he dies three days after, saying that Melo did not stab him. On the strength of such stories, the Conservador Gutiérrez, who was elected gobernador, proceeded to take informations on the matter when he came into office on 1st January, 1854. Melo, if innocent, had injuries to resent; and, whether guilty or not, punishment to fear.

It was evident, too, that the adminstration was hedged in with enemies. They had the priesthood against them, for they had imprisoned and exiled bishops, and had ended by withdrawing all support from the Church. Nearly every gobernador elected in September was an enemy to government; and in many cases I am compelled to believe that the priests interfered scandalously with the election. So the government, occupying a middle ground, had few and lukewarm supporters, and bold, active enemies. They had little to lose by a *coup d'état*, but nothing to gain from it.

Many thought differently from me in this matter. They were sure of a conspiracy about to burst. The Senate passed a resolution requesting the executive to place arms in the hands of the gobernador for the protection of the city against the soldiery. Obando assured them that their fears were groundless.

But so little satisfied were some that they even meditated a counter conspiracy to seize the barracks of San Francisco by a sudden attack with "white arms"—*i. e*, swords and poniards. This was thought too rash.

I had been invited to a party on Sunday night, which, of course, I declined attending on account of the day. Many of the bitterest enemies of the military in Congress were present there, and some also at another. A large number of the lower class, enemies to coats and gentility, and lovers of any thing new, had been put under arms before midnight, and the military proceeded thus to seize those who were obnoxious to them. Governor Gutiérrez foresaw the evil in season to escape it. He had resigned on Saturday, and left Bogotá. Colonel Emigdio Briceño, an excellent gentleman, took his place on Sunday night, and when he had been governor four hours he was a prisoner. The most extensive arrests were made, including all the males, attendants included, at the party to which I had been invited. The chief men sought for escaped. Few left Bogotá, but all hid. Samper, who was a Congress-man, and his friend Murillo, ex-Secretary of the Treasury, and now Speaker of the House of Representatives, lived together. Samper and Mrs. M. were at a ball or party, and her husband somewhere else. Their house was attacked with a volley of musketry just before their return, and they escaped. The house was treated rather roughly, but not pillaged except of eatables.

By far the worst act of the whole night, however, was firing at a French goldsmith as he stood at a window in his balcony to see what was going on. Quite a number of balls struck the frame and sash of the window, and it was indeed a wonder that he was not killed. Melo himself apologized for the act next day. Horses as well as men were seized. All stables, not the property of foreigners, were visited, and the horses taken.

I was awaked at daybreak by the sound of cannon, which were celebrating the entire success of the night's work. I rose and went to a servant, and asked what was the matter. She told me that it was a revolution. I then took my hat, and made my way to the Plaza. At the northwest corner I found a body of unwashed recruits drawn across the whole street. "You can go no farther, Señor," said one. "Yes he can, too," replied another; "we have no right to stop foreigners. Pass in, Señor."

I declined passing in, but looked around the Plaza. A large body of men were drawn up there, most of them in ruanas. They appeared much pleased with their new occupation. So I went home and completed my toilet, and went to the vice-president's house. The door was not opened to my call, but a voice behind told me that Señor Obaldía had been summoned to the palace at daybreak, and had not returned.

I went there and found a strong guard at the door. I asked permission of Major Jiron, who commanded, to enter, and was requested to wait a moment. At that instant an aid-de-camp brought him an order, to which he responded by ordering the aid into arrest. Each attempted to arrest the other, but the aid's orders prevailed. Jiron attempted to stab an officer who seized him, but instantly he had a horse-pistol at his breast, and more than one sword aimed at him. I sprang to get out of the range of the ball, and expected instantly to be covered with blood, but the Major surrendered and took his place in the ranks.

Obaldía was looking out of the window over them, and I asked him to give directions for my admission, which he did. I entered, and learned that Melo had offered Obando the dictatorship; he had consulted with his cabinet, and refused. The message which that aid brought to Jiron was to hold the President and cabinet prisoners. He refused, and now he was a prisoner without and I within. Great confusion prevailed in the palace. No one was seated; no one long remained in the same room.

I obtained my release without difficulty and with little delay. I went to the Señora de Obaldía, and conducted her to the boarding-place of Mr. Green, our minister. We went by a back street, but no one interrupted us. Others also had taken refuge there, and the house of every minister and consul had the flag flying, and persons and jewels found protection in them. It will be observed in all this that not a drop of blood was shed.

I heard afterward that Major Jiron would have been "blown through" but for the presence of a foreigner, who it was feared might be endangered in the melee. With all due respect for the

Major, I consider his seizure, his resistance, and his danger as all a farce that I had the pleasure of witnessing. Why were not the cabinet secured at the same time with other important men? What was the president doing all night? At a later hour the secretaries were carried to *secure* prisons, the president detained a professed prisoner in his palace, and the vice-president set at liberty. He immediately took refuge under the stars and stripes.

I could mention a theory that would explain every thing, even to the liberation of Obaldía, but it might be unjust. It is a little singular, but Herrera, the Designado, was also summoned to that meeting of the cabinet. Instead of complying with the message, he immediately took refuge at the American legation. Had he gone to the palace, Melo would have had every vestige of executive power—president, vice-president, Designado, and all the ministers in his power at once. Had he secured the Designado, it is not improbable that the vice-president would have been detained with the rest.

Melo assumed the dictatorship before night, "having waited in vain for Obando to change his mind." I called on him to obtain liberty for some useless persons seized last night. He assured me that orders had already been given to set them at liberty. Coarse shirts and ruanas were in great request. Few coats were seen in the streets, and those were worn by foreigners. Sudden friendships were formed by old political antagonists, now in common danger.

Some sudden changes of opinion must have occurred. The Orejon, whose portrait graces page 127, came in town to-day, and affected to be quite pleased with the new order of things. He rode home shouting, Viva la revolucion! When he got there, he found that every horse and mule capable of bearing saddle or enjalma had been carried off for the service of the glorious cause.

I see, too, that my good landlady Margarita is rather prejudiced against cachacos, but has ordered the cajera to give moderate credit to any wearers of ruanas. I must not, however, charge her with a sudden conversion entirely. Her contempt for fops, who spend freely and pay slackly, has long since attracted my attention. One of these, who is courting a girl in a house opposite ours, had at one time so many drinks of *brandi* scored against him at our tienda that he ceased to patronize it. While chatting one evening with his lady, he was surprised at the entrance of our cajera, who "presented the respects of La Señora Margarita, and advised him to pay his brandy-bill, or wear his hat with a borboquejo, as otherwise the Señora would one day seize it off his head." He squared up that night.

Melo has put forth an organic decree. All such notices are made by *bando;* that is, sending a civilian, a drum, and a squad of soldiers to various street-corners, where the civilian reads the proclamation or decree. Among other things, I perceive that Melo proclaims New Granada a Catholic nation again. It will not save him.

The great business is recruiting. All persons are invited to enroll in the national guard, and those who neglect to do so are seized and incorporated into the standing army at once. Marketmen come and go unmolested, for Bogotá must eat. A line of sentinels, posted round the city, let in all who come, and let out those that have a pass from Obregon, Melo's second. Now and then a Congressman or other person who would not be permitted to leave runs off in the night through the fields. In this way they hope to get up a force to put down the Dictator. Herrera escaped on Wednesday night.

Obregon addressed notes to the foreign representatives, who replied, generally, that it was their duty to maintain friendly relations with the government *de facto*, without taking part in domestic controversies. Obregon speaks English, so that our chargé had no need of an interpreter. All the other embassadors but ours always speak Spanish.

I could not find Samper after he hid till too late to call on him. No one, perhaps, besides him, was in so much danger as Murillo. I carried various notes between him and his wife; one of them dropped on the floor as I was talking with one of Melo's officers, who politely handed it to me without looking at it. All after that went couched in terms of a love intrigue.

What was Obando's position all this while? Professedly he was a prisoner. I do not think he was. He was not kept closely, as were the secretaries. I readily obtained admission to him, but to their prison with great difficulty. They could hold no private interviews, and were not allowed to write. No soldier or guard intruded on Obando's privacy; nay, the very window by which Bolívar escaped remained unguarded.

There was a considerable quantity of money expected soon up the river, and it behooved the Dictator to extend his field of operations; so he sent detachments to Mesa, to Facatativá, and to Guaduas. The troops guarding the Presidio at Mesa retired before superior numbers. The detachment to Guaduas, meeting no opposition, went on to Pescaderias, opposite Honda. The Gobernador of Mariquita, Mateo Viana, was at the Honda, trying to muster men enough to resist their crossing. The boats were detained on the west side while he was making the attempt. It failed, and he retired, leaving Melo's emissary to cross at leisure; but the money came only to Mompos, and returned to wait for more quiet times.

Melo must have means as well as men. There was not a large sum in the treasury when he seized on it. Forced contributions were resorted to, and sometimes with great cruelty. It was for this purpose, or some other, that an English citizen, Mr. Logan, was seized. One consequence of this, to our national honor, must not be passed by.

A guard conducting Mr. Logan was passing the American legation, then in charge of Mr. John A. Bennet, as Mr. Green had returned home. Mr. Logan sprang into Mr. Bennet's door. It was at once closed. Soon after, the legation was stormed while our flag was flying over it. The door was riddled with balls. Mr. Logan, wishing to save Mr. Bennet's life, went out and surrendered.

Mr. Bennet demanded of Melo the punishment of the assailants. All his reward was, that he had to remain in constant peril of his life, and unable to escape from Bogotá till Melo fell. He demanded again of the restored government that the criminals be tried and shot. Had this demand been enforced by a fleet off Cartagena till the miscreants had paid in their own persons the penalty, I conjecture that it would in the end save more lives of innocent American citizens than it would have cost of reckless outlaws, who, because armed with national muskets, feel freed from individual responsibility. In due time, another rewarded politician took the place of Mr. Green, and the affair was compromised by the government paying Mr. Bennet for the damage done his door, and offering him an apology for the insult of fanning him with bullets.

But I must return to my history. The most reliable part of the country for the constitutional authority was the north. In Cipaquirá was a detachment of the army schooled to Melo's purposes. There were also some conspirators in Tunja, but the dense, industrious population of these cold provinces were true to order. General Herrera escaped to Chocontá, and commenced the exercise of executive powers on the 21st of April, regarding Obando and Obaldía as prisoners in Bogotá. He appointed General Franco commander-in-chief. On the 19th of May, Franco rashly attacked Cipaquirá, fought bravely, and died. General Buitrago led the forces, over 4000 in number, out to the northern end of the Sabana, beyond Cipaquirá, where Melo fell upon them with 800 veterans, and annihilated them. The Designado was a fugitive on the plain, with victorious enemies in front and rear. He escaped through the wilds of the west to the Magdalena.

Nor did things wear a better aspect at the south. No good could of course be expected of Antonio Mateus, gobernador of Cauca. He had 800 men, but found no opportunity of doing mischief with them. In Popayan the revolution was nine days earlier than at Bogotá, but was promptly put down for the time. Again, from the 16th to the 21st of May, the friends of Melo had entire possession of Popayan, when they lost it after a severe battle. In Cali the battle lasted two days in the streets, and the conspirators capitulated. In Antioquia the movement was soon put down, but at the cost of the life of the Gobernador Pabon.

Julio Arboleda, president of the Senate, took refuge at the Danish legation till he could escape from Bogotá to Honda. This place he fortified, disinterring certain old cannon, which, had they been fired, would have been dangerous to some one. Threatened here by Melo's troops, he suddenly attacked 300 of them in Guaduas with less than 100, and routed them utterly at the point of the bayonet. There seems to me some analogy between this transaction and the capture of the Hessians at Trenton. Each was the first dawn of ultimate success.

After this he established himself at Guatequí, on the eastern bank of the Magdalena, about a day's journey below the mouth of the Coello. Here he collected men and boats, so as readily to descend the river, and defend any point more easily than Melo could attack it. In virtue of this defense, Congress assembled at Ibagué, and not at Ocaña, as had been at first intended. Almost their first act, 27th of September, was to suspend Obando from the presidency. As Vice-president Obaldía had now escaped from Bogotá, the executive power had passed from the hands of Herrera the Designado to his.

Before this, Arboleda had defeated detachments of Melo's troops at Anapoima and Anolaima, and on the 11th of September the army of the executive occupied La Mesa. Here the forces gathered from the Valley of the Cauca, and the whole were under the command of ex-President López. Some heavy pieces of artillery, brought by Arboleda, made part of their defenses. A serious discussion took place at Tena whether to spike them, or try to take them up to the Sabana. The Antioqueños were permitted to make the trial, and they succeeded.

In the previous assaults on Bogotá, it had been strongly defended at the crossing of the Bogotá, which runs along a few miles west of it through marshy ground, a terrible moat to be passed in the face of the enemy. Here, doubtless, Melo had arranged for the decisive battle, like those of Santuario and Culebrera.

In this he was not to be gratified; the troops of Congress crossed the stream in the immediate vicinity of the Falls of Tequendama. The cannon seem to have crossed below the falls, and the heroic effort of the sons of Antioquia appears to have ended in placing them in the wagon-road from the coal-mines of Cincha, mentioned on page 274.

Melo can not guard the immense circuit of the cornice of the plain. Expecting the enemy at Barro Blanco, or by the more northern ascent from Anolaima, the pass at the Hacienda of Tequendama is in the hands of his enemies before he is aware. They are advancing past Soacha, and up the east side of the Bogotá. The first point where there is any hope of resisting them is at the River Boza. He met them at the bridge of Boza, which we passed on page 273.

López was at Barro Blanco with 800 men when he saw the hopes of the nation crushed at Cipaquirá and Tiquiza in May. Now, as he stood at Boza to deliver up the command of a numerous host to General Herran, all eyes were turned to the north with hope. Mosquera was coming. He had landed on the coast early in May for commercial purposes, but was at the earliest opportunity appointed to a command by the Designado. He had advanced through Ocaña and the northern provinces toward Bogotá, not without reverses, but increasing in strength as he advanced. My friend Jiron had been defeated at Pamplona, and Melo had no troops north of Cipaquirá. These, too, had to retire, and the sole chance for the Dictator was to defeat one of the two divisions before their union.

Leaving the capital entirely unguarded, as Mosquera kept too far off with his smaller force, the Dictator marched with all his troops to meet Herran, now within five miles of Bogotá. They fought on 22d November, 1854. Long and fierce was the combat between despairing veterans and superior numbers fighting in a better cause. The day was decided by that heavy artillery brought from Honda with so much labor as to have made the transport of it almost a piece of folly.

So they advanced to Tres Esquinas, a spot where, in the southwest corner of our Plan of Bogotá, three streams and four roads seem to radiate. A detachment of Melo's best troops here availed themselves of a bend in the road, deep ditches, and thick walls of tapias, to offer a vain resistance to the cautious advance of Herran the next day. Castro led them, but here again they met the fatal artillery, were defeated, and many of them taken prisoners.

Shall Bogotá be attacked instantly? The military men advised the measure; Obaldía and the ministers feared to risk too much on it. Mosquera would soon advance, and, let Melo intrench himself as he would, the result was certain. A repulse of either division might drive both armies from the Plain before their junction.

Unhappy Bogotá! There may be found nuns now living who, from their belfries, have seen the fate of the capital decided by fire, and thunder, and blood, four times before. It was stormed in December, 1812, by Baraya, who was repulsed; stormed and carried by Bolívar in December, 1814; lost at the battle of Santuario, 27th August, 1830, and saved by that of Culebrera, 28th October, 1840; but never since the city was founded has it seen, and never may it see, a scene like that of 3d and 4th December, 1854!

On the 2d of December Mosquera was at Chapinero, just beyond the northern limits of our Plan of Bogotá. The next day, at noon, the troops of the Dictator were vainly contending with the vanguard of Herran at the suburb of Las Cruces, in the opposite extremity of the city. Step by step the besieged retired, till at midnight they were making their stand at San Agustin and San Bartolomé. For fifteen long hours they lose now a foot and now a yard, now a gun and now a tower, and the resistless foe was descending upon them from above the palace.

Nor is Mosquera idle. He has carried San Diego; he is pressing up to Las Nieves, while Melo's head-quarters are at the barracks of San Francisco. Eastward the mountain hedges him in; to the west the Sabana is in the possession of the forces of the Vice-president. Shut in thus, the Plaza of San Francisco is filled with his troops, crowding in over the bridge from the south, while at length Mosquera has carried La Tercera.

But as the last moment approached, and the end had become inevitable, the country lost a man whose life was worth as much as the death of ten like Melo. The Designado Herrera, when Obaldía assumed the executive functions, became a mere general, inferior in rank to Mosquera, whom his own decree had raised to the command, and under whose commands he now fought. He who had been the unsuccessful candidate at Obando's election, and who nevertheless had been placed second after him—who had been true to the executive in all revolutions, and had fought against Herran and Mosquera, López and Obando, now shed his blood for the cause of constitutional authority in the streets of Bogotá.

But now a dreadful sound is in the Dictator's ears. It is a loud peal from the Cathedral bells, announcing that the Plaza is lost and gained; nay, in the Calle Real a cannon is so planted as to bear upon the Barracks of San Francisco. The revolution is at its last gasp at the very spot where I had seen its birth in the bochinche of Good Friday. Now his troops are crying that this must have an end. Desperate and almost beside himself, he sends an officer to Mosquera offering to surrender if only his life is spared. Mosquera gives his word—injudiciously, perhaps, but it never will be broken. The war is at an end.

Ere the diligent reader shall have reached this paragraph, he may have heard of the election of a new president of New Granada. It will be one of three persons before mentioned. If it be T. C. Mosquera, a scene of bright hopes of future prosperity opens on us. If Mariano Ospina, our only fear will be priestly domination. But if Manuel Morillo succeed, as he probably must, then the land must be prepared to bear all that a zealous, truly patriotic, but rash and ill judged experimenter can inflict. But a happier future awaits her; soon let it come!

APPENDIX.

I. GLOSSARY.

SPANISH words, in their Peninsular acceptation, have been systematically excluded from the preceding pages. The words occurring there and below are of Indian origin, or else, being Spanish, are used in a different sense from that given in dictionaries, or applied to objects unknown in the temperate zone.

The PRONUNCIATION of the Spanish language is the easiest possible. It is readily learned, and none should shrink from it who have any occasion to use it.

ACCENT.—Two general rules include all words in which the accent is not invariably written over the word: 1. Words ending in a vowel or diphthong have the accent on the penult, as *Orinòco*. 2. Words ending in any other consonant than *s* added to form the plural, are accented on the last, as *Madrìd*. All such words are written below with the *grave* accent, to indicate that the accent is not usually to be written. All exceptions to these rules are written here and every where with the *acute* accent, as in *Bolívar*, *Panamá*.

CONSONANTS have the same power as in English, except

C before *e* and *i* has the sound of *s* lisped, or *th* in *thin;*

Z has this same sound always; neither ever sounds like *s*.

Ch (reckoned by the Spanish as one letter) has always the same sound as in *child*.

D at the end of words (and by some in the middle) is pronounced like *th* in *them*.

G before *e* and *i* has the sound of *h* in *hat*.

J always has the power of *h* in *hat*.

X never occurs in modern orthography except as *ks;* it had the power of *h* in *hat*.

H is always silent.

Ll (one letter) sounds like *lli* in *million*, which they would write *míllon*.

Ñ like *ni* in *banio*, which they write *baño*.

Qu before *e* and *i* like *k*, but

Qu before *a* and *o*, and *qü* before *e* and *i*, as in English.

Rr (one letter), a very strong *r*—an absolute rattle of the tongue.

W does not occur, and *k* rarely is found.

VOWELS have but one invariable sound each:

A like *a* in *father*.

E like *e* in *they*.

O like *o* in *no*.

U like *oo* in *pool*.

DIPHTHONGS are so accounted only in rules of accent and versification:

Au sounds like *ou* in *found*.

Ai like *i* in *pine*.

Numbers below indicate pages in the body of the work; if preceded by *f*, they refer to the *illustrations*.

Acèquia, *aqueduct*, 115.
Achicòria, *a flower*, 125.
Achiòte, *arnatto*, 141.
Achipùlla, *a plant*, 280.
Achìra, *a leaf*, 143.
Acuápar, *sandbox-tree*, 47.
Adòbe, *unburnt bricks*, 131.
Aduàna, *custom-house*, 29.
Advocaciòn, *a personality of the Virgin*, 186.
Aguacàte, *a fruit*, 410.
Ahijàda, *goddaughter*, 181.
Ahijàdo, *godson*, 181.
Ajiàco, *a stew*, 120.
Alamèda, *a walk bordered with poplars*, 164.
Albàrca, *a sandal*, 35, *f.* 292.
Alcabàla, *tax on sales*, 258.
Alcàide, *jailer*, 38.
Alcàlde, *a district officer*, 37.
Alcaldìa, *an office*, 37.
Aldéa, *an imperfect district*, 37.
Alfandòque, *a rattle*, 124, *f.* 441.
Alfandòque, *a candy*, 124.
Alférez (*ensign*), *patron*, 546.
Alma bendìta, *a ghost*, 340.
Almendròn, *palm-almond*, 400.
Almíbar, *sirup*, 122.
Almofrèz, *a bag*, 289, *f.* 288.
Almohadillàdo, *mule-ladders*, 345.
Almojávana, *a cake*, 473.
Alpargàta, } *a sandal*, 236, *f.* 236.
Alpargàte, }
Altozàno, *a platform*, 150.
Alvèrja, *pea*, 143.
Anda, *a stage*, 545.
Angelito (*little angel*), *dead child*, 446.
Anís, *a plant and seed*, 56.
Anisàdo, *a drink*, 56.
Anòn, *a fruit*, 502.
Apellìdo, *surname*, 106.
Ara, *altar-stone*, 187.
Arandèla (*flounce*), *ruff*, 145.
Arèpa, *corn-cake*, 372.
Arracàcha, *an esculent root*, 150.
Arretrànca, *breeching*, 133, *f.* 132.
Arrièro (*muleteer*), *an ant*, 64.
Arròba, *a quarter*, 487.
Arròz, *rice*, 500.
Arrozàl, *rice-field*, 500.
Atajàda, *family of a horse*, 430.
Atascadèro, *mud-hole*, 345.
Atìllo, *a hide case*, 45.
Atràso, *backwardness*, 379.
Avispa, *wasp, hornet*, 90.
Avispèro, *nest of wasp or hornet*, 90.
Azúcar, *loaf sugar*, 122.
Azucèna (*lily*), *an orchid*, 416.

Badèa, *a fruit*, 130.
Balìja, *mail-trunk*, 259.
Bambùco, *a dance*, 440, *f.* 441.
Bànco, *a bench*, 425.
Bànda, *land on a river*, 19.
Bàndo, *proclamation*, 561.
Bandòla, *small guitar*, 124, *f.* 441.
Banquìllo, *seat to be shot on*, 164.
Baquiàno, *an expert*, 49.
Barbuquèjo, *hat-string*, 133, *f.* 132.
Bàrra, *audience*, 257.
Barrigòn, *a deformed person*, 76.
Bàrrio, *ward*, 154.
Batàta, *sweet potato*, 471.
Bayetòn, *a flannel garment*, 32.
Beàta, *a devotee*, 193.
Beatèrio, *a religious house*, 516.
Bejùco, *a climber*, 417.
Bèstia, *animal for traveling*, 45.
Bìja, *arnatto*, 141.
Bochìca, *a fabulous personage*, 126.
Bochìnche, *riot*, 553.
Bodèga, *hold; store-house*, 55, 92.
Bodeguèro, *store-keeper*, 92.
Bòga, *boatman*, 39.
Bòllo, *a cake*, 108.
Bòlsa, *purse*, 101.
Bolsìllo, *pocket*, 101.
Bòngo, *a boat*, 39.
Boqueròn, *gorge*, 218.
Borrachèro, *a plant*, 131.
Bóveda, *vault; tomb*, 60.
Buìtre, *a bird*, 495.
Bùnde, *a dance*, 479.

Cabecèra, *capital of canton*, 37.
Cabèza (*head*), *seat of district government*, 37.
Cabìldo, *district Legislature*, 37.
Cabùya, *a plant; its fibre*, 246.
Cacào, *chocolate-tree*, 88.
Cachàco, *stylish fellow*, 146.
Cachimòna, *a game*, 377.
Caimàn, *a reptile*, 71.
Cajèra, *saleswoman*, 149.
Calabàza (*fruit*), calabàzo (*dish*), *calabash*, 74.
Calentàno, *lowlander*, 246.
Càlle, *block of a street; the street*, 154.
Callejòn, *deep road*, 214.
Cámara provinciàl, *provincial Legislature*, 37.
Camarìn, *image closet*, 187.
Camìsa, *under garment*, 136, *f.* 136.
Camisòn, *gown; coarse robe*, 59, *f.* 59.
Canalète, *a paddle*, 39, *f.* 70.
Canapé, *a seat*, 425.
Candèla, *a coal*, 170.
Canèlo (*cinnamon-tree*), *Winter's bark*, 238.
Canòa, *trough*, 89.
Canònigo, *prebendary*, 194.
Cantòn, *a canton*, 37.
Càña bràva, *a grass*, 71.
Càña dùlce, *sugar-cane*, 118.
Cañaveràl, *cane-field*, 118.
Capellàn, *holder of a capellanía*, 419.
Capellanía, *perpetual claim on land*, 419.
Capìlla, *chapel*, 159.
Capiròte, *a mask*, 545.
Capitàn, *a fish*, 136.
Caracolí, *cashew-tree*, 61.
Caràte, *a disease*, 151.
Càrga, *mule load*, 220.4737 *lbs. avoird.*, 45.
Carguèro, *carrier of burdens*, 93.
Càrne de menùdo, *viscera*, 177.
Carrèra, *street*, 154.
Carrièl, *a pouch*, 101, 536.
Cartìlla, *primer*, 472.
Càsa (*house*), *a group*, 183.
Càsa àlta, *two-story house*, 62.
Càsa bàja, *one-story house*, 63.
Càsa claustràda, *house with court*, 62, *f.* 139.
Cazàbe, *a kind of bread*, 62.
Cèdro, *a tree*, 389.
Cedròn, *a tree*, 457.
Cèiba, *a tree*, 506.
Cènso, *an annuity*, 419.
Céntimo, *a cent*, 119.
Cèrda, *hair rope*, 458.
Cerèzo, *cherry-tree*, 201.
Chambìmbe, *soap-berry*, 469.
Champàn, *a boat*, 81, *f.* 80.
Chapetòn, *native of Spain*, 168.
Chaquèta, *a garment*, 193.
Chàrco, *a deep spot*, 398.
Chasquí, *a messenger*, 255.
Chìcha, *a drink*, 144.
Chìnche, *bed-bug*, 49.
Chircàte, *a garment*, 136, *f.* 136.
Chirimòya, *a fruit*, 502.
Chì-to-o! *stop!* 129.
Chùlo, *a bird*, 230.
Chùsque, *a grass*, 217.
Cigarrìllo, *paper cigar*, 171.
Cilìcio, *an article for self-torture*, 189.
Cìncha, *girth of saddle*, 424.
Ciprés, *a tree*, 389.
Ciriàl, *candle-pole*, 114.

Màngle, *mangrove-tree*, 32.
Màngo, *a fruit*, 304.
Mànos muèrtas, *mortmain*, 419.
Mànta, *native cloth*, 519.
Mantèca (*butter*), *lard*, 56.
Mantellìna, *a garment*, 136, *f.* 136.
Mantèo, *priest's cloak*, 192.
Mantequìlla, *butter*, 56.
Manzanìllo, *manchineel-tree*, 32.
Manzanìllo, *a Euphorbiate bush*, 310.
Masamòrra, *a kind of food*, 371.
Matadòr, *bull-fighter*, 265.
Matràca, *a rattle*, 551.
Màure, *a sash*, 137.
Mayoràzgo, *entailment*, 419.
Mayordòmo, *steward*, 418.
Mazòrca, *fruit of maize or chocolate*, 88.
Mèdio, *a coin*, 119.
Melàdo, *sirup or molasses*, 122.
Menguànte, *waning of the moon*, 474.
Mestìzo, *mixed race*, 69, *f.* 70.
Mièl, *thin sirup*, 122.
Mièl de abèjas, *honey*, 122.
Mièl de pùrga, *molasses*, 122.
Minorìsta, *a priest-boy*, 194.
Mistèla, *cordial*, 440.
Mitàd, *eighth of a dime*, 119.
Mochìla, *a bag*, 101.
Mondòngo, *a kind of meat*, 177.
Montàña, *forest country*, 436.
Mònte, *thicket*, 436.
Montùra, *saddle, bridle, &c.*, 425.
Monumènto, *deposit of a wafer*, 550.
Mòro, *fustic*, 53.
Mòya, *a cake of salt*, 98.
Múcura, *an earthen vessel*, 115.
Mùla (*a female mule*), *mule*, 45.
Murciélago, *bat*, 140.

Nacùma, *a plant*, 63.
Naranjàda, *a drink*, 121.
Nazarèno, *a bearer*, 545.
Nème, *bitumen*, 342.
Nìgua, *an insect*, 330.
Níspero, *a fruit*, 390.
Nòmbre, *Christian name*, 106.
Ñàme, *yam*, 151.

Obìspo (*bishop*), *part of a still*, 448.
Oca, *an esculent "root,"* 150.
Olla, *an earthen pot*, 143.
Ollèta, *chocolate-pot*, 143.
Onza (*ounce*), *a coin*, 119.
O-o-ìs-te! *stop!* 129.
Oraciòn (*prayer*), *dusk*, 183.
Orejòn, *a class of men*, 132, *f.* 132.
Ornamènto, *altar-dress*, 112.

Padrìna, *godmother*, 181.
Padrinàzgo, *a relationship*, 181.
Padrìno, *godfather*, 181.
Padròte, *stud-horse*, 430.
Pàica, *worm-seed*, 445.
Pàila, *caldron*, 466.
Pàja (*straw*), *thatch*, 36.
Pàla, *push-hoe*, 487.
Palànca, *setting-pole*, 39.
Palìto, *a measure*, 487.
Palmìche, *cabbage-palm*, 149.
Pàlo bòbo, *tree-fern*, 129, *f.* 281.
Panderèta, *tamborine*, 440, *f.* 441.
Panèla, *coarse sugar*, 122.
Pàño de mànos, *towel*, 56.
Pañolòn, *a shawl*, 145.
Papàya, *papaw*, 31.
Paramèntos, *priests' robes*, 112.
Páramo, *high land*, 70.
Parròquia, *parish*, 37.
Pasàje, *ferriage*, 94.
Pasèro, *ferryman*, 94.
Pàso, *ferry*, 94.
Pàso, *part of a procession*, 545.
Pastìlla, *a pie*, 150.
Patacòn, *slice of plantain; a coin*, 119.
Patèna, *a plate*, 113.
Patíbulo, *execution place*, 164.
Pàtio, *court*, 82.
Patròn, *chief boga*, 39.
Patròna, *mistress*, 78.
Pauji, *a bird*, 127.
Pàva, *a bird*, 495.
Peàje, *transit duty*, 50.
Pèga-pèga, *a flower*, 203.
Pellòn, *a rug*, 188.
Peòn, *hired man*, 45.
Pepìno, *cucumber and another fruit*, 149.
Perìca, *drunkenness*, 453.
Perìco lijèro, *the sloth*, 388.
Perrerìsta, *whipper*, 527.
Perrèro, *whip*, 527, *f.* 288.
Persignàrse, *to cross one's self*, 184.
Personèro, *prosecuting attorney*, 407.
Pesèbre, *manger*, 467.
Pèso, *eight or ten dimes*, 119.
Pèso fuèrte, *dollar*, 119.
Petàca, *a box*, 45.
Petacòn, *a bed-bug*, 49.
Pìla, *font; fountain*, 115.
Piñuèla, *a fruit*, 103.
Pìta, *a fibre*, 247.
Pitahàya, *a fruit*, 525.
Plàta suèlta, *change*, 106.
Platanàl and platanàr, *plantain field*, 87.
Plátano, *plantain*, 87.
Plàza, *public square*, 35.
Poltròna, *easy-chair*, 425.
Pomaròsa, *a fruit*, 304.
Pòncho, *a garment*, 32.
Pontàzgo, *bridge-toll*, 50.
Pòpa, *stern*, 78.
Portòn, *front door*, 62, *f.* 156.
Posàda, *stopping-place*, 48.
Potrèro, *pasture*, 468.
Pòyo, *a bench*, 49.
Presidènte, *president*, 37.
Pretìl, *balustrade*, 62.
Pròa, *prow*, 82.
Procèso, *law-suit*, 406.
Provìncia, *province*, 37.
Puchèro, *a boiled dish*, 149.
Puèrta, *gate; door; bars*, 92.
Puèrta de gòlpe, *gate*, 92.
Puèrta de misericòrdia, *a side door*, 156.
Puèrta de tràncas, *bars*, 92.

Querème, *a flower*, 517.
Quingo, *zigzag*, 18.

Racìmo, *bunch of fruit*, 87.
Ràya, *a fish*, 341.
Ràncho, *shed, camp*, 246.
Rascadèra, *an esculent*, 538.
Raspòn, *coarse* (*hat*), 69.
Reàl, *dime*, 119.
Reinosos, *uplanders*, 246.
Rèja, *window bars*, 30.
Rèjo, *thong*, 45.
Rellèno, *a sausage*, 120.
Resbaladèro, *a slide*, 435.
Resguàrdo, *reserve*, 243.
Rodèo, *herding*, 423.
Rogaciòn, *special festival*, 444.
Rosàrio, *a set of prayers*, 183.
Ruàna, *a garment*, 32, *f.* 426.
Rúbrica, *part of signature*, 326, *f.* 326.

Sacàr, *to engage to dance*, 443.
Sacramènto del altàr, *a salutation*, 291.
Sacristàn, *sexton*, 215.
Sacristía, *vestry*, 112.
Sagràrio, *a little cupboard*, 187.
Sagù, *arrow-root*, 146.
Sàla, *main room*, 48.
Salamanquèja, *a lizard*, 35.

Salchìcha, *a sausage*, 120.
Salvàje, *a plant*, 53.
Sàlve, *Hail Mary*, 183.
Sancòcho, *a stew*, 373.
Santiguàrse, *to cross one's self*, 184.
Sàya, *a skirt*, 184.
Sìlla, *arm-chair; a saddle*, 425.
Sillèro, *bearer*, 93, 365, *f.* 364.
Sillòn, *saddle-chair*, 241, *f.* 240.
Sòbre-càrga, *a middle package*, 51.
Sofá, *sofa*, 425.
Sòpa, *soup*, 141.
Sotacuèllo, *a cravat*, 65.
Sotàna, *priests' dress*, 193.
Sudadèro, *saddle-blanket*, 425.
Suèlta, *small money*, 106.
Suspìro (*sigh*), *a cake*, 472.

Tàbla, *a cake*, 89.
Taburète, *chair*, 425.
Talèga, *money-bag*, 101.
Tamàl, *an article of food*, 143.
Tàmbo, *a shed for travelers*, 365.
Tàpa, *covering*, 69, *f.* 70.
Tàpias, *rammed earth*, 131.
Tarjàdo, *incapacitated horse*, 431.
Tàrro, *a vessel*, 109, *f.* 386.
Tasàjo, *jerked beef*, 56.
Tèja, *tile*, 67.
Templàr, *to change climate*, 241.
Tercèra, *a society*, 188.
Tèrcio, *half carga*, 45.
Tiènda, *shop*, 48.
Tièrra calièute, *lowlands*, 73.
Tièrra frìa, *uplands*, 73.
Tièrra templàda, *middle lands*, 73.
Tièrras baldías, *public domain*, 109.
Tijerèto, *a bird*, 524.
Tinàja, *a jar*, 75.
Tinajèra, *water-place*, 115.
Tinajòn, *large tinaja*, 143.
Tinièblas, *a ceremony*, 550.
Tìple, *a musical instrument*, 124.
Tìza (*chalk*), *infusorial earth*, 388.
Toàlla, *towel*, 56.
Tocàyo, *namesake*, 106.
Tòldo (*tent*), *a roof*, 81.
Tòma! *a call to animals*, 433.
Torbellìno (*whirlwind*), *a dance*, 443.
Toreadòr, *bull-fighter*, 299.
Tortìlla, *omelette*, 149.
Totùma, *a fruit; a vessel*, 74.
Tràncas, *bars*, 92.
Trènza, *braid*, 69.
Tribùna, *speaking desk*, 257.
Trisàgio, *a religious service*, 518.
Tùlpas, *three stones*, 56.
Tùna, *a fruit*, 301.

Uña-gàto (*cat-claw*), *a bush*, 413.
Uva cimarròna, *a berry*, 216.

Vàca (*cow*), *a huge bag*, 289, *f.* 288.
Vènta, *inn*, 119.
Verdolàga, *purselane*, 446.
Vìce-parròquia, *sub-parish*, 37.
Vigilància, *surveillance*, 348.
Vìsperas (*vespers*), *eve*, 183.
Vuèltas de la Virèina, *turning places*, 137.

Yùca, *an esculent root*, 62.

Zaguàn, *entry*, 62.
Zamàrros, *a garment*, 133, *f.* 132.
Zancùdo (*long legs*), *musquito*, 72.
Zapòte, *a fruit*, 390.
Zaragòza, *a flower*, 535.

II. OBSERVATIONS ON THE MAPS.

The inconvenience of consulting maps folded in the book, and their liability to mutilation, have induced the author to limit the size of the maps. Still, no important town has been omitted from them—no post-town nor seat of cantonal government. The appropriate position of every district in the nation is shown by means of the geographical index in Appendix III., which indicates the canton of each, while the cabecera of every canton is found on the map with the same number attached.

Small as are the maps, unusual care has been spent on them, and yet they must be far from accurate. No good map of New Granada exists, to the knowledge of the author. The best used in this compilation is H. S. Tanner's map of Colombia, published in New York in 1828. Brue's Colombia (Paris, 1826), Acosta's New Granada (Paris, 1847), and Mosquera's New Granada (New York, 1852), have been consulted. A rude sketch of mail-routes, prepared by Colonel Agustin Codazzi in 1853, has been used as far as possible.

The coasts and coast towns have been copied from admiralty charts, kindly furnished by the Messrs. Blunt, who have shown a lively interest in promoting the accuracy of the work. Twenty-four towns in the provinces north of Bogotá and ten in that of Antioquia are fixed from observations of the Comision Corográfica, and, from the character of Colonel Codazzi, may be relied upon as unusually accurate. They are reduced on the assumption that Bogotá is 74° 14′ 15″ west of Greenwich. Sixteen others are located according to less reliable observations. The remaining towns are from Codazzi's sketch, except Ciénega-de-oro, which is a sheer guess.

The rivers and mountains are still less accurate, as no maps have the hydrographic basins correctly shown. Besides a careful discussion of conflicting maps, the author has availed himself of his own observations and some rude copies of manuscript maps made in New Granada. In this severe task the compiler has received efficient aid from Mr. J. Wells, who drew the maps, and Mr. Charles Copley, who engraved them; yet none of the errors that shall be discovered can be attributed to either: they must be charged to the imperfection of the materials at present in reach.

The boundaries of the provinces can be but imperfectly ascertained, nor is it important, so constantly are they changing. All my applications to representatives of the Granadan government have been fruitless, and all the numerous and important changes made since 1853 have been put down from verbal statements of various gentlemen who happened to recollect most of them.

III. GEOGRAPHICAL INDEX.

New Granada has consisted of the following provinces, territories, and states, and the cantones mentioned under them were extant as territorial subdivisions. The cabecera of each bears generally the name of the canton, and in all other cases it is mentioned. In all cases the first canton contains the capital of the province. Abbreviations are affixed to the provinces, and numbers to the cantones, for convenience of reference. In the maps the names of the provinces are in Capitals, the seat of provincial government in Roman, and the other towns in *Italic*. The number of each canton is attached to its cabecera.

Antioquia. (An.)

1. Medellin.
2. Amagá.
3. Antioquia.
4. Marinilla.
5. Nordeste, *cab.* Amalfi.
6. Rio Negro.
7. Salamina, *cab.* Sonson.
8. Santa Rosa.
9. Sopetran.

Bogotá. (B.)

1. Bogotá.
2. Cáqueza.
3. Cipaquirá.
4. Chocontá.
5. Facatativá.
6. Funza.
7. Fusagasugá.
8. Guaduas.
9. Guatavita.
10. Mesa.
11. San Martin, *cab.* Medina.
12. Tocaima.
13. Ubaté.
14. Palma.

Buenaventura. (B.) *Cap.* Cali.

1. Cali.
2. Raposo, *cab.* Buenaventura.
3. Roldanillo.

Cartagena. (Ct.)

1. Cartagena.
2. Cármen.
3. Ciénega-de-oro.
4. Corozal.
5. Chinú.
6. Lorica.
7. Mahates.
8. San Andrés.
9. Sincelejo.

Casenare. (Cs.) *Cap.* Moreno.

1. Pore, *cab.* Moreno.
2. Arauca.
3. Chire.
4. Nunchía, *cab.* Labranza-grande.
5. Taguana, *cab.* Zapotosa.

Cauca. (Cc.) *Cap.* Buga.

1. Buga.
2. Anserma, *cab.* Ans. Nueva.
3. Cartago.
4. Palmira.
5. Supía.
6. Toro.
7. Tuluá.

Chocó. (Ch.) *Cap.* Quibdó.

1. Atrato, *cab.* Quibdó.
2. San Juan, *cab.* Nóvita.

Istmo. (I.)*

1. Panamá.
2. Alanje, *cab.* David.
3. Bocas del Toro.
4. Chagres.
5. Chorrera.
6. Darien, *cab.* Yavisa.
7. Natá.
8. Parita.
9. Portobello.
10. Santiago.
11. Santos.
12. Soto, *cab.* Penonomé.
13. Taboga.

Mariquita. (Mq.) *Cap.* Ibagué.

1. Ibagué.
2. Ambalema.
3. Castrolarma, *cab.* Chaparral.
4. Espinal, *cab.* Gúamo.
5. Honda.

Mocoa Terr. (Mc.)

Mompos. (Mp.)

1. Mompos.
2. Magangué.
3. Majagual.
4. Simtí.

Neiva. (Nv.)

1. Neiva.
2. Occidente, *cab.* Yaguará.
3. Plata.
4. Purificacion.
5. Timaná, *cab.* Garson.

Ocaña. (Oc.)

1. Ocaña.

Pamplona. (Pm.)

1. Pamplona.
2. Bucaramanga.
3. Concepcion.
4. Fortoul, *cab.* San Andrés.
5. Jiron.
6. Málaga.
7. Piedecuesta.
8. Rosario.
9. Salazar.
10. San José.

Pasto. (Ps.)

1. Pasto.
2. Barbacoas.
3. Ipiales.
4. Tumaco.
5. Túquerres.

Popayan. (Pp.)

1. Popayan.
2. Caldas, *cab.* Almaguer.

* The legal name is Estado de Panamá.

3. Izcuandé.
4. Micai, *cab.* Guapí.
5. Santander, *cab.* Quilichao.

RIOHACHA. (Rh.)

1. Riohacha.
2. César.

SABANILLA. (Sb.) *Cap.* Barranquilla.

1. Barranquilla.
2. Sabanalarga.
3. Soledad.

SAN MARTIN Terr. (Sn.)

SANTAMARTA. (Sm.)

1. Santamarta.
2. Ciénega.
3. Plato.
4. Remolino.
5. Tenerife, *cab.* San Antonio.

SOCORRO. (Sc.)

1. Socorro.
2. Barichara.
3. Charalá.
4. Jordan, *cab.* Aratoca.
5. Oiba.
6. Sanjil.
7. Zapatoca.

TUNDAMA. (Td.) *Cap.* Santa Rosa.

1. Santa Rosa.
2. Cocùi.
3. Ricáurte, *cab.* Sátiva Norte.
4. Soatá.
5. Sogamoso.

TUNJA. (Tj.)

1. Tunja.
2. Garagoa.
3. Guateque.
4. Leiva.
5. Miraflores.
6. Ramiriquí, *cab.* Turmequé.

VALLE DUPAR. (Vd.)

1. Valle Dupar.
2. Chiriguaná.

VELEZ. (Vz.)

1. Vélez.
2. Chiquinquirá.
3. Moniquirá.

IV. ALPHABETICAL LIST OF PLACES IN NEW GRANADA.

The territorial divisions are indicated by having attached to them their population in 1853. The abbreviations refer to the provinces, and the number annexed, the cantones in the above list. The remaining numbers refer to the pages of this work. The names of PROVINCES, STATES, and TERRITORIES are in LARGE CAPITALS, CANTONES in SMALL CAPITALS, *Aldeas* or *imperfect districts* in *Italics*, Districts in Roman letter, with the population attached. Lakes and ponds are marked L.; summits, A. (*Alto*); páramos, P.; mountains, Mt., and rivers, R. To these last are added the names of the waters into which they empty; *r* signifies from the right bank, *l* from the left. Capitals of provinces are designated by **, cabeceras of cantones by *, post-towns with weekly mail by ‡, and towns with 26 mails a year by †.

The accentuation is given on the same principle as in Appendix I.

Abejorràl †, An. 7; 6301.
Achì, Mp. 3; 1002.
Agràdo, Nv. 3; 2723.
Agua-caliènte, Mq. 1; 358
Agua-chica, Oc. 1; 701.
Aguàda, Vz. 1; 2462.
Aguàdas, An. 7; 5377.
Agua-làrga, B. 8; 125
Agua-nuèva, B. 1; 222
Aipe, Nv. 1; 3449.
ALÀNJE, I. 2; 16,654.
Alànje, I. 2; 3149.
Algarròbo, Mq. 3; 827.
Algodonàl, R., Oc., is the Catatùmbo.
Almaguèr * †, Pp. 2; 5529.
Almorzadèro, B. 10; 283
Alpujàrra, Nv. 4; 2413.
AMAGÁ, An. 2; 30,536.
Amagá * ‡, An. 2; 4717.
Amàlfi * ‡, An. 5; 2738.
AMBALÈMA, Mq. 2; 17,892.
Ambalèma * ‡, Mq. 2; 9731.
Anapòima, B. 10; 2362; 346
Ancùya, Ps. 5; 1758.
Angostùra de Nàre, Vz.; 75
Angostùra, An. 8; 2944.
Anjeles, Oc. 161.
Anolàima, B. 10; 5286.
Anorí, An. 8; 1924.
ANSÈRMA, Cc. 2; 2623.
Ansèrma-nuèvo * ‡, Cc. 2; 1609.
Ansèrma-vièjo, Cc. 2; 1014.
ANTIOQUIA, An., 243,388.
ANTIÒQUIA, An. 3; 24,439.
Antiòquia * ‡, An. 3; 8637.
Antòn, I. 12; 3711.
Anzá, An. 3; 4390.
Apopòris, R., Mc.; Caqueta, R. *l*.
Apùlo, R., B. 12; Bogotá, R. *r*. 286.
Aràma, B. 11; 100.
Aratòca * ‡, Sc. 4; 5091.
ARÀUCA, Cs. 2; 1954.
Aràuca * †, Cs. 2; 1548.
Aràuca, R., Cs.; Crinòco, R. *l*.
Arauquita, Cs. 2; 289.
Arbolèdas, Pm. 9; 1433.
Aripòro, R., Cs.; Meta, R. *l*.
Arjòna, Ct. 7; 2623; 48
Arma, R., An.; Cauca, R. *r*.
Arma, An. 7; 433.
Arrayàn, I. 5; 523.
Arrayanàl, Ch. 1; 1125.
Arròyo de Pièdra, Sb. 2; 342.
Arròyo-grande, Ct. 1; 365.
Arròyo-hondo, hacienda, Bv. 1; 524
Arròyo-hondo, Ct. 7; 363; 53
Arvèla, Pp. 2; 1542.
Arzobìspo, R. del. B.; Bogota, R. *l*.; 211
Aserradèro, B. 8; 125
Aspásica, Oc. 1; 1317.
Aspinwall, I. 9, is Colòn.
Atabàpo, R., Sn; Guaviàre, R. *r*.
Atàco, Mq. 3; 1090.
Atalàya, I. 10; 1059.
Atànques, Vd. 1; 381.
ATRÀTO, Ch. 1; 22,597.
Atràto, R., Ch.; Caribbean Sea.
Auròra, hacienda, Cc. 1; 507
Ayapèl, Ct. 5; 2015.
Azèro, Cs. 2; 44.
Azufràl de Quindìo, Mq. 1; 357

Badìllo, Vd. 1; 1098.
Baganìque, Tj., is Ramiriquí.

CARTÀGO, Cc. 3; 14,892.
Cartàgo * ‡, Cc. 3; 6744; 375
Carùpa, B. 13; 2651.
CASANARE, C. 5; 18,573; 176, 240
Casanàre, R., Cs.; Meta, R.
Cascajàl, Ct. 4; 459.
Casiquiàre, R., Cs. and Cq.; Negro R. and Orinoco.
CASTROLÀRMA, Mq. 3; 13,302.
Catatùmbo, R., Pm.; Zùlia, R. *l.*
CAUCA, Cc.; 70,748.
Càuca, R., Mp.; Magdalena, R.
Cèja, An. 6; 4108.
Cèja de Guatapé, An. 4; 1114.
Celàndia, Pp. 5; 1864.
Centino, R., Vz., is Minèro, R.
Cepitá, Pm. 7; 3363.
Ceretè, Ct. 3; 1388.
Cerrìllos, Cc. 3; 320.
Cerrìto, Cc. 1; 3331; 506
Cerrìto, R., Cc. 1; Cauca, R. *r.*; 510
Cerrìto, Pm. 3; 1945.
CESÀR, Rh. 2; 6242.
Cesàr * ‡, Rh. 2; 2550.
Cesàr, R., Sm.; Magdalena, R. *r.*
CHÁGRES, I. 4; 1340.
Chágres * ‡, I. 4; 1340.
Chágres, R., I.; Caribbean Sea.
Chaguani, B. 8; 1881.
Chàme, I. 5; 1103.
Chámeza, Tj. 5; 607.
Chaparràl * †, Mg. 3; 6210.
Chapigàna, I. 6; 268.
Chapinèro, B. 1; 201
Chaquiral, hacienda, Cc. 3; 394
CHARALÁ, Sc. 3; 19,346.
Charalá * ‡, Sc. 3; 8296.
Chèpo, I. 1; 1536.
Chìa, B. 6; 4424.
Chiapàque, B. 2; 4163.
Chicamòcha, R., Td., is the Sogamòso.
Chimá, Ct. 3; 2028.
Chìma, Sc. 1; 3010.
Chimàn, I. 13; 276.
Chìmbe, B. 8; 125
Chimichàgua, Vd. 2; 681.
Chinácota, Pm. 10; 2012.
Chinevìta, Tj. 2; 1055.
CHINÚ, Ct. 5; 24,224.
Chinú * ‡, Ct. 5; 5067.
Chipàlo, R., Mq. 1; Magdalena, R. *l.*; 337
Chiapàque, B. 2; 4163.
Chipasàque, B. 9; 5883.
Chipatá, Vz. 1; 7565.
CHIQUINQUIRÁ, Vz. 2; 24,663.
Chiquinquirá * ‡, Vz. 2; 8271; 186
Chíquisa, Tj. 1; 1414.
CHÌRE, Cs. 3; 2153.
Chìre *, Cs. 3; 404.
Chìre, R., Cs. 3; Meta, R. *l.*
CHIRIGUANÁ, Vd. 2; 6403.
Chiriguaná * ‡, Vd. 2; 3578.
Chiriquí, R., 1; Pacific.
Chirivì, Tj. 6; 3155.
Chìscas, Td. 2; 5119.
Chìta ‡, Td. 2; 7040.
Chitagá, Pm. 1; 1220.
Chitaràque, Vz. 3; 2900.
Chivatá, Tj. 1; 3045.
Choachí, B. 1; 4691; 242
Choachí, Páramo, B. 1; 237
Choachí Sulphur Spring, B. 1; 242
Chòcho, hacienda, B. 7; 301
CHOCO, Ch.; 43,649.
Chocó, Caño de, Pm. and Oc.
CHOCONTÁ, B. 4; 31,564.
Chocontá * ‡, B. 4; 8461.
Chòpo, Pm. 1; 1647.
CHORRÈRA, I. 5; 6475.
Chorrèra * ‡, I. 5; 2451.
Chorrèra, R., I.; Pacific.
Chorrèra, Rh. 1; 401.
Chòrro, Cc. 7; 493
Chucunàque, R., I.; Sabana, R. *l.*
Cibaté, B. 1; 287
CIÉNEGA, Sm. 2; 8573.
Ciénega * ‡, Sm. 2; 5078.
Ciénega, Tj. 6; 2985.
CIÉNEGA-DE-ORÒ, Ct. 3; 13,251.
Ciénega-de-orò * †, Ct. 3; 5163.
Cincelàda, Sc. 3; 3043.
Cìncha, hacienda, B. 13; 286
Cipacòn, B. 5; 1747.
CIPAQUIRÁ, B. 3; 26,994.
Cipaquirá * ‡, B. 3; 6077.
Cìte, Vz. 1; 3354.
Clàro, R., Ch.; Pacific.
Cobarachía, Td. 4; 2702.
Cocoroná, An. 4; 1304.
COCÙI, Td. 2; 29,605.
Cocùi * †, Td. 2; 5729.
Coèllo, Mq. 1; 2878; 323
Coèllo, R., Mq.; Magdalena, R. *l.*; 322
Cògua, B. 3; 3941.
Coìba, I. 10; 63.
Colèjio, B. 10; 1170.
Colòmbia, Nv. 4; 1673.
Colòn ‡, I. 9.
Colosiná, Ct. 3; 1152.
Colosò, Ct. 9; 491.
Combèima, R., Mq.; Coello, R. *l.*; 337
Cómbita, Tj. 1; 4052.
Concepciòn, An. 6; 1616.
CONCEPCIÒN, Pm. 3; 19,?25.
Concepciòn * ‡, Pm. 3; 3619.
Concòrdia, An. 2; 1747.
Conèjo, B. 14; 90
Confìnes, Sc. 1; 3376.
Consacá, Ps. 1; 2520.
Convenciòn, Oc.; 1788.
Copacabàna, An. 1; 4073.
Copèr, Vz. 2; 1040.
Córdova, An. 9; 2651.
Coromòro, Sc. 3; 2032.
COROZÀL, Ct. 4; 13,013.
Corozàl * ‡, Ct. 4; 6351.
Corràles, Td. 1; 1715.
Còta, B. 6; 1503.
Cototàma, Rh. 1; 136.
Coyàima, Nv. 4; 5544.
Crèce-nòche, Oc., is Anjeles.
Crùces, An. 8; 553.
Crùces, B. 8; 102
Crùces, I. 1; 495.
Cruz, Oc.; 2682.
Cruz, Pp. 2; 4176.
Cruz Vèrde, Páramo, B. 1; 255
Cuàtro Esquinas, B. 6; 134
Cuàtro Esquìnas, Mq. 1; 340
Cucàita, Tj. 1; 929.
Cucunubá, B. 13; 4831.
Cúcuta, Pm. 8; 602.
Cucutìlla, Pm. 1; 2344.
Cuilòto, Cs. 2; 37.
Cuitìva, Td. 5; 1446.
Culàtas, Sc. 1, is Confìnes.
Culebrèra, B. 6; 135
Cumbàl, Ps. 3; 2973.
Cunàcua, Sc. 5; 2234.
Cunàri, R., Mc.; Caquetá, R. *l.*
Cundài, B. 7; 2619.
Cùne, B. 8; 118
Cupìca, R., Ch.; Pacific.
Curití, Sc. 4; 4055.
Cùrcio, B. 10; 351

Dabèiba, An. 3; 565.
Dàgua, R., Bv. 2; Pacific; 20
DARIÈN, I. 6; 1209.
Davìd * ‡, I. 2; 4625.

Itagüí, An. 2; 5182.
Itòco, Vz. 2; 1121.
Ituàngo, An. 3; 1175.
Iza, Td. 5; 1395.
IZCUANDÉ, Pp. 3; 5441.
Izcuandó * †, Pp. 3; 5441.

Jàgua, Nv. 5; 1674.
Jàgua, Vd. 2; 524.
Jambaló, Pp. 5; 1968.
Jègua, Ct. 5; 561.
Jenesàno, Tj. 6; 4510.
Jenesèno, R., Tj., is the Boyacá.
Jericó, Td. 3; 3458.
Jesùs María, Vz. 1, is Vàlle.
Jicaramàta, Cc. 7; 496
Jigànte ‡, Nv. 5; 3213.
Jimaní, Ct. 1; 43
Jimèna, Pp. 1; 1197.
Jiradòta, An. 1; 3149.
Jiramèna, B. 11; 242.
JIRÒN, Pm. 5; 12,576.
Jiròn * ‡, Pm. 5; 9133.
Jòbo, Vd. 1; ——.
JORDÀN, Sc. 4; 9146.
Juanambú, R., Ps.; Patía, R.
Juàn de Acòsta, Sb. 1; 848.
Julumìto, Pp. 1; 1241.
Jùntas, Bv. 2; 20.
Jùntas, B. 12; 345
Júpura, R., Mc., is the Caquetá.

Labatèca, Pm. 1; 1913.
Labrànza-grànde * ‡, Cs. 4; 3379.
Lagùna, R., Pp.; Patía, R. *l.*
Lagùna-grànde, pond, B. 2; 248
Lagunètas, Cc. 3; 372
Làjas, R., Cc. 3; Càuca, R. *l.*; 394
Làjas, Ps. 3; 517
Lebrija, R., Oc.; Magdalena, R. *r.*
LÈIVA, Tj. 4; 22,219.
Lèiva * ‡, Tj. 4; 3395.
Lèiva, R., is the Moniquirá.
Lémos, Hàto de, Cc. 6; 2889.
Lenguàsaque, B. 13; 3479.
Lérida, Mq. 2; 5025.
Liborìna, An. 9; 1273.
Libràida, Cc. 3; 2151; 412
Lìmas, Nv. 5; 2576.
Limoncìto, Pm. 10; 368.
Lìpa, R., Cs.; Ele, R. *l.*
Lloró, Ch. 1; 4035.
Lòba, Mp. 1; 1039.
Lòma de Corredòr, Oc.; 401.
Lòma de Indijenas, Oc.; 513.
LORÌCA, Ct. 6; 7493.
Lorìca * ‡, Ct. 6; 3532.

Macaguàne, Cs. 3; 183.
Macanàl, Tj. 2; 2567.
Macào, R., Cs.; Sarare, R. *l.*
Macaràcas, I. 11; 2708.
Macaravìta, Pm. 3; 2550.
Machetá, B. 4; 6270.
MAGANGUÉ, Mp. 2; 6832.
Magangué * ‡, Mp. 2; 2512.
Magdalèna, R.; Caribbean Sea.
Magué, B. 7; 301
Maguí, R., Ps.; Patía, R. *l.*
MAHÀTES, Ct. 7; 12,659.
Mahàtes * ‡, Ct. 7; 1278; 50
MAJAGUÀL, Mp. 3; 5227.
Majaguàl * ‡, Mp. 3; 2409.
MÁLAGA, Pm. 6; 11,175.
Málaga * †, Pm. 6; 4410.
Malagavìta, Pm. 6; 3899.
Malàmbo, Sb. 3; 853.
Màles, Ps. 3; 1620.
Mallàma, Ps. 5; 1266.
Mamatòco, Sm. 1; 343.
Manàre, Cs. 3; 239.
Manatí, Sb. 3; 799.
Manizàles, An. 7; 2809.
Mànta, B. 4; 5303.
Maquivòr, Cs. 1; 120.
Marañòn, R., is the Amazon.
Margarìta, Mp. 1; 1827; 64
María la Bàja, Ct. 7; 266.
MARINÌLLA, An. 4; 17,909.
Marinìlla * ‡, An. 4; 3414.
Maripí, Vz. 2; 890.
MARIQUITA, Mq.; 86,985; 333
Mariquìta, Mq. 5; 1737.
Marocàso, Rh. 2; 93.
Marroquìn, Cs. 4; 469.
Matànza, Pm. 2; 3582.
Màve, B. 8; 123
Mayasquèr, Ps. 3; 212.
Màyo, R., Ps.; Patía, R. *l.*
MEDELLÌN, An. 1; 38,610.
Medellìn ** ‡, An. 1; 13,755.
Medialùna, Sm. 2; 529.
Medìna *, B. 11; 913.
Mèdio, Cc. 3; 417
Melgàr, B. 12; 2600; 318
Méndez, Mq. 5; 1043; 342
Mercadères, Pp. 2; 1712.
Merèdia, Sn. 5; 1910.
MÈSA, B. 10; 23,545.
Mèsa * ‡, B. 10; 6012; 346
Mèsa, I. 10; 2542.
Mèta, R., Cs.; Orinoco, R. *l.*; 236
MICÀI, Pp. 4; 8853.
Micài, Pp. 4; 2296.
Micài, R., Pp.; Pacific.
Micos, R., Cc. 3; Cauca, *l.*; 390
Mièl, R., Mq.; Magdalena, R. *l.*
Minas, I. 8; 1642.
Mìnas, Cc. 7; 490
Mineràl, I. 10; 282.
Mìra, R., Ps.; Pacific.
Miraflòres, Mq. 1; 680.
MIRAFLÒRES, Tj. 5; 8387.
Miraflòres * †, Tj. 5; 5002.
MOCOA Terr., Mc.
Mocòa ** †, Mc.
Mòcu, R., Cs.; Vichada, R. *l.*
Mogòtes, Sc. 6; 6568.
Molinèca, I. 6; 77.
Molino, Rh. 2; 1246.
Momìl, Ct. 6; 617.
MOMPOS, Mp.; 30,207.
MOMPÒS, Mp. 1; 13,711.
Mompòs ** ‡, Mp. 1; 7336; 60
Mòngua, Td. 5; 2461.
Mongüí, Td. 5; 1540.
MONIQUIRA, Vz. 3; 20,734.
Moniquirá * ‡, Vz. 3; 9127.
Moniquirá, R., Vz.; Fúquene, R. *r.*
Montería, Ct. 3; 2039.
Montìjo, I. 10; 2009.
Moncerràte, mountain, B. 1; 214
Moràl, Mq. 1; 357
Moràles, I., Mp. 4.
Moràles, Mp. 4; 1094.
Morcòte, Cs. 4; 721.
Morèno ** ‡, Cs. 1; 1365.
Morèno, Rh. 1; 772.
Morillo, hacienda; 455
Morillo, R., Cc.; 5 & 7; Cauca, R. *r.*; 455
Morròa, Ct. 4; 772.
Motavíta, Tj. 1; 1275.
Munèque †, Cs. ?
Murindó, Ch. 1; 2007.
Murrí, Ch. 1; 2009.
Murrí, R., Ch.; Atràto, R. *r.*
Mutìscua, Pm. 1; 982.
Mùzo †, Vz. 2; 862.

Napipí, R., Ch.; Atràto, R. *l.*

Narànjo, Cc. 3, is Obàndo.
Nàre ‡, Mq. 5; 1054; 76
Nàre, R., An.; Magdalèna, R. *l.*
Narìño, An. 7; 460.
Narìño, B. 12; 1048.
NATÁ, I. 7; 12,831.
Natá * †, I. 7; 8029.
Nátaga, Nv. 2; 471.
Natagàima ‡, Nv. 4; 4038.
Nechì, An. 5; 473.
Nechí, R., An.; Càuca, R. *r.*
Nègro, R.; Amazon, R. *l.*
Nègro, R., An., is the Nàre.
Nègro, R., Vz.; Magdalèna, R. *r.*; 90, 122
Nèira, An. 7; 3606.
Nèira, Nv. 1; 1706.
NEIVA, Nv.; 101,772.
NÈIVA, Nv. 1; 26,780.
Nèiva ** ‡, 7719.
Nèiva, R., Nv.; Magdalèna, R. *r.*
Nème, B. 8; 342
Nemocòn, B. 3; 3018.
Nepomucèno, Ct. 2; 1904.
Nervitì, Ct. 2; 113.
Nilo, B. 12; 1815.
Nimàima, B. 8; 901.
Nisperàl, Sb. 1; 30
Noanàma, Ch. 2; 3510.
Nòbsa, Td. 1; 2951.
Nocàima, B. 8; 2590.
NORDOÈSTE, An. 2; 8348.
Norosí, Mp. 4; 324.
Novillèro, hacienda, B. 7; 300
Nóvita * ‡, Ch. 2; 6097.
Nuèva Caramànta, An. 2; 1154.
NUNCHÍA, Cs. 4; 6583.
Nunchía, Cs. 4; 531.

Obàndo, Cc. 3; 2069; 290
Ocamònte, Sc. 3; 2555.
OCAÑA, Oc.; 23,450.
OCÀÑA, Oc. 1; 23,450.
Ocàna ** ‡, Oc. 1; 5046; 206
OCCIDÈNTE, Nv. 2; 9494.
Ocú, I. 8; 5580.
OÌBA, Sc. 5; 21,792.
Oìba * ‡, Sc. 5; 6376.
Oicatá, Tj. 1; 2319.
Olá, I. 7; 710.
Onzàga, Sc. 6; 6026.
Opia (ferry), Mq. 1; 341
Opía, R., Mq.; Magdalèna, R. *l.*; 340
Opòn, R., Sc.; Magdalèna, R. *l.*
Organos, Nv. 1; 510.
Orinòco, R., Cs.; Atlantic.
Oro, R., Pm. 5, is the Lebrìja.
Oro, R., Oc.; Lebrija, R. *r.*
Oro, R., Oc., is the Catatùmbo.
Oro, R., Oc.; Catatùmbo, R. *l.*
Orta, R., Vz.
Ospina, Ps. 5; 1061.
Ortèga, Mq. 3; 6002.
Otòque, I. 13; 347.
Otro Mùndo, Vz. 1.
Ovèjas, Ct. 9; 1748.
Ovèro, Cc. 7; 457

Pachavìta, Tj. 2; 3836.
Pàcho, B. 3; 3326.
Pácora, An. 7; 3610.
Pácora, I. 1; 773.
Páez, R., Nv.; Magdalèna, R. *l.*
Paicól ‡, Nv. 3; 1121.
Pàila, R., Cc.; Càuca, R. *r.*; 417
Pàila, hacienda, Cc. 3; 417
Pàime, B. 13; 731.
Pàipa, Td. 1; 6614.
Pàipa, R., Td.; Sogamoso, R. *l.*
Pajarìto, Cs. 5; 575.
Palènque, I. 9; 249.

PÀLMA, B. 14; 18,120.
Pàlma * †, B. 14; 4432.
Pàlma, Oc.; 1008.
Palmàr, Sc. 1; 2129.
Palmàr, hacienda, B. 8; 117
Palmàr de Candelària, Sb. 2; 883.
Palmàr de Varèla, Sb. 3; 1050.
Palmarìto, Mp. 3; 989.
Pàlmas, I. 10; 3004.
Pàlmas, Sc. 1; 3322.
Palmìlla, Mq. 1; 356
PALMÌRA, Cc. 4; 16,176.
Palmìra * ‡, Cc. 4; 10,055; 513
Palmìra, Vd. 1; 294.
Palmìto, Ct. 9; 772.
PAMPLONA, Pm.; 139,039.
PAMPLÒNA, Pm. 1; 22,922.
Pamplòna ** ‡, Pm. 1; 9095.
PANAMÁ, I. 1; 10,111.
Panamá ** ‡, I. 1; 6566.
Pàndi, B. 7; 2533; 310
Pàndi, bridge, B. 7; 309
Pánga, Ps. 5; 590.
Paniquitá, Pp. 1; 2413.
Panquèva, Td. 2; 1433.
Páramo, Sc. 1; 3218.
Pàre, Vz. 3; 4602.
PARÌTA, I. 8; 17,093.
Parita * †, I. 8; 3019.
Pàsacabàllos, Ct. 1; 227.
Pàsca, B. 7; 488.
Pàso, Vd. 2; 779.
PASTO, Ps.; 82,952; 251
PÀSTO, Ps. 1; 27,620.
Pàsto ** ‡, Ps. 1; 8136.
Patía, Pp. 1; 2377.
Patía, R., Ps.; Pacific.
Pàuna, Vz. 2; 2435.
Pàvas, Bv. 1; 328.
Pàya, Cs. 4; 1194.
Payandé, Mq. 1; 1584.
Paz, Td. 3; 2460.
Paz, Vd. 1; 837.
Paz, Vz. 1; 3008.
Pedasí, I. 11; 708.
Pedràl, Pm. 5; 183.
Pèña, B. 14; 3603.
Peñòl, An. 4; 5361.
Peñòn, B. 14; 1504.
Penonomé * ‡, I. 12; 8703.
Peralònso, R., Pm.
Pèsca, Td. 5; 7690.
Pescaderías, B. 8; 101
Pescàdo, R.; Caqueta, R. *l.*
Pescadòr, Bv. 3; 1752.
Pesé, I. 8; 4732.
Petaquèro, Sc. 6; 2118.
Petaquèro, A., B. 8; 121
Picàzo, hill, Cc. 7; 490
PIEDECUÈSTA, Pm. 7; 20,208.
Piedecuèsta * ‡, Pm. 7; 14,841.
Pié de la Popa, Ct. 1; 875; 46
Pièdra de Molèr, Cc. 3; 373
Pièdras, An. 2; 630.
Pièdras ‡, Mq. 1; 5575; 340
Pièdras, R., Cc. 1; Cauca, R. *r.*; 503
Piña, canal, Sb. 1; 40
Pinchòte, Sc. 6; 2602.
Pinillos, Mp. 1; 526.
Pinogàna, I. 6; 164.
Piñòn, Sm. 5; 2027.
Pintàda, I. 12; 3155.
Pìnto, Sm. 3; 367.
Piojó, Sb. 2; 604.
Pìsva, Cs. 4; 289.
Pitàl ‡, Nv. 3; 2388.
Pitalìto, Nv. 5; 1766.
Pivijài, Sm. 2; 1525.
Plàta, An. 6; 141.
PLATA, Nv. 3; 18,826.

San Càrlos, An. 4; 760.
San Càrlos, I. 5; 1111.
San Cayetàno, Ct. 7; 427.
San Cayetàno, Pm. 10; 982.
San Cristóval, An. 1; 1467.
San Estanislào, Ct. 7; 2300.
San Faustìno, Pm. 10; 544.
San Felipe de Baràjas, fort, Ct. 1; 43
San Félix, I. 2; 515.
San Fernàndo, Mp. 1; 714.
San Fernàndo, Sm. 3; 419.
San Francìsco, R., B. 1; Bogota, R. *l.*; 154
San Francìsco, I. 10; 4885.
San Jacìnto, Ct. 2; 2479.
San Jerónimo, An. 9; 2353.
Sanjìl, Sc. 6; 32,848.
Sanjìl * ‡, Sc. 6; 11,528.
San Jòrje, R., Mp.; Càuca, R. *l.*
San José, Pm. 10; 10,259.
San José * ‡, Pm. 10; 5741.
San José, Ps. 2; 3000.
San Juan, Ch. 2; 21,052.
San Juàn, Cc. 5; 1559.
San Juàn, R., An. 2; Càuca, R. *l.*
San Juàn, R., Bv.; Dàqua, R.
San Juàn, R., I.; Pacific.
San Juàn, R., Ch.; Pacific.
San Juàn, Rh. 2, is César.
San Juàn, R., Mq. 1, is the Coèllo.
San Lázaro, mount, Ct. 1; 43
San Lorènzo, I. 2; 1777.
San Lùcia, R., I.; Pacific.
San Luìs, Mq. 4; 3436.
San Màrcos, Ct. 5; 754.
San Màrcos, R., Cc. 7; Tulua, R. *r.*; 491
San Màrcos, hacienda, Bv. 1; 525
San Martin, B. 11; 2870; 240
San Martìn †, B. 11; 668.
San Matèo, An. 3; 656.
San Miguèl, I. 4 (*pop. not known*).
San Miguèl, Pm. 3; 2900.
San Miguèl, I. 13; 1941.
San Miguèl, Rh. 1; 116.
San Miguèl, R., Mc.; Putumayo, R. *r.*
San Miguèl, Cc. 3; 436, 462
San Nicholàs, Ct. 6; 349.
San Onòfre, Ct. 9; 2659.
San Pàblo, Ps. 2; 1203.
San Pàblo, I. 2; 730.
San Pàblo, Mp. 4; 233; 72
San Pèdro, An. 8; 4666.
San Pèdro, Cs. 5; 128.
San Pèdro, Cc. 1; 2137; 501
San Pèdro, Oc. 1; 342.
San Pelàyo, Ct. 3; 1481.
San Sebastiàn, An. 9; 821.
San Sebastiàn, Ct. 6; 367.
San Sebastiàn, Sm. 3; 800.
San Sebastiàn, Mp. 2; 338.
San Sebastiàn, Vd. 1; 333.
Sànta Ana, Ct. 1; 425.
Sànta Ana, Mq. 5; 2153.
Sànta Ana, Sm. 3; 708.
Sànta Ana, Vz. 3; 2153.
Sànta Bárbara, An. 6; 2225.
Sànta Catalìna, Ct. 1; 902.
Santafé, B. 1, is Bogotá.
Santafé, I. 10; 1076.
Santa Libràda, Nv. 5; 2265.
Santa María, I. 8; 2120.
Santa María, I. 6; 145.
SANTAMARTA, Sm.; 36,485.
Santamarta, Sm. 1; 5774.
Santamàrta ** ‡, Sm. 1; 4349; 27
Santandèr, Pp. 5; 19,789.
Santa Rosa, An. 8; 32,851.
Santa Ròsa * ‡, An. 8; 4996.
Santa Ròsa ‡, B 12; 2698.
Santa Ròsa, Ct. 1; 903.
Santa Rosa, Td.; 39,042.
Santa Ròsa * ‡, Td.; 4934.
Santiàgo, Ct. 5; 517.
Santiàgo, Cs. 5; 203.
Santiàgo, Pm. 9; 1249.
Santiago, I. 10; 33,864.
Santiàgo * ‡, I. 10; 6121.
Sànto Domingo, An. 1; 2235.
Sànto Tomàs, Sb. 3; 2404.
Sàntos, I. 11; 17,550.
Sàntos * ‡, I. 11; 6223.
Sàntos, Pm. 7; 2004.
Santuàrio, B. 6; 135
Santuàrio, An. 4; 2706.
San Vicènte, An. 6; 5369.
San Vicènte, Sc. 7; 88.
San Zenòn, Sm. 3; 813.
Sàpo, Ct.; 53
Sapùyes, Ps. 5; 1493.
Sajandì, R., Ps.; Patia, R. *l.*
Sarabìta, R., Vz., is the Fúquene.
Saràre, R., Cs.; Apùre, R. *r.*
Sardinàta, R., Pm.; Zùlia, R. *l.*
Sargènto, A., B. 8; 103
Sària, R., Ch.; Pacific.
Sartinajàl, haciènda, Cc. 7; 461
Sasàima, B. 8; 2255.
Satìva-nòrte * ‡, Td.; 4240.
Satìva-sur, Td.; 1048.
Sàifa, R., Pp. 4; Pacific.
Sèco, R., B. 8; Magdalena, R. *r.*; 342
Sèdros, R., Ps. 2; Pacific.
Serìnza, Td. 1; 2766.
Serrezuèla, B. 6; 1094; 133
Servièz, B. 11; 233.
Servitá, Pm. 3; 596.
Sesquilé, B. 9; 2775.
Siachòque, Tj. 1; 3001.
Sièrra, Pp. 1; 2643.
Silos, Pm. 1; 2514.
Sìlvia, Pp. 1; 3728.
Simacòta, Sc. 1; 7022.
Simàncas, Oc. 1.
Simàña, Oc. 1; 684.
Simijàca, B. 13; 3828.
Simijàca, R., Vz., is the Fúquene.
Simitàrra, R., Mp.; Magdalena, R. *l.*
Simiti, Mp. 4; 4437.
Simití * †, Mp. 4; 1980.
Sincé, Ct. 4; 4054.
Sincelejo, Ct. 9; 15,148.
Sincelèjo * ‡, Ct. 9; 6046.
Sipí, Ch. 2; 2021.
Sìquima, B. 5; 2006.
Sìte, Vz. 1, is Cite.
Sìtio nuèvo, Sm. 4; 2501.
Soàcha, B. 1; 2918; 273
Soata, Td. 4; 22,374.
Soatá * ‡, Td. 4; 9015.
Sòcha, Td. 3; 2866.
SOCORRO, Sc.; 157,085; 345
Socorro, Sc. 1; 41,761.
Socòrro ** ‡, Sc. 1; 15,015.
Socotá, Td. 3; 5306.
Sogamoso, Td. 5; 42,354.
Sogamòso * ‡, Td. 5; 6369.
Sogamòso, R., Sc.; Magdalena, R. *r.*
Solàno, R., Ch.; Pacific.
Soldàdo, Rh. 1; 210.
Soldàno, R., Mq. and Nv.; Magdalena, R. *l.*
Soledàd, An. 2; 398.
Soledàd, Sb. 3; 10,456.
Soledàd * ‡, Sb. 3; 3992.
Solimòes, R., is the Amazon.
Somondòco, Tj. 3; 5270.
Soná, I. 10; 2652.
Sonsòn * ‡, An. 7; 10,244.
Sopetràn, An. 9; 17,763.
Sopetràn * ‡, An. 9; 4573.
Sopó, B. 3; 2531.
Sòra, Tj. 1; 899.

V. MAIL ROUTES.

The following table gives the mail routes of New Granada as fixed by the decree of November 19, 1853. The distances are given in miles, together with the time allotted, both going and returning.

I. Bogotá to the Atlantic.

1. *Bogotá to*	Hours.	Hours.	Miles.
Facatativá	9 go'g.	10 ret'g.	28.0
Villeta	6	9	18.6
Guaduas	5	5	15.5
Honda	6	5	15.5
Nare	13	29	82.3
Boca del Carare	11	26	71.5
Barranca-bermeja	5	11	28.0
Puerto Nacional	17	35	97.9
Banco	14	22	59.0
Mompos	11	22	59.0
Plato	9	17	43.5
Calamar	10	20	54.4
San Antonio	1	2	4.7
Remolino (Sm.)	6	10	23.3
Soledad	5	6	17.1
Barranquilla	1	3	4.7
Sabanilla	3	4	7.8
2. *Remolino to*			
Ciénega	10	10	59.0
Santa Marta	5	5	20.2
Riohacha	40	40	102.5
3. *Calamar to*			
Mahates	10	10	31.1
Cartagena	12	11	34.2
4. *Banco to*			
Chiriguaná	26	26	59.0
Valle Dupar	39	39	87.0
César	16	16	37.3
Riohacha	32	32	87.0

II. Bogotá to Puerto Nacional.

5. *Bogotá to*	Hours.	Hours.	Miles.
Cipiquirá	11 go'g.	9 ret'g.	31.1
Ubaté	10	9	26.4
Chiquinquirá	11	9	24.9
Puente Nacional	9	8	24.9
Vélez	5	4	12.4
Suaita	6	6	18.6
Oiba	7	6	18.6
Socorro	6	6	17.1
San-jil	4	4	12.4
Aratoca	5	5	15.5
Piedecuesta	11	10	28.5
Jiron	4	4	12.4
Bucaramanga	3	3	9.3
Suratá	10	10	28.0
Ocaña	37	37	97.9
Puerto Nacional	14	14	40.4
6. *Socorro to*			
Barichara	6	6	15.5
Zapatosa	8	8	17.1
Barranca-bermeja	32	32	83.9
7. *Vélez to*			
Puerto del Carare	26	35	52.8
Boca del Carare	25	29	52.8

III. Bogotá to Venezuela.

8. *Bogotá to*	Hours.	Hours.	Miles.
Chocontá	19	22	59.0
Turmequé	9	9	24.9
Tunja	7	8	21.7
Santa Rosa	13	14	38.8

	Hours.	Hours.	Miles.
Sativa-norte	11	12	31.1
Soatá	7	7	18.6
Concepcion	15	20	43.5
Pamplona	25	23	62.1
San José	20	22	51.2
Rosario	2	2	6.2
Táchira (Venezuela)	1	1	3.1

9. *Tunja to*

	Hours.	Hours.	Miles.
Sogamoso	13	13	37.3
Lobranza-grande	19	19	51.2
Moreno	25	25	63.7
Arauca	42	42	118.1

IV. Bogotá to Ecuador.

10. *Bogotá to*

	Hours.	Hours.	Miles.
Mesa	16	13	35.7
Tocaima	8	9	23.3
Santa Rosa	11	13	?
Prado	6	5	?
Villa-vieja	13	12	?
Neiva	7	8	20.2
Yaguará	8	10	21.7
Carnicerías	10	10	24.9
Paicol	3	3	9.3
Plata	4	5	9.3
Popayan	43	47	77.6
Pasto	71	69	139.8
Túquerres	13	13	34.2
Ipiales	8	9	24.9
Tulcan (Ecuador)	4	4	7.8

V. Bogotá to the Pacific.

11. *Bogotá to*

	Hours.	Hours.	Miles.
Mesa	16	13	35.7
Tocaima	8	8	23.3
Piedras	10	10	31.1
Ibagué	9	9	28.0
Cartago	47	42	87.0
Tuluá	16	16	49.7
Buga	4	4	12.4
Palmira	9	9	26.4
Cali	7	6	18.6
Buenaventura	26	26	68.4

VI. Western Local Waters.

12. *Cartagena to*

	Hours.	Hours.	Miles.
Mahates	12	12	34.2
Cármen	5	5	?
Corozal	8	8	?
Sincelejo	4	3	9.3
Chinú	13	13	34.2
Lorica	17	17	46.6

13. *Chinú to*

	Hours.	Hours.	Miles.
Ciénega-de-oro	10	12	?

14. *Cartagena to*

	Hours.	Hours.	Miles.
Sabanalarga	20	20	55.9
Soledad	8	8	23.3
Barranquilla	1	1	4.7
Sabanilla	3	3	7.8

15. *Simití to*

	Hours.	Hours.	Miles.
Puerto-nacional	13	13	46.6

16. *Medellin to*

	Hours.	Hours.	Miles.
Santa Rosa (An.)	17	17	37.3
Amalfi	18	18	40.4
Remedios	19	19	43.5
Zaragoza	16	17	34.2
Majagual	32	73	111.8
Magangué	19	52	80.8
Tacaloa	8	16	24.9
Mompos	16	4	21.7

17. *Nare to*

	Hours.	Hours.	Miles.
Remolino (An.)	8	3	12.4
Marinilla	27	28	77.7
Rionegro	1	1	3.1
Medellin	7	6	18.6
Sopetran	11	11	28.5
Antioquia	3	4	7.8
Urrao	17	17	40.4
Bebará	31	38	55.9
Quibdó	26	26	62.2

18. *Antioquia to*

	Hours.	Hours.	Miles.
Santa Rosa (An.)	16	16	40.4

19. *Medellin to*

	Hours.	Hours.	Miles.
Amagá	9	9	21.7
Supía	25	25	52.8
Anserma-nuevo	30	30	71.5
Cartago	3	3	7.8
Toro	7	7	18.6
Roldanillo	9	9	24.9
Cali	27	27	62.1
Quilichao	9	9	24.9
Popayan	26	26	55.9

20. *Cartago to*

	Hours.	Hours.	Miles.
Anserma-nuevo	3	3	7.8
Nóvita	22	22	52.8
Quibdó	32	52	124.3

21. *Rionegro to*

	Hours.	Hours.	Miles.
Abejorral	12	12	28.0
Sonson	6	6	14.0
Salamina	22	22	40.4
Supía	11	11	20.2

22. *Honda to*

	Hours.	Hours.	Miles.
Ambalema	14	14	43.5
Ibagué	15	15	46.6
Guamo	15	16	?
Chaparral	28	28	?

23. *Buenaventura to*

	Hours.	Hours.	Miles.
Guapí	50	50	124.3
Izcuandé	6	6	15.0
Barbacoas	35	28	77.7
Túquerres	52	52	83.9

24. *Barbacoas to*

	Hours.	Hours.	Miles.
Tumaco	20	20	52.8

25. *Pasto to*

	Hours.	Hours.	Miles.
Mocoa	71	71	55.9

26. *Popayan to*

	Hours.	Hours.	Miles.
Almaguer	30	30	65.2

27. *Tocaima to*

	Hours.	Hours.	Miles.
Espinal	10	10	31.1
Guamo	2	2	6.2
Purificacion	6	6	18.6
Natagaima	6	6	18.6
Villa Vieja	9	9	28.0

VII. Routes East of the Magdalena, beginning at the North.

28. *Plata, No., to*

	Hours.	Hours.	Miles.
Pital	7	9	18.6
Garzon	10	10	21.7
Jigante	6	6	15.5
Neiva	18	18	52.8

29. *Fusagasugá to*

	Hours.	Hours.	Miles.
Mesa	17	17	38.8

30. *Bogotá to*

	Hours.	Hours.	Miles.
Fusagasugá	11	11	24.9

31. *Bogotá to*

	Hours.	Hours.	Miles.
Funza	4	4	12.4
Facatativá	5	5	15.5
Ambalema	20	20	43.5

32. *Bogotá to*

	Hours.	Hours.	Miles.
Cáquesa	11	11	24.9
Villavicencio	30	30	77.7
San Martin	20	20	52.8

33. *Moreno, Cs., to*

	Hours.	Hours.	Miles.
Cafifí	24	24	55.9

34. *Moreno, Cs.*, to	Hours.	Hours.	Miles.
Zapatosa	13	13	37.3
35. *Moreno, Cs.*, to			
Muneque	15	15	37.3
Chita	4	4	9.3
Soatá	21	21	45.0
36. *Labranza-grande, Cs.*, to			
Recetor	18	18	37.3
37. *Cipaquirá* to			
Palma	19	19	49.7
38. *Cipaquirá* to			
Guatavita	11	11	34.2
39. *Cipaquirá* to			
Chocontá	12	13	37.3
Guateque	8	8	24.9
40. *Chocontá* to			
Ubató	10	10	28.0
Muzo	19	19	55.9
41. *Tunja* to			
Garagoa	17	17	46.6
Miraflores	10	10	24.9
42. *Tunja* to			
Leiva	7	7	18.6
Moniquirá	8	8	21.7
Puente Nacional	3	3	9.3
Vélez	5	5	12.4

43. *Sogamoso, Td.*, to	Hrs.	Hours.	Miles.
Santa Rosa, Td	7	7	18.6
Charalá	16	16	45.0
Socorro	7	8	20.2
44. *Soatá* to			
Cocui	13	13	24.9
45. *Concepcion* to			
Málaga	2	2	6.2
San Andrés	10	10	24.9
46. *Pamplona* to			
Bucaramanga	24	27	71.5
47. *Zapatoca* to			
Jiron	11	11	28.0
48. *Ocaña* to			
Salazar	32	32	71.5
San José (Sd.)	12	12	28.0

VIII. Isthmus Routes.

These are under the control of the Estado de Panamá. It is intended that each distrito shall have a post-office, but all is, as yet, unsettled. The principal offices are to be at the following places. The distances of each of these from Panamá is annexed.

Panamá	0.
Colon	47.5
Natá	99.4
Pesé	149.1
Sántos	142.8
Santiago	155.3
David	310.7

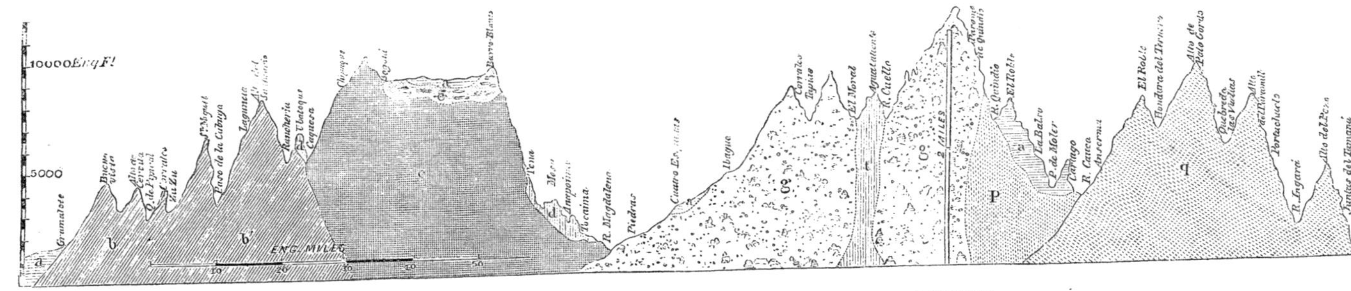

KEY.

a	Alluvium.
b	Schist, talc, and graywacke.
c	Variegated sandstone.
d	Cretaceous formation.
c	Coal, salt, and gypsum.
g	Granite.
p	Porphyry.
q	Argillaceous and quartzose schist.
t	Trachyte.

VI. GEOLOGICAL SECTION.

This geological section is copied, with some change of names only, from one published by General Acosta at Paris in 1847, in his map of New Granada. A very large drawing of this same section, but differing from this in every particular, has been recently published by Evan Hopkins, Esq., in his work "On the Connection of Geology with Terrestrial Magnetism." 2d Edition, London, 1851.

Acosta seems to me to have misapprehended the nature of the formations to a considerable degree, while of Mr. Hopkins's section I would say no more than that I saw very little indeed of all that he lays down so minutely. I copy the more convenient, and, it seems to me, the more reliable of the two, in order that future observers may have at hand the deliberate conclusions of one of the most learned natives of the country, drawn from his own observations, those of Cáldas, Humboldt, and others. Some future geologist could not render a better service to science than by retracing this same route, with time and means to throw upon these stupendous heights the light of the science of geology, as it is now developing itself.

VII. ALTITUDES, CLIMATES, AND PRODUCTIONS.

On the opposite page, the space from the top to the bottom represents the three miles of altitude that separate the limit of perpetual snow in the tropics from the level of the sea. The left-hand margin is occupied with names of places ranged at their respective altitudes. All, except four in *Italics*, are in New Granada. Next is a scale of English feet. The second scale is of mean annual temperatures, disposed in *equal* parts, and increasing downward. Between these scales lines connect the altitudes of the places named with their annual temperatures, which vary greatly from an exact correspondence. The third scale is of English miles, and the fourth the boiling-point of water at the different altitudes.

The remainder is divided into four belts of vegetation, in which lines indicate the limits of spontaneous growth or profitable cultivation of various important plants.

It would appear, from an inspection of this, that Bogotá has an altitude of a little more than 8650 feet, and a mean temperature considerably higher than might be expected, 58°. It is seen to be less than 1¾ miles above the sea, and that boiling water should have there the temperature of nearly 195°. It should be too cold for cotton, cane, pine-apples, or rice, while potatoes, barley, and cinchona would flourish.

It is much to be regretted that this table, which has cost so much to prepare, can not be made more reliable. The range of temperature which plants are capable of enduring is drawn chiefly from Boussingault and Humboldt. I have not often ventured to correct the inaccuracies I think I see in them, except when they conflict with each other; but such general statements must necessarily be but approximate; and a moderate degree of accuracy can be attained only by special observations made for this purpose. There must be great errors in the mean annual temperatures of different places, especially those in elevated regions, where observations have been made chiefly by day. With all this, I trust no man can look on it without acquiring new and more accurate ideas of the tropics.

In the accompanying map, the attempt is made to exhibit the extent of these climates, and to show what part of the surface of New Granada is occupied by each. To do this minutely in so steep and broken a country would require maps on the largest scale, and the materials for them are yet to be collected. Small as is the scale on which the attempt is here made, numerous as must be the errors that cover it, it can not but be of much utility in conveying general ideas. It claims the indulgence to which all first attempts are justly entitled.

The following tables of thermometrical observations have their chief interest from the fact that no published series is known to exist that were made in a similar location. They are from the Valley of the Cauca, and mostly made at an elevation of about 3500 feet. It is difficult to obtain suitable stations for maximum observations, where the instrument can be accessible and safe, in such a country. Mine, unfortunately, was broken before comparing it with any reliable standard. If the morning observations be found too low, and those of the warmest part of the day too high, I shall not be surprised. One A.M. observation and two P.M. were attempted, and the state of the sky noted at each time. F. signifies *fair*, S. *sun*, and R. *rain*. For the place of the observations where the date is marked with an asterisk, see Appendix VIII. All the others are at La Paila, Cauca.

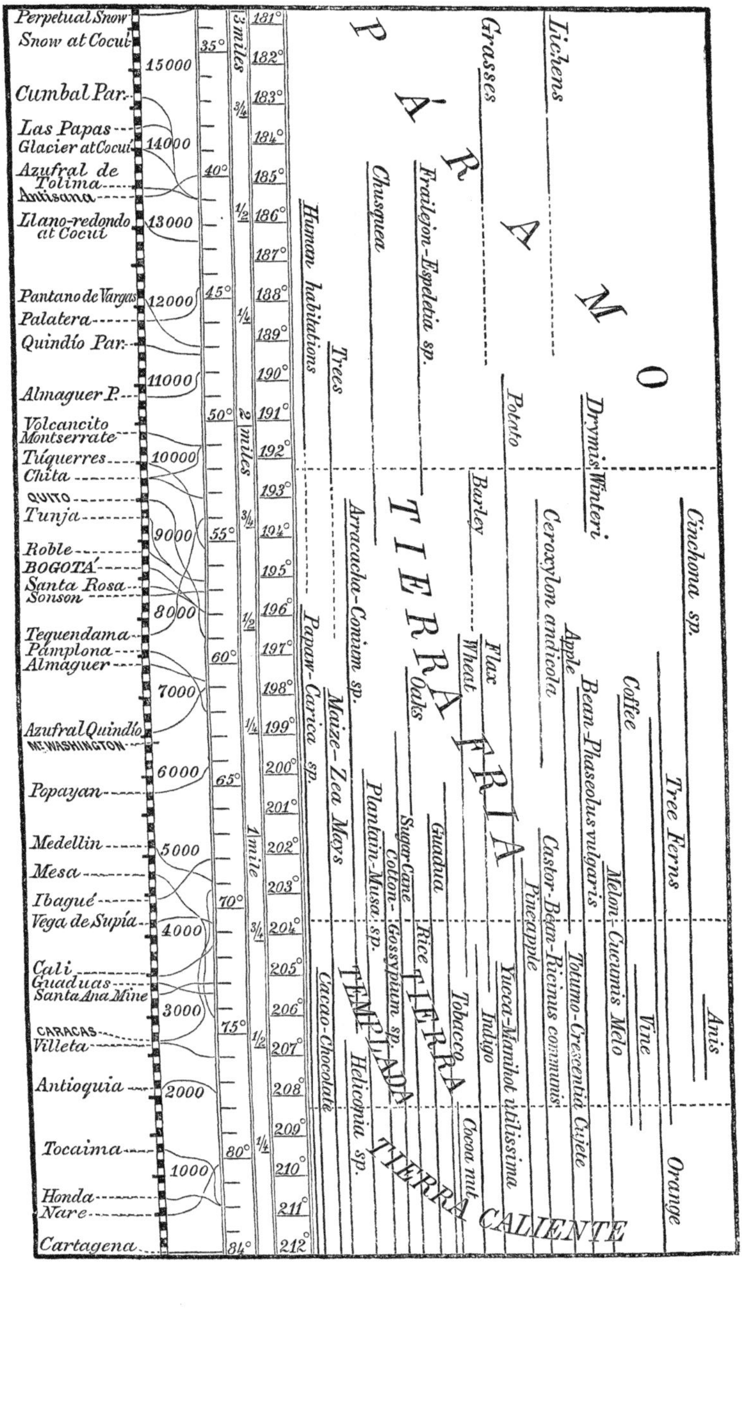

Perpetual Snow
Snow at Cocui
Cumbal Par.
Las Papas
Glacier at Cocui
Azufral de Tolima
Antisana
Llano-redondo at Cocui
Pantano de Vargas
Palatera
Quindío Par.
Almaguer P.
Volcancito
Montserrate
Túquerres
Chita
QUITO
Tunja
Roble
BOGOTÁ
Santa Rosa
Sonson
Tequendama
Pamplona
Almaguer
Azufral Quindío
MT. WASHINGTON
Popayan
Medellin
Mesa
Ibagué
Vega de Supía
Cali
Guaduas
Santa Ana Mine
CARACAS
Villeta
Antioquia
Tocaima
Honda
Nare
Cartagena

15000
14000
13000
12000
11000
10000
9000
8000
7000
6000
5000
4000
3000
2000
1000

35°
40°
45°
50°
55°
60°
65°
70°
75°
80°
84°

3 miles
3/4
1/2
1/4
2 miles
3/4
1/2
1/4
1 mile
3/4
1/2
1/4

181°
182°
183°
184°
185°
186°
187°
188°
189°
190°
191°
192°
193°
194°
195°
196°
197°
198°
199°
200°
201°
202°
203°
204°
205°
206°
207°
208°
209°
210°
211°
212°

PÁRAMO
Lichens
Grasses
Frailejon-Espeletia sp.
Chusquea
Human habitations
Trees
Potato
Drymis Winteri

TIERRA FRIA
Cinchona sp.
Ceroxylon andicola
Barley
Arracacha-Conium sp.
Papaw-Carica sp.
Apple
Flax
Wheat
Oaks
Bean-Phaseolus vulgaris
Coffee
Maize-Zea Mays
Tree Ferns
Melon-Cucumis Melo
Castor-Bean-Ricinus communis
Pineapple
Guadua
Sugar Cane
Cotton-Gossypium sp.
Plantain-Musa sp.

TIERRA TEMPLADA
Rice
Tobacco
Yucca-Manihot utilissima
Indigo
Totumo-Crescentia Cujete
Vine
Anis
Cacao-Chocolate
Heliconia sp.
Cocoa nut
Orange

TIERRA CALIENTE

THERMOMETER FOR MAY, JUNE, JULY, AUGUST, 1853.

	Morning.			Noon.			Night.		
	Hour.	°	Sky.	Hour.	°	Sky.	Hour.	°	Sky.
May 1	7	73	C.	2	76	R.	6	71	C.
2	7	67	C.	3	79	—	6	74	F.
3	6	67	F.	3	77	R.	7	71	R.
4	6	66	F.	2	79	C.	9	69	F.
5	7	68	S.	4	72	C.	7	70	R.
6	6	65	C.	3	73	R.	6	69	C.
7	6	64	S.	2	77	S.	6	73	F.
8	8	67	C.	3	75	S.	6	74	F.
9	6	64	F.	3	79	S.	6	75	F.
10	6	66	F.	3	74	C.	6	70	C.
11	6	64	C.	3	75	S.	6	73	F.
12	6	66	C.	3	76	C.	6	69	R.
13	6	64	C.	3	77	S.	6	71	F.
14	6	62	C.	3	80	S.	6	76	F.
15	7	67	S.	3	81	S.	6	74	R.
16	6	67	R.	3	71	R.	8	68	C.
17	6	63	C.	3	76	C.	6	74	C.
18	7	68	C.	3	72	C.	6	71	C.
19	6	63	C.	3	79	S.	6	75	F.
20	6	66	C.	4	79	S.	7	72	R.
21	6	67	C.	4	70	R.	7	68	R.
22	7	66	C.	3	78	F.	7	71	C.
23	6	66	R.	3	72	R.	6	67	R.
24	6	64	S.	3	76	S.	6	71	C.
25	7	65	C.	2	73	C.	6	68	R.
26	6	64	C.	4	75	S.	6	72	C.
27	6	64	S.	3	78	S.	6	74	C.
28	6	65	C.	4	78	C.	6	71	R.
29	6	68	C.	3	77	S.	7	70	F.
30	6	67	F.	4	77	C.	6	75	R.
31	6	66	S.	3	74	R.	6	71	C.
June 1	7	67	C.	4	79	S.	7	70	R.
2	7	66	C.	3	79	S.	7	73	F.
3	7	67	C.	3	79	S.	6	77	F.
4				3	79	F.	6	77	F.
5	8	72	S.			S.	6	80	F.
6	6	62	S.	3	86	S.	6	73	F.
7	6	63	F.	4	79	S.	6	76	F.
8	6	63	F.	4	79	C.	6	75	C.
9	6	66	S.	3	80	S.	6	72	R.
10	6	68	C.	12	76	S.	6	76	F.
11	6	65	C.	4	82	S.	6	76	C.
12	6	64	C.	4	82	S.	6	74	F.
13	6	66	C.	4	82	S.	6	77	C.
14	4	66	F.	3	75	S.	6	76	C.
15				4	82	S.	6	74	C.
16	6	61	F.	4	79	S.	10	67	F.
17	6	63	F.	3	80	S.	10	68	F.
18	6	66	C.	3	83	S.	10	68	F.
19	7	68	S.	5	78	C.	9	71	R.
20	6	66	C.	4	77	C.	10	69	F.
21	6	66	F.	4	80	C.	10	70	R.
22	7	69	C.	3	76	C.			
23				4	81	S.	9	67	F.
24	6	64	C.	4	80	S.	10	69	F.
25	7	65	S.	4	78	C.	11	68	C.
26	7	66	C.	4	79	S.	10	64	F.
27	7	61	S.	4	84	S.	10	67	F.

	Morning.			Noon.			Night.		
	Hour.	°	Sky.	Hour.	°	Sky.	Hour.	°	Sky.
June 28*	6	61	F.	4	82	S.	10	66	F.
29*	6	65	F.			S.	10	71	F.
30	7	66	F.	5	80	S.	9	71	C.
July 1	6	64	C.	4	80	C.	10	66	F.
2	6	61	C.	4	84	S.	10	69	F.
3	6	65	F.	4	82	S.	9	71	F.
4	6	65	F.	3	82	S.	9	68	F.
5	6	61	F.	3	84	S.	10	70	C.
6	6	67	C.	3	71	C.	10	67	R.
7	6	66	F.	3	80	S.	10	68	F.
8	6	62	F.	4	80	S.	10	68	C.
9	6	62	F.	4	74	C.	10	66	F.
10	6	62	C.	4	78	S.	10	67	F.
11	6	62	C.	2	80	S.	10	67	F.
12	6	60	C.	3	78	C.	10	70	C.
13	7	62	C.	3	81	S.	11	67	F.
14	6	59	S.	3	82	S.	9	66	F.
15	6	62	C.						
16				4	80	S.	11	70	F.
17	9	72	S.	4	79	C.	9	69	C.
18	6	66	C.	3	76	R.	10	67	C.
19*	6	66	R.	2	78	S.	9	68	F.
20*	6	64	S.	3	80	S.	9	68	F.
21*	6	62	S.	3	80	S.	9	69	F.
22*	6	64	S.	12	81	S.			
23*	7	71	C.	3	78	C.	10	72	C.
24*	7	67	C.			S.	10	70	C.
25*	6	68	F.				10	71	F.
26*	6	68	R.				9	72	F.
27*	6	71	F.	4	78	S.	9	71	F.
28*	6	70	F.	3	70	S.	10	60	C.
29*	6	58	C.	3	65	C.	10	60	F.
30*	6	56	F.	2	72	C.	10	70	F.
31*	6	68	R.	3	78	C.	10	69	F.
Aug. 1*	6	68	F.				10	70	F.
2*	6	67	C.	3	73	C.	10	71	C.
3*	6	65	C.	3	78	S.	11	69	F.
4*	6	69	F.	3	74	C.	11	68	C.
5*	6	66	F.	3	73	C.	9	68	F.
6*	6	65	S.	3	66	S.	9	56	F.
7*	6	56	C.	3	66	S.	10	56	F.
8*	6	52	F.	4	71	S.	9	58	C.
9*	6	58	C.	3		S.	9	58	C.
10*	6	55	C.	3	79	S.	9	70	F.
11*	6	65	C.	3	75	C.	9	70	F.
12*	6	66	F.	3	79	S.	9	72	F.
13*	6	66	F.	4	75	C.	9	70	F.
14*	7	66	C.	3	76	S.	9	70	F.
15*	6	68	C.			S.			F.
16*	6	62	C.	3	80	C.			
17*							10	69	F.
18*	6	61	F.	3	82	S.	9	70	F.
19*	6	68	F.	3	84	S.			
20*	6	69	F.	3	82	C.	9	70	F.
21	6	66	C.	3	82	C.	9	69	R.
22	6	66	C.	4	83	S.	10	71	F.
23	6	64	F.	3	80	S.	10	70	C.

The following special observations are of interest: May 12, 3 P.M., 76°, C.; 4.15 P.M., 70°, R.—May 23, 6 P.M., 67°, R.—May 24, 1 A.M., 63°, C.; 6 A.M. 64°, C.—June 24, 1 P.M., 124° *in the sun.*

* All but these were made at La Paila.

VIII. ITINERARY.

Names in *Italics* indicate visits to places, and a return that same day to the last place mentioned in SMALL CAPITALS.

1852.—AUGUST.

21. Off Sierra Nevada.
22. Off Santa Marta.
Harbor of SABANILLA.
23. *Sabanilla. Custom-house.*
24. Barranquilla.
25. Harbor of Sabanilla.
28. Bongo in Ciénega de Manteca.
29. Barranquilla. [la.
31. Steam-boat in Barranquil-

SEPTEMBER.

1. Remolino.
2. Calamar and above.
3. Below Mompos.
4. Mompos. [co.
5. Passed Margarita and Ban-
6. Puerto-nacional.
7. Below San Pablo.
8. San Pablo, Bodega de Sogamoso.
9. Passed Barranca-bermeja.
10. Passed I. de Rionuevo and San Bartolomé.
11. Remolino-grande, Nare.
12. Aground above Nare.
13. Champan above Nare.
14. Below Buenavista.
15. Passed Buenavista.
16. Below Conejo.
17. Passed Conejo.
18. Vuelta, Honda.
22. Pescaderías, Cruces, Sargento, Guaduas.
27. Alto del Trigo, Cune, Alto del Petaquero, Villeta, Mauve, Salitre.
28. Aserradero, Roble, Botello.
29. Facatativa, Serrezuela, Santuario, Puente-grande, Fontibon, BOGOTÁ.

OCTOBER.

5. *Boqueron.*
7. *Montserrate.*
13. *Peña.*
15. *Boqueron.*
18. *Boqueron.*
23. *Rio Arzobispo.*
27. *Rio Fucha.*
28. *Cemetery.*

NOVEMBER.

5. *Boqueron.*
6. *Rio Fucha.*
10. *Guadalupe, Boqueron.*
16. *Boqueron.*
18. *Montserrate.*
22. *Cemetery.*
23. *Rio Arzobispo.*
25. *Fucha.*
26. *Peña, Upper Fucha.*

DECEMBER.

1. *Páramo of Andres Rosas.*
3. *Boqueron.*
7. Soacha, *Hacienda de Tequendama.*
8–11. *Salto de Tequendama.*
15. Cibaté, Boca del Monte, FUSAGASUGÁ.
16. *Novillero.*
22. Pandi.
23. FUSAGASUGÁ.
25. *Chocho.*
27. *Retiro.*
28. Bogotá.
31. FUSAGASUGÁ.

1853.—JANUARY.

3. *Chocho.*
5. *La Puerta.*
7. *Chocho.*
11. La Puerta, Boqueron.
12. Passed Melgar.
13. Banks of Magdalena.
14. Espinal, Banks of the Coello.
15. Coello, Ibagué.
24. Palmilla, Tapias.
25. El Moral, Buenavista, Agua-caliente, Toche.
26. Gallego, Yerba-buena, Volcancito.
27. Páramo of Quindio, Barcinal, Boquía, El Roble.
28. Portachuelo, Cañas, Balsa.
29. Piedra de Moler, Cartago.
31. Zaragosa, Hacienda de Sanchez.

FEBRUARY.

1. Naranjo, Victoria, Las Lajas, Libraida, Las Cañas, El Medio, LA PAILA.
4. *Guavito.*
12. *Guavito.*
17. *Medio.*
21. *Cara Perro.*
26. *Medio.*

MARCH.

1. Murillo, Overo, Buga-la-grande, Tuluá, San Pedro.
2. Buga, Zonza, Cerrito, La Merced.
3. San Marcos, Cali.
10. Palmira.
12. Buga.
13. PAILA.
23. *Libraida.*

APRIL.

19. *Medio.*
30. *Guavito.*

MAY.

1. *Foot of Cara Perro.*
14. *Rio de Las Cañas.*
24. *Near Cara Perro.*

JUNE.

4. *Near Cara Perro.*
14. Roldanillo.
15. Libraida, Paila.
28. Lajas, Chaqueral.
29. Libraida, Uña-gato, PAILA.

JULY.

4. *Base of Cara Perro.*
8. Murillo.
9. Paila.
15. Lajas.
16. Paila.
19. Buga-la-grande.
20. Cerrito.
21. Cali.
25. VIJES.
26. FERRY.
28. Bolivia.
30. Vijes.

AUGUST.

3. Cali.
5. Arroyo-hondo.
6. Bolivia.
10. Vijes.
12. Espinal.
13. Vijes.
15. Cerrito.
18. Near Buga. [tas.
19. San Pedro, Tuluá, Sabale-
20. PAILA.
25. *Cara Perro.*
26. *Cienega de Burro.*
29. *Frisolar, Caracolí.*

SEPTEMBER.

7. La Cabaña.
8. Chaqueral. [elo.
9. Libraida, Paila, Portachu-
10. La Ribera.
12. Picazo, Las Minas, Rio de San Marcos, Platanal.
13. Tiemble Cul, Chorro.
14. Las Playas.
16. JICARAMATA.
17. *Guavito.*
18. Chorro.
19. LA RIBERA.
23. *Yesal.*
26. Sartinajal, Portachuelo.
27. PAILA.
30. LIBRAIDA.

OCTOBER.

4. Portachuelo.
5. Murillo.
6. PAILA.
11. *Cienega de Burro.*
14. *Las Cañas.*
17. Murillo.
18. Paila. [bera.
24. Murillo, Sabaletas, La Ri-
25. Tuluá, Tablazo, Ribera.
28. Paila.
31. Murillo.

NOVEMBER.

1. Paila.
10. Murillo.
Paila, Libraida, Cabaña.
11. Cartago, Victoria.
22. Piedra de Moler, Capote.
23. Balsa, Cañas, Portachuelo.
24. Roble, Boquía, Barcinal.
25. Páramo, Volcancito, Galle-
26. Toche, El Moral. [go.
27. IBAGUÉ.

DECEMBER.

1. *Tolima.*
6. Piedras.
7. Opía, Rio Seco, Neme.
8. Tocaima, Juntas.
9. Anapoima, Mesa.
31. Tena, Zaragoza.

14. San Antonio, Curcio, Tequendama, Zaragoza.
15. Tena, MESA.
17. *Volcan.*
19. Tena, Barro Blanco, Hacienda de Quito.
20. Bogotá.
26. Hacienda de Tequendama.
27. FUSAGASUGÁ.
29, 30. *Chocho.*

1854.—JANUARY.

3. Cibaté, BOGOTÁ.
6. *Egipto.*
14. *Guadalupe, La Peña.*
17. Cruz-verde, UBAQUE.
18. *Choachi, Thermal Spring, Laguna-grande.*
20. Cruz-verde, BOGOTÁ.

FEBRUARY.

7. *Montserrate.*
10. *Páramo of Choachi.*
25. *Rio Arzobispo.*

MARCH.

7. *Chapinero.*

APRIL.

24. Facatativá, Chimbe.
25. Guaduas.
26. Alto del Sarjento, Pescaderías.
27. Honda.

MAY.

1. La Vuelta.
3. Nare.
4. San Pedro.
5. Puerto-nacional.
6. Mompos.
7. Calamar.
8. Mahates, Arjona.
9. Turbaco, CARTAGENA.
10. *San Lázaro.*
11. Boca Chica, Caribbean Sea.

IX. CHRONOLOGICAL TABLE.

The figures in parentheses refer to pages in this work where the events are referred to.

1492. New World discovered by Columbus, October 11.
1497. Continent discovered by Cabot, June 4.
1502. New Granada discovered by Columbus, December 14.
1504. Queen Isabel died, November 26.
1506. Death of Columbus, May 20.
1510. First settlement by Nicuesa at Madre de Dios.
Turbaco plundered by Ojeda.
1513. The Pacific discovered by Balboa, September 25.
1516. Fernando V. died, January 22.
1519. Panamá founded by Arias Dávila.
1524. Peru invaded from Panamá by Pizarro.
1525. Santamarta founded by Bastidas, July 29.
1533. Cartagena founded by Heredia, Jan. 15.
1536. Quesada sets out from Santamarta, April 6 (202).
Popayan and Cali founded by Benalcázar.
1537. Quesada enters the Plain of Bogotá, March (202).
1538. Bogotá founded by Quesada, August 6.
Zaquesazipe murdered (248).
1539. Tunja, Vélez, and Mompos founded.
1544. Cartagena taken by Baal, July 27.
1555. Carlos V. abdicated, Oct. 25 (died 1558).
1558. Montaño the tyrant executed.
1564. Andres Diaz Venero de Leiva enters Bogotá (February).
1572. President Leiva founds the Cathedral, March 12 (194).
1574. Venero de Leiva, first president of Santafé, promoted.
1575. Francisco Briceño, second president, died, December 13.
1579. Quesada died, February 16 (203).
1580. Lope Diez Aux de Armendariz, third president, dies in prison.
1586. Cartagena taken by Drake, February.
1596. Cartagena taken by Robert Baal.
1597. González, fourth president, resigned.
1598. Felipe II. died, September 3.
1602. Jesuits established in Bogotá.
Francisco de Sande ("Dr. Sangre"), fifth president, died.
1608 (about). Inquisition established in Cartagena.
1620. Failure of the South Sea scheme.
1621. Felipe III. died, March 31.
1628. Juan de Borja, sixth president, died, February 12.
1638. Sancho Jiron, Marquis of Sófraga, seventh president, suspended.
1645. Martin Saavedra (Guzman), eighth president, resigned.
1653. Juan Fernández Córdoba (Coalla), Marquis de Miranda de Auta, ninth president, resigned (died 1664).
1653. Colegio del Rosario founded (263).
1662. Dionisio Pérez-Manrique, Marquis of Santiago, tenth president, removed, February.
1664. Diego de Ergües (Beaumont), eleventh president, died, December 25.
1665. John Morgan takes Portobello.
Felipe IV. died, September 17.
1667. Diego del Corro Carrascal, twelfth president, promoted.
1671. Morgan takes Panamá, January 28.
Diego de Villalba (Toledo), thirteenth president, suspended, June 12.
1674. Melchor Liñan (Cisneros), fourteenth president, promoted.
1686. Francisco Castillo (Concha), fifteenth president, died.
1695. Cartagena taken by Ducasse.
Cartagena taken by Pointis.
1700. Carlos II. died, November 1.
1703. Jil de Cabrera (Dávalos), sixteenth president, left.
1712. Diego Córdova Lasso de la Vega, seventeenth president, left.
1715. Francisco Menéses Bravo, eighteenth president, sent home, September 24.
1719. Francisco del Rincon, nineteenth president, superseded, November 27.
1724. Jorje Villalonga, first viceroy, recalled, May 17.
1731. Antonio Manso Maldonado, twentieth president, left.
1737. Rafael Eslaba, twenty-first president, died, April.
1739. Antonio González Manrique, twenty-second president, died, September 3.
Portobello taken "with six ships" by Vernon, November 22.
1740. Francisco González Manrique, last president, superseded, April 24.
Restriction of the Jesuits (508).
Gregorio Vásquez (Ceballos), painter, flourished (192).
1741. Vernon appeared before Cartagena, Mar. 13 (43).
Unsuccessful attack on San Lázaro, April 20 (43).
1746. Felipe V. died, July 9.
1749. Sebastian Eslava, second viceroy, resigned, December 6.
1753. José Alfonso Pizarro, Marquis of Villar, third viceroy, resigns.
1759. Fernando VI. died, August 10.
1761. José Solis Folch de Cardona, fourth viceroy, turned monk, February 24.
1767. Cédula expelling the Jesuits, October 18 (508).
1770. Census of the viceroyalty 806,209.

1773. Pedro Messía Cerda, Marquis de Vega de Armijo, fifth viceroy, returns.
1775. Manuel Guirior, sixth viceroy, promoted.
1781. The Socorro rebellion, March 26.
Capitulation of Cipaquirá (afterward violated), June 8.
1782. Manuel-Antonio Flóres, seventh viceroy, promoted, March 1.
Juan de Torrezal Díaz Pimienta, eighth viceroy, died, June 11.
1783. Census of the viceroyalty 1,046,641.
1785. Great earthquake at Bogotá.
1788. Carlos III. died, December 13.
1789. Antonio Caballero, ninth viceroy, resigned, January 8.
Francisco Jil (Lémus), tenth viceroy, promoted, July 31.
1795. Closure of Boca-grande (42).
1797. José Espeleta, eleventh viceroy, promoted, January 2.
1801. Humboldt arrived in New Granada.
1802. Observatory of Bogotá begun, May 24 (265).
1803. Census of the viceroyalty 2,000,000.
Pedro Mendinueta (Muzquiz), twelfth viceroy, promoted, September 17.
1808. José Celestino Mútis died, September 11 (216).
Carlos IV. resigned, March 19. No successor reigned in New Granada.
1810. Pamploneses imprisoned their corregidor, July 4.
Corregidor of Socorro imprisoned by the people, July 11.
Governor of Cartagena driven off, July 14.
Antonio Amar (Borbon), last viceroy, overthrown, July 20.
1811. General Baraya gains the battle of Palacé, Pp., March 28 (154).
General Nariño, president of Cundinamarca.
Custodio García-Rovira, president of the Provincias Unidas.
1812. Congress at Leiva.
Junta general at Bogotá.
Bolivar takes Tenerife, Sm., from the Spaniards, December 23.
Nariño attacked at Bogotá by Baraya, December 24 (565).
1813. Victory of San José, Pm., gained by Bolívar over Correa, February 28.
1814. Nariño defeated Sámano (Spaniard) at Calibio, Pp., January 15.
Antonio Ricaurte blew up himself and the enemy at San Mateo, Venezuela, March 25.
Manuel Bernardo Alvarez, president of Cundinamarca.
Camilo Tórres, president of the Congress of the United Provinces.
Bolivar stormed Bogotá and overthrew the government of Cundinamarca, December 12 (566).
1815. Cartagena shut out Bolivar. His army [dissolves.
Pablo Morillo arrived at Porto Santo, Venezuela, with 15,000 men from Spain, April 13.
Urdaneta defeated by Calzada (Spanish) at Chitagá, Pm. 1, November 30.
Morillo takes Cartagena by famine after 116 days' siege, December 5.
Morillo shot the defenders of Cartagena, December.
1816. Morillo set out from Cartagena, Janua- [ry 15.
Morillo entered Bogotá, May 30.
Morillo shot the maiden Policarpa Salavarrieta and others, June (165).
Defeat of Cuchilla del Tambo, Pp. 1; Herran, Mosquera, and López, prisoners, June 29 (266).
1816. Cáldas shot by Morillo, October 29 (266).
1819. Congress of Angostura. Union of New Granada and Venezuela, February 15.
Bolivar made president.
Bolivar defeated, and took Barreiro at Boyacá, Tj. 1, August 7.
Law of Congress of Angostura creating the nation of Colombia, December 17.
Simon Bolivar president; Zea, Santander, and Roscio vice-presidents.
1820. Calzada took Popayan, January 24.
Victory of Pitayo, Pp., June 6.
Truce with Morillo. End of the war of extermination, November 27.
1821. Congress of Cúcuta at Rosario, Pm. 8, May 6 (205).
Second battle and great victory of Carabobo, Venezuela, June 24.
First Constitution of Colombia, August 30 (205).
Cartagena taken from the Spaniards by Montilla, October 11.
1822. Bolivar gained the victory of Bomboná, Ps. 1, April 7.
Victory of Pichincha, Ecuador, May 24.
Ecuador became a part of Colombia, May 29.
Maracaibo capitulated to the Colombian arms, August 3.
1824. Last Spanish battle in Colombia at Barbacoas, Ps. 2, June 1.
Last Spanish battle in South America gained by Sucre at Ayacucho, Peru, December 9.
1825. Census of New Granada 1,258,259.
1826. Páez revolted from Colombia, April 30 (206).
Bolivar re-elected president by the people, Santander vice-president (206).
1827. Bolivar's fourth resignation (not accepted), February 6 (206).
Great earthquake at Bogotá, Nov. 16.
1828. Convention of Ocaña, Oc. 1, Mar. 2 (207).
Quorum destroyed by secession of twenty, June 10 (207).
Bolivar proclaimed dictator by Herran, June 13 (207).
War declared against Peru, July 3.
Organic decree abrogating the Constitution of 1821, August 27 (207).
Attempt to assassinate Bolivar, September 25 (207).
Battle of Ladera, Pp. 1. Obando and López against the dictator, November 12.
Unsuccessful attack of the Peruvians on Guayaquil, Ecuador, November 22.
1829. Victory over the Peruvians at Portete de Tarqui, Ecuador, February 27.
Córdova defeated by Dictatorial troops at Santuario and murdered, An. 4, October 17 (135, 209).
Secession of Venezuela under Páez, November 24.
1830. Constituent Congress of Bogotá, Jan. 20.
Fifth and last resignation of Bolivar (accepted), May 4.
Second Constitution of Colombia (209).
Congress elected Joaquin Mosquera president of Colombia, May 4 (209, 250).
Assassination of Marshal Antonio-José de Sucre at Berruecos, Ps. 1, June 4 (252).
Defeat of government at Santuario, B. 6, August 27 (250).
Rafael Urdaneta dictator, September 2.
Bolivar died at Santamarta, December 17 (210).
1831. Treaty of Juntas, B. 12. Domingo Caicedo vice-president, April 28 (250, 345).

1831. Complete dismemberment of Colombia (209).
Convention of Bogotá, October 20.
Caicedo resigns. José Maria Obando elected vice-president by Convention, November 22 (250).
1832. First Constitution of New Granada, March 1 (250).
Francisco de Paula Santander elected president by the Convention, March 9 (250).
1833. Santander, again elected by the people, took his seat, April 1.
Sardá conspiracy, 15–20 executed (250).
1835. Census of New Granada 1,687,109.
1837. José Ignacio Márquez president, April 1; (elected by the people) (251).
1839. Four convents in Pasto suppressed, June 5.
Obando defeated by government at Buesaco, Ps. 1, August 31.
1840. Government gains the battle of Culebrera, B. 6, October 28 (135, 253).
1841. Government gains the battle of Tescua, Pm. 1, April 1 (253).
Pedro Alcántara Herran president, April 1; (elected by the people) (507).
1842. Cartagena taken, and the Revolution ended, February 19 (44).
Recall of the Jesuits (508).
1843. Census of New Granada 1,932,279.
Second Constitution of New Granada, April 30 (508).
1845. Tomas Cipriano de Mosquera president, April 1; (elected by the people) (509).
1849. José Hilario López elected by Congress, March 7 (521).
1850. Re-expulsion of the Jesuits, May 18 (528).
Misgovernment in the Cauca (527).
1851. Assassination of Pinto and Morales, June 19 (529).
Seizure of Ospina at Bogotá, July 30 (192).
Battle of Rionegro, An. 6. Revolution ended,* September 7.
Census of New Granada 2,243,730.
1852. Slavery abolished, January 1 (527).
1853. José María Obando president, April 1; (elected by the people) (257).
Third Constitution of New Granada, May 21 (540).
1854. Revolution broke out in Popayan, Pp. 1, April 8 (563).
Riot at Bogotá, April 14 (555).
General José María Melo seized the executive officers, April 17 (558).
Tomas Herrera, designado, lawfully in power, April 21 (563). [562).
Melo's troops enter Honda, April 25 (104,
Franco defeated and slain at Cipaquirá, B. 3, May 19 (563).
Buitrago defeated at Tíquiza, B. 3, May 21 (563).
Battle in Cali, Bv. 1, June 16 (529).
José de Obaldía, vice-president, in supreme power.
Surprise of Guaduas by Arboleda, June 23 (563).
Battle of Palmira, Cc. 4, Aug. 31.
Battle of Boza, B. 1, November 22 (564).
Action of Tres Esquinas at Bogotá, November 23 (565).
Bogotá taken and the revolution ended, December 4 (556).
1855. Manuel María Mallarino vice-president, April 1 (522). (Obando deposed.)
Assassination of Antonio Mateus, Dec. 4.
1856. Election for president, August 31 (567).

* Neither Herran nor Mosquera were in the country during this revolution, nor was López during the one that preceded. It does not appear that either of these three presidents ever drew sword against the constitutional authority of his country. (See p. 251.) The misrepresentations on which the remarks were based were the work of political hate. This correction, thus late and out of place, is one of sheer justice.

X. WEIGHTS AND MEASURES.

Four kinds of weights and measures have been in legal use in New Granada in this century.

I. The *Castilian*, established June 26, 1801; abolished October 12, 1821.

II. The *Colombian*, established in 1821; abolished May 26, 1836.

III. The *Granadan*, established in 1836; abolished June 8, 1853.

IV. The *French*, established in 1853, now the legal system in New Granada.

The following account, calculated from official documents furnished at the last hour, must be regarded as approximate only, for the confusion is utter and inextricable. The figures preceding denominations show how many are required to make one of the next higher. The liquid gallon used below contains 231 cubic inches; the bushel, 2150.42.

I. Measures of Length.

Legal.

Miriámetro 6.214 miles.
10 Quilómetro 0.621 miles.
10 Hectómetro 19.872 rods.
10 Decámetro 10.936 yards.
10 Metro 3.28099 feet.
10 Decímetro 3.937 inches.
10 Centímetro 0.393 inches.
10 Milímetro 0.039 inches.

Castilian and Colombian.

Vara 2.742 feet.
3 Pié 0.915 feet.
12 Pulgada 0.914 inches.
12 Línea 0.076 inches.

Granadan.

Vara 2.625 feet.
4 Cuarta 7.874 inches.
2 Octava 3.937 inches.
10 Pulgada 0.787 inches.
10 Línea 0.079 inches.

II. Itinerary.

Legal.

Miriámetro 6.214 miles.
10 Quilómetro 0.621 miles.
10 Hectómetro 19.872 rods.
10 Decámetro 10.396 yards.
10 Metro 3.281 feet.

Castilian.

Legua 3.463 miles.

6666⅔ Vara 2.742 feet.
Pié 0.914 feet.

Colombian.

Legua 3.116.
3 Milla 1.039 miles.
2000 Vara 2.742 feet.
3 Pié 0.914 feet.

Granadan.

Legua 3.107 miles.
62½ Cuadra 15.907 rods.
100 Vara 2.625 feet.

III. Superficial.

Legal.

Metro cuadrada 10.764 square feet.
100 Decímetro cuadrada 15.500 square inches.
100 Centímetro cuadrada 0.155 square inches.
100 Milímetro cuadrada 0.015 square inches.

Castilian and Colombian.

Vara 7.521 square feet.
9 Pié 0.836 square feet.
144 Pulgada 0.836 square inches.
114 Línea 0.006 square inches.

Granadan.

Vara 6.889 square feet.
16 Cuarta 62.002 square inches.
4 Octava 15.501 square inches.
25 Pulgada 0.620 square inches.
100 Línea 0.006 square inches.

IV. Agrarian.

Legal.

Miriara 247.110 acres.
10 Quiloara 27.711 acres.
10 Hectoara 2.471 acres.
10 Decara 39.538 rods.
10 Ara 107.642406 feet.
10 Deciara 10.764 feet.
10 Centiara 1.076 feet.
10 Miliara 0.108 feet.

Castilian.

Fanegada 1.591 acres.
12 Celemin 21.217 rods.
4 Cuartillo 5.304 rods.
4 Estadal 188.034 feet.
25 Vara 7.521 feet.
Aranzada 1.105 acres.
Cabellaría 61.396 rods.
4 Peonía 15.349 rods.

Colombian.

Fanegada 1.727 acres.
4 Estancia 69.066 rods.
4 Celemin 17.267 rods.
4 Cuartillo 4.317 rods.
6½ Estadal 188.034 feet.
25 Vara 7.521 feet.

Granadan

Fanegada 1.582 acres.
16 Aranzada 15.815 rods.
25 Estadal 0.633 rods.
25 Vara 6.889 feet.

V. Cubic.

Legal.

Miriaesterio 39241 yards.
10 Quiloesterio 3924.1 yards.
10 Hectoesterio 392.41 yards.
10 Decaesterio 39.241 yards.
10 Esterio 35.317 feet.
10 Deciesterio 3.532 feet.
10 Centiesterio 610.278 inches.
10 Miliesterio 61.028 inches.

Castilian and Colombia

Vara 20.627 feet.
27 Pié 0.764 feet.
1728 Pulgada 0.764 inches.
1728 Línea 0.005 inches.

Granadan.

Vara 18.082 feet.
64 Cuarta 488.216 inches.
8 Octava 61.027 inches.
125 Pulgada .488 inches.
1000 Línea 0.0005 inches.

VI. Dry Measure.

Legal.

Miriálitro 283.738 bushels.
10 Quilólitro 28.374 bushels.
10 Hectólitro 2.837 bushels.
10 Decálitro 0.284 bushels.
10 Litro 0.908 quarts.
10 Decílitro 0.091 quarts.
10 Centílitro 0.009 quarts.
10 Milílitro 0.0009 quarts.

Castilian and Colombian.

Cahiz 18.658 bushels.
12 Fanega 1.555 bushels.
12 Celemin 0.518 pecks.
2 Medio celemin 2.073 quarts.
4 Cuartillo 1 quart=91.1977 pulgadas cúbicas.

Granadan.

Cahiz 73.535 bushels.
12 Fanega 6.128 bushels.
12 Almud 0.511 bushels.
2 Medio almud 1 peck=1125 pulgadas cúbicas.

VII. Liquid Measure.

Legal.

Miriálitro 2641.78 gallons.
10 Quilólitro 264.178 gallons.
10 Hectólitro 26.418 gallons.
10 Decálitro 2.642 gallons.
10 Litro 1.05672 quarts.
10 Decílitro 0.8454 gills.
10 Centílitro 0.0845 gills.
10 Milílitro 0.008 gills.

Castilian and Colombian.

Moyo 68.217 gallons.
16 Cántara 4.263 gallons.
8 Azumbre 1.066 quarts.
4 Cuartillo 2.132 gills=40.2838 pulgadas cúbicas.

Granadan.

Moyo 16.908 gallons.
8 Cántara 2.113 gallons.
8 Azumbre 1.057 quarts=125 pulgadas cúbicas.

VIII. Weights.

Legal.

Miriágramo 22.047 lbs. avoirdupois.
10 Quilógramo 2.205 lbs.
10 Hectógramo 220 lbs.
10 Decágramo 154.332 grains.
10 Gramo 15.43316 grains.
10 Decígramo 1.543 grains.
10 Centígramo 0.154 grains.
10 Milígramo 0.0015 grains.

Castilian and Colombian.

Quintal 101.418 lbs. avoirdupois.
4 Arroba 25.354 lbs.
25 Libra 1.014 lbs.
16 Onza 1.014 ounces.
16 Adarme 1.014 drachms.
3 Tomin 9.244 grains.
12 Grano 0.77033 grains.

Granadan.

Quintal 110.237 lbs. avoirdupois.
4 Arroba 27.559 lbs.
25 Libra 1.102 lbs.
16 Onza 1.102 ounces.
16 Adarme 1.102 drachms.
40 Grano 0.7633 grains.

IX. Special Castilian Weights.

Silver.

Marco 0.5070895 lbs. avoirdupois.
8 Onza 443.704 grains.
8 Ochava 55.463 grains.
6 Tomin 9.244 grains.

12 Grano 0.770 grains.

Gold.

Marco 0.507 lbs. avoirdupois.
50 Castellano 70.993 grains.
8 Tomin 8.874 grains.
12 Grano 0.74 grains.

Medicine.

Libra 0.9245 ℔ troy.
12 Onza 0.9245 ℥.
8 Dracma 0.9245 ʒ.
3 Escrúpulo 0.9245 ℈.
24 Grano 0.77033 grains.

XI. ANALYTICAL INDEX.

In the following index an attempt is made to collect the topics and things introduced into the narrative, and arrange them in the order they might occupy in a philosophical treatise on New Granada. The references are to pages, and those preceded by *f.* refer to the page where the object is *figured.* The index is arranged into thirty-two sections, as follows:

1. Physical Geography.
2. Races and Conditions of Men.
3. Dress.
4. Habitations.
5. Furniture.
6. Kitchen and Utensils.
7. Water and Drinks.
8. Food.
9. Domestic Employments.
10. Agriculture.
11. Pastoral Occupations.
12. Manufactures.
13. Transportation by Water.
14. Traveling and Transportation by Land.
15. Commerce and Trade.
16. Government.
17. Political Parties.
18. Treasury Department.
19. Foreign Relations.
20. War and Marine Departments.
21. Government Department—Law.
22. Government Department—Hospitals, Diseases, and Physicians.
23. Government Department—Schools and Literature.
24. Fine Arts.
25. Amusements, Habits, and Social Life.
26. Morals.
27. Religion—Dogmas.
28. Religion—Material Objects.
29. Religion—Persons.
30. Religion—Ceremonies.
31. Animals.
32. Plants.

Section 1.—Physical Geography.

Section 2.—Races and Conditions of Men.

Section 3.—Dress.

Section 4.—Habitations.

Section 5.—Furniture.

Section 6.—Kitchen and Utensils.

Section 7.—Water and Drinks.

SECTION 8.—FOOD.

SECTION 9.—DOMESTIC EMPLOYMENTS.

SECTION 10.—AGRICULTURE.

SECTION 11.—PASTORAL OCCUPATIONS.

SECTION 12.—MANUFACTORIES.

SECTION 13.—TRANSPORTATION BY WATER.

Section 14.—Travel and Transportation by Land.

Section 15.—Commerce and Trade.

Section 16.—Government.

Section 17.—Political Parties.

Section 18.—Treasury Department.

SECTION 24.—FINE ARTS.

SECTION 25.—AMUSEMENTS, HABITS, AND SOCIAL LIFE.

SECTION 26.—MORALS.

SECTION 27.—RELIGION—DOGMAS.

SECTION 28.—RELIGION—MATERIAL OBJECTS.

SECTION 29.—RELIGION—PERSONS.

SECTION 30.—RELIGION—CEREMONIES.

SECTION 31.—ANIMALS: CLASSIFICATION OF CUVIER.

SECTION 32.—PLANTS: ENDLICHER'S CLASSIFICATION.

* Anodonta Holtonis, *Lea*: ined. Testa lævi, oblonga, inflata, valde inæquilaterali, e natibus lineatis; valvulis subcrassis; natibus subprominentibus; epidermide tenebroso-olivacea, striata; margarita cœrulea et iridescente. Hab.—In stagno Carthaginis Novogranitensium.

THE END.

www.ingramcontent.com/pod-product-compliance
Lightning Source LLC
LaVergne TN
LVHW021219110826
845150LV00002B/204